Catechism
of the
Catholic Church

The Wanderer Press

The design of the logo on the cover is adapted from a Christian tombstone in the catacombs of Domitilla in Rome, which dates from the end of the third century A.D. This pastoral image, of pagan origin, was used by Christians to symbolize the rest and the happiness that the soul of the departed finds in eternal life.

This image also suggests certain characteristic aspects of this Catechism: Christ, the Good Shepherd who leads and protects his faithful (the lamb) by his authority (the staff), draws them by the melodious symphony of the truth (the panpipes), and makes them lie down in the shade of the tree of life, his redeeming Cross which opens paradise.

The Wanderer Press
201 Ohio Street
St. Paul, Minnesota 55107-2096

ISBN 0-915245-02-7

CONTENTS

APOSTOLIC CONSTITUTION
FIDEI DEPOSITUM

ON THE PUBLICATION OF THE
CATECHISM OF THE CATHOLIC CHURCH
PREPARED FOLLOWING THE SECOND VATICAN ECUMENICAL COUNCIL

JOHN PAUL, BISHOP
SERVANT OF THE SERVANTS OF GOD
FOR EVERLASTING MEMORY

To my Venerable Brothers the Cardinals, Patriarchs, Archbishops, Bishops, Priests, Deacons, and to all the People of God.

GUARDING THE DEPOSIT OF FAITH IS THE MISSION WHICH THE LORD ENTRUSTED TO HIS CHURCH, and which she fulfills in every age. The Second Vatican Ecumenical Council, which was opened 30 years ago by my predecessor Pope John XXIII, of happy memory, had as its intention and purpose to highlight the Church's apostolic and pastoral mission and by making the truth of the Gospel shine forth to lead all people to seek and receive Christ's love which surpasses all knowledge (cf. *Eph* 3:19).

The principal task entrusted to the Council by Pope John XXIII was to guard and present better the precious deposit of Christian doctrine in order to make it more accessible to the Christian faithful and to all people of good will. For this reason the Council was not first of all to condemn the errors of the time, but above all to strive calmly to show the strength and beauty of the doctrine of the faith. "Illumined by the light of this Council," the Pope said, "the Church . . . will become greater in spiritual riches and gaining the strength of new energies therefrom, she will look to the future without fear. . . . Our duty is to dedicate ourselves with an earnest will and without fear to that work which our era demands of us, thus pursuing the path which the Church has followed for 20 centuries."[1]

With the help of God, the Council Fathers in four years of work were able to produce a considerable number of doctrinal statements and pastoral norms which were presented to the whole Church. There the Pastors and Christian faithful find directives for that "renewal of thought, action, practices, and moral virtue, of joy and hope, which was the very purpose of the Council."[2]

After its conclusion, the Council did not cease to inspire the Church's life. In 1985 I was able to assert, "For me, then–who had the special grace of participating in it and actively collaborating in its development–Vatican II has always been, and especially during these years of my Pontificate, the constant reference point of my every pastoral action, in the conscious commitment to implement its directives concretely and faithfully at the level of each Church and the whole Church."[3]

In this spirit, on January 25, 1985, I convoked an extraordinary assembly of the Synod of Bishops for the 20th anniversary of the close of the Council. The purpose of this assembly was to celebrate the graces and spiritual fruits of Vatican II, to study its teaching in greater depth in order that all the Christian faithful might better adhere to it and to promote knowledge and application of it.

---

1   John XXIII, Discourse at the Opening of the Second Vatican Ecumenical Council, October 11, 1962: AAS 54 (1962) pp. 788-91.

2   Paul VI, Discourse at the Closing of the Second Vatican Ecumenical Council, December 7, 1965: AAS 58 (1966) pp. 7-8.

3   John Paul II, Discourse of January 25, 1985: *L'Osservatore Romano,* January 27, 1985.

On that occasion the Synod Fathers stated: "Very many have expressed the desire that a catechism or compendium of all catholic doctrine regarding both faith and morals be composed, that it might be, as it were, a point of reference for the catechisms or compendiums that are prepared in various regions. The presentation of doctrine must be biblical and liturgical. It must be sound doctrine suited to the present life of Christians."[4] After the Synod ended, I made this desire my own, considering it as "fully responding to a real need of the universal Church and of the particular Churches."[5]

For this reason we thank the Lord wholeheartedly on this day when we can offer the entire Church this "reference text" entitled the *Catechism of the Catholic Church* for a catechesis renewed at the living sources of the faith!

Following the renewal of the Liturgy and the new codification of the canon law of the Latin Church and that of the Oriental Catholic Churches, this catechism will make a very important contribution to that work of renewing the whole life of the Church, as desired and begun by the Second Vatican Council.

1. The Process and Spirit of Drafting the Text

The *Catechism of the Catholic Church* is the result of very extensive collaboration; it was prepared over six years of intense work done in a spirit of complete openness and fervent zeal.

In 1986, I entrusted a commission of twelve Cardinals and Bishops, chaired by Cardinal Joseph Ratzinger, with the task of preparing a draft of the catechism requested by the Synod Fathers. An editorial committee of seven diocesan Bishops, experts in theology and catechesis, assisted the commission in its work.

The commission, charged with giving directives and with overseeing the course of the work, attentively followed all the stages in editing the nine subsequent drafts. The editorial committee, for its part, assumed responsibility for writing the text, making the emendations requested by the commission and examining the observations of numerous theologians, exegetes and catechists, and, above all, of the Bishops of the whole world, in order to produce a better text. In the committee various opinions were compared with great profit, and thus a richer text has resulted whose unity and coherence are assured.

4　*Final Report* of the Extraordinary Synod of Bishops, December 7, 1985, *Enchiridion Vaticanum*, vol. 9, II, B, a, n. 4: p. 1758, n. 1797.

5　John Paul II, Discourse at the Closing of the Extraordinary Synod of Bishops, December 7, 1985, n. 6: AAS 78 (1986) p. 435.

The project was the object of extensive consultation among all Catholic Bishops, their Episcopal Conferences or Synods, and of theological and catechetical institutes. As a whole, it received a broadly favorable acceptance on the part of the Episcopate. It can be said that this *Catechism* is the result of the collaboration of the whole Episcopate of the Catholic Church, who generously accepted my invitation to share responsibility for an enterprise which directly concerns the life of the Church. This response elicits in me a deep feeling of joy, because the harmony of so many voices truly expresses what could be called the "symphony" of the faith. The achievement of this *Catechism* thus reflects the collegial nature of the Episcopate; it testifies to the Church's catholicity.

2.   Arrangement of the Material

A catechism should faithfully and systematically present the teaching of Sacred Scripture, the living Tradition in the Church and the authentic Magisterium, as well as the spiritual heritage of the Fathers, Doctors, and saints of the Church, to allow for a better knowledge of the Christian mystery and for enlivening the faith of the People of God. It should take into account the doctrinal statements which down the centuries the Holy Spirit has intimated to his Church. It should also help to illumine with the light of faith the new situations and problems which had not yet emerged in the past.

This catechism will thus contain both the new and the old (cf. *Mt* 13:52), because the faith is always the same yet the source of ever new light.

To respond to this twofold demand, the *Catechism of the Catholic Church* on the one hand repeats the "old," traditional order already followed by the Catechism of St. Pius V, arranging the material in four parts: the *Creed*, the *Sacred Liturgy*, with pride of place given to the sacraments, the *Christian way of life*, explained beginning with the Ten commandments, and finally, *Christian prayer*. At the same time, however, the contents are often presented in a "new" way in order to respond to the questions of our age.

The four parts are related one to another: the Christian mystery is the object of faith (first part); it is celebrated and communicated in liturgical actions (second part); it is present to enlighten and sustain the children of God in their actions (third part); it is the basis for our prayer, the privileged expression of which is the *Our Father*, and it represents the object of our supplication, our praise and our intercession (fourth part).

The Liturgy itself is prayer; the confession of faith finds its proper place in the celebration of worship. Grace, the fruit of the sacraments, is the irreplaceable condition for Christian living, just as participation in the Church's Liturgy requires faith. If faith is not expressed in works, it is dead (cf. *Jas* 2:14-16) and cannot bear fruit unto eternal life.

In reading the *Catechism of the Catholic Church* we can perceive the wonderful unity of the mystery of God, his saving will, as well as the central place of Jesus Christ, the only-begotten Son of God, sent by the Father, made man in the womb of the Blessed Virgin Mary by the power of the Holy Spirit, to be our Savior. Having died and risen, Christ is always present in his Church, especially in the sacraments; he is the source of our faith, the model of Christian conduct, and the Teacher of our prayer.

3. The Doctrinal Value of the Text

The *Catechism of the Catholic Church*, which I approved June 25th last and the publication of which I today order by virtue of my Apostolic Authority, is a statement of the Church's faith and of catholic doctrine, attested to or illumined by Sacred Scripture, the Apostolic Tradition, and the Church's Magisterium. I declare it to be a sure norm for teaching the faith and thus a valid and legitimate instrument for ecclesial communion. May it serve the renewal to which the Holy Spirit ceaselessly calls the Church of God, the Body of Christ, on her pilgrimage to the undiminished light of the Kingdom!

The approval and publication of the *Catechism of the Catholic Church* represent a service which the Successor of Peter wishes to offer to the Holy Catholic Church, to all the particular Churches in peace and communion with the Apostolic See: the service, that is, of supporting and confirming the faith of all the Lord Jesus' disciples (cf. *Lk* 22:32), as well as of strengthening the bonds of unity in the same apostolic faith.

Therefore, I ask all the Church's Pastors and the Christian faithful to receive this catechism in a spirit of communion and to use it assiduously in fulfilling their mission of proclaiming the faith and calling people to the Gospel life. This catechism is given to them that it may be a sure and authentic reference text for teaching catholic doctrine and particularly for preparing local catechisms. It is also offered to all the faithful who wish to deepen their knowledge of the unfathomable riches of salvation (cf. *Eph* 3:8). It is meant to support ecumenical efforts that are moved by the holy desire for the unity of all Christians, showing carefully the content and wondrous harmony of the catholic faith. The *Catechism of the Catholic Church*, lastly, is offered to every individual who asks us to give an account of the hope that is in us (cf. *1 Pet* 3:15) and who wants to know what the Catholic Church believes.

This catechism is not intended to replace the local catechisms duly approved by the ecclesiastical authorities, the diocesan Bishops and the Episcopal Conferences, especially if they have been approved by the Apostolic See. It is meant to encourage and assist in the writing of new local catechisms, which take into account various situations and cultures, while carefully preserving the unity of faith and fidelity to catholic doctrine.

At the conclusion of this document presenting the *Catechism of the Catholic Church*, I beseech the Blessed Virgin Mary, Mother of the Incarnate Word and Mother of the Church, to support with her powerful intercession the catechetical work of the entire Church on every level, at this time when she is called to a new effort of evangelization. May the light of the true faith free humanity from the ignorance and slavery of sin in order to lead it to the only freedom worthy of the name (cf. *Jn* 8:32): that of life in Jesus Christ under the guidance of the Holy Spirit, here below and in the Kingdom of heaven, in the fullness of the blessed vision of God face to face (cf. *1 Cor* 13:12; *2 Cor* 5:6-8)!

Given October 11, 1992, the thirtieth anniversary of the opening of the Second Vatican Ecumenical Council, in the fourteenth year of my Pontificate.

Joannes Paulus II

PROLOGUE

"FATHER, . . . this is eternal life, that they may know you, the only true God, and Jesus Christ whom you have sent.[1] God our Savior desires all men to be saved and to come to the knowledge of the truth."[2] "There is no other name under heaven given among men by which we must be saved"[3] than the name of JESUS.

I. THE LIFE OF MAN – TO KNOW AND LOVE GOD

1 God, infinitely perfect and blessed in himself, in a plan of sheer goodness freely created man to make him share in his own blessed life. For this reason, at every time and in every place, God draws close to man. He calls man to seek him, to know him, to love him with all his strength. He calls together all men, scattered and divided by sin, into the unity of his family, the Church. To accomplish this, when the fullness of time had come, God sent his Son as Redeemer and Savior. In his Son and through him, he invites men to become, in the Holy Spirit, his adopted children and thus heirs of his blessed life.

2 So that this call should resound throughout the world, Christ sent forth the apostles he had chosen, commissioning them to proclaim the gospel: "Go therefore and make disciples of all nations, baptizing them in the name of the Father and of the Son and of the Holy Spirit, teaching them to observe all that I have commanded you; and lo, I am with you always, to the close of the age."[4] Strengthened by this mission, the apostles "went forth and preached everywhere, while the Lord worked with them and confirmed the message by the signs that attended it."[5]

3 Those who with God's help have welcomed Christ's call and freely responded to it are urged on by love of Christ to proclaim the Good News everywhere in the world. This treasure, received from the apostles, has been faithfully guarded by their successors. All Christ's faithful are called to hand it on from gen-

---

1 *Jn* 17:3.
2 *1 Tim* 2:3-4.
3 *Acts* 4:12.
4 *Mt* 28:18-20.
5 *Mk* 16:20.

eration to generation, by professing the faith, by living it in fraternal sharing, and by celebrating it in liturgy and prayer.[6]

II. HANDING ON THE FAITH: CATECHESIS

4 Quite early on, the name *catechesis* was given to the totality
of the Church's efforts to make disciples, to help men believe that
Jesus is the Son of God so that believing they might have life in his
name, and to educate and instruct them in this life, thus building
up the body of Christ.[7]

5 "Catechesis is an *education in the faith* of children, young
people, and adults which includes especially the teaching of Christian doctrine imparted, generally speaking, in an organic and
systematic way, with a view to initiating the hearers into the
fullness of Christian life."[8]

6 While not being formally identified with them, catechesis
is built on a certain number of elements of the Church's pastoral
mission which have a catechetical aspect, that prepare for catfor catechesis, or spring from it. They are: the initial proclamation of the
Gospel or missionary preaching to arouse faith; examination of the
reasons for belief; experience of Christian living; celebration of the
sacraments; integration into the ecclesial community; and apostolic and missionary witness.[9]

7 "Catechesis is intimately bound up with the whole of the
Church's life. Not only her geographical extension and numerical
increase, but even more her inner growth and correspondence with
God's plan depend essentially on catechesis."[10]

8 Periods of renewal in the Church are also intense moments of
catechesis. In the great era of the Fathers of the Church, saintly bishops
devoted an important part of their ministry to catechesis. St. Cyril of
Jerusalem and St. John Chrysostom, St. Ambrose and St. Augustine, and
many other Fathers wrote catechetical works that remain models for us.[11]

9 "The ministry of catechesis draws ever fresh energy from the
councils. The Council of Trent is a noteworthy example of this. It gave
catechesis priority in its constitutions and decrees. It lies at the origin of
the *Roman Catechism*, which is also known by the name of that council and
which is a work of the first rank as a summary of Christian teaching...."[12]

---

6 Cf. *Acts* 2:42.
7 Cf. John Paul II, apostolic exhortation, *Catechesi tradendae* 1; 2.
8 *CT* 18.
9 *CT* 18.
10 *CT* 13.
11 Cf. *CT* 12.

The Council of Trent initiated a remarkable organization of the Church's catechesis. Thanks to the work of holy bishops and theologians such as St. Peter Canisius, St. Charles Borromeo, St. Turibius of Mongrovejo, or St. Robert Bellarmine, it occasioned the publication of numerous catechisms.

10 It is therefore no surprise that catechesis in the Church has again attracted attention in the wake of the Second Vatican Council, which Pope Paul VI considered the great catechism of modern times. The General Catechetical Directory (1971), the sessions of the Synod of Bishops devoted to evangelization (1974) and catechesis (1977), the apostolic exhortations *Evangelii nuntiandi* (1975) and *Catechesi tradendae* (1979) attest to this. The Extraordinary Synod of Bishops in 1985 asked "that a catechism or compendium of all Catholic doctrine regarding both faith and morals be composed."[13] The Holy Father, Pope John Paul II, made the Synod's wish his own, acknowledging that "this desire wholly corresponds to a real need of the universal Church and of the particular Churches."[14] He set in motion everything needed to carry out the Synod Fathers' wish.

III. THE AIM AND INTENDED READERSHIP OF THIS CATECHISM

11 This catechism aims at presenting an organic synthesis of the essential and fundamental contents of Catholic doctrine, as regards both faith and morals, in the light of the Second Vatican Council and the whole of the Church's Tradition. Its principal sources are the Sacred Scriptures, the Fathers of the Church, the liturgy, and the Church's Magisterium. It is intended to serve "as a point of reference for the catechisms or compendia that are composed in the various countries."[15]

12 This work is intended primarily for those responsible for catechesis: first of all the bishops, as teachers of the faith and pastors of the Church. It is offered to them as an instrument in fulfilling their responsibility of teaching the People of God. Through the bishops, it is addressed to redactors of catechisms, to priests, and to catechists. It will also be useful reading for all other Christian faithful.

IV. STRUCTURE OF THIS CATECHISM

13 The plan of this catechism is inspired by the great tradition of catechisms which build catechesis on four pillars: the baptismal profession of faith (the *Creed*), the sacraments of faith, the life of

---

12 *CT* 13.

13 Extraordinary Synod of Bishops 1985, *Final Report*, II B a, 4.

14 John Paul II, Discourse at the Closing of the Extraordinary Synod of Bishops, December 7, 1985: AAS 78 (1986).

15 Extraordinary Synod of Bishops 1985, *Final Report* II B a, 4.

faith (the *Commandments*), and the prayer of the believer (the *Lord's Prayer*).

Part One: *The profession of faith*

14   Those who belong to Christ through faith and Baptism must confess their baptismal faith before men.[16] First therefore the Catechism expounds revelation, by which God addresses and gives himself to man, and the faith by which man responds to God *(Section One)*. The profession of faith summarizes the gifts that God gives man: as the Author of all that is good; as Redeemer; and as Sanctifier. It develops these in the three chapters on our baptismal faith in the one God: the almighty *Father*, the Creator; his *Son* Jesus Christ, our Lord and Savior; and the *Holy Spirit*, the Sanctifier, in the Holy Church *(Section Two)*.

Part Two: *The sacraments of faith*

15   The second part of the Catechism explains how God's salvation, accomplished once for all through Christ Jesus and the Holy Spirit, is made present in the sacred actions of the Church's liturgy *(Section One)*, especially in the seven sacraments *(Section Two)*.

Part Three: *The life of faith*

16   The third part of the Catechism deals with the final end of man created in the image of God: beatitude, and the ways of reaching it – through right conduct freely chosen, with the help of God's law and grace *(Section One)*, and through conduct that fulfills the twofold commandment of charity, specified in God's Ten Commandments *(Section Two)*.

Part Four: *Prayer in the life of faith*

17   The last part of the Catechism deals with the meaning and importance of prayer in the life of believers *(Section One)*. It concludes with a brief commentary on the seven petitions of the Lord's Prayer *(Section Two)*, for indeed we find in these the sum of all the good things which we must hope for and which our heavenly Father wants to grant us.

---

16   Cf. *Mt* 10:32; *Rom* 10:9.

V.   PRACTICAL DIRECTIONS FOR USING THIS CATECHISM

18   This catechism is conceived as *an organic presentation* of the Catholic faith in its entirety. It should be seen therefore as a unified whole. Numerous cross-references in the margin of the text (italicized numbers referring to other paragraphs that deal with the same theme), as well as the analytical index at the end of the volume, allow the reader to view each theme in its relationship with the entirety of the faith.

19   The texts of Sacred Scripture are often not quoted word for word but are merely indicated by a reference (**cf.**). For a deeper understanding of such passages, the reader should refer to the Scriptural texts themselves. Such Biblical references are a valuable working-tool in catechesis.

20   The use of **small print** in certain passages indicates observations of an historical or apologetic nature, or supplementary doctrinal explanations.

21   The **quotations**, also in small print, from patristic, liturgical, magisterial or hagiographical sources, are intended to enrich the doctrinal presentations. These texts have often been chosen with a view to direct catechetical use.

22   At the end of each thematic unit, a series of brief texts sum up the essentials of that unit's teaching in condensed formulae. These **IN BRIEF** summaries may suggest to local catechists brief summary formulae that could be memorized.

VI.   NECESSARY ADAPTATIONS

23   The Catechism emphasizes the exposition of doctrine. It seeks to help deepen understanding of faith. In this way it is oriented toward the maturing of that faith, its putting down roots in personal life and its shining forth in personal conduct.[17]

24   By design, this Catechism does not set out to provide the adaptation of doctrinal presentations and catechetical methods required by the differences of culture, age, spiritual maturity, and social and ecclesial condition among all those to whom it is addressed. Such indispensable adaptations are the responsibility of particular catechisms and, even more, of those who instruct the faithful:

---

17   Cf. CT 20-22, 25.

> Whoever teaches must become "all things to all men" (*1 Cor*
> 9:22), to win everyone to Christ. . . . Above all, teachers must
> not imagine that a single kind of soul has been entrusted to
> them, and that consequently it is lawful to teach and form
> equally all the faithful in true piety with one and the same
> method! Let them realize that some are in Christ as newborn
> babes, others as adolescents, and still others as adults in full
> command of their powers. . . .Those who are called to the
> ministry of preaching must suit their words to the maturity
> and understanding of their hearers, as they hand on the
> teaching of the mysteries of faith and the rules of moral
> conduct.[18]

Above All – Charity

25   To conclude this Prologue, it is fitting to recall this pastoral
principle stated by the *Roman Catechism*:

> The whole concern of doctrine and its teaching must be
> directed to the love that never ends. Whether something is
> proposed for belief, for hope or for action, the love of our
> Lord must always be made accessible, so that anyone can see
> that all the works of perfect Christian virtue spring from love
> and have no other objective than to arrive at love.[19]

---

18   *Roman Catechism*, Preface, 11; cf. *1 Cor* 9:22; *1 Pet* 2:2.
19   *Roman Catechism*, Preface, 10; cf. *1 Cor* 13:8.

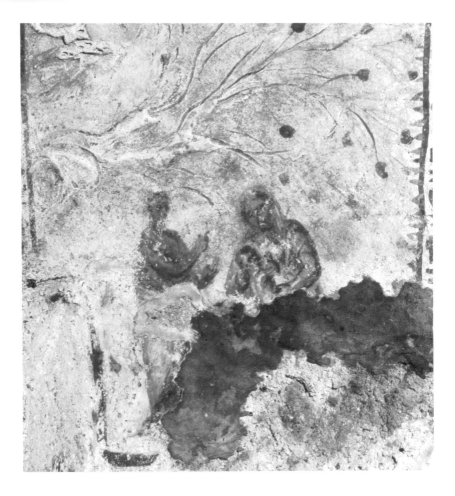

Fragment of a fresco from the catacomb of Priscilla in Rome, dating from the beginning of the third century A.D. It is the most ancient image of the Blessed Virgin.

This image, among the most ancient in Christian art, expresses a theme that lies at the heart of the Christian faith: the mystery of the incarnation of the Son of God born of the Virgin Mary.

– At the left, the figure of a man pointing to a star, located above the Virgin with the child: a prophet, probably Balaam, who announced that "a star shall come forth out of Jacob, and a scepter shall rise out of Israel" (*Num* 24:17). This is the whole expectation of the Old Covenant and the cry of a fallen humanity for a savior and redeemer (cf. §§27; 528).

– This prophecy was fulfilled in the birth of Jesus, the incarnate Son of God, conceived by the power of the Holy Spirit and born of the Virgin Mary (cf. §§27; 53; 422; 488). Mary brought him into the world and gave him to all mankind. For this reason she is the purest image of the Church (cf. §967).

PART ONE

THE PROFESSION
OF FAITH

SECTION ONE
"I BELIEVE" – "WE BELIEVE"

26   We begin our profession of faith by saying: "I believe" or "We believe." Before expounding the Church's faith, as confessed in the Creed, celebrated in the liturgy, and lived in observance of God's commandments and in prayer, we must first ask what "to believe" means. Faith is man's response to God, who reveals himself and gives himself to man, at the same time bringing man a superabundant light as he searches for the ultimate meaning of his life. Thus we shall consider first that search (*Chapter One*), then the divine Revelation by which God comes to meet man (*Chapter Two*), and finally the response of faith (*Chapter Three*).

CHAPTER ONE
MAN'S CAPACITY FOR GOD

I.   THE DESIRE FOR GOD

27   The desire for God is written in the human heart, because man is created by God and for God; and God never ceases to draw *355, 170* man to himself. Only in God will he find the truth and happiness *1718* he never stops searching for:

> The dignity of man rests above all on the fact that he is called to communion with God. This invitation to converse with God is addressed to man as soon as he comes into being. For if man exists, it is because God has created him through love, and through love continues to hold him in existence. He cannot live fully according to truth unless he freely acknowledges that love and entrusts himself to his creator.[1]

---

1   Vatican Council II, *GS* 19 § 1.

28   In many ways, throughout history down to the present
843, 2566 day, men have given expression to their quest for God in their
2095-2109 religious beliefs and behavior: in their prayers, sacrifices, rituals,
meditations, and so forth. These forms of religious expression,
despite the ambiguities they often bring with them, are so universal
that one may well call man a *religious being*:

> From one ancestor [God] made all nations to inhabit the
> whole earth, and he allotted the times of their existence and
> the boundaries of the places where they would live, so that
> they would search for God and perhaps grope for him and
> find him – though indeed he is not far from each one of us.
> For "in him we live and move and have our being."[2]

29   But this "intimate and vital bond of man to God" (*GS* 19,1)
2123-2128 can be forgotten, overlooked, or even explicitly rejected by man.[3]
Such attitudes can have different causes: revolt against evil in the
world; religious ignorance or indifference; the cares and riches of
this world; the scandal of bad example on the part of believers;
398 currents of thought hostile to religion; finally, that attitude of sinful
man which makes him hide from God out of fear and flee his call.[4]

30   "Let the hearts of those who seek the LORD rejoice."[5]
2567, 845 Although man can forget God or reject him, He never ceases to call
every man to seek him, so as to find life and happiness. But this
368 search for God demands of man every effort of intellect, a sound
will, "an upright heart," as well as the witness of others who teach
him to seek God.

> You are great, O Lord, and greatly to be praised: great is your
> power and your wisdom is without measure. And man, so
> small a part of your creation, wants to praise you: this man,
> though clothed with mortality and bearing the evidence of
> sin and the proof that you withstand the proud. Despite
> everything, man, though but a small a part of your creation,
> wants to praise you. You yourself encourage him to delight
> in your praise, for you have made us for yourself, and our
> heart is restless until it rests in you.[6]

II.   WAYS OF COMING TO KNOW GOD

31   Created in God's image and called to know and love him,
the person who seeks God discovers certain ways of coming to

---

2   *Acts* 17:26-28.
3   *GS* 19 § 1.
4   Cf. *GS* 19-21; *Mt* 13:22; *Gen* 3:8-10; *Jon* 1:3.
5   *Ps* 105:3.
6   St. Augustine, *Conf.* 1, 1, 1: PL 32, 659-661.

know him. These are also called proofs for the existence of God, not in the sense of proofs in the natural sciences, but rather in the sense of "converging and convincing arguments," which allow us to attain certainty about the truth.

These "ways" of approaching God from creation have a twofold point of departure: the physical world and the human person.

32   The *world*: starting from movement, becoming, contingency, and the world's order and beauty, one can come to a *54, 337* knowledge of God as the origin and the end of the universe.

> As St. Paul says of the Gentiles: For what can be known about God is plain to them, because God has shown it to them. Ever since the creation of the world his invisible nature, namely, his eternal power and deity, has been clearly perceived in the things that have been made.[7]

> And St. Augustine issues this challenge: Question the beauty of the earth, question the beauty of the sea, question the beauty of the air distending and diffusing itself, question the beauty of the sky . . . question all these realities. All respond: "See, we are beautiful." Their beauty is a profession [*confessio*]. These beauties are subject to change. Who made them if not the Beautiful One [*Pulcher*] who is not subject to change?[8]

33   The *human person:* With his openness to truth and beauty, his sense of moral goodness, his freedom and the voice of his *2500, 1730* conscience, with his longings for the infinite and for happiness, *1776* man questions himself about God's existence. In all this he discerns *1703* signs of his spiritual soul. The soul, the "seed of eternity we bear *366* in ourselves, irreducible to the merely material,"[9] can have its origin only in God.

34   The world, and man, attest that they contain within themselves neither their first principle nor their final end, but rather that they participate in Being itself, which alone is without origin or end. Thus, in different ways, man can come to know that there exists a reality which is the first cause and final end of all things, a reality "that everyone calls 'God.'"[10] *199*

---

7 *Rom* 1:19-20; cf. *Acts* 14:15, 17; 17:27-28; *Wis* 13:1-9.
8 St. Augustine, *Sermo* 241, 2: PL 38, 1134.
9 *GS* 18 § 1; cf. 14 § 2.
10 St. Thomas Aquinas, *STh* I, 2, 3.

35   Man's faculties make him capable of coming to a knowledge of the existence of a personal God. But for man to be able to
50 enter into real intimacy with him, God willed both to reveal himself
to man and to give him the grace of being able to welcome this
revelation in faith. The proofs of God's existence, however, can
159 predispose one to faith and help one to see that faith is not opposed
to reason.

III.   THE KNOWLEDGE OF GOD ACCORDING TO THE CHURCH

36   "Our holy mother, the Church, holds and teaches that
God, the first principle and last end of all things, can be known
with certainty from the created world by the natural light of human
reason."[11] Without this capacity, man would not be able to wel-
355 come God's revelation. Man has this capacity because he is created
"in the image of God."[12]

37   In the historical conditions in which he finds himself,
however, man experiences many difficulties in coming to know
1960 God by the light of reason alone:

> Though human reason is, strictly speaking, truly capable by
> its own natural power and light of attaining to a true and
> certain knowledge of the one personal God, who watches
> over and controls the world by his providence, and of the
> natural law written in our hearts by the Creator; yet there are
> many obstacles which prevent reason from the effective and
> fruitful use of this inborn faculty. For the truths that concern
> the relations between God and man wholly transcend the
> visible order of things, and, if they are translated into human
> action and influence it, they call for self-surrender and abne-
> gation. The human mind, in its turn, is hampered in the
> attaining of such truths, not only by the impact of the senses
> and the imagination, but also by disordered appetites which
> are the consequences of original sin. So it happens that men
> in such matters easily persuade themselves that what they
> would not like to be true is false or at least doubtful.[13]

38   This is why man stands in need of being enlightened by
God's revelation, not only about those things that exceed his
2036 understanding, but also "about those religious and moral truths
which of themselves are not beyond the grasp of human reason, so
that even in the present condition of the human race, they can be

---

11 Vatican Council I, *Dei Filius* 2: DS 3004; cf. 3026; Vatican Council II, *Dei Verbum* 6.
12 Cf. *Gen* 1:27.
13 Pius XII, *Humani Generis*, 561: DS 3875.

known by all men with ease, with firm certainty and with no admixture of error."[14]

IV. How Can We Speak about God?

39   In defending the ability of human reason to know God, the Church is expressing her confidence in the possibility of speaking   *851* about him to all men and with all men, and therefore of dialogue with other religions, with philosophy and science, as well as with unbelievers and atheists.

40   Since our knowledge of God is limited, our language about him is equally so. We can name God only by taking creatures as our starting point, and in accordance with our limited human ways of knowing and thinking.

41   All creatures bear a certain resemblance to God, most especially man, created in the image and likeness of God. The manifold perfections of creatures–their truth, their goodness, their beauty –all reflect the infinite perfection of God. Consequently we   *213, 299* can name God by taking his creatures' perfections as our starting point, "for from the greatness and beauty of created things comes a corresponding perception of their Creator."[15]

42   God transcends all creatures. We must therefore continually purify our language of everything in it that is limited, image-   *212, 300* bound or imperfect, if we are not to confuse our image of God –   *370* "the inexpressible, the incomprehensible, the invisible, the ungraspable"–with our human representations.[16] Our human words always fall short of the mystery of God.

43   Admittedly, in speaking about God like this, our language is using human modes of expression; nevertheless it really does attain to God himself, though unable to express him in his infinite simplicity. Likewise, we must recall that "between Creator and creature no similitude can be expressed without implying an even greater dissimilitude";[17] and that "concerning God, we cannot grasp what he is, but only what he is not, and how other beings   *206* stand in relation to him."[18]

---

14 Pius XII, *Humani Generis*, 561: DS 3876; cf. *Dei Filius* 2: DS 3005; *DV* 6; St. Thomas Aquinas, *STh* I, 1, 1.
15 *Wis* 13:5.
16 *Liturgy of St. John Chrysostom*, Anaphora.
17 Lateran Council IV: DS 806.
18 St. Thomas Aquinas, *SCG* I, 30.

IN BRIEF

44   Man is by nature and vocation a religious being. Coming from God, going toward God, man lives a fully human life only if he freely lives by his bond with God.

45   Man is made to live in communion with God in whom he finds happiness: "When I am completely united to you, there will be no more sorrow or trials; entirely full of you, my life will be complete" (St. Augustine, *Conf.* 10, 28, 39: PL 32, 795).

46   When he listens to the message of creation and to the voice of conscience, man can arrive at certainty about the existence of God, the cause and the end of everything.

47   The Church teaches that the one true God, our Creator and Lord, can be known with certainty from his works, by the natural light of human reason (cf. Vatican Council I, can. 2, § 1: DS 3026).

48   We really can name God, starting from the manifold perfections of his creatures, which are likenesses of the infinitely perfect God, even if our limited language cannot exhaust the mystery.

49   "Without the Creator, the creature vanishes" (*GS* 36). This is the reason why believers know that the love of Christ urges them to bring the light of the living God to those who do not know him or who reject him.

CHAPTER TWO
GOD COMES TO MEET MAN

50 By natural reason man can know God with certainty, on the basis of his works. But there is another order of knowledge, which man cannot possibly arrive at by his own powers: the order *36* of divine Revelation.[1] Through an utterly free decision, God has revealed himself and given himself to man. This he does by revealing the mystery, his plan of loving goodness, formed from all eternity in Christ, for the benefit of all men. God has fully revealed *1066* this plan by sending us his beloved Son, our Lord Jesus Christ, and the Holy Spirit.

ARTICLE 1
THE REVELATION OF GOD

I. GOD REVEALS HIS "PLAN OF LOVING GOODNESS"

51 "It pleased God, in his goodness and wisdom, to reveal himself and to make known the mystery of his will. His will was *2823* that men should have access to the Father, through Christ, the Word made flesh, in the Holy Spirit, and thus become sharers in *1996* the divine nature."[2]

52 God, who "dwells in unapproachable light," wants to communicate his own divine life to the men he freely created, in order to adopt them as his sons in his only-begotten Son.[3] By revealing himself God wishes to make them capable of responding to him, and of knowing him, and of loving him far beyond their own natural capacity.

53 The divine plan of Revelation is realized simultaneously "by deeds and words which are intrinsically bound up with each other"[4] and shed light on each other. It involves a specific divine pedagogy: God communicates himself to man gradually. He pre- *1953* pares him to welcome by stages the supernatural Revelation that *1950* is to culminate in the person and mission of the incarnate Word, Jesus Christ.

---

1 Cf. *Dei Filius:* DS 3015.
2 *DV* 2; cf. *Eph* 1:9; 2:18; *2 Pet* 1:4.
3 *1 Tim* 6:16; cf. *Eph* 1:4-5.
4 *DV* 2.

St. Irenaeus of Lyons repeatedly speaks of this divine pedagogy using the image of God and man becoming accustomed
to one another: The Word of God dwelt in man and became
the Son of man in order to accustom man to perceive God
and to accustom God to dwell in man, according to the
Father's pleasure.[5]

II.   THE STAGES OF REVELATION

In the beginning God makes himself known

54   "God, who creates and conserves all things by his Word,
32 provides men with constant evidence of himself in created realities.
And furthermore, wishing to open up the way to heavenly salvation, he manifested himself to our first parents from the very
beginning."[6] He invited them to intimate communion with himself
374 and clothed them with resplendent grace and justice.

55   This revelation was not broken off by our first parents' sin.
397, 410 "After the fall, [God] buoyed them up with the hope of salvation,
by promising redemption; and he has never ceased to show his
solicitude for the human race. For he wishes to give eternal life to
all those who seek salvation by patience in well-doing."[7]

Even when he disobeyed you and lost your friendship
you did not abandon him to the power of death . . . .
761 Again and again you offered a covenant to man.[8]

The Covenant with Noah

56   After the unity of the human race was shattered by sin God
at once sought to save humanity part by part. The covenant with
401 Noah after the flood gives expression to the principle of the divine
1219 economy toward the "nations," in other words, toward men
grouped "in their lands, each with [its] own language, by their
families, in their nations."[9]

57   This state of division into many nations, each entrusted by
divine providence to the guardianship of angels, is at once cosmic,
social, and religious. It is intended to limit the pride of fallen
humanity,[10] united only in its perverse ambition to forge its own

---

5 St. Irenaeus, *Adv. haeres.* 3, 20, 2: PG 7/1, 944; cf. 3, 17, 1; 4, 12, 4; 4, 21, 3.
6 *DV* 3; cf. *Jn* 1:3; *Rom* 1:19-20.
7 *DV* 3; cf. *Gen* 3:15; *Rom* 2:6-7.
8 *Roman Missal*, Eucharistic Prayer IV, 118.
9 *Gen* 10:5; cf. 9:9-10, 16; 10:20-31.
10 Cf. *Acts* 17:26-27; *Deut* 4: 19; *Deut* (LXX) 32: 8.

unity as at Babel.[11] But, because of sin, both polytheism and the idolatry of the nation and of its rulers constantly threaten this provisional economy with the perversion of paganism.[12]

58   The covenant with Noah remains in force during the times of the Gentiles, until the universal proclamation of the Gospel.[13] The Bible venerates several great figures among the Gentiles: Abel *674* the just, the king-priest Melchizedek – a figure of Christ – and the upright "Noah, Daniel, and Job."[14] Scripture thus expresses the heights of sanctity that can be reached by those who live according to the covenant of Noah, waiting for Christ to "gather into one the *2569* children of God who are scattered abroad."[15]

God chooses Abraham

59   In order to gather together scattered humanity God calls Abram from his country, his kindred, and his father's house,[16] and *145, 2570* makes him Abraham, that is, "the father of a multitude of nations." "In you all the nations of the earth shall be blessed."[17]

60   The people descended from Abraham would be the trustees of the promise made to the patriarchs, the chosen people, called to *760* prepare for that day when God would gather all his children into the *762, 781* unity of the Church.[18] They would be the root onto which the Gentiles would be grafted, once they came to believe.[19]

61   The patriarchs, prophets, and certain other Old Testament figures have been and always will be honored as saints in all the Church's liturgical traditions.

God forms his people Israel

62   After the patriarchs, God formed Israel as his people by *2060, 2574* freeing them from slavery in Egypt. He established with them the covenant of Mount Sinai and, through Moses, gave them his law so that they would recognize him and serve him as the one living

---

11 Cf. *Wis* 10:5; *Gen* 11:4-6.
12 Cf. *Rom* 1:18-25.
13 Cf. *Gen* 9:16; *Lk* 21:24; *DV* 3.
14 Cf. *Gen* 14:18; *Heb* 7:3; *Ezek* 14:14.
15 *Jn* 11:52.
16 *Gen* 12:1.
17 *Gen* 17:5; 12:3 (LXX); cf. *Gal* 3:8.
18 Cf. *Rom* 11:28; *Jn* 11:52; 10:16.
19 Cf. *Rom* 11:17-18, 24.

and true God, the provident Father and just judge, and so that they
1961 would look for the promised Savior.[20]

204, 2801 **63**   Israel is the priestly people of God, "called by the name of
839 the LORD," and "the first to hear the word of God,"[21] the people of
"elder brethren" in the faith of Abraham.

64   Through the prophets, God forms his people in the hope
of salvation, in the expectation of a new and everlasting Covenant
711 intended for all, to be written on their hearts.[22] The prophets
1965 proclaim a radical redemption of the People of God, purification
from all their infidelities, a salvation which will include all the
nations.[23] Above all, the poor and humble of the Lord will bear this
hope. Such holy women as Sarah, Rebecca, Rachel, Miriam, Debo-
489 rah, Hannah, Judith, and Esther kept alive the hope of Israel's
salvation. The purest figure among them is Mary.[24]

III.   CHRIST JESUS – "MEDIATOR AND FULLNESS OF ALL REVELATION"[25]

God has said everything in his Word

65   "In many and various ways God spoke of old to our fathers
by the prophets, but in these last days he has spoken to us by a
102 Son."[26] Christ, the Son of God made man, is the Father's one,
perfect, and unsurpassable Word. In him he has said everything;
there will be no other word than this one. St. John of the Cross,
among others, commented strikingly on *Hebrews* 1:1-2:

> In giving us his Son, his only Word (for he possesses no
> other), he spoke everything to us at once in this sole Word –
> and he has no more to say . . . because what he spoke before
> to the prophets in parts, he has now spoken all at once by
516 > giving us the All Who is His Son. Any person questioning
> God or desiring some vision or revelation would be guilty
> not only of foolish behavior but also of offending him, by not
> fixing his eyes entirely upon Christ and by living with the
2717 > desire for some other novelty.[27]

---

20 Cf. *DV* 3.
21 *Deut* 28:10; *Roman Missal*, Good Friday, General Intercession VI; see also *Ex* 19:6.
22 Cf. *Isa* 2:2-4; *Jer* 31:31-34; *Heb* 10:16.
23 Cf. *Ezek* 36; *Isa* 49:5-6; 53:11.
24 Cf. *Zeph* 2:3; *Lk* 1:38.
25 *DV* 2.
26 *Heb* 1:1-2.
27 St. John of the Cross, *The Ascent of Mount Carmel*, 2, 22, 3-5, in *The Collected Works*, tr. K. Kavanaugh, OCD, and O. Rodriguez, OCD (Washington DC: Institute of Carmelite Studies, 1979), 179-180: *LH*, OR Advent, wk 2, Mon.

There will be no further Revelation

66   "The Christian economy, therefore, since it is the new and definitive Covenant, will never pass away; and no new public revelation is to be expected before the glorious manifestation of our Lord Jesus Christ."[28] Yet even if Revelation is already complete, it has not been made completely explicit; it remains for Christian faith gradually to grasp its full significance over the course of the *94* centuries.

67   Throughout the ages, there have been so-called "private" revelations, some of which have been recognized by the authority of the Church. They do not belong, however, to the deposit of faith. It is not their role to *84* improve or complete Christ's definitive Revelation, but to help live more fully by it in a certain period of history. Guided by the magisterium of the Church, the *sensus fidelium* knows how to discern and welcome in these revelations whatever constitutes an authentic call of Christ or his saints to the Church.   *93*

Christian faith cannot accept "revelations" that claim to surpass or correct the Revelation of which Christ is the fulfillment, as is the case in certain non-Christian religions and also in certain recent sects which base themselves on such "revelations."

IN BRIEF

68   By love, God has revealed himself and given himself to man. He has thus provided the definitive, superabundant answer to the questions that man asks himself about the meaning and purpose of his life.

69   God has revealed himself to man by gradually communicating his own mystery in deeds and in words.

70   Beyond the witness to himself that God gives in created things, he manifested himself to our first parents, spoke to them and, after the fall, promised them salvation (cf. *Gen* 3:15) and offered them his covenant.

71   God made an everlasting covenant with Noah and with all living beings (cf. *Gen* 9:16). It will remain in force as long as the world lasts.

72   God chose Abraham and made a covenant with him and his descendants. By the covenant God formed his people and revealed his law to them through Moses.

---

28   *DV* 4; cf. *1 Tim* 6:14; *Titus* 2:13.

Through the prophets, he prepared them to accept the salvation destined for all humanity.

73   God has revealed himself fully by sending his own Son, in whom he has established his covenant for ever. The Son is his Father's definitive Word; so there will be no further Revelation after him.

ARTICLE 2
THE TRANSMISSION OF DIVINE REVELATION

74   God "desires all men to be saved and to come to the knowledge of the truth":[29] that is, of Christ Jesus.[30] Christ must be
851 proclaimed to all nations and individuals, so that this revelation may reach to the ends of the earth:

> God graciously arranged that the things he had once revealed for the salvation of all peoples should remain in their entirety, throughout the ages, and be transmitted to all generations.[31]

I.   THE APOSTOLIC TRADITION

75   "Christ the Lord, in whom the entire Revelation of the most high God is summed up, commanded the apostles to preach the Gospel, which had been promised beforehand by the prophets, and which he fulfilled in his own person and promulgated with his own lips. In preaching the Gospel, they were to communicate the gifts of God to all men. This Gospel was to be the source of all
171 saving truth and moral discipline."[32]

In the apostolic preaching . . .

76   In keeping with the Lord's command, the Gospel was handed on in two ways:

– *orally* "by the apostles who handed on, by the spoken word of their preaching, by the example they gave, by the institutions they established, what they themselves had received – whether from the

---

29 *1 Tim* 2:4
30 Cf. *Jn* 14:6.
31 *DV* 7; cf. *2 Cor* 1:20; 3:16-4:6.
32 *DV* 7; cf. *Mt* 28:19-20; *Mk* 16:15.

lips of Christ, from his way of life and his works, or whether they had learned it at the prompting of the Holy Spirit";[33]

– *in writing* "by those apostles and other men associated with the apostles who, under the inspiration of the same Holy Spirit, committed the message of salvation to writing."[34]

... continued in apostolic succession

77   "In order that the full and living Gospel might always be preserved in the Church the apostles left bishops as their successors. They gave them 'their own position of teaching authority.'"[35]   *861*
Indeed, "the apostolic preaching, which is expressed in a special way in the inspired books, was to be preserved in a continuous line of succession until the end of time."[36]

78   This living transmission, accomplished in the Holy Spirit, is called Tradition, since it is distinct from Sacred Scripture, though closely connected to it. Through Tradition, "the Church, in her *174* doctrine, life, and worship perpetuates and transmits to every *1124, 2651* generation all that she herself is, all that she believes."[37] "The sayings of the holy Fathers are a witness to the life-giving presence of this Tradition, showing how its riches are poured out in the practice and life of the Church, in her belief and her prayer."[38]

79   The Father's self-communication made through his Word in the Holy Spirit, remains present and active in the Church: "God, who spoke in the past, continues to converse with the Spouse of his beloved Son. And the Holy Spirit, through whom the living voice of the Gospel rings out in the Church – and through her in the world – leads believers to the full truth, and makes the Word of Christ dwell in them in all its richness."[39]

---

33   *DV* 7.
34   *DV* 7.
35   *DV* 7 § 2; St. Irenaeus, *Adv. haeres.* 3, 3, 1: PG 7, 848; Harvey, 2, 9.
36   *DV* 8 § 1.
37   *DV* 8 § 1.
38   *DV* 8 § 3.
39   *DV* 8 § 3; cf. *Col* 3:16.

II.   THE RELATIONSHIP BETWEEN TRADITION
         AND SACRED SCRIPTURE

One common source . . .

80   "Sacred Tradition and Sacred Scripture, then, are bound closely together and communicate one with the other. For both of them, flowing out from the same divine well-spring, come together in some fashion to form one thing and move towards the same goal."[40] Each of them makes present and fruitful in the Church the mystery of Christ, who promised to remain with his own "always, to the close of the age."[41]

. . . two distinct modes of transmission

81   "*Sacred Scripture* is the speech of God as it is put down in writing under the breath of the Holy Spirit."[42]

113   "And [Holy] *Tradition* transmits in its entirety the Word of God which has been entrusted to the apostles by Christ the Lord and the Holy Spirit. It transmits it to the successors of the apostles so that, enlightened by the Spirit of truth, they may faithfully preserve, expound, and spread it abroad by their preaching."[43]

82   As a result the Church, to whom the transmission and interpretation of Revelation is entrusted, "does not derive her certainty about all revealed truths from the holy Scriptures alone. Both Scripture and Tradition must be accepted and honored with equal sentiments of devotion and reverence."[44]

Apostolic Tradition and ecclesial traditions

83   The Tradition here in question comes from the apostles and hands on what they received from Jesus' teaching and example and what they learned from the Holy Spirit. The first generation of Christians did not yet have a written New Testament, and the New Testament itself demonstrates the process of living Tradition.

1202, 2041   Tradition is to be distinguished from the various theological,
2684 disciplinary, liturgical, or devotional traditions, born in the local churches over time. These are the particular forms, adapted to different places and

---

40   *DV* 9.
41   *Mt* 28:20.
42   *DV* 9.
43   *DV* 9.
44   *DV* 9.

times, in which the great Tradition is expressed. In the light of Tradition, these traditions can be retained, modified or even abandoned under the guidance of the Church's magisterium.

III.   THE INTERPRETATION OF THE HERITAGE OF FAITH

The heritage of faith entrusted to the whole of the Church

84   The apostles entrusted the "Sacred deposit" of the faith (the *depositum fidei*),[45] contained in Sacred Scripture and Tradition, to the whole of the Church. "By adhering to [this heritage] the *857, 871* entire holy people, united to its pastors, remains always faithful to the teaching of the apostles, to the brotherhood, to the breaking of *2033* bread and the prayers. So, in maintaining, practicing, and professing the faith that has been handed on, there should be a remarkable harmony between the bishops and the faithful."[46]

The Magisterium of the Church

85   "The task of giving an authentic interpretation of the Word of God, whether in its written form or in the form of Tradition, has been entrusted to the living, teaching office of the Church alone. Its authority in this matter is exercised in the name of Jesus *888-892* Christ."[47] This means that the task of interpretation has been *2032-2040* entrusted to the bishops in communion with the successor of Peter, the Bishop of Rome.

86   "Yet this Magisterium is not superior to the Word of God, but is its servant. It teaches only what has been handed on to it. At the divine command and with the help of the Holy Spirit, it listens to this devotedly, guards it with dedication, and expounds it *688* faithfully. All that it proposes for belief as being divinely revealed is drawn from this single deposit of faith."[48]

87   Mindful of Christ's words to his apostles: "He who hears *1548* you, hears me,"[49] the faithful receive with docility the teachings *2037* and directives that their pastors give them in different forms.

---

45   *DV* 10 § 1;cf. *1 Tim* 6:20; *2 Tim* 1:12-14 (Vulg.).
46   *DV* 10 § 1; cf. *Acts* 2:42 (Gk.); Pius XII, apostolic constitution, *Munificentissimus Deus*, November 1, 1950: AAS 42 (1950), 756, taken along with the words of St. Cyprian, *Epist.* 66, 8: CSEL 3, 2, 733: "The Church is the people united to its Priests, the flock adhering to its Shepherd."
47   *DV* 10 § 2.
48   *DV* 10 § 2.
49   *Lk* 10:16; cf. *LG* 20.

The dogmas of the faith

88   The Church's Magisterium exercises the authority it holds from Christ to the fullest extent when it defines dogmas, that is, when it proposes truths contained in divine Revelation or having a necessary connection with them, in a form obliging the Christian people to an irrevocable adherence of faith.

89   There is an organic connection between our spiritual life
2625   and the dogmas. Dogmas are lights along the path of faith; they illuminate it and make it secure. Conversely, if our life is upright, our intellect and heart will be open to welcome the light shed by the dogmas of faith.[50]

90   The mutual connections between dogmas, and their coherence, can be found in the whole of the Revelation of the mystery of
114, 158   Christ.[51] "In Catholic doctrine there exists an order or 'hierarchy'
234   of truths, since they vary in their relation to the foundation of the Christian faith."[52]

The supernatural sense of faith

91   All the faithful share in understanding and handing on
737   revealed truth. They have received the anointing of the Holy Spirit, who instructs them[53] and guides them into all truth.[54]

92   "The whole body of the faithful . . . cannot err in matters of belief. This characteristic is shown in the supernatural apprecia-
785   tion of faith (*sensus fidei*) on the part of the whole people, when, 'from the bishops to the last of the faithful,' they manifest a universal consent in matters of faith and morals."[55]

93   "By this appreciation of the faith, aroused and sustained by the Spirit of truth, the People of God, guided by the sacred
889   teaching authority (*Magisterium*), . . . receives . . . the faith, once for all delivered to the saints. . . . The People unfailingly adheres to this faith, penetrates it more deeply with right judgment, and applies it more fully in daily life."[56]

---

50   Cf. *Jn* 8:31-32.
51   Cf. Vatican Council I: DS 3016: *nexus mysteriorum; LG* 25.
52   *UR* 11.
53   Cf. *1 Jn* 2:20, 27.
54   Cf. *Jn* 16:13.
55   *LG* 12; cf. St. Augustine, *De praed. sanct.* 14, 27: PL 44, 980.
56   *LG* 12; cf. *Jude* 3.

Growth in understanding the faith

94   Thanks to the assistance of the Holy Spirit, the understanding of both the realities and the words of the heritage of faith *66* is able to grow in the life of the Church:

– "through the contemplation and study of believers who ponder *2651* these things in their hearts";[57] it is in particular "theological research [which] deepens knowledge of revealed truth."[58]

– "from the intimate sense of spiritual realities which [believers] *2038, 2518* experience,"[59] the sacred Scriptures "grow with the one who reads them."[60]

– "from the preaching of those who have received, along with their right of succession in the episcopate, the sure charism of truth."[61]

95   "It is clear therefore that, in the supremely wise arrangement of God, sacred Tradition, Sacred Scripture, and the Magisterium of the Church are so connected and associated that one of them cannot stand without the others. Working together, each in its own way, under the action of the one Holy Spirit, they all contribute effectively to the salvation of souls."[62]

IN BRIEF

96   What Christ entrusted to the apostles, they in turn handed on by their preaching and writing, under the inspiration of the Holy Spirit, to all generations, until Christ returns in glory.

97   "Sacred Tradition and Sacred Scripture make up a single sacred deposit of the Word of God" (*DV* 10), in which, as in a mirror, the pilgrim Church contemplates God, the source of all her riches.

98   "The Church, in her doctrine, life, and worship, perpetuates and transmits to every generation all that she herself is, all that she believes" (*DV* 8 §1).

---

57   *DV* 8 § 2; cf. *Lk* 2:19, 51.
58   *GS* 62 § 7; cf. *GS* 44 § 2; *DV* 23, 24; *UR* 4.
59   *DV* 8 § 2.
60   St. Gregory the Great, *Hom. in Ez.* 1, 7, 8: PL 76, 843 D.
61   *DV* 8 § 2.
62   *DV* 10 § 3.

99   Thanks to its supernatural sense of faith, the People of God as a whole never ceases to welcome, to penetrate more deeply, and to live more fully from the gift of divine Revelation.

100   The task of interpreting the Word of God authentically has been entrusted solely to the Magisterium of the Church, that is, to the Pope and to the bishops in communion with him.

ARTICLE 3
SACRED SCRIPTURE

I.   CHRIST – THE UNIQUE WORD OF SACRED SCRIPTURE

101   In order to reveal himself to men, in the condescension of his goodness God speaks to them in human words: "Indeed the words of God, expressed in the words of men, are in every way like human language, just as the Word of the eternal Father, when he took on himself the flesh of human weakness, became like men."[63]

102   Through all the words of Sacred Scripture, God speaks only one single Word, his one Utterance in whom he expresses himself completely:[64]

65, 2763

426-429
> You recall that one and the same Word of God extends throughout Scripture, that it is one and the same Utterance that resounds in the mouths of all the sacred writers, since he who was in the beginning God with God has no need of separate syllables; for he is not subject to time.[65]

103   For this reason, the Church has always venerated the Scriptures as she venerates the Lord's Body. She never ceases to present to the faithful the bread of life, taken from the one table of God's Word and Christ's Body.[66]

1100, 1184
1378

104   In Sacred Scripture, the Church constantly finds her nourishment and her strength, for she welcomes it not as a human word, "but as what it really is, the word of God."[67] "In the sacred books,

---

63 *DV* 13.
64 Cf. *Heb* 1:1-3.
65 St. Augustine, *En. in Ps.* 103, 4, 1: PL 37, 1378; cf. *Ps* 104; *Jn* 1:1.
66 Cf. *DV* 21.
67 *1 Thess* 2:13; cf. *DV* 24.

the Father who is in heaven comes lovingly to meet his children, and talks with them."[68]

II.   INSPIRATION AND TRUTH OF SACRED SCRIPTURE

105   *God is the author of Sacred Scripture.* "The divinely revealed realities, which are contained and presented in the text of Sacred Scripture, have been written down under the inspiration of the Holy Spirit."[69]

"For Holy Mother Church, relying on the faith of the apostolic age, accepts as sacred and canonical the books of the Old and the New Testaments, whole and entire, with all their parts, on the grounds that, written under the inspiration of the Holy Spirit, they have God as their author and have been handed on as such to the Church herself."[70]

106   God inspired the human authors of the sacred books. "To compose the sacred books, God chose certain men who, all the while he employed them in this task, made full use of their own faculties and powers so that, though he acted in them and by them, it was as true authors that they consigned to writing whatever he wanted written, and no more."[71]

107   The inspired books teach the truth. "Since therefore all that the inspired authors or sacred writers affirm should be regarded as affirmed by the Holy Spirit, we must acknowledge that the books of Scripture firmly, faithfully, and without error teach that truth which God, for the sake of our salvation, wished to see confided to the Sacred Scriptures."[72]   *702*

108   Still, the Christian faith is not a "religion of the book." Christianity is the religion of the "Word" of God, "not a written and mute word, but incarnate and living."[73] If the Scriptures are not to remain a dead letter, Christ, the eternal Word of the living God, must, through the Holy Spirit, "open [our] minds to understand the Scriptures."[74]

---

68   *DV* 21.
69   *DV* 11.
70   *DV* 11; cf. *Jn* 20:31; 2 *Tim* 3:16; 2 *Pet* 1:19-21; 3:15-16.
71   *DV* 11.
72   *DV* 11.
73   St. Bernard, *S. missus est hom.* 4, 11: PL 183, 86.
74   Cf. *Lk* 24:45.

III.   THE HOLY SPIRIT, INTERPRETER OF SCRIPTURE

109   In Sacred Scripture, God speaks to man in a human way. To interpret Scripture correctly, the reader must be attentive to what the human authors truly wanted to affirm and to what God wanted to reveal to us by their words.[75]

110   In order to discover *the sacred authors' intention*, the reader must take into account the conditions of their time and culture, the literary genres in use at that time, and the modes of feeling, speaking, and narrating then current. "For the fact is that truth is differently presented and expressed in the various types of historical writing, in prophetical and poetical texts, and in other forms of literary expression."[76]

111   But since Sacred Scripture is inspired, there is another and no less important principle of correct interpretation, without which Scripture would remain a dead letter. "Sacred Scripture must be read and interpreted in the light of the same Spirit by whom it was written."[77]

    The Second Vatican Council indicates three criteria for interpreting Scripture in accordance with the Spirit who inspired it.[78]

112   1. *Be especially attentive "to the content and unity of the whole Scripture."* Different as the books which comprise it may be, Scrip-
128 ture is a unity by reason of the unity of God's plan, of which Christ
368 Jesus is the center and heart, open since his Passover.[79]

> The phrase "heart of Christ" can refer to Sacred Scripture, which makes known his heart, closed before the Passion, as the Scripture was obscure. But the Scripture has been opened since the Passion; since those who from then on have understood it, consider and discern in what way the prophecies must be interpreted.[80]

113   2. *Read the Scripture within "the living Tradition of the whole Church."* According to a saying of the Fathers, Sacred Scripture is
81 written principally in the Church's heart rather than in documents and records, for the Church carries in her Tradition the living memorial of God's Word, and it is the Holy Spirit who gives her

---

75 Cf. *DV* 12 § 1.
76 *DV* 12 § 2.
77 *DV* 12 § 3.
78 Cf. *DV* 12 § 4.
79 Cf. *Lk* 24:25-27, 44-46.
80 St. Thomas Aquinas, *Expos. in Ps* 21,11; cf. *Ps* 22:15.

the spiritual interpretation of the Scripture ("according to the spiritual meaning which the Spirit grants to the Church"[81]).

114   3. *Be attentive to the analogy of faith.*[82] By "analogy of faith"   *90* we mean the coherence of the truths of faith among themselves and within the whole plan of Revelation.

The senses of Scripture

115   According to an ancient tradition, one can distinguish between two *senses* of Scripture: the literal and the spiritual, the latter being subdivided into the allegorical, moral, and anagogical senses. The profound concordance of the four senses guarantees all its richness to the living reading of Scripture in the Church.

116   The *literal sense* is the meaning conveyed by the words of Scripture and discovered by exegesis, following the rules of sound interpretation: "All other senses of Sacred Scripture are based on the literal."[83]   *110*

117   The *spiritual sense.* Thanks to the unity of God's plan, not only the text of Scripture but also the realities and events about which it speaks can   *1101* be signs.

   1. The *allegorical sense.* We can acquire a more profound understanding of events by recognizing their significance in Christ; thus the crossing of the Red Sea is a sign or type of Christ's victory and also of Christian Baptism.[84]

   2. The *moral sense.* The events reported in Scripture ought to lead us to act justly. As St. Paul says, they were written "for our instruction."[85]

   3. The *anagogical sense* (Greek: *anagoge*, "leading"). We can view realities and events in terms of their eternal significance, leading us toward our true homeland: thus the Church on earth is a sign of the heavenly Jerusalem.[86]

118   A medieval couplet summarizes the significance of the four senses:

> The Letter speaks of deeds; Allegory to faith;
> The Moral how to act; Anagogy our destiny.[87]

119   "It is the task of exegetes to work, according to these rules, toward a better understanding and explanation of the meaning of Sacred Scripture in order that their research may help the Church   *94*

---

81   Origen, *Hom. in Lev.* 5, 5: PG 12, 454D.
82   Cf. *Rom* 12:6.
83   St. Thomas Aquinas, *STh* I, 1, 10, *ad* 1.
84   Cf. *1 Cor* 10:2.
85   *1 Cor* 10:11; cf. *Heb* 3-4:11.
86   Cf. *Rev* 21:1-22:5.
87   *Lettera gesta docet, quid credas allegoria, moralis quid agas, quo tendas anagogia.*

to form a firmer judgment. For, of course, all that has been said about the manner of interpreting Scripture is ultimately subject to the judgment of the Church which exercises the divinely conferred commission and ministry of watching over and interpreting the Word of God."[88]

113
> But I would not believe in the Gospel, had not the authority of the Catholic Church already moved me.[89]

IV.   THE CANON OF SCRIPTURE

120   It was by the apostolic Tradition that the Church discerned
1117 which writings are to be included in the list of the sacred books.[90] This complete list is called the canon of Scripture. It includes 46 books for the Old Testament (45 if we count Jeremiah and Lamentations as one) and 27 for the New.[91]

> *The Old Testament:* Genesis, Exodus, Leviticus, Numbers, Deuteronomy, Joshua, Judges, Ruth, 1 *and* 2 Samuel, 1 *and* 2 Kings, 1 *and* 2 Chronicles, Ezra and Nehemiah, Tobit, Judith, Esther, 1 *and* 2 Maccabees, Job, Psalms, Proverbs, Ecclesiastes, *the* Song of Songs, *the* Wisdom of Solomon, Sirach (Ecclesiasticus), Isaiah, Jeremiah, Lamentations, Baruch, Ezekiel, Daniel, Hosea, Joel, Amos, Obadiah, Jonah, Micah, Nahum, Habakkuk, Zephaniah, Haggai, Zachariah and Malachi.

> *The New Testament: the Gospels according to* Matthew, Mark, Luke *and* John, the Acts of the Apostles, *the* Letters of St. Paul to the Romans, 1 *and* 2 Corinthians, Galatians, Ephesians, Philippians, Colossians, 1 *and* 2 Thessalonians, 1 *and* 2 Timothy, Titus, Philemon, *the* Letter to the Hebrews, *the* Letters of James, 1 *and* 2 Peter, 1, 2, *and* 3 John, *and* Jude, *and* Revelation (the Apocalypse).

The Old Testament

121   The Old Testament is an indispensable part of Sacred
1093 Scripture. Its books are divinely inspired and retain a permanent value,[92] for the Old Covenant has never been revoked.

122   Indeed, "the economy of the Old Testament was deliberately so oriented that it should prepare for and declare in prophecy
702, 763 the coming of Christ, redeemer of all men."[93] "Even though they contain matters imperfect and provisional,"[94] the books of the Old
708 Testament bear witness to the whole divine pedagogy of God's

---

88   *DV* 12 § 3.
89   St. Augustine, *Contra epistolam Manichaei,* 5, 6: PL 42, 176.
90   Cf. *DV* 8 § 3.
91   Cf. DS 179; 1334-1336; 1501-1504.
92   Cf. *DV* 14.

saving love: these writings "are a storehouse of sublime teaching on God and of sound wisdom on human life, as well as a wonderful treasury of prayers; in them, too, the mystery of our salvation is present in a hidden way."[95]   *2568*

123   Christians venerate the Old Testament as true Word of God. The Church has always vigorously opposed the idea of rejecting the Old Testament under the pretext that the New has rendered it void (Marcionism).

The New Testament

124   "The Word of God, which is the power of God for salvation to everyone who has faith, is set forth and displays its power in a most wonderful way in the writings of the New Testament"[96] which hand on the ultimate truth of God's Revelation. Their central object is Jesus Christ, God's incarnate Son: his acts, teachings, Passion and glorification, and his Church's beginnings under the Spirit's guidance.[97]

125   The *Gospels* are the heart of all the Scriptures "because they are our principal source for the life and teaching of the Incarnate   *515* Word, our Savior."[98]

126   We can distinguish three stages in the formation of the Gospels:

1. *The life and teaching of Jesus.* The Church holds firmly that the four Gospels, "whose historicity she unhesitatingly affirms, faithfully hand on what Jesus, the Son of God, while he lived among men, really did and taught for their eternal salvation, until the day when he was taken up."[99]

2. *The oral tradition.* "For, after the ascension of the Lord, the   *76* apostles handed on to their hearers what he had said and done, but with that fuller understanding which they, instructed by the glorious events of Christ and enlightened by the Spirit of truth, now enjoyed."[100]

3. *The written Gospels.* "The sacred authors, in writing the four   *76* Gospels, selected certain of the many elements which had been handed on, either orally or already in written form; others they synthesized or explained with an eye to the situation of the churches, while sustaining the

---

93   *DV* 15.
94   *DV* 15.
95   *DV* 15.
96   *DV* 17; cf. *Rom* 1:16.
97   Cf. *DV* 20.
98   *DV* 18.
99   *DV* 19; cf. *Acts* 1:1-2.
100   *DV* 19.

form of preaching, but always in such a fashion that they have told us the honest truth about Jesus."[101]

1154 **127**   The fourfold Gospel holds a unique place in the Church, as is evident both in the veneration which the liturgy accords it and in the surpassing attraction it has exercised on the saints at all times:

> There is no doctrine which could be better, more precious and more splendid than the text of the Gospel. Behold and retain what our Lord and Master, Christ, has taught by his words and accomplished by his deeds.[102]

2705

> But above all it's the Gospels that occupy my mind when I'm at prayer; my poor soul has so many needs, and yet this is the one thing needful. I'm always finding fresh lights there, hidden and enthralling meanings.[103]

The unity of the Old and New Testaments

128   The Church, as early as apostolic times,[104] and then constantly in her Tradition, has illuminated the unity of the divine plan in the two Testaments through typology, which discerns in God's *1094* works of the Old Covenant prefigurations of what he accom-*489* plished in the fullness of time in the person of his incarnate Son.

129   Christians therefore read the Old Testament in the light of Christ crucified and risen. Such typological reading discloses the *681* inexhaustible content of the Old Testament; but it must not make us forget that the Old Testament retains its own intrinsic value as Revelation reaffirmed by our Lord himself.[105] Besides, the New *2055* Testament has to be read in the light of the Old. Early Christian catechesis made constant use of the Old Testament.[106] As an old saying put it, the New Testament lies hidden in the Old and the *1968* Old Testament is unveiled in the New.[107]

130   Typology indicates the dynamic movement toward the fulfillment of the divine plan when "God [will] be everything to everyone."[108] Nor do the calling of the patriarchs and the exodus from Egypt, for example, lose their own value in God's plan, from the mere fact that they were intermediate stages.

---

101   *DV* 19.
102   St. Caesaria the Younger to St. Richildis and St. Radegunde, *SCh* 345, 480.
103   St. Thérèse of Lisieux, *ms. autob.* A 83v.
104   Cf. *1 Cor* 10:6, 11; *Heb* 10:1; *1 Pet* 3:21.
105   Cf. *Mk* 12:29-31.
106   Cf. *1 Cor* 5:6-8; 10:1-11.
107   Cf. St. Augustine, *Quaest. in Hept.* 2, 73: PL 34, 623; cf. *DV* 16.
108   *1 Cor* 15:28.

V. SACRED SCRIPTURE IN THE LIFE OF THE CHURCH

131   "And such is the force and power of the Word of God that it can serve the Church as her support and vigor and the children of the Church as strength for their faith, food for the soul, and a pure and lasting font of spiritual life."[109] Hence "access to Sacred Scripture ought to be open wide to the Christian faithful."[110]

132   "Therefore, the 'study of the sacred page' should be the very soul of sacred theology. The ministry of the Word, too — pastoral preaching, catechetics, and all forms of Christian instruc-   94
tion, among which the liturgical homily should hold pride of place — is healthily nourished and thrives in holiness through the Word of Scripture."[111]

133   The Church "forcefully and specifically exhorts all the Christian faithful . . . to learn 'the surpassing knowledge of Jesus   2653
Christ,' by frequent reading of the divine Scriptures. 'Ignorance of   1792
the Scriptures is ignorance of Christ.'"[112]

IN BRIEF

134   "All Sacred Scripture is but one book, and that one book is Christ, because all divine Scripture speaks of Christ, and all divine Scripture is fulfilled in Christ" (Hugh of St. Victor, *De arca Noe* 2, 8: PL 176, 642).

135   "The Sacred Scriptures contain the Word of God and, because they are inspired they are truly the Word of God" (*DV* 24).

136   God is the author of Sacred Scripture because he inspired its human authors; he acts in them and by means of them. He thus gives assurance that their writings teach without error his saving truth (cf. *DV* 11).

137   Interpretation of the inspired Scripture must be attentive above all to what God wants to reveal through the sacred authors for our salvation. What comes from the

---

109   *DV* 21.
110   *DV* 22.
111   *DV* 24.
112   *DV* 25; cf. *Phil* 3:8 and St. Jerome, *Commentariorum in Isaiam libri xviii* prol.: PL 24, 17b.

Spirit is not fully "understood except by the Spirit's action" (cf. Origen, *Hom. in Ex.* 4, 5: PG 12, 320).

138   The Church accepts and venerates as inspired the 46 books of the Old Testament and the 27 books of the New.

139   The four Gospels occupy a central place because Christ Jesus is their center.

140   The unity of the two Testaments proceeds from the unity of God's plan and his Revelation. The Old Testament prepares for the New and the New Testament fulfills the Old; the two shed light on each other; both are true Word of God.

141   "The Church has always venerated the divine Scriptures as she venerated the Body of the Lord" (*DV* 21): both nourish and govern the whole Christian life. "Your word is a lamp to my feet and a light to my path" (*Ps* 119:105; cf. *Isa* 50:4).

CHAPTER THREE
MAN'S RESPONSE TO GOD

142 *By his Revelation*, "the invisible God, from the fullness of his love, addresses men as his friends, and moves among them, in order to invite and receive them into his own company."[1] The adequate response to this invitation is faith.

1102

143 *By faith*, man completely submits his intellect and his will to God.[2] With his whole being man gives his assent to God the revealer. Sacred Scripture calls this human response to God, the author of revelation, "the obedience of faith."[3]

2087

ARTICLE 1
I BELIEVE

I.   THE OBEDIENCE OF FAITH

144 To obey (from the Latin *ob-audire*, to "hear or listen to") in faith is to submit freely to the word that has been heard, because its truth is guaranteed by God, who is Truth itself. Abraham is the model of such obedience offered us by Sacred Scripture. The Virgin Mary is its most perfect embodiment.

Abraham – "father of all who believe"

145 The *Letter to the Hebrews*, in its great eulogy of the faith of Israel's ancestors, lays special emphasis on Abraham's faith: "By faith, Abraham obeyed when he was called to go out to a place *59, 2570* which he was to receive as an inheritance; and he went out, not knowing where he was to go."[4] By faith, he lived as a stranger and pilgrim in the promised land.[5] By faith, Sarah was given to conceive the son of the promise. And by faith Abraham offered his only *489* son in sacrifice.[6]

146 Abraham thus fulfills the definition of faith in *Hebrews 1819* 11:1: "Faith is the assurance of things hoped for, the conviction of things not seen":[7] "Abraham believed God, and it was reckoned to

---

1   *DV* 2; cf. *Col* 1:15; *1 Tim* 1:17; *Ex* 33:11; *Jn* 15:14-15; *Bar* 3:38 (Vulg.).
2   Cf. *DV* 5.
3   Cf. *Rom* 1:5; 16:26.
4   *Heb* 11:8; cf. *Gen* 12:1-4.
5   Cf. *Gen* 23:4.
6   Cf. *Heb* 11:17.

him as righteousness."[8] Because he was "strong in his faith," Abraham became the "father of all who believe."[9]

147   The Old Testament is rich in witnesses to this faith. The
839 *Letter to the Hebrews* proclaims its eulogy of the exemplary faith of the ancestors who "received divine approval."[10] Yet "God had foreseen something better for us": the grace of believing in his Son Jesus, "the pioneer and perfecter of our faith."[11]

Mary – "Blessed is she who believed"

148   The Virgin Mary most perfectly embodies the obedience
494, 2617 of faith. By faith Mary welcomes the tidings and promise brought by the angel Gabriel, believing that "with God nothing will be impossible" and so giving her assent: "Behold I am the handmaid of the Lord; let it be [done] to me according to your word."[12]
506 Elizabeth greeted her: "Blessed is she who believed that there would be a fulfillment of what was spoken to her from the Lord."[13] It is for this faith that all generations have called Mary blessed.[14]

149   Throughout her life and until her last ordeal[15] when Jesus
969 her son died on the cross, Mary's faith never wavered. She never
507, 829 ceased to believe in the fulfillment of God's word. And so the Church venerates in Mary the purest realization of faith.

II.   "I KNOW WHOM I HAVE BELIEVED"[16]

To believe in God alone

150   Faith is first of all a personal adherence of man to God. At the same time, and inseparably, it is a *free assent to the whole truth*
222 *that God has revealed.* As personal adherence to God and assent to his truth, Christian faith differs from our faith in any human person. It is right and just to entrust oneself wholly to God and to

---

7   *Heb* 11:1.
8   *Rom* 4:3; cf. *Gen* 15:6.
9   *Rom* 4:11, 18; 4:20; cf. *Gen* 15:5.
10 *Heb* 11:2, 39.
11 *Heb* 11:40; 12:2.
12 *Lk* 1:37-38; cf. *Gen* 18:14.
13 *Lk* 1:45.
14 Cf. *Lk* 1:48.
15 Cf. *Lk* 2:35.
16 *2 Tim* 1:12.

believe absolutely what he says. It would be futile and false to place such faith in a creature.[17]

To believe in Jesus Christ, the Son of God

151   For a Christian, believing in God cannot be separated from believing in the One he sent, his "beloved Son," in whom the Father is "well pleased"; God tells us to listen to him.[18] The Lord himself said to his disciples: "Believe in God, believe also in me."[19] We can believe in Jesus Christ because he is himself God, the Word made flesh: "No one has ever seen God; the only Son, who is in the bosom of the Father, he has made him known."[20] Because he "has seen the   424 Father," Jesus Christ is the only one who knows him and can reveal him.[21]

To believe in the Holy Spirit

152   One cannot believe in Jesus Christ without sharing in his Spirit. It is the Holy Spirit who reveals to men who Jesus is. For "no   243, 683 one can say 'Jesus is Lord,' except by the Holy Spirit,"[22] who "searches everything, even the depths of God. . . . No one comprehends the thoughts of God, except the Spirit of God."[23] Only God knows God completely: we believe *in* the Holy Spirit because he is God.

    The Church never ceases to proclaim her faith in one only God: 232 *Father, Son, and Holy Spirit.*

III.   THE CHARACTERISTICS OF FAITH

Faith is a grace

153   When St. Peter confessed that Jesus is the Christ, the Son of the living God, Jesus declared to him that this revelation did not   552 come "from flesh and blood," but from "my Father who is in heaven."[24] *Faith is a gift of God, a supernatural virtue infused by him.* "Before this faith can be exercised, man must have the grace of God

---

17   Cf. *Jer* 17:5-6; *Ps* 40:5; 146:3-4.
18   *Mk* 1:11; cf. 9:7.
19   *Jn* 14:1.
20   *Jn* 1:18.
21   *Jn* 6:46; cf. *Mt* 11:27.
22   *1 Cor* 12:3.
23   *1 Cor* 2:10-11.
24   *Mt* 16:17; cf. *Gal* 1:15; *Mt* 11:25.

1814 to move and assist him; he must have the interior helps of the Holy
1996 Spirit, who moves the heart and converts it to God, who opens the
2606 eyes of the mind and 'makes it easy for all to accept and believe the
truth.'"[25]

Faith is a human act

154   Believing is possible only by grace and the interior helps
1749 of the Holy Spirit. But it is no less true that believing is an authentically human act. Trusting in God and cleaving to the truths he has
revealed are contrary neither to human freedom nor to human
reason. Even in human relations it is not contrary to our dignity to
believe what other persons tell us about themselves and their
intentions or to trust their promises (for example, when a man and
2126 a woman marry) to share a communion of life with one another. If
this is so, still less is it contrary to our dignity to "yield by faith the
full submission of . . . intellect and will to God who reveals,"[26] and
to share in an interior communion with him.

155   In faith, the human intellect and will cooperate with divine
2008 grace: "Believing is an act of the intellect assenting to the divine
truth by command of the will moved by God through grace."[27]

Faith and understanding

156   What moves us to believe is not the fact that revealed
truths appear as true and intelligible in the light of our natural
1063 reason: we believe "because of the authority of God himself who
reveals them, who can neither deceive nor be deceived."[28] So "that
the submission of our faith might nevertheless be in accordance
2465 with reason, God willed that external proofs of his Revelation
should be joined to the internal helps of the Holy Spirit."[29] Thus
548 the miracles of Christ and the saints, prophecies, the Church's
812 growth and holiness, and her fruitfulness and stability "are the
most certain signs of divine Revelation, adapted to the intelligence
of all"; they are "motives of credibility" (*motiva credibilitatis*), which
show that the assent of faith is "by no means a blind impulse of the
mind."[30]

---

25   *DV* 5; cf. DS 377; 3010.
26   *Dei Filius* 3: DS 3008.
27   St. Thomas Aquinas, *STh* II-II, 2, 9; cf. *Dei Filius* 3: DS 3010.
28   *Dei Filius* 3: DS 3008.
29   *Dei Filius* 3: DS 3009.
30   *Dei Filius* 3: DS 3008-10; cf. *Mk* 16:20; *Heb* 2:4.

157   Faith is *certain*. It is more certain than all human knowledge because it is founded on the very word of God who cannot lie. To be sure, revealed truths can seem obscure to human reason and experience, but "the certainty that the divine light gives is greater than that which the light of natural reason gives."[31] "Ten thousand difficulties do not make one doubt."[32]   *2088*

158   "Faith *seeks understanding*":[33] it is intrinsic to faith that a believer desires to know better the One in whom he has put his faith and to understand better what He has revealed; a more *2705* penetrating knowledge will in turn call forth a greater faith, increasingly set afire by love. The grace of faith opens "the eyes of *1827* your hearts"[34] to a lively understanding of the contents of Revelation: that is, of the totality of God's plan and the mysteries of faith, of their connection with each other and with Christ, the center of *90* the revealed mystery. "The same Holy Spirit constantly perfects faith by his gifts, so that Revelation may be more and more profoundly understood."[35] In the words of St. Augustine, "I believe, *2518* in order to understand; and I understand, the better to believe."[36]

159   *Faith and science*: "Though faith is above reason, there can never be any real discrepancy between faith and reason. Since the same God who reveals mysteries and infuses faith has bestowed the light of reason on the human mind, God cannot deny himself, *283* nor can truth ever contradict truth."[37] "Consequently, methodical research in all branches of knowledge, provided it is carried out in a truly scientific manner and does not override moral laws, can never conflict with the faith, because the things of the world and *2293* the things of faith derive from the same God. The humble and persevering investigator of the secrets of nature is being led, as it were, by the hand of God in spite of himself, for it is God, the conserver of all things, who made them what they are."[38]

---

31 St. Thomas Aquinas, *STh* II-II, 171, 5, obj. 3.
32 John Henry Cardinal Newman, *Apologia pro vita sua* (London: Longman, 1878), 239.
33 St. Anselm, *Prosl. prooem.*: PL 153, 225A.
34 *Eph* 1:18.
35 *DV* 5.
36 St. Augustine, *Sermo* 43, 7, 9: PL 38, 257-258.
37 *Dei Filius* 4: DS 3017.
38 *GS* 36 § 1.

The freedom of faith

160   To be human, "man's response to God by faith must be
free, and . . . therefore nobody is to be forced to embrace the faith
1738, 2106 against his will. The act of faith is of its very nature a free act."[39]
"God calls men to serve him in spirit and in truth. Consequently
they are bound to him in conscience, but not coerced. . . . This fact
received its fullest manifestation in Christ Jesus."[40] Indeed, Christ
invited people to faith and conversion, but never coerced them.
"For he bore witness to the truth but refused to use force to impose
it on those who spoke against it. His kingdom . . . grows by the love
616   with which Christ, lifted up on the cross, draws men to himself."[41]

The necessity of faith

161   Believing in Jesus Christ and in the One who sent him for
our salvation is necessary for obtaining that salvation.[42] "Since
432, 1257 'without faith it is impossible to please [God]' and to attain to the
fellowship of his sons, therefore without faith no one has ever
attained justification, nor will anyone obtain eternal life 'but he
846   who endures to the end.'"[43]

Perseverance in faith

162   Faith is an entirely free gift that God makes to man. We can
lose this priceless gift, as St. Paul indicated to St. Timothy: "Wage
2089   the good warfare, holding faith and a good conscience. By rejecting
conscience, certain persons have made shipwreck of their faith."[44]
To live, grow, and persevere in the faith until the end we must
nourish it with the word of God; we must beg the Lord to increase
1037, 2016, our faith;[45] it must be "working through charity," abounding in
2573, 2849 hope, and rooted in the faith of the Church.[46]

---

39   *DH* 10; cf. CIC, can. 748 § 2.
40   *DH* 11.
41   *DH* 11; cf. *Jn* 18:37; 12:32.
42   Cf. *Mk* 16:16; *Jn* 3:36; 6:40 *et al.*
43   *Dei Filius* 3: DS 3012; cf. *Mt* 10:22; 24:13 and *Heb* 11:6; Council of Trent: DS
     1532.
44   *1 Tim* 1:18-19.
45   Cf. *Mk* 9:24; *Lk* 17:5; 22:32.
46   *Gal* 5:6; *Rom* 15:13; cf. *Jas* 2:14-26.

Faith – the beginning of eternal life

163   Faith makes us taste in advance the light of the beatific vision, the goal of our journey here below. Then we shall see God   *1088* "face to face," "as he is."[47] So faith is already the beginning of eternal life:

> When we contemplate the blessings of faith even now, as if gazing at a reflection in a mirror, it is as if we already possessed the wonderful things which our faith assures us we shall one day enjoy.[48]

164   Now, however, "we walk by faith, not by sight";[49] we perceive God as "in a mirror, dimly" and only "in part."[50] Even though enlightened by him in whom it believes, faith is often lived in darkness and can be put to the test. The world we live in often   *2846* seems very far from the one promised us by faith. Our experiences of evil and suffering, injustice, and death, seem to contradict the Good News; they can shake our faith and become a temptation   *309* against it.   *1502, 1006*

165   It is then we must turn to the *witnesses of faith*: to Abraham, who "in hope . . . believed against hope";[51] to the Virgin Mary, who, in "her pilgrimage of faith," walked into the "night of faith"[52] in sharing the darkness of her son's suffering and death; and to so   *2719* many others: "Therefore, since we are surrounded by so great a cloud of witnesses, let us also lay aside every weight, and sin which clings so closely, and let us run with perseverance the race that is set before us, looking to Jesus the pioneer and perfecter of our faith."[53]

ARTICLE 2
WE BELIEVE

---

166   Faith is a personal act – the free response of the human person to the initiative of God who reveals himself. But faith is not   *875* an isolated act. No one can believe alone, just as no one can live alone. You have not given yourself faith as you have not given

---

47   *1 Cor* 13:12; *1 Jn* 3:2.
48   St. Basil, *De Spiritu Sancto*, 15, 36: PG 32, 132; cf. St. Thomas Aquinas, *STh* II-II, 4, 1.
49   *2 Cor* 5:7.
50   *1 Cor* 13:12.
51   *Rom* 4:18.
52   *LG* 58; John Paul II, *RMat* 18.
53   *Heb* 12:1-2.

yourself life. The believer has received faith from others and should hand it on to others. Our love for Jesus and for our neighbor impels us to speak to others about our faith. Each believer is thus a link in the great chain of believers. I cannot believe without being carried by the faith of others, and by my faith I help support others in the faith.

167 "I believe" (*Apostles' Creed*) is the faith of the Church professed personally by each believer, principally during Baptism. "We believe" (*Niceno-Constantinopolitan Creed*) is the faith of the Church confessed by the bishops assembled in council or more generally by the liturgical assembly of believers. "I believe" is also the Church, our mother, responding to God by faith as she teaches us to say both "I believe" and "We believe."

1124

2040

I.   "LORD, LOOK UPON THE FAITH OF YOUR CHURCH"

168   It is the Church that believes first, and so bears, nourishes, and sustains my faith. Everywhere, it is the Church that first confesses the Lord: "Throughout the world the holy Church acclaims you," as we sing in the hymn *"Te Deum"*; with her and in her, we are won over and brought to confess: "I believe," "We believe." It is through the Church that we receive faith and new life in Christ by Baptism. In the *Rituale Romanum*, the minister of Baptism asks the catechumen: "What do you ask of God's Church?" And the answer is: "Faith." "What does faith offer you?" "Eternal life."[54]

1253

169   Salvation comes from God alone; but because we receive the life of faith through the Church, she is our mother: "We believe the Church as the mother of our new birth, and not *in* the Church as if she were the author of our salvation."[55] Because she is our mother, she is also our teacher in the faith.

750

2030

II.   THE LANGUAGE OF FAITH

170   We do not believe in formulas, but in those realities they express, which faith allows us to touch. "The believer's act [of faith] does not terminate in the propositions, but in the realities [which they express]."[56] All the same, we do approach these realities with the help of formulations of the faith which permit us to express the

186

---

54   *Roman Ritual*, Rite of baptism of adults.
55   Faustus of Riez, *De Spiritu Sancto* 1, 2: PL 62, 11.
56   St. Thomas Aquinas, *STh* II-II, 1, 2, *ad* 2.

faith and to hand it on, to celebrate it in community, to assimilate and live on it more and more.

171 The Church, "the pillar and bulwark of the truth," faith- *78, 857, 84* fully guards "the faith which was once for all delivered to the *185* saints." She guards the memory of Christ's words; it is she who from generation to generation hands on the apostles' confession of faith.[57] As a mother who teaches her children to speak and so to understand and communicate, the Church our Mother teaches us the language of faith in order to introduce us to the understanding and the life of faith.

III.   ONLY ONE FAITH

172 Through the centuries, in so many languages, cultures, peoples, and nations, the Church has constantly confessed this one faith, received from the one Lord, transmitted by one Baptism, and grounded in the conviction that all people have only one God and *813* Father.[58] St. Irenaeus of Lyons, a witness of this faith, declared:

173 "Indeed, the Church, though scattered throughout the whole world, even to the ends of the earth, having received the faith from the apostles and their disciples . . . guards [this preaching *830* and faith] with care, as dwelling in but a single house, and similarly believes as if having but one soul and a single heart, and preaches, teaches, and hands on this faith with a unanimous voice, as if possessing only one mouth."[59]

174 "For though languages differ throughout the world, the content of the Tradition is one and the same. The Churches established in Germany have no other faith or Tradition, nor do those *78* of the Iberians, nor those of the Celts, nor those of the East, of Egypt, of Libya, nor those established at the center of the world. . . ."[60] The Church's message "is true and solid, in which one and the same way of salvation appears throughout the whole world."[61]

175 "We guard with care the faith that we have received from the Church, for without ceasing, under the action of God's Spirit, this deposit of great price, as if in an excellent vessel, is constantly being renewed and causes the very vessel that contains it to be renewed."[62]

---

57   *1 Tim* 3:15; *Jude* 3.
58   Cf. *Eph* 4:4-6.
59   St. Irenaeus, *Adv. haeres.* 1, 10, 1-2: PG 7/1, 549-552.
60   St. Irenaeus, *Adv. haeres.* 1, 10, 1-2: PG 7/1, 552-553.
61   St. Irenaeus, *Adv. haeres.* 5, 20, 1: PG 7/2, 1177.

IN BRIEF

176   Faith is a personal adherence of the whole man to God
       who reveals himself. It involves an assent of the intel-
       lect and will to the self-revelation God has made
       through his deeds and words.

177   "To believe" has thus a twofold reference: to the per-
       son and to the truth: to the truth, by trust in the person
       who bears witness to it.

178   We must believe in no one but God: the Father, the
       Son, and the Holy Spirit.

179   Faith is a supernatural gift from God. In order to
       believe, man needs the interior helps of the Holy Spirit.

180   "Believing" is a human act, conscious and free, corre-
       sponding to the dignity of the human person.

181   "Believing" is an ecclesial act. The Church's faith pre-
       cedes, engenders, supports, and nourishes our faith.
       The Church is the mother of all believers. "No one can
       have God as Father who does not have the Church as
       Mother" (St. Cyprian, *De unit.* 6: PL 4, 519).

182   We believe all "that which is contained in the word of
       God, written or handed down, and which the Church
       proposes for belief as divinely revealed" (Paul VI,
       CPG, § 20).

183   Faith is necessary for salvation. The Lord himself af-
       firms: "He who believes and is baptized will be saved;
       but he who does not believe will be condemned" (*Mk*
       16:16).

184   "Faith is a foretaste of the knowledge that will make
       us blessed in the life to come" (St. Thomas Aquinas,
       Comp. theol. 1, 2).

---

62   St. Irenaeus, *Adv. haeres.* 3, 24, 1: PG 7/1, 966.

THE CREDO

The Apostles' Creed

I believe in God,
  the Father almighty,
  creator of heaven and earth.

I believe in Jesus Christ,
  his only Son, our Lord.

He was conceived by the
  power of the Holy Spirit
  and born of the Virgin Mary.

He suffered under Pontius Pilate,
  was crucified, died, and was
  buried.
He descended into hell.

On the third day he rose again.

He ascended into heaven
  and is seated at the right
  hand of the Father.
He will come again to judge
  the living and the dead.

The Nicene Creed

We believe in one God,
  the Father, the Almighty,
  maker of heaven and earth,
  of all that is, seen and unseen.

We believe in one Lord, Jesus
  Christ,
  the only Son of God
  eternally begotten of the
  Father,
  God from God, Light from
  Light,
  true God from true God,
  begotten, not made, one in
  Being with the Father.
  Through him all things were
  made.
  For us men and for our
  salvation
  he came down from heaven:
by the power of the Holy Spirit
  he was born of the Virgin
  Mary,
  and became man.

For our sake he was crucified
  under Pontius Pilate;
  he suffered, died, and was
  buried.

On the third day he rose again
  in fulfillment of the Scriptures;

he ascended into heaven
  and is seated at the right
  hand of the Father.
  He will come again in glory
  to judge the living and the dead,
  and his kingdom will have
  no end.

The Apostles' Creed

I believe in the Holy Spirit,
the holy catholic Church,
the communion of saints,
the forgiveness of sins,
the resurrection of the body,
and the life everlasting.
Amen.

The Nicene Creed

We believe in the Holy Spirit,
the Lord, the giver of life,
who proceeds from the
Father and the Son.
With the Father and the Son
he is worshiped and
glorified.
He has spoken through the
Prophets.
We believe in one holy
catholic and apostolic
Church.
We acknowledge one
baptism for the forgiveness
of sins.
We look for the resurrection
of the dead,
and the life of the world to
come. Amen.

Section Two
The Profession
of the Christian Faith

The Creeds

185　Whoever says "I believe" says "I pledge myself to what *we* believe." Communion in faith needs a common language of faith, *171, 949* normative for all and uniting all in the same confession of faith.

186　From the beginning, the apostolic Church expressed and handed on her faith in brief formulae for all.[1] But already early on, the Church also wanted to gather the essential elements of its faith into organic and articulated summaries, intended especially for candidates for Baptism:

> This synthesis of faith was not made to accord with human opinions, but rather what was of the greatest importance was gathered from all the Scriptures, to present the one teaching of the faith in its entirety. And just as the mustard seed contains a great number of branches in a tiny grain, so too this summary of faith encompassed in a few words the whole knowledge of the true religion contained in the Old and New Testaments.[2]

187　Such syntheses are called "professions of faith" since they summarize the faith that Christians profess. They are called "creeds" on account of what is usually their first word in Latin: *credo* ("I believe"). They are also called "symbols of faith."

188　The Greek work *symbolon* meant half of a broken object, for example, a seal presented as a token of recognition. The broken parts were placed together to verify the bearer's identity. The symbol of faith, then, is a sign of recognition and communion between believers. *Symbolon* also means a gathering, collection, or summary. A symbol of faith is a summary of the principal truths of the faith and therefore serves as the first and fundamental point of reference for catechesis.

189　The first "profession of faith" is made during Baptism. The symbol of faith is first and foremost the *baptismal* creed. Since *1237, 232* Baptism is given "in the name of the Father and of the Son and of the Holy Spirit,"[3] the truths of faith professed during Baptism are

---

1 Cf. *Rom* 10:9; *1 Cor* 15:3-5, etc.
2 St. Cyril of Jerusalem, *Catech. illum.* 5, 12: PG 33, 521-524.
3 *Mt* 28:19.

articulated in terms of their reference to the three persons of the Holy Trinity.

190   And so the Creed is divided into three parts: "the first part speaks of the first divine Person and the wonderful work of creation; the next speaks of the second divine Person and the mystery of his redemption of men; the final part speaks of the third divine Person, the origin and source of our sanctification."[4] These are "the three chapters of our [baptismal] seal."[5]

191   "These three parts are distinct although connected with one another. According to a comparison often used by the Fathers, we call them *articles*. Indeed, just as in our bodily members there are certain articulations which distinguish and separate them, so too in this profession of faith, the name *articles* has justly and rightly been given to the truths we must believe particularly and distinctly."[6] In accordance with an ancient tradition, already attested to by St. Ambrose, it is also customary to reckon the articles of the Creed as *twelve*, thus symbolizing the fullness of the apostolic faith by the number of the apostles.[7]

192   Through the centuries many professions or symbols of faith have been articulated in response to the needs of the different eras: the creeds of the different apostolic and ancient Churches,[8] e.g., the *Quicumque*, also called the Athanasian Creed;[9] the professions of faith of certain Councils, such as Toledo, Lateran, Lyons, Trent;[10] or the symbols of certain popes, e.g., the *Fides Damasi*[11] or the *Credo of the People of God* of Paul VI.[12]

193   None of the creeds from the difference stages in the Church's life can be considered superseded or irrelevant. They help us today to attain and deepen the faith of all times by means of the different summaries made of it.

Among all the creeds, two occupy a special place in the Church's life:

---

4   *Roman Catechism*, I, 1, 3.
5   St. Irenaeus, *Dem. ap.* 100: SCh 62, 170.
6   *Roman Catechism*, I, 1, 4.
7   Cf. St. Ambrose, *Expl. symb.* 8.
8   Cf. DS 1-64.
9   Cf. DS 75-76.
10 Cf. DS 525-541; 800-802; 851-861; 1862-1870.
11 Cf. DS 71-72.
12 Paul VI, *CPG* (1968).

194   *The Apostles' Creed* is so called because it is rightly considered to be a faithful summary of the apostles' faith. It is the ancient baptismal symbol of the Church of Rome. Its great authority arises from this fact: it is "the Creed of the Roman Church, the See of Peter, the first of the apostles, to which he brought the common faith."[13]

195   *The Niceno-Constantinopolitan* or *Nicene Creed* draws its great authority from the fact that it stems from the first two ecumenical Councils (in 325 and 381). It remains common to all the great Churches of both East and West to this day.   *242, 245, 465*

196   Our presentation of the faith will follow the Apostles' Creed, which constitutes, as it were, "the oldest Roman catechism." The presentation will be completed however by constant references to the Nicene Creed which is often more explicit and more detailed.

197   As on the day of our Baptism, when our whole life was entrusted to the "standard of teaching,"[14] let us embrace the Creed   *1064* of our life-giving faith. To say the Credo with faith is to enter into communion with God, Father, Son, and Holy Spirit, and also with the whole Church which transmits the faith to us and in whose midst we believe:

> This Creed is the spiritual seal, our hearts's meditation and   *1274* an ever-present guardian; it is, unquestionably, the treasure of our soul.[15]

---

13   St. Ambrose, *Expl. symb.* 7: PL 17, 1196.
14   *Rom* 6:17.
15   St. Ambrose, *Expl. symb.* 1: PL 17, 1193.

CHAPTER ONE
I BELIEVE IN GOD THE FATHER

198   Our profession of faith begins with *God*, for God is the First and the Last,[1] the beginning and the end of everything. The Credo begins with God the *Father*, for the Father is the first divine person of the Most Holy Trinity; our Creed begins with the creation of heaven and earth, for creation is the beginning and the foundation of all God's works.

ARTICLE 1
"I BELIEVE IN GOD THE FATHER ALMIGHTY, CREATOR OF HEAVEN AND EARTH"

Paragraph 1. I Believe in God

199   "I believe in God": this first affirmation of the Apostles' Creed is also the most fundamental. The whole Creed speaks of God, and when it also speaks of man and of the world it does so in relation to God. The other articles of the Creed all depend on the first, just as the remaining Commandments make the first explicit.
2083 The other articles help us to know God better as he revealed himself progressively to men. "The faithful first profess their belief in God."[2]

I.   "I BELIEVE IN ONE GOD"

200   These are the words with which the Niceno-Constanti-nopolitan Creed begins. The confession of God's oneness, which
2085 has its roots in the divine revelation of the Old Covenant, is inseparable from the profession of God's existence and is equally fundamental. God is unique; there is only one God: "The Christian faith confesses that God is one in nature, substance, and essence."[3]

201   To Israel, his chosen, God revealed himself as the only One:
2083 "Hear, O Israel: The LORD our God is one LORD; and you shall love the LORD your God with all your heart, and with all your soul, and with all your might."[4] Through the prophets, God calls Israel and

---

1 Cf. *Isa* 44:6.
2 *Roman Catechism*, I, 2, 2.
3 *Roman Catechism*, I, 2, 2.
4 *Deut* 6:4-5.

all nations to turn to him, the one and only God: "Turn to me and be saved, all the ends of the earth! For I am God, and there is no other . . . . To me every knee shall bow, every tongue shall swear. 'Only in the LORD, it shall be said of me, are righteousness and strength.'"[5]

202 Jesus himself affirms that God is "the one Lord" whom you must love "with all your heart, and with all your soul, and with all your mind, and with all your strength."[6] At the same time Jesus gives us to understand that he himself is "the Lord."[7] To confess *446* that Jesus is Lord is distinctive of Christian faith. This is not contrary to belief in the One God. Nor does believing in the Holy Spirit as "Lord and giver of life" introduce any division into the *152* One God:

> We firmly believe and confess without reservation that there *42*
> is only one true God, eternal, infinite (*immensus*) and un-
> changeable, incomprehensible, almighty, and ineffable, the
> Father and the Son and the Holy Spirit; three persons indeed,
> but one essence, substance or nature entirely simple.[8]

II. GOD REVEALS HIS NAME

203 God revealed himself to his people Israel by making his name known to them. A name expresses a person's essence and identity and the meaning of this person's life. God has a name; he *2143* is not an anonymous force. To disclose one's name is to make oneself known to others; in a way it is to hand oneself over by becoming accessible, capable of being known more intimately and addressed personally.

204 God revealed himself progressively and under different names to his people, but the revelation that proved to be the fundamental one for both the Old and the New Covenants was the revelation of the divine name to Moses in the theophany of the *63* burning bush, on the threshold of the Exodus and of the covenant on Sinai.

---

5   *Isa* 45: 22-24; cf. *Phil* 2:10-11.
6   *Mk* 12:29-30.
7   Cf. *Mk* 12:35-37.
8   Lateran Council IV: DS 800.

The living God

205   God calls Moses from the midst of a bush that burns
without being consumed: "I am the God of your father, the God of
2575 Abraham, the God of Isaac, and the God of Jacob."[9] God is the God
of the fathers, the One who had called and guided the patriarchs
in their wanderings. He is the faithful and compassionate God who
remembers them and his promises; he comes to free their descendants from slavery. He is the God who, from beyond space and
268 time, can do this and wills to do it, the God who will put his
almighty power to work for this plan.

"I Am who I Am"

> Moses said to God, "If I come to the people of Israel and say
> to them, 'The God of your fathers has sent me to you', and
> they ask me, 'What is his name?' what shall I say to them?"
> God said to Moses, "I AM WHO I AM." And he said, "Say this
> to the people of Israel, 'I Am has sent me to you' . . . this is
> my name for ever, and thus I am to be remembered through-
> out all generations."[10]

206   In revealing his mysterious name, YHWH ("I AM HE WHO
IS," "I AM WHO AM" or "I AM WHO I AM"), God says who he is and
by what name he is to be called. This divine name is mysterious
just as God is mystery. It is at once a name revealed and something
like the refusal of a name, and hence it better expresses God as what
he is – infinitely above everything that we can understand or say:
he is the "hidden God," his name is ineffable, and he is the God
43 who makes himself close to men.[11]

207   By revealing his name God at the same time reveals his
faithfulness which is from everlasting to everlasting, valid for the
past ("I am the God of your fathers"), as for the future ("I will be
with you").[12] God, who reveals his name as "I AM," reveals himself
as the God who is always there, present to his people in order to
save them.

724 **208**   Faced with God's fascinating and mysterious presence,
man discovers his own insignificance. Before the burning bush,
Moses takes off his sandals and veils his face in the presence of
God's holiness.[13] Before the glory of the thrice-holy God, Isaiah

---

9   *Ex* 3:6.
10 *Ex* 3:13-15.
11 Cf. *Isa* 45:15; *Judg* 13:18.
12 *Ex* 3:6, 12.

cries out: "Woe is me! I am lost; for I am a man of unclean lips."[14] Before the divine signs wrought by Jesus, Peter exclaims: "Depart from me, for I am a sinful man, O Lord."[15] But because God is holy,   *448* he can forgive the man who realizes that he is a sinner before him: "I will not execute my fierce anger . . . for I am God and not man, the Holy One in your midst."[16] The apostle John says likewise: "We   *388* shall . . . reassure our hearts before him whenever our hearts condemn us; for God is greater than our hearts, and he knows everything."[17]

209   Out of respect for the holiness of God, the people of Israel do not pronounce his name. In the reading of Sacred Scripture, the revealed name (Yhwh) is replaced by the divine title "LORD" (in Hebrew *Adonai*, in Greek *Kyrios*). It is under this title that the divinity of Jesus will be acclaimed: "Jesus is LORD."   *446*

"A God merciful and gracious"

210   After Israel's sin, when the people had turned away from God to worship the golden calf, God hears Moses' prayer of inter- cession and agrees to walk in the midst of an unfaithful people,   *2116, 2577* thus demonstrating his love.[18] When Moses asks to see his glory, God responds "I will make all my goodness pass before you, and will proclaim before you my name 'the LORD' [YHWH]."[19] Then the LORD passes before Moses and proclaims, "YHWH, YHWH, a God merciful and gracious, slow to anger, and abounding in steadfast love and faithfulness"; Moses then confesses that the LORD is a forgiving God.[20]

211   The divine name, "I Am" or "He Is," expresses God's faithfulness: despite the faithlessness of men's sin and the punish- ment it deserves, he keeps "steadfast love for thousands."[21] By going so far as to give up his own Son for us, God reveals that he   *604* is "rich in mercy."[22] By giving his life to free us from sin, Jesus reveals that he himself bears the divine name: "When you have lifted up the Son of man, then you will realize that 'I Am.'"[23]

---

13 Cf. *Ex* 3:5-6.
14 *Isa* 6:5.
15 *Lk* 5:8.
16 *Hos* 11:9.
17 *1 Jn* 3:19-20.
18 Cf. *Ex* 32; 33:12-17.
19 *Ex* 33:18-19.
20 *Ex* 34:5-6; cf. 34:9.
21 *Ex* 34:7.
22 *Eph* 2:4.
23 *Jn* 8:28 (Gk.).

God alone IS

212   Over the centuries, Israel's faith was able to manifest and deepen realization of the riches contained in the revelation of the divine name. God is unique; there are no other gods besides him.[24] He transcends the world and history. He made heaven and earth:

42 "They will perish, but you endure; they will all wear out like a garment . . . but you are the same, and your years have no end."[25]

469, 2086 In God "there is no variation or shadow due to change."[26] God is "He who Is," from everlasting to everlasting, and as such remains ever faithful to himself and to his promises.

213   The revelation of the ineffable name "I Am who Am" contains then the truth that God alone IS. The Greek Septuagint translation of the Hebrew Scriptures, and following it the Church's Tradition, understood the divine name in this sense: God is the fullness of Being and of every perfection, without origin and

41 without end. All creatures receive all that they are and have from him; but he alone *is* his very being, and he is of himself everything that he is.

III.   GOD, "HE WHO *IS*," IS TRUTH AND LOVE

214   God, "He who is," revealed himself to Israel as the one "abounding in steadfast love and faithfulness."[27] These two terms express summarily the riches of the divine name. In all his works

1062 God displays not only his kindness, goodness, grace, and steadfast love, but also his trustworthiness, constancy, faithfulness, and truth. "I give thanks to your name for your steadfast love and your faithfulness."[28] He is the Truth, for "God is light and in him there is no darkness"; "God is love," as the apostle John teaches.[29]

---

24   Cf. *Isa* 44:6.
25   *Ps* 102:26-27
26   *Jas* 1:17.
27   *Ex* 34:6.
28   *Ps* 138:2; cf. *Ps* 85:11.
29   *1 Jn* 1:5; 4:8.

God is truth

215   "The sum of your word is truth; and every one of your righteous ordinances endures forever."[30] "And now, O LORD God, you are God, and your words are true;"[31] this is why God's *2465* promises always come true.[32] God is Truth itself, whose words *1063, 156* cannot deceive. This is why one can abandon oneself in full trust to the truth and faithfulness of his word in all things. The beginning of sin and of man's fall was due to a lie of the tempter who induced doubt of God's word, kindness, and faithfulness. *397*

216   God's truth is his wisdom, which commands the whole created order and governs the world.[33] God, who alone made *295* heaven and earth, can alone impart true knowledge of every cre- *32* ated thing in relation to himself.[34]

217   God is also truthful when he reveals himself – the teaching that comes from God is "true instruction."[35] When he sends his Son into the world it will be "to bear witness to the truth":[36] "We know that the Son of God has come and has given us understanding, to *851* know him who is true."[37] *2466*

God is love

218   In the course of its history, Israel was able to discover that God had only one reason to reveal himself to them, a single motive for choosing them from among all peoples as his special posses- sion: his sheer gratuitous love.[38] And thanks to the prophets Israel *295* understood that it was again out of love that God never stopped saving them and pardoning their unfaithfulness and sins.[39]

219   God's love for Israel is compared to a father's love for his *239* son. His love for his people is stronger than a mother's for her *796, 458* children. God loves his people more than a bridegroom his be- loved; his love will be victorious over even the worst infidelities

---

30   *Ps* 119:160.
31   *2 Sam* 7:28.
32   Cf. *Deut* 7:9.
33   Cf. *Wis* 13:1-9.
34   Cf. *Ps* 115:15; *Wis* 7:17-21.
35   *Mal* 2:6.
36   *Jn* 18:37.
37   *1 Jn* 5:20; cf. *Jn* 17:3.
38   Cf. *Deut* 4:37; 7:8; 10:15.
39   Cf. *Isa* 43:1-7; *Hos* 2.

and will extend to his most precious gift: "God so loved the world that he gave his only Son."[40]

220   God's love is "everlasting":[41] "For the mountains may depart and the hills be removed, but my steadfast love shall not depart from you."[42] Through Jeremiah, God declares to his people, "I have loved you with an everlasting love; therefore I have continued my faithfulness to you."[43]

221   But St. John goes even further when he affirms that "God
733 is love":[44] God's very being is love. By sending his only Son and
851 the Spirit of Love in the fullness of time, God has revealed his
257 innermost secret:[45] God himself is an eternal exchange of love, Father, Son, and Holy Spirit, and he has destined us to share in that exchange.

IV.   THE IMPLICATIONS OF FAITH IN ONE GOD

222   Believing in God, the only One, and loving him with all our being has enormous consequences for our whole life.

400 **223**   *It means coming to know God's greatness and majesty*: "Behold, God is great, and we know him not."[46] Therefore, we must "serve God first."[47]

2637 **224**   *It means living in thanksgiving*: if God is the only One, everything we are and have comes from him: "What have you that you did not receive?"[48] "What shall I render to the Lord for all his bounty to me?"[49]

356, 360 **225**   *It means knowing the unity and true dignity of all men*: Every-
1700, 1934 one is made in the image and likeness of God.[50]

339, 2402 **226**   *It means making good use of created things*: faith in God, the
2415 only One, leads us to use everything that is not God only insofar as it brings us closer to him, and to detach ourselves from it insofar as it turns us away from him:

---

40   *Jn* 3:16; cf. *Hos* 11:1; *Isa* 49:14-15; 62:4-5; *Ezek* 16; *Hos* 11.
41   *Isa* 54:8.
42   *Isa* 54:10; cf. 54:8.
43   *Jer* 31:3.
44   *1 Jn* 4:8, 16.
45   Cf. *1 Cor* 2:7-16; *Eph* 3:9-12.
46   *Job* 36:26.
47   St. Joan of Arc.
48   *1 Cor* 4:7.
49   *Ps* 116:12.
50   *Gen* 1:26.

> My Lord and my God, take from me everything that distances me from you.
> My Lord and my God, give me everything that brings me closer to you.
> My Lord and my God, detach me from myself to give my all to you.[51]

227   *It means trusting God in every circumstance,* even in adver-   *313, 2090*
sity. A prayer of St. Teresa of Jesus wonderfully expresses this trust:

> Let nothing trouble you / Let nothing frighten you
> Everything passes / God never changes
> Patience / Obtains all
> Whoever has God / Wants for nothing   *2830*
> God alone is enough.[52]   *1723*

IN BRIEF

228   "Hear, O Israel, the LORD our God is one LORD . . ." (*Deut* 6:4; *Mk* 12:29). "The supreme being must be unique, without equal . . . . If God is not one, he is not God" (Tertullian, *Adv. Marc.,* 1, 3, 5: PL 2, 274).

229   Faith in God leads us to turn to him alone as our first origin and our ultimate goal, and neither to prefer anything to him nor to substitute anything for him.

230   Even when he reveals himself, God remains a mystery beyond words: "If you understood him, it would not be God" (St. Augustine, *Sermo* 52, 6, 16: PL 38:360 and *Sermo* 117, 3,5: PL 38, 663).

231   The God of our faith has revealed himself as He who is; and he has made himself known as "abounding in steadfast love and faithfulness" (*Ex* 34:6). God's very being is Truth and Love.

---

51   St. Nicholas of Flüe; cf. *Mt* 5:29-30; 16:24-26.
52   St. Teresa of Jesus, *Poesías* 30, in *The Collected Works of St. Teresa of Avila,* vol. III, tr. by K. Kavanaugh, OCD, and O. Rodriguez, OCD (Washington DC: Institute of Carmelite Studies, 1985), 386 no. 9, tr. by John Wall.

Paragraph 2. The Father

I. "IN THE NAME OF THE FATHER AND OF THE SON AND OF THE HOLY SPIRIT"

232   Christians are baptized "in the name of the Father and of the Son and of the Holy Spirit."[53] Before receiving the sacrament,
189, 1223 they respond to a three-part question when asked to confess the Father, the Son, and the Spirit: "I do." "The faith of all Christians rests on the Trinity."[54]

233   Christians are baptized in the *name* of the Father and of the Son and of the Holy Spirit: not in their *names*,[55] for there is only one God, the almighty Father, his only Son, and the Holy Spirit: the Most Holy Trinity.

234   The mystery of the Most Holy Trinity is the central mystery of Christian faith and life. It is the mystery of God in himself. It is
2157 therefore the source of all the other mysteries of faith, the light that enlightens them. It is the most fundamental and essential teaching in the "hierarchy of the truths of faith."[56] The whole history of
90   salvation is identical with the history of the way and the means by
1449 which the one true God, Father, Son, and Holy Spirit, reveals himself to men "and reconciles and unites with himself those who turn away from sin."[57]

235   This paragraph expounds briefly (I) how the mystery of the Blessed Trinity was revealed, (II) how the Church has articulated the doctrine of the faith regarding this mystery, and (III) how, by the divine missions of the Son and the Holy Spirit, God the Father fulfills the "plan of his loving goodness" of creation, redemption, and sanctification.

236   The Fathers of the Church distinguish between theology (*theolo-*
1066 *gia*) and economy (*oikonomia*). "Theology" refers to the mystery of God's inmost life within the Blessed Trinity and "economy" to all the works by which God reveals himself and communicates his life. Through the *oik-onomia* the *theologia* is revealed to us; but conversely, the *theologia* illumi-
259 nates the whole *oikonomia*. God's works reveal who he is in himself; the mystery of his inmost being enlightens our understanding of all his works. So it is, analogously, among human persons. A person discloses himself

---

53 *Mt* 28:19.
54 St. Caesarius of Arles, *Sermo 9, Exp. symb.*: CCL 103, 47.
55 Cf. Profession of faith of Pope Vigilius I (552): DS 415.
56 *GCD* 43.
57 *GCD* 47.

in his actions, and the better we know a person, the better we understand his actions.

237 The Trinity is a mystery of faith in the strict sense, one of *50* the "mysteries that are hidden in God, which can never be known unless they are revealed by God."[58] To be sure, God has left traces of his Trinitarian being in his work of creation and in his Revelation throughout the Old Testament. But his inmost Being as Holy Trinity is a mystery that is inaccessible to reason alone or even to Israel's faith before the Incarnation of God's Son and the sending of the Holy Spirit.

II.   THE REVELATION OF GOD AS TRINITY

The Father revealed by the Son

238 Many religions invoke God as "Father." The deity is often considered the "father of gods and of men." In Israel, God is called "Father" inasmuch as he is Creator of the world.[59] Even more, God is Father because of the covenant and the gift of the law to Israel, "his first-born son."[60] God is also called the Father of the king of Israel. Most especially he is "the Father of the poor," of the orphaned and the widowed, who are under his loving protection.[61] *2443*

239 By calling God "Father," the language of faith indicates two main things: that God is the first origin of everything and transcendent authority; and that he is at the same time goodness and loving care for all his children. God's parental tenderness can also be expressed by the image of motherhood,[62] which emphasizes God's immanence, the intimacy between Creator and creature. The language of faith thus draws on the human experience of parents, who are in a way the first representatives of God for man. But this experience also tells us that human parents are fallible and can disfigure the face of fatherhood and motherhood. We ought therefore to recall that God transcends the human distinction between the sexes. He is neither man nor woman: he is God. He also *370, 2779* transcends human fatherhood and motherhood, although he is their origin and standard:[63] no one is father as God is Father.

240 Jesus revealed that God is Father in an unheard of sense: he is Father not only in being Creator; he is eternally Father by his relationship to his only Son who, reciprocally, is Son only in *2780* relation to his Father: "No one knows the Son except the Father, *441-445*

---

58   *Dei Filius* 4: DS 3015.
59   Cf. *Deut* 32:6; *Mal* 2:10.
60   *Ex* 4:22.
61   Cf. *2 Sam* 7:14; *Ps* 68:6.
62   Cf. *Isa* 66:13; *Ps* 131:2
63   Cf. *Ps* 27:10; *Eph* 3:14; *Isa* 49:15.

and no one knows the Father except the Son and anyone to whom the Son chooses to reveal him."[64]

241 For this reason the apostles confess Jesus to be the Word: "In the beginning was the Word, and the Word was with God, and the Word was God"; as "the image of the invisible God"; as the "radiance of the glory of God and the very stamp of his nature."[65]

242 Following this apostolic tradition, the Church confessed at the first ecumenical council at Nicaea (325) that the Son is "consubstantial" with the Father, that is, one only God with him.[66] The
465 second ecumenical council, held at Constantinople in 381, kept this expression in its formulation of the Nicene Creed and confessed "the only-begotten Son of God, eternally begotten of the Father, light from light, true God from true God, begotten not made, consubstantial with the Father."[67]

The Father and the Son revealed by the Spirit

243 Before his Passover, Jesus announced the sending of "an-
683 other Paraclete" (Advocate), the Holy Spirit. At work since creation, having previously "spoken through the prophets," the Spirit
2780 will now be with and in the disciples, to teach them and guide them
687 "into all the truth."[68] The Holy Spirit is thus revealed as another divine person with Jesus and the Father.

244 The eternal origin of the Holy Spirit is revealed in his mission in time. The Spirit is sent to the apostles and to the Church both by the Father in the name of the Son, and by the Son in person, once he had returned to the Father.[69] The sending of the person of the Spirit after Jesus' glorification[70] reveals in its fullness the mys-
732 tery of the Holy Trinity.

152 **245** The apostolic faith concerning the Spirit was confessed by the second ecumenical council at Constantinople (381): "We believe in the Holy Spirit, the Lord and giver of life, who proceeds from the Father."[71] By this confession, the Church recognizes the

---

64 *Mt* 11:27.
65 *Jn* 1:1; *Col* 1:15; *Heb* 1:3.
66 The English phrases "of one being" and "one in being" translate the Greek word *homoousios*, which was rendered in Latin by *consubstantialis*.
67 Niceno-Constantinopolitan Creed; cf. DS 150.
68 Cf. *Gen* 1:2; Nicene Creed (DS 150); *Jn* 14:17, 26; 16:13.
69 Cf. *Jn* 14:26; 15:26; 16:14.
70 Cf. *Jn* 7:39.
71 Nicene Creed; cf. DS 150.

Father as "the source and origin of the whole divinity."[72] But the eternal origin of the Spirit is not unconnected with the Son's origin: "The Holy Spirit, the third person of the Trinity, is God, one and equal with the Father and the Son, of the same substance and also of the same nature . . . . Yet he is not called the Spirit of the Father alone, . . . but the Spirit of both the Father and the Son."[73] The Creed of the Church from the Council of Constantinople confesses: "With the Father and the Son, he is worshipped and glorified."[74]

685

246 The Latin tradition of the Creed confesses that the Spirit "proceeds from the Father *and the Son (filioque)*." The Council of Florence in 1438 explains: "The Holy Spirit is eternally from Father and Son; He has his nature and subsistence at once (*simul*) from the Father and the Son. He proceeds eternally from both as from one principle and through one spiration . . . . And, since the Father has through generation given to the only-begotten Son everything that belongs to the Father, except being Father, the Son has also eternally from the Father, from whom he is eternally born, that the Holy Spirit proceeds from the Son."[75]

247 The affirmation of the *filioque* does not appear in the Creed confessed in 381 at Constantinople. But Pope St. Leo I, following an ancient Latin and Alexandrian tradition, had already confessed it dogmatically in 447,[76] even before Rome, in 451 at the Council of Chalcedon, came to recognize and receive the Symbol of 381. The use of this formula in the Creed was gradually admitted into the Latin liturgy (between the eighth and eleventh centuries). The introduction of the filioque into the Niceno-Constantinopolitan Creed by the Latin liturgy constitutes moreover, even today, a point of disagreement with the Orthodox Churches.

248 At the outset the Eastern tradition expresses the Father's character as first origin of the Spirit. By confessing the Spirit as he "who proceeds from the Father," it affirms that he *comes from* the Father *through* the Son.[77] The Western tradition expresses first the consubstantial communion between Father and Son, by saying that the Spirit proceeds from the Father and the Son (*filioque*). It says this, "legitimately and with good reason,"[78] for the eternal order of the divine persons in their consubstantial communion implies that the Father, as "the principle without principle,"[79] is the first origin of the Spirit, but also that as Father of the only Son, he is, with the Son, the single principle from which the Holy Spirit proceeds.[80] This

---

72 Council of Toledo VI (638): DS 490.
73 Council of Toledo XI (675): DS 527.
74 Nicene Creed; cf. DS 150.
75 Council of Florence (1439): DS 1300-1301.
76 Cf. Leo I, *Quam laudabiliter* (447): DS 284.
77 *Jn* 15:26; cf. *AG* 2.
78 Council of Florence (1439): DS 1302.
79 Council of Florence (1442): DS 1331.
80 Cf. Council of Lyons II (1274): DS 850.

legitimate complementarity, provided it does not become rigid, does not affect the identity of faith in the reality of the same mystery confessed.

III.   THE HOLY TRINITY IN THE TEACHING OF THE FAITH

The formation of the Trinitarian dogma

249   From the beginning, the revealed truth of the Holy Trinity has been at the very root of the Church's living faith, principally *683* by means of Baptism. It finds its expression in the rule of baptismal *189* faith, formulated in the preaching, catechesis, and prayer of the Church. Such formulations are already found in the apostolic writings, such as this salutation taken up in the Eucharistic liturgy: "The grace of the Lord Jesus Christ and the love of God and the fellowship of the Holy Spirit be with you all."[81]

250   During the first centuries the Church sought to clarify its Trinitarian faith, both to deepen its own understanding of the faith *94* and to defend it against the errors that were deforming it. This clarification was the work of the early councils, aided by the theological work of the Church Fathers and sustained by the Christian people's sense of the faith.

251   In order to articulate the dogma of the Trinity, the Church had to develop its own terminology with the help of certain notions of philosophical origin: "substance," "person" or "hypostasis," "relation," and so on. In doing this, she did not submit the faith to human wisdom, but gave a new and unprecedented meaning to these terms, which from then on would be used to signify an ineffable mystery, "infinitely beyond all that we can *170* humanly understand."[82]

252   The Church uses (I) the term "substance" (rendered also at times by "essence" or "nature") to designate the divine being in its unity, (II) the term "person" or "hypostasis" to designate the Father, Son, and Holy Spirit in the real distinction among them, and (III) the term "relation" to designate the fact that their distinction lies in the relationship of each to the others.

The dogma of the Holy Trinity

253   *The Trinity is One.* We do not confess three Gods, but one *2789* God in three persons, the "consubstantial Trinity."[83] The divine persons do not share the one divinity among themselves but each

---

81   *2 Cor* 13:13; cf. *1 Cor* 12:4-6; *Eph* 4:4-6.

82   Paul VI, *CPG* § 2.

83   Council of Constantinople II (553): DS 421.

of them is God whole and entire: "The Father is that which the Son is, the Son that which the Father is, the Father and the Son that which the Holy Spirit is, i.e., by nature one God."[84] In the words of the Fourth Lateran Council (1215): "Each of the persons is that supreme reality, viz., the divine substance, essence or nature."[85] *590*

254 *The divine persons are really distinct from one another.* "God is one but not solitary."[86] "Father," "Son," "Holy Spirit" are not simply names designating modalities of the divine being, for they *468, 689* are really distinct from one another: "He is not the Father who is the Son, nor is the Son he who is the Father, nor is the Holy Spirit he who is the Father or the Son."[87] They are distinct from one another in their relations of origin: "It is the Father who generates, the Son who is begotten, and the Holy Spirit who proceeds."[88] The divine Unity is Triune.

255 *The divine persons are relative to one another.* Because it does not divide the divine unity, the real distinction of the persons from one another resides solely in the relationships which relate them to one another: "In the relational names of the persons the Father is related to the Son, the Son to the Father, and the Holy Spirit to both. While they are called three persons in view of their relations, we *240* believe in one nature or substance."[89] Indeed "everything (in them) is one where there is no opposition of relationship."[90] "Because of that unity the Father is wholly in the Son and wholly in the Holy Spirit; the Son is wholly in the Father and wholly in the Holy Spirit; the Holy Spirit is wholly in the Father and wholly in the Son."[91]

256 St. Gregory of Nazianzus, also called "the Theologian," entrusts this summary of Trinitarian faith to the catechumens of *236, 684* Constantinople: *84*

> Above all guard for me this great deposit of faith for which I live and fight, which I want to take with me as a companion, and which makes me bear all evils and despise all pleasures: I mean the profession of faith in the Father and the Son and the Holy Spirit. I entrust it to you today. By it I am soon going to plunge you into water and raise you up from it. I give it to you as the companion and patron of your whole life. I give

---

84 Council of Toledo XI (675): DS 530:26.
85 Lateran Council IV (1215): DS 804.
86 *Fides Damasi*: DS 71.
87 Council of Toledo XI (675): DS 530:25.
88 Lateran Council IV (1215): DS 804.
89 Council of Toledo XI (675): DS 528.
90 Council of Florence (1442): DS 1330.
91 Council of Florence (1442): DS 1331.

you but one divinity and power, existing one in three, and containing the three in a distinct way. Divinity without disparity of substance or nature, without superior degree that raises up or inferior degree that casts down . . . the infinite co-naturality of three infinites. Each person considered in himself is entirely God . . . the three considered together . . . . I have not even begun to think of unity when the Trinity bathes me in its splendor. I have not even begun to think of the Trinity when unity grasps me. . . .[92]

IV.   THE DIVINE WORKS AND THE TRINITARIAN MISSIONS

257   "O blessed light, O Trinity and first Unity!"[93] God is eternal blessedness, undying life, unfading light. God is love:
221   Father, Son, and Holy Spirit. God freely wills to communicate the
758   glory of his blessed life. Such is the "plan of his loving kindness," conceived by the Father before the foundation of the world, in his beloved Son: "He destined us in love to be his sons" and "to be conformed to the image of his Son," through "the spirit of sonship."[94] This plan is a "grace [which] was given to us in Christ Jesus before the ages began," stemming immediately from Trinitarian love.[95] It unfolds in the work of creation, the whole history of
292   salvation after the fall, and the missions of the Son and the Spirit,
850   which are continued in the mission of the Church.[96]

258   The whole divine economy is the common work of the three divine persons. For as the Trinity has only one and the same nature, so too does it have only one and the same operation: "The Father, the Son, and the Holy Spirit are not three principles of
686   creation but one principle."[97] However each divine person performs the common work according to his unique personal property. Thus the Church confesses, following the New Testament, "one God and Father from whom all things are, and one Lord Jesus Christ, through whom all things are, and one Holy Spirit in whom all things are."[98] It is above all the divine missions of the Son's Incarnation and the gift of the Holy Spirit that show forth the properties of the divine persons.

---

92   St. Gregory of Nazianzus, *Oratio* 40, 41: PG 36, 417.
93   *LH,* Hymn for Evening Prayer.
94   *Eph* 1:4-5, 9; *Rom* 8:15, 29.
95   *2 Tim* 1:9-10.
96   Cf. *AG* 2-9.
97   Council of Florence (1442): DS 1331; cf. Council of Constantinople II (553): DS 421.
98   Council of Constantinople II: DS 421.

259   Being a work at once common and personal, the whole   *236*
divine economy makes known both what is proper to the divine
persons and their one divine nature. Hence the whole Christian life
is a communion with each of the divine persons, without in any
way separating them. Everyone who glorifies the Father does so
through the Son in the Holy Spirit; everyone who follows Christ
does so because the Father draws him and the Spirit moves him.[99]

260   The ultimate end of the whole divine economy is the entry
of God's creatures into the perfect unity of the Blessed Trinity.[100]
But even now we are called to be a dwelling for the Most Holy   *1050, 1721*
Trinity: "If a man loves me," says the Lord, "he will keep my word,   *1997*
and my Father will love him, and we will come to him, and make
our home with him":[101]

> O my God, Trinity whom I adore, help me forget myself   *2565*
> entirely so to establish myself in you, unmovable and peace-
> ful as if my soul were already in eternity. May nothing be
> able to trouble my peace or make me leave you, O my
> unchanging God, but may each minute bring me more
> deeply into your mystery! Grant my soul peace. Make it your
> heaven, your beloved dwelling and the place of your rest.
> May I never abandon you there, but may I be there, whole
> and entire, completely vigilant in my faith, entirely adoring,
> and wholly given over to your creative action.[102]

IN BRIEF

261   The mystery of the Most Holy Trinity is the central
mystery of the Christian faith and of Christian life.
God alone can make it known to us by revealing
himself as Father, Son, and Holy Spirit.

262   The Incarnation of God's Son reveals that God is the
eternal Father and that the Son is consubstantial with
the Father, which means that, in the Father and with
the Father, the Son is one and the same God.

263   The mission of the Holy Spirit, sent by the Father in
the name of the Son (*Jn* 14:26) and by the Son "from
the Father" (*Jn* 15:26), reveals that, with them, the
Spirit is one and the same God. "With the Father and

---

99   Cf. *Jn* 6:44; *Rom* 8:14.
100   Cf. *Jn* 17:21-23.
101   *Jn* 14:23.
102   Prayer of Blessed Elizabeth of the Trinity.

the Son he is worshipped and glorified" (Nicene Creed).

264   "The Holy Spirit proceeds from the Father as the first principle and, by the eternal gift of this to the Son, from the communion of both the Father and the Son" (St. Augustine, *De Trin.* 15, 26, 47: PL 42:1095).

265   By the grace of Baptism "in the name of the Father and of the Son and of the Holy Spirit," we are called to share in the life of the Blessed Trinity, here on earth in the obscurity of faith, and after death in eternal light (Cf. Paul VI, *CPG* § 9).

266   "Now this is the Catholic faith: We worship one God in the Trinity and the Trinity in unity, without either confusing the persons or dividing the substance; for the person of the Father is one, the Son's is another, the Holy Spirit's another; but the Godhead of the Father, Son, and Holy Spirit is one, their glory equal, their majesty coeternal" (Athanasian Creed; DS 75; ND 16).

267   Inseparable in what they are, the divine persons are also inseparable in what they do. But within the single divine operation each shows forth what is proper to him in the Trinity, especially in the divine missions of the Son's Incarnation and the gift of the Holy Spirit.

Paragraph 3. The Almighty

268   Of all the divine attributes, only God's omnipotence is named in the Creed: to confess this power has great bearing on our lives. We believe that his might is *universal,* for God who created *222* everything also rules everything and can do everything. God's power is *loving,* for he is our Father, and *mysterious,* for only faith can discern it when it "is made perfect in weakness."[103]

"He does whatever he pleases"[104]

269   The Holy Scriptures repeatedly confess the *universal* power of God. He is called the "Mighty One of Jacob," the "LORD of hosts," the "strong and mighty" one. If God is almighty "in heaven and on earth," it is because he made them.[105] Nothing is impossible with God, who disposes his works according to his will.[106] He is the Lord of the universe, whose order he established and which remains wholly subject to him and at his disposal. He *303* is master of history, governing hearts and events in keeping with his will: "It is always in your power to show great strength, and who can withstand the strength of your arm?"[107]

"You are merciful to all, for you can do all things"[108]

270   God is the *Father* Almighty, whose fatherhood and power shed light on one another: God reveals his fatherly omnipotence by the way he takes care of our needs; by the filial adoption that he *2777* gives us ("I will be a father to you, and you shall be my sons and daughters, says the Lord Almighty."):[109] finally by his infinite mercy, for he displays his power at its height by freely forgiving sins. *1441*

271   God's almighty power is in no way arbitrary: "In God, power, essence, will, intellect, wisdom, and justice are all identical. Nothing therefore can be in God's power which could not be in his just will or his wise intellect."[110]

---

103   Cf. *Gen* 1:1; *Jn* 1:3; *Mt* 6:9; *2 Cor* 12:9; cf. *1 Cor* 1:18.
104   *Ps* 115:3.
105   *Gen* 49:24; *Isa* 1:24 etc.; *Ps* 24:8-10; 135:6.
106   Cf. *Jer* 27:5; 32:17; *Lk* 1:37.
107   *Wis* 11:21; cf. *Esth* 4:17b; *Prov* 21:1; *Tob* 13:2.
108   *Wis* 11:23.
109   *2 Cor* 6:18; cf. *Mt* 6:32.
110   St. Thomas Aquinas, *STh* I, 25, 5, *ad* 1.

The mystery of God's apparent powerlessness

272   Faith in God the Father Almighty can be put to the test by
the experience of evil and suffering. God can sometimes seem to
309 be absent and incapable of stopping evil. But in the most mysterious way God the Father has revealed his almighty power in the
412 voluntary humiliation and Resurrection of his Son, by which he
conquered evil. Christ crucified is thus "the power of God and the
609 wisdom of God. For the foolishness of God is wiser than men, and
648 the weakness of God is stronger than men."[111] It is in Christ's
Resurrection and exaltation that the Father has shown forth "the
immeasurable greatness of his power in us who believe."[112]

273   Only faith can embrace the mysterious ways of God's
almighty power. This faith glories in its weaknesses in order to
148 draw to itself Christ's power.[113] The Virgin Mary is the supreme
model of this faith, for she believed that "nothing will be impossible with God," and was able to magnify the Lord: "For he who is
mighty has done great things for me, and holy is his name."[114]

274   "Nothing is more apt to confirm our faith and hope than
holding it fixed in our minds that nothing is impossible with God.
1814, 1817 Once our reason has grasped the idea of God's almighty power, it
will easily and without any hesitation admit everything that [the
Creed] will afterwards propose for us to believe – even if they be
great and marvellous things, far above the ordinary laws of nature."[115]

IN BRIEF

275   With Job, the just man, we confess: "I know that you
can do all things, and that no purpose of yours can be
thwarted" (*Job* 42:2).

276   Faithful to the witness of Scripture, the Church often
addresses its prayer to the "almighty and eternal God"
("omnipotens sempiterne Deus . . ."), believing firmly
that "nothing will be impossible with God" (*Gen* 18:14;
Lk 1:37; *Mt* 19:26).

---

111   *1 Cor* 1:24-25.
112   *Eph* 1:19-22.
113   Cf. *2 Cor* 12:9; *Phil* 4:13.
114   *Lk* 1:37, 49.
115   *Roman Catechism*, I, 2, 13.

277 God shows forth his almighty power by converting us from our sins and restoring us to his friendship by grace. "God, you show your almighty power above all in your mercy and forgiveness . . ." (*Roman Missal*, 26th Sunday, Opening Prayer).

278 If we do not believe that God's love is almighty, how can we believe that the Father could create us, the Son redeem us, and the Holy Spirit sanctify us?

Paragraph 4. The Creator

279 "In the beginning God created the heavens and the earth."[116] Holy Scripture begins with these solemn words. The profession of faith takes them up when it confesses that God the Father almighty is "Creator of heaven and earth" (*Apostles' Creed*), "of all that is, seen and unseen" (*Nicene Creed*). We shall speak first of the Creator, then of creation, and finally of the fall into sin from which Jesus Christ, the Son of God, came to raise us up again.

280 Creation is the foundation of "all God's saving plans," the "beginning of the history of salvation"[117] that culminates in Christt. Conversely, the mystery of Christ casts conclusive light on the mystery of creation and reveals the end for which "in the beginning God created the heavens and the earth": from the beginning, God envisaged the glory of the new creation in Christ.[118]   *288*   *1043*

281 And so the readings of the Easter Vigil, the celebration of the new creation in Christ, begin with the creation account; likewise in the Byzantine liturgy, the account of creation always constitutes the first reading at the vigils of the great feasts of the Lord. According to ancient witnesses the instruction of catechumens for Baptism followed the same itinerary.[119]   *1095*

I.   CATECHESIS ON CREATION

282 Catechesis on creation is of major importance. It concerns the very foundations of human and Christian life: for it makes explicit the response of the Christian faith to the basic question that

---

116   *Gen* 1:1.
117   *GCD* 51.
118   *Gen* 1:1; cf. *Rom* 8:18-23.
119   Cf. Egeria, *Peregrinatio ad loca sancta*, 46: PLS I, 1047; St. Augustine, *De catechizandis rudibus* 3, 5: PL 40, 256.

men of all times have asked themselves:[120] "Where do we come from?" "Where are we going?" "What is our origin?" "What is our end?" "Where does everything that exists come from and where is it going?" The two questions, the first about the origin and the second about the end, are inseparable. They are decisive for the
1730   meaning and orientation of our life and actions.

283   The question about the origins of the world and of man has been the object of many scientific studies which have splendidly enriched our
159   knowledge of the age and dimensions of the cosmos, the development of life-forms and the appearance of man. These discoveries invite us to even greater admiration for the greatness of the Creator, prompting us to give
341   him thanks for all his works and for the understanding and wisdom he gives to scholars and researchers. With Solomon they can say: "It is he who gave me unerring knowledge of what exists, to know the structure of the world and the activity of the elements . . . for wisdom, the fashioner of all things, taught me."[121]

284   The great interest accorded to these studies is strongly stimulated by a question of another order, which goes beyond the proper domain of the natural sciences. It is not only a question of knowing when and how the universe arose physically, or when man appeared, but rather of discovering the meaning of such an origin: is the universe governed by chance, blind fate, anonymous necessity, or by a transcendent, intelligent and good Being called "God"? And if the world does come from God's wisdom and goodness, why is there evil? Where does it come from? Who is responsible for it? Is there any liberation from it?

285   Since the beginning the Christian faith has been challenged by responses to the question of origins that differ from its own. Ancient religions and cultures produced many myths concerning origins. Some philosophers have said that everything is God, that the world is God, or that the development of the world is the development of God (Pantheism).
295   Others have said that the world is a necessary emanation arising from God and returning to him. Still others have affirmed the existence of two eternal principles, Good and Evil, Light and Darkness, locked in permanent conflict (Dualism, Manichaeism). According to some of these conceptions, the world (at least the physical world) is evil, the product of a fall, and is thus to be rejected or left behind (Gnosticism). Some admit that the world was made by God, but as by a watchmaker who, once he has made a watch, abandons it to itself (Deism). Finally, others reject any transcendent origin for the world, but see it as merely the interplay of matter that has always existed (Materialism). All these attempts bear witness to the permanence
28   and universality of the question of origins. This inquiry is distinctively human.

---

120   Cf. *NA* 2.
121   *Wis* 7:17-22.

286   Human intelligence is surely already capable of finding a *32* response to the question of origins. The existence of God the Creator can be known with certainty through his works, by the light of human reason,[122] even if this knowledge is often obscured and disfigured by error. This is why faith comes to confirm and enlighten reason in the correct understanding of this truth: "By *37* faith we understand that the world was created by the word of God, so that what is seen was made out of things which do not appear."[123]

287   The truth about creation is so important for all of human life that God in his tenderness wanted to reveal to his People everything that is salutary to know on the subject. Beyond the *107* natural knowledge that every man can have of the Creator,[124] God progressively revealed to Israel the mystery of creation. He who chose the patriarchs, who brought Israel out of Egypt, and who by choosing Israel created and formed it, this same God reveals himself as the One to whom belong all the peoples of the earth, and the whole earth itself; he is the One who alone "made heaven and earth."[125]

288   Thus the revelation of creation is inseparable from the revelation and forging of the covenant of the one God with his People. Creation is revealed as the first step toward this covenant, *280, 2569* the first and universal witness to God's all-powerful love.[126] And so, the truth of creation is also expressed with growing vigor in the message of the prophets, the prayer of the psalms and the liturgy, and in the wisdom sayings of the Chosen People.[127]

289   Among all the Scriptural texts about creation, the first three chapters of Genesis occupy a unique place. From a literary *390* standpoint these texts may have had diverse sources. The inspired authors have placed them at the beginning of Scripture to express in their solemn language the truths of creation – its origin and its end in God, its order and goodness, the vocation of man, and finally the drama of sin and the hope of salvation. Read in the light of Christ, within the unity of Sacred Scripture and in the living *111* Tradition of the Church, these texts remain the principal source for catechesis on the mysteries of the "beginning": creation, fall, and promise of salvation.

---

122 Cf. Vatican Council I, can. 2 § 1: DS 3026.
123 *Heb* 11:3.
124 Cf. *Acts* 17:24-29; *Rom* 1:19-20.
125 Cf. *Isa* 43:1; *Ps* 115:15; 124:8; 134:3.
126 Cf. *Gen* 15:5; *Jer* 33:19-26.
127 Cf. *Isa* 44:24; *Ps* 104; *Prov* 8:22-31.

II. CREATION – WORK OF THE HOLY TRINITY

290   "In the beginning God created the heavens and the earth":[128] three things are affirmed in these first words of Scripture: the eternal God gave a beginning to all that exists outside of himself; he alone is Creator (the verb "create" – Hebrew *bara* –
326 always has God for its subject). The totality of what exists (expressed by the formula "the heavens and the earth") depends on the One who gives it being.

291   "In the beginning was the Word ... and the Word was God ... all things were made through him, and without him was not
241 anything made that was made."[129] The New Testament reveals that God created everything by the eternal Word, his beloved Son. In him "all things were created, in heaven and on earth ... all things
331 were created through him and for him. He is before all things, and in him all things hold together."[130] The Church's faith likewise
703 confesses the creative action of the Holy Spirit, the "giver of life," "the Creator Spirit" ("*Veni, Creator Spiritus*"), the "source of every good."[131]

292   The Old Testament suggests and the New Covenant reveals the creative action of the Son and the Spirit,[132] inseparably one with that of the Father. This creative cooperation is clearly affirmed in the Church's rule of faith: "There exists but one God ... he is the Father, God, the Creator, the author, the giver of order. He made all things *by himself*, that is, by his Word and by his Wisdom,"
699 "by the Son and the Spirit" who, so to speak, are "his hands."[133]
257 Creation is the common work of the Holy Trinity.

III. "THE WORLD WAS CREATED FOR THE GLORY OF GOD"

293   Scripture and Tradition never cease to teach and celebrate
337, 344 this fundamental truth: "The world was made for the glory of
1361 God."[134] St. Bonaventure explains that God created all things "not to increase his glory, but to show it forth and to communicate it,"[135]

---

128   *Gen* 1:1.
129   *Jn* 1:1-3.
130   *Col* 1:16-17.
131   Cf. Nicene Creed; DS 150; Hymn "*Veni, Creator Spiritus*"; Byzantine Troparion of Pentecost vespers, "*O heavenly King, Consoler.*"
132   Cf. *Ps* 33:6; 104:30; *Gen* 1:2-3.
133   St. Irenaeus, *Adv. haeres* 2, 30, 9; 4, 20, 1: PG 7/1, 822, 1032.
134   *Dei Filius*, can. § 5: DS 3025.
135   St. Bonaventure, *In II Sent.* I, 2, 2, 1.

for God has no other reason for creating than his love and goodness: "Creatures came into existence when the key of love opened his hand."[136] The First Vatican Council explains:

> This one, true God, of his own goodness and "almighty power," not for increasing his own beatitude, nor for attaining his perfection, but in order to manifest this perfection through the benefits which he bestows on creatures, with absolute freedom of counsel "and from the beginning of time, made out of nothing both orders of creatures, the spiritual and the corporeal. . . ."[137]

759

294 The glory of God consists in the realization of this manifestation and communication of his goodness, for which the world was created. God made us "to be his sons through Jesus Christ, according to the purpose of his will, *to the praise of his glorious grace*,"[138] for "the glory of God is man fully alive; moreover man's life is the vision of God: if God's revelation through creation has already obtained life for all the beings that dwell on earth, how much more will the Word's manifestation of the Father obtain life for those who see God."[139] The ultimate purpose of creation is that God "who is the creator of all things may at last become 'all in all,' thus simultaneously assuring his own glory and our beatitude."[140]

2809

1722

1992

IV.   THE MYSTERY OF CREATION

God creates by wisdom and love

295 We believe that God created the world according to his wisdom.[141] It is not the product of any necessity whatever, nor of blind fate or chance. We believe that it proceeds from God's free will; he wanted to make his creatures share in his being, wisdom, and goodness: "For you created all things, and by your will they existed and were created."[142] Therefore the Psalmist exclaims: "O LORD, how manifold are your works! In wisdom you have made them all"; and "The LORD is good to all, and his compassion is over all that he has made."[143]

216, 1951

---

136 St. Thomas Aquinas, *Sent.* 2, Prol.
137 *Dei Filius*, 1: DS 3002; cf. Lateran Council IV (1215): DS 800.
138 *Eph* 1:5-6.
139 St. Irenaeus, *Adv. haeres* 4, 20, 7: PG 7/1, 1037.
140 *AG* 2; cf. *1 Cor* 15:28.
141 Cf. *Wis* 9:9.
142 *Rev* 4:11.
143 *Ps* 104:24; 145:9.

God creates "out of nothing"

296   We believe that God needs no pre-existent thing or any help in order to create, nor is creation any sort of necessary ema-
285 nation from the divine substance.[144] God creates freely "out of nothing":[145]

> If God had drawn the world from pre-existent matter, what would be so extraordinary in that? A human artisan makes from a given material whatever he wants, while God shows his power by starting from nothing to make all he wants.[146]

297   Scripture bears witness to faith in creation "out of nothing" as a truth full of promise and hope. Thus the mother of seven sons
338 encourages them for martyrdom:

> I do not know how you came into being in my womb. It was not I who gave you life and breath, nor I who set in order the elements within each of you. Therefore the Creator of the world, who shaped the beginning of man and devised the origin of all things, will in his mercy give life and breath back to you again, since you now forget yourselves for the sake of his laws. . . . Look at the heaven and the earth and see everything that is in them, and recognize that God did not make them out of things that existed. Thus also mankind comes into being.[147]

298   Since God could create everything out of nothing, he can also, through the Holy Spirit, give spiritual life to sinners by
1375 creating a pure heart in them[148] and bodily life to the dead through the Resurrection. God "gives life to the dead and calls into existence
992 the things that do not exist."[149] And since God was able to make light shine in darkness by his Word, he can also give the light of faith to those who do not yet know him.[150]

God creates an ordered and good world

339 **299**   Because God creates through wisdom, his creation is ordered: "You have arranged all things by measure and number and weight."[151] The universe, created in and by the eternal Word, the

---

144 Cf. *Dei Filius*, can. 2-4: DS 3022-3024.
145 Lateran Council IV (1215): DS 800; cf. DS 3025.
146 St. Theophilus of Antioch, *Ad Autolycum* II, 4: PG 6, 1052.
147 *2 Macc* 7:22-23, 28.
148 Cf. *Ps* 51:12.
149 *Rom* 4:17.
150 Cf. *Gen* 1:3; *2 Cor* 4:6.
151 *Wis* 11:20.

"image of the invisible God," is destined for and addressed to man, himself created in the "image of God" and called to a personal relationship with God.[152] Our human understanding, which shares in the light of the divine intellect, can understand what God   *41, 1147* tells us by means of his creation, though not without great effort and only in a spirit of humility and respect before the Creator and his work.[153] Because creation comes forth from God's goodness, it shares in that goodness – "And God saw that it was good . . . very good"[154] – for God willed creation as a gift addressed to man, an inheritance destined for and entrusted to him. On many occasions the Church has had to defend the goodness of creation, including   *358* that of the physical world.[155]   *2415*

God transcends creation and is present to it

300   God is infinitely greater than all his works: "You have set your glory above the heavens."[156] Indeed, God's "greatness is unsearchable."[157] But because he is the free and sovereign Creator,   *42* the first cause of all that exists, God is present to his creatures'   *223* inmost being: "In him we live and move and have our being."[158] In the words of St. Augustine, God is "higher than my highest and more inward than my innermost self."[159]

God upholds and sustains creation

301   With creation, God does not abandon his creatures to themselves. He not only gives them being and existence, but also, and at every moment, upholds and sustains them in being, enables them to act and brings them to their final end. Recognizing this   *1951* utter dependence with respect to the Creator is a source of wisdom   *396* and freedom, of joy and confidence:

> For you love all things that exist, and detest none of the things that you have made; for you would not have made anything if you had hated it. How would anything have endured, if you had not willed it? Or how would anything not called forth by you have been preserved? You spare all

---

152   *Col* 1:15; *Gen* 1:26.
153   Cf. *Ps* 19:2-5; *Job* 42:3.
154   *Gen* 1:4, 10, 12, 18, 21, 31.
155   Cf. DS 286; 455-463; 800; 1333; 3002.
156   *Ps* 8:2; cf. *Sir* 43:28.
157   *Ps* 145:3.
158   *Acts* 17:28.
159   St. Augustine, *Conf.* 3, 6, 11: PL 32, 688.

things, for they are yours, O Lord, you who love the living.[160]

V.   GOD CARRIES OUT HIS PLAN: DIVINE PROVIDENCE

302   Creation has its own goodness and proper perfection, but it did not spring forth complete from the hands of the Creator. The universe was created "in a state of journeying" (*in statu viae*) toward an ultimate perfection yet to be attained, to which God has destined it. We call "divine providence" the dispositions by which God guides his creation toward this perfection:

> By his providence God protects and governs all things which he has made, "reaching mightily from one end of the earth to the other, and ordering all things well." For "all are open and laid bare to his eyes," even those things which are yet to come into existence through the free action of creatures.[161]

303   The witness of Scripture is unanimous that the solicitude of divine providence is *concrete* and *immediate*; God cares for all, from the least things to the great events of the world and its history. The sacred books powerfully affirm God's absolute sovereignty over the course of events: "Our God is in the heavens; he does

269   whatever he pleases."[162] And so it is with Christ, "who opens and no one shall shut, who shuts and no one opens."[163] As the book of Proverbs states: "Many are the plans in the mind of a man, but it is the purpose of the Lord that will be established."[164]

304   And so we see the Holy Spirit, the principal author of Sacred Scripture, often attributing actions to God without mentioning any secondary causes. This is not a "primitive mode of speech," but a profound way of recalling God's primacy and absolute Lordship over history and the

2568   world,[165] and so of educating his people to trust in him. The prayer of the Psalms is the great school of this trust.[166]

305   Jesus asks for childlike abandonment to the providence of our heavenly Father who takes care of his children's smallest

2115   needs: "Therefore do not be anxious, saying, 'What shall we eat?' or 'What shall we drink?' . . . . Your heavenly Father knows that you need them all. But seek first his kingdom and his righteousness, and all these things shall be yours as well."[167]

---

160   *Wis* 11:24-26.
161   Vatican Council I, *Dei Filius* 1: DS 3003; cf. *Wis* 8:1; *Heb* 4:13.
162   *Ps* 115:3.
163   *Rev* 3:7.
164   *Prov* 19:21.
165   Cf. *Isa* 10:5-15; 45:5-7; *Deut* 32:39; *Sir* 11:14.
166   Cf. *Ps* 22; 32; 35; 103; 138; *et al.*

Providence and secondary causes

306   God is the sovereign master of his plan. But to carry it out he also makes use of his creatures' cooperation. This use is not a sign of weakness, but rather a token of almighty God's greatness *1884* and goodness. For God grants his creatures not only their existence, but also the dignity of acting on their own, of being causes and principles for each other, and thus of cooperating in the accom- *1951* plishment of his plan.

307   To human beings God even gives the power of freely sharing in his providence by entrusting them with the responsibil- ity of "subduing" the earth and having dominion over it.[168] God *106, 373* thus enables men to be intelligent and free causes in order to *1954* complete the work of creation, to perfect its harmony for their own *2427* good and that of their neighbors. Though often unconscious col- laborators with God's will, they can also enter deliberately into the divine plan by their actions, their prayers, and their sufferings.[169] They then fully become "God's fellow workers" and co-workers *2738* for his kingdom.[170]   *618, 1505*

308   The truth that God is at work in all the actions of his creatures is inseparable from faith in God the Creator. God is the first cause who operates in and through secondary causes: "For God is at work in you, both to will and to work for his good pleasure."[171] Far from diminishing the creature's dignity, this truth enhances it. Drawn from nothingness by God's power, wisdom, and goodness, it can do nothing if it is cut off from its origin, for *970* "without a Creator the creature vanishes."[172] Still less can a crea- ture attain its ultimate end without the help of God's grace.[173]

Providence and the scandal of evil

309   If God the Father almighty, the Creator of the ordered and good world, cares for all his creatures, why does evil exist? To this question, as pressing as it is unavoidable and as painful as it is *164, 385* mysterious, no quick answer will suffice. Only Christian faith as a *2850* whole constitutes the answer to this question: the goodness of

---

167   *Mt* 6:31-33; cf. 10:29-31.
168   Cf. *Gen* 1:26-28.
169   Cf. *Col* 1:24.
170   *1 Cor* 3:9; *1 Thess* 3:2; *Col* 4:11.
171   *Phil* 2:13; cf. *1 Cor* 12:6.
172   *GS* 36 § 3.
173   Cf. *Mt* 19:26; *Jn* 15:5; 14:13.

creation, the drama of sin, and the patient love of God who comes to meet man by his covenants, the redemptive Incarnation of his Son, his gift of the Spirit, his gathering of the Church, the power of the sacraments, and his call to a blessed life to which free creatures are invited to consent in advance, but from which, by a terrible mystery, they can also turn away in advance. *There is not a single aspect of the Christian message that is not in part an answer to the question of evil.*

310   But why did God not create a world so perfect that no evil could exist in it? With infinite power God could always create
412 something better.[174] But with infinite wisdom and goodness God
1042-1050 freely willed to create a world "in a state of journeying " toward its ultimate perfection. In God's plan this process of becoming involves the appearance of certain beings and the disappearance of
342 others, the existence of the more perfect alongside the less perfect, both constructive and destructive forces of nature. With physical good there exists also *physical evil* as long as creation has not reached perfection.[175]

311   Angels and men, as intelligent and free creatures, have to journey toward their ultimate destinies by their free choice and
396 preferential love. They can therefore go astray. Indeed, they have
1849 sinned. Thus has *moral evil*, incommensurably more harmful than physical evil, entered the world. God is in no way, directly or indirectly, the cause of moral evil.[176] He permits it, however, because he respects the freedom of his creatures and, mysteriously, knows how to derive good from it:

> For almighty God . . ., because he is supremely good, would never allow any evil whatsoever to exist in his works if he were not so all-powerful and good as to cause good to emerge from evil itself.[177]

312   In time we can discover that God in his almighty providence can bring a good from the consequences of an evil, even a moral evil, caused by his creatures: "It was not you," said Joseph to his brothers, "who sent me here, but God . . . . You meant evil against me; but God meant it for good, to bring it about that many
598-600 people should be kept alive."[178] From the greatest moral evil ever committed – the rejection and murder of God's only Son, caused

---

174   Cf. St. Thomas Aquinas, *STh* I, 25, 6.
175   Cf. St. Thomas Aquinas, *SCG* III, 71.
176   Cf. St. Augustine, *De libero arbitrio* 1, 1, 2: PL 32, 1223; St. Thomas Aquinas, *STh* I-II, 79, 1.
177   St. Augustine, *Enchiridion* 3, 11: PL 40, 236.
178   *Gen* 45:8; 50:20; cf. *Tob* 2:12-18 (Vulg.).

by the sins of all men – God, by his grace that "abounded all the more,"[179] brought the greatest of goods: the glorification of Christ and our redemption. But for all that, evil never becomes a good.   *1994*

313   "We know that in everything God works for good for those who love him."[180] The constant witness of the saints confirms this   *227* truth:

> St. Catherine of Siena said to "those who are scandalized and rebel against what happens to them": "Everything comes from love, all is ordained for the salvation of man, God does nothing without this goal in mind."[181]
>
> St. Thomas More, shortly before his martyrdom, consoled his daughter: "Nothing can come but that that God wills. And I make me very sure that whatsoever that be, seem it never so bad in sight, it shall indeed be the best."[182]
>
> Dame Julian of Norwich: "Here I was taught by the grace of God that I should steadfastly keep me in the faith . . . and that at the same time I should take my stand on and earnestly believe in what our Lord shewed in this time – that 'all manner [of] thing shall be well.'"[183]

314   We firmly believe that God is master of the world and of its history. But the ways of his providence are often unknown to us. Only at the end, when our partial knowledge ceases, when we see God "face to face,"[184] will we fully know the ways by which –   *1040* even through the dramas of evil and sin – God has guided his   *2550* creation to that definitive sabbath rest[185] for which he created heaven and earth.

IN BRIEF

315   In the creation of the world and of man, God gave the first and universal witness to his almighty love and his wisdom, the first proclamation of the "plan of his loving goodness," which finds its goal in the new creation in Christ.

---

179 Cf. *Rom* 5:20.
180 *Rom* 8:28.
181 St. Catherine of Siena, *Dialogue on Providence*, ch. IV, 138.
182 *The Correspondence of Sir Thomas More*, ed. Elizabeth F. Rogers (Princeton: Princeton University Press, 1947), letter 206, lines 661-663.
183 Julian of Norwich, *The Revelations of Divine Love*, tr. James Walshe, SJ (London: 1961), ch. 32, 99-100.
184 *1 Cor* 13:12.
185 Cf. *Gen* 2:2.

316   Though the work of creation is attributed to the Father
       in particular, it is equally a truth of faith that the
       Father, Son, and Holy Spirit together are the one,
       indivisible principle of creation.

317   God alone created the universe freely, directly, and
       without any help.

318   No creature has the infinite power necessary to "cre-
       ate" in the proper sense of the word, that is, to produce
       and give being to that which had in no way possessed
       it (to call into existence "out of nothing") (cf. DS 3624).

319   God created the world to show forth and communi-
       cate his glory. That his creatures should share in his
       truth, goodness, and beauty – this is the glory for
       which God created them.

320   God created the universe and keeps it in existence by his
       Word, the Son "upholding the universe by his word of
       power" (*Heb* 1:3) and by his Creator Spirit, the giver of life.

321   Divine providence consists of the dispositions by
       which God guides all his creatures with wisdom and
       love to their ultimate end.

322   Christ invites us to filial trust in the providence of our
       heavenly Father (cf. *Mt* 6:26-34), and St. Peter the
       apostle repeats: "Cast all your anxieties on him, for he
       cares about you" (*1 Pet* 5:7; cf. *Ps* 55:23).

323   Divine providence works also through the actions of
       creatures. To human beings God grants the ability to
       cooperate freely with his plans.

324   The fact that God permits physical and even moral evil
       is a mystery that God illuminates by his Son Jesus
       Christ who died and rose to vanquish evil. Faith gives
       us the certainty that God would not permit an evil if
       he did not cause a good to come from that very evil,
       by ways that we shall fully know only in eternal life.

Paragraph 5. Heaven and Earth

325   The Apostles' Creed professes that God is "Creator of heaven and earth." The Nicene Creed makes it explicit that this profession includes "all that is, seen and unseen."

326   The Scriptural expression "heaven and earth" means all that exists, creation in its entirety. It also indicates the bond, deep within creation, that both unites heaven and earth and distin-   *290* guishes the one from the other: "the earth" is the world of men, while "heaven" or "the heavens" can designate both the firmament and God's own "place" – "our Father in heaven" and consequently   *1023, 2794* the "heaven" too which is eschatological glory. Finally, "heaven" refers to the saints and the "place" of the spiritual creatures, the angels, who surround God.[186]

327   The profession of faith of the Fourth Lateran Council (1215) affirms that God "from the beginning of time made at once (*simul*) out of nothing both orders of creatures, the spiritual and the   *296* corporeal, that is, the angelic and the earthly, and then (*deinde*) the human creature, who as it were shares in both orders, being composed of spirit and body."[187]

I.   THE ANGELS

The existence of angels – a truth of faith

328   The existence of the spiritual, non-corporeal beings that Sacred Scripture usually calls "angels" is a truth of faith. The witness of Scripture is as clear as the unanimity of Tradition.   *150*

Who are they?

329   St. Augustine says: "'Angel' is the name of their office, not of their nature. If you seek the name of their nature, it is 'spirit'; if you seek the name of their office, it is 'angel': from what they are, 'spirit,' from what they do, 'angel.'"[188] With their whole beings the angels are *servants* and messengers of God. Because they "always behold the face of my Father who is in heaven" they are the "mighty ones who do his word, hearkening to the voice of his word."[189]

---

186   *Ps* 115:16; 19:2; *Mt* 5:16.
187   Lateran Council IV (1215): DS 800; cf. DS 3002 and Paul VI, *CPG* § 8.
188   St. Augustine, *En. in Ps.* 103, 1, 15: PL 37, 1348.

330   As purely *spiritual* creatures angels have intelligence and
will: they are personal and immortal creatures, surpassing in perfection all visible creatures, as the splendor of their glory bears
witness.[190]

Christ "with all his angels"

291 **331**   Christ is the center of the angelic world. They are *his*
angels: "When the Son of man comes in his glory, and all the angels
with him. . . ."[191] They belong to him because they were created
through and *for* him: "for in him all things were created in heaven
and on earth, visible and invisible, whether thrones or dominions
or principalities or authorities – all things were created through
him and for him."[192] They belong to him still more because he has
made them messengers of his saving plan: "Are they not all min-
istering spirits sent forth to serve, for the sake of those who are to
obtain salvation?"[193]

332   Angels have been present since creation and throughout
the history of salvation, announcing this salvation from afar or near
and serving the accomplishment of the divine plan: they closed the
earthly paradise; protected Lot; saved Hagar and her child; stayed
Abraham's hand; communicated the law by their ministry; led the
People of God; announced births and callings; and assisted the
prophets, just to cite a few examples.[194] Finally, the angel Gabriel
announced the birth of the Precursor and that of Jesus himself.[195]

333   From the Incarnation to the Ascension, the life of the Word
incarnate is surrounded by the adoration and service of angels.
When God "brings the firstborn into the world, he says: 'Let all
559 God's angels worship him.'"[196] Their song of praise at the birth of
Christ has not ceased resounding in the Church's praise: "Glory to
God in the highest!"[197] They protect Jesus in his infancy, serve him
in the desert, strengthen him in his agony in the garden, when he
could have been saved by them from the hands of his enemies as
Israel had been.[198] Again, it is the angels who "evangelize" by

---

189   *Mt* 18:10; *Ps* 103:20.
190   Cf. Pius XII, *Humani Generis*: DS 3891; *Lk* 20:36; *Dan* 10:9-12.
191   *Mt* 25:31.
192   *Col* 1:16.
193   *Heb* 1:14.
194   Cf. *Job* 38:7 (where angels are called "sons of God"); *Gen* 3:24; 19; 21:17;
      22:11; *Acts* 7:53; *Ex* 23:20-23; *Judg* 13; 6:11-24; *Isa* 6:6; *1 Kings* 19:5.
195   Cf. *Lk* 1:11, 26.
196   *Heb* 1:6.
197   *Lk* 2:14.

proclaiming the Good News of Christ's Incarnation and Resurrection.[199] They will be present at Christ's return, which they will announce, to serve at his judgment.[200]

The angels in the life of the Church

334　In the meantime, the whole life of the Church benefits from the mysterious and powerful help of angels.[201]　　*1939*

335　In her liturgy, the Church joins with the angels to adore the thrice-holy God. She invokes their assistance (in the Roman Canon's *Supplices te rogamus* . . .["Almighty God, we pray that your angel . . ."]; in the funeral liturgy's *In Paradisum deducant te angeli* . . .["May the angels lead you into Paradise . . ."]). Moreover, in the "Cherubic Hymn" of the Byzantine Liturgy, she celebrates the memory of certain angels more particularly (St. Michael, St. Gabriel, St. Raphael, and the guardian angels).　　*1138*

336　From infancy to death human life is surrounded by their watchful care and intercession.[202] "Beside each believer stands an angel as protector and shepherd leading him to life."[203] Already here on earth the Christian life shares by faith in the blessed company of angels and men united in God.　　*1020*

II.　THE VISIBLE WORLD

337　God himself created the visible world in all its richness, diversity, and order. Scripture presents the work of the Creator symbolically as a succession of six days of divine "work," concluded by the "rest" of the seventh day.[204] On the subject of creation, the sacred text teaches the truths revealed by God for our salvation,[205] permitting us to "recognize the inner nature, the value, and the ordering of the whole of creation to the praise of God."[206]　　*290*

　　293

338　*Nothing exists that does not owe its existence to God the Creator.* The world began when God's word drew it out of nothingness; all　　*297*

198　Cf. *Mt* 1:20; 2:13, 19; 4:11; 26:53; *Mk* 1:13; *Lk* 22:43; 2 *Macc* 10:29-30; 11:8.
199　Cf. *Lk* 2:8-14; *Mk* 16:5-7.
200　Cf. *Acts* 1:10-11; *Mt* 13:41; 24:31; *Lk* 12:8-9.
201　Cf. *Acts* 5:18-20; 8:26-29; 10:3-8; 12:6-11; 27:23-25.
202　Cf. *Mt* 18:10; *Lk* 16:22; *Ps* 34:7; 91:10-13; *Job* 33:23-24; *Zech* 1:12; *Tob* 12:12.
203　St. Basil, *Adv. Eunomium* III, 1: PG 29, 656B.
204　*Gen* 1:1-2:4.
205　Cf. *DV* 11.
206　*LG* 36 § 2.

existent beings, all of nature, and all human history are rooted in this primordial event, the very genesis by which the world was constituted and time begun.[207]

339   *Each creature possesses its own particular goodness and perfection.* For each one of the works of the "six days" it is said: "And
2501   God saw that it was good." "By the very nature of creation, material being is endowed with its own stability, truth, and excellence, its own order and laws."[208] Each of the various creatures, willed in its
299   own being, reflects in its own way a ray of God's infinite wisdom and goodness. Man must therefore respect the particular goodness
266   of every creature, to avoid any disordered use of things which would be in contempt of the Creator and would bring disastrous consequences for human beings and their environment.

1937 **340**   God wills the *interdependence of creatures.* The sun and the moon, the cedar and the little flower, the eagle and the sparrow: the spectacle of their countless diversities and inequalities tells us that no creature is self-sufficient. Creatures exist only in dependence on each other, to complete each other, in the service of each other.

283 **341**   The *beauty of the universe*: The order and harmony of the
2500   created world results from the diversity of beings and from the relationships which exist among them. Man discovers them progressively as the laws of nature. They call forth the admiration of scholars. The beauty of creation reflects the infinite beauty of the Creator and ought to inspire the respect and submission of man's intellect and will.

310 **342**   The *hierarchy of creatures* is expressed by the order of the "six days," from the less perfect to the more perfect. God loves all his creatures[209] and takes care of each one, even the sparrow. Nevertheless, Jesus said: "You are of more value than many sparrows," or again: "Of how much more value is a man than a sheep!"[210]

355 **343**   *Man is the summit* of the Creator's work, as the inspired account expresses by clearly distinguishing the creation of man from that of the other creatures.[211]

---

207   Cf. St. Augustine, *De Genesi adv. Man.* 1, 2, 4: PL 34, 175.
208   *GS* 36 § 1.
209   Cf. *Ps* 145:9.
210   *Lk* 12:6-7; *Mt* 12:12.
211   Cf. *Gen* 1:26.

344   There is a *solidarity among all creatures* arising from the fact   *293, 1939*
that all have the same Creator and are all ordered to his glory: *2416*

> May you be praised, O Lord, in all your creatures, especially   *1218*
> brother sun, by whom you give us light for the day; he is
> beautiful, radiating great splendor, and offering us a symbol
> of you, the Most High. . . .
> May you be praised, my Lord, for sister water, who is very
> useful and humble, precious and chaste. . . .
> May you be praised, my Lord, for sister earth, our mother,
> who bears and feeds us, and produces the variety of fruits
> and dappled flowers and grasses. . . .
> Praise and bless my Lord, give thanks and serve him in all
> humility.[212]

345   *The sabbath – the end of the work of the six days.* The sacred
text says that "on the seventh day God finished his work which he
had done," that the "heavens and the earth were finished," and that   *2168*
God "rested" on this day and sanctified and blessed it.[213] These
inspired words are rich in profitable instruction:

346   In creation God laid a foundation and established laws that
remain firm, on which the believer can rely with confidence, for they are
the sign and pledge of the unshakeable faithfulness of God's covenant.[214]   *2169*
For his part man must remain faithful to this foundation and respect the
laws which the Creator has written into it.

347   Creation was fashioned with a view to the sabbath and therefore
for the worship and adoration of God. Worship is inscribed in the order of
creation.[215] As the rule of St. Benedict says, nothing should take prece-   *1145-1152*
dence over "the work of God," that is, solemn worship.[216] This indicates
the right order of human concerns.

348   The sabbath is at the heart of Israel's law. To keep the command-   *2172*
ments is to correspond to the wisdom and the will of God as expressed in
his work of creation.

349   The *eighth day.* But for us a new day has dawned: the day
of Christ's Resurrection. The seventh day completes the first creation. The eighth day begins the new creation. Thus, the work of   *2174*
creation culminates in the greater work of redemption. The first   *1046*
creation finds its meaning and its summit in the new creation in
Christ, the splendor of which surpasses that of the first creation.[217]

---

212 St. Francis of Assisi, *Canticle of the Creatures.*
213 *Gen* 2:1-3.
214 Cf. *Heb* 4:3-4; *Jer* 31:35-37; 33:19-26.
215 Cf. *Gen* 1:14.
216 St. Benedict, *Regula* 43, 3: PL 66, 675-676.
217 Cf. *Roman Missal,* Easter Vigil 24, prayer after the first reading.

IN BRIEF

350   Angels are spiritual creatures who glorify God without ceasing and who serve his saving plans for other creatures: "The angels work together for the benefit of us all" (St. Thomas Aquinas, *STh* I, 114, 3, *ad* 3).

351   The angels surround Christ their Lord. They serve him especially in the accomplishment of his saving mission to men.

352   The Church venerates the angels who help her on her earthly pilgrimage and protect every human being.

353   God willed the diversity of his creatures and their own particular goodness, their interdependence, and their order. He destined all material creatures for the good of the human race. Man, and through him all creation, is destined for the glory of God.

354   Respect for laws inscribed in creation and the relations which derive from the nature of things is a principle of wisdom and a foundation for morality.

Paragraph 6. Man

355 "God created man in his own image, in the image of God he created him, male and female he created them."[218] Man occupies a unique place in creation: (I) he is "in the image of God"; (II) in his own nature he unites the spiritual and material worlds; (III) he is created "male and female"; (IV) God established him in his friendship.

1700, 343

I. "IN THE IMAGE OF GOD"

356 Of all visible creatures only man is "able to know and love his creator."[219] He is "the only creature on earth that God has willed for its own sake,"[220] and he alone is called to share, by knowledge and love, in God's own life. It was for this end that he was created, and this is the fundamental reason for his dignity:

1703, 2258

225

> What made you establish man in so great a dignity? Certainly the incalculable love by which you have looked on your creature in yourself! You are taken with love for her; for by love indeed you created her, by love you have given her a being capable of tasting your eternal Good.[221]

295

357 Being in the image of God the human individual possesses the dignity of a person, who is not just something, but someone. He is capable of self-knowledge, of self-possession and of freely giving himself and entering into communion with other persons. And he is called by grace to a covenant with his Creator, to offer him a response of faith and love that no other creature can give in his stead.

1935

1877

358 God created everything for man,[222] but man in turn was created to serve and love God and to offer all creation back to him:

299, 901

> What is it that is about to be created, that enjoys such honor? It is man – that great and wonderful living creature, more precious in the eyes of God than all other creatures! For him the heavens and the earth, the sea and all the rest of creation exist. God attached so much importance to his salvation that he did not spare his own Son for the sake of man. Nor does he ever cease to work, trying every possible means, until he

---

218 *Gen* 1:27.
219 *GS* 12 § 3.
220 *GS* 24 § 3.
221 St. Catherine of Siena, *Dialogue* 4, 13 "On Divine Providence": *LH*, Sunday, week 19, OR.
222 Cf. *GS* 12 § 1; 24 § 3; 39 § 1.

has raised man up to himself and made him sit at his right hand.[223]

1701 **359** "In reality it is only in the mystery of the Word made flesh that the mystery of man truly becomes clear."[224]

388, 411   St. Paul tells us that the human race takes its origin from two men: Adam and Christ . . . . The first man, Adam, he says, became a living soul, the last Adam a life-giving spirit. The first Adam was made by the last Adam, from whom he also received his soul, to give him life . . . . The second Adam stamped his image on the first Adam when he created him. That is why he took on himself the role and the name of the first Adam, in order that he might not lose what he had made in his own image. The first Adam, the last Adam: the first had a beginning, the last knows no end. The last Adam is indeed the first; as he himself says: "I am the first and the last."[225]

225, 404, 775 **360**   Because of its common origin *the human race forms a unity,* *831, 842* for "from one ancestor [God] made all nations to inhabit the whole earth":[226]

O wondrous vision, which makes us contemplate the human race in the unity of its origin in God . . . in the unity of its nature, composed equally in all men of a material body and a spiritual soul; in the unity of its immediate end and its mission in the world; in the unity of its dwelling, the earth, whose benefits all men, by right of nature, may use to sustain and develop life; in the unity of its supernatural end: God himself, to whom all ought to tend; in the unity of the means for attaining this end; . . . in the unity of the redemption wrought by Christ for all.[227]

361   "This law of human solidarity and charity,"[228] without *1939* excluding the rich variety of persons, cultures, and peoples, assures us that all men are truly brethren.

II.   "BODY AND SOUL BUT TRULY ONE"

362   The human person, created in the image of God, is a being at once corporeal and spiritual. The biblical account expresses this *1146, 2332* reality in symbolic language when it affirms that "then the LORD God formed man of dust from the ground, and breathed into his

---

223 St. John Chrysostom, *In Gen. Sermo* II, 1: PG 54, 587D-588A.
224 *GS* 22 § 1.
225 St. Peter Chrysologus, *Sermo* 117; PL 52, 520-521.
226 *Acts* 17:26; cf. *Tob* 8:6.
227 Pius XII, encyclical, *Summi Pontificatus* 3; cf. *NA* 1.
228 Pius XII, *Summi Pontificatus* 3.

nostrils the breath of life; and man became a living being."[229] Man, whole and entire, is therefore *willed* by God.

363   In Sacred Scripture the term "soul" often refers to human *life* or the entire human *person*.[230] But "soul" also refers to the *1703* innermost aspect of man, that which is of greatest value in him,[231] that by which he is most especially in God's image: "soul" signifies the *spiritual principle* in man.

364   The human body shares in the dignity of "the image of God": it is a human body precisely because it is animated by a spiritual soul, and it is the whole human person that is intended to *1004* become, in the body of Christ, a temple of the Spirit:[232]

> Man, though made of body and soul, is a unity. Through his *2289*
> very bodily condition he sums up in himself the elements of
> the material world. Through him they are thus brought to
> their highest perfection and can raise their voice in praise
> freely given to the Creator. For this reason man may not
> despise his bodily life. Rather he is obliged to regard his body
> as good and to hold it in honor since God has created it and
> will raise it up on the last day.[233]

365   The unity of soul and body is so profound that one has to consider the soul to be the "form" of the body:[234] i.e., it is because of its spiritual soul that the body made of matter becomes a living, human body; spirit and matter, in man, are not two natures united, but rather their union forms a single nature.

366   The Church teaches that every spiritual soul is created immediately by God – it is not "produced" by the parents – and *1005* also that it is immortal: it does not perish when it separates from *997* the body at death, and it will be reunited with the body at the final Resurrection.[235]

367   Sometimes the soul is distinguished from the spirit: St. Paul for instance prays that God may sanctify his people "wholly," with "spirit and soul and body" kept sound and blameless at the Lord's *2083* coming.[236] The Church teaches that this distinction does not introduce a duality into the soul.[237] "Spirit" signifies that from creation

---

229 *Gen* 2:7.
230 Cf. *Mt* 16:25-26; *Jn* 15:13; *Acts* 2:41.
231 Cf. *Mt* 10:28; 26:38; *Jn* 12:27; *2 Macc* 6:30.
232 Cf. *1 Cor* 6:19-20; 15:44-45.
233 *GS* 14 § 1; cf. *Dan* 3:57-80.
234 Cf. Council of Vienne (1312): DS 902.
235 Cf. Pius XII, *Humani Generis*: DS 3896; Paul VI, *CPG* § 8; Lateran Council V (1513): DS 1440.
236 *1 Thess* 5:23.

man is ordered to a supernatural end and that his soul can gratuitously be raised beyond all it deserves to communion with God.[238]

478,582,1431 **368**   The spiritual tradition of the Church also emphasizes the
1764,2517, *heart,* in the biblical sense of the depths of one's being, where the
2562,2843 person decides for or against God.[239]

2331-2336 **III.   "MALE AND FEMALE HE CREATED THEM"**

Equality and difference willed by God

369   Man and woman have been *created,* which is to say, *willed* by God: on the one hand, in perfect equality as human persons; on the other, in their respective beings as man and woman. "Being man" or "being woman" is a reality which is good and willed by God: man and woman possess an inalienable dignity which comes to them immediately from God their Creator.[240] Man and woman are both with one and the same dignity "in the image of God." In their "being-man" and "being-woman," they reflect the Creator's wisdom and goodness.

370   In no way is God in man's image. He is neither man nor woman. God is pure spirit in which there is no place for the difference between the
42, 239 sexes. But the respective "perfections" of man and woman reflect something of the infinite perfection of God: those of a mother and those of a father and husband.[241]

"Each for the other" – "A unity in two"

371   God created man and woman *together* and willed each *for* the other. The Word of God gives us to understand this through
1605 various features of the sacred text. "It is not good that the man should be alone. I will make him a helper fit for him."[242] None of the animals can be man's partner.[243] The woman God "fashions" from the man's rib and brings to him elicits on the man's part a cry of wonder, an exclamation of love and communion: "This at last is bone of my bones and flesh of my flesh."[244] Man discovers woman as another "I," sharing the same humanity.

---

237   Cf. Council of Constantinople IV (870): DS 657.
238   Cf. Vatican Council I, *Dei Filius:* DS 3005; *GS* 22 § 5; *Humani generis:* DS 3891.
239   Cf. *Jer* 31:33; *Deut* 6:5; 29:3; *Isa* 29:13; *Ezek* 36:26; *Mt* 6:21; *Lk* 8:15; *Rom* 5:5.
240   Cf. *Gen* 2:7, 22.
241   Cf. *Isa* 49:14-15; 66:13; *Ps* 131:2-3; *Hos* 11:1-4; *Jer* 3:4-19.
242   *Gen* 2:18.
243   *Gen* 2:19-20.

372   Man and woman were made "for each other" – not that God left them half-made and incomplete: he created them to be a communion of persons, in which each can be "helpmate" to the other, for they are equal as persons ("bone of my bones . . .") and complementary as masculine and feminine. In marriage God unites them in such a way that, by forming "one flesh,"[245] they can transmit human life: "Be fruitful and multiply, and fill the earth."[246] By transmitting human life to their descendants, man and woman as spouses and parents cooperate in a unique way in the Creator's work.[247]   *1652, 2366*

373   In God's plan man and woman have the vocation of "subduing" the earth[248] as stewards of God. This sovereignty is not to be an arbitrary and destructive domination. God calls man and woman, made in the image of the Creator "who loves everything that exists,"[249] to share in his providence toward other creatures; hence their responsibility for the world God has entrusted to them.   *307 2415*

IV.   MAN IN PARADISE

374   The first man was not only created good, but was also established in friendship with his Creator and in harmony with himself and with the creation around him, in a state that would be surpassed only by the glory of the new creation in Christ.   *54*

375   The Church, interpreting the symbolism of biblical language in an authentic way, in the light of the New Testament and Tradition, teaches that our first parents, Adam and Eve, were constituted in an original "state of holiness and justice."[250] This grace of original holiness was "to share in . . . divine life."[251]   *1997*

376   By the radiance of this grace all dimensions of man's life were confirmed. As long as he remained in the divine intimacy, man would not have to suffer or die.[252] The inner harmony of the human person, the harmony between man and woman,[253] and finally the harmony between the first couple and all creation, comprised the state called "original justice."   *1008, 1502*

---

244   *Gen* 2:23.
245   *Gen* 2:24.
246   *Gen* 1:28.
247   Cf. *GS* 50 § 1.
248   *Gen* 1:28.
249   *Wis* 11:24.
250   Cf. Council of Trent (1546): DS 1511.
251   Cf. *LG* 2.
252   Cf. *Gen* 2:17; 3:16, 19.
253   Cf. *Gen* 2:25.

2514 **377**   The "mastery" over the world that God offered man from the beginning was realized above all within man himself: *mastery of self.* The first man was unimpaired and ordered in his whole being because he was free from the triple concupiscence[254] that subjugates him to the pleasures of the senses, covetousness for earthly goods, and self-assertion, contrary to the dictates of reason.

2415 **378**   The sign of man's familiarity with God is that God places
2427 him in the garden.[255] There he lives "to till it and keep it." Work is not yet a burden,[256] but rather the collaboration of man and woman with God in perfecting the visible creation.

379   This entire harmony of original justice, foreseen for man in God's plan, will be lost by the sin of our first parents.

IN BRIEF

380   "Father, . . . you formed man in your own likeness and set him over the whole world to serve you, his creator, and to rule over all creatures" (*Roman Missal,* EP IV 118).

381   Man is predestined to reproduce the image of God's Son made man, the "image of the invisible God" (*Col* 1:15), so that Christ shall be the first-born of a multitude of brothers and sisters (cf. *Eph* 1:3-6; *Rom* 8:29).

382   "Man, though made of body and soul, is a unity " (*GS* 14 § 1). The doctrine of the faith affirms that the spiritual and immortal soul is created immediately by God.

383   "God did not create man a solitary being. From the beginning, 'male and female he created them' (*Gen* 1:27). This partnership of man and woman constitutes the first form of communion between persons" (*GS* 12 § 4).

384   Revelation makes known to us the state of original holiness and justice of man and woman before sin: from their friendship with God flowed the happiness of their existence in paradise.

---

254 Cf. *1 Jn* 2:16.
255 Cf. *Gen* 2:8.
256 *Gen* 2:15; cf. 3:17-19.

Paragraph 7. The Fall

385   God is infinitely good and all his works are good. Yet no
one can escape the experience of suffering or the evils in nature
which seem to be linked to the limitations proper to creatures: and
above all to the question of moral evil. Where does evil come from?
"I sought whence evil comes and there was no solution," said St.   *309*
Augustine,[257] and his own painful quest would only be resolved
by his conversion to the living God. For "the mystery of lawless-
ness" is clarified only in the light of the "mystery of our religion."[258] The revelation of divine love in Christ manifested at the   *457*
same time the extent of evil and the superabundance of grace.[259]   *1848*
We must therefore approach the question of the origin of evil by   *539*
fixing the eyes of our faith on him who alone is its conqueror.[260]

I.   WHERE SIN ABOUNDED, GRACE ABOUNDED
ALL THE MORE

The reality of sin

386   Sin is present in human history; any attempt to ignore it or
to give this dark reality other names would be futile. To try to
understand what sin is, one must first recognize *the profound relation of man to God*, for only in this relationship is the evil of sin
unmasked in its true identity as humanity's rejection of God and   *1847*
opposition to him, even as it continues to weigh heavy on human
life and history.

387   Only the light of divine Revelation clarifies the reality of
sin and particularly of the sin committed at mankind's origins.
Without the knowledge Revelation gives of God we cannot recognize sin clearly and are tempted to explain it as merely a develop-   *1848*
mental flaw, a psychological weakness, a mistake, or the necessary   *1739*
consequence of an inadequate social structure, etc. Only in the
knowledge of God's plan for man can we grasp that sin is an abuse
of the freedom that God gives to created persons so that they are
capable of loving him and loving one another.

---

257 St. Augustine, *Conf. 7, 7, 11: PL 32, 739.*
258 *2 Thess 2:7; 1 Tim 3:16.*
259 Cf. *Rom 5:20.*
260 Cf. *Lk 11:21-22; Jn 16:11; 1 Jn 3:8.*

Original Sin – an essential truth of the faith

388   With the progress of Revelation, the reality of sin is also
illuminated. Although to some extent the People of God in the Old
431 Testament had tried to understand the pathos of the human con-
208 dition in the light of the history of the fall narrated in Genesis, they
could not grasp this story's ultimate meaning, which is revealed
only in the light of the death and Resurrection of Jesus Christ.[261]
359 We must know Christ as the source of grace in order to know Adam
as the source of sin. The Spirit-Paraclete, sent by the risen Christ,
729 came to "convict the world concerning sin,"[262] by revealing him
who is its Redeemer.

389   The doctrine of original sin is, so to speak, the "reverse
side" of the Good News that Jesus is the Savior of all men, that all
422 need salvation, and that salvation is offered to all through Christ.
The Church, which has the mind of Christ,[263] knows very well that
we cannot tamper with the revelation of original sin without
undermining the mystery of Christ.

How to read the account of the Fall

390   The account of the fall in *Genesis* 3 uses figurative language, but affirms a primeval event, a deed that took place *at the*
289 *beginning of the history of man.*[264] Revelation gives us the certainty
of faith that the whole of human history is marked by the original
fault freely committed by our first parents.[265]

II.   THE FALL OF THE ANGELS

391   Behind the disobedient choice of our first parents lurks a
seductive voice, opposed to God, which makes them fall into death
2538 out of envy.[266] Scripture and the Church's Tradition see in this
being a fallen angel, called "Satan" or the "devil."[267] The Church
teaches that Satan was at first a good angel, made by God: "The
devil and the other demons were indeed created naturally good by
God, but they became evil by their own doing."[268]

---

261 Cf. *Rom* 5:12-21.
262 *Jn* 16:8.
263 Cf. *1 Cor* 2:16.
264 Cf. *GS* 13 § 1.
265 Cf. Council of Trent: DS 1513; Pius XII: DS 3897; Paul VI: AAS 58 (1966),
     654.
266 Cf. *Gen* 3:1-5; *Wis* 2:24.
267 Cf. *Jn* 8:44; *Rev* 12:9.

392   Scripture speaks of a sin of these angels.[269] This "fall" consists in the free choice of these created spirits, who radically and irrevocably *rejected* God and his reign. We find a reflection of that rebellion in the tempter's words to our first parents: "You will be like God."[270] The devil "has sinned from the beginning"; he is "a liar and the father of lies."[271]

1850

2482

393   It is the *irrevocable* character of their choice, and not a defect in the infinite divine mercy, that makes the angels' sin unforgivable. "There is no repentance for the angels after their fall, just as there is no repentance for men after death."[272]

1033-1037

1022

394   Scripture witnesses to the disastrous influence of the one Jesus calls "a murderer from the beginning," who would even try to divert Jesus from the mission received from his Father.[273] "The reason the Son of God appeared was to destroy the works of the devil."[274] In its consequences the gravest of these works was the mendacious seduction that led man to disobey God.

538-540

550

2846-2849

395   The power of Satan is, nonetheless, not infinite. He is only a creature, powerful from the fact that he is pure spirit, but still a creature. He cannot prevent the building up of God's reign. Although Satan may act in the world out of hatred for God and his kingdom in Christ Jesus, and although his action may cause grave injuries – of a spiritual nature and, indirectly, even of a physical nature – to each man and to society, the action is permitted by divine providence which with strength and gentleness guides human and cosmic history. It is a great mystery that providence should permit diabolical activity, but "we know that in everything God works for good with those who love him."[275]

309

1673

412

2850-2854

---

268   Lateran Council IV (1215): DS 800.
269   Cf. *2 Pet* 2:4.
270   *Gen* 3:5.
271   *1 Jn* 3:8; *Jn* 8:44.
272   St. John Damascene, *De Fide orth.* 2, 4: PG 94, 877.
273   *Jn* 8:44; cf. *Mt* 4:1-11.
274   *1 Jn* 3:8.
275   *Rom* 8:28.

III.   ORIGINAL SIN

Freedom put to the test

396   God created man in his image and established him in his
friendship. A spiritual creature, man can live this friendship only
1730 in free submission to God. The prohibition against eating "of the
311   tree of the knowledge of good and evil" spells this out: "for in the
day that you eat of it, you shall die."[276] The "tree of the knowledge
of good and evil"[277] symbolically evokes the insurmountable limits that man, being a creature, must freely recognize and respect
with trust. Man is dependent on his Creator and subject to the laws
301   of creation and to the moral norms that govern the use of freedom.

Man's first sin

1707, 2541 **397**   Man, tempted by the devil, let his trust in his Creator die
1850, 215 in his heart and, abusing his freedom, disobeyed God's command.
This is what man's first sin consisted of.[278] All subsequent sin
would be disobedience toward God and lack of trust in his goodness.

398   In that sin man *preferred* himself to God and by that very
act scorned him. He chose himself over and against God, against
2084 the requirements of his creaturely status and therefore against his
own good. Created in a state of holiness, man was destined to be
2113 fully "divinized" by God in glory. Seduced by the devil, he wanted
to "be like God," but "without God, before God, and not in accordance with God."[279]

399   Scripture portrays the tragic consequences of this first
disobedience. Adam and Eve immediately lose the grace of original
holiness.[280] They become afraid of the God of whom they have
conceived a distorted image – that of a God jealous of his prerogatives.[281]

1607 **400**   The harmony in which they had found themselves, thanks
2514 to original justice, is now destroyed: the control of the soul's
602, 1008 spiritual faculties over the body is shattered; the union of man and

---

276 *Gen* 2:17.
277 *Gen* 2:17.
278 Cf. *Gen* 3:1-11; *Rom* 5:19.
279 St. Maximus the Confessor, *Ambigua*: PG 91, 1156C; cf. *Gen* 3:5.
280 Cf. *Rom* 3:23.
281 Cf. *Gen* 3:5-10.

woman becomes subject to tensions, their relations henceforth marked by lust and domination.[282] Harmony with creation is broken: visible creation has become alien and hostile to man.[283] Because of man, creation is now subject "to its bondage to decay."[284] Finally, the consequence explicitly foretold for this disobedience will come true: man will "return to the ground,"[285] for out of it he was taken. *Death makes its entrance into human history.*[286]

401   After that first sin, the world is virtually inundated by sin. There is Cain's murder of his brother Abel and the universal corruption which follows in the wake of sin. Likewise, sin frequently manifests itself in the history of Israel, especially as infidelity to the God of the Covenant and as transgression of the Law of Moses. And even after Christ's atonement, sin raises its head in countless ways among Christians.[287] Scripture and the Church's Tradition continually recall the presence and *universality of sin in man's history:*

1865

2259

1739

> What Revelation makes known to us is confirmed by our own experience. For when man looks into his own heart he finds that he is drawn toward what is wrong and sunk in many evils which cannot come from his good creator. Often refusing to acknowledge God as his source, man has also upset the relationship which should link him to his last end; and at the same time he has broken the right order that should reign within himself as well as between himself and other men and all creatures.[288]

The consequences of Adam's sin for humanity

402   All men are implicated in Adam's sin, as St. Paul affirms: "By one man's disobedience many [that is, all men] were made sinners": "sin came into the world through one man and death through sin, and so death spread to all men because all men sinned...."[289] The Apostle contrasts the universality of sin and death with the universality of salvation in Christ. "Then as one man's trespass led to condemnation for all men, so one man's act of righteousness leads to acquittal and life for all men."[290]

430, 605

---

282 Cf. *Gen* 3:7-16.
283 Cf. *Gen* 3:17, 19.
284 *Rom* 8:21.
285 *Gen* 3:19; cf. 2:17.
286 Cf. *Rom* 5:12.
287 Cf. *Gen* 4:3-15; 6:5, 12; *Rom* 1:18-32; *1 Cor* 1-6; *Rev* 2-3.
288 *GS* 13 § 1.
289 *Rom* 5:12, 19.
290 *Rom* 5:18.

403   Following St. Paul, the Church has always taught that the
overwhelming misery which oppresses men and their inclination
2606 toward evil and death cannot be understood apart from their
connection with Adam's sin and the fact that he has transmitted to
us a sin with which we are all born afflicted, a sin which is the
"death of the soul."[291] Because of this certainty of faith, the Church
1250 baptizes for the remission of sins even tiny infants who have not
committed personal sin.[292]

404   How did the sin of Adam become the sin of all his descendants? The whole human race is in Adam "as one body of one
man."[293] By this "unity of the human race" all men are implicated
360 in Adam's sin, as all are implicated in Christ's justice. Still, the
transmission of original sin is a mystery that we cannot fully
50 understand. But we do know by Revelation that Adam had received original holiness and justice not for himself alone, but for
all human nature. By yielding to the tempter, Adam and Eve
committed a *personal sin*, but this sin affected *the human nature* that
they would then transmit *in a fallen state*.[294] It is a sin which will be
transmitted by propagation to all mankind, that is, by the transmission of a human nature deprived of original holiness and justice.
And that is why original sin is called "sin" only in an analogical
sense: it is a sin "contracted" and not "committed" – a state and not
an act.

405   Although it is proper to each individual,[295] original sin
does not have the character of a personal fault in any of Adam's
descendants. It is a deprivation of original holiness and justice, but
human nature has not been totally corrupted: it is wounded in the
natural powers proper to it; subject to ignorance, suffering, and the
dominion of death; and inclined to sin – an inclination to evil that
2515 is called "concupiscence." Baptism, by imparting the life of Christ's
1264 grace, erases original sin and turns a man back toward God, but
the consequences for nature, weakened and inclined to evil, persist
in man and summon him to spiritual battle.

406   The Church's teaching on the transmission of original sin was
articulated more precisely in the fifth century, especially under the impulse
of St. Augustine's reflections against Pelagianism, and in the sixteenth
century, in opposition to the Protestant Reformation. Pelagius held that
man could, by the natural power of free will and without the necessary

---

291 Cf. Council of Trent: DS 1512.
292 Cf. Council of Trent: DS 1514.
293 St. Thomas Aquinas, *De Malo* 4, 1.
294 Cf. Council of Trent: DS 1511-1512.
295 Cf. Council of Trent: DS 1513.

help of God's grace, lead a morally good life; he thus reduced the influence of Adam's fault to bad example. The first Protestant reformers, on the contrary, taught that original sin has radically perverted man and destroyed his freedom; they identified the sin inherited by each man with the tendency to evil (concupiscentia), which would be insurmountable. The Church pronounced on the meaning of the data of Revelation on original sin especially at the second Council of Orange (529)[296] and at the Council of Trent (1546).[297]

A hard battle . . .

407 The doctrine of original sin, closely connected with that of redemption by Christ, provides lucid discernment of man's situation and activity in the world. By our first parents' sin, the devil *2015* has acquired a certain domination over man, even though man *2852* remains free. Original sin entails "captivity under the power of him who thenceforth had the power of death, that is, the devil."[298] Ignorance of the fact that man has a wounded nature inclined to evil gives rise to serious errors in the areas of education, politics, *1888* social action,[299] and morals.

408 The consequences of original sin and of all men's personal sins put the world as a whole in the sinful condition aptly described in St. John's expression, "the sin of the world."[300] This expression can also refer to the negative influence exerted on people by communal situations and social structures that are the fruit of *1865* men's sins.[301]

409 This dramatic situation of "the whole world [which] is in the power of the evil one"[302] makes man's life a battle: *2516*

> The whole of man's history has been the story of dour combat with the powers of evil, stretching, so our Lord tells us, from the very dawn of history until the last day. Finding himself in the midst of the battlefield man has to struggle to do what is right, and it is at great cost to himself, and aided by God's grace, that he succeeds in achieving his own inner integrity.[303]

---

296 DS 371-372.
297 Cf. DS 1510-1516.
298 Council of Trent (1546): DS 1511; cf. *Heb* 2:14.
299 Cf. John Paul II, *CA* 25.
300 *Jn* 1:29.
301 Cf. John Paul II, *RP* 16.
302 *1 Jn* 5:19; cf. *1 Pet* 5:8.
303 GS 37 § 2.

IV.   "YOU DID NOT ABANDON HIM TO THE POWER OF DEATH"

410   After his fall, man was not abandoned by God. On the
contrary, God calls him and in a mysterious way heralds the
55, 705   coming victory over evil and his restoration from his fall.[304] This
1609, 2568   passage in Genesis is called the *Protoevangelium* ("first gospel"): the
first announcement of the Messiah and Redeemer, of a battle
675   between the serpent and the Woman, and of the final victory of a
descendant of hers.

411   The Christian tradition sees in this passage an announcement of the "New Adam" who, because he "became obedi-
359, 615   ent unto death, even death on a cross," makes amends
superabundantly for the disobedience of Adam.[305] Furthermore
many Fathers and Doctors of the Church have seen the woman
announced in the *Protoevangelium* as Mary, the mother of Christ,
the "new Eve." Mary benefited first of all and uniquely from
Christ's victory over sin: she was preserved from all stain of
491   original sin and by a special grace of God committed no sin of any
kind during her whole earthly life.[306]

412   But *why did God not prevent the first man from sinning?* St.
Leo the Great responds, "Christ's inexpressible grace gave us
310, 395   blessings better than those the demon's envy had taken away."[307]
And St. Thomas Aquinas wrote, "There is nothing to prevent
human nature's being raised up to something greater, even after
sin; God permits evil in order to draw forth some greater good.
272   Thus St. Paul says, 'Where sin increased, grace abounded all the
more'; and the Exultet sings, 'O happy fault, . . . which gained for
1994   us so great a Redeemer!'"[308]

IN BRIEF

413   "God did not make death, and he does not delight in
the death of the living. . . . It was through the devil's
envy that death entered the world" (*Wis* 1:13; 2:24).

414   Satan or the devil and the other demons are fallen
angels who have freely refused to serve God and his

---

304   Cf. *Gen* 3:9, 15.
305   Cf. *1 Cor* 15:21-22, 45; *Phil* 2:8; *Rom* 5:19-20.
306   Cf. Pius IX, *Ineffabilis Deus*: DS 2803; Council of Trent: DS 1573.
307   St. Leo the Great, *Sermo* 73, 4: PL 54, 396.
308   St. Thomas Aquinas, *STh* III, 1, 3, *ad* 3; cf. *Rom* 5:20.

plan. Their choice against God is definitive. They try to associate man in their revolt against God.

415 "Although set by God in a state of rectitude, man, enticed by the evil one, abused his freedom at the very start of history. He lifted himself up against God and sought to attain his goal apart from him" (*GS* 13 § 1).

416 By his sin Adam, as the first man, lost the original holiness and justice he had received from God, not only for himself but for all human beings.

417 Adam and Eve transmitted to their descendants human nature wounded by their own first sin and hence deprived of original holiness and justice; this deprivation is called "original sin."

418 As a result of original sin, human nature is weakened in its powers; subject to ignorance, suffering, and the domination of death; and inclined to sin (This inclination is called "concupiscence.").

419 "We therefore hold, with the Council of Trent, that original sin is transmitted with human nature, 'by propagation, not by imitation' and that it is . . . 'proper to each'" (Paul VI, *CPG* § 16).

420 The victory that Christ won over sin has given us greater blessings than those which sin had taken from us: "where sin increased, grace abounded all the more" (*Rom* 5:20).

421 Christians believe that "the world has been established and kept in being by the Creator's love; has fallen into slavery to sin but has been set free by Christ, crucified and risen to break the power of the evil one . . ." (*GS* 2 § 2).

Chapter Two
I Believe in Jesus Christ,
The Only Son of God

The Good News: God has sent his Son

422   "But when the time had fully come, God sent forth his Son, born of a woman, born under the law, to redeem those who were
389 under the law, so that we might receive adoption as sons."[1] This is "the gospel of Jesus Christ, the Son of God":[2] God has visited his people. He has fulfilled the promise he made to Abraham and his descendants. He acted far beyond all expectation – he has sent his
2763 own "beloved Son."[3]

423   We believe and confess that Jesus of Nazareth, born a Jew of a daughter of Israel at Bethlehem at the time of King Herod the Great and the emperor Caesar Augustus, a carpenter by trade, who died crucified in Jerusalem under the procurator Pontius Pilate during the reign of the emperor Tiberius, is the eternal Son of God made man. He "came from God,"[4] "descended from heaven,"[5] and "came in the flesh."[6] For "the Word became flesh and dwelt among us, full of grace and truth; we have beheld his glory, glory as of the only Son from the Father. . . . And from his fullness have we all received, grace upon grace."[7]

424   Moved by the grace of the Holy Spirit and drawn by the Father, we believe in Jesus and confess: "You are the Christ, the Son
683 of the living God."[8] On the rock of this faith confessed by St. Peter,
552 Christ built his Church.[9]

---

1   *Gal* 4:4-5.
2   *Mk* 1:1.
3   *Mk* 1:11; cf. *Lk* 1:55, 68.
4   *Jn* 13:3.
5   *Jn* 3:13; 6:33.
6   *1 Jn* 4:2.
7   *Jn* 1:14, 16.
8   *Mt* 16:16.
9   Cf. *Mt* 16:18; St. Leo the Great, *Sermo* 4, 3: PL 54, 150-152; 51, 1: PL 54, 308-309; 62, 2: PL 54, 350-351; 83, 3: PL 54, 431-432.

"To preach ... the unsearchable riches of Christ"[10]

425 The transmission of the Christian faith consists primarily in proclaiming Jesus Christ in order to lead others to faith in him. From the beginning, the first disciples burned with the desire to proclaim Christ: "We cannot but speak of what we have seen and heard."[11] And they invite people of every era to enter into the joy of their communion with Christ: *850, 858*

> That which was from the beginning, which we have heard, which we have seen with our eyes, which we have looked upon and touched with our hands, concerning the word of life – the life was made manifest, and we saw it, and testify to it, and proclaim to you the eternal life which was with the Father and was made manifest to us – that which we have seen and heard we proclaim also to you, so that you may have fellowship with us; and our fellowship is with the Father and with his Son Jesus Christ. And we are writing this that our joy may be complete.[12]

At the heart of catechesis: Christ

426 "At the heart of catechesis we find, in essence, a Person, the Person of Jesus of Nazareth, the only Son from the Father ... who suffered and died for us and who now, after rising, is living with us forever."[13] To catechize is "to reveal in the Person of Christ the whole of God's eternal design reaching fulfillment in that Person. It is to seek to understand the meaning of Christ's actions and words and of the signs worked by him."[14] Catechesis aims at putting "people ... in communion ... with Jesus Christ: only he can lead us to the love of the Father in the Spirit and make us share in the life of the Holy Trinity."[15] *1698* *513* *260*

427 In catechesis "Christ, the Incarnate Word and Son of God, ... is taught – everything else is taught with reference to him – and it is Christ alone who teaches – anyone else teaches to the extent that he is Christ's spokesman, enabling Christ to teach with his lips. ... Every catechist should be able to apply to himself the mysterious words of Jesus: 'My teaching is not mine, but his who sent me.'"[16] *2145* *876*

---

10 *Eph* 3:8.
11 *Acts* 4:20.
12 *1 Jn* 1:1-4.
13 *CT* 5.
14 *CT* 5.
15 *CT* 5.
16 *CT* 6; cf. *Jn* 7:16.

428   Whoever is called "to teach Christ" must first seek "the surpassing worth of knowing Christ Jesus"; he must suffer "the loss of all things . . ." in order to "gain Christ and be found in him," and "to know him and the power of his resurrection, and [to] share his sufferings, becoming like him in his death, that if possible [he] may attain the resurrection from the dead."[17]

429   From this loving knowledge of Christ springs the desire to proclaim him, to "evangelize," and to lead others to the "yes" of
851 faith in Jesus Christ. But at the same time the need to know this faith better makes itself felt. To this end, following the order of the Creed, Jesus' principal titles – "Christ," "Son of God," and "Lord" (*article 2*) – will be presented. The Creed next confesses the chief mysteries of his life – those of his Incarnation (*article 3*), Paschal mystery (*articles 4 and 5*), and glorification (*articles 6 and 7*).

ARTICLE 2
"AND IN JESUS CHRIST, HIS ONLY SON, OUR LORD"

I.   JESUS

430   Jesus means in Hebrew: "God saves." At the annunciation, the angel Gabriel gave him the name Jesus as his proper name,
210 which expresses both his identity and his mission.[18] Since God alone can forgive sins, it is God who, in Jesus his eternal Son made
402 man, "will save his people from their sins."[19] In Jesus, God recapitulates all of his history of salvation on behalf of men.

431   In the history of salvation God was not content to deliver Israel "out of the house of bondage"[20] by bringing them out of Egypt. He also saves them from their sin. Because sin is always an
1441, 1850 offense against God, only he can forgive it.[21] For this reason Israel, becoming more and more aware of the universality of sin, will no
388 longer be able to seek salvation except by invoking the name of the Redeemer God.[22]

---

17 *Phil* 3:8-11.
18 Cf. *Lk* 1:31.
19 *Mt* 1:21; cf. 2:7.
20 *Deut* 5:6.
21 Cf. *Ps* 51:4, 12.
22 Cf. *Ps* 79:9.

432   The name "Jesus" signifies that the very name of God is present in the person of his Son, made man for the universal and definitive redemption from sins. It is the divine name that alone *589, 2666* brings salvation, and henceforth all can invoke his name, for Jesus *389* united himself to all men through his Incarnation,[23] so that "there *161* is no other name under heaven given among men by which we must be saved."[24]

433   The name of the Savior God was invoked only once in the year by the high priest in atonement for the sins of Israel, after he had sprinkled the mercy seat in the Holy of Holies with the sacrificial blood. The mercy seat was the place of God's presence.[25] *615* When St. Paul speaks of Jesus whom "God put forward as an expiation by his blood," he means that in Christ's humanity "God was in Christ reconciling the world to himself."[26]

434   Jesus' Resurrection glorifies the name of the Savior God, for from that time on it is the name of Jesus that fully manifests the supreme power of the "name which is above every name."[27] The *2812* evil spirits fear his name; in his name his disciples perform miracles, for the Father grants all they ask in this name.[28] *2614*

435   The name of Jesus is at the heart of Christian prayer. All liturgical prayers conclude with the words "through our Lord Jesus Christ." The *Hail Mary* reaches its high point in the words *2667-2668* "blessed is the fruit of thy womb, Jesus." The Eastern prayer of the *2676* heart, the *Jesus Prayer*, says: "Lord Jesus Christ, Son of God, have mercy on me, a sinner." Many Christians, such as St. Joan of Arc, have died with the one word "Jesus" on their lips.

II.   CHRIST

436   The word "Christ" comes from the Greek translation of the Hebrew *Messiah*, which means "anointed." It became the name proper to Jesus only because he accomplished perfectly the divine *690, 695* mission that "Christ" signifies. In effect, in Israel those consecrated to God for a mission that he gave were anointed in his name. This was the case for kings, for priests and, in rare instances, for prophets.[29] This had to be the case all the more so for the Messiah whom

---

23   Cf. *Jn* 3:18; *Acts* 2:21; 5:41; *3 Jn* 7; *Rom* 10:6-13.
24   *Acts* 4:12; cf. 9:14; *Jas* 2:7.
25   Cf. *Ex* 25:22; *Lev* 16:2,15-16; *Num* 7:89; *Sir* 50:20; *Heb* 9:5, 7.
26   *Rom* 3:25; *2 Cor* 5:19.
27   *Phil* 2:9-10; cf. *Jn* 12:28.
28   Cf. *Acts* 16:16-18; 19:13-16; *Mk* 16:17; *Jn* 15:16.

God would send to inaugurate his kingdom definitively.[30] It was necessary that the Messiah be anointed by the Spirit of the Lord at once
711-716 as king and priest, and also as prophet.[31] Jesus fulfilled the messianic
783 hope of Israel in his threefold office of priest, prophet, and king.

437   To the shepherds, the angel announced the birth of Jesus as the Messiah promised to Israel: "To you is born this day in the
525, 486 city of David a Savior, who is Christ the Lord."[32] From the beginning he was "the one whom the Father consecrated and sent into the world," conceived as "holy" in Mary's virginal womb.[33] God called Joseph to "take Mary as your wife, for that which is conceived in her is of the Holy Spirit," so that Jesus, "who is called Christ," should be born of Joseph's spouse into the messianic lineage of David.[34]

438   Jesus' messianic consecration reveals his divine mission, "for the name 'Christ' implies 'he who anointed,' 'he who was
727 anointed' and 'the very anointing with which he was anointed.' The one who anointed is the Father, the one who was anointed is the Son, and he was anointed with the Spirit who is the anointing."[35] His eternal messianic consecration was revealed during the
535 time of his earthly life at the moment of his baptism by John, when "God anointed Jesus of Nazareth with the Holy Spirit and with power," "that he might be revealed to Israel"[36] as its Messiah. His works and words will manifest him as "the Holy One of God."[37]

439   Many Jews and even certain Gentiles who shared their hope recognized in Jesus the fundamental attributes of the messi-
528-529 anic "Son of David," promised by God to Israel.[38] Jesus accepted
547 his rightful title of Messiah, though with some reserve because it was understood by some of his contemporaries in too human a sense, as essentially political.[39]

---

29 Cf. *Ex* 29:7; *Lev* 8:12; *1 Sam* 9:16; 10:1; 16:1,12-13; *1 Kings* 1:39; 19:16.
30 Cf. *Ps* 2:2; *Acts* 4:26-27.
31 Cf. *Isa* 11:2; 61:1; *Zech* 4:14; 6:13: *Lk* 4:16-21.
32 *Lk* 2:11.
33 *Jn* 10:36: cf. *Lk* 1:35.
34 *Mt* 1:20; cf. *Mt* 1:16; *Rom* 1:1; *2 Tim* 2:8; *Rev* 22:16.
35 St. Irenaeus, *Adv. haeres.*, 3, 18, 3: PG 7/1, 934.
36 *Acts* 10:38; *Jn* 1:31.
37 *Mk* 1:24; *Jn* 6:69; *Acts* 3:14.
38 Cf. *Mt* 2:2; 9:27; 12:23; 15:22; 20:30; 21:9, 15.
39 Cf. *Jn* 4:25-26; 6:15;11:27; *Mt* 22:41-46; *Lk* 24:21.

440 Jesus accepted Peter's profession of faith, which acknowledged him to be the Messiah, by announcing the imminent Passion
of the Son of Man.[40] He unveiled the authentic content of his *552*
messianic kingship both in the transcendent identity of the Son of
Man "who came down from heaven," and in his redemptive
mission as the suffering Servant: "The Son of Man came not to be
served but to serve, and to give his life as a ransom for many."[41]
Hence the true meaning of his kingship is revealed only when he *550*
is raised high on the cross.[42] Only after his Resurrection will Peter *445*
be able to proclaim Jesus' messianic kingship to the People of God:
"Let all the house of Israel therefore know assuredly that God has
made him both Lord and Christ, this Jesus whom you crucified."[43]

III.   THE ONLY SON OF GOD

441 In the Old Testament, *"son of God"* is a title given to the
angels, the Chosen People, the children of Israel, and their kings.[44]
It signifies an adoptive sonship that establishes a relationship of
particular intimacy between God and his creature. When the promised Messiah-King is called "son of God," it does not necessarily
imply that he was more than human, according to the literal
meaning of these texts. Those who called Jesus "son of God," as the
Messiah of Israel, perhaps meant nothing more than this.[45]

442 Such is not the case for Simon Peter when he confesses
Jesus as "the Christ, the Son of the living God," for Jesus responds
solemnly: "Flesh and blood has not *revealed* this to you, but *my
Father* who is in heaven."[46] Similarly Paul will write, regarding his *552*
conversion on the road to Damascus, "When he who had set me
apart before I was born, and had called me through his grace, was
pleased to reveal his Son to me, in order that I might preach him
among the Gentiles. . . ."[47] "And in the synagogues immediately
[Paul] proclaimed Jesus, saying, 'He is the Son of God.'"[48] From
the beginning this acknowledgment of Christ's divine sonship will *424*

---

40 Cf. *Mt* 16:16-23.
41 *Jn* 3:13: *Mt* 20:28; cf. *Jn* 6:62; *Dan* 7:13; *Isa* 53:10-12.
42 Cf. *Jn* 19:19-22; *Lk* 23:39-43.
43 *Acts* 2:36.
44 Cf. *Deut* 14:1; (LXX) 32:8; *Job* 1:6; *Ex* 4:22; *Hos* 2:1; 11:1; *Jer* 3:19; *Sir* 36:11;
    Wis 18:13; *2 Sam* 7:14; *Ps* 82:6.
45 Cf. *1 Chr* 17:13; *Ps* 2:7; *Mt* 27:54; *Lk* 23:47.
46 *Mt* 16:16-17.
47 *Gal* 1:15-16.
48 *Acts* 9:20.

be the center of the apostolic faith, first professed by Peter as the Church's foundation.[49]

443   Peter could recognize the transcendent character of the Messiah's divine sonship because Jesus had clearly allowed it to be so understood. To his accusers' question before the Sanhedrin, "Are you the Son of God, then?" Jesus answered, "You say that I am."[50] Well before this, Jesus referred to himself as "the Son" who knows the Father, as distinct from the "servants" God had earlier sent to his people; he is superior even to the angels.[51] He distinguished his sonship from that of his disciples by never saying "our Father," except to command them: "You, then, pray like this: 'Our Father,'" and he
2786   emphasized this distinction, saying "my Father and your Father."[52]

444   The Gospels report that at two solemn moments, the Baptism and the Transfiguration of Christ, the voice of the Father
536, 554   designates Jesus his "beloved Son."[53] Jesus calls himself the "only Son of God," and by this title affirms his eternal preexistence.[54] He asks for faith in "the name of the only Son of God."[55] In the centurion's exclamation before the crucified Christ, "Truly this man was the Son of God,"[56] that Christian confession is already heard. Only in the Paschal mystery can the believer give the title "Son of God" its full meaning.

445   After his Resurrection, Jesus' divine sonship becomes manifest in the power of his glorified humanity. He was "desig-
653   nated Son of God in power according to the Spirit of holiness by his Resurrection from the dead."[57] The apostles can confess: "We have beheld his glory, glory as of the only Son from the Father, full of grace and truth."[58]

IV.   LORD

209 **446**   In the Greek translation of the Old Testament, the ineffable Hebrew name YHWH, by which God revealed himself to Moses,[59] is

---

49 Cf. *1 Thess* 1:10; *Jn* 20:31; *Mt* 16:18
50 *Lk* 22:70; cf. *Mt* 26:64; *Mk* 14:61-62.
51 Cf. *Mt* 11:27; 21:34-38;24:36.
52 *Mt* 5:48; 6:8-9; 7:21; *Lk* 11:13; *Jn* 20:17.
53 Cf. *Mt* 3:17; cf. *Mt* 17:5.
54 *Jn* 3:16; cf. 10:36.
55 *Jn* 3:18.
56 *Mk* 15:39.
57 *Rom* 1:3; cf. *Acts* 13:33.
58 *Jn* 1:14.
59 Cf. *Ex* 3:14.

rendered as *Kyrios*, "Lord." From then on, "*Lord*" becomes the more usual name by which to indicate the divinity of Israel's God. The New Testament uses this full sense of the title "Lord" both for the Father and – what is new – for Jesus, who is thereby recognized as God Himself.[60]

447 Jesus ascribes this title to himself in a veiled way when he disputes with the Pharisees about the meaning of *Psalm* 110, but also in an explicit way when he addresses his apostles.[61] Throughout his public life, he demonstrated his divine sovereignty by *548* works of power over nature, illnesses, demons, death, and sin.

448 Very often in the Gospels people address Jesus as "Lord." This title testifies to the respect and trust of those who approach him for help and healing.[62] At the prompting of the Holy Spirit, "Lord" expresses the recognition of the divine mystery of Jesus.[63] *208, 683* In the encounter with the risen Jesus, this title becomes adoration: "My Lord and my God!" It thus takes on a connotation of love and affection that remains proper to the Christian tradition: "It is the Lord!"[64] *641*

449 By attributing to Jesus the divine title "Lord," the first confessions of the Church's faith affirm from the beginning that the power, honor, and glory due to God the Father are due also to Jesus, because "he was in the form of God,"[65] and the Father manifested *461* the sovereignty of Jesus by raising him from the dead and exalting *653* him into his glory.[66]

450 From the beginning of Christian history, the assertion of Christ's lordship over the world and over history has implicitly recognized that man should not submit his personal freedom in an *668-672* absolute manner to any earthly power, but only to God the Father and the Lord Jesus Christ: Caesar is not "the Lord."[67] "The Church *2242* . . . believes that the key, the center, and the purpose of the whole of man's history is to be found in its Lord and Master."[68]

---

60 Cf. *1 Cor* 2:8.
61 Cf. *Mt* 22:41-46; cf. *Acts* 2:34-36; *Heb* 1:13; *Jn* 13:13.
62 Cf. *Mt* 8:2; 14:30; 15:22; *et al.*
63 Cf. *Lk* 1:43; 2:11.
64 *Jn* 20:28; *Jn* 21:7.
65 Cf. *Acts* 2:34-36; *Rom* 9:5; *Titus* 2:13; *Rev* 5:13; *Phil* 2:6.
66 Cf. *Rom* 10:9; *1 Cor* 12:3; *Phil* 2:9-11.
67 Cf. *Rev* 11:15; *Mk* 12:17; *Acts* 5:29.
68 *GS* 10 § 3; cf. 45 § 2.

451   Christian prayer is characterized by the title "Lord,"
2664-2665 whether in the invitation to prayer ("The Lord be with you."), its
2817   conclusion ("through Christ our Lord"), or the exclamation full of
trust and hope: *Maran atha* ("Our Lord, come!"), or *Marana tha*
("Come, Lord!") – "Amen. Come, Lord Jesus!"[69]

IN BRIEF

452   The name Jesus means "God saves." The child born of
the Virgin Mary is called Jesus, "for he will save his
people from their sins" (*Mt* 1:21): "there is no other
name under heaven given among men by which we
must be saved" (*Acts* 4:12).

453   The title "Christ" means "Anointed One" (Messiah).
Jesus is the Christ, for "God anointed Jesus of Nazareth with the Holy Spirit and with power" (*Acts*
10:38). He was the one "who is to come" (*Lk* 7:19), the
object of "the hope of Israel" (*Acts* 28:20).

454   The title "Son of God" signifies the unique and eternal
relationship of Jesus Christ to God his Father: he is the
only Son of the Father (cf. *Jn* 1:14,18; 3:16,18); he is God
himself (cf. *Jn* 1:1). To be a Christian, one must believe
that Jesus Christ is the Son of God (cf. *Acts* 8:37; *1 Jn*
2:23).

455   The title "Lord" indicates divine sovereignty. To con-
fess or invoke Jesus as Lord is to believe in his divinity.
"No one can say 'Jesus is Lord' except by the Holy
Spirit" (*1 Cor* 12:3).

---

69   *1 Cor* 16:22; *Rev* 22:20.

ARTICLE 3
"HE WAS CONCEIVED BY THE POWER OF THE HOLY SPIRIT, AND WAS BORN OF THE VIRGIN MARY"

Paragraph 1. The Son of God Became Man

I. WHY DID THE WORD BECOME FLESH?

456 With the Nicene Creed, we answer by confessing: "For us men and for our salvation he came down from heaven; by the power of the Holy Spirit, he became incarnate of the Virgin Mary, and was made man."

457 The Word became flesh for us *in order to save us by reconciling us with God,* who "loved us and sent his Son to be the expiation for our sins": "the Father has sent his Son as the Savior of the *607* world," and "he was revealed to take away sins":[70]

> Sick, our nature demanded to be healed; fallen, to be raised *385* up; dead, to rise again. We had lost the possession of the good; it was necessary for it to be given back to us. Closed in the darkness, it was necessary to bring us the light; captives, we awaited a Savior; prisoners, help; slaves, a liberator. Are these things minor or insignificant? Did they not move God to descend to human nature and visit it, since humanity was in so miserable and unhappy a state?[71]

458 The Word became flesh *so that thus we might know God's love:* "In this the love of God was made manifest among us, that God sent his only Son into the world, so that we might live through *219* him."[72] "For God so loved the world that he gave his only Son, that whoever believes in him should not perish but have eternal life."[73]

459 The Word became flesh *to be our model of holiness:* "Take my yoke upon you, and learn from me." "I am the way, and the truth, *520* and the life; no one comes to the Father, but by me."[74] On the *823, 2012* mountain of the Transfiguration, the Father commands: "Listen to him!"[75] Jesus is the model for the Beatitudes and the norm of the new law: "Love one another as I have loved you."[76] This love *1717, 1965* implies an effective offering of oneself, after his example.[77]

---

70 *1 Jn* 4:10; 4:14; 3:5.
71 St. Gregory of Nyssa, *Orat. catech.* 15: PG 45, 48B.
72 *1 Jn* 4:9.
73 *Jn* 3:16.
74 *Mt* 11:29; *Jn* 14:6.
75 *Mk* 9:7; cf. *Deut* 6:4-5.

460   The Word became flesh to make us *"partakers of the divine nature"*:[78] "For this is why the Word became man, and the Son of
1265, 1391 God became the Son of man: so that man, by entering into communion with the Word and thus receiving divine sonship, might
1988 become a son of God."[79] "For the Son of God became man so that we might become God."[80] "The only-begotten Son of God, wanting to make us sharers in his divinity, assumed our nature, so that he, made man, might make men gods."[81]

II.   THE INCARNATION

461   Taking up St. John's expression, "The Word became flesh,"[82]
653, 661 the Church calls "Incarnation" the fact that the Son of God assumed
449 a human nature in order to accomplish our salvation in it. In a hymn cited by St. Paul, the Church sings the mystery of the Incarnation:

> Have this mind among yourselves, which is yours in Christ Jesus, who, though he was in the form of God, did not count equality with God a thing to be grasped, but emptied himself, taking the form of a servant, being born in the likeness of men. And being found in human form he humbled himself and became obedient unto death, even death on a cross.[83]

462   The *Letter to the Hebrews* refers to the same mystery:

> Consequently, when Christ came into the world, he said, "Sacrifices and offerings you have not desired, but a body have you prepared for me; in burnt offerings and sin offerings you have taken no pleasure. Then I said, 'Lo, I have come to do your will, O God.'"[84]

463   Belief in the true Incarnation of the Son of God is the distinctive sign of Christian faith: "By this you know the Spirit of God: every
90 spirit which confesses that Jesus Christ has come in the flesh is of God."[85] Such is the joyous conviction of the Church from her beginning whenever she sings "the mystery of our religion": "He was manifested in the flesh."[86]

---

76 *Jn* 15:12.
77 Cf. *Mk* 8:34.
78 *2 Pet* 1:4.
79 St. Irenaeus, *Adv. haeres.* 3, 19, 1: PG 7/1, 939.
80 St. Athanasius, *De inc.*, 54, 3: PG 25, 192B.
81 St. Thomas Aquinas, *Opusc.* 57: 1-4.
82 *Jn* 1:14.
83 *Phil* 2:5-8; cf. *LH*, Saturday, Canticle at Evening Prayer.
84 *Heb* 10:5-7, citing *Ps* 40:6-8 ([7-9] LXX).
85 *1 Jn* 4:2.
86 *1 Tim* 3:16.

III. TRUE GOD AND TRUE MAN

464 The unique and altogether singular event of the Incarnation of the Son of God does not mean that Jesus Christ is part God and part man, nor does it imply that he is the result of a confused mixture of the divine and the human. He became truly man while remaining truly God. Jesus Christ is true God and true man. During the first centuries, the Church had to defend and clarify this truth of faith against the heresies that falsified it. *88*

465 The first heresies denied not so much Christ's divinity as his true humanity (Gnostic Docetism). From apostolic times the Christian faith has insisted on the true incarnation of God's Son "come in the flesh."[87] But already in the third century, the Church in a council at Antioch had to affirm against Paul of Samosata that Jesus Christ is Son of God by nature and not by adoption. The first ecumenical council of Nicaea in 325 confessed in its Creed that the Son of God is "begotten, not made, of the same substance (*homoousios*) as the Father," and condemned Arius, who had affirmed that the Son of God "came to be from things that were not" and that he was "from another substance" than that of the Father.[88] *242*

466 The Nestorian heresy regarded Christ as a human person joined to the divine person of God's Son. Opposing this heresy, St. Cyril of Alexandria and the third ecumenical council at Ephesus in 431 confessed "that the Word, uniting to himself in his person the flesh animated by a rational soul, became man."[89] Christ's humanity has no other subject than the divine person of the Son of God, who assumed it and made it his own, from his conception. For this reason the Council of Ephesus proclaimed in 431 that Mary truly became the Mother of God by the human conception of the Son of God in her womb: "Mother of God, not that the nature of the Word or his divinity received the beginning of its existence from the holy Virgin, but that, since the holy body, animated by a rational soul, which the Word of God united to himself according to the hypostasis, was born from her, the Word is said to be born according to the flesh."[90] *495*

467 The Monophysites affirmed that the human nature had ceased to exist as such in Christ when the divine person of God's Son assumed it. Faced with this heresy, the fourth ecumenical council, at Chalcedon in 451, confessed:

---

87 Cf. 1 Jn 4:2-3; 2 Jn 7.
88 Council of Nicaea I (325): DS 130, 126.
89 Council of Ephesus (431): DS 250.
90 Council of Ephesus: DS 251.

Following the holy Fathers, we unanimously teach and confess one and the same Son, our Lord Jesus Christ: the same perfect in divinity and perfect in humanity, the same truly God and truly man, composed of rational soul and body; consubstantial with the Father as to his divinity and consubstantial with us as to his humanity; "like us in all things but sin." He was begotten from the Father before all ages as to his divinity and in these last days, for us and for our salvation, was born as to his humanity of the virgin Mary, the Mother of God.[91]

We confess that one and the same Christ, Lord, and only-begotten Son, is to be acknowledged in two natures without confusion, change, division, or separation. The distinction between the natures was never abolished by their union, but rather the character proper to each of the two natures was preserved as they came together in one person (*prosopon*) and one hypostasis.[92]

468   After the Council of Chalcedon, some made of Christ's human nature a kind of personal subject. Against them, the fifth ecumenical council at Constantinople in 553 confessed that "there is but one *hypostasis* [or person], which is our Lord Jesus Christ, one of the Trinity."[93] Thus everything in Christ's human nature is to be
254 attributed to his divine person as its proper subject, not only his miracles but also his sufferings and even his death: "He who was
616 crucified in the flesh, our Lord Jesus Christ, is true God, Lord of glory, and *one of the Holy Trinity*."[94]

469   The Church thus confesses that Jesus is inseparably true
212 God and true man. He is truly the Son of God who, without ceasing to be God and Lord, became a man and our brother:

"What he was, he remained and what he was not, he assumed," sings the Roman Liturgy.[95] And the liturgy of St. John Chrysostom proclaims and sings: "O only-begotten Son and Word of God, immortal being, you who deigned for our salvation to become incarnate of the holy Mother of God and ever-virgin Mary, you who without change became man and were crucified, O Christ our God, you who by your death have crushed death, you who are one of the Holy Trinity, glorified with the Father and the Holy Spirit, save us!"[96]

---

91 Council of Chalcedon (451): DS 301; cf. *Heb* 4:15.
92 Council of Chalcedon: DS 302.
93 Council of Constantinople II (553): DS 424.
94 Council of Constantinople II (553): DS 432; cf. DS 424; Council of Ephesus, DS 255.
95 *LH*, January 1, Antiphon for Morning Prayer; cf. St. Leo the Great, *Sermo in nat. Dom.* 1, 2; PL 54, 191-192.
96 Liturgy of St. John Chrysostom, Troparion "*O monogenes*."

IV. How Is the Son of God Man?

470 Because "human nature was assumed, not absorbed,"[97] in the mysterious union of the Incarnation, the Church was led over the course of centuries to confess the full reality of Christ's human soul, with its operations of intellect and will, and of his human body. In parallel fashion, she had to recall on each occasion that Christ's human nature belongs, as his own, to the divine person of the Son of God, who assumed it. Everything that Christ is and does in this nature derives from "one of the Trinity." The Son of God *516* therefore communicates to his humanity his own personal mode of existence in the Trinity. In his soul as in his body, Christ thus *626* expresses humanly the divine ways of the Trinity:[98]

> The Son of God . . . worked with human hands; he thought *2599* with a human mind. He acted with a human will, and with a human heart he loved. Born of the Virgin Mary, he has truly been made one of us, like to us in all things except sin.[99]

Christ's soul and his human knowledge

471 Apollinarius of Laodicaea asserted that in Christ the divine Word had replaced the soul or spirit. Against this error the Church confessed that the eternal Son also assumed a rational, human soul.[100] *363*

472 This human soul that the Son of God assumed is endowed with a true human knowledge. As such, this knowledge could not in itself be unlimited: it was exercised in the historical conditions of his existence in space and time. This is why the Son of God could, when he became man, "increase in wisdom and in stature, and in favor with God and man,"[101] and would even have to inquire for himself about what one in the human condition can learn only from experience.[102] This corresponded to the reality of his voluntary emptying of himself, taking "the form of a slave."[103]

473 But at the same time, this truly human knowledge of God's Son expressed the divine life of his person.[104] "The human nature

---

97 *GS* 22 § 2.
98 Cf. *Jn* 14:9-10.
99 *GS* 22 § 2.
100 Cf. Damasus I: DS 149.
101 *Lk* 2:52.
102 Cf. *Mk* 6:38; 8:27; *Jn* 11:34; etc.
103 *Phil* 2:7.
104 Cf. St. Gregory the Great, *"Sicut aqua" ad Eulogium, Epist. Lib.* 10, 39: PL 77, 1097A ff.; DS 475.

of God's Son, *not by itself but by its union with the Word,* knew and showed forth in itself everything that pertains to God."[105] Such is

240   first of all the case with the intimate and immediate knowledge that the Son of God made man has of his Father.[106] The Son in his human knowledge also showed the divine penetration he had into the secret thoughts of human hearts.[107]

474   By its union to the divine wisdom in the person of the Word incarnate, Christ enjoyed in his human knowledge the fullness of understanding of the eternal plans he had come to reveal.[108] What he admitted to not knowing in this area, he elsewhere declared himself not sent to reveal.[109]

Christ's human will

475   Similarly, at the sixth ecumenical council, Constantinople III in 681, the Church confessed that Christ possesses two wills and two natural operations, divine and human. They are not opposed

2008   to each other, but cooperate in such a way that the Word made flesh
2824   willed humanly in obedience to his Father all that he had decided divinely with the Father and the Holy Spirit for our salvation.[110] Christ's human will "does not resist or oppose but rather submits to his divine and almighty will."[111]

Christ's true body

476   Since the Word became flesh in assuming a true humanity,
1159-1162   Christ's body was finite.[112] Therefore the human face of Jesus can be
2129-2132   portrayed; at the seventh ecumenical council (Nicaea II in 787) the Church recognized its representation in holy images to be legitimate.[113]

477   At the same time the Church has always acknowledged that in the body of Jesus "we see our God made visible and so are caught up in love of the God we cannot see."[114] The individual characteristics of Christ's body express the divine person of God's

---

105 St. Maximus the Confessor, *Qu. et dub.* 66: PG 90, 840A.
106 Cf. *Mk* 14:36; *Mt* 11:27; *Jn* 1:18; 8:55; etc.
107 Cf. *Mk* 2:8; *Jn* 2:25; 6:61; etc.
108 Cf. *Mk* 8:31; 9:31; 10:33-34; 14:18-20, 26-30.
109 Cf. *Mk* 13:32; *Acts* 1:7.
110 Cf. Council of Constantinople III (681): DS 556-559.
111 Council of Constantinople III: DS 556.
112 Cf. Council of the Lateran (649): DS 504.
113 Cf. *Gal* 3:1; cf. Council of Nicaea II (787): DS 600-603.
114 *Roman Missal,* Preface of Christmas I.

Son. He has made the features of his human body his own, to the point that they can be venerated when portrayed in a holy image, for the believer "who venerates the icon is venerating in it the person of the one depicted."[115]

The heart of the Incarnate Word

478   Jesus knew and loved us each and all during his life, his agony, and his Passion and gave himself up for each one of us: "The Son of God . . . loved me and gave himself for me."[116] He has loved us all with a human heart. For this reason, the Sacred Heart of Jesus, pierced by our sins and for our salvation,[117] "is quite rightly considered the chief sign and symbol of that . . . love with which the divine Redeemer continually loves the eternal Father and all human beings" without exception.[118]

487

368

2669

766

IN BRIEF

479   At the time appointed by God, the only Son of the Father, the eternal Word, that is, the Word and substantial Image of the Father, became incarnate; without losing his divine nature he has assumed human nature.

480   Jesus Christ is true God and true man, in the unity of his divine person; for this reason he is the one and only mediator between God and men.

481   Jesus Christ possesses two natures, one divine and the other human, not confused, but united in the one person of God's Son.

482   Christ, being true God and true man, has a human intellect and will, perfectly attuned and subject to his divine intellect and divine will, which he has in common with the Father and the Holy Spirit.

483   The Incarnation is therefore the mystery of the wonderful union of the divine and human natures in the one person of the Word.

---

115   Council of Nicaea II: DS 601.
116   *Gal* 2:20.
117   Cf. *Jn* 19:34.
118   Pius XII, encyclical, *Haurietis aquas* (1956): DS 3924; cf. DS 3812.

Paragraph 2. "Conceived by the Power of the Holy Spirit
and Born of the Virgin Mary"

I.   CONCEIVED BY THE POWER OF THE HOLY SPIRIT . . .

484   The Annunciation to Mary inaugurates "the fullness of
time,"[119] the time of the fulfillment of God's promises and preparations. Mary was invited to conceive him in whom the "whole
461 fullness of deity" would dwell "bodily."[120] The divine response to
her question, "How can this be, since I know not man?" was given
721 by the power of the Spirit: "The Holy Spirit will come upon
you."[121]

485   The mission of the Holy Spirit is always conjoined and
ordered to that of the Son.[122] The Holy Spirit, "the Lord, the giver
689, 723 of Life," is sent to sanctify the womb of the Virgin Mary and
divinely fecundate it, causing her to conceive the eternal Son of the
Father in a humanity drawn from her own.

486   The Father's only Son, conceived as man in the womb of
the Virgin Mary, is "Christ," that is to say, anointed by the Holy
437 Spirit, from the beginning of his human existence, though the
manifestation of this fact takes place only progressively: to the
shepherds, to the magi, to John the Baptist, to the disciples.[123] Thus
the whole life of Jesus Christ will make manifest "how God
anointed Jesus of Nazareth with the Holy Spirit and with
power."[124]

II.   . . . BORN OF THE VIRGIN MARY

963 **487**   What the Catholic faith believes about Mary is based on
what it believes about Christ, and what it teaches about Mary
illumines in turn its faith in Christ.

Mary's predestination

488   "God sent forth his Son," but to prepare a body for him,[125]
he wanted the free cooperation of a creature. For this, from all

---

119 *Gal* 4:4.
120 *Col* 2:9.
121 *Lk* 1:34-35 (Gk.).
122 Cf. *Jn* 16:14-15.
123 Cf. *Mt* 1:20; 2:1-12; *Lk* 1:35; 2:8-20; *Jn* 1:31-34; 2:11.
124 *Acts* 10:38.

eternity God chose for the mother of his Son a daughter of Israel, a young Jewish woman of Nazareth in Galilee, "a virgin betrothed to a man whose name was Joseph, of the house of David; and the virgin's name was Mary":[126]

> The Father of mercies willed that the Incarnation should be preceded by assent on the part of the predestined mother, so that just as a woman had a share in the coming of death, so also should a woman contribute to the coming of life.[127]

489 Throughout the Old Covenant the mission of many holy women *prepared* for that of Mary. At the very beginning there was Eve; despite her disobedience, she receives the promise of a pos- *722* terity that will be victorious over the evil one, as well as the promise *410* that she will be the mother of all the living.[128] By virtue of this *145* promise, Sarah conceives a son in spite of her old age.[129] Against all human expectation God chooses those who were considered powerless and weak to show forth his faithfulness to his promises: Hannah, the mother of Samuel; Deborah; Ruth; Judith and Esther; and many other women.[130] Mary "stands out among the poor and *64* humble of the Lord, who confidently hope for and receive salvation from him. After a long period of waiting the times are fulfilled in her, the exalted Daughter of Sion, and the new plan of salvation is established."[131]

The Immaculate Conception

490 To become the mother of the Savior, Mary "was enriched by God with gifts appropriate to such a role."[132] The angel Gabriel at the moment of the annunciation salutes her as "full of grace."[133] In fact, in order for Mary to be able to give the free assent of her *2676, 2853* faith to the announcement of her vocation, it was necessary that she be wholly borne by God's grace. *2001*

491 Through the centuries the Church has become ever more aware that Mary, "full of grace" through God,[134] was redeemed from the moment of her conception. That is what the dogma of the *411*

---

125 *Gal* 4:4; *Heb* 10:5.
126 *Lk* 1:26-27.
127 *LG* 56; cf. *LG* 61.
128 Cf. *Gen* 3:15, 20.
129 Cf. *Gen* 18:10-14; 21:1-2.
130 Cf. *1 Cor* 1:17; *1 Sam* 1.
131 *LG* 55.
132 *LG* 56.
133 *Lk* 1:28.
134 *Lk* 1:28.

Immaculate Conception confesses, as Pope Pius IX proclaimed in 1854:

> The most Blessed Virgin Mary was, from the first moment of her conception, by a singular grace and privilege of almighty God and by virtue of the merits of Jesus Christ, Savior of the human race, preserved immune from all stain of original sin.[135]

492   The "splendor of an entirely unique holiness" by which Mary is "enriched from the first instant of her conception" comes wholly from Christ: she is "redeemed, in a more exalted fashion, by reason of the merits of her Son."[136] The Father blessed Mary more than any other created person "in Christ with every spiritual blessing in the heavenly places" and chose her "in Christ before the foundation of the world, to be holy and blameless before him in love."[137]

2011
1077

493   The Fathers of the Eastern tradition call the Mother of God "the All-Holy" (*Panagia*) and celebrate her as "free from any stain of sin, as though fashioned by the Holy Spirit and formed as a new creature."[138] By the grace of God Mary remained free of every personal sin her whole life long.

"Let it be done to me according to your word . . ."

494   At the announcement that she would give birth to "the Son of the Most High" without knowing man, by the power of the Holy Spirit, Mary responded with the obedience of faith, certain that "with God nothing will be impossible": "Behold, I am the handmaid of the Lord; let it be [done] to me according to your word."[139] Thus, giving her consent to God's word, Mary becomes the mother of Jesus. Espousing the divine will for salvation wholeheartedly, without a single sin to restrain her, she gave herself entirely to the person and to the work of her Son; she did so in order to serve the mystery of redemption with him and dependent on him, by God's grace:[140]

2617
148

968

---

135 Pius IX, *Ineffabilis Deus*, 1854: DS 2803.
136 *LG* 53, 56.
137 Cf. *Eph* 1:3-4.
138 *LG* 56.
139 *Lk* 1:28-38; cf. *Rom* 1:5.
140 Cf. *LG* 56.

As St. Irenaeus says, "Being obedient she became the cause of salvation for herself and for the whole human race."[141] Hence not a few of the early Fathers gladly assert . . .: "The knot of Eve's disobedience was untied by Mary's obedience: what the virgin Eve bound through her disbelief, Mary loosened by her faith."[142] Comparing her with Eve, they call Mary "the Mother of the living" and frequently claim: "Death through Eve, life through Mary."[143]

726

Mary's divine motherhood

495 Called in the Gospels "the mother of Jesus," Mary is acclaimed by Elizabeth, at the prompting of the Spirit and even before the birth of her son, as "the mother of my Lord."[144] In fact, the One whom she conceived as man by the Holy Spirit, who truly became her Son according to the flesh, was none other than the Father's eternal Son, the second person of the Holy Trinity. Hence the Church confesses that Mary is truly "Mother of God" (*Theotokos*).[145]

466, 2677

Mary's virginity

496 From the first formulations of her faith, the Church has confessed that Jesus was conceived solely by the power of the Holy Spirit in the womb of the Virgin Mary, affirming also the corporeal aspect of this event: Jesus was conceived "by the Holy Spirit without human seed."[146] The Fathers see in the virginal conception the sign that it truly was the Son of God who came in a humanity like our own. Thus St. Ignatius of Antioch at the beginning of the second century says:

> You are firmly convinced about our Lord, who is truly of the race of David according to the flesh, Son of God according to the will and power of God, truly born of a virgin, . . . he was truly nailed to a tree for us in his flesh under Pontius Pilate . . . he truly suffered, as he is also truly risen.[147]

---

141 St. Irenaeus, *Adv. haeres.* 3, 22, 4: PG 7/1, 959A.

142 St. Irenaeus, *Adv. haeres.* 3, 22, 4: PG 7/1, 959A.

143 *LG* 56; Epiphanius, *Haer.* 78, 18: PG 42, 728CD-729AB; St. Jerome, *Ep.* 22, 21: PL 22, 408.

144 *Lk* 1:43; *Jn* 2:1; 19:25; cf. *Mt* 13:55; *et al.*

145 Council of Ephesus (431): DS 251.

146 Council of the Lateran (649): DS 503; cf. DS 10-64.

147 St. Ignatius of Antioch, *Ad Smyrn.* 1-2: Apostolic Fathers, ed. J. B. Lightfoot (London: Macmillan, 1889) II/2, 289-293; SCh 10, 154-156; cf. *Rom* 1:3; *Jn* 1:13.

497   The gospel accounts understand the virginal conception of Jesus as a divine work that surpasses all human understanding and possibility:[148] "That which is conceived in her is of the Holy Spirit," said the angel to Joseph about Mary his fiancée.[149] The Church sees here the fulfillment of the divine promise given through the prophet Isaiah: "Behold, a virgin shall conceive and bear a son."[150]

498   People are sometimes troubled by the silence of St. Mark's Gospel and the New Testament Epistles about Jesus' virginal conception. Some might wonder if we were merely dealing with legends or theological constructs not claiming to be history. To this we must respond: Faith in the virginal conception of Jesus met with the lively opposition, mockery, or incomprehension of non-believers, Jews and pagans alike;[151] so it could hardly have been motivated by pagan mythology or by some adaptation to the ideas of the age. The meaning of this event is accessible only to faith,

90   which understands in it the "connection of these mysteries with one another"[152] in the totality of Christ's mysteries, from his Incarnation to his Passover. St. Ignatius of Antioch already bears witness to this connection:
"Mary's virginity and giving birth, and even the Lord's death escaped the

2717   notice of the prince of this world: these three mysteries worthy of proclamation were accomplished in God's silence."[153]

Mary – "ever-virgin"

499   The deepening of faith in the virginal motherhood led the Church to confess Mary's real and perpetual virginity even in the act of giving birth to the Son of God made man.[154] In fact, Christ's birth "did not diminish his mother's virginal integrity but sanctified it."[155] And so the liturgy of the Church celebrates Mary as *Aeiparthenos*, the "Ever-virgin."[156]

500   Against this doctrine the objection is sometimes raised that the Bible mentions brothers and sisters of Jesus.[157] The Church has always understood these passages as not referring to other children of the Virgin Mary. In fact James and Joseph, "brothers of Jesus," are the sons of another Mary, a disciple of Christ, whom St. Matthew significantly calls "the other Mary."[158] They are close relations of Jesus, according to an Old Testament expression.[159]

---

148   Cf. *Mt* 1:18-25; *Lk* 1:26-38.
149   *Mt* 1:20.
150   *Isa* 7:14 in the LXX, quoted in *Mt* 1:23 (Gk.).
151   Cf. St. Justin, *Dial.*, 99, 7: PG 6, 708-709; Origen, *Contra Celsum* 1, 32, 69: PG 11, 720-721; *et al.*
152   *Dei Filius* 4: DS 3016.
153   St. Ignatius of Antioch, *Ad Eph.* 19, 1: AF II/2, 76-80; SCh 10, 88; cf. *1 Cor* 2:8.
154   Cf. DS 291; 294; 427; 442; 503; 571; 1880.
155   *LG* 57.
156   Cf. *LG* 52.
157   Cf. *Mk* 3:31-35; 6:3; *1 Cor* 9:5; *Gal* 1:19.

501 Jesus is Mary's only son, but her spiritual motherhood extends to all men whom indeed he came to save: "The Son whom she brought forth is he whom God placed as the first-born among *969* many brethren, that is, the faithful in whose generation and formu- *970* lation she cooperates with a mother's love."[160]

Mary's virginal motherhood in God's plan

502 The eyes of faith can discover in the context of the whole of Revelation the mysterious reasons why God in his saving plan wanted his Son to be born of a virgin. These reasons touch both on *90* the person of Christ and his redemptive mission, and on the welcome Mary gave that mission on behalf of all men.

503 Mary's virginity manifests God's absolute initiative in the Incarnation. Jesus has only God as Father. "He was never estranged from the Father because of the human nature which he assumed .... He is naturally *422* Son of the Father as to his divinity and naturally son of his mother as to his humanity, but properly Son of the Father in both natures."[161]

504 Jesus is conceived by the Holy Spirit in the Virgin Mary's womb because he is the New Adam, who inaugurates the new creation: "The first man was from the earth, a man of dust; the second man is from heaven."[162] *359* From his conception, Christ's humanity is filled with the Holy Spirit, for God "gives him the Spirit without measure."[163] From "his fullness" as the head of redeemed humanity "we have all received, grace upon grace."[164]

505 By his virginal conception, Jesus, the New Adam, ushers in *the new birth* of children adopted in the Holy Spirit through faith. "How can this be?"[165] Participation in the divine life arises "not of blood nor of the *1265* will of the flesh nor of the will of man, but of God."[166] The acceptance of this life is virginal because it is entirely the Spirit's gift to man. The spousal character of the human vocation in relation to God[167] is fulfilled perfectly in Mary's virginal motherhood.

506 Mary is a virgin because her virginity is *the sign of her faith* "unadulterated by any doubt," and of her undivided gift of herself to God's *148* will.[168] It is her faith that enables her to become the mother of the Savior: *1814*

---

158 *Mt* 13:55; 28:1; cf. *Mt* 27:56.
159 Cf. *Gen* 13:8; 14:16; 29:15; etc.
160 *LG* 63; cf. *Jn* 19:26-27; *Rom* 8:29; *Rev* 12:17.
161 Council of Friuli (796): DS 619; cf. *Lk* 2:48-49.
162 *1 Cor* 15:45, 47.
163 *Jn* 3:34.
164 *Jn* 1:16; cf. *Col* 1:18.
165 *Lk* 1:34; cf. *Jn* 3:9.
166 *Jn* 1:13.
167 Cf. *2 Cor* 11:2.
168 *LG* 63; cf. *1 Cor* 7:34-35.

"Mary is more blessed because she embraces faith in Christ than because she conceives the flesh of Christ."[169]

507   At once virgin and mother, Mary is the symbol and the most perfect realization of the Church: "the Church indeed . . . by receiving the word of God in faith becomes herself a mother. By preaching and Baptism she brings forth sons, who are conceived by the Holy Spirit and born of God, to a new and immortal life. She herself is a virgin, who keeps in its entirety and purity the faith she pledged to her spouse."[170]

967

149

IN BRIEF

508   From among the descendants of Eve, God chose the Virgin Mary to be the mother of his Son. "Full of grace," Mary is "the most excellent fruit of redemption" (SC 103): from the first instant of her conception, she was totally preserved from the stain of original sin and she remained pure from all personal sin throughout her life.

509   Mary is truly "Mother of God" since she is the mother of the eternal Son of God made man, who is God himself.

510   Mary "remained a virgin in conceiving her Son, a virgin in giving birth to him, a virgin in carrying him, a virgin in nursing him at her breast, always a virgin" (St. Augustine, *Serm.* 186, 1: PL 38, 999): with her whole being she is "the handmaid of the Lord" (*Lk* 1:38).

511   The Virgin Mary "cooperated through free faith and obedience in human salvation" (*LG* 56). She uttered her yes "in the name of all human nature" (St. Thomas Aquinas, *STh* III, 30, 1). By her obedience she became the new Eve, mother of the living.

---

169   St. Augustine, *De virg.*, 3: PL 40, 398.
170   *LG* 64; cf. 63.

Paragraph 3. The Mysteries of Christ's Life

512   Concerning Christ's life the Creed speaks only about the mysteries of the Incarnation (conception and birth) and Paschal mystery (passion, crucifixion, death, burial, descent into hell, resurrection, and ascension). It says nothing explicitly about the mysteries of Jesus' hidden or public life, but the articles of faith concerning his Incarnation and Passover do shed light on the *whole*   *1163* of his earthly life. "All that Jesus did and taught, from the beginning until the day when he was taken up to heaven,"[171] is to be seen in the light of the mysteries of Christmas and Easter.

513   According to circumstances catechesis will make use of all the richness of the mysteries of Jesus. Here it is enough merely to indicate some elements common to all the mysteries of Christ's life   *426, 561* (I), in order then to sketch the principal mysteries of Jesus' hidden (II) and public (III) life.

I.   CHRIST'S WHOLE LIFE IS MYSTERY

514   Many things about Jesus of interest to human curiosity do not figure in the Gospels. Almost nothing is said about his hidden life at Nazareth, and even a great part of his public life is not recounted.[172] What is written in the Gospels was set down there "so that you may believe that Jesus is the Christ, the Son of God, and that believing you may have life in his name."[173]

515   The Gospels were written by men who were among the first to have the faith[174] and wanted to share it with others. Having known in faith who Jesus is, they could see and make others see   *126* the traces of his mystery in all his earthly life. From the swaddling clothes of his birth to the vinegar of his Passion and the shroud of his Resurrection, everything in Jesus' life was a sign of his mystery.[175] His deeds, miracles, and words all revealed that "in him the whole fullness of deity dwells bodily."[176] His humanity appeared as "sacrament," that is, the sign and instrument, of his   *609, 774* divinity and of the salvation he brings: what was visible in his   *477* earthly life leads to the invisible mystery of his divine sonship and redemptive mission.

---

171 *Acts* 1:1-2.
172 Cf. *Jn* 20:30.
173 *Jn* 20:31.
174 Cf. *Mk* 1:1; *Jn* 21:24.
175 Cf. *Lk* 2:7; *Mt* 27:48; *Jn* 20:7.
176 *Col* 2:9.

Characteristics common to Jesus' mysteries

516   Christ's whole earthly life – his words and deeds, his
silences and sufferings, indeed his manner of being and speaking
65 – is *Revelation* of the Father. Jesus can say: "Whoever has seen me
has seen the Father," and the Father can say: "This is my Son, my
Chosen; listen to him!"[177] Because our Lord became man in order
to do his Father's will, even the least characteristics of his mysteries
2708 manifest "God's love . . . among us."[178]

517   Christ's whole life is a mystery of *redemption*. Redemption
606 comes to us above all through the blood of his cross,[179] but this
1115 mystery is at work throughout Christ's entire life:

– already in his Incarnation through which by becoming poor he
enriches us with his poverty;[180]

– in his hidden life which by his submission atones for our disobedience;[181]

– in his word which purifies its hearers;[182]

– in his healings and exorcisms by which "he took our infirmities
and bore our diseases";[183]

– and in his Resurrection by which he justifies us.[184]

518   Christ's whole life is a mystery of recapitulation. All Jesus
did, said, and suffered had for its aim restoring fallen man to his
original vocation:

> When Christ became incarnate and was made man, he reca-
> pitulated in himself the long history of mankind and pro-
> cured for us a 'short cut' to salvation, so that what we had
> lost in Adam, that is, being in the image and likeness of God,
> we might recover in Christ Jesus.[185] For this reason Christ
> experienced all the stages of life, thereby giving communion
668, 2748   > with God to all men.[186]

---

177 *Jn* 14:9; *Lk* 9:35; cf. *Mt* 17:5; *Mk* 9:7 ("my beloved Son").
178 *1 Jn* 4:9.
179 Cf. *Eph* 1:7; *Col* 1:13-14; *1 Pet* 1:18-19.
180 Cf. *2 Cor* 8:9.
181 Cf. *Lk* 2:51.
182 Cf. *Jn* 15:3.
183 *Mt* 8:17; cf. *Isa* 53:4.
184 Cf. *Rom* 4:25.
185 St. Irenaeus, *Adv. haeres.* 3, 18, 1: PG 7/1, 932.
186 St. Irenaeus, *Adv. haeres.* 3, 18, 7: PG 7/1, 937; cf. 2, 22, 4.

Our communion in the mysteries of Jesus

519   All Christ's riches "are for every individual and are every-
body's property."[187] Christ did not live his life for himself but *for
us*, from his Incarnation "for us men and for our salvation" to his   *793*
death "for our sins" and Resurrection "for our justification."[188] He   *602*
is still "our advocate with the Father," who "always lives to make
intercession" for us.[189] He remains ever "in the presence of God on
our behalf, bringing before him all that he lived and suffered for   *1085*
us."[190]

520   In all of his life Jesus presents himself as *our model*. He is
"the perfect man,"[191] who invites us to become his disciples and
follow him. In humbling himself, he has given us an example to   *459, 359*
imitate, through his prayer he draws us to pray, and by his poverty   *2607*
he calls us to accept freely the privation and persecutions that may
come our way.[192]

521   Christ enables us *to live in him* all that he himself lived, and   *2715*
he lives it in us. "By his Incarnation, he, the Son of God, has in a
certain way united himself with each man."[193] We are called only   *1391*
to become one with him, for he enables us as the members of his
Body to share in what he lived for us in his flesh as our model:

> We must continue to accomplish in ourselves the stages of
> Jesus' life and his mysteries and often to beg him to perfect
> and realize them in us and in his whole Church. . . . For it is
> the plan of the Son of God to make us and the whole Church
> partake in his mysteries and to extend them to and continue
> them in us and in his whole Church. This is his plan for
> fulfilling his mysteries in us.[194]

II.   THE MYSTERIES OF JESUS' INFANCY AND HIDDEN LIFE

The preparations

522   The coming of God's Son to earth is an event of such
immensity that God willed to prepare for it over centuries. He
makes everything converge on Christ: all the rituals and sacrifices,   *711, 762*

---

187 John Paul II, *RH* 11.
188 *1 Cor* 15:3; *Rom* 4:25.
189 *1 Jn* 2:1; *Heb* 7:25.
190 *Heb* 9:24.
191 *GS* 38; cf. *Rom* 15:5; *Phil* 2:5.
192 Cf. *Jn* 13:15; *Lk* 11:1; *Mt* 5:11-12.
193 *GS* 22 § 2.
194 St. John Eudes, *LH*, Week 33, Friday, OR.

figures and symbols of the "First Covenant."[195] He announces him through the mouths of the prophets who succeeded one another in Israel. Moreover, he awakens in the hearts of the pagans a dim expectation of this coming.

523   *St. John the Baptist* is the Lord's immediate precursor or forerunner, sent to prepare his way.[196] "Prophet of the Most High," *717-720* John surpasses all the prophets, of whom he is the last.[197] He inaugurates the Gospel, already from his mother's womb welcomes the coming of Christ, and rejoices in being "the friend of the bridegroom," whom he points out as "the Lamb of God, who takes away the sin of the world."[198] Going before Jesus "in the spirit and power of Elijah," John bears witness to Christ in his preaching, by his Baptism of conversion, and through his martyrdom.[199]

524   When the Church celebrates *the liturgy of Advent* each year, she makes present this ancient expectancy of the Messiah, for by *1171* sharing in the long preparation for the Savior's first coming, the faithful renew their ardent desire for his second coming.[200] By celebrating the precursor's birth and martyrdom, the Church unites herself to his desire: "He must increase, but I must decrease."[201]

The Christmas mystery

525   Jesus was born in a humble stable, into a poor family.[202] Simple shepherds were the first witnesses to this event. In this *437* poverty heaven's glory was made manifest.[203] The Church never *2443* tires of singing the glory of this night:

> The Virgin today brings into the world the Eternal
> And the earth offers a cave to the Inaccessible.
> The angels and shepherds praise him
> And the magi advance with the star,
> For you are born for us,
> Little Child, God eternal![204]

---

195   *Heb* 9:15.
196   Cf. *Acts* 13:24; *Mt* 3:3.
197   *Lk* 1:76; cf. 7:26; *Mt* 11:13.
198   *Jn* 1:29; cf. *Acts* 1:22; *Lk* 1:41; 16:16; *Jn* 3:29.
199   *Lk* 1:17; cf. *Mk* 6:17-29.
200   Cf. *Rev* 22:17.
201   *Jn* 3:30.
202   Cf. *Lk* 2:6-7.
203   Cf. *Lk* 2:8-20.
204   *Kontakion* of Romanos the Melodist.

526 To become a child in relation to God is the condition for entering the kingdom.[205] For this, we must humble ourselves and become little. Even more: to become "children of God" we must be "born from above" or "born of God."[206] Only when Christ is formed in us will the mystery of Christmas be fulfilled in us.[207] Christmas is the mystery of this "marvelous exchange":

> O marvelous exchange! Man's Creator has become man, *460* born of the Virgin. We have been made sharers in the divinity of Christ who humbled himself to share our humanity.[208]

The mysteries of Jesus' infancy

527 Jesus' *circumcision*, on the eighth day after his birth,[209] is the sign of his incorporation into Abraham's descendants, into the people of the covenant. It is the sign of his submission to the Law[210] and his deputation to Israel's worship, in which he will participate *580* throughout his life. This sign prefigures that "circumcision of *1214* Christ" which is Baptism.[211]

528 The *Epiphany* is the manifestation of Jesus as Messiah of Israel, Son of God and Savior of the world. The great feast of Epiphany celebrates the adoration of Jesus by the wise men (*magi*) *439* from the East, together with his baptism in the Jordan and the wedding feast at Cana in Galilee.[212] In the magi, representatives of the neighboring pagan religions, the Gospel sees the first-fruits of the nations, who welcome the good news of salvation through the Incarnation. The magi's coming to Jerusalem in order to pay homage to the king of the Jews shows that they seek in Israel, in the messianic light of the star of David, the one who will be king of the nations.[213] Their coming means that pagans can discover Jesus and worship him as Son of God and Savior of the world only by turning toward the Jews and receiving from them the messianic promise as contained in the Old Testament.[214] The Epiphany shows that *711-716* "the full number of the nations" now takes its "place in the family *122*

---

205 Cf. *Mt* 18:3-4.
206 *Jn* 3:7; 1:13; 1:12; cf. *Mt* 23:12.
207 Cf. *Gal* 4:19.
208 *LH,* Antiphon I of Evening Prayer for January 1st.
209 Cf. *Lk* 2:21.
210 Cf. *Gal* 4:4.
211 Cf. *Col* 2:11-13.
212 *Mt* 2:1; cf. *LH,* Epiphany, Evening Prayer II, Antiphon at the Canticle of Mary.
213 Cf. *Mt* 2:2; *Num* 24:17-19; *Rev* 22:16.
214 Cf. *Jn* 4:22; *Mt* 2:4-6.

of the patriarchs," and acquires *Israelitica dignitas*[215] (are made "worthy of the heritage of Israel").

529   The *presentation of Jesus in the temple* shows him to be the firstborn Son who belongs to the Lord.[216] With Simeon and Anna,
583 all Israel awaits its *encounter* with the Savior – the name given to
439 this event in the Byzantine tradition. Jesus is recognized as the long-expected Messiah, the "light to the nations" and the "glory of Israel," but also "a sign that is spoken against." The sword of
614 sorrow predicted for Mary announces Christ's perfect and unique oblation on the cross that will impart the salvation God had "prepared in the presence of all peoples."

530   The *flight into Egypt* and the massacre of the innocents[217] make manifest the opposition of darkness to the light: "He came to his own home, and his own people received him not."[218] Christ's
574 whole life was lived under the sign of persecution. His own share it with him.[219] Jesus' departure from Egypt recalls the exodus and presents him as the definitive liberator of God's people.[220]

The mysteries of Jesus' hidden life

531   During the greater part of his life Jesus shared the condition of the vast majority of human beings: a daily life spent without evident greatness, a life of manual labor. His religious life was that
2427 of a Jew obedient to the law of God,[221] a life in the community. From this whole period it is revealed to us that Jesus was "obedient" to his parents and that he "increased in wisdom and in stature, and in favor with God and man."[222]

532   Jesus' obedience to his mother and legal father fulfills the fourth commandment perfectly and was the temporal image of his
2214-2220 filial obedience to his Father in heaven. The everyday obedience of Jesus to Joseph and Mary both announced and anticipated the obedience of Holy Thursday: "Not my will. . . ."[223] The obedience
612 of Christ in the daily routine of his hidden life was already inaugu-

---

215 St. Leo the Great, *Sermo 3 in epiphania Domini* 1-3,5: PL 54, 242; *LH*,
       Epiphany, OR; *Roman Missal*, Easter Vigil 26, Prayer after the third reading.
216 Cf. *Lk* 2:22-39; *Ex* 13:2, 12-13.
217 Cf. *Mt* 2:13-18.
218 *Jn* 1:11.
219 Cf. *Jn* 15:20.
220 Cf. *Mt* 2:15; *Hos* 11:1.
221 Cf. *Gal* 4:4.
222 *Lk* 2:51-52.
223 *Lk* 22:42.

rating his work of restoring what the disobedience of Adam had destroyed.[224]

533 The hidden life at Nazareth allows everyone to enter into fellowship with Jesus by the most ordinary events of daily life:

> The home of Nazareth is the school where we begin to understand the life of Jesus – the school of the Gospel. First, then, a lesson of silence. May esteem for *silence*, that admira-   2712
> ble and indispensable condition of mind, revive in us . . . A lesson on *family life*. May Nazareth teach us what family life is, its communion of love, its austere and simple beauty, and its sacred and inviolable character . . . A lesson of *work*.   2204
> Nazareth, home of the "Carpenter's Son," in you I would choose to understand and proclaim the severe and redeeming law of human work. . . . To conclude, I want to greet all the workers of the world, holding up to them their great pattern, their brother who is God.[225]   2427

534 The *finding of Jesus in the temple* is the only event that breaks the silence of the Gospels about the hidden years of Jesus.[226] Here Jesus lets us catch a glimpse of the mystery of his total consecration   583 to a mission that flows from his divine sonship: "Did you not know   2599 that I must be about my Father's work?"[227] Mary and Joseph did not understand these words, but they accepted them in faith. Mary "kept all these things in her heart" during the years Jesus remained   964 hidden in the silence of an ordinary life.

---

224 Cf. *Rom* 5:19.
225 Paul VI at Nazareth, January 5, 1964: *LH*, Feast of the Holy Family, OR.
226 Cf. *Lk* 2:41-52.
227 *Lk* 2:49 alt.

III.   THE MYSTERIES OF JESUS' PUBLIC LIFE

The baptism of Jesus

535   Jesus' public life begins with his baptism by John in the Jordan.[228] John preaches "a baptism of repentance for the forgive-
719-720   ness of sins."[229] A crowd of sinners[230] – tax collectors and soldiers, Pharisees and Sadducees, and prostitutes – come to be baptized by him. "Then Jesus appears." The Baptist hesitates, but Jesus insists and receives baptism. Then the Holy Spirit, in the form of a dove,
701   comes upon Jesus and a voice from heaven proclaims, "This is my
438   beloved Son."[231] This is the manifestation ("Epiphany") of Jesus as Messiah of Israel and Son of God.

536   The baptism of Jesus is on his part the acceptance and inauguration of his mission as God's suffering Servant. He allows
606   himself to be numbered among sinners; he is already "the Lamb of God, who takes away the sin of the world."[232] Already he is anticipating the "baptism" of his bloody death.[233] Already he is
1224   coming to "fulfill all righteousness," that is, he is submitting him-self entirely to his Father's will: out of love he consents to this baptism of death for the remission of our sins.[234] The Father's voice responds to the Son's acceptance, proclaiming his entire delight in
444   his Son.[235] The Spirit whom Jesus possessed in fullness from his conception comes to "rest on him."[236] Jesus will be the source of the Spirit for all mankind. At his baptism "the heavens were
727   opened"[237] – the heavens that Adam's sin had closed – and the
739   waters were sanctified by the descent of Jesus and the Spirit, a prelude to the new creation.

537   Through Baptism the Christian is sacramentally assimi-
1262   lated to Jesus, who in his own baptism anticipates his death and resurrection. The Christian must enter into this mystery of humble self-abasement and repentance, go down into the water with Jesus in order to rise with him, be reborn of water and the Spirit so as to

---

228   Cf. *Lk* 3:23; *Acts* 1:22.
229   *Lk* 3:3.
230   Cf. *Lk* 3:10-14; *Mt* 3:7; 21:32.
231   *Mt* 3:13-17.
232   *Jn* 1:29; cf. *Isa* 53:12.
233   Cf. *Mk* 10:38; *Lk* 12:50.
234   *Mt* 3:15; cf. 26:39.
235   Cf. *Lk* 3:22; *Isa* 42:1.
236   *Jn* 1:32-33; cf. *Isa* 11:2.
237   *Mt* 3:16.

become the Father's beloved son in the Son and "walk in newness of life":[238]

> Let us be buried with Christ by Baptism to rise with him; let   *628*
> us go down with him to be raised with him; and let us rise
> with him to be glorified with him.[239]

> Everything that happened to Christ lets us know that, after
> the bath of water, the Holy Spirit swoops down upon us from
> high heaven and that, adopted by the Father's voice, we
> become sons of God.[240]

Jesus' temptations

538   The Gospels speak of a time of solitude for Jesus in the desert immediately after his baptism by John. Driven by the Spirit into the desert, Jesus remains there for forty days without eating; he lives among wild beasts, and angels minister to him.[241] At the end of this time Satan tempts him three times, seeking to compromise his filial attitude toward God. Jesus rebuffs these attacks,   *394* which recapitulate the temptations of Adam in Paradise and of   *518* Israel in the desert, and the devil leaves him "until an opportune time."[242]

539   The evangelists indicate the salvific meaning of this mys-   *397* terious event: Jesus is the new Adam who remained faithful just where the first Adam had given in to temptation. Jesus fulfills Israel's vocation perfectly: in contrast to those who had once provoked God during forty years in the desert, Christ reveals himself as God's Servant, totally obedient to the divine will. In this,   *385* Jesus is the devil's conqueror: he "binds the strong man" to take back his plunder.[243] Jesus' victory over the tempter in the desert anticipates victory at the Passion, the supreme act of obedience of   *609* his filial love for the Father.

---

238   *Rom* 6:4.
239   St. Gregory of Nazianzus, *Oratio.* 40, 9: PG 36, 369.
240   St. Hilary of Poitiers, *In Matth.* 2, 5: PL 9, 927.
241   Cf. *Mk* 1:12-13.
242   *Lk* 4:13.
243   Cf. *Ps* 95:10; *Mk* 3:27.

540   Jesus' temptation reveals the way in which the Son of God
2119   is Messiah, contrary to the way Satan proposes to him and the way
519-2849   men wish to attribute to him.[244] This is why Christ vanquished the
Tempter *for us*: "For we have not a high priest who is unable to
sympathize with our weaknesses, but one who in every respect has
been tested as we are, yet without sinning."[245] By the solemn forty
days of *Lent* the Church unites herself each year to the mystery of
1438   Jesus in the desert.

"The Kingdom of God is at hand"

541   "Now after John was arrested, Jesus came into Galilee,
preaching the gospel of God, and saying: 'The time is fulfilled, and
the kingdom of God is at hand: repent, and believe in the gos-
2816   pel.'"[246] "To carry out the will of the Father Christ inaugurated the
763   kingdom of heaven on earth."[247] Now the Father's will is "to raise
669, 768   up men to share in his own divine life."[248] He does this by gather-
865   ing men around his Son Jesus Christ. This gathering is the Church,
"on earth the seed and beginning of that kingdom."[249]

542   Christ stands at the heart of this gathering of men into the
"family of God." By his word, through signs that manifest the reign
2233   of God, and by sending out his disciples, Jesus calls all people to
come together around him. But above all in the great Paschal
mystery – his death on the cross and his Resurrection – he would
accomplish the coming of his kingdom. "And I, when I am lifted
up from the earth, will draw all men to myself." Into this union
789   with Christ all men are called.[250]

---

244   Cf. *Mt* 16:21-23.
245   *Heb* 4:15.
246   *Mk* 1:14-15.
247   *LG* 3.
248   *LG* 2.
249   *LG* 5.
250   *Jn* 12:32; cf. *LG* 3.

The proclamation of the Kingdom of God

543   *Everyone* is called to enter the kingdom. First announced
to the children of Israel, this messianic kingdom is intended to
accept men of all nations.[251] To enter it, one must first accept Jesus'
word: *764*

> The word of the Lord is compared to a seed which is sown
> in a field; those who hear it with faith and are numbered
> among the little flock of Christ have truly received the king-
> dom. Then, by its own power, the seed sprouts and grows
> until the harvest.[252]

544   The kingdom belongs *to the poor and lowly,* which means
those who have accepted it with humble hearts. Jesus is sent to
"preach good news to the poor";[253] he declares them blessed, for *709*
"theirs is the kingdom of heaven."[254] To them – the "little ones" – *2443*
the Father is pleased to reveal what remains hidden from the wise *2546*
and the learned.[255] Jesus shares the life of the poor, from the cradle
to the cross; he experiences hunger, thirst, and privation.[256] Jesus
identifies himself with the poor of every kind and makes active
love toward them the condition for entering his kingdom.[257]

545   Jesus invites *sinners* to the table of the kingdom: "I came
not to call the righteous, but sinners."[258] He invites them to that
conversion without which one cannot enter the kingdom, but *1443*
shows them in word and deed his Father's boundless mercy for *588, 1846*
them and the vast "joy in heaven over one sinner who repents."[259] *1439*
The supreme proof of his love will be the sacrifice of his own life
"for the forgiveness of sins."[260]

546   Jesus' invitation to enter his kingdom comes in the form of
parables, a characteristic feature of his teaching.[261] Through his *2613*
parables he invites people to the feast of the kingdom, but he also
asks for a radical choice: to gain the kingdom, one must give *542*
everything.[262] Words are not enough; deeds are required.[263] The

---

251 Cf. *Mt* 8:11; 10:5-7; 28:19.
252 *LG* 5; cf. *Mk* 4:14, 26-29; *Lk* 12:32.
253 *Lk* 4:18; cf. 7:22.
254 *Mt* 5:3.
255 Cf. *Mt* 11:25.
256 Cf. *Mt* 21:18; *Mk* 2:23-26; *Jn* 4:6-7; 19:28; *Lk* 9:58.
257 Cf. *Mt* 25:31-46.
258 *Mk* 2:17; cf. *1 Tim* 1:15.
259 *Lk* 15:7; cf. 7:11-32.
260 *Mt* 26:28.
261 Cf. *Mk* 4:33-34.
262 Cf. *Mt* 13:44-45; 22:1-14.

parables are like mirrors for man: will he be hard soil or good earth for the word?[264] What use has he made of the talents he has received?[265] Jesus and the presence of the kingdom in this world are secretly at the heart of the parables. One must enter the kingdom, that is, become a disciple of Christ, in order to "know the secrets of the kingdom of heaven."[266] For those who stay "outside," everything remains enigmatic.[267]

The signs of the Kingdom of God

670, 439

547 Jesus accompanies his words with many "mighty works and wonders and signs," which manifest that the kingdom is present in him and attest that he was the promised Messiah.[268]

156, 2616

574

447

548 The signs worked by Jesus attest that the Father has sent him. They invite belief in him.[269] To those who turn to him in faith, he grants what they ask.[270] So miracles strengthen faith in the One who does his Father's works; they bear witness that he is the Son of God.[271] But his miracles can also be occasions for "offense";[272] they are not intended to satisfy people's curiosity or desire for magic. Despite his evident miracles some people reject Jesus; he is even accused of acting by the power of demons.[273]

1503

440

549 By freeing some individuals from the earthly evils of hunger, injustice, illness, and death,[274] Jesus performed messianic signs. Nevertheless he did not come to abolish all evils here below,[275] but to free men from the gravest slavery, sin, which thwarts them in their vocation as God's sons and causes all forms of human bondage.[276]

---

263 Cf. *Mt* 21:28-32.
264 Cf. *Mt* 13:3-9.
265 Cf. *Mt* 25:14-30.
266 *Mt* 13:11.
267 *Mk* 4:11; cf. *Mt* 13:10-15.
268 *Acts* 2:22; cf. *Lk* 7:18-23.
269 Cf. *Jn* 5:36; 10:25, 38.
270 Cf. *Mk* 5:25-34; 10:52; etc.
271 Cf. *Jn* 10:31-38.
272 *Mt* 11:6.
273 Cf. *Jn* 11:47-48; *Mk* 3:22.
274 Cf. *Jn* 6:5-15; *Lk* 19:8; *Mt* 11:5.
275 Cf. *Lk* 12:13-14; *Jn* 18:36.
276 Cf. *Jn* 8:34-36.

550   The coming of God's kingdom means the defeat of Satan's: "If it is by the Spirit of God that I cast out demons, then the kingdom of God has come upon you."[277] Jesus' *exorcisms* free some individu-   *394* als from the domination of demons. They anticipate Jesus' great *1673* victory over "the ruler of this world."[278] The kingdom of God will *440, 2816* be definitively established through Christ's cross: "God reigned from the wood."[279]

"The keys of the kingdom"

551   From the beginning of his public life Jesus chose certain men, twelve in number, to be with him and to participate in his mission.[280] He gives the Twelve a share in his authority and "sent *858* them out to preach the kingdom of God and to heal."[281] They *765* remain associated for ever with Christ's kingdom, for through them he directs the Church:

> As my Father appointed a kingdom for me, so do I appoint for you that you may eat and drink at my table in my kingdom, and sit on thrones judging the twelve tribes of Israel.[282]

552   Simon Peter holds the first place in the college of the Twelve;[283] Jesus entrusted a unique mission to him. Through a revelation from the Father, Peter had confessed: "You are the *880* Christ, the Son of the living God." Our Lord then declared to him: *153, 442* "You are Peter, and on this rock I will build my Church, and the gates of Hades will not prevail against it."[284] Christ, the "living stone,"[285] thus assures his Church, built on Peter, of victory over the powers of death. Because of the faith he confessed Peter will remain the unshakeable rock of the Church. His mission will be to keep this faith from every lapse and to strengthen his brothers in *424* it.[286]

---

277   *Mt* 12:26, 28.
278   *Jn* 12:31; cf. *Lk* 8:26-39.
279   *LH*, Lent, Holy Week, Evening Prayer, Hymn *Vexilla Regis*: *"Regnavit a ligno Deus."*
280   Cf. *Mk* 3:13-19.
281   *Lk* 9:2.
282   *Lk* 22:29-30.
283   Cf. *Mk* 3:16; 9:2; *Lk* 24:34; *1 Cor* 15:5.
284   *Mt* 16:18.
285   *1 Pet* 2:4.
286   Cf. *Lk* 22:32.

553   Jesus entrusted a specific authority to Peter: "I will give
you the keys of the kingdom of heaven, and whatever you bind on
881   earth shall be bound in heaven, and whatever you loose on earth
shall be loosed in heaven."[287] The "power of the keys" designates
authority to govern the house of God, which is the Church. Jesus,
the Good Shepherd, confirmed this mandate after his Resurrection:
1445   "Feed my sheep."[288] The power to "bind and loose" connotes the
authority to absolve sins, to pronounce doctrinal judgments, and
to make disciplinary decisions in the Church. Jesus entrusted this
authority to the Church through the ministry of the apostles[289] and
641, 881   in particular through the ministry of Peter, the only one to whom
he specifically entrusted the keys of the kingdom.

A foretaste of the Kingdom: the Transfiguration

554   From the day Peter confessed that Jesus is the Christ, the
Son of the living God, the Master "began to show his disciples that
he must go to Jerusalem and suffer many things . . . and be killed,
and on the third day be raised."[290] Peter scorns this prediction, nor
do the others understand it any better than he.[291] In this context
the mysterious episode of Jesus' Transfiguration takes place on a
high mountain,[292] before three witnesses chosen by himself: Peter,
697, 2600   James, and John. Jesus' face and clothes become dazzling with
light, and Moses and Elijah appear, speaking "of his departure,
which he was to accomplish at Jerusalem."[293] A cloud covers him
440   and a voice from heaven says: "This is my Son, my Chosen; listen
to him!"[294]

555   For a moment Jesus discloses his divine glory, confirming
Peter's confession. He also reveals that he will have to go by the
way of the cross at Jerusalem in order to "enter into his glory."[295]
2576, 2583   Moses and Elijah had seen God's glory on the Mountain; the Law
and the Prophets had announced the Messiah's sufferings.[296]
Christ's Passion is the will of the Father: the Son acts as God's
257   servant;[297] the cloud indicates the presence of the Holy Spirit. "The

---

287   *Mt* 16:19.
288   *Jn* 21:15-17; cf. 10:11.
289   Cf. *Mt* 18:18.
290   *Mt* 16:21.
291   Cf. *Mt* 16:22-23; *Mt* 17:23; *Lk* 9:45.
292   Cf. *Mt* 17:1-8 and parallels; 2 *Pet* 1:16-18.
293   *Lk* 9:31.
294   *Lk* 9:35.
295   *Lk* 24:26.
296   Cf. *Lk* 24:27.

whole Trinity appeared: the Father in the voice; the Son in the man; the Spirit in the shining cloud."[298]

> You were transfigured on the mountain, and your disciples, as much as they were capable of it, beheld your glory, O Christ our God, so that when they should see you crucified they would understand that your Passion was voluntary, and proclaim to the world that you truly are the splendor of the Father.[299]

556 On the threshold of the public life: the baptism; on the threshold of the Passover: the Transfiguration. Jesus' baptism proclaimed "the mystery of the first regeneration," namely, our Baptism; the Transfiguration "is the sacrament of the second regeneration": our own Resurrection.[300] From now on we share in the Lord's Resurrection through the Spirit who acts in the sacraments of the Body of Christ. The Transfiguration gives us a foretaste of Christ's glorious coming, when he "will change our lowly body to be like his glorious body."[301] But it also recalls that "it is through many persecutions that we must enter the kingdom of God".[302]

1003

> Peter did not yet understand this when he wanted to remain with Christ on the mountain. It has been reserved for you, Peter, but for after death. For now, Jesus says: "Go down to toil on earth, to serve on earth, to be scorned and crucified on earth. Life goes down to be killed; Bread goes down to suffer hunger; the Way goes down to be exhausted on his journey; the Spring goes down to suffer thirst; and you refuse to suffer?"[303]

297 Cf. *Isa* 42:1.
298 St. Thomas Aquinas, *STh* III, 45, 4, *ad* 2.
299 Byzantine Liturgy, Feast of the Transfiguration, *Kontakion*.
300 St. Thomas Aquinas, *STh* III, 45, 4, *ad* 2.
301 *Phil* 3:21.
302 *Acts* 14:22.
303 St. Augustine, *Sermo* 78, 6: PL 38, 492-493; cf. *Lk* 9:33.

Jesus' ascent to Jerusalem

557   "When the days drew near for him to be taken up [Jesus] set his face to go to Jerusalem."[304] By this decision he indicated that he was going up to Jerusalem prepared to die there. Three times he had announced his Passion and Resurrection; now, heading toward Jerusalem, Jesus says: "It cannot be that a prophet should perish away from Jerusalem."[305]

558   Jesus recalls the martyrdom of the prophets who had been put to death in Jerusalem. Nevertheless he persists in calling Jerusalem to gather around him: "How often would I have gathered your children together as a hen gathers her brood under her wings, and you would not!"[306] When Jerusalem comes into view he weeps over her and expresses once again his heart's desire: "Would that even today you knew the things that make for peace! But now they are hid from your eyes."[307]

Jesus' messianic entrance into Jerusalem

559   How will Jerusalem welcome her Messiah? Although Jesus had always refused popular attempts to make him king, he chooses the time and prepares the details for his messianic entry into the city of "his father David."[308] Acclaimed as son of David, as the one who brings salvation (*Hosanna* means "Save!" or "Give salvation!"), the "King of glory" enters his City "riding on an ass."[309] Jesus conquers the Daughter of Zion, a figure of his Church, neither by ruse nor by violence, but by the humility that bears witness to the truth.[310] And so the subjects of his kingdom on that day are children and God's poor, who acclaim him as had the angels when they announced him to the shepherds.[311] Their
333 acclamation, "Blessed be he who comes in the name of the
1352 LORD,"[312] is taken up by the Church in the "*Sanctus*" of the Eucharistic liturgy that introduces the memorial of the Lord's Passover.

---

304   *Lk* 9:51; cf. *Jn* 13:1.
305   *Lk* 13:33; cf. *Mk* 8:31-33; 9:31-32; 10:32-34.
306   *Mt* 23:37.
307   *Lk* 19:41-42.
308   *Lk* 1:32; cf. *Mt* 21:1-11; *Jn* 6:15.
309   *Ps* 24:7-10; *Zech* 9:9.
310   Cf. *Jn* 18:37.
311   Cf. *Mt* 21:15-16; cf. *Ps* 8:3; *Lk* 19:38; 2:14.
312   Cf. *Ps* 118:26.

560 *Jesus' entry into Jerusalem* manifested the coming of the kingdom that the King-Messiah was going to accomplish by the Passover of his Death and Resurrection. It is with the celebration *550, 2816* of that entry on Palm Sunday that the Church's liturgy solemnly opens Holy Week.

IN BRIEF

561 "The whole of Christ's life was a continual teaching: his silences, his miracles, his gestures, his prayer, his love for people, his special affection for the little and the poor, his acceptance of the total sacrifice on the Cross for the redemption of the world, and his Resurrection are the actualization of his word and the fulfillment of Revelation" (John Paul II, *CT* 9).

562 Christ's disciples are to conform themselves to him until he is formed in them (cf. *Gal* 4:19). "For this reason we, who have been made like to him, who have died with him and risen with him, are taken up into the mysteries of his life, until we reign together with him" (*LG* 7 § 4).

563 No one, whether shepherd or wise man, can approach God here below except by kneeling before the manger at Bethlehem and adoring him hidden in the weakness of a new-born child.

564 By his obedience to Mary and Joseph, as well as by his humble work during the long years in Nazareth, Jesus gives us the example of holiness in the daily life of family and work.

565 From the beginning of his public life, at his baptism, Jesus is the "Servant," wholly consecrated to the redemptive work that he will accomplish by the "baptism" of his Passion.

566 The temptation in the desert shows Jesus, the humble Messiah, who triumphs over Satan by his total adherence to the plan of salvation willed by the Father.

567 The Kingdom of heaven was inaugurated on earth by Christ. "This kingdom shone out before men in the word, in the works, and in the presence of Christ" (*LG* 5). The Church is the seed and beginning of this kingdom. Her keys are entrusted to Peter.

568   Christ's Transfiguration aims at strengthening the apostles' faith in anticipation of his Passion: the ascent onto the "high mountain" prepares for the ascent to Calvary. Christ, Head of the Church, manifests what his Body contains and radiates in the sacraments: "the hope of glory" (*Col* 1:27; cf. St. Leo the Great, *Sermo* 51, 3: PL 54, 310c).

569   Jesus went up to Jerusalem voluntarily, knowing well that there he would die a violent death because of the opposition of sinners (cf. *Heb* 12:3).

570   Jesus' entry into Jerusalem manifests the coming of the kingdom that the Messiah-King, welcomed into his city by children and the humble of heart, is going to accomplish by the Passover of his Death and Resurrection.

ARTICLE 4
"JESUS CHRIST SUFFERED UNDER PONTIUS PILATE, WAS CRUCIFIED, DIED, AND WAS BURIED"

571   The Paschal mystery of Christ's cross and Resurrection stands at the center of the Good News that the apostles, and the
1067   Church following them, are to proclaim to the world. God's saving plan was accomplished "once for all"[313] by the redemptive death of his Son Jesus Christ.

572   The Church remains faithful to the interpretation of "all the Scriptures" that Jesus gave both before and after his Passover:
599   "Was it not necessary that the Christ should suffer these things and enter into his glory?"[314] Jesus' sufferings took their historical, concrete form from the fact that he was "rejected by the elders and the chief priests and the scribes," who handed "him to the Gentiles to be mocked and scourged and crucified."[315]

573   Faith can therefore try to examine the circumstances of Jesus' death, faithfully handed on by the Gospels[316] and illuminated by

---

313   *Heb* 9:26.
314   *Lk* 24:26-27, 44-45.
315   *Mk* 8:31; *Mt* 20:19.
316   Cf. *DV* 19.

other historical sources, the better to understand the meaning of
the Redemption. *158*

Paragraph 1. Jesus and Israel

574   From the beginning of Jesus' public ministry, certain
Pharisees and partisans of Herod together with priests and scribes
agreed together to destroy him.[317] Because of certain of his acts – *530*
expelling demons, forgiving sins, healing on the sabbath day, his
novel interpretation of the precepts of the Law regarding purity,
and his familiarity with tax collectors and public sinners[318] – some
ill-intentioned persons suspected Jesus of demonic possession.[319]
He is accused of blasphemy and false prophecy, religious crimes *591*
which the Law punished with death by stoning.[320]

575   Many of Jesus' deeds and words constituted a "sign of contradiction,"[321] but more so for the religious authorities in Jerusalem, whom the
Gospel according to John often calls simply "the Jews,"[322] than for the
ordinary People of God.[323] To be sure, Christ's relations with the Pharisees
were not exclusively polemical. Some Pharisees warned him of the danger
he was courting;[324] Jesus praises some of them, like the scribe of *Mark*
12:34, and dines several times at their homes.[325] Jesus endorses some of
the teachings imparted by this religious elite of God's people: the resurrection of the dead,[326] certain forms of piety (almsgiving, fasting, and
prayer),[327] the custom of addressing God as Father, and the centrality of *993*
the commandment to love God and neighbor.[328]

576   In the eyes of many in Israel, Jesus seems to be acting
against essential institutions of the Chosen People:

– submission to the whole of the Law in its written commandments
and, for the Pharisees, in the interpretation of oral tradition;

– the centrality of the Temple at Jerusalem as the holy place where
God's presence dwells in a special way;

– faith in the one God whose glory no man can share.

---

317   Cf. *Mk* 3:6; 14:1.
318   Cf. *Mt* 12:24: *Mk* 2:7, 14-17; 3:1-6; 7:14-23.
319   Cf. *Mk* 3:22; *Jn* 8:48; 10:20.
320   Cf. *Mk* 2:7; *Jn* 5:18; *Jn* 7:12; 7:52; 8:59; 10:31, 33.
321   *Lk* 2:34.
322   Cf. *Jn* 1:19; 2:18; 5:10; 7:13; 9:22; 18:12; 19:38; 20:19.
323   *Jn* 7:48-49.
324   Cf. *Lk* 13:31.
325   Cf. *Lk* 7:36; 14:1.
326   Cf. *Mt* 22:23-34; *Lk* 20:39.
327   Cf. *Mt* 6:18.
328   Cf. *Mk* 12:28-34.

I.   JESUS AND THE LAW

577   At the beginning of the Sermon on the Mount Jesus issued
1965   a solemn warning in which he presented God's law, given on Sinai
during the first covenant, in light of the grace of the New Covenant:

> Do not think that I have come to abolish the law or the
> prophets: I have come not to abolish but to fulfill. For truly
1967   I tell you, until heaven and earth pass away, not one letter,
> not one stroke of a letter, will pass from the law, until all is
> accomplished. Therefore, whoever breaks one of the least of
> these commandments, and teaches others to do the same,
> will be called least in the kingdom of heaven; but whoever
> does them and teaches them will be called great in the
> kingdom of heaven.[329]

578   Jesus, Israel's Messiah and therefore the greatest in the
kingdom of heaven, was to fulfill the Law by keeping it in its
1953   all-embracing detail – according to his own words, down to "the
least of these commandments."[330] He is in fact the only one who
could keep it perfectly.[331] On their own admission the Jews were
never able to observe the Law in its entirety without violating the
least of its precepts.[332] This is why every year on the Day of
Atonement the children of Israel ask God's forgiveness for their
transgressions of the Law. The Law indeed makes up one inseparable whole, and St. James recalls, "Whoever keeps the whole law
but fails in one point has become guilty of all of it."[333]

579   This principle of integral observance of the Law not only in letter
but in spirit was dear to the Pharisees. By giving Israel this principle they
had led many Jews of Jesus' time to an extreme religious zeal.[334] This zeal,
were it not to lapse into "hypocritical" casuistry,[335] could only prepare the
People for the unprecedented intervention of God through the perfect
fulfillment of the Law by the only Righteous One in place of all sinners.[336]

580   The perfect fulfillment of the Law could be the work of
none but the divine legislator, born subject to the Law in the person
527   of the Son.[337] In Jesus, the Law no longer appears engraved on
tables of stone but "upon the heart" of the Servant who becomes
"a covenant to the people," because he will "faithfully bring forth

---

329   *Mt* 5:17-19.
330   *Mt* 5:19.
331   Cf. *Jn* 8:46.
332   Cf. *Jn* 7:19; *Acts* 13:38-41; 15:10.
333   *Jas* 2:10; cf. *Gal* 3:10; 5:3.
334   Cf. *Rom* 10:2.
335   Cf. *Mt* 15:3-7, *Lk* 11:39-54.
336   Cf. *Isa* 53:11; *Heb* 9:15.
337   Cf. *Gal* 4:4.

justice."[338] Jesus fulfills the Law to the point of taking upon himself "the curse of the Law" incurred by those who do not "abide by the things written in the book of the Law, and do them," for his death took place to redeem them "from the transgressions under the first covenant."[339]

581 The Jewish people and their spiritual leaders viewed Jesus as a rabbi.[340] He often argued within the framework of rabbinical interpretation of the Law.[341] Yet Jesus could not help but offend the teachers of the Law, for he was not content to propose his interpretation alongside theirs but taught the people "as one who had authority, and not as their *2054* scribes."[342] In Jesus, the same Word of God, that had resounded on Mount Sinai to give the written Law to Moses, made itself heard anew on the Mount of the Beatitudes.[343] Jesus did not abolish the Law but fulfilled it by giving its ultimate interpretation in a divine way: "You have heard that it was said to the men of old . . . . But I say to you. . . ."[344] With this same divine authority, he disavowed certain human traditions of the Pharisees that were "making void the word of God."[345]

582 Going even further, Jesus perfects the dietary law, so important in Jewish daily life, by revealing its pedagogical meaning through a divine interpretation: "Whatever goes into a man from outside cannot defile him . . . (Thus he declared all foods clean.). What comes out of a man is what defiles a man. For from within, out of the heart of man, come evil thoughts. . . ."[346] In presenting with divine authority the definitive interpretation of the Law, Jesus found himself confronted by *368* certain teachers of the Law who did not accept his interpretation of the Law, guaranteed though it was by the divine signs that accompanied *548* it.[347] This was the case especially with the sabbath laws, for he recalls often with rabbinical arguments, that the sabbath rest is not violated by *2173* serving God and neighbor,[348] which his own healings did.

II.   JESUS AND THE TEMPLE

583 Like the prophets before him Jesus expressed the deepest respect for the Temple in Jerusalem. It was in the Temple that Joseph and Mary presented him forty days after his birth.[349] At the *529* age of twelve he decided to remain in the Temple to remind his *534*

---

338 *Jer* 31:33; *Isa* 42:3, 6.
339 *Gal* 3:13; 3:10; *Heb* 9:15.
340 Cf. *Jn* 11:28; 3:2; *Mt* 22:23-24, 34-36.
341 Cf. *Mt* 12:5; 9:12; *Mk* 2:23-27; *Lk* 6:6-9; *Jn* 7:22-23.
342 *Mt* 7:28-29.
343 Cf. *Mt* 5:1.
344 *Mt* 5:33-34.
345 *Mk* 7:13; cf. 3:8.
346 *Mk* 7:18- 21; cf. *Gal* 3:24.
347 Cf. *Jn* 5:36; 10:25, 37-38; 12:37.
348 Cf. *Num* 28:9; *Mt* 12:5; *Mk* 2:25-27; *Lk* 13:15-16; 14:3-4; *Jn* 7:22-24.
349 *Lk* 2:22-39.

parents that he must be about his Father's business.[350] He went there each year during his hidden life at least for Passover.[351] His public ministry itself was patterned by his pilgrimages to Jerusalem for the great Jewish feasts.[352]

584   Jesus went up to the Temple as the privileged place of encounter with God. For him, the Temple was the dwelling of his

2599 Father, a house of prayer, and he was angered that its outer court had become a place of commerce.[353] He drove merchants out of it because of jealous love for his Father: "You shall not make my Father's house a house of trade. His disciples remembered that it was written, 'Zeal for your house will consume me.'"[354] After his Resurrection his apostles retained their reverence for the Temple.[355]

585   On the threshold of his Passion Jesus announced the coming destruction of this splendid building, of which there would not remain "one stone upon another."[356] By doing so, he announced a sign of the last days, which were to begin with his own Passover.[357] But this prophecy would be distorted in its telling by false witnesses during his interrogation at the high priest's house and would be thrown back at him as an insult when he was nailed to the cross.[358]

586   Far from having been hostile to the Temple, where he gave the essential part of his teaching, Jesus was willing to pay the temple-tax, associating with him Peter, whom he had just made the foundation of his future Church.[359] He even identified himself with the Temple by presenting himself as God's definitive dwell-

797 ing-place among men.[360] Therefore his being put to bodily death[361] presaged the destruction of the Temple, which would manifest the dawning of a new age in the history of salvation: "The hour is coming when neither on this mountain nor in Jerusalem will you

1179 worship the Father."[362]

---

350   Cf. *Lk* 2:46-49.
351   Cf. *Lk* 2:41.
352   Cf. *Jn* 2:13-14; 5:1, 14; 7:1, 10, 14; 8:2; 10:22-23.
353   Cf. *Mt* 21:13
354   *Jn* 2:16-17; cf. *Ps* 69:10.
355   Cf. *Acts* 2:46; 3:1; 5:20, 21; etc.
356   Cf. *Mt* 24:1-2.
357   Cf. *Mt* 24:3; *Lk* 13:35.
358   Cf. *Mk* 14:57-58: *Mt* 27:39-40.
359   Cf. *Mt* 8:4; 16:18; 17:24-27; *Lk* 17:14; *Jn* 4:22; 18:20.
360   Cf. *Jn* 2:21; *Mt* 12:6.
361   Cf. *Jn* 2:18-22.
362   *Jn* 4:21; cf. *Jn* 4:23-24; *Mt* 27:51; *Heb* 9:11; *Rev* 21:22.

III.   JESUS AND ISRAEL'S FAITH IN THE ONE GOD AND SAVIOR

587   If the Law and the Jerusalem Temple could be occasions of opposition to Jesus by Israel's religious authorities, his role in the redemption of sins, the divine work par excellence, was the true stumbling-block for them.[363]

588   Jesus scandalized the Pharisees by eating with tax collectors and sinners as familiarly as with themselves.[364] Against those among them "who trusted in themselves that they were righteous and despised others," Jesus affirmed: "I have not come to call the *545* righteous, but sinners to repentance."[365] He went further by proclaiming before the Pharisees that, since sin is universal, those who pretend not to need salvation are blind to themselves.[366]

589   Jesus gave scandal above all when he identified his merciful conduct toward sinners with God's own attitude toward them.[367] He went so far as to hint that by sharing the table of sinners he was admitting them to the messianic banquet.[368] But it was most especially by forgiving sins that Jesus placed the religious authorities of Israel on the horns of a dilemma. Were they not entitled to demand in consternation, "Who can forgive sins but God alone?"[369] By forgiving sins Jesus either is blaspheming as a man *431, 1441* who made himself God's equal or is speaking the truth, and his *432* person really does make present and reveal God's name.[370]

590   Only the divine identity of Jesus' person can justify so absolute a claim as "He who is not with me is against me"; and his saying that there was in him "something greater than Jonah, . . . greater than Solomon,"something "greater than the Temple"; his reminder that David had called the Messiah his Lord,[371] and his affirmations, "Before Abraham was, I AM"; and even "I and the Father are one."[372]   *253*

---

363   Cf. *Lk* 2:34; 20:17-18; *Ps* 118:22.
364   Cf. *Lk* 5:30; 7:36; 11:37; 14:1.
365   *Lk* 18:9; 5:32; cf. *Jn* 7:49; 9:34.
366   Cf. *Jn* 8:33-36; 9:40-41.
367   Cf. *Mt* 9:13; *Hos* 6:6.
368   Cf. *Lk* 15:1-2, 22-32.
369   *Mk* 2:7.
370   Cf. *Jn* 5:18;10:33;17:6, 26.
371   Cf. *Mt* 12:6, 30, 36, 37, 41-42.
372   *Jn* 8:58; 10:30.

591   Jesus asked the religious authorities of Jerusalem to believe in him because of the Father's works which he accomplished.[373] But such an act of faith must go through a mysterious death to self,
526 for a new "birth from above" under the influence of divine grace.[374] Such a demand for conversion in the face of so surprising a fulfillment of the promises[375] allows one to understand the Sanhedrin's tragic misunderstanding of Jesus: they judged that he deserved the death sentence as a blasphemer.[376] The members of the Sanhedrin were thus acting at the same time out of "ignorance" and the
574 "hardness" of their "unbelief."[377]

IN BRIEF

592   Jesus did not abolish the Law of Sinai, but rather fulfilled it (cf. *Mt* 5:17-19) with such perfection (cf. *Jn* 8:46) that he revealed its ultimate meaning (cf. *Mt* 5:33) and redeemed the transgressions against it (cf. *Heb* 9:15).

593   Jesus venerated the Temple by going up to it for the Jewish feasts of pilgrimage, and with a jealous love he loved this dwelling of God among men. The Temple prefigures his own mystery. When he announces its destruction, it is as a manifestation of his own execution and of the entry into a new age in the history of salvation, when his Body would be the definitive Temple.

594   Jesus performed acts, such as pardoning sins, that manifested him to be the Savior God himself (cf. *Jn* 5:16-18). Certain Jews, who did not recognize God made man (cf. *Jn* 1:14), saw in him only a man who made himself God (*Jn* 10:33), and judged him as a blasphemer.

---

373   *Jn* 10:36-38.
374   Cf. *Jn* 3:7; 6:44.
375   Cf. *Isa* 53:1.
376   Cf. *Mk* 3:6; *Mt* 26:64-66.
377   Cf. *Lk* 23:34; *Acts* 3:17-18; *Mk* 3:5; *Rom* 11:25, 20.

Paragraph 2. Jesus Died Crucified

I.   THE TRIAL OF JESUS

Divisions among the Jewish authorities concerning Jesus

595   Among the religious authorities of Jerusalem, not only were the Pharisee Nicodemus and the prominent Joseph of Arimathea both secret disciples of Jesus, but there was also long-standing dissension about him, so much so that St. John says of these authorities on the very eve of Christ's Passion, "many . . . believed in him," though very imperfectly.[378] This is not surprising, if one recalls that on the day after Pentecost "a great many of the priests were obedient to the faith" and "some believers . . . belonged to the party of the Pharisees," to the point that St. James could tell St. Paul, "How many thousands there are among the Jews of those who have believed; and they are all zealous for the Law."[379]

596   The religious authorities in Jerusalem were not unanimous about what stance to take toward Jesus.[380] The Pharisees threatened to excommunicate his followers.[381] To those who feared that "everyone will believe in him, and the Romans will come and destroy both our holy place and our nation," the high priest Caiaphas replied by prophesying: "It is expedient for you that one man should die for the people, and that the whole *1753* nation should not perish."[382] The Sanhedrin, having declared Jesus deserving of death as a blasphemer but having lost the right to put anyone to death, hands him over to the Romans, accusing him of political revolt, a charge that puts him in the same category as Barabbas who had been accused of sedition.[383] The high priests also threatened Pilate politically so that he would condemn Jesus to death.[384]

Jews are not collectively responsible for Jesus' death

597   The historical complexity of Jesus' trial is apparent in the Gospel accounts. The personal sin of the participants (Judas, the Sanhedrin, Pilate) is known to God alone. Hence we cannot lay responsibility for the trial on the Jews in Jerusalem as a whole, despite the outcry of a manipulated crowd and the global reproaches contained in the apostles' calls to conversion after Pentecost.[385] Jesus himself, in forgiving them on the cross, and Peter in *1735*

---

378   *Jn* 12:42; cf. 7:50; 9:16-17; 10:19-21; 19:38-39.
379   *Acts* 6:7; 15:5; 21:20.
380   Cf. *Jn* 9:16; *Jn* 10:19.
381   Cf. *Jn* 9:22.
382   *Jn* 11:48-50.
383   Cf. *Mt* 26:66; *Jn* 18:31; *Lk* 23:2, 19.
384   Cf. *Jn* 19:12, 15, 21.
385   Cf. *Mk* 15:11; *Acts* 2:23, 36; 3:13-14; 4:10; 5:30; 7:52; 10:39; 13:27-28; 1 *Thess* 2:14-15.

following suit, both accept "the ignorance" of the Jews of Jerusalem and even of their leaders.[386] Still less can we extend responsibility to other Jews of different times and places, based merely on the crowd's cry: "His blood be on us and on our children!" a formula for ratifying a judicial sentence.[387] As the Church declared at the Second Vatican Council:

839

> ... [N]either all Jews indiscriminately at that time, nor Jews today, can be charged with the crimes committed during his Passion. . . . [T]he Jews should not be spoken of as rejected or accursed as if this followed from holy Scripture.[388]

All sinners were the authors of Christ's Passion

598   In her Magisterial teaching of the faith and in the witness of her saints, the Church has never forgotten that "sinners were the authors and the ministers of all the sufferings that the divine Redeemer endured."[389] Taking into account the fact that our sins affect Christ himself,[390] the Church does not hesitate to impute to Christians the gravest responsibility for the torments inflicted upon Jesus, a responsibility with which they have all too often burdened the Jews alone:

1851

> We must regard as guilty all those who continue to relapse into their sins. Since our sins made the Lord Christ suffer the torment of the cross, those who plunge themselves into disorders and crimes crucify the Son of God anew in their hearts (for he is in them) and hold him up to contempt. And it can be seen that our crime in this case is greater in us than in the Jews. As for them, according to the witness of the Apostle, "None of the rulers of this age understood this; for if they had, they would not have crucified the Lord of glory." We, however, profess to know him. And when we deny him by our deeds, we in some way seem to lay violent hands on him.[391]
>
> Nor did demons crucify him; it is you who have crucified him and crucify him still, when you delight in your vices and sins.[392]

---

386   Cf. *Lk* 23:34; *Acts* 3:17.
387   *Mt* 27:25; cf. *Acts* 5:28; 18:6.
388   *NA* 4.
389   *Roman Catechism* I, 5, 11; cf. *Heb* 12:3.
390   Cf. *Mt* 25:45; *Acts* 9:4-5.
391   *Roman Catechism* I, 5, 11; cf. *Heb* 6:6; *1 Cor* 2:8.
392   St. Francis of Assisi, *Admonitio* 5, 3.

II. CHRIST'S REDEMPTIVE DEATH IN GOD'S PLAN OF SALVATION

"Jesus handed over according to the definite plan of God"

599   Jesus' violent death was not the result of chance in an unfortunate coincidence of circumstances, but is part of the mystery of God's plan, as St. Peter explains to the Jews of Jerusalem in his first *517* sermon on Pentecost: "This Jesus [was] delivered up according to the definite plan and foreknowledge of God."[393] This Biblical language does not mean that those who handed him over were merely passive players in a scenario written in advance by God.[394]

600   To God, all moments of time are present in their immediacy. When therefore he establishes his eternal plan of "predestination," he includes in it each person's free response to his grace: "In this city, in fact, both Herod and Pontius Pilate, with the Gentiles and the peoples of Israel, gathered together against your holy servant Jesus, whom you anointed, to do whatever your hand and your plan had predestined to take place."[395] For the sake of accomplishing his plan of salvation, God permitted the acts that flowed *312* from their blindness.[396]

"He died for our sins in accordance with the Scriptures"

601   The Scriptures had foretold this divine plan of salvation through the putting to death of "the righteous one, my Servant" as a mystery of universal redemption, that is, as the ransom that would free men from the slavery of sin.[397] Citing a confession of faith that he himself had "received," St. Paul professes that "Christ died for our sins in accordance with the scriptures."[398] In particular Jesus' redemptive death fulfills Isaiah's prophecy of the suffering *652* Servant.[399] Indeed Jesus himself explained the meaning of his life and death in the light of God's suffering Servant.[400] After his *713* Resurrection he gave this interpretation of the Scriptures to the disciples at Emmaus, and then to the apostles.[401]

---

393   *Acts* 2:23.
394   Cf. *Acts* 3:13.
395   *Acts* 4:27-28; cf. *Ps* 2:1-2.
396   Cf. *Mt* 26:54; *Jn* 18:36; 19:11; *Acts* 3:17-18.
397   *Isa* 53:11; cf. 53:12; *Jn* 8:34-36; *Acts* 3:14.
398   *1 Cor* 15:3; cf. also *Acts* 3:18; 7:52; 13:29; 26:22-23.
399   Cf. *Isa* 53:7-8 and *Acts* 8:32-35.
400   Cf. *Mt* 20:28.
401   Cf. *Lk* 24:25-27, 44-45.

"For our sake God made him to be sin"

602   Consequently, St. Peter can formulate the apostolic faith in the divine plan of salvation in this way: "You were ransomed from the futile ways inherited from your fathers . . . with the precious blood of Christ, like that of a lamb without blemish or spot. He was destined before the foundation of the world but was made manifest at the end of the times for your sake."[402] Man's sins, following on
400 original sin, are punishable by death.[403] By sending his own Son
519 in the form of a slave, in the form of a fallen humanity, on account of sin, God "made him to be sin who knew no sin, so that in him we might become the righteousness of God."[404]

603   Jesus did not experience reprobation as if he himself had sinned.[405] But in the redeeming love that always united him to the Father, he assumed us in the state of our waywardness of sin, to the point that he could say in our name from the cross: "My God, my God, why have you forsaken me?"[406] Having thus established
2572 him in solidarity with us sinners, God "did not spare his own Son but gave him up for us all," so that we might be "reconciled to God by the death of his Son."[407]

God takes the initiative of universal redeeming love

604   By giving up his own Son for our sins, God manifests that his plan for us is one of benevolent love, prior to any merit on our part:
211, 2009 "In this is love, not that we loved God but that he loved us and sent
1825 his Son to be the expiation for our sins."[408] God "shows his love for us in that while we were yet sinners Christ died for us."[409]

605   At the end of the parable of the lost sheep Jesus recalled that God's love excludes no one: "So it is not the will of your Father who is in heaven that one of these little ones should perish."[410] He affirms that he came "to give his life as a ransom for many"; this last term is not restrictive, but contrasts the whole of humanity with
402 the unique person of the redeemer who hands himself over to save

---

402   *1 Pet* 1:18-20.
403   Cf. *Rom* 5:12; *1 Cor* 15:56.
404   *2 Cor* 5:21; cf. *Phil* 2:7; *Rom* 8:3.
405   Cf. *Jn* 8:46.
406   *Mk* 15:34; *Ps* 22:2; cf. *Jn* 8:29.
407   *Rom* 8:32, 5:10.
408   *1 Jn* 4:10; 4:19.
409   *Rom* 5:8.
410   *Mt* 18:14.

us.[411] The Church, following the apostles, teaches that Christ died for all men without exception: "There is not, never has been, and never will be a single human being for whom Christ did not suffer."[412]   *634, 2793*

III.   CHRIST OFFERED HIMSELF TO HIS FATHER FOR OUR SINS

Christ's whole life is an offering to the Father

606   The Son of God, who came down "from heaven, not to do [his] own will, but the will of him who sent [him],"[413] said on coming into the world, "Lo, I have come to do your will, O God."   *517* "And by that will we have been sanctified through the offering of the body of Jesus Christ once for all."[414] From the first moment of his Incarnation the Son embraces the Father's plan of divine salvation in his redemptive mission: "My food is to do the will of him who sent me, and to accomplish his work."[415] The sacrifice of Jesus "for the sins of the whole world"[416] expresses his loving commun-   *536* ion with the Father. "The Father loves me, because I lay down my life," said the Lord, "[for] I do as the Father has commanded me, so that the world may know that I love the Father."[417]

607   The desire to embrace his Father's plan of redeeming love inspired Jesus' whole life,[418] for his redemptive passion was the very reason for his Incarnation. And so he asked, "And what shall   *457* I say? 'Father, save me from this hour'? No, for this purpose I have come to this hour."[419] And again, "Shall I not drink the cup which the Father has given me?"[420] From the cross, just before "It is finished," he said, "I thirst."[421]

"The Lamb who takes away the sin of the world"

608   After agreeing to baptize him along with the sinners, John the Baptist looked at Jesus and pointed him out as the "Lamb of God, who takes away the sin of the world."[422] By doing so, he   *523*

---

411   *Mt* 20:28; cf. *Rom* 5:18-19.
412   Council of Quiercy (853): DS 624; cf. *2 Cor* 5:15; *1 Jn* 2:2.
413   *Jn* 6:38.
414   *Heb* 10:5-10.
415   *Jn* 4:34.
416   *1 Jn* 2:2.
417   *Jn* 10:17; 14:31.
418   Cf. *Lk* 12:50; 22:15; *Mt* 16:21-23.
419   *Jn* 12:27.
420   *Jn* 18:11.
421   *Jn* 19:30; 19:28.

reveals that Jesus is at the same time the suffering Servant who silently allows himself to be led to the slaughter and who bears the sin of the multitudes, and also the Paschal Lamb, the symbol of Israel's redemption at the first Passover.[423] Christ's whole life expresses his mission: "to serve and to give his life as a ransom for many."[424]

517

Jesus freely embraced the Father's redeeming love

609 By embracing in his human heart the Father's love for men, Jesus "loved them to the end," for "greater love has no man than this, that a man lay down his life for his friends."[425] In suffering and death his humanity became the free and perfect instrument of his divine love which desires the salvation of men.[426] Indeed, out of love for his Father and for men, whom the Father wants to save, Jesus freely accepted his Passion and death: "No one takes [my life] from me, but I lay it down of my own accord."[427] Hence the sovereign freedom of God's Son as he went out to his death.[428]

478
515
272, 539

At the Last Supper Jesus anticipated the free offering of his life

610 Jesus gave the supreme expression of his free offering of himself at the meal shared with the twelve Apostles "on the night he was betrayed."[429] On the eve of his Passion, while still free, Jesus transformed this Last Supper with the apostles into the memorial of his voluntary offering to the Father for the salvation of men: "This is my body which is given for you." "This is my blood of the covenant, which is poured out for many for the forgiveness of sins."[430]

766
1337

611 The Eucharist that Christ institutes at that moment will be the memorial of his sacrifice.[431] Jesus includes the apostles in his own offering and bids them perpetuate it.[432] By doing so, the Lord institutes his apostles as priests of the New Covenant: "For their sakes I sanctify myself, so that they also may be sanctified in truth."[433]

1364
1341, 1566

---

422 *Jn* 1:29; cf. *Lk* 3:21; *Mt* 3:14-15; *Jn* 1:36.
423 *Isa* 53:7, 12; cf. *Jer* 11:19; *Ex* 12:3-14; *Jn* 19:36; *1 Cor* 5:7.
424 *Mk* 10:45.
425 *Jn* 13:1;15:13.
426 Cf. *Heb* 2:10, 17-18; 4:15; 5:7-9.
427 *Jn* 10:18.
428 Cf. *Jn* 18:4-6; *Mt* 26:53.
429 *Roman Missal*, EP 111; cf. *Mt* 26:20; *1 Cor* 11:23.
430 *Lk* 22:19; *Mt* 26:28; cf. *1 Cor* 5:7.
431 *1 Cor* 11:25.
432 Cf. *Lk* 22:19.

The agony at Gethsemani

612   The cup of the New Covenant, which Jesus anticipated when he offered himself at the Last Supper, is afterwards accepted by him from his Father's hands in his agony in the garden at Gethsemani,[434] making himself "obedient unto death." Jesus *532, 2600* prays: "My Father, if it be possible, let this cup pass from me...."[435] Thus he expresses the horror that death represented for his human nature. Like ours, his human nature is destined for eternal life; but unlike ours, it is perfectly exempt from sin, the cause of death.[436] Above all, his human nature has been assumed by the divine person of the "Author of life," the "Living One."[437] By accepting in his human will that the Father's will be done, he accepts his death as redemptive, for "he himself bore our sins in his body on the tree."[438]   *1009*

Christ's death is the unique and definitive sacrifice

613   Christ's death is both the *Paschal sacrifice* that accomplishes the definitive redemption of men, through "the Lamb of God, who takes away the sin of the world,"[439] and the *sacrifice of the New* *1366* *Covenant*, which restores man to communion with God by recon- *2009* ciling him to God through the "blood of the covenant, which was poured out for many for the forgiveness of sins."[440]

614   This sacrifice of Christ is unique; it completes and sur- *529, 1330* passes all other sacrifices.[441] First, it is a gift from God the Father *2100* himself, for the Father handed his Son over to sinners in order to reconcile us with himself. At the same time it is the offering of the Son of God made man, who in freedom and love offered his life to his Father through the Holy Spirit in reparation for our disobedience.[442]

---

433   *Jn* 17:19; cf. Council of Trent: DS 1752; 1764.
434   Cf. *Mt* 26:42; *Lk* 22:20.
435   *Phil* 2:8; *Mt* 26:39; cf. *Heb* 5:7-8.
436   Cf. *Rom* 5:12; *Heb* 4:15.
437   Cf. *Acts* 3:15; *Rev* 1:17; *Jn* 1:4; 5:26.
438   *1 Pet* 2:24; cf. *Mt* 26:42.
439   *Jn* 1:29; cf. 8:34-36; *1 Cor* 5:7; *1 Pet* 1:19.
440   *Mt* 26:28; cf. *Ex* 24:8; *Lev* 16:15-16; *1 Cor* 11:25.
441   Cf. *Heb* 10:10.
442   Cf. *Jn* 10:17-18; 15:13; *Heb* 9:14; *1 Jn* 4:10.

Jesus substitutes his obedience for our disobedience

615 "For as by one man's disobedience many were made sinners, so by one man's obedience many will be made righteous."[443] By his
1850 obedience unto death, Jesus accomplished the substitution of the suffering Servant, who "makes himself an *offering for sin,*" when "he
433 bore the sin of many," and who "shall make many to be accounted
411 righteous," for "he shall bear their iniquities."[444] Jesus atoned for our faults and made satisfaction for our sins to the Father.[445]

Jesus consummates his sacrifice on the Cross

616 It is love "to the end"[446] that confers on Christ's sacrifice its value as redemption and reparation, as atonement and satisfaction. He knew and loved us all when he offered his life.[447] Now
478 "the love of Christ controls us, because we are convinced that one has died for all; therefore all have died."[448] No man, not even the holiest, was ever able to take on himself the sins of all men and offer himself as a sacrifice for all. The existence in Christ of the divine
468 person of the Son, who at once surpasses and embraces all human
519 persons and constitutes himself as the Head of all mankind, makes possible his redemptive sacrifice *for all.*

617 The Council of Trent emphasizes the unique character of Christ's sacrifice as "the source of eternal salvation"[449] and teaches
1992 that "his most holy Passion on the wood of the cross merited
1235 justification for us."[450] And the Church venerates his cross as it sings: "Hail, O Cross, our only hope."[451]

Our participation in Christ's sacrifice

618 The cross is the unique sacrifice of Christ, the "one mediator between God and men."[452] But because in his incarnate divine person he has in some way united himself to every man, "the possibility of being made partners, in a way known to God, in the

---

443 *Rom* 5:19.
444 *Isa* 53:10-12.
445 Cf. Council of Trent (1547): DS 1529.
446 *Jn* 13:1.
447 Cf. *Gal* 2:20; *Eph* 5:2, 25.
448 *2 Cor* 5:14.
449 *Heb* 5:9.
450 Council of Trent: DS 1529.
451 *LH*, Lent, Holy Week, Evening Prayer, Hymn *Vexilla regis*.
452 *1 Tim* 2:5.

paschal mystery" is offered to all men.[453] He calls his disciples to   *1368, 1460*
"take up [their] cross and follow [him],"[454] for "Christ also suffered   *307, 2100*
for [us], leaving [us] an example so that [we] should follow in his
steps."[455] In fact Jesus desires to associate with his redeeming
sacrifice those who were to be its first beneficiaries.[456] This is   *964*
achieved supremely in the case of his mother, who was associated
more intimately than any other person in the mystery of his redemptive suffering.[457]

> Apart from the cross there is no other ladder by which we
> may get to heaven.[458]

IN BRIEF

619   "Christ died for our sins in accordance with the scrip-
            tures" (*1 Cor* 15:3).

620   Our salvation flows from God's initiative of love for
            us, because "he loved us and sent his Son to be the
            expiation for our sins" (*1 Jn* 4:10). "God was in Christ
            reconciling the world to himself" (*2 Cor* 5:19).

621   Jesus freely offered himself for our salvation. Before-
            hand, during the Last Supper, he both symbolized this
            offering and made it really present: "This is my body
            which is given for you" (*Lk* 22:19).

622   The redemption won by Christ consists in this, that he
            came "to give his life as a ransom for many" (*Mt* 20:28),
            that is, he "loved [his own] to the end" (*Jn* 13:1), so that
            they might be "ransomed from the futile ways inher-
            ited from [their] fathers"(*1 Pet* 1:18).

623   By his loving obedience to the Father, "unto death,
            even death on a cross" (*Phil* 2:8), Jesus fulfills the
            atoning mission (cf. *Isa* 53:10) of the suffering Servant,
            who will "make many righteous; and he shall bear
            their iniquities" (*Isa* 53:11; cf. *Rom* 5:19).

---

453   *GS* 22 § 5; cf. § 2.
454   *Mt* 16:24.
455   *1 Pet* 2:21.
456   Cf. *Mk* 10:39; *Jn* 21:18-19; *Col* 1:24.
457   Cf. *Lk* 2:35.
458   St. Rose of Lima, cf. P. Hansen, *Vita mirabilis* (Louvain, 1668).

Paragraph 3. Jesus Christ Was Buried

624   "By the grace of God" Jesus tasted death "for every one."[459] In his plan of salvation, God ordained that his Son should not only "die for our sins"[460] but should also "taste death," expe-
1005, 362   rience the condition of death, the separation of his soul from his body, between the time he expired on the cross and the time he was raised from the dead. The state of the dead Christ is the mystery of the tomb and the descent into hell. It is the mystery of Holy Saturday, when Christ, lying in the tomb,[461] reveals God's great
349   sabbath rest[462] after the fulfillment[463] of man's salvation, which brings peace to the whole universe.[464]

Christ in the tomb in his body

625   Christ's stay in the tomb constitutes the real link between his passible state before Easter and his glorious and risen state today. The same person of the "Living One" can say, "I died, and behold I am alive for evermore":[465]

> God [the Son] did not impede death from separating his soul from his body according to the necessary order of nature, but has reunited them to one another in the Resurrection, *so that he himself might be, in his person, the meeting point for death and life*, by arresting in himself the decomposition of nature produced by death and so becoming the source of reunion for the separated parts.[466]

626   Since the "Author of life" who was killed[467] is the same
470, 650   "living one [who has] risen,"[468] the divine person of the Son of God necessarily continued to possess his human soul and body, separated from each other by death:

> By the fact that at Christ's death his soul was separated from his flesh, his one person is not itself divided into two persons; for the human body and soul of Christ have existed in the same way from the beginning of his earthly existence, in the divine person of the Word; and in death, although separated

---

459   *Heb* 2:9.
460   *1 Cor* 15:3.
461   Cf. *Jn* 19:42.
462   Cf. *Heb* 4:7-9.
463   Cf. *Jn* 19:30.
464   Cf. *Col* 1:18-20.
465   *Rev* 1:18.
466   St. Gregory of Nyssa, *Orat. catech.*, 16: PG 45, 52D.
467   *Acts* 3:15.
468   *Lk* 24:5-6.

from each other, both remained with one and the same person of the Word.[469]

"You will not let your Holy One see corruption"

627   Christ's death was a real death in that it put an end to his earthly human existence. But because of the union his body retained with the person of the Son, his was not a mortal corpse like others, for "divine power preserved Christ's body from corruption."[470] Both of these statements can be said of Christ: "He was cut off out of the land of the living,"[471] and "My flesh will dwell in hope. For you will not abandon my soul to Hades, nor let your Holy One see corruption."[472] Jesus' Resurrection "on the third day" was the proof of this, for bodily decay was held to begin on the fourth day after death.[473]

1009

1683

"Buried with Christ . . ."

628   Baptism, the original and full sign of which is immersion, efficaciously signifies the descent into the tomb by the Christian who dies to sin with Christ in order to live a new life. "We were buried therefore with him by baptism into death, so that as Christ was raised from the dead by the glory of the Father, we too might walk in newness of life."[474]

537

1214

IN BRIEF

629   To the benefit of every man, Jesus Christ tasted death (cf. *Heb* 2:9). It is truly the Son of God made man who died and was buried.

630   During Christ's period in the tomb, his divine person continued to assume both his soul and his body, although they were separated from each other by death. For this reason the dead Christ's body "saw no corruption" (*Acts* 13:37).

---

469 St. John Damascene, *De fide orth.*, 3, 27: PG 94, 1098A.
470 St. Thomas Aquinas, *STh* III, 51, 3.
471 *Isa* 53:8.
472 *Acts* 2:26-27; cf. *Ps* 16:9-10.
473 Cf. *1 Cor* 15:4; *Lk* 24:46; *Mt* 12:40; *Jon* 2:1; *Hos* 6:2; cf. *Jn* 11:39.
474 *Rom* 6:4; cf. *Col* 2:12; *Eph* 5:26.

ARTICLE 5
"HE DESCENDED INTO HELL
ON THE THIRD DAY HE ROSE AGAIN"

631 Jesus "descended into the lower parts of the earth. He who descended is he who also ascended far above all the heavens."[475] The Apostles' Creed confesses in the same article Christ's descent into hell and his Resurrection from the dead on the third day, because in his Passover it was precisely out of the depths of death that he made life spring forth:

> Christ, that Morning Star, who came back from the dead,
> and shed his peaceful light on all mankind,
> your Son who lives and reigns for ever and ever. Amen.[476]

Paragraph 1. Christ Descended into Hell

632 The frequent New Testament affirmations that Jesus was "raised from the dead" presuppose that the crucified one sojourned in the realm of the dead prior to his resurrection.[477] This was the first meaning given in the apostolic preaching to Christ's descent into hell: that Jesus, like all men, experienced death and in his soul joined the others in the realm of the dead. But he descended there as Savior, proclaiming the Good News to the spirits imprisoned there.[478]

633 Scripture calls the abode of the dead, to which the dead Christ went down, "hell" – *Sheol* in Hebrew or *Hades* in Greek – because those who are there are deprived of the vision of God.[479] Such is the case for all the dead, whether evil or righteous, while they await the redeemer: which does not mean that their lot is identical, as Jesus shows through the parable of the poor man Lazarus who was received into "Abraham's bosom":[480] "It is precisely these holy souls, who awaited their Savior in Abraham's bosom, whom Christ the Lord delivered when he descended into
1033 hell."[481] Jesus did not descend into hell to deliver the damned, nor to destroy the hell of damnation, but to free the just who had gone before him.[482]

---

475 *Eph* 4:9-10.
476 *Roman Missal*, Easter Vigil 18, *Exsultet*.
477 *Acts* 3:15; *Rom* 8:11; *1 Cor* 15:20; cf. *Heb* 13:20.
478 Cf. *1 Pet* 3:18-19.
479 Cf. *Phil* 2:10; *Acts* 2:24; *Rev* 1:18; *Eph* 4:9; *Pss* 6:6; 88:11-13.
480 Cf. *Ps* 89:49; *1 Sam* 28:19; *Ezek* 32:17-32; *Lk* 16:22-26.
481 *Roman Catechism* I, 6, 3.
482 Cf. Council of Rome (745): DS 587; Benedict XII, *Cum dudum* (1341): DS

634   "The gospel was preached even to the dead."[483] The descent
into hell brings the Gospel message of salvation to complete fulfillment. This is the last phase of Jesus' messianic mission, a phase which
is condensed in time but vast in its real significance: the spread of
Christ's redemptive work to all men of all times and all places, for all
who are saved have been made sharers in the redemption.   *605*

635   Christ went down into the depths of death so that "the
dead will hear the voice of the Son of God, and those who hear will
live."[484] Jesus, "the Author of life," by dying destroyed "him who
has the power of death, that is, the devil, and [delivered] all those
who through fear of death were subject to lifelong bondage."[485]
Henceforth the risen Christ holds "the keys of Death and Hades,"
so that "at the name of Jesus every knee should bow, in heaven and
on earth and under the earth."[486]

> Today a great silence reigns on earth, a great silence and a great
> stillness. A great silence because the King is asleep. The earth
> trembled and is still because God has fallen asleep in the flesh
> and he has raised up all who have slept ever since the world
> began.... He has gone to search for Adam, our first father, as
> for a lost sheep. Greatly desiring to visit those who live in
> darkness and in the shadow of death, he has gone to free from
> sorrow Adam in his bonds and Eve, captive with him – He who
> is both their God and the son of Eve.... "I am your God, who
> for your sake have become your son.... I order you, O sleeper,
> to awake. I did not create you to be a prisoner in hell. Rise from
> the dead, for I am the life of the dead."[487]

IN BRIEF

636   By the expression "He descended into hell," the Apostles' Creed confesses that Jesus did really die and
through his death for us conquered death and the
devil "who has the power of death" (*Heb* 2:14).

637   In his human soul united to his divine person, the dead
Christ went down to the realm of the dead. He opened
heaven's gates for the just who had gone before him.

1011; Clement VI, *Super quibusdam* (1351): DS 1077; Council of Toledo IV
(625): DS 485; *Mt* 27:52-53.

483 *1 Pet* 4:6.
484 *Jn* 5:25; cf. *Mt* 12:40; *Rom* 10:7; *Eph* 4:9.
485 *Heb* 2:14-15; cf. *Acts* 3:15.
486 *Rev* 1:18; *Phil* 2:10.
487 Ancient Homily for Holy Saturday: PG 43, 440A, 452C: *LH*, Holy Saturday, OR.

Paragraph 2. On the Third Day He Rose from the Dead

638   "We bring you the good news that what God promised to
the fathers, this day he has fulfilled to us their children by raising
Jesus."[488] The Resurrection of Jesus is the crowning truth of our faith
90 in Christ, a faith believed and lived as the central truth by the first
651 Christian community; handed on as fundamental by Tradition; estab-
991 lished by the documents of the New Testament; and preached as an
essential part of the Paschal mystery along with the cross:

> Christ is risen from the dead!
> Dying, he conquered death;
> To the dead, he has given life.[489]

I.   THE HISTORICAL AND TRANSCENDENT EVENT

639   The mystery of Christ's resurrection is a real event, with
manifestations that were historically verified, as the New Testament bears witness. In about a.d. 56, St. Paul could already write
to the Corinthians: "I delivered to you as of first importance what
I also received, that Christ died for our sins in accordance with the
scriptures, and that he was buried, that he was raised on the third
day in accordance with the scriptures, and that he appeared to
Cephas, then to the Twelve . . ."[490] The Apostle speaks here of the
living tradition of the Resurrection which he had learned after his
conversion at the gates of Damascus.[491]

The empty tomb

640   "Why do you seek the living among the dead? He is not
here, but has risen."[492] The first element we encounter in the
framework of the Easter events is the empty tomb. In itself it is not
a direct proof of Resurrection; the absence of Christ's body from
the tomb could be explained otherwise.[493] Nonetheless the empty
tomb was still an essential sign for all. Its discovery by the disciples
was the first step toward recognizing the very fact of the Resurrection. This was the case, first with the holy women, and then with
Peter.[494] The disciple "whom Jesus loved" affirmed that when he

---

488   *Acts* 13:32-33.
489   Byzantine Liturgy, Troparion of Easter.
490   *1 Cor* 15:3-4.
491   Cf. *Acts* 9:3-18.
492   *Lk* 24:5-6.
493   Cf. *Jn* 20:13; *Mt* 28:11-15.
494   Cf. *Lk* 24:3, 12, 22-23.

entered the empty tomb and discovered "the linen cloths lying there," "he saw and believed."[495] This suggests that he realized from the empty tomb's condition that the absence of Jesus' body could not have been of human doing and that Jesus had not simply returned to earthly life as had been the case with Lazarus.[496]

999

The appearances of the Risen One

641   Mary Magdalene and the holy women who came to finish anointing the body of Jesus, which had been buried in haste because the Sabbath began on the evening of Good Friday, were the first to encounter the Risen One.[497] Thus the women were the first messengers of Christ's Resurrection for the apostles themselves.[498] They were the next to whom Jesus appears: first Peter, then the Twelve. Peter had been called to strengthen the faith of his brothers,[499] and so sees the Risen One before them; it is on the basis of his testimony that the community exclaims: "The Lord has risen indeed, and has appeared to Simon!"[500]

553

448

642   Everything that happened during those Paschal days involves each of the apostles – and Peter in particular – in the building of the new era begun on Easter morning. As witnesses of the Risen One, they remain the foundation stones of his Church. The faith of the first community of believers is based on the witness of concrete men known to the Christians and for the most part still living among them. Peter and the Twelve are the primary "witnesses to his Resurrection," but they are not the only ones – Paul speaks clearly of more than five hundred persons to whom Jesus appeared on a single occasion and also of James and of all the apostles.[501]

659, 881

860

643   Given all these testimonies, Christ's Resurrection cannot be interpreted as something outside the physical order, and it is impossible not to acknowledge it as an historical fact. It is clear from the facts that the disciples' faith was drastically put to the test by their master's Passion and death on the cross, which he had foretold.[502] The shock provoked by the Passion was so great that at least some of the disciples did not at once believe in the news of the Resurrection. Far from showing us a community seized by a mystical exaltation, the Gospels present us with disciples demoralized ("looking sad"[503]) and frightened. For they had not believed the holy women returning

---

495   *Jn* 20:2, 6, 8.
496   Cf. *Jn* 11:44; 20:5-7.
497   *Mk* 16:1; *Lk* 24:1; *Jn* 19:31, 42.
498   Cf. *Lk* 24:9-10; *Mt* 28:9-10; *Jn* 20:11-18.
499   Cf. *1 Cor* 15:5; *Lk* 22:31-32.
500   *Lk* 24:34, 36.
501   *1 Cor* 15:4-8; cf. *Acts* 1:22.
502   Cf. *Lk* 22:31-32.

from the tomb and had regarded their words as an "idle tale."[504] When Jesus reveals himself to the Eleven on Easter evening, "he upbraided them for their unbelief and hardness of heart, because they had not believed those who saw him after he had risen."[505]

644   Even when faced with the reality of the risen Jesus the disciples are still doubtful, so impossible did the thing seem: they thought they were seeing a ghost. "In their joy they were still disbelieving and still wondering."[506] Thomas will also experience the test of doubt and St. Matthew relates that during the risen Lord's last appearance in Galilee "some doubted."[507] Therefore the hypothesis that the Resurrection was produced by the apostles' faith (or credulity) will not hold up. On the contrary their faith in the Resurrection was born, under the action of divine grace, from their direct experience of the reality of the risen Jesus.

The condition of Christ's risen humanity

645   By means of touch and the sharing of a meal, the risen Jesus establishes direct contact with his disciples. He invites them in this way to recognize that he is not a ghost and above all to verify that 999 the risen body in which he appears to them is the same body that had been tortured and crucified, for it still bears the traces of his passion.[508] Yet at the same time this authentic, real body possesses the new properties of a glorious body: not limited by space and time but able to be present how and when he wills; for Christ's humanity can no longer be confined to earth and belongs henceforth only to the Father's divine realm.[509] For this reason too the risen Jesus enjoys the sovereign freedom of appearing as he wishes: in the guise of a gardener or in other forms familiar to his disciples, precisely to awaken their faith.[510]

646   Christ's Resurrection was not a return to earthly life, as was the case with the raisings from the dead that he had performed before Easter: Jairus' daughter, the young man of Naim, Lazarus. These actions were miraculous events, but the persons miraculously raised 934 returned by Jesus' power to ordinary earthly life. At some particular 549 moment they would die again. Christ's Resurrection is essentially different. In his risen body he passes from the state of death to another life beyond time and space. At Jesus' Resurrection his body is filled

---

503   *Lk* 24:17; cf. *Jn* 20:19.
504   *Lk* 24:11; cf. *Mk* 16:11, 13.
505   *Mk* 16:14.
506   *Lk* 24:38-41.
507   Cf. *Jn* 20:24-27; *Mt* 28:17.
508   Cf. *Lk* 24:30, 39-40, 41-43; *Jn* 20:20, 27; 21:9, 13-15.
509   Cf. *Mt* 28:9, 16-17; *Lk* 24:15, 36; *Jn* 20:14, 17, 19, 26; 21:4.
510   Cf. *Mk* 16:12; *Jn* 20:14-16; 21:4, 7.

with the power of the Holy Spirit: he shares the divine life in his glorious state, so that St. Paul can say that Christ is "the man of heaven."[511]

The Resurrection as transcendent event

647 O truly blessed Night, sings the Exsultet of the Easter Vigil, which alone deserved to know the time and the hour when Christ rose from the realm of the dead![512] But no one was an eyewitness to Christ's Resurrection and no evangelist describes it. No one can say how it came about physically. Still less was its innermost *1000* essence, his passing over to another life, perceptible to the senses. Although the Resurrection was an historical event that could be verified by the sign of the empty tomb and by the reality of the apostles' encounters with the risen Christ, still it remains at the very heart of the mystery of faith as something that transcends and surpasses history. This is why the risen Christ does not reveal himself to the world, but to his disciples, "to those who came up with him from Galilee to Jerusalem, who are now his witnesses to the people."[513]

II.   The Resurrection – A Work of the Holy Trinity

648 Christ's Resurrection is an object of faith in that it is a transcendent intervention of God himself in creation and history. In it the three divine persons act together as one, and manifest their own *258, 989* proper characteristics. The Father's power "raised up" Christ his Son and by doing so perfectly introduced his Son's humanity, including *663* his body, into the Trinity. Jesus is conclusively revealed as "Son of *445* God in power according to the Spirit of holiness by his Resurrection *272* from the dead."[514] St. Paul insists on the manifestation of God's power[515] through the working of the Spirit who gave life to Jesus' dead humanity and called it to the glorious state of Lordship.

649 As for the Son, he effects his own Resurrection by virtue of his divine power. Jesus announces that the Son of man will have to suffer much, die, and then rise.[516] Elsewhere he affirms explicitly: "I lay down my life, that I may take it again. . . . I have power to lay it down, and I have power to take it again."[517] "We believe that Jesus died and rose again."[518]

---

511 Cf. *1 Cor* 15:35-50.
512 "*O vere beata nox, quae sola meruit scire tempus et horam, in qua Christus ab inferis resurrexit!*"
513 *Acts* 13:31; cf. *Jn* 14:22.
514 *Rom* 1:3-4; cf. *Acts* 2:24.
515 Cf. *Rom* 6:4; *2 Cor* 13:4; *Phil* 3:10; *Eph* 1:19-22; *Heb* 7:16.
516 Cf. *Mk* 8:31; 9:9-31; 10:34.

626 **650**   The Fathers contemplate the Resurrection from the per-
1005 spective of the divine person of Christ who remained united to his
soul and body, even when these were separated from each other
by death: "By the unity of the divine nature, which remains present
in each of the two components of man, these are reunited. For as
death is produced by the separation of the human components, so
Resurrection is achieved by the union of the two."[519]

III.   THE MEANING AND SAVING SIGNIFICANCE
    OF THE RESURRECTION

651   "If Christ has not been raised, then our preaching is in vain
and your faith is in vain."[520] The Resurrection above all constitutes
the confirmation of all Christ's works and teachings. All truths,
129 even those most inaccessible to human reason, find their justifica-
274 tion if Christ by his Resurrection has given the definitive proof of
his divine authority, which he had promised.

652   Christ's Resurrection is the fulfillment of the promises
994, 601 both of the Old Testament and of Jesus himself during his earthly
life.[521] The phrase "in accordance with the Scriptures"[522] indicates
that Christ's Resurrection fulfilled these predictions.

445 **653**   The truth of Jesus' divinity is confirmed by his Resurrection. He had said: "When you have lifted up the Son of man, then
you will know that I am he."[523] The Resurrection of the crucified
one shows that he was truly "I Am," the Son of God and God
himself. So St. Paul could declare to the Jews: "What God promised
to the fathers, this he has fulfilled to us their children by raising
Jesus; as also it is written in the second psalm, 'You are my Son,
today I have begotten you.'"[524] Christ's Resurrection is closely
linked to the Incarnation of God's Son and is its fulfillment in
461, 422 accordance with God's eternal plan.

654   The Paschal mystery has two aspects: by his death, Christ
liberates us from sin; by his Resurrection, he opens for us the way
to a new life. This new life is above all justification that reinstates

---

517   *Jn* 10:17-18.
518   *1 Thess* 4:14.
519   St. Gregory of Nyssa, *In Christi res. orat.* 1: PG 46:617B; cf. also DS 325; 359;
      369.
520   *1 Cor* 15:14.
521   Cf. *Mt* 28:6; *Mk* 16:7; *Lk* 24:6-7, 26-27, 44-48.
522   Cf. *1 Cor* 15:3-4; cf. the Nicene Creed.
523   *Jn* 8:28.
524   *Acts* 13:32-34; cf. *Ps* 2:7.

us in God's grace, "so that as Christ was raised from the dead by *1987*
the glory of the Father, we too might walk in newness of life."[525]
Justification consists in both victory over the death caused by sin
and a new participation in grace.[526] It brings about filial adoption
so that men become Christ's brethren, as Jesus himself called his *1996*
disciples after his Resurrection: "Go and tell my brethren."[527] We
are brethren not by nature, but by the gift of grace, because that
adoptive filiation gains us a real share in the life of the only Son,
which was fully revealed in his Resurrection.

655 Finally, Christ's Resurrection – and the risen Christ himself
– is the principle and source of our future resurrection: "Christ has
been raised from the dead, the first fruits of those who have fallen *989*
asleep. . . . For as in Adam all die, so also in Christ shall all be made
alive."[528] The risen Christ lives in the hearts of his faithful while they
await that fulfillment. In Christ, Christians "have tasted . . . the powers
of the age to come"[529] and their lives are swept up by Christ into the *1002*
heart of divine life, so that they may "live no longer for themselves
but for him who for their sake died and was raised."[530]

IN BRIEF

656 Faith in the Resurrection has as its object an event
which is historically attested to by the disciples, who
really encountered the Risen One. At the same time,
this event is mysteriously transcendent insofar as it is
the entry of Christ's humanity into the glory of God.

657 The empty tomb and the linen cloths lying there signify in themselves that by God's power Christ's body
had escaped the bonds of death and corruption. They
prepared the disciples to encounter the Risen Lord.

658 Christ, "the first-born from the dead" (*Col* 1:18), is the
principle of our own resurrection, even now by the
justification of our souls (cf. *Rom* 6:4), and one day by
the new life he will impart to our bodies (cf. *Rom* 8:11).

---

525 *Rom* 6:4; cf. 4:25.
526 Cf. *Eph* 2:4-5; *1 Pet* 1:3.
527 *Mt* 28:10; *Jn* 20:17.
528 *1 Cor* 15:20-22.
529 *Heb* 6:5.
530 *2 Cor* 5:15; cf. *Col* 3:1-3.

ARTICLE 6
"HE ASCENDED INTO HEAVEN AND IS SEATED AT THE RIGHT HAND OF THE FATHER"

659   "So then the Lord Jesus, after he had spoken to them, was taken up into heaven, and sat down at the right hand of God."[531] Christ's body was glorified at the moment of his Resurrection, as
645 proved by the new and supernatural properties it subsequently and permanently enjoys.[532] But during the forty days when he eats and drinks familiarly with his disciples and teaches them about the kingdom, his glory remains veiled under the appearance of ordinary humanity.[533] Jesus' final apparition ends with the irreversible
66 entry of his humanity into divine glory, symbolized by the cloud
697 and by heaven, where he is seated from that time forward at God's
642 right hand.[534] Only in a wholly exceptional and unique way would Jesus show himself to Paul "as to one untimely born," in a last apparition that established him as an apostle.[535]

660   The veiled character of the glory of the Risen One during this time is intimated in his mysterious words to Mary Magdalene: "I have not yet ascended to the Father; but go to my brethren and say to them, I am ascending to my Father and your Father, to my God and your God."[536] This indicates a difference in manifestation between the glory of the risen Christ and that of the Christ exalted to the Father's right hand, a transition marked by the historical and transcendent event of the Ascension.

661   This final stage stays closely linked to the first, that is, to his descent from heaven in the Incarnation. Only the one who
461 "came from the Father" can return to the Father: Christ Jesus.[537] "No one has ascended into heaven but he who descended from heaven, the Son of man."[538] Left to its own natural powers humanity does not have access to the "Father's house," to God's life and
792 happiness.[539] Only Christ can open to man such access that we, his members, might have confidence that we too shall go where he, our Head and our Source, has preceded us.[540]

---

531 *Mk* 16:19.
532 Cf. *Lk* 24:31; *Jn* 20:19, 26.
533 Cf. *Acts* 1:3; 10:41; *Mk* 16:12; *Lk* 24:15; *Jn* 20:14-15; 21:4.
534 Cf. *Acts* 1:9; 2:33; 7:56; *Lk* 9:34-35; 24:51; *Ex* 13:22; *Mk* 16:19; *Ps* 110:1.
535 *1 Cor* 15:8; cf. 9:1; *Gal* 1:16.
536 *Jn* 20:17.
537 Cf. *Jn* 16:28.
538 *Jn* 3:13; cf. *Eph* 4:8-10.
539 *Jn* 14:2.

662   "And I, when I am lifted up from the earth, will draw all men to myself."[541] The lifting up of Jesus on the cross signifies and announces his lifting up by his Ascension into heaven, and indeed begins it. Jesus Christ, the one priest of the new and eternal Cove- *1545* nant, "entered, not into a sanctuary made by human hands . . . but into heaven itself, now to appear in the presence of God on our behalf."[542] There Christ permanently exercises his priesthood, for he "always lives to make intercession" for "those who draw near to God through him."[543] As "high priest of the good things to come" he is the center and the principal actor of the liturgy that *1137* honors the Father in heaven.[544]

663   Henceforth Christ is *seated at the right hand of the Father*: "By 'the Father's right hand' we understand the glory and honor of divinity, where he who exists as Son of God before all ages, indeed as God, of one being with the Father, is seated bodily after he became incarnate and his flesh was glorified."[545] *648*

664   Being seated at the Father's right hand signifies the inauguration of the Messiah's kingdom, the fulfillment of the prophet Daniel's vision concerning the Son of man: "To him was *541* given dominion and glory and kingdom, that all peoples, nations, and languages should serve him; his dominion is an everlasting dominion, which shall not pass away, and his kingdom one that shall not be destroyed."[546] After this event the apostles became witnesses of the "kingdom [that] will have no end."[547]

IN BRIEF

665   Christ's ascension marks the definitive entrance of Jesus' humanity into God's heavenly domain, whence he will come again (cf. *Acts* 1:11); this humanity in the meantime hides him from the eyes of men (cf. *Col* 3:3).

666   Jesus Christ, the head of the Church, precedes us into the Father's glorious kingdom so that we, the mem-

---

540 *Roman Missal*, Preface of the Ascension: *"sed ut illuc confideremus, sua membra, nos subsequi quo ipse, caput nostrum principiumque, praecessit."*
541 *Jn* 12:32.
542 *Heb* 9:24.
543 *Heb* 7:25.
544 *Heb* 9:11; cf. *Rev* 4:6-11.
545 St. John Damascene, *De fide orth.*, 4, 2: PG 94, 1104C.
546 *Dan* 7:14.
547 Nicene Creed.

bers of his Body, may live in the hope of one day being with him for ever.

667   Jesus Christ, having entered the sanctuary of heaven once and for all, intercedes constantly for us as the mediator who assures us of the permanent outpouring of the Holy Spirit.

ARTICLE 7
"FROM THENCE HE WILL COME AGAIN TO JUDGE THE LIVING AND THE DEAD"

I.   HE WILL COME AGAIN IN GLORY

Christ already reigns through the Church . . .

668   "Christ died and lived again, that he might be Lord both of the dead and of the living."[548] Christ's Ascension into heaven signifies his participation, in his humanity, in God's power and
450 authority. Jesus Christ is Lord: he possesses all power in heaven and on earth. He is "far above all rule and authority and power and dominion," for the Father "has put all things under his feet."[549] Christ is Lord of the cosmos and of history. In him human history
518 and indeed all creation are "set forth" and transcendently fulfilled.[550]

669   As Lord, Christ is also head of the Church, which is his Body.[551] Taken up to heaven and glorified after he had thus fully
792, 1088 accomplished his mission, Christ dwells on earth in his Church. The redemption is the source of the authority that Christ, by virtue
541 of the Holy Spirit, exercises over the Church. "The kingdom of Christ [is] already present in mystery," "on earth, the seed and the beginning of the kingdom."[552]

---

548   *Rom* 14:9.
549   *Eph* 1:20-22.
550   *Eph* 1:10; cf. *Eph* 4:10; *1 Cor* 15:24, 27-28.
551   Cf. *Eph* 1:22.
552   *LG* 3; 5; cf. *Eph* 4:11-13.

670   Since the Ascension God's plan has entered into its fulfillment. We are already at "the last hour."[553] "Already the final age of the world is with us, and the renewal of the world is irrevocably *1042* under way; it is even now anticipated in a certain real way, for the Church on earth is endowed already with a sanctity that is real but imperfect."[554] Christ's kingdom already manifests its presence *825* through the miraculous signs that attend its proclamation by the *547* Church.[555]

... until all things are subjected to him

671   Though already present in his Church, Christ's reign is nevertheless yet to be fulfilled "with power and great glory" by the king's return to earth.[556] This reign is still under attack by the evil powers, even though they have been defeated definitively by Christ's Passover.[557] Until everything is subject to him, "until there be realized new heavens and a new earth in which justice dwells, *1043* the pilgrim Church, in her sacraments and institutions, which *769, 773* belong to this present age, carries the mark of this world which will pass, and she herself takes her place among the creatures which groan and travail yet and await the revelation of the sons of God."[558] That is why Christians pray, above all in the Eucharist, to *1043, 2046* hasten Christ's return by saying to him:[559] *Marana tha!* "Our Lord, *2817* come!"[560]

672   Before his Ascension Christ affirmed that the hour had not yet come for the glorious establishment of the messianic kingdom awaited by Israel[561] which, according to the prophets, was to bring all men the definitive order of justice, love, and peace.[562] According to the Lord, the present time is the time of the Spirit and of witness, but also a time still marked by "distress" and the trial of evil which *732* does not spare the Church[563] and ushers in the struggles of the last *2612* days. It is a time of waiting and watching.[564]

---

553   *1 Jn* 2:18; cf. *1 Pet* 4:7.
554   *LG* 48 § 3; cf. *1 Cor* 10:11.
555   Cf. *Mk* 16:17-18, 20.
556   *Lk* 21:27; cf. *Mt* 25:31.
557   Cf. *2 Thess* 2:7.
558   *LG* 48 § 3; cf. *2 Pet* 3:13; *Rom* 8:19-22; *1 Cor* 15:28.
559   Cf. *1 Cor* 11:26; *2 Pet* 3:11-12.
560   *1 Cor* 16:22; *Rev* 22:17, 20.
561   Cf. *Acts* 1:6-7.
562   Cf. *Isa* 11:1-9.
563   Cf. *Acts* 1:8; *1 Cor* 7:26; *Eph* 5:16; *1 Pet* 4:17.
564   Cf. *Mt* 25:1, 13; *Mk* 13:33-37; *1 Jn* 2:18; 4:3; *1 Tim* 4:1.

The glorious advent of Christ, the hope of Israel

673   Since the Ascension Christ's coming in glory has been imminent,[565] even though "it is not for you to know times or seasons which the Father has fixed by his own authority."[566] This eschatological coming could be accomplished at any moment, even if both it and the final trial that will precede it are "delayed."[567]

1040, 1048

674   The glorious Messiah's coming is suspended at every moment of history until his recognition by "all Israel," for "a hardening has come upon part of Israel" in their "unbelief" toward Jesus.[568] St. Peter says to the Jews of Jerusalem after Pentecost: "Repent therefore, and turn again, that your sins may be blotted out, that times of refreshing may come from the presence of the Lord, and that he may send the Christ appointed for you, Jesus, whom heaven must receive until the time for establishing all that God spoke by the mouth of his holy prophets from of old."[569] St. Paul echoes him: "For if their rejection means the reconciliation of the world, what will their acceptance mean but life from the dead?"[570] The "full inclusion" of the Jews in the Messiah's salvation, in the wake of "the full number of the Gentiles,"[571] will enable the People of God to achieve "the measure of the stature of the fullness of Christ," in which "God may be all in all."[572]

840

58

The Church's ultimate trial

675   Before Christ's second coming the Church must pass through a final trial that will shake the faith of many believers.[573] The persecution that accompanies her pilgrimage on earth[574] will unveil the "mystery of iniquity" in the form of a religious deception offering men an apparent solution to their problems at the price of apostasy from the truth. The supreme religious deception is that of the Antichrist, a pseudo-messianism by which man glorifies himself in place of God and of his Messiah come in the flesh.[575]

769

---

565 Cf. *Rev* 22:20.
566 *Acts* 1:7; cf. *Mk* 13:32.
567 Cf. *Mt* 24:44; *1 Thess* 5:2; *2 Thess* 2:3-12.
568 *Rom* 11:20-26; cf. *Mt* 23:39.
569 *Acts* 3:19-21.
570 *Rom* 11:15.
571 *Rom* 11:12, 25; cf. *Lk* 21:24.
572 *Eph* 4:13; *1 Cor* 15:28.
573 Cf. *Lk* 18:8; *Mt* 24:12.
574 Cf. *Lk* 21:12; *Jn* 15:19-20.
575 Cf. *2 Thess* 2:4-12; *1 Thess* 5:2-3; *2 Jn* 7; *1 Jn* 2:18, 22.

676 The Antichrist's deception already begins to take shape in the world every time the claim is made to realize within history that messianic hope which can only be realized beyond history through the eschatalogical judgment. The Church has rejected even modified forms of this falsification of the kingdom to come under the name of millenarianism,[576] especially the "intrinsically perverse" political form of a secular messianism.[577] *2425*

677 The Church will enter the glory of the kingdom only through this final Passover, when she will follow her Lord in his death and Resurrection.[578] The kingdom will be fulfilled, then, not *1340* by a historic triumph of the Church through a progressive ascendancy, but only by God's victory over the final unleashing of evil, which will cause his Bride to come down from heaven.[579] God's *2853* triumph over the revolt of evil will take the form of the Last Judgment after the final cosmic upheaval of this passing world.[580]

II. TO JUDGE THE LIVING AND THE DEAD   *1038-1041*

678 Following in the steps of the prophets and John the Baptist, Jesus announced the judgment of the Last Day in his preaching.[581] *1470* Then will the conduct of each one and the secrets of hearts be brought to light.[582] Then will the culpable unbelief that counted the offer of God's grace as nothing be condemned.[583] Our attitude about our neighbor will disclose acceptance or refusal of grace and divine love.[584] On the last day Jesus will say: "Truly I say to you, as you did it to one of the least of these my brethren, you did it to me."[585]

679 Christ is Lord of eternal life. Full right to pass definitive judgment on the works and hearts of men belongs to him as redeemer of the world. He "acquired" this right by his cross. The Father has given "all judgment to the Son."[586] Yet the Son did not *1021* come to judge, but to save and to give the life he has in himself.[587]

---

576 Cf. DS 3839.
577 Pius XI, *Divini Redemptoris*, condemning the "false mysticism" of this "counterfeit of the redemption of the lowly"; cf. *GS* 20-21.
578 Cf. *Rev* 19:1-9.
579 Cf. *Rev* 13:8; 20:7-10; 21:2-4.
580 Cf. *Rev* 20:12; *2 Pet* 3:12-13.
581 Cf. *Dan* 7:10; *Joel* 3-4; *Mal* 3:19; *Mt* 3:7-12.
582 Cf. *Mk* 12:38-40; *Lk* 12:1-3; *Jn* 3:20-21; *Rom* 2:16; *1 Cor* 4:5.
583 Cf. *Mt* 11:20-24; 12:41-42.
584 Cf. *Mt* 5:22; 7:1-5.
585 *Mt* 25:40.
586 *Jn* 5:22; cf. 5:27; *Mt* 25:31; *Acts* 10:42; 17:31; *2 Tim* 4:1.
587 Cf. *Jn* 3:17; 5:26.

By rejecting grace in this life, one already judges oneself, receives according to one's works, and can even condemn oneself for all eternity by rejecting the Spirit of love.[588]

IN BRIEF

680 Christ the Lord already reigns through the Church, but all the things of this world are not yet subjected to him. The triumph of Christ's kingdom will not come about without one last assault by the powers of evil.

681 On Judgment Day at the end of the world, Christ will come in glory to achieve the definitive triumph of good over evil which, like the wheat and the tares, have grown up together in the course of history.

682 When he comes at the end of time to judge the living and the dead, the glorious Christ will reveal the secret disposition of hearts and will render to each man according to his works and according to his acceptance or refusal of grace.

---

588 Cf. *Jn* 3:18; 12:48; *Mt* 12:32; *1 Cor* 3:12-15; *Heb* 6:4-6; 10:26-31.

CHAPTER THREE
I BELIEVE IN THE HOLY SPIRIT

683   "No one can say 'Jesus is Lord' except by the Holy Spirit."[1] "God has sent the Spirit of his Son into our hearts, crying, '*Abba! Father!*'"[2] This knowledge of faith is possible only in the Holy Spirit: to be in touch with Christ, we must first have been touched by the Holy Spirit. He comes to meet us and kindles faith in us. By virtue of our Baptism, the first sacrament of the faith, the Holy Spirit in the Church communicates to us, intimately and personally, the life that originates in the Father and is offered to us in the Son.

424, 2670
152

> Baptism gives us the grace of new birth in God the Father, through his Son, in the Holy Spirit. For those who bear God's Spirit are led to the Word, that is, to the Son, and the Son presents them to the Father, and the Father confers incorruptibility on them. And it is impossible to see God's Son without the Spirit, and no one can approach the Father without the Son, for the knowledge of the Father is the Son, and the knowledge of God's Son is obtained through the Holy Spirit.[3]

249

684   Through his grace, the Holy Spirit is the first to awaken faith in us and to communicate to us the new life, which is to "know the Father and the one whom he has sent, Jesus Christ."[4] But the Spirit is the last of the persons of the Holy Trinity to be revealed. St. Gregory of Nazianzus, the Theologian, explains this progression in terms of the pedagogy of divine "condescension":

236

> The Old Testament proclaimed the Father clearly, but the Son more obscurely. The New Testament revealed the Son and gave us a glimpse of the divinity of the Spirit. Now the Spirit dwells among us and grants us a clearer vision of himself. It was not prudent, when the divinity of the Father had not yet been confessed, to proclaim the Son openly and, when the divinity of the Son was not yet admitted, to add the Holy Spirit as an extra burden, to speak somewhat daringly.... By advancing and progressing "from glory to glory," the light of the Trinity will shine in ever more brilliant rays.[5]

---

1   *1 Cor* 12:3.
2   *Gal* 4:6.
3   St. Irenæus, *Dem. ap.* 7: SCh 62, 41-42.
4   *Jn* 17:3.
5   St. Gregory of Nazianzus, *Oratio theol.,* 5, 26 (= *Oratio* 31, 26): PG 36, 161-163.

685   To believe in the Holy Spirit is to profess that the Holy
Spirit is one of the persons of the Holy Trinity, consubstantial with
the Father and the Son: "with the Father and the Son he is worshipped and glorified."[6] For this reason, the divine mystery of the
Holy Spirit was already treated in the context of Trinitarian "the-
236 ology." Here, however, we have to do with the Holy Spirit only in
the divine "economy."

686   The Holy Spirit is at work with the Father and the Son from
the beginning to the completion of the plan for our salvation. But
258 in these "end times," ushered in by the Son's redeeming Incarnation, the Spirit is revealed and given, recognized and welcomed as
a person. Now can this divine plan, accomplished in Christ, the
firstborn and head of the new creation, be embodied in mankind
by the outpouring of the Spirit: as the Church, the communion of
saints, the forgiveness of sins, the resurrection of the body, and the
life everlasting.

ARTICLE 8
"I BELIEVE IN THE HOLY SPIRIT"

687   "No one comprehends the thoughts of God except the
Spirit of God."[7] Now God's Spirit, who reveals God, makes known
243 to us Christ, his Word, his living Utterance, but the Spirit does not
speak of himself. The Spirit who "has spoken through the prophets" makes us hear the Father's Word, but we do not hear the Spirit
himself. We know him only in the movement by which he reveals
the Word to us and disposes us to welcome him in faith. The Spirit
of truth who "unveils" Christ to us "will not speak on his own."[8]
Such properly divine self-effacement explains why "the world
cannot receive [him], because it neither sees him nor knows him,"
while those who believe in Christ know the Spirit because he
dwells with them.[9]

688   The Church, a communion living in the faith of the apostles which she transmits, is the place where we know the Holy
Spirit:

– in the Scriptures he inspired;

---

6   Nicene Creed; see above, par. 465.
7   *1 Cor* 2:11.
8   *Jn* 16:13.
9   *Jn* 14:17.

– in the Tradition, to which the Church Fathers are always timely witnesses;

– in the Church's Magisterium, which he assists;

– in the sacramental liturgy, through its words and symbols, in which the Holy Spirit puts us into communion with Christ;

– in prayer, wherein he intercedes for us;

– in the charisms and ministries by which the Church is built up;

– in the signs of apostolic and missionary life;

– in the witness of saints through whom he manifests his holiness and continues the work of salvation.

I.   THE JOINT MISSION OF THE SON AND THE SPIRIT

689   The One whom the Father has sent into our hearts, the Spirit of his Son, is truly God.[10] Consubstantial with the Father and the Son, the Spirit is inseparable from them, in both the inner life *245* of the Trinity and his gift of love for the world. In adoring the Holy Trinity, life-giving, consubstantial, and indivisible, the Church's faith also professes the distinction of persons. When the Father sends his Word, he always sends his Breath. In their joint mission, *254* the Son and the Holy Spirit are distinct but inseparable. To be sure, *485* it is Christ who is seen, the visible image of the invisible God, but it is the Spirit who reveals him.

690   Jesus is Christ, "anointed," because the Spirit is his anointing, and everything that occurs from the Incarnation on derives from this fullness.[11] When Christ is finally glorified,[12] he can in *436* turn send the Spirit from his place with the Father to those who believe in him: he communicates to them his glory,[13] that is, the Holy Spirit who glorifies him.[14] From that time on, this joint mission will be manifested in the children adopted by the Father in the Body of his Son: the mission of the Spirit of adoption is to *788* unite them to Christ and make them live in him:

---

10   Cf. *Gal* 4:6.
11   Cf. *Jn* 3:34.
12   *Jn* 7:39.
13   Cf. *Jn* 17:22.
14   Cf. *Jn* 16:14.

> The notion of anointing suggests . . . that there is no distance
> between the Son and the Spirit. Indeed, just as between the
> surface of the body and the anointing with oil neither reason
> nor sensation recognizes any intermediary, so the contact of
> the Son with the Spirit is immediate, so that anyone who
> would make contact with the Son by faith must first encoun-
> ter the oil by contact. In fact there is no part that is not covered
> by the Holy Spirit. That is why the confession of the Son's
> Lordship is made in the Holy Spirit by those who receive
> him, the Spirit coming from all sides to those who approach
> the Son in faith.[15]

448

II.   THE NAME, TITLES, AND SYMBOLS
OF THE HOLY SPIRIT

The proper name of the Holy Spirit

691   "Holy Spirit" is the proper name of the one whom we
adore and glorify with the Father and the Son. The Church has
received this name from the Lord and professes it in the Baptism
of her new children.[16]

> The term "Spirit" translates the Hebrew word *ruah,* which,
> in its primary sense, means breath, air, wind. Jesus indeed
> uses the sensory image of the wind to suggest to Nicodemus
> the transcendent newness of him who is personally God's
> breath, the divine Spirit.[17] On the other hand, "Spirit" and
> "Holy" are divine attributes common to the three divine
> persons. By joining the two terms, Scripture, liturgy, and
> theological language designate the inexpressible person of
> the Holy Spirit, without any possible equivocation with
> other uses of the terms "spirit" and "holy."

Titles of the Holy Spirit

692   When he proclaims and promises the coming of the Holy
Spirit, Jesus calls him the "Paraclete," literally, "he who is called to
1433 one's side," *ad-vocatus.*[18] "Paraclete" is commonly translated by
"consoler," and Jesus is the first consoler.[19] The Lord also called
the Holy Spirit "the Spirit of truth."[20]

---

15   St. Gregory of Nyssa, *De Spiritu Sancto,* 16: PG 45, 1321A-B.
16   Cf. *Mt* 28:19.
17   *Jn* 3:5-8.
18   *Jn* 14:16, 26; 15:26; 16:7.
19   Cf. *1 Jn* 2:1.
20   *Jn* 16:13.

693   Besides the proper name of "Holy Spirit," which is most frequently used in the *Acts of the Apostles* and in the Epistles, we also find in St. Paul the titles: the Spirit of the promise,[21] the Spirit of adoption,[22] the Spirit of Christ,[23] the Spirit of the Lord,[24] and the Spirit of God[25] – and, in St. Peter, the Spirit of glory.[26]

Symbols of the Holy Spirit

694   *Water.* The symbolism of water signifies the Holy Spirit's action in Baptism, since after the invocation of the Holy Spirit it becomes the efficacious sacramental sign of new birth: just as the gestation of our first   *1218* birth took place in water, so the water of Baptism truly signifies that our birth into the divine life is given to us in the Holy Spirit. As "by one Spirit we were all baptized," so we are also "made to drink of one Spirit."[27] Thus the Spirit is also personally the living water welling up from Christ crucified[28] as its source and welling up in us to eternal life.[29]   *2652*

695   *Anointing.* The symbolism of anointing with oil also signifies the Holy Spirit,[30] to the point of becoming a synonym for the Holy Spirit. In Christian initiation, anointing is the sacramental sign of Confirmation,   *1293* called "chrismation" in the Churches of the East. Its full force can be grasped only in relation to the primary anointing accomplished by the Holy Spirit, that of Jesus. Christ (in Hebrew *"messiah"*) means the one "anointed" by God's Spirit. There were several anointed ones of the Lord   *436* in the Old Covenant, pre-eminently King David.[31] But Jesus is God's Anointed in a unique way: the humanity the Son assumed was entirely anointed by the Holy Spirit. The Holy Spirit established him as "Christ."[32] The Virgin Mary conceived Christ by the Holy Spirit who, through the angel, proclaimed him the Christ at his birth, and prompted Simeon to come to the temple to see the Christ of the Lord.[33] The Spirit filled Christ and the power   *1504* of the Spirit went out from him in his acts of healing and of saving.[34] Finally, it was the Spirit who raised Jesus from the dead.[35] Now, fully established as "Christ" in his humanity victorious over death, Jesus pours out the Holy Spirit abundantly until "the saints" constitute - in their union with the humanity of the Son of God - that perfect man "to the measure of the stature of the fullness of Christ":[36] "the whole Christ," in St. Augustine's expression.   *794*

---

21 Cf. *Gal* 3:14; *Eph* 1:13.
22 *Rom* 8:15; *Gal* 4:6.
23 *Rom* 8:9.
24 *2 Cor* 3:17.
25 *Rom* 8:9, 14; 15:19; *1 Cor* 6:11; 7:40.
26 *1 Pet* 4:14.
27 *1 Cor* 12:13.
28 *Jn* 19:34; *1 Jn* 5:8.
29 Cf. *Jn* 4:10-14; 7:38; *Ex* 17:1-6; *Isa* 55:1; *Zech* 14:8; *1 Cor* 10:4; *Rev* 21:6; 22:17.
30 Cf. *1 Jn* 2:20:27; *2 Cor* 1:21.
31 Cf. *Ex* 30:22-32; *1 Sam* 16:13.
32 Cf. *Lk* 4:18-19; *Isa* 61:1.
33 Cf. *Lk* 2:11, 26-27.
34 Cf. *Lk* 4:1; 6:19; 8:46.

696   *Fire.* While water signifies birth and the fruitfulness of life given
in the Holy Spirit, fire symbolizes the transforming energy of the Holy
1127   Spirit's actions. The prayer of the prophet Elijah, who "arose like fire" and
whose "word burned like a torch," brought down fire from heaven on the
2586   sacrifice on Mount Carmel.[37] This event was a "figure" of the fire of the
Holy Spirit, who transforms what he touches. John the Baptist, who goes
718   "before [the Lord] in the spirit and power of Elijah," proclaims Christ as
the one who "will baptize you with the Holy Spirit and with fire."[38] Jesus
will say of the Spirit: "I came to cast fire upon the earth; and would that it
were already kindled!"[39] In the form of tongues "as of fire," the Holy Spirit
rests on the disciples on the morning of Pentecost and fills them with
himself.[40] The spiritual tradition has retained this symbolism of fire as one
of the most expressive images of the Holy Spirit's actions.[41] "Do not
quench the Spirit."[42]

697   *Cloud and light.* These two images occur together in the manifestations of the Holy Spirit. In the theophanies of the Old Testament, the
cloud, now obscure, now luminous, reveals the living and saving God,
while veiling the transcendence of his glory – with Moses on Mount
Sinai,[43] at the tent of meeting,[44] and during the wandering in the desert,[45]
and with Solomon at the dedication of the Temple.[46] In the Holy Spirit,
Christ fulfills these figures. The Spirit comes upon the Virgin Mary and
484   "overshadows" her, so that she might conceive and give birth to Jesus.[47]
554   On the mountain of Transfiguration, the Spirit in the "cloud came and
overshadowed" Jesus, Moses and Elijah, Peter, James and John, and "a
voice came out of the cloud, saying, 'This is my Son, my Chosen; listen to
him!' "[48] Finally, the cloud took Jesus out of the sight of the disciples on
the day of his ascension and will reveal him as Son of man in glory on the
659   day of his final coming.[49]

---

35   Cf. *Rom* 1:4; 8:11.

36   *Eph* 4:13; cf. *Acts* 2:36.

37   *Sir* 48:1; cf. *1 Kings* 18:38-39.

38   *Lk* 1:17; 3:16.

39   *Lk* 12:49.

40   *Acts* 2:3-4.

41   Cf. St. John of the Cross, *The Living Flame of Love,* in *The Collected Works of
St. John of the Cross,* tr. K. Kavanaugh, OCD, and O. Rodriguez, OCD
(Washington DC: Institute of Carmelite Studies, 1979), 577 ff.

42   *1 Thess* 5:19.

43   Cf. *Ex* 24:15-18.

44   Cf. *Ex* 33:9-10.

45   Cf. *Ex* 40:36-38; *1 Cor* 10:1-2.

46   Cf. *1 Kings* 8:10-12.

47   *Lk* 1:35.

48   *Lk* 9:34-35.

49   Cf. *Acts* 1:9; cf. *Lk* 21:27.

698   *The seal* is a symbol close to that of anointing. "The Father has set his seal" on Christ and also seals us in him.[50] Because this seal indicates the indelible effect of the anointing with the Holy Spirit in the sacraments   *1295-1296* of Baptism, Confirmation, and Holy Orders, the image of the seal (*sphragis*) has been used in some theological traditions to express the indelible   *1121* "character" imprinted by these three unrepeatable sacraments.

699   *The hand.* Jesus heals the sick and blesses little children by laying   *292* hands on them.[51] In his name the apostles will do the same.[52] Even more   *1288* pointedly, it is by the Apostles' imposition of hands that the Holy Spirit is   *1300, 1573,* given.[53] The *Letter to the Hebrews* lists the imposition of hands among the   *1668* "fundamental elements" of its teaching.[54] The Church has kept this sign of the all-powerful outpouring of the Holy Spirit in its sacramental epiclesis.

700   *The finger.* "It is by the finger of God that [Jesus] cast out demons."[55] If God's law was written on tablets of stone "by the finger of God," then the "letter from Christ" entrusted to the care of the apostles, is   *2056* written "with the Spirit of the living God, not on tablets of stone, but on tablets of human hearts."[56] The hymn *Veni Creator Spiritus* invokes the Holy Spirit as the *"finger of the Father's right hand."*[57]

701   *The dove.* At the end of the flood, whose symbolism refers to Baptism, a dove released by Noah returns with a fresh olive-tree branch in its beak as a sign that the earth was again habitable.[58] When Christ   *1219* comes up from the water of his baptism, the Holy Spirit, in the form of a   *535* dove, comes down upon him and remains with him.[59] The Spirit comes down and remains in the purified hearts of the baptized. In certain churches, the Eucharist is reserved in a metal receptacle in the form of a dove (*columbarium*) suspended above the altar. Christian iconography traditionally uses a dove to suggest the Spirit.

---

50 *Jn* 6:27; cf. *2 Cor* 1:22; *Eph* 1:13; 4:30.
51 Cf. *Mk* 6:5; 8:23; 10:16.
52 Cf. *Mk* 16:18; *Acts* 5:12; 14:3.
53 Cf. *Acts* 8:17-19; 13:3; 19:6.
54 Cf. *Heb* 6:2.
55 *Lk* 11:20.
56 *Ex* 31:18; *2 Cor* 3:3.
57 *LH*, Easter Season after Ascension, Hymn at Vespers: *digitus paternae dexterae.*
58 Cf. *Gen* 8:8-12.
59 Cf. *Mt* 3:16 and parallels.

III.   GOD'S SPIRIT AND WORD IN THE TIME OF THE PROMISES

702   From the beginning until "the fullness of time,"[60] the joint
mission of the Father's Word and Spirit remains *hidden*, but it is at
122   work. God's Spirit prepares for the time of the Messiah. Neither is
fully revealed but both are already promised, to be watched for and
welcomed at their manifestation. So, for this reason, when the
Church reads the Old Testament, she searches there for what the
107   Spirit, "who has spoken through the prophets," wants to tell us
about Christ.[61]

243   By "prophets" the faith of the Church here understands all whom
the Holy Spirit inspired in the composition of the sacred books, both of the
Old and the New Testaments. Jewish tradition distinguishes first the Law
(the five first books or Pentateuch), then the Prophets (our historical and
prophetic books) and finally the Writings (especially the wisdom litera-
ture, in particular the Psalms).[62]

In creation

292 **703**   The Word of God and his Breath are at the origin of the
being and life of every creature:[63]

              It belongs to the Holy Spirit to rule, sanctify, and animate
              creation, for he is God, consubstantial with the Father and
              the Son. . . . Power over life pertains to the Spirit, for being
291   God he preserves creation in the Father through the Son.[64]

704   "God fashioned man with his own hands [that is, the Son
and the Holy Spirit] and impressed his own form on the flesh he
had fashioned, in such a way that even what was visible might bear
356   the divine form."[65]

The Spirit of the promise

705   Disfigured by sin and death, man remains "in the image
410   of God," in the image of the Son, but is deprived "of the glory of
2809 God,"[66] of his "likeness." The promise made to Abraham inaugurates the economy of salvation, at the culmination of which the Son

---

60   *Gal* 4:4.
61   Cf. *2 Cor* 3:14; *Jn* 5:39, 46.
62   Cf. *Lk* 24:44.
63   Cf. *Pss* 33:6; 104:30; *Gen* 1:2; 2:7; *Eccl* 3:20-21; *Ezek* 37:10.
64   Byzantine liturgy, Sundays of the second mode, *Troparion* of Morning
      Prayer.
65   St. Irenæus, *Dem ap.* 11: SCh 62, 48-49.
66   *Rom* 3:23.

himself will assume that "image"[67] and restore it in the Father's "likeness" by giving it again its Glory, the Spirit who is "the giver of life."

706   Against all human hope, God promises descendants to Abraham, as the fruit of faith and of the power of the Holy Spirit.[68] In Abraham's progeny all the nations of the earth will be blessed. *60* This progeny will be Christ himself,[69] in whom the outpouring of the Holy Spirit will "gather into one the children of God who are scattered abroad."[70] God commits himself by his own solemn oath to giving his beloved Son and "the promised Holy Spirit . . . [who is] the guarantee of our inheritance until we acquire possession of it."[71]

In Theophanies and the Law

707   Theophanies (manifestations of God) light up the way of the promise, from the patriarchs to Moses and from Joshua to the visions that inaugurated the missions of the great prophets. Christian tradition has always recognized that God's Word allowed himself to be seen and heard in these theophanies, in which the cloud of the Holy Spirit both revealed him and concealed him in its shadow.

708   This divine pedagogy appears especially in the gift of the Law.[72] God gave the letter of the Law as a "pedagogue" to lead his people towards Christ.[73] But the Law's powerlessness to save man *1961-1964* deprived of the divine "likeness," along with the growing aware- *122* ness of sin that it imparts,[74] enkindles a desire for the Holy Spirit. *2585* The lamentations of the Psalms bear witness to this.

In the Kingdom and the Exile

709   The Law, the sign of God's promise and covenant, ought to have governed the hearts and institutions of that people to *2579* whom Abraham's faith gave birth. "If you will obey my voice and *544* keep my covenant, . . . you shall be to me a kingdom of priests and

---

67   Cf. *Jn* 1:14; *Phil* 2:7.
68   Cf. *Gen* 18:1-15; *Lk* 1:26-38. 54-55; *Jn* 1:12-13; *Rom* 4:16-21.
69   Cf. *Gen* 12:3; *Gal* 3:16.
70   Cf. *Jn* 11:52.
71   *Eph* 1:13-14; cf. *Gen* 22:17-19; *Lk* 1:73; *Jn* 3:16; *Rom* 8:32; *Gal* 3:14.
72   Cf. *Ex* 19-20; *Deut* 1-11; 29-30.
73   *Gal* 3:24.
74   Cf. *Rom* 3:20.

a holy nation."[75] But after David, Israel gave in to the temptation of becoming a kingdom like other nations. The Kingdom, however, the object of the promise made to David,[76] would be the work of the Holy Spirit; it would belong to the poor according to the Spirit.

710   The forgetting of the Law and the infidelity to the covenant end in death: it is the Exile, apparently the failure of the promises, which is in fact the mysterious fidelity of the Savior God and the beginning of a promised restoration, but according to the Spirit. The People of God had to suffer this purification.[77] In God's plan, the Exile already stands in the shadow of the Cross, and the Remnant of the poor that returns from the Exile is one of the most transparent prefigurations of the Church.

Expectation of the Messiah and his Spirit

711   "Behold, I am doing a new thing."[78] Two prophetic lines
64 were to develop, one leading to the expectation of the Messiah, the
522 other pointing to the announcement of a new Spirit. They converge in the small Remnant, the people of the poor, who await in hope the "consolation of Israel" and "the redemption of Jerusalem."[79]

We have seen earlier how Jesus fulfills the prophecies concerning himself. We limit ourselves here to those in which the relationship of the Messiah and his Spirit appears more clearly.

712   The characteristics of the awaited *Messiah* begin to appear in the "Book of Emmanuel" ("Isaiah said this when he saw his
439 glory,"[80] speaking of Christ), especially in the first two verses of *Isaiah* 11:

> There shall come forth a shoot from the stump of Jesse,
> and a branch shall grow out of his roots.
> And the Spirit of the LORD shall rest upon him,
> the spirit of wisdom and understanding,
> the spirit of counsel and might,
> the spirit of knowledge and the fear of the LORD.[81]

---

75 *Ex* 19:5-6; Cf. *1 Pet* 2:9.
76 Cf. *2 Sam* 7; *Ps* 89; *Lk* 1:32-33.
77 Cf. *Lk* 24:26.
78 *Isa* 43:19.
79 Cf. *Zeph* 2:3; *Lk* 2:25, 38.
80 *Jn* 12:41; cf. *Isa* 6-12.
81 *Isa* 11:1-2.

713 The Messiah's characteristics are revealed above all in the "Servant songs."[82] These songs proclaim the meaning of Jesus' *601* Passion and show how he will pour out the Holy Spirit to give life to the many: not as an outsider, but by embracing our "form as slave."[83] Taking our death upon himself, he can communicate to us his own Spirit of life.

714 This is why Christ inaugurates the proclamation of the Good News by making his own the following passage from Isaiah:[84]

> The Spirit of the LORD God is upon me,
> because the LORD has anointed me
> to bring good tidings to the afflicted;
> he has sent me to bind up the broken hearted,
> to proclaim liberty to the captives,
> and the opening of the prison to those who are bound;
> to proclaim the year of the LORD's favor.

715 The prophetic texts that directly concern the sending of the Holy Spirit are oracles by which God speaks to the heart of his people in the language of the promise, with the accents of "love and fidelity."[85] St. Peter will proclaim their fulfillment on the *214* morning of Pentecost.[86] According to these promises, at the "end time" the Lord's Spirit will renew the hearts of men, engraving a new law in them. He will gather and reconcile the scattered and divided peoples; he will transform the first creation, and God will *1965* dwell there with men in peace.

716 The People of the "poor"[87] – those who, humble and meek, rely solely on their God's mysterious plans, who await the justice, not of men but of the Messiah – are in the end the great achievement of the Holy Spirit's hidden mission during the time of the promises that prepare for Christ's coming. It is this quality of heart, purified and enlightened by the Spirit, which is expressed in the Psalms. In these poor, the Spirit is making ready "a people prepared for the *368* Lord."[88]

---

82 Cf. *Isa* 42:1-9; cf. *Mt* 12:18-21; *Jn* 1:32-34; then cf. *Isa* 49:1-6; cf. *Mt* 3:17; *Lk* 2:32; finally cf. *Isa* 50:4-10 and *Isa* 52:13 - 53:12.
83 *Phil* 2:7.
84 *Isa* 61:1-2; cf. *Lk* 4:18-19.
85 Cf. *Ezek* 11:19; 36:25-28; 37:1-14; *Jer* 31:31-34; and cf. *Joel* 3:1-5.
86 Cf. *Acts* 2:17-21.
87 Cf. *Zeph* 2:3; *Pss* 22:27; 34:3; *Isa* 49:13; 61:1; etc.
88 *Lk* 1:17.

IV. THE SPIRIT OF CHRIST IN THE FULLNESS OF TIME

John, precursor, prophet, and baptist

717 "There was a man sent from God, whose name was
John."[89] John was "filled with the Holy Spirit even from his
523 mother's womb"[90] by Christ himself, whom the Virgin Mary had
just conceived by the Holy Spirit. Mary's visitation to Elizabeth
thus became a visit from God to his people.[91]

718 John is "Elijah [who] must come."[92] The fire of the Spirit
dwells in him and makes him the forerunner of the coming Lord.
696 In John, the precursor, the Holy Spirit completes the work of
"[making] ready a people prepared for the Lord."[93]

719 John the Baptist is "more than a prophet."[94] In him, the
Holy Spirit concludes his speaking through the prophets. John
completes the cycle of prophets begun by Elijah.[95] He proclaims
the imminence of the consolation of Israel; he is the "voice" of the
Consoler who is coming.[96] As the Spirit of truth will also do, John
2684 "came to bear witness to the light."[97] In John's sight, the Spirit thus
brings to completion the careful search of the prophets and fulfills
the longing of the angels.[98] "He on whom you see the Spirit
descend and remain, this is he who baptizes with the Holy Spirit.
And I have seen and have borne witness that this is the Son of
536 God. . . . Behold, the Lamb of God."[99]

720 Finally, with John the Baptist, the Holy Spirit begins the
535 restoration to man of "the divine likeness," prefiguring what he
would achieve with and in Christ. John's baptism was for repentance; baptism in water and the Spirit will be a new birth.[100]

---

89 *Jn* 1:6.
90 *Lk* 1:15, 41.
91 Cf. *Lk* 1:68.
92 *Mt* 17:10-13; cf. *Lk* 1:78.
93 *Lk* 1:17.
94 *Lk* 7:26.
95 Cf. *Mt* 11:13-14.
96 *Jn* 1:23; cf. *Isa* 40:1-3.
97 *Jn* 1:7; cf. *Jn* 15:26; 5:35.
98 Cf. *1 Pet* 1:10-12.
99 *Jn* 1:33-36.
100 Cf. *Jn* 3:5.

"Rejoice, you who are full of grace"

721   Mary, the all-holy ever-virgin Mother of God, is the masterwork of the mission of the Son and the Spirit in the fullness of time. For the first time in the plan of salvation and because his Spirit had prepared her, the Father found the *dwelling place* where his Son 484
and his Spirit could dwell among men. In this sense the Church's Tradition has often read the most beautiful texts on wisdom in relation to Mary.[101] Mary is acclaimed and represented in the liturgy as the "Seat of Wisdom."

In her, the "wonders of God" that the Spirit was to fulfill in Christ and the Church began to be manifested:

722   The Holy Spirit *prepared* Mary by his grace. It was fitting 489
that the mother of him in whom "the whole fullness of deity dwells bodily"[102] should herself be "full of grace." She was, by sheer grace, conceived without sin as the most humble of creatures, the most capable of welcoming the inexpressible gift of the Almighty. It was quite correct for the angel Gabriel to greet her as the "Daughter of Zion": "Rejoice."[103] It is the thanksgiving of the whole People 2676
of God, and thus of the Church, which Mary in her canticle[104] lifts up to the Father in the Holy Spirit while carrying within her the eternal Son.

723   In Mary, the Holy Spirit *fulfills* the plan of the Father's loving goodness. With and through the Holy Spirit, the Virgin conceives and gives birth to the Son of God. By the Holy Spirit's 485
power and her faith, her virginity became uniquely fruitful.[105]   506

724   In Mary, the Holy Spirit *manifests* the Son of the Father, now become the Son of the Virgin. She is the burning bush of the definitive theophany. Filled with the Holy Spirit she makes the 963
Word visible in the humility of his flesh. It is to the poor and the first representatives of the gentiles that she makes him known.[106]

725   Finally, through Mary, the Holy Spirit begins to bring men, the objects of God's merciful love,[107] *into communion* with Christ. And the humble are always the first to accept him: shepherds, 208, 2619

---

101   Cf. *Prov* 8:1-9:6; *Sir* 24.
102   *Col* 2:9.
103   Cf. *Zeph* 3:14; *Zech* 2:14.
104   Cf. *Lk* 1:46-55.
105   Cf. *Lk* 1:26-38; *Rom* 4:18-21; *Gal* 4:26-28.
106   Cf. *Lk* 1:15-19; *Mt* 2:11.
107   Cf. *Lk* 2:14.

magi, Simeon and Anna, the bride and groom at Cana, and the first disciples.

726   At the end of this mission of the Spirit, Mary became the Woman, the new Eve ("mother of the living"), the mother of the "whole Christ."[108] As such, she was present with the Twelve, who "with one accord devoted themselves to prayer,"[109] at the dawn of the "end time" which the Spirit was to inaugurate on the morning of Pentecost with the manifestation of the Church.

494, 2618

Christ Jesus

727   The entire mission of the Son and the Holy Spirit, in the fullness of time, is contained in this: that the Son is the one anointed by the Father's Spirit since his Incarnation – Jesus is the Christ, the Messiah.

438, 695
536

Everything in the second chapter of the Creed is to be read in this light. Christ's whole work is in fact a joint mission of the Son and the Holy Spirit. Here, we shall mention only what has to do with Jesus' promise of the Holy Spirit and the gift of him by the glorified Lord.

728   Jesus does not reveal the Holy Spirit fully, until he himself has been glorified through his Death and Resurrection. Nevertheless, little by little he alludes to him even in his teaching of the multitudes, as when he reveals that his own flesh will be food for the life of the world.[110] He also alludes to the Spirit in speaking to Nicodemus,[111] to the Samaritan woman,[112] and to those who take part in the feast of Tabernacles.[113] To his disciples he speaks openly of the Spirit in connection with prayer[114] and with the witness they will have to bear.[115]

2615

729   Only when the hour has arrived for his glorification does Jesus *promise* the coming of the Holy Spirit, since his Death and Resurrection will fulfill the promise made to the fathers.[116] The Spirit of truth, the other Paraclete, will be given by the Father in answer to Jesus' prayer; he will be sent by the Father in Jesus' name;

---

108   Cf. *Jn* 19:25-27.
109   *Acts* 1:14.
110   Cf. *Jn* 6:27, 51, 62-63.
111   Cf. *Jn* 3:5-8.
112   Cf. *Jn* 4:10, 14, 23-24.
113   Cf. *Jn* 7:37-39.
114   Cf. *Lk* 11:13.
115   Cf. *Mt* 10:19-20.
116   Cf. *Jn* 14:16-17, 26; 15:26; 16:7-15; 17:26.

and Jesus will send him from the Father's side, since he comes from the Father. The Holy Spirit will come and we shall know him; he will be with us for ever; he will remain with us. The Spirit will teach us everything, remind us of all that Christ said to us and bear witness to him. The Holy Spirit will lead us into all truth and will glorify Christ. He will prove the world wrong about sin, righteousness, and judgment. *388, 1433*

730 At last Jesus' hour arrives:[117] he commends his spirit into the Father's hands[118] at the very moment when by his death he conquers death, so that, "raised from the dead by the glory of the Father,"[119] he might immediately *give* the Holy Spirit by "breathing" on his disciples.[120] From this hour onward, the mission of Christ and the Spirit becomes the mission of the Church: "As the Father has sent me, even so I send you."[121] *850*

V. THE SPIRIT AND THE CHURCH IN THE LAST DAYS

Pentecost

731 On the day of Pentecost when the seven weeks of Easter had come to an end, Christ's Passover is fulfilled in the outpouring of the Holy Spirit, manifested, given, and communicated as a *2623, 767* divine person: of his fullness, Christ, the Lord, pours out the Spirit in abundance.[122] *1302*

732 On that day, the Holy Trinity is fully revealed. Since that day, the Kingdom announced by Christ has been open to those who believe in him: in the humility of the flesh and in faith, they *244* already share in the communion of the Holy Trinity. By his coming, which never ceases, the Holy Spirit causes the world to enter into *672* the "last days," the time of the Church, the Kingdom already inherited though not yet consummated.

> We have seen the true Light, we have received the heavenly Spirit, we have found the true faith: we adore the indivisible Trinity, who has saved us.[123]

---

117 Cf. *Jn* 13:1; 17:1.
118 Cf. *Lk* 23:46; *Jn* 19:30.
119 *Rom* 6:4.
120 Cf. *Jn* 20:22.
121 *Jn* 20:21; cf. *Mt* 28:19; *Lk* 24:47-48; *Acts* 1:8.
122 Cf. *Acts* 2:33-36.
123 Byzantine liturgy, Pentecost, Vespers, *Troparion*, repeated after communion.

The Holy Spirit – God's gift

733   "God is Love"[124] and love is his first gift, containing all
218   others. "God's love has been poured into our hearts through the
Holy Spirit who has been given to us."[125]

734   Because we are dead or at least wounded through sin, the
1987 first effect of the gift of love is the forgiveness of our sins. The
communion of the Holy Spirit[126] in the Church restores to the
baptized the divine likeness lost through sin.

735   He, then, gives us the "pledge" or "first fruits" of our
1822 inheritance: the very life of the Holy Trinity, which is to love as
"God [has] loved us."[127] This love (the "charity" of *1 Cor* 13) is the
source of the new life in Christ, made possible because we have
received "power" from the Holy Spirit.[128]

736   By this power of the Spirit, God's children can bear much
1832 fruit. He who has grafted us onto the true vine will make us bear
"the fruit of the Spirit: . . . love, joy, peace, patience, kindness,
goodness, faithfulness, gentleness, self-control."[129] "We live by the
Spirit"; the more we renounce ourselves, the more we "walk by the
Spirit."[130]

> Through the Holy Spirit we are restored to paradise, led back
> to the Kingdom of heaven, and adopted as children, given
> confidence to call God "Father" and to share in Christ's
> grace, called children of light and given a share in eternal
> glory.[131]

The Holy Spirit and the Church

737   The mission of Christ and the Holy Spirit is brought to
completion in the Church, which is the Body of Christ and the
787-798 Temple of the Holy Spirit. This joint mission henceforth brings
Christ's faithful to share in his communion with the Father in the
1093-1109 Holy Spirit. The Spirit *prepares* men and goes out to them with his
grace, in order to draw them to Christ. The Spirit *manifests* the risen
Lord to them, recalls his word to them and opens their minds to

---

124   *1 Jn* 4:8, 16.
125   *Rom* 5:5.
126   *2 Cor* 13:14.
127   *1 Jn* 4:11-12; cf. *Rom* 8:23; *2 Cor* 1:21.
128   *Acts* 1:8; cf. *1 Cor* 13.
129   *Gal* 5:22-23.
130   *Gal* 5:25; cf. *Mt* 16:24-26.
131   St. Basil, *De Spiritu Sancto*, 15, 36: PG 32, 132.

the understanding of his Death and Resurrection. He *makes present* the mystery of Christ, supremely in the Eucharist, in order to reconcile them, to *bring them into communion* with God, that they may "bear much fruit."[132]

738   Thus the Church's mission is not an addition to that of Christ and the Holy Spirit, but is its sacrament: in her whole being and in all her members, the Church is sent to announce, bear *850, 777* witness, make present, and spread the mystery of the communion of the Holy Trinity (the topic of the next article):

> All of us who have received one and the same Spirit, that is, the Holy Spirit, are in a sense blended together with one another and with God. For if Christ, together with the Father's and his own Spirit, comes to dwell in each of us, though we are many, still the Spirit is one and undivided. He binds together the spirits of each and every one of us, . . . and makes all appear as one in him. For just as the power of Christ's sacred flesh unites those in whom it dwells into one body, I think that in the same way the one and undivided Spirit of God, who dwells in all, leads all into spiritual unity.[133]

739   Because the Holy Spirit is the anointing of Christ, it is Christ who, as the head of the Body, pours out the Spirit among his members to nourish, heal, and organize them in their mutual *1076* functions, to give them life, send them to bear witness, and associate them to his self-offering to the Father and to his intercession for the whole world. Through the Church's sacraments, Christ communicates his Holy and sanctifying Spirit to the members of his Body. (This will be the topic of Part Two of the Catechism.)

740   These "mighty works of God," offered to believers in the sacraments of the Church, bear their fruit in the new life in Christ, according to the Spirit. (This will be the topic of Part Three.)

741   "The Spirit helps us in our weakness; for we do not know how to pray as we ought, but the Spirit himself intercedes with sighs too deep for words."[134] The Holy Spirit, the artisan of God's works, is the master of prayer. (This will be the topic of Part Four.)

---

132 *Jn* 15:8, 16.
133 St. Cyril of Alexandria, *In Jo. ev.*, 11, 11: PG 74, 561.
134 *Rom* 8:26.

IN BRIEF

742   "Because you are sons, God has sent the Spirit of his
Son into our hearts, crying, 'Abba! Father!'" (*Gal* 4:6).

743   From the beginning to the end of time, whenever God
sends his Son, he always sends his Spirit: their mission
is conjoined and inseparable.

744   In the fullness of time the Holy Spirit completes in
Mary all the preparations for Christ's coming among
the People of God. By the action of the Holy Spirit in
her, the Father gives the world Emmanuel, "God-
with-us" (*Mt* 1:23).

745   The Son of God was consecrated as Christ (Messiah)
by the anointing of the Holy Spirit at his Incarnation
(cf. *Ps* 2:6-7).

746   By his Death and his Resurrection, Jesus is constituted
in glory as Lord and Christ (cf. *Acts* 2:36). From his
fullness, he poured out the Holy Spirit on the apostles
and the Church.

747   The Holy Spirit, whom Christ the head pours out on
his members, builds, animates, and sanctifies the
Church. She is the sacrament of the Holy Trinity's
communion with men.

ARTICLE 9
"I BELIEVE IN THE HOLY CATHOLIC CHURCH"

748   "Christ is the light of humanity; and it is, accordingly, the heart-felt desire of this sacred Council, being gathered together in the Holy Spirit, that, by proclaiming his Gospel to every creature, it may bring to all men that light of Christ which shines out visibly from the Church."[135] These words open the Second Vatican Council's *Dogmatic Constitution on the Church.* By choosing this starting point, the Council demonstrates that the article of faith about the Church depends entirely on the articles concerning Christ Jesus. The Church has no other light than Christ's; according to a favorite image of the Church Fathers, the Church is like the moon, all its light reflected from the sun.

749   The article concerning the Church also depends entirely on the article about the Holy Spirit, which immediately precedes it. "Indeed, having shown that the Spirit is the source and giver of all holiness, we now confess that it is he who has endowed the Church with holiness."[136] The Church is, in a phrase used by the Fathers, the place "where the Spirit flourishes."[137]

750   To believe that the Church is "holy" and "catholic," and that she is "one" and "apostolic" (as the Nicene Creed adds), is inseparable from belief in God, the Father, the Son, and the Holy *811* Spirit. In the Apostles' Creed we profess "one Holy Church" (*Credo ... Ecclesiam*), and not to believe *in* the Church, so as not to confuse God with his works and to attribute clearly to God's goodness *all 169* the gifts he has bestowed on his Church.[138]

Paragraph 1. The Church in God's Plan

I.   NAMES AND IMAGES OF THE CHURCH

751   The word "Church" (Latin *ecclesia*, from the Greek *ek-ka-lein*, to "call out of") means a convocation or an assembly. It designates the assemblies of the people, usually for a religious purpose.[139] *Ekklesia* is used frequently in the Greek Old Testament for the assembly of the Chosen People before God, above all for

---

135   *LG* 1; cf. *Mk* 16:15.
136   *Roman Catechism* I, 10, 1.
137   St. Hippolytus, *Trad. Ap.* 35: SCh 11, 118.
138   *Roman Catechism* I, 10, 22.
139   Cf. *Acts* 19:39.

their assembly on Mount Sinai where Israel received the Law and was established by God as his holy people.[140] By calling itself "Church," the first community of Christian believers recognized itself as heir to that assembly. In the Church, God is "calling together" his people from all the ends of the earth. The equivalent Greek term *Kyriake,* from which the English word *Church* and the German *Kirche* are derived, means "what belongs to the Lord."

752   In Christian usage, the word "church" designates the liturgical assembly,[141] but also the local community[142] or the whole *1140, 832* universal community of believers.[143] These three meanings are *830* inseparable. "The Church" is the People that God gathers in the whole world. She exists in local communities and is made real as a liturgical, above all a Eucharistic, assembly. She draws her life from the word and the Body of Christ and so herself becomes Christ's Body.

Symbols of the Church

753   In Scripture, we find a host of interrelated images and figures through which Revelation speaks of the inexhaustible mystery of the Church. The images taken from the Old Testament are variations on a profound theme: the People of God. In the New *781, 789* Testament, all these images find a new center because Christ has become the head of this people, which henceforth is his Body.[144] Around this center are grouped images taken "from the life of the shepherd or from cultivation of the land, from the art of building or from family life and marriage."[145]

857 **754**   "The Church is, accordingly, a *sheepfold,* the sole and necessary gateway to which is Christ. It is also the flock of which God himself foretold that he would be the shepherd, and whose sheep, even though governed by human shepherds, are unfailingly nourished and led by Christ himself, the Good Shepherd and Prince of Shepherds, who gave his life for his sheep.[146]

---

140   Cf. *Ex* 19.
141   Cf. *1 Cor* 11:18; 14:19, 28, 34, 35.
142   Cf. *1 Cor* 1:2; 16:1.
143   Cf. *1 Cor* 15:9; *Gal* 1:13; *Phil* 3:6.
144   Cf. *Eph* 1:22; *Col* 1:18; *LG* 9.
145   *LG* 6.
146   *LG* 6; cf. *Jn* 10:1-10; *Isa* 40:11; *Ezek* 34:11-31; *Jn* 10:11; *1 Pet* 5:4; *Jn* 10:11-16.

755   "The Church is a *cultivated field*, the tillage of God. On that land
the ancient olive tree grows whose holy roots were the prophets and in
which the reconciliation of Jews and Gentiles has been brought about and
will be brought about again. That land, like a choice vineyard, has been
planted by the heavenly cultivator. Yet the true vine is Christ who gives
life and fruitfulness to the branches, that is, to us, who through the Church
remain in Christ, without whom we can do nothing.[147]   795

756   "Often, too, the Church is called the *building* of God. The Lord
compared himself to the stone which the builders rejected, but which was
made into the corner-stone. On this foundation the Church is built by the   797
apostles and from it the Church receives solidity and unity. This edifice
has many names to describe it: the house of God in which his *family* dwells;
the household of God in the Spirit; the dwelling-place of God among men;   857
and, especially, the holy *temple*. This temple, symbolized in places of
worship built out of stone, is praised by the Fathers and, not without
reason, is compared in the liturgy to the Holy City, the New Jerusalem. As   1045
living stones we here on earth are built into it. It is this holy city that is seen
by John as it comes down out of heaven from God when the world is made
anew, prepared like a bride adorned for her husband.[148]

757   "The Church, further, which is called 'that Jerusalem which is
above' and 'our mother', is described as the spotless spouse of the spotless 507, 796
lamb. It is she whom Christ 'loved and for whom he delivered himself up
that he might sanctify her.' It is she whom he unites to himself by an   1616
unbreakable alliance, and whom he constantly 'nourishes and cherishes.'"[149]

II.   THE CHURCH'S ORIGIN, FOUNDATION, AND MISSION

758   We begin our investigation of the Church's mystery by   257
meditating on her origin in the Holy Trinity's plan and her progressive realization in history.

A plan born in the Father's heart

759   "The eternal Father, in accordance with the utterly gratuitous and mysterious design of his wisdom and goodness, created
the whole universe and chose to raise up men to share in his own   293
divine life,"[150] to which he calls all men in his Son. "The Father . . .
determined to call together in a holy Church those who should
believe in Christ."[151] This "family of God" is gradually formed and   1655
takes shape during the stages of human history, in keeping with
the Father's plan. In fact, "already present in figure at the beginning

---

147   *LG* 6; cf. *1 Cor* 3:9; *Rom* 11:13-26; *Mt* 21:33-43 and parallels; *Isa* 5:1-7; *Jn* 15:1-5.
148   *LG* 6; cf. *1 Cor* 3:9; *Mt* 21:42 and parallels; *Acts* 4:11; *1 Pet* 2:7; *Ps* 118:22;
      1 Cor 3:11; *1 Tim* 3:15; *Eph* 2:19-22; *Rev* 21:3; *1 Pet* 2:5; *Rev* 21:1-2.
149   *LG* 6; cf. *Gal* 4:26; *Rev* 12:17; 19:7; 21:2, 9; 22:17; *Eph* 5:25-26, 29.
150   *LG* 2.
151   *LG* 2.

of the world, this Church was prepared in marvellous fashion in the history of the people of Israel and the old Alliance. Established in this last age of the world and made manifest in the outpouring of the Spirit, it will be brought to glorious completion at the end of time."[152]

The Church – foreshadowed from the world's beginning

760   Christians of the first centuries said, "The world was created for the sake of the Church."[153] God created the world for the sake of communion with his divine life, a communion brought

294 about by the "convocation" of men in Christ, and this "convocation" is the Church. The Church is the goal of all things,[154] and God permitted such painful upheavals as the angels' fall and man's sin

309 only as occasions and means for displaying all the power of his arm and the whole measure of the love he wanted to give the world:

> Just as God's will is creation and is called "the world," so his intention is the salvation of men, and it is called "the Church."[155]

The Church – prepared for in the Old Covenant

761   The gathering together of the People of God began at the moment when sin destroyed the communion of men with God, and that of men among themselves. The gathering together of the Church

55 is, as it were, God's reaction to the chaos provoked by sin. This reunification is achieved secretly in the heart of all peoples: "In every nation anyone who fears him and does what is right is acceptable" to God.[156]

762   The remote *preparation* for this gathering together of the People of God begins when he calls Abraham and promises that

122, 522 he will become the father of a great people.[157] Its immediate

60 preparation begins with Israel's election as the People of God. By this election, Israel is to be the sign of the future gathering of all nations.[158] But the prophets accuse Israel of breaking the covenant

64 and behaving like a prostitute. They announce a new and eternal covenant. "Christ instituted this New Covenant."[159]

---

152 *LG* 2.
153 *Pastor Hermæ*, Vision 2, 4, 1: PG 2, 899; cf. Aristides, *Apol.* 16, 6; St. Justin, *Apol.* 2, 7: PG 6, 456; Tertullian, *Apol.* 31, 3; 32, 1: PL 1, 508-509.
154 Cf. St. Epiphanius, *Panarion* 1, 1, 5: PG 41, 181C.
155 Clement of Alex., *Pæd. 1, 6, 27: PG 8, 281.*
156 *Acts* 10:35; cf. *LG* 9; 13; 16.
157 Cf. *Gen* 12:2; 15:5-6.
158 Cf. *Ex* 19:5-6; *Deut* 7:6; *Isa* 2:2-5; *Mic* 4:1-4.
159 *LG* 9; cf. *Hos* 1; *Isa* 1:2-4; *Jer* 2; 31:31-34; *Isa* 55:3.

The Church – instituted by Christ Jesus

763   It was the Son's task to accomplish the Father's plan of salvation in the fullness of time. Its accomplishment was the reason for his being sent.[160] "The Lord Jesus inaugurated his Church by preaching the Good News, that is, the coming of the Reign of God, promised over the ages in the scriptures."[161] To fulfill the Father's   *541* will, Christ ushered in the Kingdom of heaven on earth. The Church "is the Reign of Christ already present in mystery."[162]

764   "This Kingdom shines out before men in the word, in the works and in the presence of Christ."[163] To welcome Jesus' word is to welcome "the Kingdom itself."[164] The seed and beginning of   *543* the Kingdom are the "little flock" of those whom Jesus came to gather around him, the flock whose shepherd he is.[165] They form Jesus' true family.[166] To those whom he thus gathered around him,   *1691* he taught a new "way of acting" and a prayer of their own.[167]   *2558*

765   The Lord Jesus endowed his community with a structure that will remain until the Kingdom is fully achieved. Before all else there is the choice of the Twelve with Peter as their head.[168] Representing the twelve tribes of Israel, they are the foundation   *610* stones of the new Jerusalem.[169] The Twelve and the other disciples   *551* share in Christ's mission and his power, but also in his lot.[170] By all his actions, Christ prepares and builds his Church.

766   The Church is born primarily of Christ's total self-giving for our salvation, anticipated in the institution of the Eucharist and fulfilled on the cross. "The origin and growth of the Church are   *813, 860* symbolized by the blood and water which flowed from the open   *1340* side of the crucified Jesus."[171] "For it was from the side of Christ   *617* as he slept the sleep of death upon the cross that there came forth   *478* the 'wondrous sacrament of the whole Church.'"[172] As Eve was

---

160 Cf. *LG* 3; *AG* 3.
161 *LG* 5.
162 *LG* 3.
163 *LG* 5.
164 *LG* 5.
165 *Lk* 12:32; cf. *Mt* 10:16; 26:31; *Jn* 10:1-21.
166 Cf. *Mt* 12:49.
167 Cf. *Mt* 5-6.
168 Cf. *Mk* 3:14-15.
169 Cf. *Mt* 19:28; *Lk* 22:30; *Rev* 21:12-14.
170 Cf. *Mk* 6:7; *Lk* 10:1-2; *Mt* 10:25; *Jn* 15:20.
171 *LG* 3; cf. *Jn* 19:34.
172 *SC* 5.

formed from the sleeping Adam's side, so the Church was born from the pierced heart of Christ hanging dead on the cross.[173]

The Church – revealed by the Holy Spirit

767   "When the work which the Father gave the Son to do on earth was accomplished, the Holy Spirit was sent on the day of
731 Pentecost in order that he might continually sanctify the Church."[174] Then "the Church was openly displayed to the crowds and the spread of the Gospel among the nations, through preaching, was begun."[175] As the "convocation" of all men for salvation,
849 the Church in her very nature is missionary, sent by Christ to all the nations to make disciples of them.[176]

768   So that she can fulfill her mission, the Holy Spirit "bestows upon [the Church] varied hierarchic and charismatic gifts, and in this way directs her."[177] "Henceforward the Church, endowed with the gifts of her founder and faithfully observing his precepts of charity, humility and self-denial, receives the mission of proclaiming and establishing among all peoples the Kingdom of Christ and of God,
541 and she is on earth the seed and the beginning of that kingdom."[178]

The Church – perfected in glory

769   "The Church . . . will receive its perfection only in the glory of heaven,"[179] at the time of Christ's glorious return. Until that day,
671, 2818 "the Church progresses on her pilgrimage amidst this world's persecutions and God's consolations."[180] Here below she knows that she is in exile far from the Lord, and longs for the full coming
675 of the Kingdom, when she will "be united in glory with her king."[181] The Church, and through her the world, will not be perfected in glory without great trials. Only then will "all the just from the time of Adam, 'from Abel, the just one, to the last of the elect,'
1045 . . . be gathered together in the universal Church in the Father's presence."[182]

---

173   Cf. St. Ambrose, *In Luc.* 2, 85-89: PL 15, 1666-1668.
174   *LG* 4; cf. *Jn* 17:4.
175   *AG* 4.
176   Cf. *Mt* 28:19-20; *AG* 2; 5-6.
177   *LG* 4.
178   *LG* 5.
179   *LG* 48.
180   St. Augustine, *De civ. Dei,* 18, 51: PL 41, 614; cf. *LG* 8.
181   *LG* 5; cf. 6; 2 *Cor* 5:6.
182   *LG* 2.

III. THE MYSTERY OF THE CHURCH

770   The Church is in history, but at the same time she transcends it. It is only "with the eyes of faith"[183] that one can see her in her visible reality and at the same time in her spiritual reality as *812* bearer of divine life.

The Church – both visible and spiritual

771   "The one mediator, Christ, established and ever sustains *827* here on earth his holy Church, the community of faith, hope, and charity, as a visible organization through which he communicates truth and grace to all men."[184] The Church is at the same time:

– a "society structured with hierarchical organs and the mystical *1880* body of Christ;

– the visible society and the spiritual community;

– the earthly Church and the Church endowed with heavenly *954* riches."[185]

These dimensions together constitute "one complex reality which comes together from a human and a divine element":[186]

> The Church is essentially both human and divine, visible but endowed with invisible realities, zealous in action and dedicated to contemplation, present in the world, but as a pilgrim, so constituted that in her the human is directed toward and subordinated to the divine, the visible to the invisible, action to contemplation, and this present world to that city yet to come, the object of our quest.[187]
>
> O humility! O sublimity! Both tabernacle of cedar and sanctuary of God; earthly dwelling and celestial palace; house of clay and royal hall; body of death and temple of light; and at last both object of scorn to the proud and bride of Christ! She is black but beautiful, O daughters of Jerusalem, for even if the labor and pain of her long exile may have discolored her, yet heaven's beauty has adorned her.[188]

---

183   *Roman Catechism* I, 10, 20.
184   *LG* 8 § 1.
185   *LG* 8.
186   *LG* 8.
187   *SC* 2; cf. *Heb* 13:14.
188   St. Bernard of Clairvaux, *In Cant. Sermo* 27:14: PL 183:920D.

The Church – mystery of man's union with God

518 **772**   It is in the Church that Christ fulfills and reveals his own
796 mystery as the purpose of God's plan: "to unite all things in
him."[189] St. Paul calls the nuptial union of Christ and the Church
"a great mystery." Because she is united to Christ as to her bridegroom, she becomes a mystery in her turn.[190] Contemplating this
mystery in her, Paul exclaims: "Christ in you, the hope of glory."[191]

773   In the Church this communion of men with God, in the
"love [that] never ends," is the purpose which governs everything
in her that is a sacramental means, tied to this passing world.[192]
"[The Church's] structure is totally ordered to the holiness of
671 Christ's members. And holiness is measured according to the
'great mystery' in which the Bride responds with the gift of love to
972 the gift of the Bridegroom."[193] Mary goes before us all in the
holiness that is the Church's mystery as "the bride without spot or
wrinkle."[194] This is why the "Marian" dimension of the Church
precedes the "Petrine."[195]

The universal Sacrament of Salvation

774   The Greek word *mysterion* was translated into Latin by two terms:
mysterium and *sacramentum*. In later usage the term *sacramentum* empha-
1075 sizes the visible sign of the hidden reality of salvation which was indicated
by the term *mysterium*. In this sense, Christ himself is the mystery of
salvation: "For there is no other mystery of God, except Christ."[196] The
saving work of his holy and sanctifying humanity is the sacrament of
salvation, which is revealed and active in the Church's sacraments (which
515 the Eastern Churches also call "the holy mysteries"). The seven sacraments
2014 are the signs and instruments by which the Holy Spirit spreads the grace of
1116 Christ the head throughout the Church which is his Body. The Church, then,
both contains and communicates the invisible grace she signifies. It is in this
analogical sense, that the Church is called a "sacrament."

775   "The Church, in Christ, is like a sacrament – a sign and
instrument, that is, of communion with God and of unity among
all men."[197] The Church's first purpose is to be the sacrament of

---

189 *Eph* 1:10.
190 *Eph* 5:32; 3:9-11; 5:25-27.
191 *Col* 1:27.
192 *1 Cor* 13:8; cf. *LG* 48.
193 John Paul II, *MD* 27.
194 *Eph* 5:27.
195 Cf. John Paul II, *MD* 27.
196 St. Augustine, *Ep.* 187, 11, 34: PL 33, 846.
197 *LG* 1.

the *inner union of men with God.* Because men's communion with one another is rooted in that union with God, the Church is also the sacrament of the *unity of the human race.* In her, this unity is already begun, since she gathers men "from every nation, from all tribes and peoples and tongues";[198] at the same time, the Church is the "sign and instrument" of the full realization of the unity yet to come.

360

776   As sacrament, the Church is Christ's instrument. "She is taken up by him also as the instrument for the salvation of all," "the universal sacrament of salvation," by which Christ is "at once manifesting and actualizing the mystery of God's love for men."[199] The Church "is the visible plan of God's love for humanity," because God desires "that the whole human race may become one People of God, form one Body of Christ, and be built up into one temple of the Holy Spirit."[200]

1088

IN BRIEF

777   The word "Church" means "convocation." It designates the assembly of those whom God's Word "convokes," i.e., gathers together to form the People of God, and who themselves, nourished with the Body of Christ, become the Body of Christ.

778   The Church is both the means and the goal of God's plan: prefigured in creation, prepared for in the Old Covenant, founded by the words and actions of Jesus Christ, fulfilled by his redeeming cross and his Resurrection, the Church has been manifested as the mystery of salvation by the outpouring of the Holy Spirit. She will be perfected in the glory of heaven as the assembly of all the redeemed of the earth (cf. *Rev* 14:4).

779   The Church is both visible and spiritual, a hierarchical society and the Mystical Body of Christ. She is one, yet formed of two components, human and divine. That is her mystery, which only faith can accept.

780   The Church in this world is the sacrament of salvation, the sign and the instrument of the communion of God and men.

---

198   *Rev* 7:9.
199   *LG* 9 § 2, 48 § 2; GS 45 § 1.
200   Paul VI, June 22, 1973; *AG* 7 § 2; cf. *LG* 17.

Paragraph 2. The Church – People of God, Body of Christ,
Temple of the Holy Spirit

I.   THE CHURCH – PEOPLE OF GOD

781   "At all times and in every race, anyone who fears God and
does what is right has been acceptable to him. He has, however,
willed to make men holy and save them, not as individuals without
any bond or link between them, but rather to make them into a
people who might acknowledge him and serve him in holiness. He
therefore chose the Israelite race to be his own people and established a covenant with it. He gradually instructed this people. . . .
All these things, however, happened as a preparation for and
figure of that new and perfect covenant which was to be ratified in
Christ . . . the New Covenant in his blood; he called together a race
made up of Jews and Gentiles which would be one, not according
to the flesh, but in the Spirit."[201]

Characteristics of the People of God

871 **782**   The People of God is marked by characteristics that clearly
distinguish it from all other religious, ethnic, political, or cultural
groups found in history:

2787 – It is the People *of God:* God is not the property of any one people.
But he acquired a people for himself from those who previously
were not a people: "a chosen race, a royal priesthood, a holy
nation."[202]

1267 – One becomes a *member* of this people not by a physical birth, but
by being "born anew," a birth "of water and the Spirit,"[203] that is,
by faith in Christ, and Baptism.

695 – This People has for its Head Jesus the Christ (the anointed, the
Messiah). Because the same anointing, the Holy Spirit, flows from
the head into the body, this is "the messianic people."

1741 – "The *status* of this people is that of the dignity and freedom of the
sons of God, in whose hearts the Holy Spirit dwells as in a temple."

1972 – "Its *law* is the new commandment to love as Christ loved us."[204]
This is the "new" law of the Holy Spirit.[205]

---

201   *LG* 9; cf. *Acts* 10:35; *1 Cor* 11:25.
202   *1 Pet* 2:9.
203   *Jn* 3:3-5.
204   Cf. *Jn* 13:34.

– Its *mission* is to be salt of the earth and light of the world.[206] This 849
people is "a most sure seed of unity, hope, and salvation for the
whole human race."

– Its *destiny*, finally, "is the Kingdom of God which has been begun 769
by God himself on earth and which must be further extended until
it has been brought to perfection by him at the end of time."[207]

A priestly, prophetic, and royal people

783   Jesus Christ is the one whom the Father anointed with the
Holy Spirit and established as priest, prophet, and king. The whole 436
People of God participates in these three offices of Christ and bears 873
the responsibilities for mission and service that flow from them.[208]

784   On entering the People of God through faith and Baptism,
one receives a share in this people's unique, *priestly* vocation:
"Christ the Lord, high priest taken from among men, has made this 1268
new people 'a kingdom of priests to God, his Father.' The baptized,
by regeneration and the anointing of the Holy Spirit, are *consecrated* 1546
to be a spiritual house and a holy priesthood."[209]

785   "The holy People of God shares also in Christ's *prophetic*
office," above all in the supernatural sense of faith that belongs to
the whole People, lay and clergy, when it "unfailingly adheres to 92
this faith . . . once for all delivered to the saints,"[210] and when it
deepens its understanding and becomes Christ's witness in the
midst of this world.

786   Finally, the People of God shares in the *royal* office of
Christ. He exercises his kingship by drawing all men to himself
through his death and Resurrection.[211] Christ, King and Lord of
the universe, made himself the servant of all, for he came "not to
be served but to serve, and to give his life as a ransom for many."[212]
For the Christian, "to reign is to serve him," particularly when
serving "the poor and the suffering, in whom the Church recognizes the image of her poor and suffering founder."[213] The People 2449

---

205   *Rom* 8:2; *Gal* 5:25.
206   Cf. *Mt* 5:13-16.
207   *LG* 9 § 2.
208   Cf. John Paul II, *RH* 18-21.
209   *LG* 10; cf. *Heb* 5:1-5; *Rev* 1:6.
210   *LG* 12; cf. *Jude* 3.
211   Cf. *Jn* 12:32.
212   *Mt* 20:28.
213   *LG* 8; cf. 36.

of God fulfills its royal dignity by a life in keeping with its vocation
2443 to serve with Christ.

> The sign of the cross makes kings of all those reborn in Christ
> and the anointing of the Holy Spirit consecrates them as
> priests, so that, apart from the particular service of our
> ministry, all spiritual and rational Christians are recognized
> as members of this royal race and sharers in Christ's priestly
> office. What, indeed, is as royal for a soul as to govern the
> body in obedience to God? And what is as priestly as to
> dedicate a pure conscience to the Lord and to offer the
> spotless offerings of devotion on the altar of the heart?[214]

II.   THE CHURCH – BODY OF CHRIST

The Church is communion with Jesus

787   From the beginning, Jesus associated his disciples with his
own life, revealed the mystery of the Kingdom to them, and gave
them a share in his mission, joy, and sufferings.[215] Jesus spoke of
a still more intimate communion between him and those who
would follow him: "Abide in me, and I in you. . . . I am the vine,
755 you are the branches."[216] And he proclaimed a mysterious and real
communion between his own body and ours: "He who eats my
flesh and drinks my blood abides in me, and I in him."[217]

788   When his visible presence was taken from them, Jesus did
not leave his disciples orphans. He promised to remain with them
until the end of time; he sent them his Spirit.[218] As a result com-
690 munion with Jesus has become, in a way, more intense: "By communicating his Spirit, Christ mystically constitutes as his body
those brothers of his who are called together from every nation."[219]

789   The comparison of the Church with the body casts light on
the intimate bond between Christ and his Church. Not only is she
521 gathered *around him*; she is united *in him*, in his body. Three aspects
of the Church as the Body of Christ are to be more specifically
noted: the unity of all her members with each other as a result of
their union with Christ; Christ as head of the Body; and the Church
as bride of Christ.

---

214   St. Leo the Great, *Sermo* 4, 1: PL 54, 149.
215   Cf. *Mk* 1:16-20; 3:13-19; *Mt* 13:10-17; *Lk* 10:17-20; 22:28-30.
216   *Jn* 15:4-5.
217   *Jn* 6:56.
218   Cf. *Jn* 14:18; 20:22; *Mt* 28:20; *Acts* 2:33.
219   *LG* 7.

"One Body"

790   Believers who respond to God's word and become members of Christ's Body, become intimately united with him: "In that body the life of Christ is communicated to those who believe, and *947* who, through the sacraments, are united in a hidden and real way to Christ in his Passion and glorification."[220] This is especially true of Baptism, which unites us to Christ's death and Resurrection, and *1227* the Eucharist, by which "really sharing in the body of the Lord, . . . we *1329* are taken up into communion with him and with one another."[221]

791   The body's unity does not do away with the diversity of its members: "In the building up of Christ's Body there is engaged a diversity of members and functions. There is only one Spirit who, *814* according to his own richness and the needs of the ministries, gives *1937* his different gifts for the welfare of the Church."[222] The unity of the Mystical Body produces and stimulates charity among the faithful: "From this it follows that if one member suffers anything, all the members suffer with him, and if one member is honored, all the members together rejoice."[223] Finally, the unity of the Mystical Body triumphs over all human divisions: "For as many of you as were baptized into Christ have put on Christ. There is neither Jew nor Greek, there is neither slave nor free, there is neither male nor female; for you are all one in Christ Jesus."[224]

"Christ is the Head of this Body"

792   Christ "is the head of the body, the Church."[225] He is the *669* principle of creation and redemption. Raised to the Father's glory, *1119* "in everything he [is] preeminent,"[226] especially in the Church, through whom he extends his reign over all things.

793   *Christ unites us with his Passover:* all his members must *661* strive to resemble him, "until Christ be formed" in them.[227] "For *519* this reason we . . . are taken up into the mysteries of his life, . . .

---

220   *LG* 7.
221   *LG* 7; cf. *Rom* 6:4-5; *1 Cor* 12:13.
222   *LG* 7 § 3.
223   *LG* 7 § 3; cf. *1 Cor* 12:26.
224   *Gal* 3:27-28.
225   *Col* 1:18.
226   *Col* 1:18.
227   *Gal* 4:19.

associated with his sufferings as the body with its head, suffering with him, that with him we may be glorified."[228]

794   *Christ provides for our growth:* to make us grow toward him, our head,[229] he provides in his Body, the Church, the gifts and
872 assistance by which we help one another along the way of salvation.

795   Christ and his Church thus together make up the "whole Christ" (*Christus totus*). The Church is one with Christ. The saints
695 are acutely aware of this unity:

> Let us rejoice then and give thanks that we have become not only Christians, but Christ himself. Do you understand and grasp, brethren, God's grace toward us? Marvel and rejoice: we have become Christ. For if he is the head, we are the members; he and we together are the whole man. . . . The fullness of Christ then is the head and the members. But what does "head and members" mean? Christ and the Church.[230]

> Our redeemer has shown himself to be one person with the holy Church whom he has taken to himself.[231]

1474
> Head and members form as it were one and the same mystical person.[232]

> A reply of St. Joan of Arc to her judges sums up the faith of the holy doctors and the good sense of the believer: "About Jesus Christ and the Church, I simply know they're just one thing, and we shouldn't complicate the matter."[233]

The Church is the Bride of Christ

796   The unity of Christ and the Church, head and members of one Body, also implies the distinction of the two within a personal relationship. This aspect is often expressed by the image of bride-
757 groom and bride. The theme of Christ as Bridegroom of the Church was prepared for by the prophets and announced by John the
219 Baptist.[234] The Lord referred to himself as the "bridegroom."[235] The Apostle speaks of the whole Church and of each of the faithful, members of his Body, as a bride "betrothed" to Christ the Lord so
772 as to become but one spirit with him.[236] The Church is the spotless

---

228   *LG* 7 § 4; cf. *Phil* 3:21; *Rom* 8:17.
229   Cf. *Col* 2:19; *Eph* 4:11-16.
230   St. Augustine, *In Jo. ev.* 21, 8: PL 35, 1568.
231   Pope St. Gregory the Great, *Moralia in Job, præf.*, 14: PL 75, 525A.
232   St. Thomas Aquinas, *STh* III, 48, 2.
233   Acts of the Trial of Joan of Arc.
234   *Jn* 3:29.
235   *Mk* 2:19.
236   Cf. *Mt* 22:1-14; 25:1-13; *1 Cor* 6:15-17; *2 Cor* 11:2.

bride of the spotless Lamb.[237] "Christ loved the Church and gave *1602* himself up for her, that he might sanctify her."[238] He has joined her with himself in an everlasting covenant and never stops caring for *1616* her as for his own body:[239]

> This is the whole Christ, head and body, one formed from many . . . whether the head or members speak, it is Christ who speaks. He speaks in his role as the head (*ex persona capitis*) and in his role as body (*ex persona corporis*). What does this mean? "The two will become one flesh. This is a great mystery, and I am applying it to Christ and the Church."[240] And the Lord himself says in the Gospel: "So they are no longer two, but one flesh."[241] They are, in fact, two different persons, yet they are one in the conjugal union, . . . *as head, he calls himself the bridegroom, as body, he calls himself "bride."*[242]

III.   The Church Is the Temple of the Holy Spirit

797   "What the soul is to the human body, the Holy Spirit is to the Body of Christ, which is the Church."[243] "To this Spirit of Christ, as an invisible principle, is to be ascribed the fact that all the *813* parts of the body are joined one with the other and with their exalted head; for the whole Spirit of Christ is in the head, the whole Spirit is in the body, and the whole Spirit is in each of the members."[244] The Holy Spirit makes the Church "the temple of the living God":[245]   *586*

> Indeed, it is to the Church herself that the "Gift of God" has been entrusted. . . . In it is in her that communion with Christ has been deposited, that is to say: the Holy Spirit, the pledge of incorruptibility, the strengthening of our faith and the ladder of our ascent to God. . . . For where the Church is, there also is God's Spirit; where God's Spirit is, there is the Church and every grace.[246]

---

237   Cf. *Rev* 22:17; *Eph* 1:4. 5:27.
238   *Eph* 5:25-26.
239   Cf. *Eph* 5:29.
240   *Eph* 5:31-32.
241   *Mt* 19:6.
242   St. Augustine, *En. in Ps.* 74:4: PL 36, 948-949.
243   St. Augustine, *Sermo* 267, 4: PL 38, 1231D.
244   Pius XII, encyclical, *Mystici Corporis*: DS 3808.
245   *2 Cor* 6:16; cf. *1 Cor* 3:16-17; *Eph* 2:21.
246   St. Irenaeus, *Adv. haeres.* 3, 24, 1: PG 7/1, 966.

798   The Holy Spirit is "the principle of every vital and truly
saving action in each part of the Body."[247] He works in many ways
737   to build up the whole Body in charity:[248] by God's Word "which
is able to build you up";[249] by Baptism, through which he forms
1091-1109   Christ's Body;[250] by the sacraments, which give growth and healing to Christ's members; by "the grace of the apostles, which holds
first place among his gifts";[251] by the virtues, which make us act
according to what is good; finally, by the many special graces
(called "charisms"), by which he makes the faithful "fit and ready
791   to undertake various tasks and offices for the renewal and building
up of the Church."[252]

Charisms

799   Whether extraordinary or simple and humble, charisms
are graces of the Holy Spirit which directly or indirectly benefit the
951, 2003 Church, ordered as they are to her building up, to the good of men,
and to the needs of the world.

800   Charisms are to be accepted with gratitude by the person
who receives them and by all members of the Church as well. They
are a wonderfully rich grace for the apostolic vitality and for the
holiness of the entire Body of Christ, provided they really are
genuine gifts of the Holy Spirit and are used in full conformity with
authentic promptings of this same Spirit, that is, in keeping with
charity, the true measure of all charisms.[253]

801   It is in this sense that discernment of charisms is always
necessary. No charism is exempt from being referred and submit-
894   ted to the Church's shepherds. "Their office [is] not indeed to
extinguish the Spirit, but to test all things and hold fast to what is
good,"[254] so that all the diverse and complementary charisms work
1905   together "for the common good."[255]

---

247 Pius XII, encyclical, *Mystici Corporis*: DS 3808.
248 Cf. *Eph* 4:16.
249 *Acts* 20:32.
250 Cf. *1 Cor* 12:13.
251 *LG* 7 § 2.
252 *LG* 12 § 2; cf. *AA* 3.
253 Cf. *1 Cor* 13.
254 *LG* 12; cf. 30; *1 Thess* 5:12, 19-21; John Paul II, *Christifideles Laici*, 24.
255 *1 Cor* 12:7.

IN BRIEF

802 Christ Jesus "gave himself for us to redeem us from all iniquity and to purify for himself a people of his own" (*Titus* 2:14).

803 "You are a chosen race, a royal priesthood, a holy nation, God's own people" (*1 Pet* 2:9).

804 One enters into the People of God by faith and Baptism. "All men are called to belong to the new People of God" (*LG* 13), so that, in Christ, "men may form one family and one People of God" (*AG* 1).

805 The Church is the Body of Christ. Through the Spirit and his action in the sacraments, above all the Eucharist, Christ, who once was dead and is now risen, establishes the community of believers as his own Body.

806 In the unity of this Body, there is a diversity of members and functions. All members are linked to one another, especially to those who are suffering, to the poor and persecuted.

807 The Church is this Body of which Christ is the head: she lives from him, in him, and for him; he lives with her and in her.

808 The Church is the Bride of Christ: he loved her and handed himself over for her. He has purified her by his blood and made her the fruitful mother of all God's children.

809 The Church is the Temple of the Holy Spirit. The Spirit is the soul, as it were, of the Mystical Body, the source of its life, of its unity in diversity, and of the riches of its gifts and charisms.

810 "Hence the universal Church is seen to be 'a people brought into unity from the unity of the Father, the Son, and the Holy Spirit'" (*LG* 4 citing St. Cyprian, *De Dom. orat.* 23: PL 4, 553).

Paragraph 3. The Church Is One, Holy, Catholic, and Apostolic

811   "This is the sole Church of Christ, which in the Creed we profess to be one, holy, catholic and apostolic."[256] These four
750 characteristics, inseparably linked with each other,[257] indicate essential features of the Church and her mission. The Church does
832, 865 not possess them of herself; it is Christ who, through the Holy Spirit, makes his Church one, holy, catholic, and apostolic, and it is he who calls her to realize each of these qualities.

812   Only faith can recognize that the Church possesses these properties from her divine source. But their historical manifesta-
156, 770 tions are signs that also speak clearly to human reason. As the First Vatican Council noted, the "Church herself, with her marvellous propagation, eminent holiness, and inexhaustible fruitfulness in everything good, her catholic unity and invincible stability, is a great and perpetual motive of credibility and an irrefutable witness of her divine mission."[258]

I.   THE CHURCH IS ONE

"The sacred mystery of the Church's unity" (UR 2)

813   *The Church is one because of her source:* "the highest exemplar and source of this mystery is the unity, in the Trinity of Persons, of
172 one God, the Father and the Son in the Holy Spirit."[259] The Church
766 is one *because of her founder:* for "the Word made flesh, the prince of peace, reconciled all men to God by the cross, . . . restoring the unity
797 of all in one people and one body."[260] The Church is one *because of her "soul":* "It is the Holy Spirit, dwelling in those who believe and pervading and ruling over the entire Church, who brings about that wonderful communion of the faithful and joins them together so intimately in Christ that he is the principle of the Church's unity."[261] Unity is of the essence of the Church:

> What an astonishing mystery! There is one Father of the universe, one Logos of the universe, and also one Holy Spirit,

---

256   *LG* 8.
257   Cf. DS 2888.
258   Vatican Council I, *Dei Filius* 3: DS 3013.
259   *UR* 2 § 5.
260   *GS* 78 § 3.
261   *UR* 2 § 2.

everywhere one and the same; there is also one virgin become mother, and I should like to call her "Church."[262]

814 From the beginning, this one Church has been marked by a great *diversity* which comes from both the variety of God's gifts and the diversity of those who receive them. Within the unity of *791, 873* the People of God, a multiplicity of peoples and cultures is gathered together. Among the Church's members, there are different gifts, offices, conditions, and ways of life. "Holding a rightful place *1202* in the communion of the Church there are also particular Churches that retain their own traditions."[263] The great richness of such diversity is not opposed to the Church's unity. Yet sin and the *832* burden of its consequences constantly threaten the gift of unity. And so the Apostle has to exhort Christians to "maintain the unity of the Spirit in the bond of peace."[264]

815 What are these bonds of unity? Above all, charity "binds *1827* everything together in perfect harmony."[265] But the unity of the *830, 837* pilgrim Church is also assured by visible bonds of communion: *173*

– profession of one faith received from the Apostles;

– common celebration of divine worship, especially of the sacraments;

– apostolic succession through the sacrament of Holy Orders, maintaining the fraternal concord of God's family.[266]

816 "The sole Church of Christ [is that] which our Savior, after his Resurrection, entrusted to Peter's pastoral care, commissioning him and the other apostles to extend and rule it. . . . This Church, constituted and organized as a society in the present world, subsists in (*subsistit in*) the Catholic Church, which is governed by the successor of Peter and by the bishops in communion with him."[267]

> The Second Vatican Council's *Decree on Ecumenism* explains: *830*
> "For it is through Christ's Catholic Church alone, which is the universal help toward salvation, that the fullness of the means of salvation can be obtained. It was to the apostolic college alone, of which Peter is the head, that we believe that our Lord entrusted all the blessings of the New Covenant, in order to establish on earth the one Body of Christ into which all those should be fully incorporated who belong in any way to the People of God."[268]

---

262 St. Clement of Alexandria, *Paed.* 1, 6, 42: PG 8, 300.
263 *LG* 13 § 2.
264 *Eph* 4:3.
265 *Col* 3:14.
266 Cf. *UR* 2; *LG* 14; CIC, can. 205.
267 *LG* 8 § 2.

Wounds to unity

817   In fact, "in this one and only Church of God from its very
beginnings there arose certain rifts, which the Apostle strongly
censures as damnable. But in subsequent centuries much more
serious dissensions appeared and large communities became separated from full communion with the Catholic Church – for which,
often enough, men of both sides were to blame."[269] The ruptures
that wound the unity of Christ's Body – here we must distinguish
2089   heresy, apostasy, and schism[270] – do not occur without human sin:

> Where there are sins, there are also divisions, schisms, here-
> sies, and disputes. Where there is virtue, however, there also
> are harmony and unity, from which arise the one heart and
> one soul of all believers.[271]

818   "However, one cannot charge with the sin of the separation those who at present are born into these communities [that
resulted from such separation] and in them are brought up in the
faith of Christ, and the Catholic Church accepts them with respect
and affection as brothers . . . . All who have been justified by faith
1271   in Baptism are incorporated into Christ; they therefore have a right
to be called Christians, and with good reason are accepted as
brothers in the Lord by the children of the Catholic Church."[272]

819   "Furthermore, many elements of sanctification and of
truth"[273] are found outside the visible confines of the Catholic
Church: "the written Word of God; the life of grace; faith, hope,
and charity, with the other interior gifts of the Holy Spirit, as well
as visible elements."[274] Christ's Spirit uses these Churches and
ecclesial communities as means of salvation, whose power derives
from the fullness of grace and truth that Christ has entrusted to the
Catholic Church. All these blessings come from Christ and lead to
him,[275] and are in themselves calls to "Catholic unity."[276]

---

268   *UR* 3 § 5.
269   *UR* 3 § 1.
270   Cf. CIC, can. 751.
271   Origen, *Hom. in Ezech.* 9, 1: PG 13, 732.
272   *UR* 3 § 1.
273   *LG* 8 § 2.
274   *UR* 3 § 2; cf. *LG* 15.
275   Cf. *UR* 3.
276   Cf. *LG* 8.

Toward unity

820   "Christ bestowed unity on his Church from the beginning. This unity, we believe, subsists in the Catholic Church as something she can never lose, and we hope that it will continue to increase until the end of time."[277] Christ always gives his Church the gift of unity, but the Church must always pray and work to maintain, reinforce, and perfect the unity that Christ wills for her. This is why Jesus himself prayed at the hour of his Passion, and *2748* does not cease praying to his Father, for the unity of his disciples: "That they may all be one. As you, Father, are in me and I am in you, may they also be one in us, . . . so that the world may know that you have sent me."[278] The desire to recover the unity of all Christians is a gift of Christ and a call of the Holy Spirit.[279]

821   Certain things are required in order to respond adequately to this call:

– a permanent *renewal* of the Church in greater fidelity to her vocation; such renewal is the driving-force of the movement toward unity;[280]

– *conversion of heart* as the faithful "try to live holier lives according to the *827* Gospel",[281] for it is the unfaithfulness of the members to Christ's gift which causes divisions;

– *prayer in common*, because "change of heart and holiness of life, along *2791* with public and private prayer for the unity of Christians, should be regarded as the soul of the whole ecumenical movement, and merits the name 'spiritual ecumenism;'"[282]

– *fraternal knowledge of each other;*[283]

– *ecumenical formation* of the faithful and especially of priests;[284]

– *dialogue* among theologians and meetings among Christians of the different churches and communities;[285]

– *collaboration* among Christians in various areas of service to mankind.[286] "Human service" is the idiomatic phrase.

---

277   *UR* 4 § 3.
278   *Jn* 17:21; cf. *Heb* 7:25.
279   Cf. *UR* 1.
280   Cf. *UR* 6.
281   *UR* 7 § 3.
282   *UR* 8 § 1.
283   Cf. *UR* 9.
284   Cf. *UR* 10.
285   Cf. *UR* 4; 9; 11.
286   Cf. *UR* 12.

822   Concern for achieving unity "involves the whole Church, faithful and clergy alike."[287] But we must realize "that this holy objective – the reconciliation of all Christians in the unity of the one and only Church of Christ – transcends human powers and gifts." That is why we place all our hope "in the prayer of Christ for the Church, in the love of the Father for us, and in the power of the Holy Spirit."[288]

II.   THE CHURCH IS HOLY

         823   "The Church . . . is held, as a matter of faith, to be unfailingly holy. This is because Christ, the Son of God, who with the
459 Father and the Spirit is hailed as 'alone holy,' loved the Church as
796 his Bride, giving himself up for her so as to sanctify her; he joined her to himself as his body and endowed her with the gift of the Holy Spirit for the glory of God."[289] The Church, then, is "the holy
946 People of God,"[290] and her members are called "saints."[291]

824   United with Christ, the Church is sanctified by him; through him and with him she becomes sanctifying. "All the activities of the Church are directed, as toward their end, to the sanctification of men in Christ and the glorification of God."[292] It is in the Church that "the fullness of the means of salvation"[293] has
816 been deposited. It is in her that "by the grace of God we acquire holiness."[294]

825   "The Church on earth is endowed already with a sanctity that is real though imperfect."[295] In her members perfect holiness
670 is something yet to be acquired: "Strengthened by so many and such great means of salvation, all the faithful, whatever their
2013 condition or state – though each in his own way – are called by the Lord to that perfection of sanctity by which the Father himself is perfect."[296]

1827, 2658 **826**   Charity is the soul of the holiness to which all are called: it "governs, shapes, and perfects all the means of sanctification."[297]

---

287   *UR* 5.
288   *UR* 24 § 2.
289   *LG* 39; cf. *Eph* 5:25-26.
290   *LG* 12.
291   *Acts* 9:13; *1 Cor* 6:1; 16:1.
292   *SC* 10.
293   *UR* 3 § 5.
294   *LG* 48.
295   *LG* 48 § 3.
296   *LG* 11 § 3.

> If the Church was a body composed of different members, it couldn't lack the noblest of all; *it must have a Heart, and a Heart BURNING WITH LOVE.* And I realized that *this love alone* was the true motive force which enabled the other members of the Church to act; if it ceased to function, the Apostles would forget to preach the gospel, the Martyrs would refuse to shed their blood. LOVE, IN FACT, IS THE VOCATION WHICH INCLUDES ALL OTHERS; IT'S A UNIVERSE OF ITS OWN, COMPRISING ALL TIME AND SPACE – IT'S ETERNAL![298]

864

827 "Christ, 'holy, innocent, and undefiled,' knew nothing of sin, but came only to expiate the sins of the people. The Church, however, clasping sinners to her bosom, at once holy and always in need of purification, follows constantly the path of penance and renewal."[299] All members of the Church, including her ministers, must acknowledge that they are sinners.[300] In everyone, the weeds of sin will still be mixed with the good wheat of the Gospel until the end of time.[301] Hence the Church gathers sinners already caught up in Christ's salvation but still on the way to holiness:

1425-1429
821

> The Church is therefore holy, though having sinners in her midst, because she herself has no other life but the life of grace. If they live her life, her members are sanctified; if they move away from her life, they fall into sins and disorders that prevent the radiation of her sanctity. This is why she suffers and does penance for those offenses, of which she has the power to free her children through the blood of Christ and the gift of the Holy Spirit.[302]

828 By *canonizing* some of the faithful, i.e., by solemnly proclaiming that they practiced heroic virtue and lived in fidelity to God's grace, the Church recognizes the power of the Spirit of holiness within her and sustains the hope of believers by proposing the saints to them as models and intercessors.[303] "The saints have always been the source and origin of renewal in the most difficult moments in the Church's history."[304] Indeed, "holiness is the hidden source and infallible measure of her apostolic activity and missionary zeal."[305]

1173

2045

---

297 *LG* 42.
298 St. Thérèse of Lisieux, *Autobiography of a Saint*, tr. Ronald Knox (London: Harvill, 1958) 235.
299 *LG* 8 § 3; cf. *UR* 3; 6; *Heb* 2:17; 7:26; 2 *Cor* 5:21.
300 Cf. *1 Jn* 1:8-10.
301 Cf. *Mt* 13:24-30.
302 Paul VI, *CPG* § 19.
303 Cf. *LG* 40; 48-51.
304 John Paul II, *CL* 16, 3.
305 *CL* 17, 3.

829   "But while in the most Blessed Virgin the Church has
1172 already reached that perfection whereby she exists without spot or
972   wrinkle, the faithful still strive to conquer sin and increase in
holiness. And so they turn their eyes to Mary":[306] in her, the
Church is already the "all-holy."

III.   THE CHURCH IS CATHOLIC

What does "catholic" mean?

830   The word "catholic" means "universal," in the sense of
"according to the totality" or "in keeping with the whole." The
Church is catholic in a double sense:

> First, the Church is catholic because Christ is present in
795   her. "Where there is Christ Jesus, there is the Catholic Church."[307]
815-816 In her subsists the fullness of Christ's body united with its head;
this implies that she receives from him "the fullness of the means
of salvation"[308] which he has willed: correct and complete confession of faith, full sacramental life, and ordained ministry in apostolic succession. The Church was, in this fundamental sense,
catholic on the day of Pentecost[309] and will always be so until the
day of the Parousia.

831   Secondly, the Church is catholic because she has been sent
849   out by Christ on a mission to the whole of the human race:[310]

> All men are called to belong to the new People of God. This
> People, therefore, while remaining one and only one, is to be
> spread throughout the whole world and to all ages in order
> that the design of God's will may be fulfilled: he made
> 360   human nature one in the beginning and has decreed that all
> his children who were scattered should be finally gathered
> together as one. . . . The character of universality which
> adorns the People of God is a gift from the Lord himself
> 518   whereby the Catholic Church ceaselessly and efficaciously
> seeks for the return of all humanity and all its goods, under
> Christ the Head in the unity of his Spirit.[311]

---

306   *LG* 65; cf. *Eph* 5:26-27.
307   St. Ignatius of Antioch, *Ad Smyrn.* 8, 2: *Apostolic Fathers,* II/2, 311.
308   *UR* 3; *AG* 6; *Eph* 1:22-23.
309   Cf. *AG* 4.
310   Cf. *Mt* 28:19.
311   *LG* 13 §§ 1-2; cf. *Jn* 11:52.

Each particular Church is "catholic"

832   "The Church of Christ is really present in all legitimately *814* organized local groups of the faithful, which, in so far as they are *811* united to their pastors, are also quite appropriately called Churches in the New Testament. . . . In them the faithful are gathered together through the preaching of the Gospel of Christ, and the mystery of the Lord's Supper is celebrated. . . . In these communities, though they may often be small and poor, or existing in the diaspora, Christ is present, through whose power and influence the One, Holy, Catholic, and Apostolic Church is constituted."[312]

833   The phrase "particular church," which is the diocese (or eparchy), refers to a community of the Christian faithful in communion of faith and sacraments with their bishop ordained in apostolic succession.[313] These particular Churches "are constituted after the *886* model of the universal Church; it is in these and formed out of them that the one and unique Catholic Church exists."[314]

834   Particular Churches are fully catholic through their communion with one of them, the Church of Rome "which presides in charity."[315] "For with this church, by reason of its pre-eminence, *882, 1369* the whole Church, that is the faithful everywhere, must necessarily be in accord."[316] Indeed, "from the incarnate Word's descent to us, all Christian churches everywhere have held and hold the great Church that is here [at Rome] to be their only basis and foundation since, according to the Savior's promise, the gates of hell have never prevailed against her."[317]

835   "Let us be very careful not to conceive of the universal Church as the simple sum, or . . . the more or less anomalous federation of essentially different particular churches. In the mind of the Lord the Church is universal by vocation and mission, but when she puts down her roots in a variety of cultural, social, and human terrains, she takes on different external expressions and appearances in each part of the world."[318] The rich variety of ecclesiastical disciplines, liturgical rites, and theological and spiritual heritages proper to the local churches "unified in a common effort, shows all the more resplendently the catholicity of the undivided *1202* Church."[319]

---

312   *LG* 26.
313   Cf. *CD* 11; CIC, cann. 368-369.
314   *LG* 23.
315   St. Ignatius of Antioch, *Ad Rom.* 1, 1: *Apostolic Fathers*, II/2, 192; cf. *LG* 13.
316   St. Irenaeus, *Adv. haeres.* 3, 3, 2: PG 7/1, 849; cf. Vatican Council I: DS 3057.
317   St. Maximus the Confessor, *Opuscula theo.*: PG 91:137-140.
318   Paul VI, *EN* 62.

Who belongs to the Catholic Church?

836   "All men are called to this catholic unity of the People of
God. . . . And to it, in different ways, belong or are ordered: the
831 Catholic faithful, others who believe in Christ, and finally all
mankind, called by God's grace to salvation."[320]

837   "Fully incorporated into the society of the Church are
those who, possessing the Spirit of Christ, accept all the means of
771 salvation given to the Church together with her entire organiza-
815 tion, and who – by the bonds constituted by the profession of faith,
the sacraments, ecclesiastical government, and communion – are
joined in the visible structure of the Church of Christ, who rules
her through the Supreme Pontiff and the bishops. Even though
incorporated into the Church, one who does not however perse-
882 vere in charity is not saved. He remains indeed in the bosom of the
Church, but 'in body' not 'in heart.'"[321]

838   "The Church knows that she is joined in many ways to the
baptized who are honored by the name of Christian, but do not
818 profess the Catholic faith in its entirety or have not preserved unity
or communion under the successor of Peter."[322] Those "who believe in Christ and have been properly baptized are put in a certain,
1271 although imperfect, communion with the Catholic Church."[323]
With the Orthodox Churches, this communion is so profound "that
it lacks little to attain the fullness that would permit a common
1399 celebration of the Lord's Eucharist."[324]

The Church and non-Christians

856 **839**   "Those who have not yet received the Gospel are related
to the People of God in various ways."[325]

The relationship of the Church with the Jewish People. When
she delves into her own mystery, the Church, the People of God in
the New Covenant, discovers her link with the Jewish People,[326]
63 "the first to hear the Word of God."[327] The Jewish faith, unlike
147 other non-Christian religions, is already a response to God's reve-

---

319 *LG* 23.
320 *LG* 13.
321 *LG* 14.
322 *LG* 15.
323 *UR* 3.
324 Paul VI, Discourse, December 14, 1975; cf. *UR* 13-18.
325 *LG* 16.
326 Cf. *NA* 4.

lation in the Old Covenant. To the Jews "belong the sonship, the glory, the covenants, the giving of the law, the worship, and the promises; to them belong the patriarchs, and of their race, according to the flesh, is the Christ";[328] "for the gifts and the call of God are irrevocable."[329]

840   And when one considers the future, God's People of the Old Covenant and the new People of God tend towards similar goals: expectation of the coming (or the return) of the Messiah. But one awaits the *674* return of the Messiah who died and rose from the dead and is recognized as Lord and Son of God; the other awaits the coming of a Messiah, whose features remain hidden till the end of time; and the latter waiting is accompanied by the drama of not knowing or of misunderstanding Christ *597* Jesus.

841   *The Church's relationship with the Muslims.* "The plan of salvation also includes those who acknowledge the Creator, in the first place amongst whom are the Muslims; these profess to hold the faith of Abraham, and together with us they adore the one, merciful God, mankind's judge on the last day."[330]

842   *The Church's bond with non-Christian religions* is in the first place the common origin and end of the human race: *360*

> All nations form but one community. This is so because all stem from the one stock which God created to people the entire earth, and also because all share a common destiny, namely God. His providence, evident goodness, and saving designs extend to all against the day when the elect are gathered together in the holy city. . . .[331]

843   The Catholic Church recognizes in other religions that search, among shadows and images, for the God who is unknown yet near since he gives life and breath and all things and wants all men to *28* be saved. Thus, the Church considers all goodness and truth found in *856* these religions as "a preparation for the Gospel and given by him who enlightens all men that they may at length have life."[332]

844   In their religious behavior, however, men also display the limits and errors that disfigure the image of God in them: *29*

> Very often, deceived by the Evil One, men have become vain in their reasonings, and have exchanged the truth of God for a lie, and served the creature rather than the Creator. Or else,

---

327 *Roman Missal*, Good Friday 13: General Intercessions, VI.
328 *Rom* 9:4-5.
329 *Rom* 11:29.
330 *LG* 16; cf. *NA* 3.
331 *NA* 1.
332 *LG* 16; cf. *NA* 2; *EN* 53.

living and dying in this world without God, they are exposed to ultimate despair.[333]

845   To reunite all his children, scattered and led astray by sin, the Father willed to call the whole of humanity together into his
30   Son's Church. The Church is the place where humanity must
953 rediscover its unity and salvation. The Church is "the world reconciled." She is that bark which "in the full sail of the Lord's cross, by the breath of the Holy Spirit, navigates safely in this world."
1219 According to another image dear to the Church Fathers, she is prefigured by Noah's ark, which alone saves from the flood.[334]

"Outside the Church there is no salvation"

846   How are we to understand this affirmation, often repeated by the Church Fathers?[335] Re-formulated positively, it means that all salvation comes from Christ the Head through the Church which is his Body:

> Basing itself on Scripture and Tradition, the Council teaches that the Church, a pilgrim now on earth, is necessary for salvation: the one Christ is the mediator and the way of salvation; he is present to us in his body which is the Church. He himself explicitly asserted the necessity of faith and
161, 1257   Baptism, and thereby affirmed at the same time the necessity of the Church which men enter through Baptism as through a door. Hence they could not be saved who, knowing that the Catholic Church was founded as necessary by God through Christ, would refuse either to enter it or to remain in it.[336]

847   This affirmation is not aimed at those who, through no fault of their own, do not know Christ and his Church:

> Those who, through no fault of their own, do not know the Gospel of Christ or his Church, but who nevertheless seek God with a sincere heart, and, moved by grace, try in their actions to do his will as they know it through the dictates of their conscience – those too may achieve eternal salvation.[337]

848   "Although in ways known to himself God can lead those who, through no fault of their own, are ignorant of the Gospel, to
1260 that faith without which it is impossible to please him, the Church

---

333 *LG* 16; cf. *Rom* 1:21, 25.
334 St. Augustine, *Serm.* 96, 7, 9: PL 38, 588; St. Ambrose, *De virg.* 18, 118: PL 16, 297B; cf. already *1 Pet* 3:20-21.
335 Cf. Cyprian, *Ep.* 73.21: PL 3, 1169; *De unit.*: PL 4, 509-536.
336 *LG* 14; cf. *Mk* 16:16; *Jn* 3:5.
337 *LG* 16; cf. DS 3866-3872.

still has the obligation and also the sacred right to evangelize all men."[338]

Mission – a requirement of the Church's catholicity

849   *The missionary mandate.* "Having been divinely sent to the nations that she might be 'the universal sacrament of salvation,' the Church, in obedience to the command of her founder and *738, 767* because it is demanded by her own essential universality, strives to preach the Gospel to all men":[339] "Go therefore and make disciples of all nations, baptizing them in the name of the Father and of the Son and of the Holy Spirit, teaching them to observe all that I have commanded you; and Lo, I am with you always, until the close of the age."[340]

850   *The origin and purpose of mission.* The Lord's missionary mandate is ultimately grounded in the eternal love of the Most Holy Trinity: "The Church on earth is by her nature missionary *257* since, according to the plan of the Father, she has as her origin the mission of the Son and the Holy Spirit."[341] The ultimate purpose *730* of mission is none other than to make men share in the communion between the Father and the Son in their Spirit of love.[342]

851   *Missionary motivation.* It is from God's love for all men that the Church in every age receives both the obligation and the vigor of her missionary dynamism, "for the love of Christ urges us on."[343] Indeed, God "desires all men to be saved and to come to *221, 429* the knowledge of the truth";[344] that is, God wills the salvation of *74, 217* everyone through the knowledge of the truth. Salvation is found *2104* in the truth. Those who obey the prompting of the Spirit of truth are already on the way of salvation. But the Church, to whom this truth has been entrusted, must go out to meet their desire, so as to bring them the truth. Because she believes in God's universal plan *890* of salvation, the Church must be missionary.

852   *Missionary paths.* The Holy Spirit is the protagonist, "the principal agent of the whole of the Church's mission."[345] It is he *2044* who leads the Church on her missionary paths. "This mission *2473*

---

338   *AG* 7; cf. *Heb* 11:6; *1 Cor* 9:16.
339   *AG* 1; cf. *Mt* 16:15.
340   *Mt* 28:19-20.
341   *AG* 2.
342   Cf. John Paul II, *RMiss* 23.
343   *2 Cor* 5:14 ; cf. *AA* 6; *RMiss* 11.
344   *1 Tim* 2:4.
345   John Paul II, *RMiss* 21.

continues and, in the course of history, unfolds the mission of Christ, who was sent to evangelize the poor; so the Church, urged on by the Spirit of Christ, must walk the road Christ himself walked, a way of poverty and obedience, of service and self-sacrifice even to death, a death from which he emerged victorious by his resurrection."[346] So it is that "the blood of martyrs is the seed of Christians."[347]

853 On her pilgrimage, the Church has also experienced the "discrepancy existing between the message she proclaims and the human weakness of those to whom the Gospel has been entrusted."[348] Only by taking the "way of penance and renewal," the "narrow way of the cross," can the

1428 People of God extend Christ's reign.[349] For "just as Christ carried out the work of redemption in poverty and oppression, so the Church is called to

2443 follow the same path if she is to communicate the fruits of salvation to men."[350]

854 By her very mission, "the Church ... travels the same journey as all humanity and shares the same earthly lot with the world: she is to be a leaven and, as it were, the soul of human society in its renewal by Christ and transformation into the family of God."[351] Missionary endeavor requires *patience*. It begins with the proclamation of the Gospel to peoples

2105 and groups who do not yet believe in Christ,[352] continues with the establishment of Christian communities that are "a sign of God's presence in the world,"[353] and leads to the foundation of local churches.[354] It must

1204 involve a process of inculturation if the Gospel is to take flesh in each people's culture.[355] There will be times of defeat. "With regard to individuals, groups, and peoples it is only by degrees that [the Church] touches and penetrates them, and so receives them into a fullness which is Catholic."[356]

855 The Church's mission stimulates efforts *towards Christian unity*.[357] Indeed, "divisions among Christians prevent the Church from

821 realizing in practice the fullness of catholicity proper to her in those of her sons who, though joined to her by Baptism, are yet separated from full communion with her. Furthermore, the Church herself finds it more difficult to express in actual life her full catholicity in all its aspects."[358]

---

346   *AG* 5.
347   Tertullian, *Apol.* 50, 13: PL 1, 603.
348   *GS* 43 § 6.
349   *LG* 8 § 3; 15; *AG* 1 § 3; cf. *RMiss* 12-20.
350   *LG* 8 § 3.
351   *GS* 40 § 2.
352   Cf. *RMiss* 42-47.
353   *AG* 15 § 1.
354   Cf. *RMiss* 48-49.
355   Cf. *RMiss* 52-54.
356   *AG* 6 § 2.
357   Cf. *RMiss* 50.
358   *UR* 4 § 8.

856   The missionary task implies a *respectful dialogue* with those who do not yet accept the Gospel.[359] Believers can profit from this dialogue by learning to appreciate better "those elements of truth and grace which are *839* found among peoples, and which are, as it were, a secret presence of God."[360] They proclaim the Good News to those who do not know it, in order to consolidate, complete, and raise up the truth and the goodness that God has distributed among men and nations, and to purify them from *843* error and evil "for the glory of God, the confusion of the demon, and the happiness of man."[361]

IV.   THE CHURCH IS APOSTOLIC

857   The Church is apostolic because she is founded on the *75* apostles, in three ways:

– she was and remains built on "the foundation of the Apostles,"[362] the witnesses chosen and sent on mission by Christ himself;[363]

– with the help of the Spirit dwelling in her, the Church keeps and *171* hands on the teaching,[364] the "good deposit," the salutary words she has heard from the apostles;[365]

– she continues to be taught, sanctified, and guided by the apostles until Christ's return, through their successors in pastoral office: the college of bishops, "assisted by priests, in union with the successor *880* of Peter, the Church's supreme pastor":[366] *1575*

> You are the eternal Shepherd
> who never leaves his flock untended.
> Through the apostles
> you watch over us and protect us always.
> You made them shepherds of the flock
> to share in the work of your Son. . . .[367]

The Apostles' mission

858   Jesus is the Father's Emissary. From the beginning of his ministry, he "called to him those whom he desired; . . . . And he appointed twelve, whom also he named apostles, to be with him, *551* and to be sent out to preach."[368] From then on, they would also be

---

359   Cf. *RMiss* 55.
360   *AG* 9.
361   *AG* 9.
362   *Eph* 2:20; *Rev* 21:14.
363   Cf. *Mt* 28:16-20; *Acts* 1:8; *1 Cor* 9:1; 15:7-8; *Gal* 1:1; etc.
364   Cf. *Acts* 2:42.
365   Cf. *2 Tim* 1:13-14.
366   *AG* 5.
367   *Roman Missal*, Preface of the Apostles I.

his "emissaries" (Greek *apostoloi*). In them, Christ continues his own mission: "As the Father has sent me, even so I send you."[369]

425, 1086 The apostles' ministry is the continuation of his mission; Jesus said to the Twelve: "he who receives you receives me."[370]

859   Jesus unites them to the mission he received from the Father. As "the Son can do nothing of his own accord," but receives everything from the Father who sent him, so those whom Jesus sends can do nothing apart from him,[371] from whom they received both the mandate for their mission and the power to carry it out. Christ's apostles knew that they were called by God as "ministers

876 of a new covenant," "servants of God," "ambassadors for Christ," "servants of Christ and stewards of the mysteries of God."[372]

860   In the office of the apostles there is one aspect that cannot be transmitted: to be the chosen witnesses of the Lord's Resurrection and so the foundation stones of the Church. But their office also has a permanent aspect. Christ promised to remain with them

642 always. The divine mission entrusted by Jesus to them "will continue to the end of time, since the Gospel they handed on is the

765 lasting source of all life for the Church. Therefore, . . . the apostles

1087 took care to appoint successors."[373]

The bishops – successors of the apostles

861   "In order that the mission entrusted to them might be continued after their death, [the apostles] consigned, by will and

77 testament, as it were, to their immediate collaborators the duty of completing and consolidating the work they had begun, urging them to tend to the whole flock, in which the Holy Spirit had appointed them to shepherd the Church of God. They accordingly

1087 designated such men and then made the ruling that likewise on their death other proven men should take over their ministry."[374]

---

368 *Mk* 3:13-14.
369 *Jn* 20:21; cf. 13:20; 17:18.
370 *Mt* 10:40; cf. *Lk* 10:16.
371 *Jn* 5:19, 30; cf. *Jn* 15:5.
372 *2 Cor* 3:6; 6:4; 5:20; *1 Cor* 4:1.
373 *LG* 20; cf. *Mt* 28:20.
374 *LG* 20; cf. *Acts* 20:28; St. Clement of Rome, *Ad Cor.* 42, 44: PG 1, 291-300.

862   "Just as the office which the Lord confided to Peter alone, as first of the apostles, destined to be transmitted to his successors, is a permanent one, so also endures the office, which the apostles *880* received, of shepherding the Church, a charge destined to be exercised without interruption by the sacred order of bishops."[375] *1556* Hence the Church teaches that "the bishops have by divine institution taken the place of the apostles as pastors of the Church, in such wise that whoever listens to them is listening to Christ and whoever despises them despises Christ and him who sent Christ."[376]

The apostolate

863   The whole Church is apostolic, in that she remains, through the successors of St. Peter and the other apostles, in communion of faith and life with her origin: and in that she is "sent *900* out" into the whole world. All members of the Church share in this mission, though in various ways. "The Christian vocation is, of its nature, a vocation to the apostolate as well." Indeed, we call an *2472* apostolate "every activity of the Mystical Body" that aims "to spread the Kingdom of Christ over all the earth."[377]

864   "Christ, sent by the Father, is the source of the Church's whole apostolate"; thus the fruitfulness of apostolate for ordained ministers as well as for lay people clearly depends on their vital *828* union with Christ.[378] In keeping with their vocations, the demands of the times and the various gifts of the Holy Spirit, the apostolate assumes the most varied forms. But charity, drawn from the Eucha- *824* rist above all, is always "as it were, the soul of the whole aposto- *1324* late."[379]

865   The Church is ultimately *one, holy, catholic, and apostolic* in her deepest and ultimate identity, because it is in her that "the Kingdom of heaven," the "Reign of God,"[380] already exists and will *811, 541* be fulfilled at the end of time. The kingdom has come in the person of Christ and grows mysteriously in the hearts of those incorporated into him, until its full eschatological manifestation. Then all those he has redeemed and made "holy and blameless before him in love,"[381] will be gathered together as the one People of God, the

---

375   *LG* 20 § 2.
376   *LG* 20 § 2.
377   *AA* 2.
378   *AA* 4; cf. *Jn* 15:5.
379   *AA* 3.
380   *Rev* 19:6.

"Bride of the Lamb,"[382] "the holy city Jerusalem coming down out of heaven from God, having the glory of God."[383] For "the wall of the city had twelve foundations, and on them the twelve names of the *twelve apostles of the Lamb.*"[384]

IN BRIEF

866   The Church is one: she acknowledges one Lord, confesses one faith, is born of one Baptism, forms only one Body, is given life by the one Spirit, for the sake of one hope (cf. *Eph* 4:3-5), at whose fulfillment all divisions will be overcome.

867   The Church is holy: the Most Holy God is her author; Christ, her bridegroom, gave himself up to make her holy; the Spirit of holiness gives her life. Since she still includes sinners, she is "the sinless one made up of sinners." Her holiness shines in the saints; in Mary she is already all-holy.

868   The Church is catholic: she proclaims the fullness of the faith. She bears in herself and administers the totality of the means of salvation. She is sent out to all peoples. She speaks to all men. She encompasses all times. She is "missionary of her very nature" (*AG* 2).

869   The Church is apostolic. She is built on a lasting foundation: "the twelve apostles of the Lamb" (*Rev* 21:14). She is indestructible (cf. *Mt* 16:18). She is upheld infallibly in the truth: Christ governs her through Peter and the other apostles, who are present in their successors, the Pope and the college of bishops.

870   "The sole Church of Christ which in the Creed we profess to be one, holy, catholic, and apostolic, . . . subsists in the Catholic Church, which is governed by the successor of Peter and by the bishops in communion with him. Nevertheless, many elements of sanctification and of truth are found outside its visible confines"(*LG* 8).

---

381   *Eph* 1:4.
382   *Rev* 21:9.
383   *Rev* 21:10-11.
384   *Rev* 21:14.

Paragraph 4. Christ's Faithful – Hierarchy, Laity, Consecrated Life

871   "The Christian faithful are those who, inasmuch as they have been incorporated in Christ through Baptism, have been constituted as the people of God; for this reason, since they have *1268-1269* become sharers in Christ's priestly, prophetic, and royal office in their own manner, they are called to exercise the mission which *782-786* God has entrusted to the Church to fulfill in the world, in accord with the condition proper to each one."[385]

872   "In virtue of their rebirth in Christ there exists among all the Christian faithful a true equality with regard to dignity and the activity whereby all cooperate in the building up of the Body of *1934* Christ in accord with each one's own condition and function."[386]   *794*

873   The very differences which the Lord has willed to put between the members of his body serve its unity and mission. For "in the Church there is diversity of ministry but unity of mission. *814, 1937* To the apostles and their successors Christ has entrusted the office of teaching, sanctifying, and governing in his name and by his power. But the laity are made to share in the priestly, prophetical, and kingly office of Christ; they have therefore, in the Church and in the world, their own assignment in the mission of the whole People of God."[387] Finally, "from both groups [hierarchy and laity] there exist Christian faithful who are consecrated to God in their own special manner and serve the salvific mission of the Church through the profession of the evangelical counsels."[388]

I.   THE HIERARCHICAL CONSTITUTION OF THE CHURCH

Why the ecclesial ministry?

874   Christ is himself the source of ministry in the Church. He instituted the Church. He gave her authority and mission, orienta- *1544* tion and goal:

> In order to shepherd the People of God and to increase its numbers without cease, Christ the Lord set up in his Church a variety of offices which aim at the good of the whole body. The holders of office, who are invested with a sacred power,

---

385   CIC, can. 204 § 1; cf. *LG* 31.
386   CIC, can. 208; cf. *LG* 32.
387   *AA* 2.
388   CIC, can. 207 § 2.

are, in fact, dedicated to promoting the interests of their
brethren, so that all who belong to the People of God . . . may
attain to salvation.[389]

875   "How are they to believe in him of whom they have never
heard? And how are they to hear without a preacher? And how
166 can men preach unless they are sent?"[390] No one – no individual
and no community – can proclaim the Gospel to himself: "Faith
comes from what is heard."[391] No one can give himself the mandate and the mission to proclaim the Gospel. The one sent by the
Lord does not speak and act on his own authority, but by virtue of
Christ's authority; not as a member of the community, but speaking to it in the name of Christ. No one can bestow grace on himself;
it must be given and offered. This fact presupposes ministers of
grace, authorized and empowered by Christ. From him, they re-
1548 ceive the mission and faculty ("the sacred power") to act *in persona*
1536 *Christi Capitis.* The ministry in which Christ's emissaries do and
give by God's grace what they cannot do and give by their own
powers, is called a "sacrament" by the Church's tradition. Indeed,
the ministry of the Church is conferred by a special sacrament.

876   Intrinsically linked to the sacramental nature of ecclesial
ministry is *its character as service.* Entirely dependent on Christ who
1551 gives mission and authority, ministers are truly "slaves of
Christ,"[392] in the image of him who freely took "the form of a slave"
for us.[393] Because the word and grace of which they are ministers
427 are not their own, but are given to them by Christ for the sake of
others, they must freely become the slaves of all.[394]

877   Likewise, it belongs to the sacramental nature of ecclesial
ministry that it have a *collegial character.* In fact, from the beginning
1559 of his ministry, the Lord Jesus instituted the Twelve as "the seeds
of the new Israel and the beginning of the sacred hierarchy."[395]
Chosen together, they were also sent out together, and their fraternal unity would be at the service of the fraternal communion of all
the faithful: they would reflect and witness to the communion of
the divine persons.[396] For this reason every bishop exercises his
ministry from within the episcopal college, in communion with the

---

389   *LG* 18.
390   *Rom* 10:14-15.
391   *Rom* 10:17.
392   Cf. *Rom* 1:1.
393   *Phil* 2:7.
394   Cf. *1 Cor* 9:19.
395   *AG* 5.
396   Cf. *Jn* 17:21-23.

bishop of Rome, the successor of St. Peter and head of the college. So also priests exercise their ministry from within the *presbyterium* of the diocese, under the direction of their bishop.

878 Finally, it belongs to the sacramental nature of ecclesial ministry that it have a *personal character.* Although Christ's ministers act in communion with one another, they also always act in a personal way. Each one is called personally: "You, follow me"[397] in order to be a personal witness within the common mission, to bear personal responsibility before him who gives the mission, acting "in his person" and for other persons: "I baptize you in the name of the Father 1484 and of the Son and of the Holy Spirit . . ."; "I absolve you. . . ."

879 Sacramental ministry in the Church, then, is at once a collegial and a personal service, exercised in the name of Christ. This is evidenced by the bonds between the episcopal college and its head, the successor of St. Peter, and in the relationship between the bishop's pastoral responsibility for his particular church and the common solicitude of the episcopal college for the universal Church.

The episcopal college and its head, the Pope

880 When Christ instituted the Twelve, "he constituted [them] in the form of a college or permanent assembly, at the head of which he placed Peter, chosen from among them."[398] Just as "by 552, 862 the Lord's institution, St. Peter and the rest of the apostles constitute a single apostolic college, so in like fashion the Roman Pontiff, Peter's successor, and the bishops, the successors of the apostles, are related with and united to one another."[399]

881 The Lord made Simon alone, whom he named Peter, the "rock" of his Church. He gave him the keys of his Church and instituted him shepherd of the whole flock.[400] "The office of bind- 553 ing and loosing which was given to Peter was also assigned to the college of apostles united to its head."[401] This pastoral office of Peter and the other apostles belongs to the Church's very founda- 642 tion and is continued by the bishops under the primacy of the Pope.

---

397 *Jn* 21:22; Cf. *Mt* 4:19. 21; *Jn* 1:4.
398 *LG* 19; cf. *Lk* 6:13; *Jn* 21:15-17.
399 *LG* 22; cf. CIC, can. 330.
400 Cf. *Mt* 16:18-19; *Jn* 21:15-17.
401 *LG* 22 § 2.

882   The *Pope,* Bishop of Rome and Peter's successor, "is the
perpetual and visible source and foundation of the unity both of
834, 1369 the bishops and of the whole company of the faithful."[402] "For the
837 Roman Pontiff, by reason of his office as Vicar of Christ, and as
pastor of the entire Church has full, supreme, and universal power
over the whole Church, a power which he can always exercise
unhindered."[403]

883   "The *college or body of bishops* has no authority unless united
with the Roman Pontiff, Peter's successor, as its head." As such,
this college has "supreme and full authority over the universal
Church; but this power cannot be exercised without the agreement
of the Roman Pontiff."[404]

884   "The college of bishops exercises power over the universal
Church in a solemn manner in an ecumenical council."[405] But
"there never is an ecumenical council which is not confirmed or at
least recognized as such by Peter's successor."[406]

885   "This college, in so far as it is composed of many members,
is the expression of the variety and universality of the People of
God; and of the unity of the flock of Christ, in so far as it is
assembled under one head."[407]

886   "The individual *bishops* are the visible source and foundation of unity in their own particular Churches."[408] As such, they
1560, 833 "exercise their pastoral office over the portion of the People of God
assigned to them,"[409] assisted by priests and deacons. But, as a
member of the episcopal college, each bishop shares in the concern
for all the Churches.[410] The bishops exercise this care first "by
ruling well their own Churches as portions of the universal
Church," and so contributing "to the welfare of the whole Mystical
Body, which, from another point of view, is a corporate body of
Churches."[411] They extend it especially to the poor,[412] to those
2448 persecuted for the faith, as well as to missionaries who are working
throughout the world.

---

402   *LG* 23.
403   *LG* 22; cf. *CD* 2, 9.
404   *LG* 22; cf. CIC, can. 336.
405   CIC, can. 337 § 1.
406   *LG* 22.
407   *LG* 22.
408   *LG* 23.
409   *LG* 23.
410   Cf. *CD* 3.
411   *LG* 23.
412   Cf. *Gal* 2:10.

887   Neighboring particular Churches who share the same culture form ecclesiastical provinces or larger groupings called patriarchates or regions.[413] The bishops of these groupings can meet in synods or provincial councils. "In a like fashion, the episcopal conferences at the present time are in a position to contribute in many and fruitful ways to the concrete realization of the collegiate spirit."[414]

The teaching office

85-87, 2032-2040

888   Bishops, with priests as co-workers, have as their first task "to preach the Gospel of God to all men," in keeping with the Lord's command.[415] They are "heralds of faith, who draw new *2068* disciples to Christ; they are authentic teachers" of the apostolic faith "endowed with the authority of Christ."[416]

889   In order to preserve the Church in the purity of the faith handed on by the apostles, Christ who is the Truth willed to confer on her a share in his own infallibility. By a "supernatural sense of *92* faith" the People of God, under the guidance of the Church's living Magisterium, "unfailingly adheres to this faith."[417]

890   The mission of the Magisterium is linked to the definitive nature of the covenant established by God with his people in Christ. It is this Magisterium's task to preserve God's people from deviations and defections and to guarantee them the objective *851* possibility of professing the true faith without error. Thus, the pastoral duty of the Magisterium is aimed at seeing to it that the People of God abides in the truth that liberates. To fulfill this service, Christ endowed the Church's shepherds with the charism of infallibility in matters of faith and morals. The exercise of this *1785* charism takes several forms:

891   "The Roman Pontiff, head of the college of bishops, enjoys this infallibility in virtue of his office, when, as supreme pastor and teacher of all the faithful – who confirms his brethren in the faith – he proclaims by a definitive act a doctrine pertaining to faith or morals. . . . The infallibility promised to the Church is also present in the body of bishops when, together with Peter's successor, they exercise the supreme Magisterium," above all in an Ecumenical Council.[418] When the Church through its supreme Magisterium

---

413   Cf. *Apostolic Constitutions* 34.
414   *LG* 23 § 3.
415   *PO* 4; cf. *Mk* 16:15.
416   *LG* 25.
417   *LG* 12; cf. *DV* 10.

proposes a doctrine "for belief as being divinely revealed,"[419] and as the teaching of Christ, the definitions "must be adhered to with the obedience of faith."[420] This infallibility extends as far as the deposit of divine Revelation itself.[421]

892   Divine assistance is also given to the successors of the apostles, teaching in communion with the successor of Peter, and, in a particular way, to the bishop of Rome, pastor of the whole Church, when, without arriving at an infallible definition and without pronouncing in a "definitive manner," they propose in the exercise of the ordinary Magisterium a teaching that leads to better understanding of Revelation in matters of faith and morals. To this ordinary teaching the faithful "are to adhere to it with religious assent"[422] which, though distinct from the assent of faith, is nonetheless an extension of it.

The sanctifying office

893   The bishop is "the steward of the grace of the supreme priesthood,"[423] especially in the Eucharist which he offers person-
1561 ally or whose offering he assures through the priests, his co-workers. The Eucharist is the center of the life of the particular Church. The bishop and priests sanctify the Church by their prayer and work, by their ministry of the word and of the sacraments. They sanctify her by their example, "not as domineering over those in your charge but being examples to the flock."[424] Thus, "together with the flock entrusted to them, they may attain to eternal life."[425]

The governing office

894   "The bishops, as vicars and legates of Christ, govern the particular Churches assigned to them by their counsels, exhortations, and example, but over and above that also by the authority
801 and sacred power" which indeed they ought to exercise so as to edify, in the spirit of service which is that of their Master.[426]

---

418 *LG* 25; cf. Vatican Council I: DS 3074.
419 *DV* 10 § 2.
420 *LG* 25 § 2.
421 Cf. *LG* 25.
422 *LG* 25.
423 *LG* 26.
424 *1 Pet* 5:3.
425 *LG* 26 § 3.
426 *LG* 27; cf. *Lk* 22:26-27.

895   "The power which they exercise personally in the name of Christ, is proper, ordinary, and immediate, although its exercise is ultimately controlled by the supreme authority of the Church."[427]   *1558* But the bishops should not be thought of as vicars of the Pope. His ordinary and immediate authority over the whole Church does not annul, but on the contrary confirms and defends that of the bishops. Their authority must be exercised in communion with the whole Church under the guidance of the Pope.

896   The Good Shepherd ought to be the model and "form" of the bishop's pastoral office. Conscious of his own weaknesses, "the bishop . . . can have compassion for those who are ignorant and erring. He should not refuse to listen to his subjects whose welfare   *1550* he promotes as of his very own children. . . . The faithful . . . should be closely attached to the bishop as the Church is to Jesus Christ, and as Jesus Christ is to the Father":[428]

> Let all follow the bishop, as Jesus Christ follows his Father, and the college of presbyters as the apostles; respect the deacons as you do God's law. Let no one do anything concerning the Church in separation from the bishop.[429]

II.   THE LAY FAITHFUL

897   "The term 'laity' is here understood to mean all the faithful except those in Holy Orders and those who belong to a religious state approved by the Church. That is, the faithful, who by Baptism   *873* are incorporated into Christ and integrated into the People of God, are made sharers in their particular way in the priestly, prophetic, and kingly office of Christ, and have their own part to play in the mission of the whole Christian people in the Church and in the world."[430]

The vocation of lay people

898   "By reason of their special vocation it belongs to the laity to seek the kingdom of God by engaging in temporal affairs and directing them according to God's will. . . . It pertains to them in a   *2105* special way so to illuminate and order all temporal things with which they are closely associated that these may always be effected

---

427   *LG* 27.
428   *LG* 27 § 2.
429   St. Ignatius of Antioch, *Ad Smyrn.* 8, 1: *Apostolic Fathers*, II/2, 309.
430   *LG* 31.

and grow according to Christ and may be to the glory of the Creator and Redeemer."[431]

899   The initiative of lay Christians is necessary especially when the matter involves discovering or inventing the means for
2442   permeating social, political, and economic realities with the demands of Christian doctrine and life. This initiative is a normal element of the life of the Church:

> Lay believers are in the front line of Church life; for them the Church is the animating principle of human society. Therefore, they in particular ought to have an ever-clearer consciousness not only of belonging to the Church, but of being the Church, that is to say, the community of the faithful on earth under the leadership of the Pope, the common Head, and of the bishops in communion with him. They are the Church.[432]

900   Since, like all the faithful, lay Christians are entrusted by God with the apostolate by virtue of their Baptism and Confirma-
863   tion, they have the right and duty, individually or grouped in associations, to work so that the divine message of salvation may be known and accepted by all men throughout the earth. This duty is the more pressing when it is only through them that men can hear the Gospel and know Christ. Their activity in ecclesial communities is so necessary that, for the most part, the apostolate of the pastors cannot be fully effective without it.[433]

The participation of lay people in Christ's priestly office

901   "Hence the laity, dedicated as they are to Christ and anointed by the Holy Spirit, are marvellously called and prepared
784, 1268   so that even richer fruits of the Spirit may be produced in them. For all their works, prayers, and apostolic undertakings, family and married life, daily work, relaxation of mind and body, if they are accomplished in the Spirit – indeed even the hardships of life if patiently born – all these become spiritual sacrifices acceptable to God through Jesus Christ. In the celebration of the Eucharist these may most fittingly be offered to the Father along with the body of the Lord. And so, worshipping everywhere by their holy actions,
358   the laity consecrate the world itself to God, everywhere offering worship by the holiness of their lives."[434]

---

431   *LG* 31 § 2.
432   Pius XII, Discourse, February 20, 1946: AAS 38 (1946) 149; quoted by John Paul II, *CL* 9.
433   Cf. *LG* 33.
434   *LG* 34; cf. *LG* 10; 1 *Pet* 2:5.

902   In a very special way, parents share in the office of sanctifying "by leading a conjugal life in the Christian spirit and by seeing to the Christian education of their children."[435]

903   Lay people who possess the required qualities can be admitted permanently to the ministries of lector and acolyte.[436] When the necessity of the Church warrants it and when ministers are lacking, lay persons, *1143* even if they are not lectors or acolytes, can also supply for certain of their offices, namely, to exercise the ministry of the word, to preside over liturgical prayers, to confer Baptism, and to distribute Holy Communion in accord with the prescriptions of law."[437]

Participation in Christ's prophetic office

904   "Christ . . . fulfills this prophetic office, not only by the hierarchy . . . but also by the laity. He accordingly both establishes *785* them as witnesses and provides them with the sense of the faith *92* [*sensus fidei*] and the grace of the word"[438]

> To teach in order to lead others to faith is the task of every preacher and of each believer.[439]

905   Lay people also fulfill their prophetic mission by evangeli- *2044* zation, "that is, the proclamation of Christ by word and the testimony of life." For lay people, "this evangelization . . . acquires a specific property and peculiar efficacy because it is accomplished in the ordinary circumstances of the world."[440]

> This witness of life, however, is not the sole element in the apostolate; the true apostle is on the lookout for occasions of announcing Christ by word, either to unbelievers . . . or to the faithful.[441]   *2472*

906   Lay people who are capable and trained may also collaborate in *2495* catechetical formation, in teaching the sacred sciences, and in use of the communications media.[442]

907   "In accord with the knowledge, competence, and preeminence which they possess, [lay people] have the right and even at times a duty to manifest to the sacred pastors their opinion on matters which pertain to the good of the Church, and they have a right to make their opinion known to the other Christian faithful, with due regard to the integrity of faith and

---

435   CIC, can. 835 § 4.
436   Cf. CIC, can. 230 § 1.
437   CIC, can. 230 § 3.
438   *LG* 35.
439   St. Thomas Aquinas, *STh.* III, 71, 4 *ad* 3.
440   *LG* 35 § 1, § 2.
441   *AA* 6 § 3; cf. *AG* 15.
442   Cf. CIC, cann. 229; 774; 776; 780; 823 § 1.

morals and reverence toward their pastors, and with consideration for the common good and the dignity of persons."[443]

Participation in Christ's kingly office

908   By his obedience unto death,[444] Christ communicated to his disciples the gift of royal freedom, so that they might "by the *786* self-abnegation of a holy life, overcome the reign of sin in them-selves":[445]

> That man is rightly called a king who makes his own body an obedient subject and, by governing himself with suitable rigor, refuses to let his passions breed rebellion in his soul, for he exercises a kind of royal power over himself. And because he knows how to rule his own person as king, so too does he sit as its judge. He will not let himself be imprisoned by sin, or thrown headlong into wickedness.[446]

909   "Moreover, by uniting their forces let the laity so remedy the institutions and conditions of the world when the latter are an *1887* inducement to sin, that these may be conformed to the norms of justice, favoring rather than hindering the practice of virtue. By so doing they will impregnate culture and human works with a moral value."[447]

910   "The laity can also feel called, or be in fact called, to cooperate with their pastors in the service of the ecclesial commu-*799* nity, for the sake of its growth and life. This can be done through the exercise of different kinds of ministries according to the grace and charisms which the Lord has been pleased to bestow on them."[448]

911   In the Church, "lay members of the Christian faithful can cooperate in the exercise of this power [of governance] in accord with the norm of law."[449] And so the Church provides for their presence at particular councils, diocesan synods, pastoral councils; the exercise in solidum of the pastoral care of a parish, collaboration in finance committees, and participation in ecclesiastical tribunals, etc.[450]

---

443   CIC, can. 212 § 3.
444   Cf. *Phil* 2:8-9.
445   *LG* 36.
446   St. Ambrose, *Psal. 118*:14:30: PL 15:1476.
447   *LG* 36 § 3.
448   Paul VI, *EN* 73.
449   CIC, can. 129 § 2.
450   Cf. CIC, cann. 443 § 4; 463 §§ 1 and 2; 492 § 1; 511; 517 § 2; 536; 1421 § 2.

912 The faithful should "distinguish carefully between the rights and the duties which they have as belonging to the Church and those which fall to them as members of the human society. *2245* They will strive to unite the two harmoniously, remembering that in every temporal affair they are to be guided by a Christian conscience, since no human activity, even of the temporal order, can be withdrawn from God's dominion."[451]

913 "Thus, every person, through these gifts given to him, is at once the witness and the living instrument of the mission of the Church itself 'according to the measure of Christ's bestowal.'"[452]

III. THE CONSECRATED LIFE

914 "The state of life which is constituted by the profession of the evangelical counsels, while not entering into the hierarchical structure of the Church, belongs undeniably to her life and holi- *2103* ness."[453]

Evangelical counsels, consecrated life

915 Christ proposes the evangelical counsels, in their great variety, to every disciple. The perfection of charity, to which all the faithful are called, entails for those who freely follow the call to *1973-1974* consecrated life the obligation of practicing chastity in celibacy for the sake of the Kingdom, poverty and obedience. It is the *profession* of these counsels, within a permanent state of life recognized by the Church, that characterizes the life consecrated to God.[454]

916 The religious state is thus one way of experiencing a "more intimate" consecration, rooted in Baptism and dedicated totally to God.[455] In the consecrated life, Christ's faithful, moved by the Holy *2687* Spirit, propose to follow Christ more nearly, to give themselves to God who is loved above all and, pursuing the perfection of charity in the service of the Kingdom, to signify and proclaim in the *933* Church the glory of the world to come.[456]

---

451 *LG* 36 § 4.
452 *LG* 33 § 2; cf. *Eph* 4:7.
453 *LG* 44 § 4.
454 Cf. *LG* 42-43; *PC* 1.
455 Cf. *PC* 5.
456 Cf. *CIC,* can. 573.

One great tree, with many branches

917   "From the God-given seed of the counsels a wonderful and wide-spreading tree has grown up in the field of the Lord, branch-
2684 ing out into various forms of the religious life lived in solitude or in community. Different religious families have come into exist-ence in which spiritual resources are multiplied for the progress in holiness of their members and for the good of the entire Body of Christ."[457]

918   From the very beginning of the Church there were men and women who set out to follow Christ with greater liberty, and to imitate him more closely, by practicing the evangelical counsels. They led lives dedicated to God, each in his own way. Many of them, under the inspira-tion of the Holy Spirit, became hermits or founded religious families. These the Church, by virtue of her authority, gladly accepted and approved.[458]

919   Bishops will always strive to discern new gifts of conse-crated life granted to the Church by the Holy Spirit; the approval of new forms of consecrated life is reserved to the Apostolic See.[459]

The eremitic life

920   Without always professing the three evangelical counsels publicly, hermits "devote their life to the praise of God and salva-tion of the world through a stricter separation from the world, the silence of solitude and assiduous prayer and penance."[460]

921   They manifest to everyone the interior aspect of the mys-tery of the Church, that is, personal intimacy with Christ. Hidden
2719 from the eyes of men, the life of the hermit is a silent preaching of the Lord, to whom he has surrendered his life simply because he
2015 is everything to him. Here is a particular call to find in the desert, in the thick of spiritual battle, the glory of the Crucified One.

Consecrated virgins

922   From apostolic times Christian virgins, called by the Lord to cling only to him with greater freedom of heart, body, and spirit,
1618-1620 have decided with the Church's approval to live in a state of virginity "for the sake of the Kingdom of heaven."[461]

---

457 *LG* 43.
458 *PC* 1.
459 Cf. CIC, can. 605.
460 CIC, can. 603 § 1.
461 *Mt* 19:12; cf. *1 Cor* 7:34-36.

923   "Virgins who, committed to the holy plan of following Christ more closely, are consecrated to God by the diocesan bishop according to the approved liturgical rite, are betrothed mystically   *1537* to Christ, the Son of God, and are dedicated to the service of the Church."[462] By this solemn rite (*Consecratio Virginum*), the virgin   *1672* is "constituted . . . a sacred person, a transcendent sign of the Church's love for Christ, and an eschatological image of this heavenly Bride of Christ and of the life to come."[463]

924   "As with other forms of consecrated life," the order of virgins establishes the woman living in the world (or the nun) in prayer, penance, service of her brethren, and apostolic activity, according to the state of life and spiritual gifts given to her.[464] Consecrated virgins can form themselves into associations to observe their commitment more faithfully.[465]

Religious life

925   Religious life was born in the East during the first centuries of Christianity. Lived within institutes canonically erected by the Church, it is distinguished from other forms of consecrated life by its liturgical character, public profession of the evangelical coun-   *1672* sels, fraternal life led in common, and witness given to the union of Christ with the Church.[466]

926   Religious life derives from the mystery of the Church. It is a gift she has received from her Lord, a gift she offers as a stable way of life to the faithful called by God to profess the counsels. Thus, the Church can both show forth Christ and acknowledge herself to be the Savior's bride. Religious life in its various forms is   *796* called to signify the very charity of God in the language of our time.

927   All religious, whether exempt or not, take their place among the collaborators of the diocesan bishop in his pastoral duty.[467] From the outset of the work of evangelization, the missionary "planting" and expansion of the Church require the presence   *854* of the religious life in all its forms.[468] "History witnesses to the outstanding service rendered by religious families in the propaga-

---

462   CIC, can. 604 § 1.
463   *Ordo Consecrationis Virginum, Praenotanda* 1.
464   Cf. CIC, can. 604 § 1; *OCV Praenotanda* 2.
465   Cf. CIC, can. 604 § 2.
466   Cf. CIC, cann. 607; 573; UR 15.
467   Cf. *CD* 33-35; CIC, can. 591.
468   Cf. *AG* 18; 40.

tion of the faith and in the formation of new Churches: from the ancient monastic institutions to the medieval orders, all the way to the more recent congregations."[469]

Secular institutes

928   "A secular institute is an institute of consecrated life in which the Christian faithful living in the world strive for the perfection of charity and work for the sanctification of the world especially from within."[470]

929   By a "life perfectly and entirely consecrated to [such] sanctification," the members of these institutes share in the Church's task of evangelization, "in the world and from within the 901 world," where their presence acts as "leaven in the world."[471] "Their witness of a Christian life" aims "to order temporal things according to God and inform the world with the power of the gospel." They commit themselves to the evangelical counsels by sacred bonds and observe among themselves the communion and fellowship appropriate to their "particular secular way of life."[472]

Societies of apostolic life

930   Alongside the different forms of consecrated life are "societies of apostolic life whose members without religious vows pursue the particular apostolic purpose of their society, and lead a life as brothers or sisters in common according to a particular manner of life, strive for the perfection of charity through the observance of the constitutions. Among these there are societies in which the members embrace the evangelical counsels" according to their constitutions.[473]

Consecration and mission: proclaiming the King who is coming

931   Already dedicated to him through Baptism, the person who surrenders himself to the God he loves above all else thereby consecrates himself more intimately to God's service and to the good of the Church. By this state of life consecrated to God, the Church manifests Christ and shows us how the Holy Spirit acts so wonderfully in her. And so the first mission of those who profess the evangelical counsels is to live out their consecration. Moreover,

---

469   John Paul II, *RMiss* 69.
470   CIC, can. 710.
471   Pius XII, *Provida Mater*; cf. PC 11.
472   Cf. CIC, can. 713 § 2.
473   Cf. CIC, can. 731 §§ 1 and 2.

"since members of institutes of consecrated life dedicate themselves through their consecration to the service of the Church they are obliged in a special manner to engage in missionary work, in accord with the character of the institute."[474]

932   In the Church, which is like the sacrament – the sign and instrument – of God's own life, the consecrated life is seen as a special sign of the mystery of redemption. To follow and imitate Christ more *775* nearly and to manifest more clearly his self-emptying is to be more deeply present to one's contemporaries, in the heart of Christ. For those who are on this "narrower" path encourage their brethren by their example, and bear striking witness "that the world cannot be transfigured and offered to God without the spirit of the Beatitudes."[475]

933   Whether their witness is public, as in the religious state, or less public, or even secret, Christ's coming remains for all those consecrated both the origin and rising sun of their life: *672*

> For the People of God has here no lasting city, . . . [and this *769* state] reveals more clearly to all believers the heavenly goods which are already present in this age, witnessing to the new and eternal life which we have acquired through the redemptive work of Christ and preluding our future resurrection and the glory of the heavenly kingdom.[476]

IN BRIEF

934   "Among the Christian faithful by divine institution there exist in the Church sacred ministers, who are also called clerics in law, and other Christian faithful who are also called laity." In both groups there are those Christian faithful who, professing the evangelical counsels, are consecrated to God and so serve the Church's saving mission (cf. CIC, can. 207 § 1, 2).

935   To proclaim the faith and to plant his reign, Christ sends his apostles and their successors. He gives them a share in his own mission. From him they receive the power to act in his person.

936   The Lord made St. Peter the visible foundation of his Church. He entrusted the keys of the Church to him. The bishop of the Church of Rome, successor to St. Peter, is "head of the college of bishops, the Vicar of Christ and

---

474   CIC, can. 783; cf. *RM* 69.
475   *LG* 31 § 2.
476   *LG* 44 § 3.

Pastor of the universal Church on earth" (CIC, can. 331).

937   The Pope enjoys, by divine institution, "supreme, full, immediate, and universal power in the care of souls" (*CD* 2).

938   The Bishops, established by the Holy Spirit, succeed the apostles. They are "the visible source and foundation of unity in their own particular Churches" (*LG* 23).

939   Helped by the priests, their co-workers, and by the deacons, the bishops have the duty of authentically teaching the faith, celebrating divine worship, above all the Eucharist, and guiding their Churches as true pastors. Their responsibility also includes concern for all the Churches, with and under the Pope.

940   "The characteristic of the lay state being a life led in the midst of the world and of secular affairs, lay people are called by God to make of their apostolate, through the vigor of their Christian spirit, a leaven in the world" (*AA* 2 § 2).

941   Lay people share in Christ's priesthood: ever more united with him, they exhibit the grace of Baptism and Confirmation in all dimensions of their personal, family, social, and ecclesial lives, and so fulfill the call to holiness addressed to all the baptized.

942   By virtue of their prophetic mission, lay people "are called ... to be witnesses to Christ in all circumstances and at the very heart of the community of mankind" (*GS* 43 § 4).

943   By virtue of their kingly mission, lay people have the power to uproot the rule of sin within themselves and in the world, by their self-denial and holiness of life (cf. *LG* 36).

944   The life consecrated to God is characterized by the public profession of the evangelical counsels of poverty, chastity, and obedience, in a stable state of life recognized by the Church.

945   Already destined for him through Baptism, the person who surrenders himself to the God he loves above all else thereby consecrates himself more intimately to God's service and to the good of the whole Church.

Paragraph 5. The Communion of Saints *1474-1477*

946   After confessing "the holy catholic Church," the Apostles' Creed adds "the communion of saints." In a certain sense this article is a further explanation of the preceding: "What is the *823* Church if not the assembly of all the saints?"[477] The communion of saints is the Church.

947   "Since all the faithful form one body, the good of each is communicated to the others. . . . We must therefore believe that there exists a communion of goods in the Church. But the most important member is Christ, since he is the head. . . . Therefore, the *790* riches of Christ are communicated to all the members, through the sacraments."[478] "As this Church is governed by one and the same Spirit, all the goods she has received necessarily become a common fund."[479]

948   The term "communion of saints" therefore has two closely linked meanings: communion "in holy things (*sancta*)" and *1331* "among holy persons (*sancti*)."

> *Sancta sanctis!* ("God's holy gifts for God's holy people") is proclaimed by the celebrant in most Eastern liturgies during the elevation of the holy Gifts before the distribution of communion. The faithful (*sancti*) are fed by Christ's holy body and blood (*sancta*) to grow in the communion of the Holy Spirit (*koinonia*) and to communicate it to the world.

I.   COMMUNION IN SPIRITUAL GOODS

949   In the primitive community of Jerusalem, the disciples "devoted themselves to the apostles' teaching and fellowship, to the breaking of the bread and the prayers."[480]

Communion in the faith. The faith of the faithful is the faith *185* of the Church, received from the apostles. Faith is a treasure of life which is enriched by being shared.

---

477 Nicetas, *Expl. symb.* 10: PL 52:871B.
478 St. Thomas Aquinas, *Symb.*, 10.
479 *Roman Catechism* I, 10, 24.
480 *Acts* 2:42.

950   *Communion of the sacraments.* "The fruit of all the sacra-
1130   ments belongs to all the faithful. All the sacraments are sacred links
uniting the faithful with one another and binding them to Jesus
Christ, and above all Baptism, the gate by which we enter into the
Church. The communion of saints must be understood as the
communion of the sacraments. . . . The name 'communion' can be
1331   applied to all of them, for they unite us to God. . . . But this name
is better suited to the Eucharist than to any other, because it is
primarily the Eucharist that brings this communion about."[481]

951   *Communion of charisms.* Within the communion of the
Church, the Holy Spirit "distributes special graces among the
799   faithful of every rank" for the building up of the Church.[482] Now,
"to each is given the manifestation of the Spirit for the common
good."[483]

952   *"They had everything in common."*[484] "Everything the true
Christian has is to be regarded as a good possessed in common
2402   with everyone else. All Christians should be ready and eager to
come to the help of the needy . . . and of their neighbors in want."[485]
A Christian is a steward of the Lord's goods.[486]

953   *Communion in charity.* In the sanctorum communio, "None
1827   of us lives to himself, and none of us dies to himself."[487] "If one
member suffers, all suffer together; if one member is honored, all
rejoice together. Now you are the body of Christ and individually
2011   members of it."[488] "Charity does not insist on its own way."[489] In
this solidarity with all men, living or dead, which is founded on
845, 1469   the communion of saints, the least of our acts done in charity
redounds to the profit of all. Every sin harms this communion.

---

481   *Roman Catechism* I, 10, 24.
482   *LG* 12 § 2.
483   *1 Cor* 12:7.
484   *Acts* 4:32.
485   *Roman Catechism* I, 10, 27.
486   Cf. *Lk* 16:1, 3.
487   *Rom* 14:7.
488   *1 Cor* 12:26-27.
489   *1 Cor* 13:5; cf. 10:24.

II. THE COMMUNION OF THE CHURCH OF HEAVEN AND EARTH

954 *The three states of the Church.* "When the Lord comes in glory, and all his angels with him, death will be no more and all things will be subject to him. But at the present time some of his *771* disciples are pilgrims on earth. Others have died and are being *1031* purified, while still others are in glory, contemplating 'in full light, *1023* God himself triune and one, exactly as he is'":[490]

> All of us, however, in varying degrees and in different ways share in the same charity towards God and our neighbours, and we all sing the one hymn of glory to our God. All, indeed, who are of Christ and who have his Spirit form one Church and in Christ cleave together.[491]

955 "So it is that the union of the wayfarers with the brethren who sleep in the peace of Christ is in no way interrupted, but on the contrary, according to the constant faith of the Church, this union is reinforced by an exchange of spiritual goods."[492]

956 *The intercession of the saints.* "Being more closely united to Christ, those who dwell in heaven fix the whole Church more firmly in holiness. . . . [T]hey do not cease to intercede with the *1370* Father for us, as they proffer the merits which they acquired on *2683* earth through the one mediator between God and men, Christ Jesus. . . . So by their fraternal concern is our weakness greatly helped."[493]

> Do not weep, for I shall be more useful to you after my death and I shall help you then more effectively than during my life.[494]

> I want to spend my heaven in doing good on earth.[495]

957 *Communion with the saints.* "It is not merely by the title of example that we cherish the memory of those in heaven; we seek, rather, that by this devotion to the exercise of fraternal charity the *1173* union of the whole Church in the Spirit may be strengthened. Exactly as Christian communion among our fellow pilgrims brings us closer to Christ, so our communion with the saints joins us to

---

490 *LG* 49; cf. *Mt* 25:31; *1 Cor* 15:26-27; Council of Florence (1439): DS 1305.
491 *LG* 49; cf. *Eph* 4:16.
492 *LG* 49.
493 *LG* 49; cf. *1 Tim* 2:5.
494 St. Dominic, dying, to his brothers.
495 St. Thérèse of Lisieux, *The Final Conversations,* tr. John Clarke (Washington: ICS, 1977), 102.

Christ, from whom as from its fountain and head issues all grace, and the life of the People of God itself"[496]:

> We worship Christ as God's Son; we love the martyrs as the Lord's disciples and imitators, and rightly so because of their matchless devotion towards their king and master. May we also be their companions and fellow disciples![497]

958   *Communion with the dead.* "In full consciousness of this
1371   communion of the whole Mystical Body of Jesus Christ, the Church
1032, 1689   in its pilgrim members, from the very earliest days of the Christian religion, has honored with great respect the memory of the dead; and 'because it is a holy and a wholesome thought to pray for the dead that they may be loosed from their sins' she offers her suffrages for them."[498] Our prayer for them is capable not only of helping them, but also of making their intercession for us effective.

959   *In the one family of God.* "For if we continue to love one another and to join in praising the Most Holy Trinity – all of us who
1027   are sons of God and form one family in Christ – we will be faithful to the deepest vocation of the Church."[499]

IN BRIEF

960   The Church is a "communion of saints": this expression refers first to the "holy things" (*sancta*), above all the Eucharist, by which "the unity of believers, who form one body in Christ, is both represented and brought about" (*LG* 3).

961   The term "communion of saints" refers also to the communion of "holy persons" (*sancti*) in Christ who "died for all," so that what each one does or suffers in and for Christ bears fruit for all.

962   "We believe in the communion of all the faithful of Christ, those who are pilgrims on earth, the dead who are being purified, and the blessed in heaven, all together forming one Church; and we believe that in this communion, the merciful love of God and his saints is always [attentive] to our prayers" (Paul VI, *CPG* § 30).

---

496 *LG* 50; cf. *Eph* 4:1-6.
497 *Martyrium Polycarpi*, 17: *Apostolic Fathers* II/3, 396.
498 *LG* 50; cf. *2 Macc* 12:45.
499 *LG* 51; cf. *Heb* 3:6.

Paragraph 6. Mary – Mother of Christ, Mother of the Church

963   Since the Virgin Mary's role in the mystery of Christ and the Spirit has been treated, it is fitting now to consider her place in the mystery of the Church. "The Virgin Mary . . . is acknowledged *484-507,* and honored as being truly the Mother of God and of the re- *721-726* deemer. . . . She is 'clearly the mother of the members of Christ' . . . since she has by her charity joined in bringing about the birth of believers in the Church, who are members of its head."[500] "Mary, Mother of Christ, Mother of the Church."[501]

I.   MARY'S MOTHERHOOD WITH REGARD TO THE CHURCH

Wholly united with her Son . . .

964   Mary's role in the Church is inseparable from her union with Christ and flows directly from it. "This union of the mother with the Son in the work of salvation is made manifest from the time of Christ's virginal conception up to his death";[502] it is made manifest above all at the hour of his Passion:

> Thus the Blessed Virgin advanced in her pilgrimage of faith,   *534* and faithfully persevered in her union with her Son unto the cross. There she stood, in keeping with the divine plan, enduring with her only begotten Son the intensity of his suffering, joining herself with his sacrifice in her mother's heart, and lovingly consenting to the immolation of this victim, born of her: to be given, by the same Christ Jesus   *618* dying on the cross, as a mother to his disciple, with these words: "Woman, behold your son."[503]

965   After her Son's Ascension, Mary "aided the beginnings of the Church by her prayers."[504] In her association with the apostles and several women, "we also see Mary by her prayers imploring the gift of the Spirit, who had already overshadowed her in the Annunciation."[505]

---

500   *LG* 53; cf. St. Augustine, *De virg.* 6: PL 40, 399.
501   Paul VI, Discourse, November 21, 1964.
502   *LG* 57.
503   *LG* 58; cf. *Jn* 19:26-27.
504   *LG* 69.
505   *LG* 59.

... also in her Assumption

966   "Finally the Immaculate Virgin, preserved free from all stain of original sin, when the course of her earthly life was fin-
491 ished, was taken up body and soul into heavenly glory, and exalted by the Lord as Queen over all things, so that she might be the more fully conformed to her Son, the Lord of lords and conqueror of sin and death."[506] The Assumption of the Blessed Virgin is a singular participation in her Son's Resurrection and an anticipation of the resurrection of other Christians:

> In giving birth you kept your virginity; in your Dormition you did not leave the world, O Mother of God, but were joined to the source of Life. You conceived the living God and, by your prayers, will deliver our souls from death.[507]

... she is our Mother in the order of grace

967   By her complete adherence to the Father's will, to his Son's redemptive work, and to every prompting of the Holy Spirit, the
2679 Virgin Mary is the Church's model of faith and charity. Thus she is a "preeminent and ... wholly unique member of the Church";
507 indeed, she is the "exemplary realization" (*typus*)[508] of the Church.

968   Her role in relation to the Church and to all humanity goes still further. "In a wholly singular way she cooperated by her
494 obedience, faith, hope, and burning charity in the Savior's work of restoring supernatural life to souls. For this reason she is a mother to us in the order of grace."[509]

969   "This motherhood of Mary in the order of grace continues
149, 501 uninterruptedly from the consent which she loyally gave at the Annunciation and which she sustained without wavering beneath the cross, until the eternal fulfilment of all the elect. Taken up to heaven she did not lay aside this saving office but by her manifold
1370 intercession continues to bring us the gifts of eternal salvation .... Therefore the Blessed Virgin is invoked in the Church under the titles of Advocate, Helper, Benefactress, and Mediatrix."[510]

---

506   *LG* 59; cf. Pius XII, *Munificentissimus Deus* (1950): DS 3903; cf. *Rev* 19:16.
507   Byzantine Liturgy, *Troparion,* Feast of the Dormition, August 15th.
508   *LG* 53; 63.
509   *LG* 61.
510   *LG* 62.

970   "Mary's function as mother of men in no way obscures or dimin-
ishes this unique mediation of Christ, but rather shows its power. But the
Blessed Virgin's salutary influence on men . . . flows forth from the   *2008*
superabundance of the merits of Christ, rests on his mediation, depends
entirely on it, and draws all its power from it."[511] "No creature could ever
be counted along with the Incarnate Word and Redeemer; but just as the   *1545*
priesthood of Christ is shared in various ways both by his ministers and
the faithful, and as the one goodness of God is radiated in different ways
among his creatures, so also the unique mediation of the Redeemer does
not exclude but rather gives rise to a manifold cooperation which is but a
sharing in this one source."[512]   *308*

II.   DEVOTION TO THE BLESSED VIRGIN   *2673-2679*

971   *"All generations will call me blessed"*: "The Church's devotion to the Blessed Virgin is intrinsic to Christian worship."[513] The
Church rightly honors "the Blessed Virgin with special devotion.   *1172*
From the most ancient times the Blessed Virgin has been honored
with the title of 'Mother of God,' to whose protection the faithful
fly in all their dangers and needs. . . . This very special devotion . . .
differs essentially from the adoration which is given to the incarnate Word and equally to the Father and the Holy Spirit, and   *2678*
greatly fosters this adoration."[514] The liturgical feasts dedicated to
the Mother of God and Marian prayer, such as the rosary, an
"epitome of the whole Gospel," express this devotion to the Virgin
Mary.[515]

III.   MARY – ESCHATOLOGICAL ICON OF THE CHURCH

972   After speaking of the Church, her origin, mission, and
destiny, we can find no better way to conclude than by looking to
Mary. In her we contemplate what the Church already is in her
mystery on her own "pilgrimage of faith," and what she will be in   *773*
the homeland at the end of her journey. There, "in the glory of the
Most Holy and Undivided Trinity," "in the communion of all the
saints,"[516] the Church is awaited by the one she venerates as   *829*
Mother of her Lord and as her own mother.

> In the meantime the Mother of Jesus, in the glory which she   *2853*
> possesses in body and soul in heaven, is the image and
> beginning of the Church as it is to be perfected in the world

---

511 *LG* 60.
512 *LG* 62.
513 *Lk* 1:48; Paul VI, *MC* 56.
514 *LG* 66.
515 Cf. Paul VI, *MC* 42; *SC* 103.
516 *LG* 69.

to come. Likewise she shines forth on earth, until the day of the Lord shall come, a sign of certain hope and comfort to the pilgrim People of God.[517]

IN BRIEF

973   By pronouncing her "fiat" at the Annunciation and giving her consent to the Incarnation, Mary was already collaborating with the whole work her Son was to accomplish. She is mother wherever he is Savior and head of the Mystical Body.

974   The Most Blessed Virgin Mary, when the course of her earthly life was completed, was taken up body and soul into the glory of heaven, where she already shares in the glory of her Son's Resurrection, anticipating the resurrection of all members of his Body.

975   "We believe that the Holy Mother of God, the new Eve, Mother of the Church, continues in heaven to exercise her maternal role on behalf of the members of Christ" (Paul VI, *CPG* § 15).

ARTICLE 10
"I BELIEVE IN THE FORGIVENESS OF SINS"

976   The Apostle's Creed associates faith in the forgiveness of sins not only with faith in the Holy Spirit, but also with faith in the Church and in the communion of saints. It was when he gave the Holy Spirit to his apostles that the risen Christ conferred on them his own divine power to forgive sins: "Receive the Holy Spirit. If you forgive the sins of any, they are forgiven; if you retain the sins of any, they are retained."[518]

> (Part Two of the catechism will deal explicitly with the forgiveness of sins through Baptism, the sacrament of Penance, and the other sacraments, especially the Eucharist. Here it will suffice to suggest some basic facts briefly.)

---

517 *LG* 68; cf. *2 Pet* 3:10.
518 *Jn* 20:22-23.

I.   ONE BAPTISM FOR THE FORGIVENESS OF SINS   *1263*

977   Our Lord tied the forgiveness of sins to faith and Baptism: "Go into all the world and preach the gospel to the whole creation. He who believes and is baptized will be saved."[519] Baptism is the first and chief sacrament of forgiveness of sins because it unites us with Christ, who died for our sins and rose for our justification, so that "we too might walk in newness of life."[520]

978   "When we made our first profession of faith while receiving the holy Baptism that cleansed us, the forgiveness we received then was so full and complete that there remained in us absolutely nothing left to efface, neither original sin nor offenses committed by our own will, nor was there left any penalty to suffer in order to expiate them. . . . Yet the grace of Baptism delivers no one from all the weakness of nature. On the contrary, we must still combat the movements of concupiscence that never cease leading us into *1264* evil."[521]

979   In this battle against our inclination towards evil, who could be brave and watchful enough to escape every wound of sin? "If the Church has the power to forgive sins, then Baptism cannot be her only means of using the keys of the Kingdom of heaven received from Jesus Christ. The Church must be able to forgive all *1446* penitents their offenses, even if they should sin until the last moment of their lives."[522]

980   It is through the sacrament of Penance that the baptized can be reconciled with God and with the Church: *1422-1484*

> Penance has rightly been called by the holy Fathers "a laborious kind of baptism." This sacrament of Penance is necessary for salvation for those who have fallen after Baptism, just as Baptism is necessary for salvation for those who have not yet been reborn.[523]

---

519   *Mk* 16:15-16.
520   *Rom* 6:4; cf. 4:25.
521   *Roman Catechism* I, 11, 3.
522   *Roman Catechism* I, 11, 4.
523   Council of Trent (1551): DS 1672; cf. St. Gregory of Nazianzus, *Oratio* 39, 17: PG 36, 356.

II.   THE POWER OF THE KEYS

981   After his Resurrection, Christ sent his apostles "so that repentance and forgiveness of sins should be preached in his name to all nations."[524] The apostles and their successors carry out this "ministry of reconciliation," not only by announcing to men God's forgiveness merited for us by Christ, and calling them to conversion and faith; but also by communicating to them the forgiveness

1444 of sins in Baptism, and reconciling them with God and with the Church through the power of the keys, received from Christ:[525]

553   [The Church] has received the keys of the Kingdom of heaven so that, in her, sins may be forgiven through Christ's blood and the Holy Spirit's action. In this Church, the soul dead through sin comes back to life in order to live with Christ, whose grace has saved us.[526]

982   There is no offense, however serious, that the Church cannot forgive. "There is no one, however wicked and guilty, who

1463 may not confidently hope for forgiveness, provided his repentance
605   is honest."[527] Christ who died for all men desires that in his Church the gates of forgiveness should always be open to anyone who turns away from sin.[528]

983   Catechesis strives to awaken and nourish in the faithful

1442 faith in the incomparable greatness of the risen Christ's gift to his Church: the mission and the power to forgive sins through the ministry of the apostles and their successors:

1465   The Lord wills that his disciples possess a tremendous power: that his lowly servants accomplish in his name all that he did when he was on earth.[529]

Priests have received from God a power that he has given neither to angels nor to archangels.... God above confirms what priests do here below.[530]

Were there no forgiveness of sins in the Church, there would be no hope of life to come or eternal liberation. Let us thank God who has given his Church such a gift.[531]

---

524   *Lk* 24:47.
525   *2 Cor* 5:18.
526   St. Augustine, *Sermo* 214, 11: PL 38, 1071-1072.
527   *Roman Catechism* I, 11, 5.
528   Cf. *Mt* 18:21-22.
529   Cf. St. Ambrose, *De poenit.* I, 15: PL 16, 490.
530   St. John Chrysostom, *De sac.* 3, 5: PG 48, 643.
531   St. Augustine, *Sermo* 213, 8: PL 38,1064.

IN BRIEF

984 The Creed links "the forgiveness of sins" with its profession of faith in the Holy Spirit, for the risen Christ entrusted to the apostles the power to forgive sins when he gave them the Holy Spirit.

985 Baptism is the first and chief sacrament of the forgiveness of sins: it unites us to Christ, who died and rose, and gives us the Holy Spirit.

986 By Christ's will, the Church possesses the power to forgive the sins of the baptized and exercises it through bishops and priests normally in the sacrament of Penance.

987 "In the forgiveness of sins, both priests and sacraments are instruments which our Lord Jesus Christ, the only author and liberal giver of salvation, wills to use in order to efface our sins and give us the grace of justification" (*Roman Catechism*, I, 11, 6).

ARTICLE 11
"I BELIEVE IN THE RESURRECTION OF THE BODY"

988   The Christian Creed – the profession of our faith in God, the Father, the Son, and the Holy Spirit, and in God's creative, saving, and sanctifying action – culminates in the proclamation of the resurrection of the dead on the last day and in life everlasting.

989   We firmly believe, and hence we hope that, just as Christ is truly risen from the dead and lives for ever, so after death the *655* righteous will live for ever with the risen Christ and he will raise *648* them up on the last day.[532] Our resurrection, like his own, will be the work of the Most Holy Trinity:

> If the Spirit of him who raised Jesus from the dead dwells in you, he who raised Christ Jesus from the dead will give life to your mortal bodies also through his Spirit who dwells in you.[533]

990   The term "flesh" refers to man in his state of weakness and mortality.[534] The "resurrection of the flesh" (the literal formulation of the Apostles' Creed) means not only that the immortal soul will live on after *364* death, but that even our "mortal body" will come to life again.[535]

991   Belief in the resurrection of the dead has been an essential *638* element of the Christian faith from its beginnings. "The confidence of Christians is the resurrection of the dead; believing this we live."[536]

> How can some of you say that there is no resurrection of the dead? But if there is no resurrection of the dead, then Christ has not been raised; if Christ has not been raised, then our preaching is in vain and your faith is in vain. . . . But in fact Christ has been raised from the dead, the first fruits of those who have fallen asleep.[537]

---

532 Cf. *Jn* 6:39-40.
533 *Rom* 8:11; cf. *1 Thess* 4:14; *1 Cor* 6:14; *2 Cor* 4:14; *Phil* 3:10-11.
534 Cf. *Gen* 6:3; *Ps* 56:5; *Isa* 40:6.
535 *Rom* 8:11.
536 Tertullian, *De res.* 1, 1: PL 2, 841.
537 *1 Cor* 15:12-14.

I. CHRIST'S RESURRECTION AND OURS

The progressive revelation of the Resurrection

992   God revealed the resurrection of the dead to his people progressively. Hope in the bodily resurrection of the dead established itself as a consequence intrinsic to faith in God as creator of the whole man, soul and body. The creator of heaven and earth is also the one who faithfully maintains his covenant with Abraham and his posterity. It was in this double perspective that faith in the   *297* resurrection came to be expressed. In their trials, the Maccabean martyrs confessed:

> The King of the universe will raise us up to an everlasting renewal of life, because we have died for his laws.[538] One cannot but choose to die at the hands of men and to cherish the hope that God gives of being raised again by him.[539]

993   The Pharisees and many of the Lord's contemporaries hoped for the resurrection. Jesus teaches it firmly. To the Sadducees who deny it he answers, "Is not this why you are wrong, that you   *575* know neither the scriptures nor the power of God?"[540] Faith in the resurrection rests on faith in God who "is not God of the dead, but of the living."[541]   *205*

994   But there is more. Jesus links faith in the resurrection to his own person: "I am the Resurrection and the life."[542] It is Jesus himself who on the last day will raise up those who have believed in him, who have eaten his body and drunk his blood.[543] Already now in this present life he gives a sign and pledge of this by restoring some of the dead to life,[544] announcing thereby his own   *646* Resurrection, though it was to be of another order. He speaks of this unique event as the "sign of Jonah,"[545] the sign of the temple: he announces that he will be put to death but rise thereafter on the third day.[546]

995   To be a witness to Christ is to be a "witness to his Resur-   *860* rection," to "[have eaten and drunk] with him after he rose from   *655*

---

538 *2 Macc* 7:9.
539 *2 Macc* 7:14; cf. 7:29; *Dan* 12:1-13.
540 *Mk* 12:24; cf. *Jn* 11:24; *Acts* 23:6.
541 *Mk* 12:27.
542 *Jn* 11:25.
543 Cf. *Jn* 5:24-25; 6:40, 54.
544 Cf. *Mk* 5:21-42; *Lk* 7:11-17; *Jn* 11.
545 *Mt* 12:39.
546 Cf. *Mk* 10:34; *Jn* 2:19-22.

the dead."[547] Encounters with the risen Christ characterize the Christian hope of resurrection. We shall rise like Christ, with him, and through him.

996   From the beginning, Christian faith in the resurrection has met with incomprehension and opposition.[548] "On no point does
643 the Christian faith encounter more opposition than on the resurrection of the body."[549] It is very commonly accepted that the life of the human person continues in a spiritual fashion after death. But how can we believe that this body, so clearly mortal, could rise to everlasting life?

How do the dead rise?

997   *What is "rising"?* In death, the separation of the soul from the body, the human body decays and the soul goes to meet God,
366 while awaiting its reunion with its glorified body. God, in his almighty power, will definitively grant incorruptible life to our bodies by reuniting them with our souls, through the power of Jesus' Resurrection.

998   *Who will rise?* All the dead will rise, "those who have done good, to the resurrection of life, and those who have done evil, to
1038 the resurrection of judgment."[550]

999   *How?* Christ is raised with his own body: "See my hands and my feet, that it is I myself";[551] but he did not return to an earthly life. So, in him, "all of them will rise again with their own bodies
640 which they now bear," but Christ "will change our lowly body to
645 be like his glorious body," into a "spiritual body":[552]

> But someone will ask, "How are the dead raised? With what kind of body do they come?" You foolish man! What you sow does not come to life unless it dies. And what you sow is not the body which is to be, but a bare kernel . . . .What is sown is perishable, what is raised is imperishable. . . . The dead will be raised imperishable. . . . For this perishable nature must put on the imperishable, and this mortal nature must put on immortality.[553]

---

547   *Acts* 1:22; 10:41; cf. 4:33.
548   Cf. *Acts* 17:32; *1 Cor* 15:12-13.
549   St. Augustine, *En. in Ps.* 88, 5: PL 37, 1134.
550   *Jn* 5:29; cf. *Dan* 12:2.
551   *Lk* 24:39.
552   Lateran Council IV (1215): DS 801; *Phil* 3:21; *1 Cor* 15:44.
553   *1 Cor* 15:35-37, 42, 52, 53.

1000   This "how" exceeds our imagination and understanding; it is accessible only to faith. Yet our participation in the Eucharist already gives us a foretaste of Christ's transfiguration of our bodies: *647*

> Just as bread that comes from the earth, after God's blessing   *1405*
> has been invoked upon it, is no longer ordinary bread, but
> Eucharist, formed of two things, the one earthly and the
> other heavenly: so too our bodies, which partake of the
> Eucharist, are no longer corruptible, but possess the hope of
> resurrection.[554]

1001   *When?* Definitively "at the last day," "at the end of the   *1038*
world."[555] Indeed, the resurrection of the dead is closely associated   *673*
with Christ's Parousia:

> For the Lord himself will descend from heaven, with a cry
> of command, with the archangel's call, and with the sound
> of the trumpet of God. And the dead in Christ will rise
> first.[556]

Risen with Christ

1002   Christ will raise us up "on the last day"; but it is also true that, in a certain way, we have already risen with Christ. For, by virtue of the Holy Spirit, Christian life is already now on earth a   *655*
participation in the death and Resurrection of Christ:

> And you were buried with him in Baptism, in which you
> were also raised with him through faith in the working of
> God, who raised him from the dead . . . . If then you have
> been raised with Christ, seek the things that are above, where
> Christ is, seated at the right hand of God.[557]

1003   United with Christ by Baptism, believers already truly participate in the heavenly life of the risen Christ, but this life remains "hidden with Christ in God."[558] The Father has already   *1227*
"raised us up with him, and made us sit with him in the heavenly   *2796*
places in Christ Jesus."[559] Nourished with his body in the Eucharist, we already belong to the Body of Christ. When we rise on the last day we "also will appear with him in glory."[560]

---

554   St. Irenaeus, *Adv. haeres.* 4, 18, 4-5: PG 7/1, 1028-1029.
555   *Jn* 6: 39-40, 44, 54; 11:24; *LG* 48 § 3.
556   *1 Thess* 4:16.
557   *Col* 2:12; 3:1.
558   *Col* 3:3; cf. *Phil* 3:20.
559   *Eph* 2:6.
560   *Col* 3:4.

1004   In expectation of that day, the believer's body and soul already participate in the dignity of belonging to Christ. This
364 dignity entails the demand that he should treat with respect his
1397 own body, but also the body of every other person, especially the suffering:

> The body [is meant] for the Lord, and the Lord for the body. And God raised the Lord and will also raise us up by his power. Do you not know that your bodies are members of Christ? . . . . You are not your own; . . . . So glorify God in your body.[561]

II.   DYING IN CHRIST JESUS

1005   To rise with Christ, we must die with Christ: we must "be away from the body and at home with the Lord."[562] In that "departure" which is death the soul is separated from the body.[563] It will be reunited with the body on the day of resurrection of the
650 dead.[564]

Death

1006   "It is in regard to death that man's condition is most shrouded in doubt."[565] In a sense bodily death is natural, but for faith it is in fact "the wages of sin."[566] For those who die in Christ's grace it is a participation in the death of the Lord, so that they can also share his Resurrection.[567]

1007   *Death is the end of earthly life.* Our lives are measured by time, in the course of which we change, grow old and, as with all living beings on earth, death seems like the normal end of life. That aspect of death lends urgency to our lives: remembering our mortality helps us realize that we have only a limited time in which to bring our lives to fulfillment:

> Remember also your Creator in the days of your youth, . . . before the dust returns to the earth as it was, and the spirit returns to God who gave it.[568]

---

561   *1 Cor* 6:13-15, 19-20.
562   *2 Cor* 5:8.
563   Cf. *Phil* 1:23.
564   Cf. Paul VI, *CPG* § 28.
565   *GS* 18.
566   *Rom* 6:23; cf. *Gen* 2:17.
567   Cf. *Rom* 6:3-9; *Phil* 3:10-11.
568   *Eccl* 12:1, 7.

1008   *Death is a consequence of sin.* The Church's Magisterium, as
authentic interpreter of the affirmations of Scripture and Tradition,
teaches that death entered the world on account of man's sin.[569]
Even though man's nature is mortal, God had destined him not to   *401*
die. Death was therefore contrary to the plans of God the Creator
and entered the world as a consequence of sin.[570] "Bodily death,
from which man would have been immune had he not sinned" is   *376*
thus "the last enemy" of man left to be conquered.[571]

1009   *Death is transformed by Christ.* Jesus, the Son of God, also
himself suffered the death that is part of the human condition. Yet,
despite his anguish as he faced death, he accepted it in an act of   *612*
complete and free submission to his Father's will.[572] The obedience
of Jesus has transformed the curse of death into a blessing.[573]

The meaning of Christian death   *1681-1690*

1010   Because of Christ, Christian death has a positive meaning:
"For to me to live is Christ, and to die is gain."[574] "The saying is
sure: if we have died with him, we will also live with him."[575] What
is essentially new about Christian death is this: through Baptism,
the Christian has already "died with Christ" sacramentally, in
order to live a new life; and if we die in Christ's grace, physical   *1220*
death completes this "dying with Christ" and so completes our
incorporation into him in his redeeming act:

> It is better for me to die in (*eis*) Christ Jesus than to reign over
> the ends of the earth. Him it is I seek – who died for us. Him
> it is I desire – who rose for us. I am on the point of giving
> birth . . . . Let me receive pure light; when I shall have arrived
> there, then shall I be a man.[576]

1011   In death, God calls man to himself. Therefore the Christian
can experience a desire for death like St. Paul's: "My desire is to
depart and be with Christ."[577] He can transform his own death into
an act of obedience and love towards the Father, after the example   *1025*
of Christ:[578]

---

569   Cf. *Gen* 2:17; 3:3; 3:19; *Wis* 1:13; *Rom* 5:12; 6:23; DS 1511.
570   Cf. *Wis* 2:23-24.
571   *GS* 18 § 2; cf. *1 Cor* 15:26.
572   Cf. *Mk* 14:33-34; *Heb* 5:7-8.
573   Cf. *Rom* 5:19-21.
574   *Phil* 1:21.
575   *2 Tim* 2:11.
576   St. Ignatius of Antioch, *Ad Rom.*, 6, 1-2: *Apostolic Fathers*, II/2, 217-220.
577   *Phil* 1:23.

> My earthly desire has been crucified; . . . there is living water in me, water that murmurs and says within me: Come to the Father.[579]

> I want to see God and, in order to see him, I must die.[580]

> I am not dying; I am entering life.[581]

1012 The Christian vision of death receives privileged expression in the liturgy of the Church:[582]

> Lord, for your faithful people life is changed, not ended.
> When the body of our earthly dwelling lies in death
> we gain an everlasting dwelling place in heaven.[583]

1013 Death is the end of man's earthly pilgrimage, of the time of grace and mercy which God offers him so as to work out his earthly life in keeping with the divine plan, and to decide his ultimate destiny. When "the single course of our earthly life" is completed,[584] we shall not return to other earthly lives: "It is appointed for men to die once."[585] There is no "reincarnation" after death.

1014 The Church encourages us to prepare ourselves for the hour of our death. In the litany of the saints, for instance, she has us pray: "From a sudden and unforeseen death, deliver us, O Lord";[586] to ask the Mother of God to intercede for us "at the hour of our death" in the *Hail Mary*; and to entrust ourselves to St.

2676-2677 Joseph, the patron of a happy death.

> Every action of yours, every thought, should be those of one who expects to die before the day is out. Death would have no great terrors for you if you had a quiet conscience . . . . Then why not keep clear of sin instead of running away from death? If you aren't fit to face death today, it's very unlikely you will be tomorrow . . . .[587]

> Praised are you, my Lord, for our sister bodily Death,
> from whom no living man can escape.
> Woe on those who will die in mortal sin!
> Blessed are they who will be found
> in your most holy will,
> for the second death will not harm them.[588]

---

578 Cf. *Lk* 23:46.
579 St. Ignatius of Antioch, *Ad Rom.*, 6, 1- 2: *Apostolic Fathers*, II/2, 223-224.
580 St. Teresa of Avila, *Life*, chap. 1.
581 St. Thérèse of Lisieux, *The Last Conversations*.
582 Cf. *1 Thess* 4:13-14.
583 *Roman Missal*, Preface of Christian Death I.
584 *LG* 48 § 3.
585 *Heb* 9:27.
586 *Roman Missal*, Litany of the Saints.
587 *The Imitation of Christ*, 1, 23, 1.

IN BRIEF

1015   "The flesh is the hinge of salvation" (Tertullian, *De res.* 8, 2: PL 2, 852). We believe in God who is creator of the flesh; we believe in the Word made flesh in order to redeem the flesh; we believe in the resurrection of the flesh, the fulfillment of both the creation and the redemption of the flesh.

1016   By death the soul is separated from the body, but in the resurrection God will give incorruptible life to our body, transformed by reunion with our soul. Just as Christ is risen and lives for ever, so all of us will rise at the last day.

1017   "We believe in the true resurrection of this flesh that we now possess" (Council of Lyons II: DS 854). We sow a corruptible body in the tomb, but he raises up an incorruptible body, a "spiritual body" (cf. *1 Cor* 15:42-44).

1018   As a consequence of original sin, man must suffer "bodily death, from which man would have been immune had he not sinned" (*GS* § 18).

1019   Jesus, the Son of God, freely suffered death for us in complete and free submission to the will of God, his Father. By his death he has conquered death, and so opened the possibility of salvation to all men.

---

588   St. Francis of Assisi, *Canticle of the Creatures.*

ARTICLE 12
"I BELIEVE IN LIFE EVERLASTING"

1523-1525 **1020**   The Christian who unites his own death to that of Jesus
views it as a step towards him and an entrance into everlasting life.
When the Church for the last time speaks Christ's words of pardon
and absolution over the dying Christian, seals him for the last time
with a strengthening anointing, and gives him Christ in viaticum
as nourishment for the journey, she speaks with gentle assurance:

> Go forth, Christian soul, from this world
> in the name of God the almighty Father,
> who created you,
> in the name of Jesus Christ, the Son of the living God,
> who suffered for you,
> in the name of the Holy Spirit,
> who was poured out upon you.
> Go forth, faithful Christian!
>
> May you live in peace this day,
> may your home be with God in Zion,
> with Mary, the virgin Mother of God,
> with Joseph, and all the angels and saints. . . .

2677, 336
> May you return to [your Creator]
> who formed you from the dust of the earth.
> May holy Mary, the angels, and all the saints
> come to meet you as you go forth from this life. . . .
> May you see your Redeemer face to face. . . .[589]

I.   THE PARTICULAR JUDGMENT

1021   Death puts an end to human life as the time open to either
accepting or rejecting the divine grace manifested in Christ.[590] The
New Testament speaks of judgment primarily in its aspect of the
final encounter with Christ in his second coming, but also repeatedly affirms that each will be rewarded immediately after death in
679 accordance with his works and faith. The parable of the poor man
Lazarus and the words of Christ on the cross to the good thief, as
well as other New Testament texts speak of a final destiny of the
soul—a destiny which can be different for some and for others.[591]

1022   Each man receives his eternal retribution in his immortal
393 soul at the very moment of his death, in a particular judgment that

---

589   *OCF*, Prayer of Commendation.
590   Cf. *2 Tim* 1:9-10.
591   Cf. *Lk* 16:22; 23:43; *Mt* 16:26; *2 Cor* 5:8; *Phil* 1:23; *Heb* 9:27; 12:23.

refers his life to Christ: either entrance into the blessedness of heaven—through a purification[592] or immediately,[593]—or immediate and everlasting damnation.[594]

At the evening of life, we shall be judged on our love.[595]   *1470*

II.   HEAVEN

1023   Those who die in God's grace and friendship and are perfectly purified live for ever with Christ. They are like God for *954* ever, for they "see him as he is," face to face:[596]

> By virtue of our apostolic authority, we define the following: According to the general disposition of God, the souls of all the saints . . . and other faithful who died after receiving Christ's holy Baptism (provided they were not in need of purification when they died, . . . or, if they then did need or will need some purification, when they have been purified after death, . . .) already before they take up their bodies again and before the general judgment – and this since the Ascension of our Lord and Savior Jesus Christ into heaven – have been, are and will be in heaven, in the heavenly Kingdom and celestial paradise with Christ, joined to the company of the holy angels. Since the Passion and death of our Lord Jesus Christ, these souls have seen and do see the divine essence with an intuitive vision, and even face to face, without the mediation of any creature.[597]

1024   This perfect life with the Most Holy Trinity – this communion of life and love with the Trinity, with the Virgin Mary, the angels and all the blessed – is called "heaven." Heaven is the *260, 326* ultimate end and fulfillment of the deepest human longings, the *2794, 1718* state of supreme, definitive happiness.

1025   To live in heaven is "to be with Christ." The elect live "in Christ,"[598] but they retain, or rather find, their true identity, their *1011* own name.[599]

> For life is to be with Christ; where Christ is, there is life, there is the kingdom.[600]

---

592   Cf. Council of Lyons II (1274): DS 857-858; Council of Florence (1439): DS 1304-1306; Council of Trent (1563): DS 1820.
593   Cf. Benedict XII, *Benedictus Deus* (1336): DS 1000-1001; John XXII, *Ne super his* (1334): DS 990.
594   Cf. Benedict XII, *Benedictus Deus* (1336): DS 1002.
595   St. John of the Cross, *Dichos* 64.
596   *1 Jn* 3:2; cf. *1 Cor* 13:12; *Rev* 22:4.
597   Benedict XII, *Benedictus Deus* (1336): DS 1000; cf. *LG* 49.
598   *Phil* 1:23; cf. *Jn* 14:3; *1 Thess* 4:17.
599   Cf. *Rev* 2:17.

1026   By his death and Resurrection, Jesus Christ has "opened" heaven to us. The life of the blessed consists in the full and perfect possession of the fruits of the redemption accomplished by Christ. He makes partners in his heavenly glorification those who have 793 believed in him and remained faithful to his will. Heaven is the blessed community of all who are perfectly incorporated into Christ.

1027   This mystery of blessed communion with God and all who are in Christ is beyond all understanding and description. Scrip-
959, 1720 ture speaks of it in images: life, light, peace, wedding feast, wine of the kingdom, the Father's house, the heavenly Jerusalem, paradise: "no eye has seen, nor ear heard, nor the heart of man conceived, what God has prepared for those who love him."[601]

1028   Because of his transcendence, God cannot be seen as he is, 1722, unless he himself opens up his mystery to man's immediate con-
163 templation and gives him the capacity for it. The Church calls this contemplation of God in his heavenly glory "the beatific vision":

> How great will your glory and happiness be, to be allowed to see God, to be honored with sharing the joy of salvation and eternal light with Christ your Lord and God, . . . to delight in the joy of immortality in the Kingdom of heaven with the righteous and God's friends.[602]

956 **1029**   In the glory of heaven the blessed continue joyfully to 668 fulfill God's will in relation to other men and to all creation. Already they reign with Christ; with him "they shall reign for ever and ever."[603]

III.   THE FINAL PURIFICATION, OR PURGATORY

1030   All who die in God's grace and friendship, but still imper-fectly purified, are indeed assured of their eternal salvation; but after death they undergo purification, so as to achieve the holiness necessary to enter the joy of heaven.

1031   The Church gives the name *Purgatory* to this final purifi-
954, 1472 cation of the elect, which is entirely different from the punishment of the damned.[604] The Church formulated her doctrine of faith on

---

600 St. Ambrose, *In Luc.*, 10, 121: PL 15, 1834A.
601 *1 Cor* 2:9.
602 St. Cyprian, *Ep.* 58, 10,1: CSEL 3/2, 665.
603 *Rev* 22:5; cf. *Mt* 25:21, 23.
604 Cf. Council of Florence (1439): DS 1304; Council of Trent (1563): DS 1820;
     (1547): 1580; see also Benedict XII, *Benedictus Deus* (1336): DS 1000.

Purgatory especially at the Councils of Florence and Trent. The tradition of the Church, by reference to certain texts of Scripture, speaks of a cleansing fire:[605]

> As for certain lesser faults, we must believe that, before the Final Judgment, there is a purifying fire. He who is truth says that whoever utters blasphemy against the Holy Spirit will be pardoned neither in this age nor in the age to come. From this sentence we understand that certain offenses can be forgiven in this age, but certain others in the age to come.[606]

1032 This teaching is also based on the practice of prayer for the dead, already mentioned in Sacred Scripture: "Therefore [Judas Maccabeus] made atonement for the dead, that they might be delivered from their sin."[607] From the beginning the Church has honored the memory of the dead and offered prayers in suffrage for them, above all the Eucharistic sacrifice, so that, thus purified, they may attain the beatific vision of God.[608] The Church also commends almsgiving, indulgences, and works of penance undertaken on behalf of the dead:

958

1371

1479

> Let us help and commemorate them. If Job's sons were purified by their father's sacrifice, why would we doubt that our offerings for the dead bring them some consolation? Let us not hesitate to help those who have died and to offer our prayers for them.[609]

IV. HELL

1033 We cannot be united with God unless we freely choose to love him. But we cannot love God if we sin gravely against him, against our neighbor or against ourselves: "He who does not love remains in death. Anyone who hates his brother is a murderer, and you know that no murderer has eternal life abiding in him."[610] Our Lord warns us that we shall be separated from him if we fail to meet the serious needs of the poor and the little ones who are his brethren.[611] To die in mortal sin without repenting and accepting God's merciful love means remaining separated from him for ever by our own free choice. This state of definitive self-exclusion from communion with God and the blessed is called "hell."

1861

393

633

---

605 Cf. *1 Cor* 3:15; *1 Pet* 1:7.
606 St. Gregory the Great, *Dial.* 4, 39: PL 77, 396; cf. *Mt* 12:31.
607 *2 Macc* 12:46.
608 Cf. Council of Lyons II (1274): DS 856.
609 St. John Chrysostom, *Hom. in 1 Cor.* 41, 5: PG 61, 361; cf. *Job* 1:5.
610 *1 Jn* 3:14-15.
611 Cf. *Mt* 25:31-46.

1034   Jesus often speaks of "Gehenna," of "the unquenchable fire" reserved for those who to the end of their lives refuse to believe and be converted, where both soul and body can be lost.[612] Jesus solemnly proclaims that he "will send his angels, and they will gather . . . all evil doers, and throw them into the furnace of fire,"[613] and that he will pronounce the condemnation: "Depart from me, you cursed, into the eternal fire!"[614]

1035   The teaching of the Church affirms the existence of hell and its eternity. Immediately after death the souls of those who die in a state of mortal sin descend into hell, where they suffer the punishments of hell, "eternal fire."[615] The chief punishment of hell

393   is eternal separation from God, in whom alone man can possess the life and happiness for which he was created and for which he longs.

1036   The affirmations of Sacred Scripture and the teachings of the Church on the subject of hell are a *call to the responsibility*

1734   incumbent upon man to make use of his freedom in view of his

1428   eternal destiny. They are at the same time an urgent *call to conversion:* "Enter by the narrow gate; for the gate is wide and the way is easy, that leads to destruction, and those who enter by it are many. For the gate is narrow and the way is hard, that leads to life, and those who find it are few."[616]

> Since we know neither the day nor the hour, we should follow the advice of the Lord and watch constantly so that, when the single course of our earthly life is completed, we may merit to enter with him into the marriage feast and be numbered among the blessed, and not, like the wicked and slothful servants, be ordered to depart into the eternal fire, into the outer darkness where "men will weep and gnash their teeth."[617]

1037   God predestines no one to go to hell;[618] for this, a willful

162   turning away from God (a mortal sin) is necessary, and persistence

1014, 1821   in it until the end. In the Eucharistic liturgy and in the daily prayers of her faithful, the Church implores the mercy of God, who does not want "any to perish, but all to come to repentance":[619]

---

612   Cf. *Mt* 5:22, 29; 10:28; 13:42, 50; *Mk* 9:43-48.

613   *Mt* 13:41-42.

614   *Mt* 25:41.

615   Cf. DS 76; 409; 411; 801; 858; 1002; 1351; 1575; Paul VI, *CPG* § 12.

616   *Mt* 7:13-14.

617   *LG* 48 § 3; *Mt* 22:13; cf. *Heb* 9:27; *Mt* 25:13, 26, 30, 31-46.

618   Cf. Council of Orange II (529): DS 397; Council of Trent (1547):1567.

619   *2 Pet* 3:9.

Father, accept this offering
from your whole family.
Grant us your peace in this life,
save us from final damnation,
and count us among those you have chosen.[620]

678-679

V.   THE LAST JUDGMENT

1038   The resurrection of all the dead, "of both the just and the unjust,"[621] will precede the Last Judgment. This will be "the hour *1001, 998* when all who are in the tombs will hear [the Son of man's] voice and come forth, those who have done good, to the resurrection of life, and those who have done evil, to the resurrection of judgment."[622] Then Christ will come "in his glory, and all the angels with him . . . . Before him will be gathered all the nations, and he will separate them one from another as a shepherd separates the sheep from the goats, and he will place the sheep at his right hand, but the goats at the left. . . . And they will go away into eternal punishment, but the righteous into eternal life."[623]

1039   In the presence of Christ, who is Truth itself, the truth of each man's relationship with God will be laid bare.[624] The Last Judgment will reveal even to its furthest consequences the good each person has done or failed to do during his earthly life: *678*

All that the wicked do is recorded, and they do not know. When "our God comes, he does not keep silence.". . . he will turn towards those at his left hand: . . . "I placed my poor little ones on earth for you. I as their head was seated in heaven at the right hand of my Father – but on earth my members were suffering, my members on earth were in need. If you gave anything to my members, what you gave would reach their Head. Would that you had known that my little ones were in need when I placed them on earth for you and appointed them your stewards to bring your good works into my treasury. But you have placed nothing in their hands; therefore you have found nothing in my presence."[625]

---

620   *Roman Missal*, EP I (Roman Canon) 88.
621   *Acts* 24:15.
622   *Jn* 5:28-29.
623   *Mt* 25:31, 32, 46.
624   Cf. *Jn* 12:49.
625   St. Augustine, *Sermo* 18, 4: PL 38, 130-131; cf. *Ps* 50:3.

1040   The Last Judgment will come when Christ returns in glory.
Only the Father knows the day and the hour; only he determines
637   the moment of its coming. Then through his Son Jesus Christ he
will pronounce the final word on all history. We shall know the
ultimate meaning of the whole work of creation and of the entire
economy of salvation and understand the marvellous ways by
314   which his Providence led everything towards its final end. The Last
Judgment will reveal that God's justice triumphs over all the
injustices committed by his creatures and that God's love is
stronger than death.[626]

1041   The message of the Last Judgment calls men to conversion
while God is still giving them "the acceptable time, . . . the day of
1432   salvation."[627] It inspires a holy fear of God and commits them to
the justice of the Kingdom of God. It proclaims the "blessed hope"
of the Lord's return, when he will come "to be glorified in his saints,
and to be marvelled at in all who have believed."[628]

2854   **VI.   THE HOPE OF THE NEW HEAVEN AND THE NEW EARTH**

1042   At the end of time, the Kingdom of God will come in its
fullness. After the universal judgment, the righteous will reign for
769   ever with Christ, glorified in body and soul. The universe itself will
670   be renewed:

> The Church . . . will receive her perfection only in the glory
> of heaven, when will come the time of the renewal of all
310   > things. At that time, together with the human race, the
> universe itself, which is so closely related to man and which
> attains its destiny through him, will be perfectly re-estab-
> lished in Christ.[629]

1043   Sacred Scripture calls this mysterious renewal, which will
transform humanity and the world, "new heavens and a new
671   earth."[630] It will be the definitive realization of God's plan to bring
280, 518   under a single head "all things in [Christ], things in heaven and
things on earth."[631]

1044   In this new universe, the heavenly Jerusalem, God will
have his dwelling among men.[632] "He will wipe away every tear

---

626   Cf. *Song* 8:6.
627   *2 Cor* 6:2.
628   *Titus* 2:13; *2 Thess* 1:10.
629   *LG* 48; cf. *Acts* 3:21; *Eph* 1:10; *Col* 1:20; *2 Pet* 3:10-13.
630   *2 Pet* 3:13; cf. *Rev* 21:1.
631   *Eph* 1:10.

from their eyes, and death shall be no more, neither shall there be mourning nor crying nor pain any more, for the former things have passed away."[633]

1045 *For man,* this consummation will be the final realization of the unity of the human race, which God willed from creation and of which the pilgrim Church has been "in the nature of sacra- *775* ment."[634] Those who are united with Christ will form the community of the redeemed, "the holy city" of God, "the Bride, the wife *1404* of the Lamb."[635] She will not be wounded any longer by sin, stains, self-love, that destroy or wound the earthly community.[636] The beatific vision, in which God opens himself in an inexhaustible way to the elect, will be the ever-flowing well-spring of happiness, peace, and mutual communion.

1046 *For the cosmos,* Revelation affirms the profound common destiny of the material world and man:

> For the creation waits with eager longing for the revealing *349* of the sons of God . . . in hope because the creation itself will be set free from its bondage to decay. . . . We know that the whole creation has been groaning in travail together until now; and not only the creation, but we ourselves, who have the first fruits of the Spirit, groan inwardly as we wait for adoption as sons, the redemption of our bodies.[637]

1047 The visible universe, then, is itself destined to be transformed, "so that the world itself, restored to its original state, facing no further obstacles, should be at the service of the just," sharing their glorification in the risen Jesus Christ.[638]

1048 *"We know neither the moment of the consummation* of the earth and of man, nor the way in which the universe will be transformed. The form of this world, distorted by sin, is passing away, and we *673* are taught that God is preparing a new dwelling and a new earth in which righteousness dwells, in which happiness will fill and surpass all the desires of peace arising in the hearts of men."[639]

---

632 Cf. *Rev* 21:5.
633 *Rev* 21:4.
634 Cf. *LG* 1.
635 *Rev* 21:2, 9.
636 Cf. *Rev* 21:27.
637 *Rom* 8:19-23.
638 St. Irenaeus, *Adv. haeres.* 5, 32, 1: PG 7/2, 210.
639 *GS* 39 § 1.

1049   "Far from diminishing our concern to develop this earth, the expectancy of a new earth should spur us on, for it is here that the body of a new human family grows, foreshadowing in some way the age which is to come. That is why, although we must be careful to distinguish earthly progress clearly from the increase of

2820   the kingdom of Christ, such progress is of vital concern to the kingdom of God, insofar as it can contribute to the better ordering of human society."[640]

1050   "When we have spread on earth the fruits of our nature and our enterprise . . . according to the command of the Lord and

1709   in his Spirit, we will find them once again, cleansed this time from the stain of sin, illuminated and transfigured, when Christ presents

260   to his Father an eternal and universal kingdom."[641] God will then be "all in all" in eternal life:[642]

> True and subsistent life consists in this: the Father, through the Son and in the Holy Spirit, pouring out his heavenly gifts on all things without exception. Thanks to his mercy, we too, men that we are, have received the inalienable promise of eternal life.[643]

IN BRIEF

1051   Every man receives his eternal recompense in his immortal soul from the moment of his death in a particular judgment by Christ, the judge of the living and the dead.

1052   "We believe that the souls of all who die in Christ's grace . . . are the People of God beyond death. On the day of resurrection, death will be definitively conquered, when these souls will be reunited with their bodies" (Paul VI, *CPG* § 28).

1053   "We believe that the multitude of those gathered around Jesus and Mary in Paradise forms the Church of heaven, where in eternal blessedness they see God as he is and where they are also, to various degrees, associated with the holy angels in the divine governance exercised by Christ in glory, by interceding for us

---

640   *GS* 39 § 2.
641   *GS* 39 § 3.
642   *1 Cor* 5:28.
643   St. Cyril of Jerusalem, *Catech. illum.* 18, 29: PG 33, 1049.

and helping our weakness by their fraternal concern" (Paul VI, *CPG* § 29).

1054 Those who die in God's grace and friendship imperfectly purified, although they are assured of their eternal salvation, undergo a purification after death, so as to achieve the holiness necessary to enter the joy of God.

1055 By virtue of the "communion of saints," the Church commends the dead to God's mercy and offers her prayers, especially the holy sacrifice of the Eucharist, on their behalf.

1056 Following the example of Christ, the Church warns the faithful of the "sad and lamentable reality of eternal death" (*GCD* 69), also called "hell."

1057 Hell's principal punishment consists of eternal separation from God in whom alone man can have the life and happiness for which he was created and for which he longs.

1058 The Church prays that no one should be lost: "Lord, let me never be parted from you." If it is true that no one can save himself, it is also true that God "desires all men to be saved" (*1 Tim* 2:4), and that for him "all things are possible" (*Mt* 19:26).

1059 "The holy Roman Church firmly believes and confesses that on the Day of Judgment all men will appear in their own bodies before Christ's tribunal to render an account of their own deeds" (Council of Lyons II [1274]: DS 859; cf. DS 1549).

1060 At the end of time, the Kingdom of God will come in its fullness. Then the just will reign with Christ for ever, glorified in body and soul, and the material universe itself will be transformed. God will then be "all in all" (*1 Cor* 15:28), in eternal life.

"AMEN"

1061   The Creed, like the last book of the Bible,[644] ends with the
Hebrew word amen. This word frequently concludes prayers in
2856 the New Testament. The Church likewise ends her prayers with
"Amen."

1062   In Hebrew, amen comes from the same root as the word
"believe." This root expresses solidity, trustworthiness, faithful-
214 ness. And so we can understand why "Amen" may express both
God's faithfulness towards us and our trust in him.

1063   In the book of the prophet Isaiah, we find the expression
"God of truth" (literally "God of the Amen"), that is, the God who
215 is faithful to his promises: "He who blesses himself in the land shall
bless himself by the God of truth [amen]."[645] Our Lord often used
156 the word "Amen," sometimes repeated,[646] to emphasize the trustworthiness of his teaching, his authority founded on God's truth.

1064   Thus the Creed's final "Amen" repeats and confirms its
first words: "I believe." To believe is to say "Amen" to God's
197, 2101 words, promises and commandments; to entrust oneself completely to him who is the "Amen" of infinite love and perfect
faithfulness. The Christian's everyday life will then be the "Amen"
to the "I believe" of our baptismal profession of faith:

> May your Creed be for you as a mirror. Look at yourself in
> it, to see if you believe everything you say you believe. And
> rejoice in your faith each day.[647]

1065   Jesus Christ himself is the "Amen."[648] He is the definitive
"Amen" of the Father's love for us. He takes up and completes our
"Amen" to the Father: "For all the promises of God find their Yes
in him. That is why we utter the Amen through him, to the glory
of God":[649]

> Through him, with him, in him,
> in the unity of the Holy Spirit,
> all glory and honor is yours,
> almighty Father,
> God, for ever and ever.
> AMEN.

---

644 Cf. *Rev* 22:21.
645 *Isa* 65:16.
646 Cf. *Mt* 6:2, 5, 16; *Jn* 5:19.
647 St. Augustine, *Sermo* 58, 11, 13: PL 38, 399.
648 *Rev* 3:14.
649 *2 Cor* 1:20.

Fresco from the catacomb of Saints Marcellinus and Peter, Rome, from the beginning of the fourth century A.D.

The scene depicts the encounter of Jesus with the woman with the hemorrhage. This woman who had suffered for many years was healed by touching the cloak of Jesus through the power that "had gone forth from him" (cf. *Mk* 5:25-34).

The sacraments of the Church now continue the works which Christ had performed during his earthly life (cf. § 1115). The sacraments are as it were "powers that go forth" from the Body of Christ to heal the wounds of sin and to give us the new life of Christ (cf. §1116).

This image thus symbolizes the divine and saving power of the Son of God who heals the whole man, soul and body, through the sacramental life.

PART TWO

THE CELEBRATION OF THE CHRISTIAN MYSTERY

Why the liturgy?

1066   In the Symbol of the faith the Church confesses the mystery of the Holy Trinity and of the plan of God's "good pleasure" for all creation: the Father accomplishes the "mystery of his will" by *50* giving his beloved Son and his Holy Spirit for the salvation of the world and for the glory of his name.[1] Such is the mystery of Christ, revealed and fulfilled in history according to the wisely ordered plan that St. Paul calls the "plan of the mystery"[2] and the patristic *236* tradition will call the "economy of the Word incarnate" or the "economy of salvation."

1067   "The wonderful works of God among the people of the Old Testament were but a prelude to the work of Christ the Lord in redeeming mankind and giving perfect glory to God. He accomplished this work principally by the Paschal mystery of his blessed Passion, Resurrection from the dead, and glorious Ascension, whereby 'dying he destroyed our death, rising he restored our life.' For it was from the side of Christ as he slept the sleep of death upon the cross that there came forth 'the wondrous sacrament of the whole Church.'"[3] For this reason, the Church celebrates in the liturgy above all the Paschal mystery by which Christ accomplished the work of our salvation.   *571*

1068   It is this mystery of Christ that the Church proclaims and celebrates in her liturgy so that the faithful may live from it and bear witness to it in the world:

---

1   *Eph* 1:9.
2   *Eph* 3:9; cf. 3:4.
3   *SC* 5 § 2; cf. St. Augustine, *En. in Ps.* 138, 2: PL 37, 1784-1785.

For it is in the liturgy, especially in the divine sacrifice of the Eucharist, that "the work of our redemption is accomplished," and it is through the liturgy especially that the faithful are enabled to express in their lives and manifest to others the mystery of Christ and the real nature of the true Church.[4]

What does the word liturgy mean?

1069   The word "liturgy" originally meant a "public work" or a "service in the name of/on behalf of the people." In Christian tradition it means the participation of the People of God in "the work of God."[5] Through the liturgy Christ, our redeemer and high priest, continues the work of our redemption in, with, and through his Church.

1070   In the New Testament the word "liturgy" refers not only to the celebration of divine worship but also to the proclamation of the Gospel and to active charity.[6] In all of these situations it is a question of the service of God and neighbor. In a liturgical celebration the Church is servant in the image of her Lord, the one

783   "*leitourgos*";[7] she shares in Christ's priesthood (worship), which is both prophetic (proclamation) and kingly (service of charity):

The liturgy then is rightly seen as an exercise of the priestly office of Jesus Christ. It involves the presentation of man's sanctification under the guise of signs perceptible by the senses and its accomplishment in ways appropriate to each of these signs. In it full public worship is performed by the Mystical Body of Jesus Christ, that is, by the Head and his members. From this it follows that every liturgical celebration, because it is an action of Christ the priest and of his Body which is the Church, is a sacred action surpassing all others. No other action of the Church can equal its efficacy by the same title and to the same degree.[8]

Liturgy as source of life

1071   As the work of Christ liturgy is also an action of his *Church*. It makes the Church present and manifests her as the visible sign of the communion in Christ between God and men. It engages the faithful in the new life of the community and involves the "con-

1692   scious, active, and fruitful participation" of everyone.[9]

---

4   *SC* 2.
5   Cf. *Jn* 17:4.
6   Cf. *Lk* 1:23; *Acts* 13:2; *Rom* 15:16, 27; *2 Cor* 9:12; *Phil* 2:14-17, 25, 30.
7   Cf. *Heb* 8:2, 6.
8   *SC* 7 § 2-3.
9   *SC* 11.

1072 "The sacred liturgy does not exhaust the entire activity of the Church":[10] it must be preceded by evangelization, faith, and conversion. It can then produce its fruits in the lives of the faithful: new life in the Spirit, involvement in the mission of the Church, and service to her unity.

Prayer and liturgy

1073 The liturgy is also a participation in Christ's own prayer addressed to the Father in the Holy Spirit. In the liturgy, all Christian prayer finds its source and goal. Through the liturgy the inner man is rooted and grounded in "the great love with which [the Father] loved us" in his beloved Son.[11] It is the same "marvelous work of God" that is lived and internalized by all prayer, "at all times in the Spirit."[12]   *2558*

Catechesis and liturgy

1074 "The liturgy is the summit toward which the activity of the Church is directed; it is also the font from which all her power flows."[13] It is therefore the privileged place for catechizing the People of God. "Catechesis is intrinsically linked with the whole of liturgical and sacramental activity, for it is in the sacraments, especially in the Eucharist, that Christ Jesus works in fullness for the transformation of men."[14]

1075 Liturgical catechesis aims to initiate people into the mys- *426* tery of Christ (It is "mystagogy.") by proceeding from the visible to the invisible, from the sign to the thing signified, from the "sacraments" to the "mysteries." Such catechesis is to be presented *774* by local and regional catechisms. This Catechism, which aims to serve the whole Church in all the diversity of her rites and cultures,[15] will present what is fundamental and common to the whole Church in the liturgy as mystery and as celebration (*Section One*), and then the seven sacraments and the sacramentals (*Section Two*).

---

10 *SC* 9.
11 *Eph* 2:4; 3:16-17.
12 *Eph* 6:18.
13 *SC* 10.
14 John Paul II, *CT* 23.
15 Cf. *SC* 3-4.

SECTION ONE
THE SACRAMENTAL ECONOMY

1076 The Church was made manifest to the world on the day of Pentecost by the outpouring of the Holy Spirit.[1] The gift of the Spirit ushers in a new era in the "dispensation of the mystery" – the age of the Church, during which Christ manifests, makes

739 present, and communicates his work of salvation through the liturgy of his Church, "until he comes."[2] In this age of the Church Christ now lives and acts in and with his Church, in a new way appropriate to this new age. He acts through the sacraments in what the common Tradition of the East and the West calls "the sacramental economy"; this is the communication (or "dispensation") of the fruits of Christ's Paschal mystery in the celebration of the Church's "sacramental" liturgy.

It is therefore important first to explain this "sacramental dispensation" (*chapter one*). The nature and essential features of liturgical celebration will then appear more clearly (*chapter two*).

CHAPTER ONE
THE PASCHAL MYSTERY IN THE AGE OF THE CHURCH

ARTICLE 1
THE LITURGY – WORK OF THE HOLY TRINITY

I.   THE FATHER – SOURCE AND GOAL OF THE LITURGY

1077 "Blessed be the God and Father of our Lord Jesus Christ, who has blessed us in Christ with every spiritual blessing in the

492 heavenly places, even as he chose us in him before the foundation of the world, that we should be holy and blameless before him. He destined us before him in love to be his sons through Jesus Christ, according to the purpose of his will, to the praise of his glorious grace which he freely bestowed on us in the Beloved."[3]

2626 **1078** Blessing is a divine and life-giving action, the source of which is the Father; his blessing is both word and gift.[4] When

---

1 Cf. *SC* 6; *LG* 2.
2 *1 Cor* 11:26.
3 *Eph* 1:3-6.
4 *eu-logia, bene-dictio.*

applied to man, the word "blessing" means adoration and surrender to his Creator in thanksgiving.

1079 From the beginning until the end of time the whole of God's work is a *blessing*. From the liturgical poem of the first creation to the canticles of the heavenly Jerusalem, the inspired authors proclaim the plan of salvation as one vast divine blessing.

1080 From the very beginning God blessed all living beings, especially man and woman. The covenant with Noah and with all living things renewed this blessing of fruitfulness despite man's sin which had brought a curse on the ground. But with Abraham, the divine blessing entered into human history which was moving toward death, to redirect it toward life, toward its source. By the faith of "the father of all believers," who embraced the blessing, the history of salvation is inaugurated.

1081 The divine blessings were made manifest in astonishing and saving events: the birth of Isaac, the escape from Egypt (Passover and Exodus), the gift of the promised land, the election of David, the presence of God in the Temple, the purifying exile, and return of a "small remnant." The Law, the Prophets, and the Psalms, interwoven in the liturgy of the Chosen People, recall these divine blessings and at the same time respond to them with blessings of praise and thanksgiving.

1082 In the Church's liturgy the divine blessing is fully revealed and communicated. The Father is acknowledged and adored as the source and the end of all the blessings of creation and salvation. In his Word who became incarnate, died, and rose for us, he fills us with his blessings. Through his Word, he pours into our hearts the Gift that contains all gifts, the Holy Spirit.

1083 The dual dimension of the Christian liturgy as a response of faith and love to the spiritual blessings the Father bestows on us is thus evident. On the one hand, the Church, united with her Lord and "in the Holy Spirit,"[5] blesses the Father "for his inexpressible gift"[6] in her adoration, praise, and thanksgiving. On the other hand, until the consummation of God's plan, the Church never ceases to present to the Father the offering of his own gifts and to beg him to send the Holy Spirit upon that offering, upon herself, upon the faithful, and upon the whole world, so that through communion in the death and resurrection of Christ the Priest, and by the power of the Spirit, these divine blessings will bring forth the fruits of life "to the praise of his glorious grace."[7]

2627
1360

---

5   *Lk* 10:21.
6   *2 Cor* 9:15.

II.   CHRIST'S WORK IN THE LITURGY

Christ glorified . . .

662 **1084**   "Seated at the right hand of the Father" and pouring out the
Holy Spirit on his Body which is the Church, Christ now acts through
the sacraments he instituted to communicate his grace. The sacra-
1127 ments are perceptible signs (words and actions) accessible to our
human nature. By the action of Christ and the power of the Holy Spirit
they make present efficaciously the grace that they signify.

1085   In the liturgy of the Church, it is principally his own
Paschal mystery that Christ signifies and makes present. During
his earthly life Jesus announced his Paschal mystery by his teaching
and anticipated it by his actions. When his Hour comes, he lives
out the unique event of history which does not pass away: Jesus
dies, is buried, rises from the dead, and is seated at the right hand
of the Father "once for all."[8] His Paschal mystery is a real event that
occurred in our history, but it is unique: all other historical events
happen once, and then they pass away, swallowed up in the past.
The Paschal mystery of Christ, by contrast, cannot remain only in
519 the past, because by his death he destroyed death, and all that
Christ is – all that he did and suffered for all men – participates in
the divine eternity, and so transcends all times while being made
1165 present in them all. The event of the Cross and Resurrection *abides*
and draws everything toward life.

. . . from the time of the Church of the Apostles . . .

858 **1086**   "Accordingly, just as Christ was sent by the Father so also
he sent the apostles, filled with the Holy Spirit. This he did so that
they might preach the Gospel to every creature and proclaim that
the Son of God by his death and resurrection had freed us from the
power of Satan and from death and brought us into the Kingdom
of his Father. But he also willed that the work of salvation which
they preached should be set in train through the sacrifice and
sacraments, around which the entire liturgical life revolves."[9]

1087   Thus the risen Christ, by giving the Holy Spirit to the
apostles, entrusted to them his power of sanctifying:[10] they
became sacramental signs of Christ. By the power of the same
861 Holy Spirit they entrusted this power to their successors. This

---

7 *Eph* 1:6.
8 *Rom* 6:10; *Heb* 7:27; 9:12; cf. *Jn* 13:1; 17:1.
9 *SC* 6.

"apostolic succession" structures the whole liturgical life of the Church and is itself sacramental, handed on by the sacrament of Holy Orders.

1536

... is present in the earthly liturgy ...

1088   "To accomplish so great a work" – the dispensation or communication of his work of salvation – "Christ is always present in his Church, especially in her liturgical celebrations. He is present in the *776* Sacrifice of the Mass not only in the person of his minister, 'the same *669* now offering, through the ministry of priests, who formerly offered himself on the cross,' but especially in the Eucharistic species. By his power he is present in the sacraments so that when anybody baptizes, *1373* it is really Christ himself who baptizes. He is present in his word since it is he himself who speaks when the holy Scriptures are read in the Church. Lastly, he is present when the Church prays and sings, for he has promised 'where two or three are gathered together in my name there am I in the midst of them.'"[11]

1089   "Christ, indeed, always associates the Church with himself in this great work in which God is perfectly glorified and men are sanctified. The Church is his beloved Bride who calls to her Lord *796* and through him offers worship to the eternal Father."[12]

... which participates in the liturgy of heaven

1090   "In the earthly liturgy we share in a foretaste of that *1137-1139* heavenly liturgy which is celebrated in the Holy City of Jerusalem toward which we journey as pilgrims, where Christ is sitting at the right hand of God, Minister of the sanctuary and of the true tabernacle. With all the warriors of the heavenly army we sing a hymn of glory to the Lord; venerating the memory of the saints, we hope for some part and fellowship with them; we eagerly await the Savior, our Lord Jesus Christ, until he, our life, shall appear and we too will appear with him in glory."[13]

III.   THE HOLY SPIRIT AND THE CHURCH IN THE LITURGY

1091   In the liturgy the Holy Spirit is teacher of the faith of the People of God and artisan of "God's masterpieces," the sacraments of the New Covenant. The desire and work of the Spirit in the heart *798*

---

10   Cf. *Jn* 20:21-23.
11   *SC* 7; *Mt* 18:20.
12   *SC* 7.
13   *SC* 8; cf. *LG* 50.

of the Church is that we may live from the life of the risen Christ. When the Spirit encounters in us the response of faith which he has aroused in us, he brings about genuine cooperation. Through it, the liturgy becomes the common work of the Holy Spirit and the Church.

1092   In this sacramental dispensation of Christ's mystery the Holy Spirit acts in the same way as at other times in the economy
737 of salvation: he prepares the Church to encounter her Lord; he recalls and makes Christ manifest to the faith of the assembly. By his transforming power, he makes the mystery of Christ present here and now. Finally the Spirit of communion unites the Church to the life and mission of Christ.

The Holy Spirit prepares for the reception of Christ

1093   In the sacramental economy the Holy Spirit fulfills what was prefigured in *the Old Covenant*. Since Christ's Church was
762 "prepared in marvellous fashion in the history of the people of Israel and in the Old Covenant,"[14] the Church's liturgy has retained certain elements of the worship of the Old Covenant as integral and irreplaceable, adopting them as her own:

121 –notably, reading the Old Testament;

2585 –praying the Psalms;

1081 –above all, recalling the saving events and significant realities which have found their fulfillment in the mystery of Christ (promise and covenant, Exodus and Passover, kingdom and temple, exile and return).

128-130 **1094**   It is on this harmony of the two Testaments that the Paschal catechesis of the Lord is built,[15] and then, that of the Apostles and the Fathers of the Church. This catechesis unveils what lay hidden under the letter of the Old Testament: the mystery of Christ. It is called "typological" because it reveals the newness of Christ on the basis of the "figures" (types) which announce him in the deeds, words, and symbols of the first covenant. By this re-reading in the Spirit of Truth, starting from Christ, the figures are unveiled.[16] Thus the flood and Noah's ark prefigured salvation by Baptism,[17] as did the cloud and the crossing of the Red Sea. Water from the rock was the figure of the spiritual gifts of Christ, and manna in the desert prefigured the Eucharist, "the true bread from heaven."[18]

---

14   *LG* 2.

15   Cf. *DV* 14-16; *Lk* 24:13-49.

16   Cf. *2 Cor* 3:14-16.

17   Cf. *1 Pet* 3:21.

18   *Jn* 6:32; cf. *1 Cor* 10:1-6.

1095 For this reason the Church, especially during Advent and Lent and above all at the Easter Vigil, re-reads and re-lives the great events of salvation history in the "today" of her liturgy. But this *281* also demands that catechesis help the faithful to open themselves to this spiritual understanding of the economy of salvation as the *117* Church's liturgy reveals it and enables us to live it.

1096 *Jewish liturgy and Christian liturgy.* A better knowledge of the Jewish people's faith and religious life as professed and lived even now can help our better understanding of certain aspects of Christian liturgy. For both Jews and Christians Sacred Scripture is an essential part of their respective liturgies: in the proclamation of the Word of God, the response to this word, prayer of praise and intercession for the living and the dead, invocation of God's mercy. In its characteristic structure the Liturgy of the Word originates in Jewish prayer. The Liturgy of the Hours and other liturgical texts and formularies, as well as those of our most venerable *1174* prayers, including the Lord's Prayer, have parallels in Jewish prayer. The Eucharistic Prayers also draw their inspiration from the Jewish tradition. The relationship between Jewish liturgy and Christian liturgy, but also their *1352* differences in content, are particularly evident in the great feasts of the liturgical year, such as Passover. Christians and Jews both celebrate the Passover. For Jews, it is the Passover of history, tending toward the future; for *840* Christians, it is the Passover fulfilled in the death and Resurrection of Christ, though always in expectation of its definitive consummation.

1097 In the *liturgy of the New Covenant* every liturgical action, especially the celebration of the Eucharist and the sacraments, is an encounter between Christ and the Church. The liturgical assembly derives its unity from the "communion of the Holy Spirit" who gathers the children of God into the one Body of Christ. This assembly transcends racial, cultural, social – indeed, all human affinities.

1098 The assembly should *prepare* itself to encounter its Lord and to become "a people well disposed." The preparation of hearts is the joint work of the Holy Spirit and the assembly, especially of its ministers. The grace of the Holy Spirit seeks to awaken faith, conversion of heart, and adherence to the Father's will. These *1430* dispositions are the precondition both for the reception of other graces conferred in the celebration itself and the fruits of new life which the celebration is intended to produce afterward.

The Holy Spirit recalls the mystery of Christ

1099 The Spirit and the Church cooperate to manifest Christ and his work of salvation in the liturgy. Primarily in the Eucharist, and by analogy in the other sacraments, the liturgy is the *memorial* of the mystery of salvation. The Holy Spirit is the Church's living memory.[19] *91*

---

19 Cf. *Jn* 14:26.

1134 **1100**   *The Word of God.* The Holy Spirit first recalls the meaning of the salvation event to the liturgical assembly by giving life to the Word of God, which is proclaimed so that it may be received and lived:

103, 131   In the celebration of the liturgy, Sacred Scripture is extremely important. From it come the lessons that are read and explained in the homily and the psalms that are sung. It is from the Scriptures that the prayers, collects, and hymns draw their inspiration and their force, and that actions and signs derive their meaning.[20]

117 **1101**   The Holy Spirit gives a spiritual understanding of the Word of God to those who read or hear it, according to the dispositions of their hearts. By means of the words, actions, and symbols that form the structure of a celebration, the Spirit puts both the faithful and the ministers into a living relationship with Christ, the Word and Image of the Father, so that they can live out the meaning of what they hear, contemplate, and do in the celebration.

1102   "By the saving word of God, faith . . . is nourished in the hearts of believers. By this faith then the congregation of the faithful begins and grows."[21] The proclamation does not stop with a teaching; it elicits the *response of faith* as consent and commitment,
143 directed at the covenant between God and his people. Once again it is the Holy Spirit who gives the grace of faith, strengthens it and makes it grow in the community. The liturgical assembly is first of all a communion in faith.

1362 **1103**   *Anamnesis.* The liturgical celebration always refers to God's saving interventions in history. "The economy of Revelation is realized by deeds and words which are intrinsically bound up with each other. . . . [T]he words for their part proclaim the works and bring to light the mystery they contain."[22] In the Liturgy of the Word the Holy Spirit "recalls" to the assembly all that Christ has done for us. In keeping with the nature of liturgical actions and the ritual traditions of the churches, the celebration "makes a remembrance" of the marvelous works of God in an anamnesis which may be more or less developed. The Holy Spirit who thus awakens the memory of the Church then inspires thanksgiving and praise (*doxology*).

---

20   *SC* 24.
21   *PO* 4.
22   *DV* 2.

The Holy Spirit makes present the mystery of Christ

1104   Christian liturgy not only recalls the events that saved us but actualizes them, makes them present. The Paschal mystery of Christ is celebrated, not repeated. It is the celebrations that are *1085* repeated, and in each celebration there is an outpouring of the Holy Spirit that makes the unique mystery present.

1105   The *Epiclesis* ("invocation upon") is the intercession in which the priest begs the Father to send the Holy Spirit, the Sanctifier, so that the offerings may become the body and blood of *1153* Christ and that the faithful, by receiving them, may themselves become a living offering to God.[23]

1106   Together with the anamnesis, the epiclesis is at the heart of each sacramental celebration, most especially of the Eucharist:

> You ask how the bread becomes the Body of Christ, and the *1375*
> wine ... the Blood of Christ. I shall tell you: the Holy Spirit comes
> upon them and accomplishes what surpasses every word and
> thought. . . . Let it be enough for you to understand that it is by
> the Holy Spirit, just as it was of the Holy Virgin and by the Holy
> Spirit that the Lord, through and in himself, took flesh.[24]

1107   The Holy Spirit's transforming power in the liturgy hastens the coming of the kingdom and the consummation of the mystery of salvation. While we wait in hope he causes us really to anticipate the fullness of communion with the Holy Trinity. Sent *2816* by the Father who hears the epiclesis of the Church, the Spirit gives life to those who accept him and is, even now, the "guarantee" of their inheritance.[25]

The communion of the Holy Spirit

1108   In every liturgical action the Holy Spirit is sent in order to bring us into communion with Christ and so to form his Body. The Holy Spirit is like the sap of the Father's vine which bears fruit on *788* its branches.[26] The most intimate cooperation of the Holy Spirit *1091* and the Church is achieved in the liturgy. The Spirit, who is the Spirit of communion, abides indefectibly in the Church. For this reason the Church is the great sacrament of divine communion *775* which gathers God's scattered children together. Communion with

---

23   Cf. *Rom* 12:1.
24   St. John Damascene, *De fide orth.* 4, 13: PG 94, 1145A.
25   Cf. *Eph* 1:14; *2 Cor* 1:22.
26   Cf. *Jn* 15:1-17; *Gal* 5:22.

the Holy Trinity and fraternal communion are inseparably the fruit of the Spirit in the liturgy.[27]

1109 The epiclesis is also a prayer for the full effect of the assembly's communion with the mystery of Christ. "The grace of the Lord Jesus Christ and the love of God and the fellowship of the Holy Spirit"[28] have to remain with us always and bear fruit beyond the Eucharistic celebration. The Church therefore asks the Father to send the Holy Spirit to make the lives of the faithful a living 1368 sacrifice to God by their spiritual transformation into the image of Christ, by concern for the Church's unity, and by taking part in her mission through the witness and service of charity.

IN BRIEF

1110 In the liturgy of the Church, God the Father is blessed and adored as the source of all the blessings of creation and salvation with which he has blessed us in his Son, in order to give us the Spirit of filial adoption.

1111 Christ's work in the liturgy is sacramental: because his mystery of salvation is made present there by the power of his Holy Spirit; because his Body, which is the Church, is like a sacrament (sign and instrument) in which the Holy Spirit dispenses the mystery of salvation; and because through her liturgical actions the pilgrim Church already participates, as by a fore-taste, in the heavenly liturgy.

1112 The mission of the Holy Spirit in the liturgy of the Church is to prepare the assembly to encounter Christ; to recall and manifest Christ to the faith of the assembly; to make the saving work of Christ present and active by his transforming power; and to make the gift of communion bear fruit in the Church.

---

27 Cf. *1 Jn* 1:3-7.
28 *2 Cor* 13:13.

ARTICLE 2
THE PASCHAL MYSTERY IN THE CHURCH'S SACRAMENTS

1113   The whole liturgical life of the Church revolves around the   *1210*
Eucharistic sacrifice and the sacraments.[29] There are seven sacraments
in the Church: Baptism, Confirmation or Chrismation, Eucharist,
Penance, Anointing of the Sick, Holy Orders, and Matrimony.[30] This
article will discuss what is common to the Church's seven sacraments
from a doctrinal point of view. What is common to them in terms of
their celebration will be presented in the second chapter, and what is
distinctive about each will be the topic of the *Section Two*.

I.   THE SACRAMENTS OF CHRIST

1114   "Adhering to the teaching of the Holy Scriptures, to the
apostolic traditions, and to the consensus . . . of the Fathers," we
profess that "the sacraments of the new law were . . . all instituted
by Jesus Christ our Lord."[31]

1115   Jesus' words and actions during his hidden life and public
ministry were already salvific, for they anticipated the power of his
Paschal mystery. They announced and prepared what he was going
to give the Church when all was accomplished. The mysteries of   *512-560*
Christ's life are the foundations of what he would henceforth dispense
in the sacraments, through the ministers of his Church, for "what was
visible in our Savior has passed over into his mysteries."[32]

1116   Sacraments are "powers that comes forth" from the Body   *1504*
of Christ,[33] which is ever-living and life-giving. They are actions of   *774*
the Holy Spirit at work in his Body, the Church. They are "the
masterworks of God" in the new and everlasting covenant.

II.   THE SACRAMENTS OF THE CHURCH

1117   As she has done for the canon of Sacred Scripture and for   *120*
the doctrine of the faith, the Church, by the power of the Spirit who
guides her "into all truth," has gradually recognized this treasure

---

29 Cf. *SC* 6.
30 Cf. Council of Lyons II (1274) DS 860; Council of Florence (1439): DS 1310;
    Council of Trent (1547): DS 1601.
31 Council of Trent (1547): DS 1600-1601.
32 St. Leo the Great, *Sermo.* 74, 2: PL 54, 398.
33 Cf. *Lk* 5:17; 6:19; 8:46.

received from Christ and, as the faithful steward of God's mysteries, has determined its "dispensation."[34] Thus the Church has discerned over the centuries that among liturgical celebrations there are seven that are, in the strict sense of the term, sacraments instituted by the Lord.

1118   The sacraments are "of the Church" in the double sense that they are "by her" and "for her." They are "by the Church," for she is the sacrament of Christ's action at work in her through the
1396   mission of the Holy Spirit. They are "for the Church" in the sense that "the sacraments make the Church,"[35] since they manifest and communicate to men, above all in the Eucharist, the mystery of communion with the God who is love, One in three persons.

792 **1119**   Forming "as it were, one mystical person" with Christ the head, the Church acts in the sacraments as "an organically structured priestly community."[36] Through Baptism and Confirmation the priestly people is enabled to celebrate the liturgy, while those of the faithful "who have received Holy Orders, are appointed to nourish the Church with the word and grace of God in the name of Christ."[37]

1547 **1120**   The ordained ministry or *ministerial* priesthood is at the service of the baptismal priesthood.[38] The ordained priesthood guarantees that it really is Christ who acts in the sacraments through the Holy Spirit for the Church. The saving mission entrusted by the Father to his incarnate Son was committed to the apostles and through them to their successors: they receive the Spirit of Jesus to act in his name and in his person.[39] The ordained minister is the sacramental bond that ties the liturgical action to what the apostles said and did and, through them, to the words and actions of Christ, the source and foundation of the sacraments.

1121   The three sacraments of Baptism, Confirmation, and Holy Orders confer, in addition to grace, a sacramental *character* or "seal"
1272, 1304, by which the Christian shares in Christ's priesthood and is made
1582 a member of the Church according to different states and functions. This configuration to Christ and to the Church, brought about by the Spirit, is indelible;[40] it remains for ever in the Christian as a

---

34 *Jn* 16:13; cf. *Mt* 13:52; *1 Cor* 4:1.
35 St. Augustine, *De civ. Dei*, 22, 17: PL 41, 779; cf. St. Thomas Aquinas, *STh* III, 64, 2 *ad* 3.
36 *LG* 11; cf. Pius XII, *Mystici Corporis* (1943).
37 *LG* 11 § 2.
38 Cf. *LG* 10 § 2.
39 Cf. *Jn* 20:21-23; *Lk* 24:47; *Mt* 28:18-20.
40 Cf. Council of Trent (1547): DS 1609.

positive disposition for grace, a promise and guarantee of divine protection, and as a vocation to divine worship and to the service of the Church. Therefore these sacraments can never be repeated.

III.   THE SACRAMENTS OF FAITH

1122   Christ sent his apostles so that "repentance and forgiveness of sins should be preached in his name to all nations."[41] "Go therefore and make disciples of all nations, baptizing them in the name of the Father and of the Son and of the Holy Spirit."[42] The mission to baptize, and so the sacramental mission, is implied in the mission to evangelize, because the sacrament is prepared for *849* by *the word of God and by the faith* which is assent to this word: *1236*

> The People of God is formed into one in the first place by the Word of the living God. . . . The preaching of the Word is required for the sacramental ministry itself, since the sacraments are sacraments of faith, drawing their origin and nourishment from the Word.[43]

1123   "The purpose of the sacraments is to sanctify men, to build up the Body of Christ and, finally, to give worship to God. Because they are signs they also instruct. They not only presuppose faith, but by words and objects they also nourish, strengthen, and ex- *1154* press it. That is why they are called 'sacraments *of faith*.'"[44]

1124   The Church's faith precedes the faith of the believer who *166* is invited to adhere to it. When the Church celebrates the sacraments, she confesses the faith received from the apostles – whence the ancient saying: *lex orandi, lex credendi* (or: *legem credendi lex* *1327* *statuat supplicandi,* according to Prosper of Aquitaine [5th cent.]).[45] The law of prayer is the law of faith: the Church believes as she *78* prays. Liturgy is a constitutive element of the holy and living Tradition.[46]

1125   For this reason no sacramental rite may be modified or *1205* manipulated at the will of the minister or the community. Even the supreme authority in the Church may not change the liturgy arbitrarily, but only in the obedience of faith and with religious respect for the mystery of the liturgy.

---

41   *Lk* 24:47.
42   *Mt* 28:19.
43   *PO* 4 §§ 1, 2.
44   *SC* 59.
45   *Ep.* 8.
46   Cf. *DV* 8.

1126   Likewise, since the sacraments express and develop the communion of faith in the Church, the *lex orandi* is one of the essential
815 criteria of the dialogue that seeks to restore the unity of Christians.[47]

IV.   THE SACRAMENTS OF SALVATION

1127   Celebrated worthily in faith, the sacraments confer the grace that they signify.[48] They are *efficacious* because in them Christ
1084 himself is at work: it is he who baptizes, he who acts in his sacraments in order to communicate the grace that each sacrament signifies. The Father always hears the prayer of his Son's Church
1105 which, in the epiclesis of each sacrament, expresses her faith in the
696 power of the Spirit. As fire transforms into itself everything it touches, so the Holy Spirit transforms into the divine life whatever is subjected to his power.

1128   This is the meaning of the Church's affirmation[49] that the sacraments act *ex opere operato* (literally: "by the very fact of the action's being performed"), i.e., by virtue of the saving work of Christ, accomplished once for all. It follows that "the sacrament is not wrought by the righteousness of either the celebrant or the
1584 recipient, but by the power of God."[50] From the moment that a sacrament is celebrated in accordance with the intention of the Church, the power of Christ and his Spirit acts in and through it, independently of the personal holiness of the minister. Nevertheless, the fruits of the sacraments also depend on the disposition of the one who receives them.

1257 **1129**   The Church affirms that for believers the sacraments of the
2003 New Covenant are *necessary for salvation*.[51] "Sacramental grace" is the grace of the Holy Spirit, given by Christ and proper to each sacrament. The Spirit heals and transforms those who receive him by conforming
460 them to the Son of God. The fruit of the sacramental life is that the Spirit of adoption makes the faithful partakers in the divine nature[52] by uniting them in a living union with the only Son, the Savior.

V.   THE SACRAMENTS OF ETERNAL LIFE

1130   The Church celebrates the mystery of her Lord "until he comes," when God will be "everything to everyone."[53] Since the

---

47 Cf. *UR* 2; 15.
48 Cf. Council of Trent (1547): DS 1605; DS 1606.
49 Cf. Council of Trent (1547): DS 1608.
50 St. Thomas Aquinas, *STh* III, 68, 8.
51 Cf. Council of Trent (1547): DS 1604.
52 Cf. 2 *Pet* 1:4.

apostolic age the liturgy has been drawn toward its goal by the Spirit's groaning in the Church: *Marana tha!*[54] The liturgy thus shares in Jesus' desire: "I have earnestly desired to eat this Passover with you . . . until it is fulfilled in the kingdom of God."[55] In the sacraments of Christ the Church already receives the guarantee of her inheritance and even now shares in everlasting life, while "awaiting our blessed hope, the appearing of the glory of our great God and Savior Christ Jesus."[56] The "Spirit and the Bride say, 'Come . . . Come, Lord Jesus!'"[57]

2817

950

> St. Thomas sums up the various aspects of sacramental signs: "Therefore a sacrament is a sign that commemorates what precedes it – Christ's Passion; demonstrates what is accomplished in us through Christ's Passion – grace; and prefigures what that Passion pledges to us – future glory."[58]

IN BRIEF

1131 The sacraments are efficacious signs of grace, instituted by Christ and entrusted to the Church, by which divine life is dispensed to us. The visible rites by which the sacraments are celebrated signify and make present the graces proper to each sacrament. They bear fruit in those who receive them with the required dispositions.

1132 The Church celebrates the sacraments as a priestly community structured by the baptismal priesthood and the priesthood of ordained ministers.

1133 The Holy Spirit prepares the faithful for the sacraments by the Word of God and the faith which welcomes that word in well-disposed hearts. Thus the sacraments strengthen faith and express it.

1134 The fruit of sacramental life is both personal and ecclesial. For every one of the faithful on the one hand, this fruit is life for God in Christ Jesus; for the Church, on the other, it is an increase in charity and in her mission of witness.

---

53   *1 Cor* 11:26; 15:28.
54   *1 Cor* 16:22.
55   *Lk* 22:15.
56   *Titus* 2:13.
57   *Rev* 22:17, 20.
58   St. Thomas Aquinas, *STh* III, 60, 3.

CHAPTER TWO
THE SACRAMENTAL CELEBRATION
OF THE PASCHAL MYSTERY

1135   The catechesis of the liturgy entails first of all an understanding of the sacramental economy (Chapter One). In this light, the innovation of its *celebration* is revealed. This chapter will therefore treat of the celebration of the sacraments of the Church. It will consider that which, through the diversity of liturgical traditions, is common to the celebration of the seven sacraments. What is proper to each will be treated later. This fundamental catechesis on the sacramental celebrations responds to the first questions posed by the faithful regarding this subject:

– Who celebrates the liturgy?

– How is the liturgy celebrated?

– When is the liturgy celebrated?

– Where is the liturgy celebrated?

ARTICLE 1
CELEBRATING THE CHURCH'S LITURGY

I.   WHO CELEBRATES?

795   **1136**   Liturgy is an "action" of the *whole Christ* (*Christus totus*).
1090   Those who even now celebrate it without signs are already in the heavenly liturgy, where celebration is wholly communion and feast.

2642   **The celebrants of the heavenly liturgy**

1137   The book of *Revelation* of St. John, read in the Church's liturgy, first reveals to us, "A throne stood in heaven, with one seated on the throne": "the Lord God."[1] It then shows the Lamb, "standing, as though it had been slain": Christ crucified and risen, the one high priest of the true sanctuary, the same one "who offers
662   and is offered, who gives and is given."[2] Finally it presents "the river of the water of life . . . flowing from the throne of God and of the Lamb," one of most beautiful symbols of the Holy Spirit.[3]

---

1   *Rev* 4:2, 8; *Isa* 6:1; cf. *Ezek* 1:26-28.
2   *Rev* 5:6; *Liturgy of St. John Chrysostom*, Anaphora; cf. *Jn* 1:29;
    Heb 4:14-15; 10:19-2.
3   *Rev* 22:1; cf. 21:6; *Jn* 4:10-14.

1138   "Recapitulated in Christ," these are the ones who take part in the service of the praise of God and the fulfillment of his plan: the heavenly powers, all creation (the four living beings), the servants of the Old and New Covenants (the twenty-four elders), the new People of God (the one hundred and forty-four thousand),[4] especially the martyrs "slain for the word of God," and the all-holy Mother of God (the Woman), the Bride of the Lamb,[5] and finally "a great multitude which no one could number, from every nation, from all tribes, and peoples and tongues."[6]

335

1370

1139   It is in this eternal liturgy that the Spirit and the Church enable us to participate whenever we celebrate the mystery of salvation in the sacraments.

The celebrants of the sacramental liturgy

1140   It is the whole *community*, the Body of Christ united with its Head, that celebrates. "Liturgical services are not private functions but are celebrations of the Church which is 'the sacrament of unity,' namely, the holy people united and organized under the authority of the bishops. Therefore, liturgical services pertain to the whole Body of the Church. They manifest it, and have effects upon it. But they touch individual members of the Church in different ways, depending on their orders, their role in the liturgical services, and their actual participation in them."[7] For this reason, "rites which are meant to be celebrated in common, with the faithful present and actively participating, should as far as possible be celebrated in that way rather than by an individual and quasi-privately."[8]

752, 1348

1372

1141   The celebrating assembly is the community of the baptized who, "by regeneration and the anointing of the Holy Spirit, are consecrated to be a spiritual house and a holy priesthood, that . . . they may offer spiritual sacrifices."[9] This "common priesthood" is that of Christ the sole priest, in which all his members participate:[10]

1120

> Mother Church earnestly desires that all the faithful should be led to that full, conscious, and active participation in liturgical celebrations which is demanded by the very nature of the liturgy, and to which the Christian people, "a chosen

---

4   Cf. *Rev* 4-5; 7:1-8; 14:1; *Isa* 6:2-3.
5   *Rev* 6:9-11; *Rev* 21:9; cf. 12.
6   *Rev* 7:9.
7   *SC* 26.
8   *SC* 27.
9   *LG* 10; cf. *1 Pet* 2:4-5.
10   Cf. *LG* 10; 34; *PO* 2.

1268   ·   race, a royal priesthood, a holy nation, a redeemed people,"
                        have a right and an obligation by reason of their Baptism.[11]

1142   But "the members do not all have the same function."[12]
Certain members are called by God, in and through the Church, to
a special service of the community. These servants are chosen and
consecrated by the sacrament of Holy Orders, by which the Holy
Spirit enables them to act in the person of Christ the head, for the
service of all the members of the Church.[13] The ordained minister
1549 is, as it were, an "icon" of Christ the priest. Since it is in the
Eucharist that the sacrament of the Church is made fully visible, it
is in his presiding at the Eucharist that the bishop's ministry is most
1561 evident, as well as, in communion with him, the ministry of priests
and deacons.

1143   For the purpose of assisting the work of the common
priesthood of the faithful, other *particular ministries* also exist, not
903 consecrated by the sacrament of Holy Orders; their functions are
determined by the bishops, in accord with liturgical traditions and
pastoral needs. "Servers, readers, commentators, and members of
1672 the choir also exercise a genuine liturgical function."[14]

1144   In the celebration of the sacraments it is thus the whole
assembly that is *leitourgos*, each according to his function, but in
the "unity of the Spirit" who acts in all. "In liturgical celebrations
each person, minister or layman, who has an office to perform,
should carry out *all* and *only* those parts which pertain to his office
by the nature of the rite and the norms of the liturgy."[15]

II.   How Is the Liturgy Celebrated?

1333-1340 **Signs and symbols**

53 **1145**   A sacramental celebration is woven from signs and symbols. In keeping with the divine pedagogy of salvation, their meaning is rooted in the work of creation and in human culture,
specified by the events of the Old Covenant and fully revealed in
the person and work of Christ.

---

11   *SC* 14; cf. *1 Pet* 2:9; 2:4-5.
12   *Rom* 12:4.
13   Cf. *PO* 2; 15.
14   *SC* 29.
15   *SC* 28.

1146   *Signs of the human world.* In human life, signs and symbols occupy an important place. As a being at once body and spirit, man expresses and perceives spiritual realities through physical signs *362, 2702* and symbols. As a social being, man needs signs and symbols to communicate with others, through language, gestures, and actions. The same holds true for his relationship with God.   *1879*

1147   God speaks to man through the visible creation. The ma- *299* terial cosmos is so presented to man's intelligence that he can read there traces of its Creator.[16] Light and darkness, wind and fire, water and earth, the tree and its fruit speak of God and symbolize both his greatness and his nearness.

1148   Inasmuch as they are creatures, these perceptible realities can become means of expressing the action of God who sanctifies men, and the action of men who offer worship to God. The same is true of signs and symbols taken from the social life of man: washing and anointing, breaking bread and sharing the cup can express the sanctifying presence of God and man's gratitude toward his Creator.

1149   The great religions of mankind witness, often impres- *843* sively, to this cosmic and symbolic meaning of religious rites. The liturgy of the Church presupposes, integrates and sanctifies elements from creation and human culture, conferring on them the dignity of signs of grace, of the new creation in Jesus Christ.

1150   *Signs of the covenant.* The Chosen People received from God *1334* distinctive signs and symbols that marked its liturgical life. These are no longer solely celebrations of cosmic cycles and social gestures, but signs of the covenant, symbols of God's mighty deeds for his people. Among these liturgical signs from the Old Covenant are circumcision, anointing and consecration of kings and priests, laying on of hands, sacrifices, and above all the Passover. The Church sees in these signs a prefiguring of the sacraments of the New Covenant.

1151   *Signs taken up by Christ.* In his preaching the Lord Jesus *1335* often makes use of the signs of creation to make known the mysteries of the Kingdom of God.[17] He performs healings and illustrates his preaching with physical signs or symbolic gestures.[18] He gives new meaning to the deeds and signs of the Old Covenant, above all to the Exodus and the Passover,[19] for he himself is the meaning of all these signs.

---

16 Cf. *Wis* 13:1; *Rom* 1:19 f.; *Acts* 14:17.
17 Cf. *Lk* 8:10.
18 Cf. *Jn* 9:6; *Mk* 7:33 ff.; 8:22 ff.

1152   *Sacramental signs.* Since Pentecost, it is through the sacramental signs of his Church that the Holy Spirit carries on the work of sanctification. The sacraments of the Church do not abolish but purify and integrate all the richness of the signs and symbols of the cosmos and of social life. Further, they fulfill the types and figures of the Old Covenant, signify and make actively present the salvation wrought by Christ, and prefigure and anticipate the glory of heaven.

Words and actions

1153   A sacramental celebration is a meeting of God's children with their Father, in Christ and the Holy Spirit; this meeting takes
53   the form of a dialogue, through actions and words. Admittedly, the symbolic actions are already a language, but the Word of God and the response of faith have to accompany and give life to them, so that the seed of the Kingdom can bear its fruit in good soil. The liturgical actions signify what the Word of God expresses: both his free initiative and his people's response of faith.

1100 **1154**   The *liturgy of the Word* is an integral part of sacramental celebrations. To nourish the faith of believers, the signs which accompany the Word of God should be emphasized: the book of
103   the Word (a lectionary or a book of the Gospels), its veneration (procession, incense, candles), the place of its proclamation (lectern or ambo), its audible and intelligible reading, the minister's homily which extends its proclamation, and the responses of the assembly (acclamations, meditation psalms, litanies, and profession of faith).

1155   The liturgical word and action are inseparable both insofar
1127   as they are signs and instruction and insofar as they accomplish what they signify. When the Holy Spirit awakens faith, he not only gives an understanding of the Word of God, but through the sacraments also makes present the "wonders" of God which it proclaims. The Spirit makes present and communicates the Father's work, fulfilled by the beloved Son.

Singing and music

1156   "The musical tradition of the universal Church is a treasure of inestimable value, greater even than that of any other art. The main reason for this pre-eminence is that, as a combination of sacred music and words, it forms a necessary or integral part of solemn liturgy."[20] The composition and singing of inspired

---

19   Cf. *Lk* 9:31; 22:7-20.

psalms, often accompanied by musical instruments, were already closely linked to the liturgical celebrations of the Old Covenant. The Church continues and develops this tradition: "Address . . . one another in psalms and hymns and spiritual songs, singing and making melody to the Lord with all your heart." "He who sings prays twice."[21]

1157 Song and music fulfill their function as signs in a manner all the more significant when they are "more closely connected . . . with the liturgical action,"[22] according to three principal criteria: beauty expressive of prayer, the unanimous participation of the assembly at the designated moments, and the solemn character of the cele-   *2502* bration. In this way they participate in the purpose of the liturgical words and actions: the glory of God and the sanctification of the faithful:[23]

> How I wept, deeply moved by your hymns, songs, and the voices that echoed through your Church! What emotion I experienced in them! Those sounds flowed into my ears, distilling the truth in my heart. A feeling of devotion surged within me, and tears streamed down my face – tears that did me good.[24]

1158 The harmony of signs (song, music, words, and actions) is all the more expressive and fruitful when expressed in the *cultural* *1201* *richness* of the People of God who celebrate.[25] Hence "religious singing by the faithful is to be intelligently fostered so that in *1674* devotions and sacred exercises as well as in liturgical services," in conformity with the Church's norms, "the voices of the faithful may be heard." But "the texts intended to be sung must always be in conformity with Catholic doctrine. Indeed they should be drawn chiefly from the Sacred Scripture and from liturgical sources."[26]

Holy images   *476-477*
                                                                   2129-2132

1159 The sacred image, the liturgical icon, principally repre-sents *Christ*. It cannot represent the invisible and incomprehensible God, but the incarnation of the Son of God has ushered in a new "economy" of images:

---

20 *SC* 112.
21 *Eph* 5:19; St. Augustine, *En. in Ps.* 72, 1: PL 36, 914; cf. *Col* 3:16.
22 *SC* 112 § 3.
23 Cf. *SC* 112.
24 St. Augustine, *Conf.* 9, 6, 14: PL 32, 769-770.
25 Cf. *SC* 119.
26 *SC* 118; 121.

Previously God, who has neither a body nor a face, absolutely could not be represented by an image. But now that he has made himself visible in the flesh and has lived with men, I can make an image of what I have seen of God . . . and contemplate the glory of the Lord, his face unveiled.[27]

1160   Christian iconography expresses in images the same Gospel message that Scripture communicates by words. Image and word illuminate each other:

We declare that we preserve intact all the written and unwritten traditions of the Church which have been entrusted to us. One of these traditions consists in the production of representational artwork, which accords with the history of the preaching of the Gospel. For it confirms that the incarnation of the Word of God was real and not imaginary, and to our benefit as well, for realities that illustrate each other undoubtedly reflect each other's meaning.[28]

1161   All the signs in the liturgical celebrations are related to Christ: as are sacred images of the holy Mother of God and of the saints as well. They truly signify Christ, who is glorified in them. They make manifest the "cloud of witnesses"[29] who continue to participate in the salvation of the world and to whom we are united, above all in sacramental celebrations. Through their icons, it is man "in the image of God," finally transfigured "into his likeness,"[30] who is revealed to our faith. So too are the angels, who also are recapitulated in Christ:

Following the divinely inspired teaching of our holy Fathers and the tradition of the Catholic Church (for we know that this tradition comes from the Holy Spirit who dwells in her) we rightly define with full certainty and correctness that, like the figure of the precious and life-giving cross, venerable and holy images of our Lord and God and Savior, Jesus Christ, our inviolate Lady, the holy Mother of God, and the venerated angels, all the saints and the just, whether painted or made of mosaic or another suitable material, are to be exhibited in the holy churches of God, on sacred vessels and vestments, walls and panels, in houses and on streets.[31]

2502 **1162**   "The beauty of the images moves me to contemplation, as a meadow delights the eyes and subtly infuses the soul with the glory of God."[32] Similarly, the contemplation of sacred icons,

---

27 St. John Damascene, *De imag.* 1, 16: PG 96:1245-1248.
28 Council of Nicaea II (787): COD 111.
29 *Heb* 12:1.
30 Cf. *Rom* 8:29; *1 Jn* 3:2.
31 Council of Nicaea II: DS 600.
32 St. John Damascene, *De imag.* 1, 27: PG 94, 1268A, B.

united with meditation on the Word of God and the singing of liturgical hymns, enters into the harmony of the signs of celebration so that the mystery celebrated is imprinted in the heart's memory and is then expressed in the new life of the faithful.

III. WHEN IS THE LITURGY CELEBRATED?

Liturgical seasons

1163 "Holy Mother Church believes that she should celebrate the saving work of her divine Spouse in a sacred commemoration on certain days throughout the course of the year. Once each week, on the day which she has called the Lord's Day, she keeps the memory of the Lord's resurrection. She also celebrates it once every year, together with his blessed Passion, at Easter, that most solemn of all feasts. In the course of the year, moreover, she unfolds the whole mystery of Christ . . . . Thus recalling the mysteries of the *512* redemption, she opens up to the faithful the riches of her Lord's powers and merits, so that these are in some way made present in every age; the faithful lay hold of them and are filled with saving grace."[33]

1164 From the time of the Mosaic law, the People of God have observed fixed feasts, beginning with Passover, to commemorate the astonishing actions of the Savior God, to give him thanks for them, to perpetuate their remembrance, and to teach new generations to conform their conduct to them. In the age of the Church, between the Passover of Christ already accomplished once for all, and its consummation in the kingdom of God, the liturgy celebrated on fixed days bears the imprint of the newness of the mystery of Christ.

1165 When the Church celebrates the mystery of Christ, there is *2659-2836* a word that marks her prayer: "Today!" – a word echoing the prayer her Lord taught her and the call of the Holy Spirit.[34] This "today" of the living God which man is called to enter is "the hour" of Jesus' Passover, which reaches across and underlies all history: *1085*

> Life extends over all beings and fills them with unlimited light; the Orient of orients pervades the universe, and he who was "before the daystar" and before the heavenly bodies, immortal and vast, the great Christ, shines over all beings more brightly than the sun. Therefore a day of long, eternal light is ushered in for us who believe in him, a day which is never blotted out: the mystical Passover.[35]

---

33 *SC* 102.
34 Cf. *Mt* 6:11; *Heb* 3:7-4:11; *Ps* 95:7.

2174-2188 **The Lord's day**

1166   "By a tradition handed down from the apostles which took its origin from the very day of Christ's Resurrection, the Church celebrates the Paschal mystery every seventh day, which day is
1343 appropriately called the Lord's Day or Sunday."[36] The day of Christ's Resurrection is both the first day of the week, the memorial of the first day of creation, and the "eighth day," on which Christ after his "rest" on the great sabbath inaugurates the "day that the Lord has made," the "day that knows no evening."[37] The Lord's Supper is its center, for there the whole community of the faithful encounters the risen Lord who invites them to his banquet:[38]

> The Lord's day, the day of Resurrection, the day of Christians, is our day. It is called the Lord's day because on it the Lord rose victorious to the Father. If pagans call it the "day of the sun," we willingly agree, for today the light of the world is raised, today is revealed the sun of justice with healing in his rays.[39]

1167   Sunday is the pre-eminent day for the liturgical assembly, when the faithful gather "to listen to the word of God and take part in the Eucharist, thus calling to mind the Passion, Resurrection, and glory of the Lord Jesus, and giving thanks to God who 'has begotten them again, by the resurrection of Jesus Christ from the dead' unto a living hope":[40]

> When we ponder, O Christ, the marvels accomplished on this day, the Sunday of your holy resurrection, we say: "Blessed is Sunday, for on it began creation . . . the world's salvation . . . the renewal of the human race . . . . On Sunday heaven and earth rejoiced and the whole universe was filled with light. Blessed is Sunday, for on it were opened the gates of paradise so that Adam and all the exiles might enter it without fear.[41]

---

35 St. Hippolytus, *De pasch.* 1-2: SCh 27, 117.
36 *SC* 106.
37 Byzantine liturgy.
38 Cf. *Jn* 21:12; *Lk* 24:30.
39 St. Jerome, *Pasch.*: CCL 78, 550.
40 *SC* 106.
41 Fanqîth, *The Syriac Office of Antioch*, vol. VI, first part of Summer, 193 B.

The liturgical year

1168   Beginning with the Easter Triduum as its source of light, the new age of the Resurrection fills the whole liturgical year with its brilliance. Gradually, on either side of this source, the year is transfigured by the liturgy. It really is a "year of the Lord's favor."[42] The economy of salvation is at work within the framework of time, but since its fulfillment in the Passover of Jesus and the outpouring of the Holy Spirit, the culmination of history is anticipated "as a foretaste," and the kingdom of God enters into our time.

2698

1169   Therefore *Easter* is not simply one feast among others, but the "Feast of feasts," the "Solemnity of solemnities," just as the Eucharist is the "Sacrament of sacraments" (the Great Sacrament). St. Athanasius calls Easter "the Great Sunday"[43] and the Eastern Churches call Holy Week "the Great Week." The mystery of the Resurrection, in which Christ crushed death, permeates with its powerful energy our old time, until all is subjected to him.

1330

560

1170   At the Council of Nicaea in 325, all the Churches agreed that Easter, the Christian Passover, should be celebrated on the Sunday following the first full moon (14 Nisan) after the vernal equinox. The reform of the Western calendar, called "Gregorian" after Pope Gregory XIII (1582), caused a discrepancy of several days with the Eastern calendar. Today, the Western and Eastern Churches are seeking an agreement in order once again to celebrate the day of the Lord's Resurrection on a common date.

1171   In the liturgical year the various aspects of the one Paschal mystery unfold. This is also the case with the cycle of feasts surrounding the mystery of the incarnation (Annunciation, Christmas, Epiphany). They commemorate the beginning of our salvation and communicate to us the first fruits of the Paschal mystery.

524

The sanctoral in the liturgical year

1172   "In celebrating this annual cycle of the mysteries of Christ, Holy Church honors the Blessed Mary, Mother of God, with a special love. She is inseparably linked with the saving work of her Son. In her the Church admires and exalts the most excellent fruit of redemption and joyfully contemplates, as in a faultless image, that which she herself desires and hopes wholly to be."[44]

971

2030

---

42   *Lk* 4:19.
43   St. Athanasius (*ad* 329) *ep. fest.* 1: PG 24, 1366.
44   *SC* 103.

957 **1173**   When the Church keeps the memorials of martyrs and other saints during the annual cycle, she proclaims the Paschal mystery in those "who have suffered and have been glorified with Christ. She proposes them to the faithful as examples who draw all men to the Father through Christ, and through their merits she begs for God's favors."[45]

The Liturgy of the Hours

1174   The mystery of Christ, his Incarnation and Passover, which we celebrate in the Eucharist especially at the Sunday assembly, permeates and transfigures the time of each day, through the celebration of the Liturgy of the Hours, "the divine office."[46]
2698 This celebration, faithful to the apostolic exhortations to "pray constantly," is "so devised that the whole course of the day and night is made holy by the praise of God."[47] In this "public prayer of the Church,"[48] the faithful (clergy, religious, and lay people) exercise the royal priesthood of the baptized. Celebrated in "the form approved" by the Church, the Liturgy of the Hours "is truly the voice of the Bride herself addressed to her Bridegroom. It is the very prayer which Christ himself together with his Body addresses to the Father."[49]

1175   The Liturgy of the Hours is intended to become the prayer of the whole People of God. In it Christ himself "continues his priestly work through his Church."[50] His members participate according to their own place in the Church and the circumstances of their lives: priests devoted to the pastoral ministry, because they are called to remain diligent in prayer and the service of the word; religious, by the charism of their consecrated lives; all the faithful as much as possible: "Pastors of souls should see to it that the principal hours, especially Vespers, are celebrated in common in church on Sundays and on the more solemn feasts. The laity, too, are encouraged to recite the divine office, either with the priests, or among themselves, or even individually."[51]

1176   The celebration of the Liturgy of the Hours demands not
2700 only harmonizing the voice with the praying heart, but also a deeper "understanding of the liturgy and of the Bible, especially of the Psalms."[52]

---

45 *SC* 104; cf. *SC* 108, 111.
46 Cf. *SC*, ch. IV, 83-101.
47 *SC* 84; *1 Thess* 5:17; *Eph* 6:18.
48 *SC* 98.
49 *SC* 84.
50 *SC* 83.
51 *SC* 100; cf. 86; 96; 98; *PO* 5.
52 *SC* 90.

1177   The hymns and litanies of the Liturgy of the Hours integrate the prayer of the psalms into the age of the Church, expressing the symbolism of the time of day, the liturgical season, or the feast being celebrated. Moreover, the reading from the Word of God at each Hour (with the subsequent responses or *troparia*) and readings from the Fathers and spiritual masters at certain Hours, reveal more deeply the meaning of the mystery being celebrated, assist in understanding the psalms, and prepare for silent prayer. The *lectio divina*, where the Word of God is so read and meditated that it becomes prayer, is thus rooted in the liturgical celebration.

2586

1178   The Liturgy of the Hours, which is like an extension of the Eucharistic celebration, does not exclude but rather in a complementary way calls forth the various devotions of the People of God, especially adoration and worship of the Blessed Sacrament.

1378

IV.   WHERE IS THE LITURGY CELEBRATED?

1179   The worship "in Spirit and in truth"[53] of the New Covenant is not tied exclusively to any one place. The whole earth is sacred and entrusted to the children of men. What matters above all is that, when the faithful assemble in the same place, they are the "living stones," gathered to be "built into a spiritual house."[54] For the Body of the risen Christ is the spiritual temple from which the source of living water springs forth: incorporated into Christ by the Holy Spirit, "we are the temple of the living God."[55]

586

1180   When the exercise of religious liberty is not thwarted,[56] Christians construct buildings for divine worship. These visible churches are not simply gathering places but signify and make visible the Church living in this place, the dwelling of God with men reconciled and united in Christ.

2106

1181   A church, "a house of prayer in which the Eucharist is celebrated and reserved, where the faithful assemble, and where is worshipped the presence of the Son of God our Savior, offered for us on the sacrificial altar for the help and consolation of the faithful – this house ought to be in good taste and a worthy place for prayer and sacred ceremonial."[57] In this "house of God" the truth and the harmony of the signs that make it up should show Christ to be present and active in this place.[58]

2691

---

53   *Jn* 4:24.
54   *1 Pet* 2:4-5.
55   *2 Cor* 6:16.
56   Cf. *DH* 4.
57   *PO* 5; cf. *SC* 122-127.

617, 1383 **1182**   The *altar* of the New Covenant is the Lord's Cross,[59] from which the sacraments of the Paschal mystery flow. On the altar, which is the center of the church, the sacrifice of the Cross is made present under sacramental signs. The altar is also the table of the Lord, to which the People of God are invited.[60] In certain Eastern liturgies, the altar is also the symbol of the tomb (Christ truly died and is truly risen).

1379 **1183**   The *tabernacle* is to be situated "in churches in a most worthy place
2120 with the greatest honor."[61] The dignity, placing, and security of the Eucharistic tabernacle should foster adoration before the Lord really present in the Blessed Sacrament of the altar.[62]

1241   The *sacred chrism* (*myron*), used in anointings as the sacramental sign of the seal of the gift of the Holy Spirit, is traditionally reserved and venerated in a secure place in the sanctuary. The oil of catechumens and the oil of the sick may also be placed there.

1184   The *chair* (*cathedra*) of the bishop or the priest "should express his office of presiding over the assembly and of directing prayer."[63]

103   The *lectern* (*ambo*): "The dignity of the Word of God requires the church to have a suitable place for announcing his message so that the attention of the people may be easily directed to that place during the liturgy of the Word."[64]

1185   The gathering of the People of God begins with Baptism; a church must have a place for the celebration of *Baptism* (baptistry) and for fostering remembrance of the baptismal promises (holy water font).

The renewal of the baptismal life requires *penance*. A church, then, must lend itself to the expression of repentance and the reception of forgiveness, which requires an appropriate place to receive penitents.

2717   A church must also be a space that invites us to the recollection and silent prayer that extend and internalize the great prayer of the Eucharist.

1186   Finally, the church has an eschatological significance. To enter into the house of God, we must cross a *threshold*, which
1130 symbolizes passing from the world wounded by sin to the world of the new Life to which all men are called. The visible church is a symbol of the Father's house toward which the People of God is journeying and where the Father "will wipe every tear from their eyes."[65] Also for this reason, the Church is the house of *all* God's children, open and welcoming.

---

58 Cf. *SC* 7.
59 Cf. *Heb* 13:10.
60 Cf. GIRM 259.
61 Paul VI, *Mysterium Fidei*: AAS (1965) 771.
62 Cf. *SC* 128.
63 GIRM 271.
64 GIRM 272.

IN BRIEF

1187 The liturgy is the work of the whole Christ, head and body. Our high priest celebrates it unceasingly in the heavenly liturgy, with the holy Mother of God, the apostles, all the saints, and the multitude of those who have already entered the kingdom.

1188 In a liturgical celebration, the whole assembly is *leitourgos,* each member according to his own function. The baptismal priesthood is that of the whole Body of Christ. But some of the faithful are ordained through the sacrament of Holy Orders to represent Christ as head of the Body.

1189 The liturgical celebration involves signs and symbols relating to creation (candles, water, fire), human life (washing, anointing, breaking bread) and the history of salvation (the rites of the Passover). Integrated into the world of faith and taken up by the power of the Holy Spirit, these cosmic elements, human rituals, and gestures of remembrance of God become bearers of the saving and sanctifying action of Christ.

1190 The Liturgy of the Word is an integral part of the celebration. The meaning of the celebration is expressed by the Word of God which is proclaimed and by the response of faith to it.

1191 Song and music are closely connected with the liturgical action. The criteria for their proper use are the beauty expressive of prayer, the unanimous participation of the assembly, and the sacred character of the celebration.

1192 Sacred images in our churches and homes are intended to awaken and nourish our faith in the mystery of Christ. Through the icon of Christ and his works of salvation, it is he whom we adore. Through sacred images of the holy Mother of God, of the angels and of the saints, we venerate the persons represented.

1193 Sunday, the "Lord's Day," is the principal day for the celebration of the Eucharist because it is the day of the Resurrection. It is the pre-eminent day of the liturgical

---

65 *Rev* 21:4.

assembly, the day of the Christian family, and the day of joy and rest from work. Sunday is "the foundation and kernel of the whole liturgical year" (*SC* 106).

1194   The Church, "in the course of the year, . . . unfolds the whole mystery of Christ from his Incarnation and Nativity through his Ascension, to Pentecost and the expectation of the blessed hope of the coming of the Lord" (*SC* 102 § 2).

1195   By keeping the memorials of the saints – first of all the holy Mother of God, then the apostles, the martyrs, and other saints – on fixed days of the liturgical year, the Church on earth shows that she is united with the liturgy of heaven. She gives glory to Christ for having accomplished his salvation in his glorified members; their example encourages her on her way to the Father.

1196   The faithful who celebrate the Liturgy of the Hours are united to Christ our high priest, by the prayer of the Psalms, meditation on the Word of God, and canticles and blessings, in order to be joined with his unceasing and universal prayer that gives glory to the Father and implores the gift of the Holy Spirit on the whole world.

1197   Christ is the true temple of God, "the place where his glory dwells"; by the grace of God, Christians also become temples of the Holy Spirit, living stones out of which the Church is built.

1198   In its earthly state the Church needs places where the community can gather together. Our visible churches, holy places, are images of the holy city, the heavenly Jerusalem, toward which we are making our way on pilgrimage.

1199   It is in these churches that the Church celebrates public worship to the glory of the Holy Trinity, hears the word of God and sings his praise, lifts up her prayer, and offers the sacrifice of Christ sacramentally present in the midst of the assembly. These churches are also places of recollection and personal prayer.

Article 2
LITURGICAL DIVERSITY AND THE UNITY OF THE MYSTERY

Liturgical traditions and the catholicity of the Church

1200 From the first community of Jerusalem until the parousia, it is the same Paschal mystery that the Churches of God, faithful to the apostolic faith, celebrate in every place. The mystery celebrated in the liturgy is one, but the forms of its celebration are diverse.   *2625*

1201 The mystery of Christ is so unfathomably rich that it cannot be exhausted by its expression in any single liturgical tradition. The history of the blossoming and development of these *2663* rites witnesses to a remarkable complementarity. When the Churches lived their respective liturgical traditions in the communion of the faith and the sacraments of the faith, they enriched *1158* one another and grew in fidelity to Tradition and to the common mission of the whole Church.[66]

1202 The diverse liturgical traditions have arisen by very reason *814* of the Church's mission. Churches of the same geographical and cultural area came to celebrate the mystery of Christ through particular expressions characterized by the culture: in the tradition *1674* of the "deposit of faith,"[67] in liturgical symbolism, in the organization of fraternal communion, in the theological understanding of the mysteries, and in various forms of holiness. Through the liturgical life of a local church, Christ, the light and salvation of all peoples, is made manifest to the particular people and culture to which that Church is sent and in which she is rooted. The Church is catholic, capable of integrating into her unity, while purifying *835* them, all the authentic riches of cultures.[68] *1937*

1203 The liturgical traditions or rites presently in use in the Church are the Latin (principally the Roman rite, but also the rites of certain local churches, such as the Ambrosian rite, or those of certain religious orders) and the Byzantine, Alexandrian or Coptic, Syriac, Armenian, Maronite, and Chaldean rites. In "faithful obedience to tradition, the sacred Council declares that Holy Mother Church holds all lawfully recognized rites to be of equal right and dignity, and that she wishes to preserve them in the future and to foster them in every way."[69]

---

66   Cf. Paul VI, *EN* 63-64.
67   *2 Tim* 1:14 (Vulg.).
68   Cf. *LG* 23; *UR* 4.
69   *SC* 4.

Liturgy and culture

2684 **1204**   The celebration of the liturgy, therefore, should correspond to the genius and culture of the different peoples.[70] In order
that the mystery of Christ be "made known to all the nations . . . to
bring about the obedience of faith,"[71] it must be proclaimed, celebrated, and lived in all cultures in such a way that they themselves
854, 1232 are not abolished by it, but redeemed and fulfilled:[72] It is with and
2527 through their own human culture, assumed and transfigured by
Christ, that the multitude of God's children has access to the Father,
in order to glorify him in the one Spirit.

1125 **1205**   "In the liturgy, above all that of the sacraments, there is an
immutable part, a part that is divinely instituted and of which the
Church is the guardian, and parts that *can be changed*, which the
Church has the power and on occasion also the duty to adapt to
the cultures of recently evangelized peoples."[73]

1206   "Liturgical diversity can be a source of enrichment, but it
can also provoke tensions, mutual misunderstandings, and even
schisms. In this matter it is clear that diversity must not damage
unity. It must express only fidelity to the common faith, to the
sacramental signs that the Church has received from Christ, and to
hierarchical communion. Cultural adaptation also requires a conversion of heart and even, where necessary, a breaking with ances-
tral customs incompatible with the Catholic faith."[74]

IN BRIEF

1207   It is fitting that liturgical celebration tends to express itself
in the culture of the people where the Church finds herself,
though without being submissive to it. Moreover, the
liturgy itself generates cultures and shapes them.

1208   The diverse liturgical traditions or rites, legitimately recognized, manifest the catholicity of the Church, because
they signify and communicate the same mystery of Christ.

1209   The criterion that assures unity amid the diversity of
liturgical traditions is fidelity to apostolic Tradition, i.e.,
the communion in the faith and the sacraments received
from the apostles, a communion that is both signified
and guaranteed by apostolic succession.

---

70 Cf. *SC* 37-40.
71 *Rom* 16:26.
72 Cf. *CT* 53.
73 John Paul II, *Vicesimus quintus annus,* 16; cf. *SC* 21.
74 John Paul II, *Vicesimus quintus annus,* 16.

SECTION TWO
THE SEVEN SACRAMENTS
OF THE CHURCH

1210   Christ instituted the sacraments of the new law. There are   *1113*
seven: Baptism, Confirmation (or Chrismation), the Eucharist, Penance, the Anointing of the Sick, Holy Orders and Matrimony. The
seven sacraments touch all the stages and all the important moments
of Christian life:[1] they give birth and increase, healing and mission to
the Christian's life of faith. There is thus a certain resemblance between the stages of natural life and the stages of the spiritual life.

1211   Following this analogy, the *first chapter* will expound the
three sacraments of Christian initiation; the *second*, the sacraments
of healing; and the *third*, the sacraments at the service of communion and the mission of the faithful. This order, while not the only
one possible, does allow one to see that the sacraments form an
organic whole in which each particular sacrament has its own vital
place. In this organic whole, the Eucharist occupies a unique place
as the "Sacrament of sacraments": "all the other sacraments are   *1374*
ordered to it as to their end."[2]

CHAPTER ONE
THE SACRAMENTS OF CHRISTIAN INITIATION

1212   The sacraments of Christian initiation – Baptism, Confirmation, and the Eucharist – lay the *foundations* of every Christian
life. "The sharing in the divine nature given to men through the
grace of Christ bears a certain likeness to the origin, development,
and nourishing of natural life. The faithful are born anew by
Baptism, strengthened by the sacrament of Confirmation, and
receive in the Eucharist the food of eternal life. By means of these
sacraments of Christian initiation, they thus receive in increasing
measure the treasures of the divine life and advance toward the
perfection of charity."[3]

---

1   Cf. St. Thomas Aquinas, *STh* III, 65, 1.
2   St. Thomas Aquinas, *STh* III, 65, 3.
3   Paul VI, apostolic constitution, *Divinae consortium naturae*: AAS 63 (1971)
    657; cf. RCIA Introduction 1-2.

ARTICLE 1
THE SACRAMENT OF BAPTISM

1213 Holy Baptism is the basis of the whole Christian life, the gateway to life in the Spirit (*vitae spiritualis ianua*),[4] and the door which gives access to the other sacraments. Through Baptism we are freed from sin and reborn as sons of God; we become members of Christ, are incorporated into the Church and made sharers in her mission: "Baptism is the sacrament of regeneration through water in the word."[5]

I.   WHAT IS THIS SACRAMENT CALLED?

1214 This sacrament is called *Baptism*, after the central rite by which it is carried out: to baptize (Greek *baptizein*) means to "plunge" or "immerse"; the "plunge" into the water symbolizes
628   the catechumen's burial into Christ's death, from which he rises up by resurrection with him, as "a new creature."[6]

1215 This sacrament is also called *"the washing of regeneration and renewal by the Holy Spirit,"* for it signifies and actually brings about
1257   the birth of water and the Spirit without which no one "can enter the kingdom of God."[7]

1216 "This bath is called *enlightenment*, because those who receive this [catechetical] instruction are enlightened in their understanding . . . ."[8] Having received in Baptism the Word, "the true light that enlightens every man," the person baptized has been "enlightened,"
1243   he becomes a "son of light," indeed, he becomes "light" himself:[9]

> Baptism is God's most beautiful and magnificent gift. . . . We call it gift, grace, anointing, enlightenment, garment of immortality, bath of rebirth, seal, and most precious gift. It is called *gift* because it is conferred on those who bring nothing of their own; *grace* since it is given even to the guilty; *Baptism* because sin is buried in the water; *anointing* for it is priestly and royal as are those who are anointed; *enlightenment* because it radiates light; *clothing* since it veils our shame; *bath* because it washes; and *seal* as it is our guard and the sign of God's Lordship.[10]

---

4   Cf. Council of Florence: DS 1314: *vitae spiritualis ianua*.
5   *Roman Catechism* II, 2, 5; cf. Council of Florence: DS 1314; CIC, cann. 204 § 1; 849; CCEO, can. 675 § 1.
6   *2 Cor* 5:17; *Gal* 6:15; cf. *Rom* 6:3-4; *Col* 2:12.
7   *Titus* 3:5; *Jn* 3:5.
8   St. Justin, *Apol.* 1, 61, 12: PG 6, 421.
9   *Jn* 1:9; *1 Thess* 5:5; *Heb* 10:32; *Eph* 5:8.
10   St. Gregory of Nazianzus, *Oratio* 40, 3-4: PG 36, 361C.

II.   BAPTISM IN THE ECONOMY OF SALVATION

Prefigurations of Baptism in the Old Covenant

1217   In the liturgy of the Easter Vigil, during the *blessing of the baptismal water*, the Church solemnly commemorates the great events in salvation history that already prefigured the mystery of Baptism:

> Father, you give us grace through sacramental signs,
>   which tell us of the wonders of your unseen power.
>
> In Baptism we use your gift of water,
>   which you have made a rich symbol
>   of the grace you give us in this sacrament.[11]

1218   Since the beginning of the world, water, so humble and   *344* wonderful a creature, has been the source of life and fruitfulness.   *694* Sacred Scripture sees it as "overshadowed" by the Spirit of God:[12]

> At the very dawn of creation
>   your Spirit breathed on the waters,
>   making them the wellspring of all holiness.[13]

1219   The Church has seen in Noah's ark a prefiguring of salva-   *701, 845* tion by Baptism, for by it "a few, that is, eight persons, were saved through water":[14]

> The waters of the great flood
>   you made a sign of the waters of Baptism,
>   that make an end of sin and a new beginning of goodness.[15]

1220   If water springing up from the earth symbolizes life, the water of the sea is a symbol of death and so can represent the mystery of the cross. By this symbolism Baptism signifies commun-   *1010* ion with Christ's death.

1221   But above all, the crossing of the Red Sea, literally the liberation of Israel from the slavery of Egypt, announces the liberation wrought by Baptism:

> You freed the children of Abraham from the slavery of Pharaoh,
>   bringing them dry-shod through the waters of the Red Sea,
>   to be an image of the people set free in Baptism.[16]

1222   Finally, Baptism is prefigured in the crossing of the Jordan River by which the People of God received the gift of the land

---

11 *Roman Missal*, Easter Vigil 42: Blessing of Water.
12 Cf. *Gen* 1:2.
13 *Roman Missal*, Easter Vigil 42: Blessing of Water.
14 *1 Pet* 3:20.
15 *Roman Missal*, Easter Vigil 42: Blessing of Water.
16 *Roman Missal*, Easter Vigil 42: Blessing of Water: "Abrahae filios per mare Rubrum sicco vestigio transire fecisti, ut plebs, a Pharaonis servitute liberata, populum baptizatorum præfiguraret."

promised to Abraham's descendants, an image of eternal life. The promise of this blessed inheritance is fulfilled in the New Covenant.

Christ's Baptism

1223   All the Old Covenant prefigurations find their fulfillment in Christ Jesus. He begins his public life after having himself baptized by St. John the Baptist in the Jordan.[17] After his resurrection Christ gives this mission to his apostles: "Go therefore and make disciples of all nations, baptizing them in the name of the
232 Father and of the Son and of the Holy Spirit, teaching them to observe all that I have commanded you."[18]

536 **1224**   Our Lord voluntarily submitted himself to the baptism of St. John, intended for sinners, in order to "fulfill all righteousness."[19] Jesus' gesture is a manifestation of his self-emptying.[20] The Spirit who had hovered over the waters of the first creation descended then on the Christ as a prelude of the new creation, and the Father revealed Jesus as his "beloved Son."[21]

1225   In his Passover Christ opened to all men the fountain of Baptism. He had already spoken of his Passion, which he was about to suffer in Jerusalem, as a "Baptism" with which he had to
766 be baptized.[22] The blood and water that flowed from the pierced side of the crucified Jesus are types of Baptism and the Eucharist, the sacraments of new life.[23] From then on, it is possible "to be born of water and the Spirit"[24] in order to enter the Kingdom of God.

> See where you are baptized, see where Baptism comes from, if not from the cross of Christ, from his death. There is the whole mystery: he died for you. In him you are redeemed, in him you are saved.[25]

Baptism in the Church

1226   From the very day of Pentecost the Church has celebrated and administered holy Baptism. Indeed St. Peter declares to the crowd astounded by his preaching: "Repent, and be baptized every
849 one of you in the name of Jesus Christ for the forgiveness of your

---

17 Cf. *Mt* 3:13.
18 *Mt* 28:19-20; cf. *Mk* 16:15-16.
19 *Mt* 3:15.
20 Cf. *Phil* 2:7.
21 *Mt* 3:16-17.
22 *Mk* 10:38; cf. *Lk* 12:50.
23 Cf. *Jn* 19:34; *1 Jn* 5:6-8.
24 Cf. *Jn* 3:5.
25 St. Ambrose, *De sacr.* 2, 2, 6: PL 16, 444; cf. *Jn* 3:5.

sins; and you shall receive the gift of the Holy Spirit."[26] The apostles and their collaborators offer Baptism to anyone who believed in Jesus: Jews, the God-fearing, pagans.[27] Always, Baptism is seen as connected with faith: "Believe in the Lord Jesus, and you will be saved, you and your household," St. Paul declared to his jailer in Philippi. And the narrative continues, the jailer "was baptized at once, with all his family."[28]

1227   According to the Apostle Paul, the believer enters through Baptism into communion with Christ's death, is buried with him,   *790* and rises with him:

> Do you not know that all of us who have been baptized into Christ Jesus were baptized into his death? We were buried therefore with him by baptism into death, so that as Christ was raised from the dead by the glory of the Father, we too might walk in newness of life.[29]

The baptized have "put on Christ."[30] Through the Holy Spirit, Baptism is a bath that purifies, justifies, and sanctifies.[31]

1228   Hence Baptism is a bath of water in which the "imperishable seed" of the Word of God produces its life-giving effect.[32] St. Augustine says of Baptism: "The word is brought to the material element, and it becomes a sacrament."[33]

III.   HOW IS THE SACRAMENT OF BAPTISM CELEBRATED?

Christian Initiation

1229   From the time of the apostles, becoming a Christian has been accomplished by a journey and initiation in several stages. This journey can be covered rapidly or slowly, but certain essential elements will always have to be present: proclamation of the Word, acceptance of the Gospel entailing conversion, profession of faith, Baptism itself, the outpouring of the Holy Spirit, and admission to Eucharistic communion.

1230   This initiation has varied greatly through the centuries according to circumstances. In the first centuries of the Church, Christian initiation saw considerable development. A long period of *catechumenate* included a series of preparatory rites, which were liturgical landmarks along the path   *1248*

---

26   *Acts* 2:38.
27   Cf. *Acts* 2:41; 8:12-13; 10:48; 16:15.
28   *Acts* 16:31-33.
29   *Rom* 6:3-4; cf. *Col* 2:12.
30   *Gal* 3:27.
31   Cf. *1 Cor* 6:11; 12:13.
32   *1 Pet* 1:23; cf. *Eph* 5:26.
33   St. Augustine, *In Jo. ev.* 80, 3: PL 35, 1840.

of catechumenal preparation and culminated in the celebration of the sacraments of Christian initiation.

1231   Where infant Baptism has become the form in which this sacrament is usually celebrated, it has become a single act encapsulating the preparatory stages of Christian initiation in a very abridged way. By its very nature infant Baptism requires a *post-baptismal catechumenate*. Not only is there a need for instruction after Baptism, but also for the necessary

13   flowering of baptismal grace in personal growth. The *catechism* has its proper place here.

1232   The second Vatican Council restored for the Latin Church "the catechumenate for adults, comprising several distinct steps."[34] The rites for these stages are to be found in the *Rite of Christian Initiation of Adults* (*RCIA*).[35] The Council also gives permission that: "In mission countries, in addition to what is furnished by the Christian tradition, those elements

1204   of initiation rites may be admitted which are already in use among some peoples insofar as they can be adapted to the Christian ritual."[36]

1233   Today in all the rites, Latin and Eastern, the Christian initiation of adults begins with their entry into the catechumenate and reaches its culmination in a single celebration of the three sacraments of initiation: Baptism, Confirmation, and the Eucharist.[37] In the Eastern rites the Christian initiation of infants also begins with Baptism followed immediately by Confirmation and the Eucharist, while in the Roman rite it is followed by years of catechesis before being completed later by Confirmation and the Eucharist, the summit of their Christian initiation.[38]

The mystagogy of the celebration

1234   The meaning and grace of the sacrament of Baptism are clearly seen in the rites of its celebration. By following the gestures and words of this celebration with attentive participation, the faithful are initiated into the riches this sacrament signifies and actually brings about in each newly baptized person.

617   **1235**   The *sign of the cross*, on the threshold of the celebration, marks with the imprint of Christ the one who is going to belong to him and
2157   signifies the grace of the redemption Christ won for us by his cross.

1236   The proclamation of the Word of God enlightens the candidates and the assembly with the revealed truth and elicits the
1112   response of faith, which is inseparable from Baptism. Indeed Baptism is "the sacrament of faith" in a particular way, since it is the sacramental entry into the life of faith.

---

34   *SC* 64.
35   Cf. RCIA (1972).
36   *SC* 65; cf. *SC* 37-40.
37   Cf. AG 14; CIC, cann. 851; 865; 866.
38   Cf. CIC, cann. 851, 2°; 868.

1237   Since Baptism signifies liberation from sin and from its instigator the devil, one or more *exorcisms* are pronounced over the candidate. The celebrant then anoints him with the oil of catechu-   *1673* mens, or lays his hands on him, and he explicitly renounces Satan. Thus prepared, he is able to *confess the faith of the Church*, to which   *189* he will be "entrusted" by Baptism.[39]

1238   The *baptismal water* is consecrated by a prayer of epiclesis   *1217* (either at this moment or at the Easter Vigil). The Church asks God that through his Son the power of the Holy Spirit may be sent upon the water, so that those who will be baptized in it may be "born of water and the Spirit."[40]

1239   The *essential rite* of the sacrament follows: *Baptism* properly   *1214* speaking. It signifies and actually brings about death to sin and entry into the life of the Most Holy Trinity through configuration to the Paschal mystery of Christ. Baptism is performed in the most expressive way by triple immersion in the baptismal water. However, from ancient times it has also been able to be conferred by pouring the water three times over the candidate's head.

1240   In the Latin Church this triple infusion is accompanied by the minister's words: "N., I baptize you in the name of the Father, and of the Son, and of the Holy Spirit." In the Eastern liturgies the catechumen turns toward the East and the priest says: "The servant of God, N., is baptized in the name of the Father, and of the Son, and of the Holy Spirit." At the invocation of each person of the Most Holy Trinity, the priest immerses the candidate in the water and raises him up again.

1241   The *anointing with sacred chrism*, perfumed oil consecrated by   *1294, 1574* the bishop, signifies the gift of the Holy Spirit to the newly baptized, who has become a Christian, that is, one "anointed" by the Holy Spirit, incorporated into Christ who is anointed priest, prophet, and king.[41]   *783*

1242   In the liturgy of the Eastern Churches, the post-baptismal anointing is the sacrament of Chrismation (Confirmation). In the Roman liturgy the post-baptismal anointing announces a second anointing with sacred chrism to be conferred later by the bishop – Confirmation, which will as it were "confirm" and complete the   *1291* baptismal anointing.

1243   The white garment symbolizes that the person baptized has "put on Christ,"[42] has risen with Christ. The *candle*, lit from the Easter candle, signifies that Christ has enlightened the neophyte. In him the baptized are "the light of the world."[43]   *1216*

---

39   Cf. *Rom* 6:17.
40   *Jn* 3:5.
41   Cf. RBC 62.

The newly baptized is now, in the only Son, a child of God
2769 entitled to say the prayer of the children of God: "Our Father."

1244   *First Holy Communion.* Having become a child of God
clothed with the wedding garment, the neophyte is admitted "to
the marriage supper of the Lamb"[44] and receives the food of the
new life, the body and blood of Christ. The Eastern Churches
maintain a lively awareness of the unity of Christian initiation by
giving Holy Communion to all the newly baptized and confirmed,
1292 even little children, recalling the Lord's words: "Let the children
come to me, do not hinder them."[45] The Latin Church, which
reserves admission to Holy Communion to those who have attained the age of reason, expresses the orientation of Baptism to the
Eucharist by having the newly baptized child brought to the altar
for the praying of the Our Father.

1245   The *solemn blessing* concludes the celebration of Baptism.
At the Baptism of newborns the blessing of the mother occupies a
special place.

IV.   WHO CAN RECEIVE BAPTISM?

1246   "Every person not yet baptized and only such a person is
able to be baptized."[46]

The Baptism of adults

1247   Since the beginning of the Church, adult Baptism is the
common practice where the proclamation of the Gospel is still new.
The catechumenate (preparation for Baptism) therefore occupies
an important place. This initiation into Christian faith and life
should dispose the catechumen to receive the gift of God in Baptism, Confirmation, and the Eucharist.

1230 **1248**   The catechumenate, or formation of catechumens, aims at
bringing their conversion and faith to maturity, in response to the
divine initiative and in union with an ecclesial community. The
catechumenate is to be "a formation in the whole Christian life . . .
during which the disciples will be joined to Christ their teacher.
The catechumens should be properly initiated into the mystery of
salvation and the practice of the evangelical virtues, and they

---

42   *Gal* 3:27.
43   *Mt* 5:14; cf. *Phil* 2:15.
44   *Rev* 19:9.
45   *Mk* 10:14.
46   CIC, can. 864; cf. CCEO, can. 679.

should be introduced into the life of faith, liturgy, and charity of the People of God by successive sacred rites."[47]

1249   Catechumens "are already joined to the Church, they are   *1259* already of the household of Christ, and are quite frequently already living a life of faith, hope, and charity."[48] "With love and solicitude mother Church already embraces them as her own."[49]

The Baptism of infants

1250   Born with a fallen human nature and tainted by original   *403* sin, children also have need of the new birth in Baptism to be freed from the power of darkness and brought into the realm of the freedom of the children of God, to which all men are called.[50] The sheer gratuitousness of the grace of salvation is particularly mani-   *1996* fest in infant Baptism. The Church and the parents would deny a child the priceless grace of becoming a child of God were they not to confer Baptism shortly after birth.[51]

1251   Christian parents will recognize that this practice also accords with their role as nurturers of the life that God has entrusted to them.[52]

1252   The practice of infant Baptism is an immemorial tradition of the Church. There is explicit testimony to this practice from the second century on, and it is quite possible that, from the beginning of the apostolic preaching, when whole "households" received baptism, infants may also have been baptized.[53]

Faith and Baptism

1253   Baptism is the sacrament of faith.[54] But faith needs the   *1123* community of believers. It is only within the faith of the Church that each of the faithful can believe. The faith required for Baptism is not a perfect and mature faith, but a beginning that is called to develop. The catechumen or the godparent is asked: "What do you   *168* ask of God's Church?" The response is: "Faith!"

---

47   *AG* 14; cf. RCIA 19; 98.
48   *AG* 14 § 5.
49   *LG* 14 § 3; cf. CIC, cann. 206; 788 § 3.
50   Cf. Council of Trent (1546): DS 1514; cf. *Col* 1:12-14.
51   Cf. CIC, can. 867; CCEO, cann. 681; 686, 1.
52   Cf. *LG* 11; 41; *GS* 48; CIC, can. 868.
53   Cf. *Acts* 16:15, 33; 18:8; *1 Cor* 1:16; CDF, instruction, *Pastoralis actio* : AAS 72 (1980) 1137-1156.
54   Cf. *Mk* 16:16.

1254   For all the baptized, children or adults, faith must grow *after* Baptism. For this reason the Church celebrates each year at the Easter Vigil the renewal of baptismal promises. Preparation for Baptism
2101   leads only to the threshold of new life. Baptism is the source of that new life in Christ from which the entire Christian life springs forth.

1255   For the grace of Baptism to unfold, the parents' help is important. So too is the role of the *godfather* and *godmother*, who must be firm
1311   believers, able and ready to help the newly baptized – child or adult – on the road of Christian life.[55] Their task is a truly ecclesial function (*officium*).[56] The whole ecclesial community bears some responsibility for the development and safeguarding of the grace given at Baptism.

V.   Who Can Baptize?

1256   The ordinary ministers of Baptism are the bishop and priest and, in the Latin Church, also the deacon.[57] In case of necessity, any person, even someone not baptized, can baptize, if he has the required intention. The intention required is to will to do what the Church does when she baptizes, and to apply the
1752   Trinitarian baptismal formula. The Church finds the reason for this possibility in the universal saving will of God and the necessity of Baptism for salvation.[58]

VI.   The Necessity of Baptism

1129   **1257**   The Lord himself affirms that Baptism is necessary for salvation.[59] He also commands his disciples to proclaim the Gospel to all nations and to baptize them.[60] Baptism is necessary for salvation for those to whom the Gospel has been proclaimed and
161, 846   who have had the possibility of asking for this sacrament.[61] The Church does not know of any means other than Baptism that assures entry into eternal beatitude; this is why she takes care not to neglect the mission she has received from the Lord to see that all who can be baptized are "reborn of water and the Spirit." *God has bound salvation to the sacrament of Baptism, but he himself is not bound by his sacraments.*

---

55   Cf. CIC, cann. 872-874.
56   Cf. *SC* 67.
57   Cf. CIC, can. 861 § 1; CCEO, can. 677 § 1.
58   Cf. *1 Tim* 2:4.
59   Cf. *Jn* 3:5.
60   Cf. *Mt* 28:19-20; cf. Council of Trent (1547) DS 1618; *LG* 14; *AG* 5.
61   Cf. *Mk* 16:16.

1258   The Church has always held the firm conviction that those who suffer death for the sake of the faith without having received Baptism are baptized by their death for and with Christ. This *Baptism of blood*, like the *desire for Baptism*, brings about the fruits of   *2473* Baptism without being a sacrament.

1259   For *catechumens* who die before their Baptism, their explicit   *1249* desire to receive it, together with repentance for their sins, and charity, assures them the salvation that they were not able to receive through the sacrament.

1260   "Since Christ died for all, and since all men are in fact called to one and the same destiny, which is divine, we must hold that the Holy Spirit offers to all the possibility of being made partakers, in a way known to God, of the Paschal mystery."[62] Every man who is   *848* ignorant of the Gospel of Christ and of his Church, but seeks the truth and does the will of God in accordance with his understanding of it, can be saved. It may be supposed that such persons would have *desired Baptism explicitly* if they had known its necessity.

1261   As regards *children who have died without Baptism*, the Church can only entrust them to the mercy of God, as she does in her funeral rites for them. Indeed, the great mercy of God who desires that all men should be saved, and Jesus' tenderness toward children which caused him to say: "Let the children come to me, do not hinder them,"[63] allow us to hope that there is a way of salvation for children who have died without Baptism. All the more urgent is the Church's call not to prevent little children   *1250* coming to Christ through the gift of holy Baptism.

VII.   THE GRACE OF BAPTISM

1262   The different effects of Baptism are signified by the percep-   *1234* tible elements of the sacramental rite. Immersion in water symbolizes not only death and purification, but also regeneration and renewal. Thus the two principal effects are purification from sins and new birth in the Holy Spirit.[64]

For the forgiveness of sins . . .

1263   By Baptism *all sins* are forgiven, original sin and all per-   *977* sonal sins, as well as all punishment for sin.[65] In those who have   *1425*

---

62   *GS* 22 § 5; cf. *LG* 16; *AG* 7.
63   *Mk* 10:14; cf. *1 Tim* 2:4.
64   Cf. *Acts* 2:38; *Jn* 3:5.
65   Cf. Council of Florence (1439): DS 1316.

been reborn nothing remains that would impede their entry into the Kingdom of God, neither Adam's sin, nor personal sin, nor the consequences of sin, the gravest of which is separation from God.

1264   Yet certain temporal consequences of sin remain in the baptized, such as suffering, illness, death, and such frailties inherent in life as weaknesses of character, and so on, as well as an *975, 2514* inclination to sin that Tradition calls *concupiscence*, or metaphori-*1426* cally, "the tinder for sin" (*fomes peccati*); since concupiscence "is left for us to wrestle with, it cannot harm those who do not consent but manfully resist it by the grace of Jesus Christ."[66] Indeed, "an athlete *405* is not crowned unless he competes according to the rules."[67]

"A new creature"

505 **1265**   Baptism not only purifies from all sins, but also makes the *460* neophyte "a new creature," an adopted son of God, who has become a "partaker of the divine nature,"[68] member of Christ and co-heir with him,[69] and a temple of the Holy Spirit.[70]

1266   The Most Holy Trinity gives the baptized sanctifying grace, the grace of *justification*:
1992 – enabling them to believe in God, to hope in him, and to love him through the theological virtues;
1812 – giving them the power to live and act under the prompting of the Holy Spirit through the gifts of the Holy Spirit;
1831 – allowing them to grow in goodness through the moral virtues.
1810 Thus the whole organism of the Christian's supernatural life has its roots in Baptism.

Incorporated into the Church, the Body of Christ

782 **1267**   Baptism makes us members of the Body of Christ: "Therefore . . . we are members one of another."[71] Baptism incorporates us *into the Church*. From the baptismal fonts is born the one People of God of the New Covenant, which transcends all the natural or human limits of nations, cultures, races, and sexes: "For by one Spirit we were all baptized into one body."[72]

---

66 Council of Trent (1546): DS 1515.
67 *2 Tim* 2:5.
68 *2 Cor* 5:17; *2 Pet* 1:4; cf. *Gal* 4:5-7.
69 Cf. *1 Cor* 6:15; 12:27; *Rom* 8:17.
70 Cf. *1 Cor* 6:19.
71 *Eph* 4:25.
72 *1 Cor* 12:13.

1268   The baptized have become "living stones" to be "built into a spiritual house, to be a holy priesthood."[73] By Baptism they share in the priesthood of Christ, in his prophetic and royal mission. They are "a chosen race, a royal priesthood, a holy nation, God's own people, that [they] may declare the wonderful deeds of him who called [them] out of darkness into his marvelous light."[74] *Baptism gives a share in the common priesthood of all believers.*   *1141*

784

1269   Having become a member of the Church, the person baptized belongs no longer to himself, but to him who died and rose for us.[75] From now on, he is called to be subject to others, to serve them in the communion of the Church, and to "obey and submit" to the Church's leaders,[76] holding them in respect and affection.[77]   *871* Just as Baptism is the source of responsibilities and duties, the baptized person also enjoys rights within the Church: to receive the sacraments, to be nourished with the Word of God and to be sustained by the other spiritual helps of the Church.[78]

1270   "Reborn as sons of God, [the baptized] must profess before men the faith they have received from God through the Church" and participate in the apostolic and missionary activity of the People of God.[79]

The sacramental bond of the unity of Christians

1271   Baptism constitutes the foundation of communion among all Christians, including those who are not yet in full communion with the Catholic Church: "For men who believe in Christ and have been properly baptized are put in some, though imperfect, communion with the Catholic Church. Justified by faith in Baptism, [they] are incorporated into Christ; they therefore have a right to be called Christians, and with good reason are accepted as brothers by the children of the Catholic Church."[80] "Baptism therefore constitutes *the sacramental bond of unity* existing among all who through it are reborn."[81]

---

73 *1 Pet* 2:5.
74 *1 Pet* 2:9.
75 Cf. *1 Cor* 6:19; *2 Cor* 5:15.
76 *Heb* 13:17.
77 Cf. *Eph* 5:21; *1 Cor* 16:15-16; *1 Thess* 5:12-13; *Jn* 13:12-15.
78 Cf. *LG* 37; CIC, cann. 208-223; CCEO, can. 675:2.
79 *LG* 11; cf. *LG* 17; *AG* 7; 23.
80 *UR* 3.
81 *UR* 22 § 2.

An indelible spiritual mark . . .

1272 Incorporated into Christ by Baptism, the person baptized is configured to Christ. Baptism seals the Christian with the indelible spiritual mark (*character*) of his belonging to Christ. No sin can erase this mark, even if sin prevents Baptism from bearing the fruits of salvation.[82] Given once for all, Baptism cannot be repeated.

1273 Incorporated into the Church by Baptism, the faithful have received the sacramental character that consecrates them for Christian religious worship.[83] The baptismal seal enables and commits Christians to serve God by a vital participation in the holy liturgy of the Church and to exercise their baptismal priesthood by the witness of holy lives and practical charity.[84]

1274 The Holy Spirit has marked us with the *seal of the Lord* (*"Dominicus character"*) "for the day of redemption."[85] "Baptism indeed is the seal of eternal life."[86] The faithful Christian who has "kept the seal" until the end, remaining faithful to the demands of his Baptism, will be able to depart this life "marked with the sign of faith,"[87] with his baptismal faith, in expectation of the blessed vision of God – the consummation of faith – and in the hope of resurrection.

197
2016

IN BRIEF

1275 Christian initiation is accomplished by three sacraments together: Baptism which is the beginning of new life; Confirmation which is its strengthening; and the Eucharist which nourishes the disciple with Christ's Body and Blood for his transformation in Christ.

1276 "Go therefore and make disciples of all nations, baptizing them in the name of the Father and of the Son and of the Holy Spirit, teaching them to observe all that I have commanded you" (*Mt* 28:19-20).

1277 Baptism is birth into the new life in Christ. In accordance with the Lord's will, it is necessary for salvation, as is the Church herself, which we enter by Baptism.

---

82 Cf. *Rom* 8:29; Council of Trent (1547): DS 1609-1619.
83 Cf. *LG* 11.
84 Cf. *LG* 10.
85 St. Augustine, *Ep.* 98, 5: PL 33, 362; *Eph* 4:30; cf. 1:13-14; 2 *Cor* 1:21-22.
86 St. Irenaeus, *Dem ap.* 3: SCh 62, 32.
87 *Roman Missal*, EP I (Roman Canon) 97.

1278 The essential rite of Baptism consists in immersing the candidate in water or pouring water on his head, while pronouncing the invocation of the Most Holy Trinity: the Father, the Son, and the Holy Spirit.

1279 The fruit of Baptism, or baptismal grace, is a rich reality that includes forgiveness of original sin and all personal sins, birth into the new life by which man becomes an adoptive son of the Father, a member of Christ and a temple of the Holy Spirit. By this very fact the person baptized is incorporated into the Church, the Body of Christ, and made a sharer in the priesthood of Christ.

1280 Baptism imprints on the soul an indelible spiritual sign, the character, which consecrates the baptized person for Christian worship. Because of the character Baptism cannot be repeated (cf. DS 1609 and DS 1624).

1281 Those who die for the faith, those who are catechumens, and all those who, without knowing of the Church but acting under the inspiration of grace, seek God sincerely and strive to fulfill his will, are saved even if they have not been baptized (cf. *LG* 16).

1282 Since the earliest times, Baptism has been administered to children, for it is a grace and a gift of God that does not presuppose any human merit; children are baptized in the faith of the Church. Entry into Christian life gives access to true freedom.

1283 With respect to children who have died without Baptism, the liturgy of the Church invites us to trust in God's mercy and to pray for their salvation.

1284 In case of necessity, any person can baptize provided that he have the intention of doing that which the Church does and provided that he pours water on the candidate's head while saying: "I baptize you in the name of the Father, and of the Son, and of the Holy Spirit."

ARTICLE 2
THE SACRAMENT OF CONFIRMATION

1285 Baptism, the Eucharist, and the sacrament of Confirmation together constitute the "sacraments of Christian initiation," whose unity must be safeguarded. It must be explained to the faithful that the reception of the sacrament of Confirmation is necessary for the completion of baptismal grace.[88] For "by the sacrament of Confirmation, [the baptized] are more perfectly bound to the Church and are enriched with a special strength of the Holy Spirit. Hence they are, as true witnesses of Christ, more strictly obliged to spread and defend the faith by word and deed."[89]

I.   CONFIRMATION IN THE ECONOMY OF SALVATION

1286   In the Old Testament the prophets announced that the Spirit of the Lord would rest on the hoped-for Messiah for his 702-716 saving mission.[90] The descent of the Holy Spirit on Jesus at his baptism by John was the sign that this was he who was to come, the Messiah, the Son of God.[91] He was conceived of the Holy Spirit; his whole life and his whole mission are carried out in total communion with the Holy Spirit whom the Father gives him "without measure."[92]

1287   This fullness of the Spirit was not to remain uniquely the Messiah's, but was to be communicated to *the whole messianic* 739 *people.*[93] On several occasions Christ promised this outpouring of the Spirit,[94] a promise which he fulfilled first on Easter Sunday and then more strikingly at Pentecost.[95] Filled with the Holy Spirit the apostles began to proclaim "the mighty works of God," and Peter declared this outpouring of the Spirit to be the sign of the messianic age.[96] Those who believed in the apostolic preaching and were baptized received the gift of the Holy Spirit in their turn.[97]

1288   "From that time on the apostles, in fulfillment of Christ's will, imparted to the newly baptized by the laying on of hands the gift of the Spirit that completes the grace of Baptism. For this reason 699 in the *Letter to the Hebrews* the doctrine concerning Baptism and the laying on of hands is listed among the first elements of Christian instruction. The imposition of hands is rightly recognized by the Catholic tradition as the origin of the sacrament of Confirmation, which in a certain way perpetuates the grace of Pentecost in the Church."[98]

---

88   Cf. *Roman Ritual*, Rite of Confirmation (*OC*), Introduction 1.
89   *LG* 11; cf. *OC*, Introduction 2.
90   Cf. *Isa* 11:2; 61:1; *Lk* 4:16-22.
91   Cf. *Mt* 3:13-17; *Jn* 1:33-34.
92   *Jn* 3:34.
93   Cf. *Ezek* 36:25-27; *Joel* 3:1-2.
94   Cf. *Lk* 12:12; *Jn* 3:5-8; 7:37-39; 16:7-15; *Acts* 1:8.
95   Cf. *Jn* 20:22; *Acts* 2:1-4.
96   *Acts* 2:11; cf. 2:17-18.
97   Cf. *Acts* 2:38.

1289   Very early, the better to signify the gift of the Holy Spirit, an anointing with perfumed oil (*chrism*) was added to the laying   *695* on of hands. This anointing highlights the name "Christian," which means "anointed" and derives from that of Christ himself whom God "anointed with the Holy Spirit."[99] This rite of anointing has   *436* continued ever since, in both East and West. For this reason the Eastern Churches call this sacrament *Chrismation*, anointing with chrism, or *myron* which means "chrism." In the West, *Confirmation*   *1297* suggests both the ratification of Baptism, thus completing Christian initiation, and the strengthening of baptismal grace – both fruits of the Holy Spirit.

Two traditions: East and West

1290   In the first centuries Confirmation generally comprised one single celebration with Baptism, forming with it a "double sacrament," according to the expression of St. Cyprian. Among other reasons, the multiplication of infant baptisms all through the year, the increase of rural parishes, and the growth of dioceses often prevented the bishop from being present at all baptismal celebrations. In the West the desire to reserve the completion of Baptism to the bishop caused the temporal separation of the two sacraments. The East has kept them united, so that Confirmation is conferred by the priest who baptizes. But he can do so only with the   *1233* "myron" consecrated by a bishop.[100]

1291   A custom of the Roman Church facilitated the development of   *1242* the Western practice: a double anointing with sacred chrism after Baptism. The first anointing of the neophyte on coming out of the baptismal bath was performed by the priest; it was completed by a second anointing on the forehead of the newly baptized by the bishop.[101] The first anointing with sacred chrism, by the priest, has remained attached to the baptismal rite; it signifies the participation of the one baptized in the prophetic, priestly, and kingly offices of Christ. If Baptism is conferred on an adult, there is only one post-baptismal anointing, that of Confirmation.

1292   The practice of the Eastern Churches gives greater emphasis to   *1244* the unity of Christian initiation. That of the Latin Church more clearly expresses the communion of the new Christian with the bishop as guarantor and servant of the unity, catholicity and apostolicity of his Church, and hence the connection with the apostolic origins of Christ's Church.

II.   THE SIGNS AND THE RITE OF CONFIRMATION

1293   In treating the rite of Confirmation, it is fitting to consider the sign of *anointing* and what it signifies and imprints: a spiritual *seal*.

---

98   Paul VI, *Divinae consortium naturae*, 659; cf. *Acts* 8:15-17; 19:5-6; *Heb* 6:2.
99   *Acts* 10:38.
100   Cf. CCEO, can. 695 § 1; 696 § 1.
101   Cf. St. Hippolytus, *Trad. Ap.* 21: SCh 11, 80-95.

695   Anointing, in Biblical and other ancient symbolism, is rich in meaning: oil is a sign of abundance and joy;[102] it cleanses (anointing before and after a bath) and limbers (the anointing of athletes and wrestlers); oil is a sign of healing, since it is soothing to bruises and wounds;[103] and it makes radiant with beauty, health, and strength.

1152 **1294**   Anointing with oil has all these meanings in the sacramental life. The pre-baptismal anointing with the oil of catechumens signifies cleansing and strengthening; the anointing of the sick expresses healing and comfort. The post-baptismal anointing with sacred chrism in Confirmation and ordination is the sign of consecration. By Confirmation Christians, that is, those who are anointed, share more completely in the mission of Jesus Christ and the fullness of the Holy Spirit with which he is filled, so that their lives may give off "the aroma of Christ."[104]

698 **1295**   By this anointing the confirmand receives the "mark," the *seal* of the Holy Spirit. A seal is a symbol of a person, a sign of personal authority, or ownership of an object.[105] Hence soldiers were marked with their leader's seal and slaves with their master's. A seal authenticates a juridical act or document and occasionally makes it secret.[106]

1296   Christ himself declared that he was marked with his Father's seal.[107] Christians are also marked with a seal: "It is God who 1121 establishes us with you in Christ and has commissioned us; he has put his seal on us and given us his Spirit in our hearts as a guarantee."[108] This seal of the Holy Spirit marks our total belonging to Christ, our enrollment in his service for ever, as well as the promise of divine protection in the great eschatological trial.[109]

The celebration of Confirmation

1183 **1297**   *The consecration of the sacred chrism* is an important action that precedes the celebration of Confirmation, but is in a certain way a part of it. It is the bishop who, in the course of the Chrism Mass of Holy Thursday, consecrates the sacred chrism for his whole diocese. In 1241 some Eastern Churches this consecration is even reserved to the patriarch:

---

102   Cf. *Deut* 11:14; *Pss* 23:5; 104:15.
103   Cf. *Isa* 1:6; *Lk* 10:34.
104   *2 Cor* 2:15.
105   Cf. *Gen* 38:18; 41:42; *Deut* 32:34; *CT* 8:6.
106   Cf. *1 Kings* 21:8; *Jer* 32:10; *Isa* 29:11.
107   Cf. *Jn* 6:27.
108   *2 Cor* 1:21-22; cf. *Eph* 1:13; 4, 30.
109   Cf. *Rev* 7:2-3; 9:4; *Ezek* 9:4-6.

> The Syriac liturgy of Antioch expresses the epiclesis for the consecration of the sacred chrism (myron) in this way: "[Father . . . send your Holy Spirit] on us and on this oil which is before us and consecrate it, so that it may be for all who are anointed and marked with it holy myron, priestly myron, royal myron, anointing with gladness, clothing with light, a cloak of salvation, a spiritual gift, the sanctification of souls and bodies, imperishable happiness, the indelible seal, a buckler of faith, and a fearsome helmet against all the works of the adversary."

1298 When Confirmation is celebrated separately from Baptism, as is the case in the Roman Rite, the Liturgy of Confirmation begins with the renewal of baptismal promises and the profession of faith by the confirmands. This clearly shows that Confirmation follows Baptism.[110] When adults are baptized, they immediately receive Confirmation and participate in the Eucharist.[111]

1299 In the Roman Rite the bishop extends his hands over the whole group of the confirmands. Since the time of the apostles this gesture has signified the gift of the Spirit. The bishop invokes the outpouring of the Spirit in these words:

> All-powerful God, Father of our Lord Jesus Christ,
> by water and the Holy Spirit
> you freed your sons and daughters from sin
> and gave them new life.
> Send your Holy Spirit upon them
> to be their helper and guide.
> Give them the spirit of wisdom and understanding,
> the spirit of right judgment and courage,
> the spirit of knowledge and reverence.
> Fill them with the spirit of wonder and awe in your presence.
> We ask this through Christ our Lord.[112]

1831

1300 The *essential rite* of the sacrament follows. In the Latin rite, "the sacrament of Confirmation is conferred through the anointing with chrism on the forehead, which is done by the laying on of the hand, and through the words: '*Accipe signaculum doni Spiritus Sancti*' [Be sealed with the Gift of the Holy Spirit.]."[113] In the Eastern Churches, after a prayer of epiclesis the more significant parts of the body are anointed with myron: forehead, eyes, nose, ears, lips, breast, back, hands, and feet. Each anointing is accompanied by the formula: "The seal of the gift that is the Holy Spirit."

699

---

110 Cf. *SC* 71.
111 Cf. CIC, can. 866.
112 OC 25.
113 Paul VI, apostolic constitution, *Divinae consortium naturae*, 663.

1301   The sign of peace that concludes the rite of the sacrament signifies and demonstrates ecclesial communion with the bishop and with all the faithful.[114]

III.   THE EFFECTS OF CONFIRMATION

1302   It is evident from its celebration that the effect of the sacrament of Confirmation is the full outpouring of the Holy Spirit
731   as once granted to the apostles on the day of Pentecost.

1262-1274   **1303**   From this fact, Confirmation brings an increase and deepening of baptismal grace:
– it roots us more deeply in the divine filiation which makes us cry, "Abba! Father!";[115]
– it unites us more firmly to Christ;
– it increases the gifts of the Holy Spirit in us;
– it renders our bond with the Church more perfect;[116]
– it gives us a special strength of the Holy Spirit to spread and defend
2044   the faith by word and action as true witnesses of Christ, to confess the name of Christ boldly, and never to be ashamed of the Cross:[117]

> Recall then that you have received the spiritual seal, the spirit of wisdom and understanding, the spirit of right judgment and courage, the spirit of knowledge and reverence, the spirit of holy fear in God's presence. Guard what you have received. God the Father has marked you with his sign; Christ the Lord has confirmed you and has placed his pledge, the Spirit, in your hearts.[118]

1121   **1304**   Like Baptism which it completes, Confirmation is given only once, for it too imprints on the soul an *indelible spiritual mark*, the "character," which is the sign that Jesus Christ has marked a Christian with the seal of his Spirit by clothing him with power from on high so that he may be his witness.[119]

1268   **1305**   This "character" perfects the common priesthood of the faithful, received in Baptism, and "the confirmed person receives the power to profess faith in Christ publicly and as it were officially (*quasi ex officio*)."[120]

---

114   Cf. St. Hippolytus, *Trad. Ap.* 21: SCh 11, 80-95.
115   *Rom* 8:15.
116   Cf. *LG* 11.
117   Cf. Council of Florence (1439): DS 1319; *LG* 11; 12.
118   St. Ambrose, De myst. 7, 42: PL 16, 402-403.
119   Cf. Council of Trent (1547): DS 1609; *Lk* 24:48-49.
120   St. Thomas Aquinas, *STh III, 72, 5, ad* 2.

IV. WHO CAN RECEIVE THIS SACRAMENT?

1306 Every baptized person not yet confirmed can and should receive the sacrament of Confirmation.[121] Since Baptism, Confirmation, and Eucharist form a unity, it follows that "the faithful are *1212* obliged to receive this sacrament at the appropriate time,"[122] for without Confirmation and Eucharist, Baptism is certainly valid and efficacious, but Christian initiation remains incomplete.

1307 The Latin tradition gives "the age of discretion" as the reference point for receiving Confirmation. But in danger of death children should be confirmed even if they have not yet attained the age of discretion.[123]

1308 Although Confirmation is sometimes called the "sacrament of Christian maturity," we must not confuse adult faith with the adult age of natural growth, nor forget that the baptismal grace is a grace of free, unmerited election and does not need "ratifica- *1250* tion" to become effective. St. Thomas reminds us of this:

> Age of body does not determine age of soul. Even in child-hood man can attain spiritual maturity: as the book of *Wisdom* says: "For old age is not honored for length of time, or measured by number of years." Many children, through the strength of the Holy Spirit they have received, have bravely fought for Christ even to the shedding of their blood.[124]

1309 *Preparation* for Confirmation should aim at leading the Christian toward a more intimate union with Christ and a more lively familiarity with the Holy Spirit – his actions, his gifts, and his biddings – in order to be more capable of assuming the apostolic responsibilities of Christian life. To this end catechesis for Confirmation should strive to awaken a sense of belonging to the Church of Jesus Christ, the universal Church as well as the parish community. The latter bears special responsibility for the preparation of confirmands.[125]

1310 To receive Confirmation one must be in a state of grace. One should receive the sacrament of Penance in order to be cleansed for the gift of the Holy Spirit. More intense prayer should *2670* prepare one to receive the strength and graces of the Holy Spirit with docility and readiness to act.[126]

---

121 Cf. CIC, can. 889 § 1.
122 CIC, can. 890.
123 Cf. CIC, cann. 891; 883, 3°.
124 St. Thomas Aquinas, *STh* III, 72, 8, *ad* 2; cf. *Wis* 4:8.
125 Cf. *OC* Introduction 3.
126 Cf. *Acts* 1:14.

1311   Candidates for Confirmation, as for Baptism, fittingly seek
the spiritual help of a *sponsor*. To emphasize the unity of the two
1255 sacraments, it is appropriate that this be one of the baptismal
godparents.[127]

V.   THE MINISTER OF CONFIRMATION

1312   The *original minister* of Confirmation is the bishop.[128]
1233   In the East, ordinarily the priest who baptizes also immediately confers Confirmation in one and the same celebration. But
he does so with sacred chrism consecrated by the patriarch or the
bishop, thus expressing the apostolic unity of the Church whose
bonds are strengthened by the sacrament of Confirmation. In the
Latin Church, the same discipline applies to the Baptism of adults
or to the reception into full communion with the Church of a
person baptized in another Christian community that does not
have valid Confirmation.[129]

1290 **1313**   In the Latin Rite, the ordinary minister of Confirmation is
the bishop.[130] Although the bishop may for grave reasons concede
to priests the faculty of administering Confirmation,[131] it is appropriate from the very meaning of the sacrament that he should
confer it himself, mindful that the celebration of Confirmation has
been temporally separated from Baptism for this reason. Bishops
are the successors of the apostles. They have received the fullness
of the sacrament of Holy Orders. The administration of this sacrament by them demonstrates clearly that its effect is to unite those
who receive it more closely to the Church, to her apostolic origins,
1285 and to her mission of bearing witness to Christ.

1307 **1314**   If a Christian is in danger of death, any priest should give him
Confirmation.[132] Indeed the Church desires that none of her children,
even the youngest, should depart this world without having been
perfected by the Holy Spirit with the gift of Christ's fullness.

IN BRIEF

1315   "Now when the apostles at Jerusalem heard that
Samaria had received the word of God, they sent to
them Peter and John, who came down and prayed for

---

127 Cf. *OC* Introduction 5; 6; CIC, can. 893 §§ 1- 2.
128 Cf. *LG* 26.
129 Cf. CIC, can. 883 § 2.
130 Cf. CIC, can. 882.
131 Cf. CIC, can. 884 § 2.
132 Cf. CIC, can. 883 § 3.

them that they might receive the Holy Spirit; for it had not yet fallen on any of them, but they had only been baptized in the name of the Lord Jesus. Then they laid their hands on them and they received the Holy Spirit" (*Acts* 8:14-17).

1316   Confirmation perfects Baptismal grace; it is the sacrament which gives the Holy Spirit in order to root us more deeply in the divine filiation, incorporate us more firmly into Christ, strengthen our bond with the Church, associate us more closely with her mission, and help us bear witness to the Christian faith in words accompanied by deeds.

1317   Confirmation, like Baptism, imprints a spiritual mark or indelible character on the Christian's soul; for this reason one can receive this sacrament only once in one's life.

1318   In the East this sacrament is administered immediately after Baptism and is followed by participation in the Eucharist; this tradition highlights the unity of the three sacraments of Christian initiation. In the Latin Church this sacrament is administered when the age of reason has been reached, and its celebration is ordinarily reserved to the bishop, thus signifying that this sacrament strengthens the ecclesial bond.

1319   A candidate for Confirmation who has attained the age of reason must profess the faith, be in the state of grace, have the intention of receiving the sacrament, and be prepared to assume the role of disciple and witness to Christ, both within the ecclesial community and in temporal affairs.

1320   The essential rite of Confirmation is anointing the forehead of the baptized with sacred chrism (in the East other sense-organs as well), together with the laying on of the minister's hand and the words: "*Accipe signaculum doni Spiritus Sancti*" (Be sealed with the Gift of the Holy Spirit.) in the Roman Rite, or "The seal of the gift that is the Holy Spirit" in the Byzantine rite.

1321   When Confirmation is celebrated separately from Baptism, its connection with Baptism is expressed, among other ways, by the renewal of baptismal promises. The celebration of Confirmation during the Eucharist helps underline the unity of the sacraments of Christian initiation.

ARTICLE 3
THE SACRAMENT OF THE EUCHARIST

1212 **1322**   The holy Eucharist completes Christian initiation. Those who have been raised to the dignity of the royal priesthood by Baptism and configured more deeply to Christ by Confirmation participate with the whole community in the Lord's own sacrifice by means of the Eucharist.

1323   "At the Last Supper, on the night he was betrayed, our Savior instituted the Eucharistic sacrifice of his Body and Blood. This he did in order to perpetuate the sacrifice of the cross throughout the ages until he should come again, and so to entrust to his beloved Spouse, the Church, a memorial of his death and resurrection: a sacrament of love, a sign of unity, a bond of charity, a Paschal

1402 banquet 'in which Christ is consumed, the mind is filled with grace, and a pledge of future glory is given to us.'"[133]

I.   THE EUCHARIST – SOURCE AND SUMMIT
OF ECCLESIAL LIFE

864 **1324**   The Eucharist is "the source and summit of the Christian life."[134] "The other sacraments, and indeed all ecclesiastical ministries and works of the apostolate, are bound up with the Eucharist and are oriented toward it. For in the blessed Eucharist is contained the whole spiritual good of the Church, namely Christ himself, our Pasch."[135]

1325   "The Eucharist is the efficacious sign and sublime cause of that communion in the divine life and that unity of the People of God

775 by which the Church is kept in being. It is the culmination both of God's action sanctifying the world in Christ and of the worship men offer to Christ and through him to the Father in the Holy Spirit."[136]

1090 **1326**   Finally, by the Eucharistic celebration we already unite ourselves with the heavenly liturgy and anticipate eternal life, when God will be all in all.[137]

1327   In brief, the Eucharist is the sum and summary of our faith:

1124 "Our way of thinking is attuned to the Eucharist, and the Eucharist in turn confirms our way of thinking."[138]

---

133   *SC* 47.
134   *LG* 11.
135   *PO* 5.
136   Congregation of Rites, instruction, *Eucharisticum mysterium,* 6.
137   Cf. *1 Cor* 15:28.
138   St. Irenaeus, *Adv. haeres.* 4, 18, 5: PG 7/1, 1028.

II.   WHAT IS THIS SACRAMENT CALLED?

1328   The inexhaustible richness of this sacrament is expressed in the different names we give it. Each name evokes certain aspects of it. It is called:

Eucharist, because it is an action of thanksgiving to God. *2637* The Greek words *eucharistein*[139] and *eulogein*[140] recall the Jewish *1082* blessings that proclaim – especially during a meal – God's works: *1359* creation, redemption, and sanctification.

1329   The Lord's Supper, because of its connection with the *1382* supper which the Lord took with his disciples on the eve of his Passion and because it anticipates the wedding feast of the Lamb in the heavenly Jerusalem.[141]

The *Breaking of Bread*, because Jesus used this rite, part of a Jewish meal, when as master of the table he blessed and distributed the bread,[142] above all at the Last Supper.[143] It is by this action that his disciples will recognize him after his Resurrection,[144] and it is this expression that the first Christians will use to designate their Eucharistic assemblies;[145] by doing so they signified that all who *790* eat the one broken bread, Christ, enter into communion with him and form but one body in him.[146]

The *Eucharistic assembly* (*synaxis*), because the Eucharist is *1348* celebrated amid the assembly of the faithful, the visible expression of the Church.[147]

1330   The *memorial* of the Lord's Passion and Resurrection. *1341*

The *Holy Sacrifice*, because it makes present the one sacrifice of Christ the Savior and includes the Church's offering. The terms *holy sacrifice of the Mass*, "*sacrifice of praise*," *spiritual sacrifice*, *pure and holy sacrifice* are also used,[148] since it completes and *614, 2643* surpasses all the sacrifices of the Old Covenant.

The *Holy and Divine Liturgy*, because the Church's whole liturgy finds its center and most intense expression in the celebration of this sacrament; in the same sense we also call its celebration the *Sacred Mysteries*. We speak of the *Most Blessed Sacrament* because *1169*

---

139   Cf. *Lk* 22:19; *1 Cor* 11:24.
140   Cf. *Mt* 26:26; *Mk* 14:22.
141   Cf. *1 Cor* 11:20; *Rev* 19:9.
142   Cf. *Mt* 14:19; 15:36; *Mk* 8:6, 19.
143   Cf. *Mt* 26:26; *1 Cor* 11:24.
144   Cf. *Lk* 24:13-35.
145   Cf. *Acts* 2:42, 46; 20:7, 11.
146   Cf. *1 Cor* 10:16-17.
147   Cf. *1 Cor* 11:17-34.
148   *Heb* 13:15; cf. *1 Pet* 2:5; *Ps* 116:13, 17; *Mal* 1:11.

it is the Sacrament of sacraments. The Eucharistic species reserved in the tabernacle are designated by this same name.

950 **1331** *Holy Communion,* because by this sacrament we unite ourselves to Christ, who makes us sharers in his Body and Blood to form a single body.[149] We also call it: *the holy things (ta hagia;*
948 *sancta)*[150] – the first meaning of the phrase "communion of saints"
1405 in the Apostles' Creed – *the bread of angels, bread from heaven, medicine of immortality,*[151] *viaticum.* . . .

1332 *Holy Mass (Missa),* because the liturgy in which the mystery of salvation is accomplished concludes with the sending forth (*missio*)
849 of the faithful, so that they may fulfill God's will in their daily lives.

III. THE EUCHARIST IN THE ECONOMY OF SALVATION

The signs of bread and wine

1350 **1333** At the heart of the Eucharistic celebration are the bread and wine that, by the words of Christ and the invocation of the Holy Spirit, become Christ's Body and Blood. Faithful to the Lord's command the Church continues to do, in his memory and until his glorious return, what he did on the eve of his Passion: "He took bread. . . ." "He took the cup filled with wine. . . ." The signs of bread and wine become, in a way surpassing understanding, the Body and Blood of Christ; they continue also to signify the goodness of creation. Thus in the Offertory we give thanks to
1147 the Creator for bread and wine,[152] fruit of the "work of human hands," but above all as "fruit of the earth" and "of the vine" – gifts of the Creator.
1148 The Church sees in the gesture of the king-priest Melchizedek, who "brought out bread and wine," a prefiguring of her own offering.[153]

1150 **1334** In the Old Covenant bread and wine were offered in sacrifice among the first fruits of the earth as a sign of grateful acknowledgment to the Creator. But they also received a new
1363 significance in the context of the Exodus: the unleavened bread that Israel eats every year at Passover commemorates the haste of the departure that liberated them from Egypt; the remembrance of the manna in the desert will always recall to Israel that it lives by the bread of the Word of God;[154] their daily bread is the fruit of the promised land, the pledge of God's faithfulness to his promises.

---

149   Cf. *1 Cor* 10:16-17.
150   *Apostolic Constitutions* 8, 13, 12: PG 1, 1108; *Didache* 9, 5; 10:6: SCh 248, 176-178.
151   St. Ignatius of Antioch, *Ad Eph.* 20, 2: SCh 10, 76.
152   Cf. *Ps* 104:13-15.
153   *Gen* 14:18; cf. *Roman Missal,* EP I (Roman Canon) 95.
154   Cf. *Deut* 8:3.

The "cup of blessing"[155] at the end of the Jewish Passover meal adds to the festive joy of wine an eschatological dimension: the messianic expectation of the rebuilding of Jerusalem. When Jesus instituted the Eucharist, he gave a new and definitive meaning to the blessing of the bread and the cup.

1335   The miracles of the multiplication of the loaves, when the *1151* Lord says the blessing, breaks and distributes the loaves through his disciples to feed the multitude, prefigure the superabundance of this unique bread of his Eucharist.[156] The sign of water turned into wine at Cana already announces the Hour of Jesus' glorification. It makes manifest the fulfillment of the wedding feast in the Father's kingdom, where the faithful will drink the new wine that has become the Blood of Christ.[157]

1336   The first announcement of the Eucharist divided the disciples, just as the announcement of the Passion scandalized them: "This is a hard saying; who can listen to it?"[158] The Eucharist and the Cross are stumbling blocks. It is the same mystery and it never ceases to be an occasion of division. "Will you also go away?":[159] the Lord's question echoes through the ages, as a loving invitation to discover that only he has "the words of eternal life"[160] and that to receive in faith the gift of his Eucharist is to receive the Lord himself.   *1327*

The institution of the Eucharist

1337   The Lord, having loved those who were his own, loved *610* them to the end. Knowing that the hour had come to leave this world and return to the Father, in the course of a meal he washed their feet and gave them the commandment of love.[161] In order to leave them a pledge of this love, in order never to depart from his own and to make them sharers in his Passover, he instituted the Eucharist as the memorial of his death and Resurrection, and commanded his apostles to celebrate it until his return; "thereby he constituted them priests of the New Testament."[162]   *611*

1338   The three synoptic Gospels and St. Paul have handed on to us the account of the institution of the Eucharist; St. John, for his part, reports the words of Jesus in the synagogue of Capernaum that prepare for the

---

155   *1 Cor* 10:16.
156   Cf. *Mt* 14:13-21; 15:32-39.
157   Cf. *Jn* 2:11; *Mk* 14:25.
158   *Jn* 6:60.
159   *Jn* 6:67.
160   *Jn* 6:68.
161   Cf. *Jn* 13:1-17; 34-35.
162   Council of Trent (1562): DS 1740.

institution of the Eucharist: Christ calls himself the bread of life, come down from heaven.[163]

1169 **1339**   Jesus chose the time of Passover to fulfill what he had announced at Capernaum: giving his disciples his Body and his Blood:

> Then came the day of Unleavened Bread, on which the passover lamb had to be sacrificed. So Jesus sent Peter and John, saying, "Go and prepare the passover meal for us, that we may eat it...." They went... and prepared the passover. And when the hour came, he sat at table, and the apostles with him. And he said to them, "I have earnestly desired to eat this passover with you before I suffer; for I tell you I shall not eat it again until it is fulfilled in the kingdom of God.".... And he took bread, and when he had given thanks he broke it and gave it to them, saying, "This is my body which is given for you. Do this in remembrance of me." And likewise the cup after supper, saying, "This cup which is poured out for you is the New Covenant in my blood."[164]

1340   By celebrating the Last Supper with his apostles in the course of the Passover meal, Jesus gave the Jewish Passover its definitive
1151 meaning. Jesus' passing over to his father by his death and Resurrection, the new Passover, is anticipated in the Supper and celebrated in the Eucharist, which fulfills the Jewish Passover and anticipates the
677   final Passover of the Church in the glory of the kingdom.

"Do this in memory of me"

611   **1341**   The command of Jesus to repeat his actions and words "until he comes" does not only ask us to remember Jesus and what he did. It is directed at the liturgical celebration, by the apostles and their
1363 successors, of the *memorial* of Christ, of his life, of his death, of his Resurrection, and of his intercession in the presence of the Father.[165]

2624 **1342**   From the beginning the Church has been faithful to the Lord's command. Of the Church of Jerusalem it is written:

> They devoted themselves to the apostles' teaching and fellowship, to the breaking of bread and the prayers.... Day by day, attending the temple together and breaking bread in their homes, they partook of food with glad and generous hearts.[166]

1166, 2177 **1343**   It was above all on "the first day of the week," Sunday, the day of Jesus' resurrection, that the Christians met "to break bread."[167] From that time on down to our own day the celebration

---

163 Cf. *Jn* 6.
164 *Lk* 22:7-20; cf. *Mt* 26:17-29; *Mk* 14:12-25; *1 Cor* 11:23-26.
165 Cf. *1 Cor* 11:26.
166 *Acts* 2:42, 46.
167 *Acts* 20:7.

of the Eucharist has been continued so that today we encounter it everywhere in the Church with the same fundamental structure. It remains the center of the Church's life.

1344   Thus from celebration to celebration, as they proclaim the   *1404* Paschal mystery of Jesus "until he comes," the pilgrim People of God advances, "following the narrow way of the cross,"[168] toward the heavenly banquet, when all the elect will be seated at the table of the kingdom.

IV.   The Liturgical Celebration of the Eucharist

The Mass of all ages

1345   As early as the second century we have the witness of St. Justin Martyr for the basic lines of the order of the Eucharistic celebration. They have stayed the same until our own day for all the great liturgical families. St. Justin wrote to the pagan emperor Antoninus Pius (138-161) around the year 155, explaining what Christians did:

> On the day we call the day of the sun, all who dwell in the city or country gather in the same place.
>
> The memoirs of the apostles and the writings of the prophets are read, as much as time permits.
>
> When the reader has finished, he who presides over those gathered admonishes and challenges them to imitate these beautiful things.
>
> Then we all rise together and offer prayers* for ourselves . . . and for all others, wherever they may be, so that we may be found righteous by our life and actions, and faithful to the commandments, so as to obtain eternal salvation.
>
> When the prayers are concluded we exchange the kiss.
>
> Then someone brings bread and a cup of water and wine mixed together to him who presides over the brethren.
>
> He takes them and offers praise and glory to the Father of the universe, through the name of the Son and of the Holy Spirit and for a considerable time he gives thanks (in Greek: *eucharistian*) that we have been judged worthy of these gifts.
>
> When he has concluded the prayers and thanksgivings, all present give voice to an acclamation by saying: 'Amen.'
>
> When he who presides has given thanks and the people have responded, those whom we call deacons give to those present the "eucharisted" bread, wine and water and take them to those who are absent.[169]

---

168 *AG* 1; cf. *1 Cor* 11:26.

169 St. Justin, *Apol.* 1, 65-67: PG 6, 428-429; the text before the asterisk (*) is from chap. 67.

1346   The liturgy of the Eucharist unfolds according to a fundamental structure which has been preserved throughout the centuries down to our own day. It displays two great parts that form a
fundamental unity:
– the gathering, the liturgy of the Word, with readings, homily and
general intercessions;
– the liturgy of the Eucharist, with the presentation of the bread
and wine, the consecratory thanksgiving, and communion.
            The liturgy of the Word and liturgy of the Eucharist together
form "one single act of worship";[170] the Eucharistic table set for us is
103   the table both of the Word of God and of the Body of the Lord.[171]

1347   Is this not the same movement as the Paschal meal of the
risen Jesus with his disciples? Walking with them he explained the
Scriptures to them; sitting with them at table "he took bread,
blessed and broke it, and gave it to them."[172]

The movement of the celebration

1348   *All gather together.* Christians come together in one place
for the Eucharistic assembly. At its head is Christ himself, the
1140   principal agent of the Eucharist. He is high priest of the New
Covenant; it is he himself who presides invisibly over every
Eucharistic celebration. It is in representing him that the bishop or
1548   priest acting *in the person of Christ the head (in persona Christi capitis)*
presides over the assembly, speaks after the readings, receives the
offerings, and says the Eucharistic Prayer. *All* have their own active
parts to play in the celebration, each in his own way: readers, those
who bring up the offerings, those who give communion, and the
whole people whose "Amen" manifests their participation.

1184   **1349**   The *Liturgy of the Word* includes "the writings of the prophets," that is, the Old Testament, and "the memoirs of the apostles"
(their letters and the Gospels). After the homily, which is an exhortation to accept this Word as what it truly is, the Word of God,[173]
and to put it into practice, come the intercessions for all men,
according to the Apostle's words: "I urge that supplications,
prayers, intercessions, and thanksgivings be made for all men, for
kings, and all who are in high positions."[174]

---

170   *SC* 56.
171   Cf. *DV* 21.
172   Cf. *Lk* 24:13-35.
173   Cf. *1 Thess* 2:13.
174   *1 Tim* 2:1-2.

1350   The *presentation of the offerings* (the Offertory). Then, sometimes in procession, the bread and wine are brought to the altar; they will be offered by the priest in the name of Christ in the Eucharistic sacrifice in which they will become his body and blood. It is the very action of Christ at the Last Supper – "taking the bread and a cup." "The Church alone offers this pure oblation to the Creator, when she offers what comes forth from his creation with *1359* thanksgiving."[175] The presentation of the offerings at the altar takes up the gesture of Melchizedek and commits the Creator's gifts into the hands of Christ who, in his sacrifice, brings to perfection all human attempts to offer sacrifices.   *614*

1351   From the very beginning Christians have brought, along with the bread and wine for the Eucharist, gifts to share with those in need. This custom of the *collection*, ever appropriate, is inspired *1397* by the example of Christ who became poor to make us rich:[176]   *2186*

> Those who are well off, and who are also willing, give as each chooses. What is gathered is given to him who presides to assist orphans and widows, those whom illness or any other cause has deprived of resources, prisoners, immigrants and, in a word, all who are in need.[177]

1352   The *anaphora*: with the Eucharistic Prayer – the prayer of thanksgiving and consecration – we come to the heart and summit of the celebration:

> In the *preface,* the Church gives thanks to the Father, through Christ,   *559*
> in the Holy Spirit, for all his works: creation, redemption, and sanctification. The whole community thus joins in the unending praise that the Church in heaven, the angels and all the saints, sing to the thrice-holy God.

1353   In the *epiclesis,* the Church asks the Father to send his Holy Spirit   *1105*
(or the power of his blessing[178]) on the bread and wine, so that by his power they may become the body and blood of Jesus Christ and so that those who take part in the Eucharist may be one body and one spirit (some liturgical traditions put the epiclesis after the anamnesis).

> In the *institution narrative,* the power of the words and the action   *1375*
of Christ, and the power of the Holy Spirit, make sacramentally present under the species of bread and wine Christ's body and blood, his sacrifice offered on the cross once for all.

1354   In the *anamnesis* that follows, the Church calls to mind the Pas-   *1103*
sion, resurrection, and glorious return of Christ Jesus; she presents to the Father the offering of his Son which reconciles us with him.

---

175 St. Irenaeus, *Adv. haeres.* 4, 18, 4: PG 7/1, 1027; cf. *Mal* 1:11.
176 Cf. *1 Cor* 16:1; *2 Cor* 8:9.
177 St. Justin, *Apol.* 1, 67: PG 6, 429.
178 Cf. *Roman Missal*, EP I (Roman Canon) 90.

In the *intercessions*, the Church indicates that the Eucharist is
954   celebrated in communion with the whole Church in heaven and on earth,
the living and the dead, and in communion with the pastors of the Church,
the Pope, the diocesan bishop, his presbyterium and his deacons, and all
the bishops of the whole world together with their Churches.

1382   **1355**   In the communion, preceded by the Lord's prayer and the
breaking of the bread, the faithful receive "the bread of heaven"
and "the cup of salvation," the body and blood of Christ who
offered himself "for the life of the world":[179]

1327   Because this bread and wine have been made Eucharist
("eucharisted," according to an ancient expression), "we call
this food *Eucharist*, and no one may take part in it unless he
believes that what we teach is true, has received baptism for
the forgiveness of sins and new birth, and lives in keeping
with what Christ taught."[180]

V.   THE SACRAMENTAL SACRIFICE: THANKSGIVING, MEMORIAL, PRESENCE

1356   If from the beginning Christians have celebrated the
Eucharist and in a form whose substance has not changed despite
the great diversity of times and liturgies, it is because we know
ourselves to be bound by the command the Lord gave on the eve
of his Passion: "Do this in remembrance of me."[181]

1357   We carry out this command of the Lord by celebrating the
memorial of his sacrifice. In so doing, *we offer to the Father* what he has
himself given us: the gifts of his creation, bread and wine which,
by the power of the Holy Spirit and by the words of Christ, have
become the body and blood of Christ. Christ is thus really and
mysteriously made *present*.

1358   We must therefore consider the Eucharist as:
– thanksgiving and praise to the *Father*;
– the sacrificial memorial of *Christ* and his Body;
– the presence of Christ by the power of his word and of his *Spirit*.

Thanksgiving and praise to the Father

1359   The Eucharist, the sacrament of our salvation accomplished
293   by Christ on the cross, is also a sacrifice of praise in thanksgiving for
the work of creation. In the Eucharistic sacrifice the whole of creation

---

179   *Jn* 6:51.
180   St. Justin, *Apol.* 1, 66, 1-2: PG 6, 428.
181   *1 Cor* 11:24-25.

loved by God is presented to the Father through the death and the Resurrection of Christ. Through Christ the Church can offer the sacrifice of praise in thanksgiving for all that God has made good, beautiful, and just in creation and in humanity.

1360   The Eucharist is a sacrifice of thanksgiving to the Father, a *1083* blessing by which the Church expresses her gratitude to God for all his benefits, for all that he has accomplished through creation, redemption, and sanctification. Eucharist means first of all "thanksgiving."

1361   The Eucharist is also the sacrifice of praise by which the Church sings the glory of God in the name of all creation. This sacrifice of praise is possible only through Christ: he unites the *294* faithful to his person, to his praise, and to his intercession, so that the sacrifice of praise to the Father is offered *through* Christ and *with* him, to be accepted *in* him.

The sacrificial memorial of Christ and of his Body, the Church

1362   The Eucharist is the memorial of Christ's Passover, the making present and the sacramental offering of his unique sacrifice, in the liturgy of the Church which is his Body. In all the Eucharistic Prayers we find after the words of institution a prayer called the *anamnesis* or memorial. *1103*

1363   In the sense of Sacred Scripture the *memorial* is not merely *1099* the recollection of past events but the proclamation of the mighty works wrought by God for men.[182] In the liturgical celebration of these events, they become in a certain way present and real. This is how Israel understands its liberation from Egypt: every time Passover is celebrated, the Exodus events are made present to the memory of believers so that they may conform their lives to them.

1364   In the New Testament, the memorial takes on new meaning. When the Church celebrates the Eucharist, she commemorates Christ's Passover, and it is made present: the sacrifice Christ offered once for all *611* on the cross remains ever present.[183] "As often as the sacrifice of the *1085* Cross by which 'Christ our Pasch has been sacrificed' is celebrated on the altar, the work of our redemption is carried out."[184]

1365   Because it is the memorial of Christ's Passover, the Eucha- *2100* rist is also a sacrifice. The sacrificial character of the Eucharist is manifested in the very words of institution: "This is my body which

---

182 Cf. *Ex* 13:3.
183 Cf. *Heb* 7:25-27.
184 *LG* 3; cf. *1 Cor* 5:7.

is given for you" and "This cup which is poured out for you is the New Covenant in my blood."[185] In the Eucharist Christ gives us the very body which he gave up for us on the cross, the very blood

1846 which he "poured out for many for the forgiveness of sins."[186]

613 **1366**   The Eucharist is thus a sacrifice because it *re-presents* (makes present) the sacrifice of the cross, because it is its *memorial* and because it *applies* its fruit:

> [Christ], our Lord and God, was once and for all to offer himself to God the Father by his death on the altar of the cross, to accomplish there an everlasting redemption. But because his priesthood was not to end with his death, at the Last Supper "on the night when he was betrayed," [he wanted] to leave to his beloved spouse the Church a visible sacrifice (as the nature of man demands) by which the bloody sacrifice which he was to accomplish once for all on the cross would be re-presented, its memory perpetuated until the end of the world, and its salutary power be applied to the forgiveness of the sins we daily commit.[187]

1545 **1367**   The sacrifice of Christ and the sacrifice of the Eucharist are *one single sacrifice*: "The victim is one and the same: the same now offers through the ministry of priests, who then offered himself on the cross; only the manner of offering is different." "In this divine sacrifice which is celebrated in the Mass, the same Christ who offered himself once in a bloody manner on the altar of the cross is contained and is offered in an unbloody manner."[188]

1368   *The Eucharist is also the sacrifice of the Church.* The Church which is the Body of Christ participates in the offering of her Head. With him, she herself is offered whole and entire. She unites herself to his intercession with the Father for all men. In the Eucharist the sacrifice of Christ becomes also the sacrifice of the members of his

618 Body. The lives of the faithful, their praise, sufferings, prayer, and
2031 work, are united with those of Christ and with his total offering, and
1109 so acquire a new value. Christ's sacrifice present on the altar makes it possible for all generations of Christians to be united with his offering.

> In the catacombs the Church is often represented as a woman in prayer, arms outstretched in the praying position. Like Christ who stretched out his arms on the cross, through him, with him, and in him, she offers herself and intercedes for all men.

---

185   *Lk* 22:19-20.
186   *Mt* 26:28.
187   Council of Trent (1562): DS 1740; cf. *1 Cor* 11:23; *Heb* 7:24, 27.
188   Council of Trent (1562): DS 1743; cf. *Heb* 9:14, 27.

1369   *The whole Church is united with the offering and intercession of Christ.* Since he has the ministry of Peter in the Church, the *Pope* is associated with every celebration of the Eucharist, wherein he is *834, 882* named as the sign and servant of the unity of the universal Church. The *bishop* of the place is always responsible for the Eucharist, even when a *priest* presides; the bishop's name is mentioned to signify *1561, 1566* his presidency over the particular Church, in the midst of his presbyterium and with the assistance of *deacons.* The community intercedes also for all ministers who, for it and with it, offer the Eucharistic sacrifice:

> Let only that Eucharist be regarded as legitimate, which is celebrated under [the presidency of] the bishop or him to whom he has entrusted it.[189]

> Through the ministry of priests the spiritual sacrifice of the faithful is completed in union with the sacrifice of Christ the only Mediator, which in the Eucharist is offered through the priests' hands in the name of the whole Church in an unbloody and sacramental manner until the Lord himself comes.[190]

1370   To the offering of Christ are united not only the members still here on earth, but also those already *in the glory of heaven.* In communion with and commemorating the Blessed Virgin Mary *956* and all the saints, the Church offers the Eucharistic sacrifice. In the *969* Eucharist the Church is as it were at the foot of the cross with Mary, united with the offering and intercession of Christ.

1371   The Eucharistic sacrifice is also offered for *the faithful de-* *958, 1689* *parted* who "have died in Christ but are not yet wholly purified,"[191] *1032* so that they may be able to enter into the light and peace of Christ:

> Put this body anywhere! Don't trouble yourselves about it! I simply ask you to remember me at the Lord's altar wherever you are.[192]

> Then, we pray [in the anaphora] for the holy fathers and bishops who have fallen asleep, and in general for all who have fallen asleep before us, in the belief that it is a great benefit to the souls on whose behalf the supplication is offered, while the holy and tremendous Victim is present. . . . By offering to God our supplications for those who have fallen asleep, if they have sinned, we . . . offer Christ sacrificed for the sins of all, and so render favorable, for them and for us, the God who loves man.[193]

---

189   St. Ignatius of Antioch, *Ad Smyrn.* 8:1; SCh 10, 138.
190   *PO* 2 § 4.
191   Council of Trent (1562): DS 1743.
192   St. Monica, before her death, to her sons, St. Augustine and his brother; *Conf.* 9, 11, 27: PL 32, 775.
193   St. Cyril of Jerusalem, *Catech. myst.* 5, 9. 10: PG 33, 1116-1117.

1372   St. Augustine admirably summed up this doctrine that
moves us to an ever more complete participation in our Redeemer's
1140 sacrifice which we celebrate in the Eucharist:

> This wholly redeemed city, the assembly and society of the
> saints, is offered to God as a universal sacrifice by the high priest
> who in the form of a slave went so far as to offer himself for us
> in his Passion, to make us the Body of so great a head. . . . Such
> is the sacrifice of Christians: "we who are many are one Body in
> Christ." The Church continues to reproduce this sacrifice in the
> sacrament of the altar so well-known to believers wherein it is
> evident to them that in what she offers she herself is offered.[194]

The presence of Christ by the power of his word and the Holy Spirit

1373   "Christ Jesus, who died, yes, who was raised from the dead,
who is at the right hand of God, who indeed intercedes for us," is
present in many ways to his Church:[195] in his word, in his Church's
prayer, "where two or three are gathered in my name,"[196] in the poor,
the sick, and the imprisoned,[197] in the sacraments of which he is the
author, in the sacrifice of the Mass, and in the person of the minister.
1088 But "he is present . . . most *especially in the Eucharistic species.*"[198]

1374   The mode of Christ's presence under the Eucharistic species is unique. It raises the Eucharist above all the sacraments as
1211 "the perfection of the spiritual life and the end to which all the
sacraments tend."[199] In the most blessed sacrament of the Eucharist "the body and blood, together with the soul and divinity, of
our Lord Jesus Christ and, therefore, *the whole Christ is truly, really,
and substantially* contained."[200] "This presence is called 'real' – by
which is not intended to exclude the other types of presence as if
they could not be 'real' too, but because it is presence in the fullest
sense: that is to say, it is a *substantial* presence by which Christ, God
and man, makes himself wholly and entirely present."[201]

1375   It is by the conversion of the bread and wine into Christ's
body and blood that Christ becomes present in this sacrament. The
Church Fathers strongly affirmed the faith of the Church in the
1105 efficacy of the Word of Christ and of the action of the Holy Spirit
to bring about this conversion. Thus St. John Chrysostom declares:

---

194   St. Augustine, *De civ. Dei*, 10, 6: PL 41, 283; cf. *Rom* 12:5.
195   *Rom* 8:34; cf. *LG* 48.
196   *Mt* 18:20.
197   Cf. *Mt* 25:31-46.
198   *SC* 7.
199   St. Thomas Aquinas, *STh* III, 73, 3c.
200   Council of Trent (1551): DS 1651.
201   Paul VI, *MF* 39.

> It is not man that causes the things offered to become the
> Body and Blood of Christ, but he who was crucified for us,
> Christ himself. The priest, in the role of Christ, pronounces
> these words, but their power and grace are God's. This is my   *1128*
> body, he says. This word transforms the things offered.[202]

And St. Ambrose says about this conversion:

> Be convinced that this is not what nature has formed, but what
> the blessing has consecrated. The power of the blessing prevails
> over that of nature, because by the blessing nature itself is
> changed. . . . Could not Christ's word, which can make from
> nothing what did not exist, change existing things into what   *298*
> they were not before? It is no less a feat to give things their
> original nature than to change their nature.[203]

1376   The Council of Trent summarizes the Catholic faith by
declaring: "Because Christ our Redeemer said that it was truly his
body that he was offering under the species of bread, it has always
been the conviction of the Church of God, and this holy Council
now declares again, that by the consecration of the bread and wine
there takes place a change of the whole substance of the bread into
the substance of the body of Christ our Lord and of the whole
substance of the wine into the substance of his blood. This change
the holy Catholic Church has fittingly and properly called transubstantiation."[204]

1377   The Eucharistic presence of Christ begins at the moment
of the consecration and endures as long as the Eucharistic species
subsist. Christ is present whole and entire in each of the species
and whole and entire in each of their parts, in such a way that the
breaking of the bread does not divide Christ.[205]

1378   *Worship of the Eucharist.* In the liturgy of the Mass we express *1178*
our faith in the real presence of Christ under the species of bread and
wine by, among other ways, genuflecting or bowing deeply as a sign
of adoration of the Lord. "The Catholic Church has always offered *103*
and still offers to the sacrament of the Eucharist the cult of adoration, *2628*
not only during Mass, but also outside of it, reserving the consecrated
hosts with the utmost care, exposing them to the solemn veneration
of the faithful, and carrying them in procession."[206]

---

202 St. John Chrysostom, *prod. Jud.* 1:6: PG 49, 380.
203 St. Ambrose, *De myst.* 9, 50; 52: PL 16, 405-407.
204 Council of Trent (1551): DS 1642; cf. *Mt* 26:26 ff.; *Mk* 14:22 ff.; *Lk* 22:19 ff.;
      1 Cor 11:24 ff.
205 Cf. Council of Trent: DS 1641.
206 Paul VI, *MF* 56.

1183 **1379** The tabernacle was first intended for the reservation of the Eucharist in a worthy place so that it could be brought to the sick and those absent, outside of Mass. As faith in the real presence of Christ in his Eucharist deepened, the Church became conscious of the meaning of silent adoration of the Lord present under the Eucharistic species. It is for this reason that the tabernacle should be located in an especially worthy place in the church and should be constructed in such a way that it emphasizes and manifests the truth
2691 of the real presence of Christ in the Blessed Sacrament.

1380 It is highly fitting that Christ should have wanted to remain present to his Church in this unique way. Since Christ was about to take his departure from his own in his visible form, he wanted to give us his sacramental presence; since he was about to
669 offer himself on the cross to save us, he wanted us to have the memorial of the love with which he loved us "to the end,"[207] even to the giving of his life. In his Eucharistic presence he remains mysteriously in our midst as the one who loved us and gave
478 himself up for us,[208] and he remains under signs that express and communicate this love:

> The Church and the world have a great need for Eucharistic
> worship. Jesus awaits us in this sacrament of love. Let us not
2715 > refuse the time to go to meet him in adoration, in contemplation
> full of faith, and open to making amends for the serious offenses
> and crimes of the world. Let our adoration never cease.[209]

1381 "That in this sacrament are the true Body of Christ and his true Blood is something that 'cannot be apprehended by the
156 senses,' says St. Thomas, 'but *only by faith*, which relies on divine
215 authority.' For this reason, in a commentary on *Luke* 22:19 ('This is my body which is given for you.'), St. Cyril says: 'Do not doubt whether this is true, but rather receive the words of the Savior in faith, for since he is the truth, he cannot lie.'"[210]

> Godhead here in hiding, whom I do adore
> Masked by these bare shadows, shape and nothing more,
> See, Lord, at thy service low lies here a heart
> Lost, all lost in wonder at the God thou art.
>
> Seeing, touching, tasting are in thee deceived;
> How says trusty hearing? that shall be believed;
> What God's Son has told me, take for truth I do;
> Truth himself speaks truly or there's nothing true.[211]

---

207 *Jn* 13:1.
208 Cf. *Gal* 2:20.
209 John Paul II, *Dominicae cenae*, 3.
210 St. Thomas Aquinas, *STh* III, 75, 1; cf. Paul VI, *MF* 18; St. Cyril of Alexandria, *In Luc.* 22, 19: PG 72, 912; cf. Paul VI, *MF* 18.
211 St. Thomas Aquinas (attr.), *Adoro te devote*; tr. Gerard Manley Hopkins.

VI. THE PASCHAL BANQUET

1382   The Mass is at the same time, and inseparably, the sacrificial memorial in which the sacrifice of the cross is perpetuated and the sacred banquet of communion with the Lord's body and blood. But the celebration of the Eucharistic sacrifice is wholly directed toward the intimate union of the faithful with Christ through communion. To receive communion is to receive Christ himself who has offered himself for us.

950

1383   *The altar,* around which the Church is gathered in the celebration of the Eucharist, represents the two aspects of the same mystery: the altar of the sacrifice and the table of the Lord. This is all the more so since the Christian altar is the symbol of Christ himself, present in the midst of the assembly of his faithful, both as the victim offered for our reconciliation and as food from heaven who is giving himself to us. "For what is the altar of Christ if not the image of the Body of Christ?"[212] asks St. Ambrose. He says elsewhere, "The altar represents the body [of Christ] and the Body of Christ is on the altar."[213] The liturgy expresses this unity of sacrifice and communion in many prayers. Thus the Roman Church prays in its anaphora:

1182

> We entreat you, almighty God,
> that by the hands of your holy Angel
> this offering may be borne to your altar in heaven
> in the sight of your divine majesty,
> so that as we receive in communion at this altar
> the most holy Body and Blood of your Son,
> we may be filled with every heavenly blessing and grace.[214]

"Take this and eat it, all of you": communion

1384   The Lord addresses an invitation to us, urging us to receive him in the sacrament of the Eucharist: "Truly, I say to you, unless you eat the flesh of the Son of man and drink his blood, you have no life in you."[215]

2835

---

212 St. Ambrose, *De Sacr.* 5, 2, 7: PL 16, 447C.
213 St. Ambrose, *De Sacr.* 4, 2, 7: PL 16, 437D.
214 *Roman Missal,* EP I (Roman Canon) 96: Supplices te rogamus, omnipotens Deus: iube hæc perferri per manus sancti Angeli tui in sublime altare tuum, in conspectu divinae maiestatis tuae: ut, quotquot ex hac altaris participatione sacrosanctum Filii Corpus et Sanguinem sumpserimus, omni benedictione cælesti et gratia repleamur.
215 *Jn* 6:53.

1385   To respond to this invitation we must *prepare ourselves* for so great and so holy a moment. St. Paul urges us to examine our conscience: "Whoever, therefore, eats the bread or drinks the cup of the Lord in an unworthy manner will be guilty of profaning the body and blood of the Lord. Let a man examine himself, and so eat of the bread and drink of the cup. For any one who eats and drinks without discerning the body eats and drinks judgment upon him-
1457   self."[216] Anyone conscious of a grave sin must receive the sacrament of Reconciliation before coming to communion.

1386   Before so great a sacrament, the faithful can only echo humbly and with ardent faith the words of the Centurion: *"Domine, non sum dignus ut intres sub tectum meum, sed tantum dic verbo, et sanabitur anima mea"* ("Lord, I am not worthy that you should enter under my roof, but only say the word and my soul will be healed.").[217] And in the Divine Liturgy of St. John Chrysostom the faithful pray in the same spirit:

732   O Son of God, bring me into communion today with your
              mystical supper. I shall not tell your enemies the secret, nor
              kiss you with Judas' kiss. But like the good thief I cry, "Jesus,
              remember me when you come into your kingdom."

1387   To prepare for worthy reception of this sacrament, the faithful should observe the fast required in their Church.[218] Bodily demeanor
2043   (gestures, clothing) ought to convey the respect, solemnity, and joy of this moment when Christ becomes our guest.

1388   It is in keeping with the very meaning of the Eucharist that the faithful, if they have the required dispositions, *receive communion each time* they participate in the Mass.[219] As the Second Vatican Council says: "That more perfect form of participation in the Mass whereby the faithful, after the priest's communion, receive the Lord's Body from the same sacrifice, is warmly recommended."[220]

2042 **1389**   The Church obliges the faithful "to take part in the Divine Liturgy on Sundays and feast days" and, prepared by the sacrament of Reconciliation, to receive the Eucharist at least once a year, if possible during the Easter season.[221] But the Church strongly encourages the faithful to receive the holy Eucharist on Sundays
2837   and feast days, or more often still, even daily.

---

216   1 Cor 11:27-29.
217   *Roman Missal*, response to the invitation to communion; cf. *Mt* 8:8.
218   Cf. CIC, can. 919.
219   Cf. CIC, can. 917; AAS 76 (1984) 746-747.
220   *SC* 55.
221   *OE* 15; CIC, can. 920.

1390   Since Christ is sacramentally present under each of the species, communion under the species of bread alone makes it possible to receive all the fruit of Eucharistic grace. For pastoral reasons this manner of receiving communion has been legitimately established as the most common form in the Latin rite. But "the sign of communion is more complete when given under both kinds, since in that form the sign of the Eucharistic meal appears more clearly."[222] This is the usual form of receiving communion in the Eastern rites.

The fruits of Holy Communion

1391   *Holy Communion augments our union with Christ.* The principal fruit of receiving the Eucharist in Holy Communion is an intimate union with Christ Jesus. Indeed, the Lord said: "He who   460 eats my flesh and drinks my blood abides in me, and I in him."[223] Life in Christ has its foundation in the Eucharistic banquet: "As the living Father sent me, and I live because of the Father, so he who eats me will live because of me."[224]   521

> On the feasts of the Lord, when the faithful receive the Body of the Son, they proclaim to one another the Good News that the first fruits of life have been given, as when the angel said to Mary Magdalene, "Christ is risen!" Now too are life and resurrection conferred on whoever receives Christ.[225]

1392   What material food produces in our bodily life, Holy   1212 Communion wonderfully achieves in our spiritual life. Communion with the flesh of the risen Christ, a flesh "given life and giving life through the Holy Spirit,"[226] preserves, increases, and renews the life of grace received at Baptism. This growth in Christian life needs the nourishment of Eucharistic Communion, the bread for our pilgrimage until the moment of death, when it will be given to us as viaticum.   1524

1393   *Holy Communion separates us from sin.* The body of Christ we receive in Holy Communion is "given up for us," and the blood we drink "shed for the many for the forgiveness of sins." For this reason the Eucharist cannot unite us to Christ without at the same   613 time cleansing us from past sins and preserving us from future sins:

---

222   GIRM 240.
223   *Jn* 6:56.
224   *Jn* 6:57.
225   Fanqîth, Syriac Office of Antioch, Vol. I, Commun., 237 a-b.
226   *PO* 5.

> For as often as we eat this bread and drink the cup, we proclaim the death of the Lord. If we proclaim the Lord's death, we proclaim the forgiveness of sins. If, as often as his blood is poured out, it is poured for the forgiveness of sins, I should always receive it, so that it may always forgive my sins. Because I always sin, I should always have a remedy.[227]

1394 As bodily nourishment restores lost strength, so the Eucharist strengthens our charity, which tends to be weakened in
1863 daily life; and this living charity *wipes away venial sins*.[228] By giving
1436 himself to us Christ revives our love and enables us to break our disordered attachments to creatures and root ourselves in him:

> Since Christ died for us out of love, when we celebrate the memorial of his death at the moment of sacrifice we ask that love may be granted to us by the coming of the Holy Spirit. We humbly pray that in the strength of this love by which Christ willed to die for us, we, by receiving the gift of the Holy Spirit, may be able to consider the world as crucified for us, and to be ourselves as crucified to the world. . . . Having received the gift of love, let us die to sin and live for God.[229]

1395 By the same charity that it enkindles in us, the Eucharist *preserves us from future mortal sins*. The more we share the life of
1855 Christ and progress in his friendship, the more difficult it is to break away from him by mortal sin. The Eucharist is not ordered to the forgiveness of mortal sins – that is proper to the sacrament of
1446 Reconciliation. The Eucharist is properly the sacrament of those who are in full communion with the Church.

1118 **1396** *The unity of the Mystical Body: the Eucharist makes the Church.* Those who receive the Eucharist are united more closely to Christ. Through it Christ unites them to all the faithful in one body – the Church. Communion renews, strengthens, and deepens this incorporation into the Church, already achieved by Baptism. In Baptism we have been called to form but one body.[230] The Eucharist fulfills
1267 this call: "The cup of blessing which we bless, is it not a participation in the blood of Christ? The bread which we break, is it not a participation in the body of Christ? Because there is one bread, we
790 who are many are one body, for we all partake of the one bread:"[231]

> If you are the body and members of Christ, then it is your
1064 sacrament that is placed on the table of the Lord; it is your

---

227 St. Ambrose, *De Sacr.* 4, 6, 28: PL 16, 446; cf. *1 Cor* 11:26.
228 Cf. Council of Trent (1551): DS 1638.
229 St. Fulgentius of Ruspe, *Contra Fab.* 28, 16-19: CCL 19A, 813-814.
230 Cf. *1 Cor* 12:13.
231 *1 Cor* 10:16-17.

sacrament that you receive. To that which you are you respond "Amen" ("yes, it is true!") and by responding to it you assent to it. For you hear the words, "the Body of Christ" and respond "Amen." Be then a member of the Body of Christ that your *Amen* may be true.[232]

1397   *The Eucharist commits us to the poor.* To receive in truth the Body and Blood of Christ given up for us, we must recognize Christt   *2449* in the poorest, his brethren:

> You have tasted the Blood of the Lord, yet you do not recognize your brother,. . . . You dishonor this table when you do not judge worthy of sharing your food someone judged worthy to take part in this meal. . . . God freed you from all your sins and invited you here, but you have not become more merciful.[233]

1398   *The Eucharist and the unity of Christians.* Before the greatness of this mystery St. Augustine exclaims, "*O sacrament of devotion! O sign of unity! O bond of charity!*"[234] The more painful the experience   *817* of the divisions in the Church which break the common participation in the table of the Lord, the more urgent are our prayers to the Lord that the time of complete unity among all who believe in him may return.

1399   The Eastern churches that are not in full communion with the   *838* Catholic Church celebrate the Eucharist with great love. "These Churches, although separated from us, yet possess true sacraments, above all – by apostolic succession – the priesthood and the Eucharist, whereby they are still joined to us in closest intimacy." A certain communion *in sacris*, and so in the Eucharist, "given suitable circumstances and the approval of Church authority, is not merely possible but is encouraged."[235]

1400   Ecclesial communities derived from the Reformation and separated from the Catholic Church, "have not preserved the proper reality of the Eucharistic mystery in its fullness, especially because of the absence of the sacrament of Holy Orders."[236] It is for this reason that Eucharistic intercommunion with these communities is not possible for the Catholic   *1536* Church. However these ecclesial communities, "when they commemorate the Lord's death and resurrection in the Holy Supper . . . profess that it signifies life in communion with Christ and await his coming in glory."[237]

1401   When, in the Ordinary's judgment, a grave necessity arises,   *1483* Catholic ministers may give the sacraments of Eucharist, Penance, and Anointing of the Sick to other Christians not in full communion with the Catholic Church, who ask for them of their own will, provided they give

232   St. Augustine, *Sermo* 272: PL 38, 1247.
233   St. John Chrysostom, *Hom. in 1 Cor.* 27, 4: PG 61, 229-230; cf. *Mt* 25:40.
234   St. Augustine, *In Jo. ev.* 26, 13: PL 35, 1613; cf. *SC* 47.
235   *UR* 15 § 2; cf. CIC, can. 844 § 3.
236   *UR* 22 § 3.
237   *UR* 22 § 3.

1385   evidence of holding the Catholic faith regarding these sacraments and possess the required dispositions.[238]

VII.   THE EUCHARIST – "PLEDGE OF THE GLORY TO COME"

1402   In an ancient prayer the Church acclaims the mystery of the Eucharist: "O sacred banquet in which Christ is received as
1323   food, the memory of his Passion is renewed, the soul is filled with grace and a pledge of the life to come is given to us." If the Eucharist is the memorial of the Passover of the Lord Jesus, if by our communion at the altar we are filled "with every heavenly blessing and grace,"[239]
1130   then the Eucharist is also an anticipation of the heavenly glory.

1403   At the Last Supper the Lord himself directed his disciples' attention toward the fulfillment of the Passover in the kingdom of God: "I tell you I shall not drink again of this fruit of the vine until that day when I drink it new with you in my Father's kingdom."[240] Whenever the Church celebrates the Eucharist she remembers this promise and turns her gaze "to him who is to come." In her prayer
671   she calls for his coming: *"Marana tha!"* "Come, Lord Jesus!"[241] "May your grace come and this world pass away!"[242]

1404   The Church knows that the Lord comes even now in his Eucharist and that he is there in our midst. However, his presence is veiled. Therefore we celebrate the Eucharist "awaiting the blessed hope and the coming of our Savior, Jesus Christ,"[243] asking
1041   "to share in your glory when every tear will be wiped away. On
1028   that day we shall see you, our God, as you are. We shall become like you and praise you for ever through Christ our Lord."[244]

1042   **1405**   There is no surer pledge or clearer sign of this great hope in the new heavens and new earth "in which righteousness dwells,"[245] than the Eucharist. Every time this mystery is celebrated, "the work of our redemption is carried on" and we "break the one bread that provides the medicine of immortality, the anti-
1000   dote for death, and the food that makes us live for ever in Jesus Christ."[246]

---

238   Cf. CIC, can. 844 § 4.
239   *Roman Missal*, EP I (Roman Canon) 96: *Supplices te rogamus.*
240   *Mt* 26:29; cf. *Lk* 22:18; *Mk* 14:25.
241   *Rev* 1:4; 22:20; 1 *Cor* 16:22.
242   *Didache* 10, 6: SCh 248, 180.
243   *Roman Missal* 126, embolism after the Our Father: *expectantes beatam spem et adventum Salvatoris nostri Jesu Christi;* cf. *Titus* 2:13.
244   EP III 116: prayer for the dead.
245   2 *Pet* 3:13.

IN BRIEF

1406　Jesus said: "I am the living bread that came down from heaven; if any one eats of this bread, he will live for ever; . . . he who eats my flesh and drinks my blood has eternal life and . . . abides in me, and I in him" (*Jn* 6:51, 54, 56).

1407　The Eucharist is the heart and the summit of the Church's life, for in it Christ associates his Church and all her members with his sacrifice of praise and thanksgiving offered once for all on the cross to his Father; by this sacrifice he pours out the graces of salvation on his Body which is the Church.

1408　The Eucharistic celebration always includes: the proclamation of the Word of God; thanksgiving to God the Father for all his benefits, above all the gift of his Son; the consecration of bread and wine; and participation in the liturgical banquet by receiving the Lord's body and blood. These elements constitute one single act of worship.

1409　The Eucharist is the memorial of Christ's Passover, that is, of the work of salvation accomplished by the life, death, and resurrection of Christ, a work made present by the liturgical action.

1410　It is Christ himself, the eternal high priest of the New Covenant who, acting through the ministry of the priests, offers the Eucharistic sacrifice. And it is the same Christ, really present under the species of bread and wine, who is the offering of the Eucharistic sacrifice.

1411　Only validly ordained priests can preside at the Eucharist and consecrate the bread and the wine so that they become the Body and Blood of the Lord.

1412　The essential signs of the Eucharistic sacrament are wheat bread and grape wine, on which the blessing of the Holy Spirit is invoked and the priest pronounces the words of consecration spoken by Jesus during the Last Supper: "This is my body which will be given up for you. . . . This is the cup of my blood. . . ."

246　*LG* 3; St. Ignatius of Antioch, *Ad Eph.* 20, 2: SCh 10, 76.

1413   By the consecration the transubstantiation of the bread and wine into the Body and Blood of Christ is brought about. Under the consecrated species of bread and wine Christ himself, living and glorious, is present in a true, real, and substantial manner: his Body and his Blood, with his soul and his divinity (cf. Council of Trent: DS 1640; 1651).

1414   As sacrifice, the Eucharist is also offered in reparation for the sins of the living and the dead and to obtain spiritual or temporal benefits from God.

1415   Anyone who desires to receive Christ in Eucharistic communion must be in the state of grace. Anyone aware of having sinned mortally must not receive communion without having received absolution in the sacrament of penance.

1416   Communion with the Body and Blood of Christ increases the communicant's union with the Lord, forgives his venial sins, and preserves him from grave sins. Since receiving this sacrament strengthens the bonds of charity between the communicant and Christ, it also reinforces the unity of the Church as the Mystical Body of Christ.

1417   The Church warmly recommends that the faithful receive Holy Communion each time they participate in the celebration of the Eucharist; she obliges them to do so at least once a year.

1418   Because Christ himself is present in the sacrament of the altar, he is to be honored with the worship of adoration. "To visit the Blessed Sacrament is . . . a proof of gratitude, an expression of love, and a duty of adoration toward Christ our Lord" (Paul VI, *MF* 66).

1419   Having passed from this world to the Father, Christ gives us in the Eucharist the pledge of glory with him. Participation in the Holy Sacrifice identifies us with his Heart, sustains our strength along the pilgrimage of this life, makes us long for eternal life, and unites us even now to the Church in heaven, the Blessed Virgin Mary, and all the saints.

Chapter Two
The Sacraments of Healing

1420   Through the sacraments of Christian initiation, man receives the new life of Christ. Now we carry this life "in earthen vessels," and it remains "hidden with Christ in God."[1] We are still in our "earthly tent," subject to suffering, illness, and death.[2] This new life as a child of God can be weakened and even lost by sin.

1421   The Lord Jesus Christ, physician of our souls and bodies, who forgave the sins of the paralytic and restored him to bodily health,[3] has willed that his Church continue, in the power of the Holy Spirit, his work of healing and salvation, even among her own members. This is the purpose of the two sacraments of healing: the sacrament of Penance and the sacrament of Anointing of the Sick.

Article 4
THE SACRAMENT OF PENANCE AND RECONCILIATION

1422   "Those who approach the sacrament of Penance obtain   *980* pardon from God's mercy for the offense committed against him, and are, at the same time, reconciled with the Church which they have wounded by their sins and which by charity, by example, and by prayer labors for their conversion."[4]

I.   What Is This Sacrament Called?

1423   It is called the *sacrament of conversion* because it makes   *1989* sacramentally present Jesus' call to conversion, the first step in returning to the Father[5] from whom one has strayed by sin.

It is called the *sacrament of Penance,* since it consecrates the   *1440* Christian sinner's personal and ecclesial steps of conversion, penance, and satisfaction.

1424   It is called the *sacrament of confession,* since the disclosure   *1456* or confession of sins to a priest is an essential element of this sacrament. In a profound sense it is also a "confession" – acknow-

---

1   *2 Cor* 4:7; *Col* 3:3.
2   *2 Cor* 5:1.
3   Cf. *Mk* 2:1-12.
4   *LG* 11 § 2.
5   Cf. *Mk* 1:15; *Lk* 15:18.

ledgment and praise – of the holiness of God and of his mercy toward sinful man.

1449	It is called the *sacrament of forgiveness*, since by the priest's sacramental absolution God grants the penitent "pardon and peace."[6]

1442	It is called the *sacrament of Reconciliation*, because it imparts to the sinner the love of God who reconciles: "Be reconciled to God."[7] He who lives by God's merciful love is ready to respond to the Lord's call: "Go; first be reconciled to your brother."[8]

## II.	WHY A SACRAMENT OF RECONCILIATION AFTER BAPTISM?

1263 **1425**	"You were washed, you were sanctified, you were justified in the name of the Lord Jesus Christ and in the Spirit of our God."[9] One must appreciate the magnitude of the gift God has given us in the sacraments of Christian initiation in order to grasp the degree to which sin is excluded for him who has "put on Christ."[10] But the apostle John also says: "If we say we have no sin, we deceive ourselves, and the truth is not in us."[11] And the Lord himself taught 2838	us to pray: "Forgive us our trespasses,"[12] linking our forgiveness of one another's offenses to the forgiveness of our sins that God will grant us.

1426	*Conversion* to Christ, the new birth of Baptism, the gift of the Holy Spirit and the Body and Blood of Christ received as food have made us "holy and without blemish," just as the Church herself, the Bride of Christ, is "holy and without blemish."[13] Nevertheless the new life received in Christian initiation has not abolished the frailty and weakness of human nature, nor the inclination 405, 978	to sin that tradition calls *concupiscence*, which remains in the bap-1264	tized such that with the help of the grace of Christ they may prove themselves in the struggle of Christian life.[14] This is the struggle of *conversion* directed toward holiness and eternal life to which the Lord never ceases to call us.[15]

6	*OP* 46: formula of absolution.
7	*2 Cor* 5:20.
8	*Mt* 5:24.
9	*1 Cor* 6:11.
10	*Gal* 3:27.
11	*1 Jn* 1:8.
12	Cf. *Lk* 11:4; *Mt* 6:12.
13	*Eph* 1:4; 5:27.
14	Cf. Council of Trent (1546): DS 1515.

III.   THE CONVERSION OF THE BAPTIZED

1427   Jesus calls to conversion. This call is an essential part of the   *541*
proclamation of the kingdom: "The time is fulfilled, and the kingdom of God is at hand; repent, and believe in the gospel."[16] In the
Church's preaching this call is addressed first to those who do not
yet know Christ and his Gospel. Also, Baptism is the principal
place for the first and fundamental conversion. It is by faith in the
Gospel and by Baptism[17] that one renounces evil and gains salva-   *1226*
tion, that is, the forgiveness of all sins and the gift of new life.

1428   Christ's call to conversion continues to resound in the lives
of Christians. This *second conversion* is an uninterrupted task for the
whole Church who, "clasping sinners to her bosom, [is] at once holy   *1036*
and always in need of purification, [and] follows constantly the path
of penance and renewal."[18] This endeavor of conversion is not just a   *853*
human work. It is the movement of a "contrite heart," drawn and
moved by grace to respond to the merciful love of God who loved us   *1996*
first.[19]

1429   St. Peter's conversion after he had denied his master three
times bears witness to this. Jesus' look of infinite mercy drew tears
of repentance from Peter and, after the Lord's resurrection, a
threefold affirmation of love for him.[20] The second conversion also
has a *communitarian* dimension, as is clear in the Lord's call to a
whole Church: "Repent!"[21]

> St. Ambrose says of the two conversions that, in the Church,
> "there are water and tears: the water of Baptism and the tears
> of repentance."[22]

IV.   INTERIOR PENANCE

1430   Jesus' call to conversion and penance, like that of the
prophets before him, does not aim first at outward works, "sack-
cloth and ashes," fasting and mortification, but at the *conversion of
the heart, interior conversion.* Without this, such penances remain
sterile and false; however, interior conversion urges expression in   *1098*
visible signs, gestures and works of penance.[23]

---

15   Cf. Council of Trent (1547): DS 1545; *LG* 40.
16   *Mk* 1:15.
17   Cf. *Acts* 2:38.
18   *LG* 8 § 3.
19   *Ps* 51:17; cf. *Jn* 6:44; 12:32; *1 Jn* 4:10.
20   Cf. *Lk* 22:61; *Jn* 21:15-17.
21   *Rev* 2:5, 16.
22   St. Ambrose, *ep.* 41, 12: PL 16, 1116.

1431   Interior repentance is a radical reorientation of our whole
life, a return, a conversion to God with all our heart, an end of sin,
1451 a turning away from evil, with repugnance toward the evil actions
we have committed. At the same time it entails the desire and
resolution to change one's life, with hope in God's mercy and trust
in the help of his grace. This conversion of heart is accompanied by
a salutary pain and sadness which the Fathers called *animi cruciatus*
368 (affliction of spirit) and *compunctio cordis* (repentance of heart).[24]

1432   The human heart is heavy and hardened. God must give
man a new heart.[25] Conversion is first of all a work of the grace of
1989 God who makes our hearts return to him: "Restore us to thyself, O
LORD, that we may be restored!"[26] God gives us the strength to
begin anew. It is in discovering the greatness of God's love that our
heart is shaken by the horror and weight of sin and begins to fear
offending God by sin and being separated from him. The human
heart is converted by looking upon him whom our sins have
pierced:[27]

> Let us fix our eyes on Christ's blood and understand how
> precious it is to his Father, for, poured out for our salvation,
> it has brought to the whole world the grace of repentance.[28]

729 **1433**   Since Easter, the Holy Spirit has proved "the world wrong
about sin,"[29] i.e., proved that the world has not believed in him
whom the Father has sent. But this same Spirit who brings sin to
692, 1848 light is also the Consoler who gives the human heart grace for
repentance and conversion.[30]

V.   THE MANY FORMS OF PENANCE IN CHRISTIAN LIFE

1969 **1434**   The interior penance of the Christian can be expressed in many
and various ways. Scripture and the Fathers insist above all on three forms,
fasting, prayer, and *almsgiving,*[31] which express conversion in relation to
oneself, to God, and to others. Alongside the radical purification brought
about by Baptism or martyrdom they cite as means of obtaining forgiveness of sins: efforts at reconciliation with one's neighbor, tears of repentance, concern for the salvation of one's neighbor, the intercession of the
saints, and the practice of charity "which covers a multitude of sins."[32]

---

23   Cf. *Joel* 2:12-13; *Isa* 1:16-17; *Mt* 6:1-6; 16-18.
24   Cf. Council of Trent (1551): DS 1676-1678; 1705; cf. *Roman Catechism,* II, V, 4.
25   Cf. *Ezek* 36:26-27.
26   *Lam* 5:21.
27   Cf. *Jn* 19:37; *Zech* 12:10.
28   St. Clement of Rome, *Ad Cor.* 7, 4: PG 1, 224.
29   Cf. *Jn* 16:8-9.
30   Cf. *Jn* 15:26; *Acts* 2:36-38; John Paul II, *DeV* 27-48.
31   Cf. *Tob* 12:8; *Mt* 6:1-18.

1435   Conversion is accomplished in daily life by gestures of reconciliation, concern for the poor, the exercise and defense of justice and right,[33] by the admission of faults to one's brethren, fraternal correction, revision of life, examination of conscience, spiritual direction, acceptance of suffering, endurance of persecution for the sake of righteousness. Taking up one's cross each day and following Jesus is the surest way of penance.[34]

1436   *Eucharist and Penance.* Daily conversion and penance find their source and nourishment in the Eucharist, for in it is made present the sacrifice of Christ which has reconciled us with God. Through the Eucharist those who live from the life of Christ are fed and strengthened. "It is a remedy to free us from our daily faults and to preserve us from mortal sins."[35]

1394

1437   Reading Sacred Scripture, praying the Liturgy of the Hours and the Our Father – every sincere act of worship or devotion revives the spirit of conversion and repentance within us and contributes to the forgiveness of our sins.

1438   *The seasons and days of penance* in the course of the liturgical year   *540* (Lent, and each Friday in memory of the death of the Lord) are intense moments of the Church's penitential practice.[36] These times are particularly appropriate for spiritual exercises, penitential liturgies, pilgrimages as signs of penance, voluntary self-denial such as fasting and almsgiving, and fraternal sharing (charitable and missionary works).

2043

1439   *The process of conversion and repentance* was described by Jesus in the parable of the prodigal son, the center of which is the merciful father:[37] the fascination of illusory freedom, the abandonment of the father's house;   *545* the extreme misery in which the son finds himself after squandering his fortune; his deep humiliation at finding himself obliged to feed swine, and still worse, at wanting to feed on the husks the pigs ate; his reflection on all he has lost; his repentance and decision to declare himself guilty before his father; the journey back; the father's generous welcome; the father's joy – all these are characteristic of the process of conversion. The beautiful robe, the ring, and the festive banquet are symbols of that new life – pure, worthy, and joyful – of anyone who returns to God and to the bosom of his family, which is the Church. Only the heart of Christ who knows the depths of his Father's love could reveal to us the abyss of his mercy in so simple and beautiful a way.

VI.   THE SACRAMENT OF PENANCE AND RECONCILIATION

1440   Sin is before all else an offense against God, a rupture of   *1850* communion with him. At the same time it damages communion with the Church. For this reason conversion entails both God's

---

32   *1 Pet* 4:8; cf. *Jas* 5:20.
33   Cf. *Am* 5:24; *Isa* 1:17.
34   Cf. *Lk* 9:23.
35   Council of Trent (1551): DS 1638.
36   Cf. *SC* 109-110; CIC, cann. 1249-1253; CCEO, cann. 880-883.
37   Cf. *Lk* 15:11-24.

forgiveness and reconciliation with the Church, which are expressed and accomplished liturgically by the sacrament of Penance and Reconciliation.[38]

Only God forgives sin

270, 431 **1441**   Only God forgives sins.[39] Since he is the Son of God, Jesus says of himself, "The Son of man has authority on earth to forgive *589* sins" and exercises this divine power: "Your sins are forgiven."[40] Further, by virtue of his divine authority he gives this power to men to exercise in his name.[41]

1442   Christ has willed that in her prayer and life and action his whole Church should be the sign and instrument of the forgiveness and reconciliation that he acquired for us at the price of his blood. But he entrusted the exercise of the power of absolution to the *983* apostolic ministry which he charged with the "ministry of reconciliation."[42] The apostle is sent out "on behalf of Christ" with "God making his appeal" through him and pleading: "Be reconciled to God."[43]

Reconciliation with the Church

1443   During his public life Jesus not only forgave sins, but also made plain the effect of this forgiveness: he reintegrated forgiven sinners into the community of the People of God from which sin *545* had alienated or even excluded them. A remarkable sign of this is the fact that Jesus receives sinners at his table, a gesture that expresses in an astonishing way both God's forgiveness and the return to the bosom of the People of God.[44]

981 **1444**   In imparting to his apostles his own power to forgive sins the Lord also gives them the authority to reconcile sinners with the Church. This ecclesial dimension of their task is expressed most notably in Christ's solemn words to Simon Peter: "I will give you the keys of the kingdom of heaven, and whatever you bind on earth shall be bound in heaven, and whatever you loose on earth shall be loosed in heaven."[45] "The office of binding and loosing which

---

38   Cf. *LG* 11.
39   Cf. *Mk* 2:7.
40   *Mk* 2:5, 10; *Lk* 7:48.
41   Cf. *Jn* 20:21-23.
42   *2 Cor* 5:18.
43   *2 Cor* 5:20.
44   Cf. *Lk* 15; 19:9.
45   *Mt* 16:19; cf. *Mt* 18:18; 28:16-20.

was given to Peter was also assigned to the college of the apostles united to its head."[46]

1445   The words *bind and loose* mean: whomever you exclude   553 from your communion, will be excluded from communion with God; whomever you receive anew into your communion, God will welcome back into his. *Reconciliation with the Church is inseparable from reconciliation with God.*

The sacrament of forgiveness

1446   Christ instituted the sacrament of Penance for all sinful   979 members of his Church: above all for those who, since Baptism, have fallen into grave sin, and have thus lost their baptismal grace   1856 and wounded ecclesial communion. It is to them that the sacrament of Penance offers a new possibility to convert and to recover the grace of justification. The Fathers of the Church present this sacra-   1990 ment as "the second plank [of salvation] after the shipwreck which is the loss of grace."[47]

1447   Over the centuries the concrete form in which the Church has exercised this power received from the Lord has varied considerably. During the first centuries the reconciliation of Christians who had committed particularly grave sins after their Baptism (for example, idolatry, murder, or adultery) was tied to a very rigorous discipline, according to which penitents had to do public penance for their sins, often for years, before receiving reconciliation. To this "order of penitents" (which concerned only certain grave sins), one was only rarely admitted and in certain regions only once in a lifetime. During the seventh century Irish missionaries, inspired by the Eastern monastic tradition, took to continental Europe the "private" practice of penance, which does not require public and prolonged completion of penitential works before reconciliation with the Church. From that time on, the sacrament has been performed in secret between penitent and priest. This new practice envisioned the possibility of repetition and so opened the way to a regular frequenting of this sacrament. It allowed the forgiveness of grave sins and venial sins to be integrated into one sacramental celebration. In its main lines this is the form of penance that the Church has practiced down to our day.

1448   Beneath the changes in discipline and celebration that this sacrament has undergone over the centuries, the same *fundamental structure* is to be discerned. It comprises two equally essential elements: on the one hand, the acts of the man who undergoes conversion through the action of the Holy Spirit: namely, contrition, confession, and satisfaction; on the other, God's action through the intervention of the Church. The Church, who through

---

46   *LG* 22 § 2.
47   Tertullian, *De Pænit.* 4, 2: PL 1, 1343; cf. Council of Trent (1547): DS 1542.

the bishop and his priests forgives sins in the name of Jesus Christ and determines the manner of satisfaction, also prays for the sinner and does penance with him. Thus the sinner is healed and re-established in ecclesial communion.

1481 **1449**   The formula of absolution used in the Latin Church expresses the essential elements of this sacrament: the Father of mercies is the source of all forgiveness. He effects the reconciliation

234 of sinners through the Passover of his Son and the gift of his Spirit, through the prayer and ministry of the Church:

> God, the Father of mercies,
> through the death and the resurrection of his Son
> has reconciled the world to himself
> and sent the Holy Spirit among us
> for the forgiveness of sins;
> through the ministry of the Church
> may God give you pardon and peace,
> and I absolve you from your sins
> in the name of the Father, and of the Son, and of the Holy
> Spirit.[48]

VII.   THE ACTS OF THE PENITENT

1450   "Penance requires . . . the sinner to endure all things willingly, be contrite of heart, confess with the lips, and practice complete humility and fruitful satisfaction."[49]

Contrition

1451   Among the penitent's acts contrition occupies first place. Contrition is "sorrow of the soul and detestation for the sin com-

431 mitted, together with the resolution not to sin again."[50]

1822 **1452**   When it arises from a love by which God is loved above all else, contrition is called "perfect" (contrition of charity). Such contrition remits venial sins; it also obtains forgiveness of mortal sins if it includes the firm resolution to have recourse to sacramental confession as soon as possible.[51]

1453   The contrition called "imperfect" (or "attrition") is also a gift of God, a prompting of the Holy Spirit. It is born of the consideration of sin's ugliness or the fear of eternal damnation and the other penalties threatening the sinner (contrition of fear). Such

---

48   *OP* 46: formula of absolution.
49   *Roman Catechism* II, V, 21; cf. Council of Trent (1551): DS 1673.
50   Council of Trent (1551): DS 1676.
51   Cf. Council of Trent (1551): DS 1677.

a stirring of conscience can initiate an interior process which, under the prompting of grace, will be brought to completion by sacramental absolution. By itself however, imperfect contrition cannot obtain the forgiveness of grave sins, but it disposes one to obtain forgiveness in the sacrament of Penance.[52]

1454   The reception of this sacrament ought to be prepared for by an *examination of conscience* made in the light of the Word of God. The passages best suited to this can be found in the moral catechesis of the Gospels and the apostolic Letters, such as the Sermon on the Mount and the apostolic teachings.[53]

The confession of sins

1455   The confession (or disclosure) of sins, even from a simply *1424* human point of view, frees us and facilitates our reconciliation with others. Through such an admission man looks squarely at the sins he is guilty of, takes responsibility for them, and thereby opens *1734* himself again to God and to the communion of the Church in order to make a new future possible.

1456   Confession to a priest is an essential part of the sacrament of Penance: "All mortal sins of which penitents after a diligent self-examination are conscious must be recounted by them in *1855* confession, even if they are most secret and have been committed against the last two precepts of the Decalogue; for these sins sometimes wound the soul more grievously and are more dangerous than those which are committed openly."[54]

> When Christ's faithful strive to confess all the sins that they can remember, they undoubtedly place all of them before the divine mercy for pardon. But those who fail to do so and *1505* knowingly withhold some, place nothing before the divine goodness for remission through the mediation of the priest, "for if the sick person is too ashamed to show his wound to the doctor, the medicine cannot heal what it does not know."[55]

1457   According to the Church's command, "after having attained the *2042* age of discretion, each of the faithful is bound by an obligation faithfully to confess serious sins at least once a year."[56] Anyone who is aware of having committed a mortal sin must not receive Holy Communion, even if he experiences deep contrition, without having first received sacramen- *1385*

---

52 Cf. Council of Trent (1551): DS 1678; 1705.
53 Cf. *Mt* 5-7; *Rom* 12-15; *1 Cor* 12-13; *Gal* 5; *Eph* 4-6; etc.
54 Council of Trent (1551): DS 1680 (ND 1626); cf. *Ex* 20:17; *Mt* 5:28.
55 Council of Trent (1551): DS 1680 (ND 1626); cf. St. Jerome, *In Eccl.* 10, 11: PL 23:1096.
56 Cf. CIC, can. 989; Council of Trent (1551): DS 1683; DS 1708.

tal absolution, unless he has a grave reason for receiving Communion and there is no possibility of going to confession.[57] Children must go to the sacrament of Penance before receiving Holy Communion for the first time.[58]

1458   Without being strictly necessary, confession of everyday faults (venial sins) is nevertheless strongly recommended by the Church.[59] Indeed the regular confession of our venial sins helps us

1783   form our conscience, fight against evil tendencies, let ourselves be healed by Christ and progress in the life of the Spirit. By receiving more frequently through this sacrament the gift of the Father's mercy, we are spurred to be merciful as he is merciful:[60]

> Whoever confesses his sins . . . is already working with God. God indicts your sins; if you also indict them, you are joined with God. Man and sinner are, so to speak, two realities: when you hear "man" – this is what God has made; when you hear "sinner" – this is what man himself has made. Destroy what you have made, so that God may save what he has made . . . . When you begin to abhor what you have made, it is then that your good works are beginning, since you are accusing yourself of your evil works. The beginning of good works is the confession of evil works. You do the truth and come to the light.[61]

2468

Satisfaction

1459   Many sins wrong our neighbor. One must do what is possible in order to repair the harm (e.g., return stolen goods,

2412   restore the reputation of someone slandered, pay compensation for

2487   injuries). Simple justice requires as much. But sin also injures and weakens the sinner himself, as well as his relationships with God and neighbor. Absolution takes away sin, but it does not remedy all the disorders sin has caused.[62] Raised up from sin, the sinner must still recover his full spiritual health by doing something more to make amends for the sin: he must "make satisfaction for" or

1473   "expiate" his sins. This satisfaction is also called "penance."

---

57   Cf. Council of Trent (1551): DS 1647; 1661; CIC, can. 916; CCEO, can. 711.

58   Cf. CIC, can. 914.

59   Cf. Council of Trent: DS 1680; CIC, can. 988 § 2.

60   Cf. *Lk* 6:36.

61   St. Augustine, *In Jo. ev.* 12, 13: PL 35, 1491.

62   Cf. Council of Trent (1551): DS 1712.

1460 The *penance* the confessor imposes must take into account the penitent's personal situation and must seek his spiritual good. It must correspond as far as possible with the gravity and nature of the sins committed. It can consist of prayer, an offering, works *2447* of mercy, service of neighbor, voluntary self-denial, sacrifices, and above all the patient acceptance of the cross we must bear. Such penances help configure us to Christ, who alone expiated our sins *618* once for all. They allow us to become co-heirs with the risen Christ, "provided we suffer with him."[63]

> The satisfaction that we make for our sins, however, is not so much ours as though it were not done through Jesus Christ. We who can do nothing ourselves, as if just by ourselves, can do all things with the cooperation of "him who strengthens" us. Thus man has nothing of which to boast, but all our boasting is in Christ . . . in whom we make satisfaction by bringing forth "fruits that befit repentance." *2011* These fruits have their efficacy from him, by him they are offered to the Father, and through him they are accepted by the Father.[64]

VIII. THE MINISTER OF THIS SACRAMENT

1461 Since Christ entrusted to his apostles the ministry of rec- *981* onciliation,[65] bishops who are their successors, and priests, the bishops' collaborators, continue to exercise this ministry. Indeed bishops and priests, by virtue of the sacrament of Holy Orders, have the power to forgive all sins "in the name of the Father, and of the Son, and of the Holy Spirit."

1462 Forgiveness of sins brings reconciliation with God, but also with the Church. Since ancient times the bishop, visible head of a particular Church, has thus rightfully been considered to be *886* the one who principally has the power and ministry of reconciliation: he is the moderator of the penitential discipline.[66] Priests, his *1567* collaborators, exercise it to the extent that they have received the commission either from their bishop (or religious superior) or the Pope, according to the law of the Church.[67]

---

63 *Rom* 8:17; *Rom* 3:25; *1 Jn* 2:1-2; cf. Council of Trent (1551): DS 1690.
64 Council of Trent (1551): DS 1691; cf. *Phil* 4:13; *1 Cor* 1:31; *2 Cor* 10:17; *Gal* 6:14; *Lk* 3:8.
65 Cf. *Jn* 20:23; *2 Cor* 5:18.
66 Cf. *LG* 26 § 3.
67 Cf. CIC, cann. 844; 967-969; 972; CCEO, can. 722 §§ 3-4.

1463   Certain particularly grave sins incur excommunication, the most severe ecclesiastical penalty, which impedes the reception of the sacraments and the exercise of certain ecclesiastical acts, and for which absolution consequently cannot be granted, according to canon law, except by the Pope, the bishop of the place or priests authorized by them.[68] In danger of death any priest, even if deprived of faculties for hearing confessions,

982   can absolve from every sin and excommunication.[69]

1464   Priests must encourage the faithful to come to the sacrament of Penance and must make themselves available to celebrate this sacrament each time Christians reasonably ask for it.[70]

1465   When he celebrates the sacrament of Penance, the priest is fulfilling the ministry of the Good Shepherd who seeks the lost

983   sheep, of the Good Samaritan who binds up wounds, of the Father who awaits the prodigal son and welcomes him on his return, and of the just and impartial judge whose judgment is both just and merciful. The priest is the sign and the instrument of God's merciful love for the sinner.

1551   **1466**   The confessor is not the master of God's forgiveness, but its servant. The minister of this sacrament should unite himself to the intention and charity of Christ.[71] He should have a proven

2690   knowledge of Christian behavior, experience of human affairs, respect and sensitivity toward the one who has fallen; he must love the truth, be faithful to the Magisterium of the Church, and lead the penitent with patience toward healing and full maturity. He must pray and do penance for his penitent, entrusting him to the Lord's mercy.

1467   Given the delicacy and greatness of this ministry and the respect due to persons, the Church declares that every priest who hears confessions is bound under very severe penalties to keep absolute secrecy regarding the sins that his penitents have con-

2490   fessed to him. He can make no use of knowledge that confession gives him about penitents' lives.[72] This secret, which admits of no exceptions, is called the "sacramental seal," because what the penitent has made known to the priest remains "sealed" by the sacrament.

---

68   Cf. CIC, cann. 1331; 1354-1357; CCEO, can. 1431; 1434; 1420.
69   Cf. CIC, can. 976; CCEO, can. 725.
70   Cf. CIC, can. 986; CCEO, can. 735; *PO* 13.
71   Cf. *PO* 13.
72   Cf. CIC, can. 1388 § 1; CCEO, can. 1456.

IX.   THE EFFECTS OF THIS SACRAMENT

1468   "The whole power of the sacrament of Penance consists in restoring us to God's grace and joining us with him in an intimate friendship."[73] Reconciliation with God is thus the purpose and effect of this sacrament. For those who receive the sacrament of Penance with contrite heart and religious disposition, reconciliation "is usually followed by peace and serenity of conscience with strong spiritual consolation."[74] Indeed the sacrament of Reconciliation with God brings about a true "spiritual resurrection," restoration of the dignity and blessings of the life of the children of God, of which the most precious is friendship with God.[75]

2305

1469   This sacrament *reconciles us with the Church.* Sin damages or even breaks fraternal communion. The sacrament of Penance repairs or restores it. In this sense it does not simply heal the one restored to ecclesial communion, but has also a revitalizing effect on the life of the Church which suffered from the sin of one of her members.[76] Re-established or strengthened in the communion of saints, the sinner is made stronger by the exchange of spiritual goods among all the living members of the Body of Christ, whether still on pilgrimage or already in the heavenly homeland:[77]

953

949

> It must be recalled that . . . this reconciliation with God leads, as it were, to other reconciliations, which repair the other breaches caused by sin. The forgiven penitent is reconciled with himself in his inmost being, where he regains his innermost truth. He is reconciled with his brethren whom he has in some way offended and wounded. He is reconciled with the Church. He is reconciled with all creation.[78]

1470   In this sacrament, the sinner, placing himself before the merciful judgment of God, *anticipates* in a certain way *the judgment* to which he will be subjected at the end of his earthly life. For it is now, in this life, that we are offered the choice between life and death, and it is only by the road of conversion that we can enter the Kingdom, from which one is excluded by grave sin.[79] In converting to Christ through penance and faith, the sinner passes from death to life and "does not come into judgment."[80]

678, 1039

---

73   *Roman Catechism*, II, V, 18.
74   Council of Trent (1551): DS 1674.
75   Cf. *Lk* 15:32.
76   Cf. *1 Cor* 12:26.
77   Cf. *LG* 48-50.
78   John Paul II, *RP* 31, 5.
79   Cf. *1 Cor* 5:11; *Gal* 5:19-21; *Rev* 22:15.
80   *Jn* 5:24.

X.   INDULGENCES

1471   The doctrine and practice of indulgences in the Church are closely linked to the effects of the sacrament of Penance.

What is an indulgence?

"An indulgence is a remission before God of the temporal punishment due to sins whose guilt has already been forgiven, which the faithful Christian who is duly disposed gains under certain prescribed conditions through the action of the Church which, as the minister of redemption, dispenses and applies with authority the treasury of the satisfactions of Christ and the saints."[81]

"An indulgence is partial or plenary according as it removes either part or all of the temporal punishment due to sin."[82] Indulgences may be applied to the living or the dead.

The punishments of sin

1472   To understand this doctrine and practice of the Church, it is necessary to understand that sin has *a double consequence.* Grave sin deprives us of communion with God and therefore makes us incapable of eternal life, the privation of which is called the "eternal punishment" of sin. On the other hand every sin, even venial, entails an unhealthy attachment to creatures, which must be purified either here on earth, or after death in the state called Purgatory. This purification frees one from what is called the "temporal punishment" of sin. These two punishments must not be conceived of as a kind of vengeance inflicted by God from without, but as following from the very nature of sin. A conversion which proceeds from a fervent charity can attain the complete purification of the sinner in such a way that no punishment would remain.[83]

1861

1031

1473   The forgiveness of sin and restoration of communion with God entail the remission of the eternal punishment of sin, but temporal punishment of sin remains. While patiently bearing sufferings and trials of all kinds and, when the day comes, serenely facing death, the Christian must strive to accept this temporal punishment of sin as a grace. He should strive by works of mercy and charity, as well as by prayer and the various practices of penance, to put off completely the "old man" and to put on the "new man."[84]

2447

---

81 Paul VI, apostolic constitution, *Indulgentiarum doctrina*, Norm 1.
82 *Indulgentiarum doctrina*, Norm 2; cf. Norm 3.
83 Cf. Council of Trent (1551): DS 1712-1713; (1563): 1820.
84 *Eph* 4:22, 24.

In the Communion of Saints

1474   The Christian who seeks to purify himself of his sin and to *946-959* become holy with the help of God's grace is not alone. "The life of each of God's children is joined in Christ and through Christ in a wonderful way to the life of all the other Christian brethren in the supernatural unity of the Mystical Body of Christ, as in a single mystical person."[85]   *795*

1475   In the communion of saints, "a perennial link of charity exists between the faithful who have already reached their heavenly home, those who are expiating their sins in purgatory and those who are still pilgrims on earth. Between them there is, too, an abundant exchange of all good things."[86] In this wonderful exchange, the holiness of one profits others, well beyond the harm that the sin of one could cause others. Thus recourse to the communion of saints lets the contrite sinner be more promptly and efficaciously purified of the punishments for sin.

1476   We also call these spiritual goods of the communion of saints the *Church's treasury*, which is "not the sum total of the material goods which have accumulated during the course of the centuries. On the contrary the 'treasury of the Church' is the infinite value, which can never be exhausted, which Christ's merits have before God. They were offered so that the whole of mankind could be set free from sin and attain communion with the *617* Father. In Christ, the Redeemer himself, the satisfactions and merits of his Redemption exist and find their efficacy."[87]

1477   "This treasury includes as well the prayers and good works of *969* the Blessed Virgin Mary. They are truly immense, unfathomable, and even pristine in their value before God. In the treasury, too, are the prayers and good works of all the saints, all those who have followed in the footsteps of Christ the Lord and by his grace have made their lives holy and carried out the mission the Father entrusted to them. In this way they attained their own salvation and at the same time cooperated in saving their brothers in the unity of the Mystical Body."[88]

Obtaining indulgence from God through the Church

1478   An indulgence is obtained through the Church who, by virtue of *981* the power of binding and loosing granted her by Christ Jesus, intervenes in favor of individual Christians and opens for them the treasury of the merits of Christ and the saints to obtain from the Father of mercies the remission of the temporal punishments due for their sins. Thus the Church does not want simply to come to the aid of these Christians, but also to spur them to works of devotion, penance, and charity.[89]

1479   Since the faithful departed now being purified are also members *1032* of the same communion of saints, one way we can help them is to obtain

---

85 *Indulgentiarum doctrina,* 5.
86 *Indulgentiarum doctrina,* 5.
87 *Indulgentiarum doctrina,* 5.
88 *Indulgentiarum doctrina,* 5.
89 Cf. *Indulgentiarum doctrina,* 5.

indulgences for them, so that the temporal punishments due for their sins may be remitted.

XI.   THE CELEBRATION OF THE SACRAMENT OF PENANCE

1480   Like all the sacraments, Penance is a liturgical action. The elements of the celebration are ordinarily these: a greeting and blessing from the priest, reading the word of God to illuminate the conscience and elicit contrition, and an exhortation to repentance; the confession, which acknowledges sins and makes them known to the priest; the imposition and acceptance of a penance; the priest's absolution; a prayer of thanksgiving and praise and dismissal with the blessing of the priest.

1449   **1481**   The Byzantine Liturgy recognizes several formulas of absolution, in the form of invocation, which admirably express the mystery of forgiveness: "May the same God, who through the Prophet Nathan forgave David when he confessed his sins, who forgave Peter when he wept bitterly, the prostitute when she washed his feet with her tears, the Pharisee, and the prodigal son, through me, a sinner, forgive you both in this life and in the next and enable you to appear before his awe-inspiring tribunal without condemnation, he who is blessed for ever and ever. Amen."

1482   The sacrament of Penance can also take place in the framework of a *communal celebration* in which we prepare ourselves together for confession and give thanks together for the forgiveness received. Here, the personal confession of sins and individual absolution are inserted into a liturgy of the word of God with readings and a homily, an examination of conscience conducted in common, a communal request for forgiveness, the Our Father and a thanksgiving in common. This communal celebration expresses more clearly the ecclesial character of penance. However, regardless of its manner of celebration the sacrament of Penance is always, by its very nature, a
1140   liturgical action, and therefore an ecclesial and public action.[90]

1401   **1483**   In case of grave necessity recourse may be had to a *communal celebration of reconciliation with general confession and general absolution*. Grave necessity of this sort can arise when there is imminent danger of death without sufficient time for the priest or priests to hear each penitent's confession. Grave necessity can also exist when, given the number of penitents, there are not enough confessors to hear individual confessions properly in a reasonable time, so that the penitents through no fault of their own would be deprived of sacramental grace or Holy Communion for a long time. In this case, for the absolution to be valid the faithful must have the intention of individually confessing their sins in the time required.[91] The diocesan bishop is the judge of whether or not the conditions required for general absolution exist.[92] A large gathering of the faithful on the occasion of major feasts or pilgrimages does not constitute a case of grave necessity.[93]

---

90   Cf. *SC* 26-27.
91   Cf. CIC, can. 962 § 1.
92   Cf. CIC, can. 961 § 2.

1484　　"Individual, integral confession and absolution remain the only ordinary way for the faithful to reconcile themselves with God and the Church, unless physical or moral impossibility excuses from this kind of confession."[94] There are profound reasons for this. Christ is at work in each of the sacraments. He personally addresses every sinner: "My son, your sins are forgiven."[95] He is　*878* the physician tending each one of the sick who need him to cure them.[96] He raises them up and reintegrates them into fraternal communion. Personal confession is thus the form most expressive of reconciliation with God and with the Church.

IN BRIEF

1485　　"On the evening of that day, the first day of the week," Jesus showed himself to his apostles. "He breathed on them, and said to them: 'Receive the Holy Spirit. If you forgive the sins of any, they are forgiven; if you retain the sins of any, they are retained'" (*Jn* 20:19, 22-23).

1486　　The forgiveness of sins committed after Baptism is conferred by a particular sacrament called the sacrament of conversion, confession, penance, or reconciliation.

1487　　The sinner wounds God's honor and love, his own human dignity as a man called to be a son of God, and the spiritual well-being of the Church, of which each Christian ought to be a living stone.

1488　　To the eyes of faith no evil is graver than sin and nothing has worse consequences for sinners themselves, for the Church, and for the whole world.

1489　　To return to communion with God after having lost it through sin is a process born of the grace of God who is rich in mercy and solicitous for the salvation of men. One must ask for this precious gift for oneself and for others.

1490　　The movement of return to God, called conversion and repentance, entails sorrow for and abhorrence of sins committed, and the firm purpose of sinning no more in the future. Conversion touches the past and the future and is nourished by hope in God's mercy.

93　Cf. CIC, can. 961 § 1.
94　*OP* 31.
95　*Mk* 2:5.
96　Cf. *Mk* 2:17.

1491   The sacrament of Penance is a whole consisting in three actions of the penitent and the priest's absolution. The penitent's acts are repentance, confession or disclosure of sins to the priest, and the intention to make reparation and do works of reparation.

1492   Repentance (also called contrition) must be inspired by motives that arise from faith. If repentance arises from love of charity for God, it is called "perfect" contrition; if it is founded on other motives, it is called "imperfect."

1493   One who desires to obtain reconciliation with God and with the Church, must confess to a priest all the unconfessed grave sins he remembers after having carefully examined his conscience. The confession of venial faults, without being necessary in itself, is nevertheless strongly recommended by the Church.

1494   The confessor proposes the performance of certain acts of "satisfaction" or "penance" to be performed by the penitent in order to repair the harm caused by sin and to re-establish habits befitting a disciple of Christ.

1495   Only priests who have received the faculty of absolving from the authority of the Church can forgive sins in the name of Christ.

1496   The spiritual effects of the sacrament of Penance are:
        – reconciliation with God by which the penitent recovers grace;
        – reconciliation with the Church;
        – remission of the eternal punishment incurred by mortal sins;
        – remission, at least in part, of temporal punishments resulting from sin;
        – peace and serenity of conscience, and spiritual consolation;
        – an increase of spiritual strength for the Christian battle.

1497   Individual and integral confession of grave sins followed by absolution remains the only ordinary means of reconciliation with God and with the Church.

1498   Through indulgences the faithful can obtain the remission of temporal punishment resulting from sin for themselves and also for the souls in Purgatory.

ARTICLE 5
THE ANOINTING OF THE SICK

1499 "By the sacred anointing of the sick and the prayer of the priests the whole Church commends those who are ill to the suffering and glorified Lord, that he may raise them up and save them. And indeed she exhorts them to contribute to the good of the People of God by freely uniting themselves to the Passion and death of Christ."[97]

I. ITS FOUNDATIONS IN THE ECONOMY OF SALVATION

Illness in human life

1500 Illness and suffering have always been among the gravest problems confronted in human life. In illness, man experiences his powerlessness, his limitations, and his finitude. Every illness can make us glimpse death.

1006

1501 Illness can lead to anguish, self-absorption, sometimes even despair and revolt against God. It can also make a person more mature, helping him discern in his life what is not essential so that he can turn toward that which is. Very often illness provokes a search for God and a return to him.

The sick person before God

1502 The man of the Old Testament lives his sickness in the presence of God. It is before God that he laments his illness, and it is of God, Master of life and death, that he implores healing.[98] Illness becomes a way to conversion; God's forgiveness initiates the healing.[99] It is the experience of Israel that illness is mysteriously linked to sin and evil, and that faithfulness to God according *164* to his law restores life: "For I am the Lord, your healer."[100] The *376* prophet intuits that suffering can also have a redemptive meaning for the sins of others.[101] Finally Isaiah announces that God will usher in a time for Zion when he will pardon every offense and heal every illness.[102]

---

97 *LG* 11; cf. *Jas* 5:14-16; *Rom* 8:17; *Col* 1:24; *2 Tim* 2:11-12; *1 Pet* 4:13.
98 Cf. *Pss* 6:3; 38; *Isa* 38.
99 Cf. *Pss* 32:5; 38:5; 39:9, 12; 107:20; cf. *Mk* 2:5-12.
100 *Ex* 15:26.
101 Cf. *Isa* 53:11.
102 Cf. *Isa* 33:24.

Christ the physician

549 **1503**   Christ's compassion toward the sick and his many healings of every kind of infirmity are a resplendent sign that "God has
visited his people"[103] and that the Kingdom of God is close at hand.
Jesus has the power not only to heal, but also to forgive sins;[104] he
has come to heal the whole man, soul and body; he is the physician
1421 the sick have need of.[105] His compassion toward all who suffer
goes so far that he identifies himself with them: "I was sick and you
visited me."[106] His preferential love for the sick has not ceased
through the centuries to draw the very special attention of Chris-
2288 tians toward all those who suffer in body and soul. It is the source
of tireless efforts to comfort them.

1504   Often Jesus asks the sick to believe.[107] He makes use of
signs to heal: spittle and the laying on of hands,[108] mud and
washing.[109] The sick try to touch him, "for power came forth from
695 him and healed them all."[110] And so in the sacraments Christ
1116 continues to "touch" us in order to heal us.

1505   Moved by so much suffering Christ not only allows himself to be touched by the sick, but he makes their miseries his own:
"He took our infirmities and bore our diseases."[111] But he did not
heal all the sick. His healings were signs of the coming of the
Kingdom of God. They announced a more radical healing: the
440 victory over sin and death through his Passover. On the cross
Christ took upon himself the whole weight of evil and took away
the "sin of the world,"[112] of which illness is only a consequence.
By his passion and death on the cross Christ has given a new
meaning to suffering: it can henceforth configure us to him and
307 unite us with his redemptive Passion.

---

103   *Lk* 7:16; cf. *Mt* 4:24.
104   Cf. *Mk* 2:5-12.
105   Cf. *Mk* 2:17.
106   *Mt* 25:36.
107   Cf. *Mk* 5:34, 36; 9:23.
108   Cf. *Mk* 7:32-36; 8:22-25.
109   Cf. *Jn* 9:6-7.
110   *Lk* 6:19; cf. *Mk* 1:41; 3:10; 6:56.
111   *Mt* 8:17; cf. *Isa* 53:4.
112   *Jn* 1:29; cf. *Isa* 53:4-6.

"Heal the sick . . ."

1506   Christ invites his disciples to follow him by taking up their cross in their turn.[113] By following him they acquire a new outlook on illness and the sick. Jesus associates them with his own life of poverty and service. He makes them share in his ministry of compassion and healing: "So they went out and preached that men *859* should repent. And they cast out many demons, and anointed with oil many that were sick and healed them."[114]

1507   The risen Lord renews this mission ("In my name . . . they will lay their hands on the sick, and they will recover."[115]) and confirms it through the signs that the Church performs by invoking his name.[116] These signs demonstrate in a special way that Jesus is truly "God who saves."[117]   *430*

1508   The Holy Spirit gives to some a special charism of heal- *798* ing[118] so as to make manifest the power of the grace of the risen Lord. But even the most intense prayers do not always obtain the healing of all illnesses. Thus St. Paul must learn from the Lord that "my grace is sufficient for you, for my power is made perfect in *618* weakness," and that the sufferings to be endured can mean that "in my flesh I complete what is lacking in Christ's afflictions for the sake of his Body, that is, the Church."[119]

1509   "Heal the sick!"[120] The Church has received this charge from the Lord and strives to carry it out by taking care of the sick as well as by accompanying them with her prayer of intercession. She believes in the life-giving presence of Christ, the physician of souls and bodies. This presence is particularly active through the sacraments, and in an altogether special way through the Eucharist, the bread that gives eternal life and that St. Paul suggests is *1405* connected with bodily health.[121]

---

113 Cf. *Mt* 10:38.
114 *Mk* 6:12-13.
115 *Mk* 16:17-18.
116 Cf. *Acts* 9:34; 14:3.
117 Cf. *Mt* 1:21; *Acts* 4:12.
118 Cf. *1 Cor* 12:9, 28, 30.
119 *2 Cor* 12:9; *Col* 1:24.
120 *Mt* 10:8.
121 Cf. *Jn* 6:54, 58; *1 Cor* 11:30.

1510   However, the apostolic Church has its own rite for the sick, attested to by St. James: "Is any among you sick? Let him call for the elders [*presbyters*] of the Church and let them pray over him, anointing him with oil in the name of the Lord; and the prayer of faith will save the sick man, and the Lord will raise him up; and if he has committed sins, he will be forgiven."[122] Tradition has *1117* recognized in this rite one of the seven sacraments.[123]

A sacrament of the sick

1511   The Church believes and confesses that among the seven sacraments there is one especially intended to strengthen those who are being tried by illness, the Anointing of the Sick:

> This sacred anointing of the sick was instituted by Christ our Lord as a true and proper sacrament of the New Testament. It is alluded to indeed by Mark, but is recommended to the faithful and promulgated by James the apostle and brother of the Lord.[124]

1512   From ancient times in the liturgical traditions of both East and West, we have testimonies to the practice of anointings of the sick with blessed oil. Over the centuries the Anointing of the Sick was conferred more and more exclusively on those at the point of death. Because of this it received the name "Extreme Unction." Notwithstanding this evolution the liturgy has never failed to beg the Lord that the sick person may recover his health if it would be conducive to his salvation.[125]

1513   The Apostolic Constitution *Sacram unctionem infirmorum*,[126] following upon the Second Vatican Council,[127] established that henceforth, in the Roman Rite, the following be observed:

> The sacrament of Anointing of the Sick is given to those who are seriously ill by anointing them on the forehead and hands with duly blessed oil – pressed from olives or from other plants – saying, only once: "Through this holy anointing may the Lord in his love and mercy help you with the grace of the Holy Spirit. May the Lord who frees you from sin save you and raise you up."[128]

---

122 *Jas* 5:14-15.
123 Cf. Council of Constantinople II (553): DS 216; Council of Florence (1439): 1324-1325; Council of Trent (1551) 1695-1696; 1716-1717.
124 Council of Trent (1551): DS 1695; cf. *Mk* 6:13; *Jas* 5:14-15.
125 Cf. Council of Trent (1551): DS 1696.
126 Paul VI, apostolic constitution, *Sacram unctionem infirmorum*, November 30, 1972.
127 Cf. *SC* 73.
128 Cf. CIC, can. 847 § 1.

II. WHO RECEIVES AND WHO ADMINISTERS THIS SACRAMENT?

In case of grave illness . . .

1514 The Anointing of the Sick "is not a sacrament for those only who are at the point of death. Hence, as soon as anyone of the faithful begins to be in danger of death from sickness or old age, the fitting time for him to receive this sacrament has certainly already arrived."[129]

1515 If a sick person who received this anointing recovers his health, he can in the case of another grave illness receive this sacrament again. If during the same illness the person's condition becomes more serious, the sacrament may be repeated. It is fitting to receive the Anointing of the Sick just prior to a serious operation. The same holds for the elderly whose frailty becomes more pronounced.

" . . . let him call for the presbyters of the Church"

1516 Only priests (bishops and presbyters) are ministers of the Anointing of the Sick.[130] It is the duty of pastors to instruct the faithful on the benefits of this sacrament. The faithful should encourage the sick to call for a priest to receive this sacrament. The sick should prepare themselves to receive it with good dispositions, assisted by their pastor and the whole ecclesial community, which is invited to surround the sick in a special way through their prayers and fraternal attention.

III. HOW IS THIS SACRAMENT CELEBRATED?

1517 Like all the sacraments the Anointing of the Sick is a *1140* liturgical and communal celebration,[131] whether it takes place in the family home, a hospital or church, for a single sick person or a whole group of sick persons. It is very fitting to celebrate it within the Eucharist, the memorial of the Lord's Passover. If circumstances suggest it, the celebration of the sacrament can be preceded by the sacrament of Penance and followed by the sacrament of the Eucharist. As the sacrament of Christ's Passover the Eucharist should always be the last sacrament of the earthly journey, the "viaticum" for "passing over" to eternal life. *1524*

---

129 *SC* 73; cf. CIC, cann. 1004 § 1; 1005; 1007; CCEO, can. 738.
130 Cf. Council of Trent (1551): DS 1697; 1719; CIC, can. 1003; CCEO, can. 739 § 1.
131 Cf. *SC* 27.

1518 Word and sacrament form an indivisible whole. The Liturgy of the Word, preceded by an act of repentance, opens the celebration. The words of Christ, the witness of the apostles, awaken the faith of the sick person and of the community to ask the Lord for the strength of his Spirit.

1519 The celebration of the sacrament includes the following principal elements: the "priests of the Church"[132] – in silence – lay hands on the sick; they pray over them in the faith of the Church[133] – this is the epiclesis proper to this sacrament; they then anoint them with oil blessed, if possible, by the bishop.

These liturgical actions indicate what grace this sacrament confers upon the sick.

IV.   THE EFFECTS OF THE CELEBRATION OF THIS SACRAMENT

733 **1520** *A particular gift of the Holy Spirit.* The first grace of this sacrament is one of strengthening, peace and courage to overcome the difficulties that go with the condition of serious illness or the frailty of old age. This grace is a gift of the Holy Spirit, who renews trust and faith in God and strengthens against the temptations of the evil one, the temptation to discouragement and anguish in the face of death.[134] This assistance from the Lord by the power of his Spirit is meant to lead the sick person to healing of the soul, but also of the body if such is God's will.[135] Furthermore, "if he has committed sins, he will be forgiven."[136]

1521 *Union with the passion of Christ.* By the grace of this sacrament the sick person receives the strength and the gift of uniting himself more closely to Christ's Passion: in a certain way he is

1535 *consecrated* to bear fruit by configuration to the Savior's redemptive Passion. Suffering, a consequence of original sin, acquires a new

1499 meaning; it becomes a participation in the saving work of Jesus.

1522 An *ecclesial grace.* The sick who receive this sacrament, "by freely uniting themselves to the passion and death of Christ," "contribute to the good of the People of God."[137] By celebrating this sacrament the Church, in the communion of saints, intercedes

953 for the benefit of the sick person, and he, for his part, though the

---

132 *Jas* 5:14.
133 Cf. *Jas* 5:15.
134 Cf. *Heb* 2:15.
135 Cf. Council of Florence (1439): DS 1325.
136 *Jas* 5:15; cf. Council of Trent (1551): DS 1717.

grace of this sacrament, contributes to the sanctification of the Church and to the good of all men for whom the Church suffers and offers herself through Christ to God the Father.

1523 *A preparation for the final journey.* If the sacrament of anointing   *1020* of the sick is given to all who suffer from serious illness and infirmity, even more rightly is it given to those at the point of departing this life; so it is also called *sacramentum exeuntium* (the sacrament of those departing).[138] The Anointing of the Sick completes our conformity to the death and Resurrection of Christ, just as Baptism began it. It completes the holy anointings that mark the whole Christian life: that of Baptism which sealed the new life in us, and that of Confirmation which strengthened us for the combat of this life. This last anointing   *1294* fortifies the end of our earthly life like a solid rampart for the final   *1020* struggles before entering the Father's house.[139]

V.   VIATICUM, THE LAST SACRAMENT OF THE CHRISTIAN

1524 In addition to the Anointing of the Sick, the Church offers   *1392* those who are about to leave this life the Eucharist as viaticum. Communion in the body and blood of Christ, received at this moment of "passing over" to the Father, has a particular significance and importance. It is the seed of eternal life and the power of resurrection, according to the words of the Lord: "He who eats my flesh and drinks my blood has eternal life, and I will raise him up at the last day."[140] The sacrament of Christ once dead and now risen, the Eucharist is here the sacrament of passing over from death to life, from this world to the Father.[141]

1525 Thus, just as the sacraments of Baptism, Confirmation, and   *1680* the Eucharist form a unity called "the sacraments of Christian initiation," so too it can be said that Penance, the Anointing of the Sick and the Eucharist as viaticum constitute at the end of Christian life "the sacraments that prepare for our heavenly homeland" or the sacraments that complete the earthly pilgrimage.   *2299*

---

137 *LG* 11 § 2.
138 Council of Trent (1551): DS 1698.
139 Council of Trent (1551): DS 1694.
140 *Jn* 6:54.
141 Cf. *Jn* 13:1.

IN BRIEF

1526 "Is any among you sick? Let him call for the presbyters of the Church, and let them pray over him, anointing him with oil in the name of the Lord; and the prayer of faith will save the sick man, and the Lord will raise him up; and if he has committed sins, he will be forgiven" (*Jas* 5:14-15).

1527 The sacrament of Anointing of the Sick has as its purpose the conferral of a special grace on the Christian experiencing the difficulties inherent in the condition of grave illness or old age.

1528 The proper time for receiving this holy anointing has certainly arrived when the believer begins to be in danger of death because of illness or old age.

1529 Each time a Christian falls seriously ill, he may receive the Anointing of the Sick, and also when, after he has received it, the illness worsens.

1530 Only priests (presbyters and bishops) can give the sacrament of the Anointing of the Sick, using oil blessed by the bishop, or if necessary by the celebrating presbyter himself.

1531 The celebration of the Anointing of the Sick consists essentially in the anointing of the forehead and hands of the sick person (in the Roman Rite) or of other parts of the body (in the Eastern rite), the anointing being accompanied by the liturgical prayer of the celebrant asking for the special grace of this sacrament.

1532 The special grace of the sacrament of the Anointing of the Sick has as its effects:
– the uniting of the sick person to the passion of Christ, for his own good and that of the whole Church;
– the strengthening, peace, and courage to endure in a Christian manner the sufferings of illness or old age;
– the forgiveness of sins, if the sick person was not able to obtain it through the sacrament of Penance;
– the restoration of health, if it is conducive to the salvation of his soul;
– the preparation for passing over to eternal life.

CHAPTER THREE
THE SACRAMENTS AT THE SERVICE OF COMMUNION

1533   Baptism, Confirmation, and Eucharist are sacraments of   *1212*
Christian initiation. They ground the common vocation of all
Christ's disciples, a vocation to holiness and to the mission of
evangelizing the world. They confer the graces needed for the life
according to the Spirit during this life as pilgrims on the march
towards the homeland.

1534   Two other sacraments, Holy Orders and Matrimony, are
directed towards the salvation of others; if they contribute as well to
personal salvation, it is through service to others that they do so. They
confer a particular mission in the Church and serve to build up the
People of God.

1535   Through these sacraments those already *consecrated* by   *784*
Baptism and Confirmation[1] for the common priesthood of all the
faithful can receive particular *consecrations*. Those who receive the
sacrament of Holy Orders are *consecrated* in Christ's name "to feed
the Church by the word and grace of God."[2] On their part, "Christian spouses are fortified and, as it were, *consecrated* for the duties
and dignity of their state by a special sacrament."[3]

ARTICLE 6
THE SACRAMENT OF HOLY ORDERS

1536   Holy Orders is the sacrament through which the mission
entrusted by Christ to his apostles continues to be exercised in the
Church until the end of time: thus it is the sacrament of apostolic   *860*
ministry. It includes three degrees: episcopate, presbyterate, and diaconate.

(On the institution and mission of the apostolic ministry by
Christ, see above, no. 874 ff. Here only the sacramental means by which
this ministry is handed on will be treated.)

---

1   Cf. *LG* 10.
2   *LG* 11 § 2.
3   *GS* 48 § 2.

I.   WHY IS THIS SACRAMENT CALLED "ORDERS"?

1537   The word *order* in Roman antiquity designated an established civil body, especially a governing body. *Ordinatio* means
incorporation into an *ordo*. In the Church there are established
bodies which Tradition, not without a basis in Sacred Scripture,[4]
has since ancient times called *taxeis* (Greek) or *ordines*. And so the
liturgy speaks of the *ordo episcoporum*, the *ordo presbyterorum*, the
923, 1631   *ordo diaconorum*. Other groups also receive this name of *ordo*: catechumens, virgins, spouses, widows,. . . .

1538   Integration into one of these bodies in the Church was accomplished by a rite called *ordinatio*, a religious and liturgical act which
was a consecration, a blessing or a sacrament. Today the word *"ordination"* is reserved for the sacramental act which integrates a man into
the order of bishops, presbyters, or deacons, and goes beyond a simple
election, designation, delegation, or *institution* by the community, for it
confers a gift of the Holy Spirit that permits the exercise of a "sacred
power" (*sacra potestas*)[5] which can come only from Christ himself
875   through his Church. Ordination is also called *consecratio,* for it is a
setting apart and an investiture by Christ himself for his Church. The
699   *laying on of hands* by the bishop, with the consecratory prayer, constitutes the visible sign of this ordination.

II.   THE SACRAMENT OF HOLY ORDERS IN THE ECONOMY OF SALVATION

The priesthood of the Old Covenant

1539   The chosen people was constituted by God as "a kingdom
of priests and a holy nation."[6] But within the people of Israel, God
chose one of the twelve tribes, that of Levi, and set it apart for
liturgical service; God himself is its inheritance.[7] A special rite
consecrated the beginnings of the priesthood of the Old Covenant.
The priests are "appointed to act on behalf of men in relation to
God, to offer gifts and sacrifices for sins."[8]

2099   **1540**   Instituted to proclaim the Word of God and to restore communion with God by sacrifices and prayer,[9] this priesthood nevertheless

---

4   Cf. *Heb* 5:6; 7:11; *Ps* 110:4.
5   Cf. *LG* 10.
6   *Ex* 19:6; cf. *Isa* 61:6.
7   Cf. *Num* 1:48-53; *Josh* 13:33.
8   *Heb* 5:1; cf. *Ex* 29:1-30; *Lev* 8.
9   Cf. *Mal* 2:7-9.

remains powerless to bring about salvation, needing to repeat its sacrifices ceaselessly and being unable to achieve a definitive sanctification, which only the sacrifice of Christ would accomplish.[10]

1541 The liturgy of the Church, however, sees in the priesthood of Aaron and the service of the Levites, as in the institution of the seventy elders,[11] a prefiguring of the ordained ministry of the New Covenant. Thus in the Latin Rite the Church prays in the consecratory preface of the ordination of bishops:

> God the Father of our Lord Jesus Christ, . . .
> by your gracious word
> you have established the plan of your Church.

> From the beginning,
> you chose the descendants of Abraham to be your holy nation.
> You established rulers and priests,
> and did not leave your sanctuary without ministers to serve you. . . .[12]

1542 At the ordination of priests, the Church prays:

> Lord, holy Father, . . .
> when you had appointed high priests to rule your people,
> you chose other men next to them in rank and dignity
> to be with them and to help them in their task. . . .

> you extended the spirit of Moses to seventy wise men. . . .
> You shared among the sons of Aaron
> the fullness of their father's power.[13]

1543 In the consecratory prayer for ordination of deacons, the Church confesses:

> Almighty God . . . ,
> You make the Church, Christ's body,
> grow to its full stature as a new and greater temple.
> You enrich it with every kind of grace
> and perfect it with a diversity of members
> to serve the whole body in a wonderful pattern of unity.

> You established a threefold ministry of worship and service,
> for the glory of your name.
> As ministers of your tabernacle you chose the sons of Levi
> and gave them your blessing as their everlasting inheritance.[14]

---

10 Cf. *Heb* 5:3; 7:27; 10:1-4.

11 Cf. *Num* 11:24-25.

12 *Roman Pontifical,* Ordination of Bishops 26, Prayer of Consecration.

13 *Roman Pontifical,* Ordination of Priests 22, Prayer of Consecration.

14 *Roman Pontifical,* Ordination of Deacons 21, Prayer of Consecration.

The one priesthood of Christ

1544   Everything that the priesthood of the Old Covenant prefigured finds its fulfillment in Christ Jesus, the "one mediator
between God and men."[15] The Christian tradition considers Mel-
874 chizedek, "priest of God Most High," as a prefiguration of the
priesthood of Christ, the unique "high priest after the order of
Melchizedek";[16] "holy, blameless, unstained,"[17] "by a single offering he has perfected for all time those who are sanctified,"[18] that
is, by the unique sacrifice of the cross.

1367 **1545**   The redemptive sacrifice of Christ is unique, accomplished
once for all; yet it is made present in the Eucharistic sacrifice of the
Church. The same is true of the one priesthood of Christ; it is made
662 present through the ministerial priesthood without diminishing
the uniqueness of Christ's priesthood: "Only Christ is the true
priest, the others being only his ministers."[19]

Two participations in the one priesthood of Christ

1546   Christ, high priest and unique mediator, has made of the
Church "a kingdom, priests for his God and Father."[20] The whole
community of believers is, as such, priestly. The faithful exercise
their baptismal priesthood through their participation, each ac-
1268 cording to his own vocation, in Christ's mission as priest, prophet,
and king. Through the sacraments of Baptism and Confirmation
the faithful are "consecrated to be . . . a holy priesthood."[21]

1142 **1547**   The ministerial or hierarchical priesthood of bishops and
priests, and the common priesthood of all the faithful participate,
"each in its own proper way, in the one priesthood of Christ."
While being "ordered one to another," they differ essentially.[22] In
what sense? While the common priesthood of the faithful is exercised by the unfolding of baptismal grace —a life of faith, hope,
and charity, a life according to the Spirit—, the ministerial priesthood is at the service of the common priesthood. It is directed at
1120 the unfolding of the baptismal grace of all Christians. The ministerial priesthood is a *means* by which Christ unceasingly builds up

---

15   *1 Tim* 2:5.
16   *Heb* 5:10; cf. 6:20; *Gen* 14:18.
17   *Heb* 7:26.
18   *Heb* 10:14.
19   St. Thomas Aquinas, *Hebr.* 8, 4.
20   *Rev* 1:6; cf. *Rev* 5:9-10; *1 Pet* 2:5, 9.
21   *LG* 10 § 1.
22   *LG* 10 § 2.

and leads his Church. For this reason it is transmitted by its own sacrament, the sacrament of Holy Orders.

In the person of Christ the Head . . .

1548   In the ecclesial service of the ordained minister, it is Christ   *875*
himself who is present to his Church as Head of his Body, Shepherd   *792*
of his flock, high priest of the redemptive sacrifice, Teacher of Truth.
This is what the Church means by saying that the priest, by virtue of
the sacrament of Holy Orders, acts *in persona Christi Capitis:*[23]

> It is the same priest, Christ Jesus, whose sacred person his
> minister truly represents. Now the minister, by reason of the
> sacerdotal consecration which he has received, is truly made
> like to the high priest and possesses the authority to act in
> the power and place of the person of Christ himself (*virtute
> ac persona ipsius Christi*).[24]

> Christ is the source of all priesthood: the priest of the old law
> was a figure of Christ, and the priest of the new law acts in
> the person of Christ.[25]

1549   Through the ordained ministry, especially that of bishops
and priests, the presence of Christ as head of the Church is made
visible in the midst of the community of believers.[26] In the beautiful
expression of St. Ignatius of Antioch, the bishop is *typos tou Patros:*   *1142*
he is like the living image of God the Father.[27]

1550   This presence of Christ in the minister is not to be understood
as if the latter were preserved from all human weaknesses, the spirit
of domination, error, even sin. The power of the Holy Spirit does not   *896*
guarantee all acts of ministers in the same way. While this guarantee
extends to the sacraments, so that even the minister's sin cannot
impede the fruit of grace, in many other acts the minister leaves   *1128*
human traces that are not always signs of fidelity to the Gospel and   *1584*
consequently can harm the apostolic fruitfulness of the Church.

1551   This priesthood is ministerial. "That office . . . which the
Lord committed to the pastors of his people, is in the strict sense of
the term a *service.*"[28] It is entirely related to Christ and to men. It   *876*

---

23   Cf. *LG* 10; 28; *SC* 33; *CD* 11; *PO* 2; 6.
24   Pius XII, encyclical, *Mediator Dei* : AAS, 39 (1947) 548.
25   St. Thomas Aquinas, *STh* III, 22 , 4c.
26   Cf. *LG* 21.
27   St. Ignatius of Antioch, *Ad Trall.* 3, 1: SCh 10, 96; cf. *Ad Magn.* 6, 1: SCh 10, 82-84.
28   *LG* 24.

depends entirely on Christ and on his unique priesthood; it has been instituted for the good of men and the communion of the Church. The sacrament of Holy Orders communicates a "sacred

1538 power" which is none other than that of Christ. The exercise of this
608   authority must therefore be measured against the model of Christ, who by love made himself the least and the servant of all.[29] "The Lord said clearly that concern for his flock was proof of love for him."[30]

... "in the name of the whole Church"

1552   The ministerial priesthood has the task not only of representing Christ – Head of the Church – before the assembly of the faithful, but also of acting in the name of the whole Church when presenting to God the prayer of the Church, and above all when offering the Eucharistic sacrifice.[31]

1553   "In the name of the *whole* Church" does not mean that priests are the delegates of the community. The prayer and offering of the Church are inseparable from the prayer and offering of Christ, her head; it is always the case that Christ worships in and through his Church. The whole Church, the Body of Christ, prays and offers herself "through him, with him, in him," in the unity of

795   the Holy Spirit, to God the Father. The whole Body, *caput et membra*, prays and offers itself, and therefore those who in the Body are especially his ministers are called ministers not only of Christ, but also of the Church. It is because the ministerial priesthood represents Christ that it can represent the Church.

III.   THE THREE DEGREES OF THE SACRAMENT OF HOLY ORDERS

1554   "The divinely instituted ecclesiastical ministry is exercised in different degrees by those who even from ancient times have

1536 been called bishops, priests, and deacons."[32] Catholic doctrine, expressed in the liturgy, the Magisterium, and the constant practice of the Church, recognizes that there are two degrees of ministerial participation in the priesthood of Christ: the episcopacy and the presbyterate. The diaconate is intended to help and serve them. For this reason the term *sacerdos* in current usage denotes bishops and priests but not deacons. Yet Catholic doctrine teaches that the degrees of priestly participation (episcopate and presbyterate) and the degree of

---

29   Cf. *Mk* 10:43-45; *1 Pet* 5:3.
30   St. John Chrysostom, *De sac.* 2, 4: PG 48, 636; cf. *Jn* 21:15-17.
31   Cf. *SC* 33N; *LG* 10.
32   *LG* 28.

service (diaconate) are all three conferred by a sacramental act
called "ordination," that is, by the sacrament of Holy Orders: *1538*

> Let everyone revere the deacons as Jesus Christ, the bishop
> as the image of the Father, and the presbyters as the senate
> of God and the assembly of the apostles. For without them
> one cannot speak of the Church.[33]

Episcopal ordination – fullness of the sacrament of Holy Orders

1555   "Amongst those various offices which have been exercised
in the Church from the earliest times the chief place, according to
the witness of tradition, is held by the function of those who,
through their appointment to the dignity and responsibility of
bishop, and in virtue consequently of the unbroken succession
going back to the beginning, are regarded as transmitters of the   *861*
apostolic line."[34]

1556   To fulfil their exalted mission, "the apostles were endowed
by Christ with a special outpouring of the Holy Spirit coming upon
them, and by the imposition of hands they passed on to their   *862*
auxiliaries the gift of the Spirit, which is transmitted down to our
day through episcopal consecration."[35]

1557   The Second Vatican Council "teaches . . . that *the fullness of
the sacrament of Holy Orders* is conferred by episcopal consecration,
that fullness namely which, both in the liturgical tradition of the
Church and the language of the Fathers of the Church, is called the
high priesthood, the acme (*summa*) of the sacred ministry."[36]

1558   "Episcopal consecration confers, together with the office   *895*
of sanctifying, also the offices of teaching and ruling. . . . In fact . . . by
the imposition of hands and through the words of the consecration,   *1121*
the grace of the Holy Spirit is given, and a sacred character is
impressed in such wise that bishops, in an eminent and visible
manner, take the place of Christ himself, teacher, shepherd, and
priest, and act as his representative (*in Eius persona agant*)."[37] "By
virtue, therefore, of the Holy Spirit who has been given to them,
bishops have been constituted true and authentic teachers of the
faith and have been made pontiffs and pastors."[38]

---

33   St. Ignatius of Antioch, *Ad Trall.* 3, 1: SCh 10, 96.
34   *LG* 20.
35   *LG* 21; cf. *Acts* 1:8; 2:4; *Jn* 20:22-23; *1 Tim* 4:14; *2 Tim* 1:6-7.
36   *LG* 21 § 2.
37   *LG* 21.

1559   "One is constituted a member of the episcopal body in virtue of the sacramental consecration and by the hierarchical communion with the head and members of the college."[39] The character and *collegial nature* of the episcopal order are evidenced
877   among other ways by the Church's ancient practice which calls for several bishops to participate in the consecration of a new bishop.[40] In our day, the lawful ordination of a bishop requires a special intervention of the Bishop of Rome, because he is the supreme
882   visible bond of the communion of the particular Churches in the one Church and the guarantor of their freedom.

833   **1560**   As Christ's vicar, each bishop has the pastoral care of the particular Church entrusted to him, but at the same time he bears collegially with all his brothers in the episcopacy the *solicitude for*
886   *all the Churches*: "Though each bishop is the lawful pastor only of the portion of the flock entrusted to his care, as a legitimate successor of the apostles he is, by divine institution and precept, responsible with the other bishops for the apostolic mission of the Church."[41]

1369   **1561**   The above considerations explain why the Eucharist celebrated by the bishop has a quite special significance as an expression of the Church gathered around the altar, with the one who represents Christ, the Good Shepherd and Head of his Church, presiding.[42]

The ordination of priests – co-workers of the bishops

1562   "Christ, whom the Father hallowed and sent into the world, has, through his apostles, made their successors, the bishops namely, sharers in his consecration and mission; and these, in their turn, duly entrusted in varying degrees various members of the Church with the office of their ministry."[43] "The function of the bishops' ministry was handed over in a subordinate degree to priests so that they might be appointed in the order of the priesthood and be *co-workers of the episcopal order* for the proper fulfillment of the apostolic mission that had been entrusted to it by Christ."[44]

---

38   *CD* 2 § 2.
39   *LG* 22.
40   Cf. *LG* 22.
41   Pius XII, *Fidei donum*: AAS 49 (1957) 237; cf. *LG* 23; *CD* 4; 36; 37; *AG* 5; 6; 38.
42   Cf. *SC* 41; *LG* 26.
43   *LG* 28; cf. *Jn* 10:36.
44   *PO* 2 § 2.

1563 "Because it is joined with the episcopal order the office of priests shares in the authority by which Christ himself builds up and sanctifies and rules his Body. Hence the priesthood of priests, while presupposing the sacraments of initiation, is nevertheless conferred by its own particular sacrament. Through that sacrament priests by the anointing of the Holy Spirit are signed with a special character and so are configured to Christ the priest in such a way that they are able to act in the person of Christ the head."[45]

1121

1564 "Whilst not having the supreme degree of the pontifical office, and notwithstanding the fact that they depend on the bishops in the exercise of their own proper power, the priests are for all that associated with them by reason of their sacerdotal dignity; and in virtue of the sacrament of Holy Orders, after the image of Christ, the supreme and eternal priest, they are consecrated in order to preach the Gospel and shepherd the faithful as well as to celebrate divine worship *as true priests of the New Testament*."[46]

611

1565 Through the sacrament of Holy Orders priests share in the universal dimensions of the mission that Christ entrusted to the apostles. The spiritual gift they have received in ordination prepares them, not for a limited and restricted mission, "but for the fullest, in fact the universal mission of salvation 'to the end of the earth,'"[47] "prepared in spirit to preach the Gospel everywhere."[48]

849

1566 "It is in the Eucharistic cult or in the *Eucharistic assembly* of the faithful (*synaxis*) that they exercise in a supreme degree their sacred office; there, acting in the person of Christ and proclaiming his mystery, they unite the votive offerings of the faithful to the sacrifice of Christ their head, and in the sacrifice of the Mass they make present again and apply, until the coming of the Lord, the unique sacrifice of the New Testament, that namely of Christ offering himself once for all a spotless victim to the Father."[49] From this unique sacrifice their whole priestly ministry draws its strength.[50]

1369

611

---

45 *PO* 2.
46 *LG* 28; cf. *Heb* 5:1-10; 7:24; 9:11-28; Innocent I, *Epist. ad Decentium*: PL 20, 554 A; St. Gregory of Nazianzus, *Oratio* 2, 22: PG 35, 432B.
47 *PO* 10; *OT* 20; cf. *Acts* 1:8.
48 *OT* 20.
49 *LG* 28; cf. *1 Cor* 11:26.
50 Cf. *PO* 2.

1462 **1567**   "The priests, prudent cooperators of the episcopal college and its support and instrument, called to the service of the People of God, constitute, together with their bishop, a unique sacerdotal college (*presbyterium*) dedicated, it is, true to a variety of distinct duties. In each local assembly of the faithful they represent, in a
2179 certain sense, the bishop, with whom they are associated in all trust and generosity; in part they take upon themselves his duties and solicitude and in their daily toils discharge them."[51] Priests can exercise their ministry only in dependence on the bishop and in communion with him. The promise of obedience they make to the bishop at the moment of ordination and the kiss of peace from him at the end of the ordination liturgy mean that the bishop considers them his co-workers, his sons, his brothers and his friends, and that they in return owe him love and obedience.

1537 **1568**   "All priests, who are constituted in the order of priesthood by the sacrament of Order, are bound together by an intimate sacramental brotherhood, but in a special way they form one priestly body in the diocese to which they are attached under their own bishop. . . ."[52] The unity of the presbyterium finds liturgical expression in the custom of the presbyters' imposing hands, after the bishop, during the rite of ordination.

The ordination of deacons – "in order to serve"

1569   "At a lower level of the hierarchy are to be found deacons, who receive the imposition of hands 'not unto the priesthood, but unto the ministry.'"[53] At an ordination to the diaconate only the bishop lays hands on the candidate, thus signifying the deacon's special attachment to the bishop in the tasks of his "diakonia."[54]

1570   Deacons share in Christ's mission and grace in a special
1121 way.[55] The sacrament of Holy Orders marks them with an *imprint* ("character") which cannot be removed and which configures them to Christ, who made himself the "deacon" or servant of all.[56] Among other tasks, it is the task of deacons to assist the bishop and priests in the celebration of the divine mysteries, above all the Eucharist, in the distribution of Holy Communion, in assisting at and blessing marriages, in the proclamation of the Gospel and

---

51 *LG* 28 § 2.
52 *PO* 8.
53 *LG* 29; cf. *CD* 15.
54 Cf. St. Hippolytus, *Trad. ap.* 8: SCh 11, 58-62.
55 Cf. *LG* 41; *AA* 16.
56 Cf. *Mk* 10:45; *Lk* 22:27; St. Polycarp, *Ad Phil.* 5, 2: SCh 10, 182.

preaching, in presiding over funerals, and in dedicating themselves to the various ministries of charity.[57]

1571 Since the Second Vatican Council the Latin Church has restored the diaconate "as a proper and permanent rank of the hierarchy,"[58] while the Churches of the East had always maintained it. This *permanent diaconate*, which can be conferred on married men, constitutes an important enrichment for the Church's mission. Indeed it is appropriate and useful *1579* that men who carry out a truly diaconal ministry in the Church, whether in its liturgical and pastoral life or whether in its social and charitable works, should "be strengthened by the imposition of hands which has come down from the apostles. They would be more closely bound to the altar and their ministry would be made more fruitful through the sacramental grace of the diaconate."[59]

IV. THE CELEBRATION OF THIS SACRAMENT

1572 Given the importance that the ordination of a bishop, a priest, or a deacon has for the life of the particular Church, its celebration calls for as many of the faithful as possible to take part. It should take place preferably on Sunday, in the cathedral, with solemnity appropriate to the occasion. All three ordinations, of the bishop, of the priest, and of the deacon, follow the same movement. Their proper place is within the Eucharistic liturgy.

1573 The *essential rite* of the sacrament of Holy Orders for all three degrees consists in the bishop's imposition of hands on the head of the ordinand and in the bishop's specific consecratory prayer asking *699* God for the outpouring of the Holy Spirit and his gifts proper to the *1585* ministry to which the candidate is being ordained.[60]

1574 As in all the sacraments additional rites surround the celebration. Varying greatly among the different liturgical traditions, these rites have in common the expression of the multiple aspects of sacramental grace. Thus in the Latin Church, the initial rites – presentation and election of the ordinand, instruction by the bishop, examination of the candidate, litany of the saints – attest that the choice of the candidate is made in keeping with the practice of the Church and prepare for the solemn act of consecration, after which several rites symbolically express and complete the mystery accomplished: for bishop and priest, an anointing with holy chrism, a sign of the special anointing of the Holy Spirit who makes their *1294* ministry fruitful; giving the book of the Gospels, the ring, the miter, and the crosier to the bishop as the sign of his apostolic mission to proclaim the Word of God, of his fidelity to the Church, the bride of Christ, and his office as shepherd of the Lord's flock; presentation to the priest of the paten and *796* chalice, "the offering of the holy people" which he is called to present to

---

57 Cf. *LG* 29; *SC* 35 § 4; *AG* 16.
58 *LG* 29 § 2.
59 *AG* 16 § 6.
60 Cf. Pius XII, apostolic constitution, *Sacramentum Ordinis: DS 3858.*

God; giving the book of the Gospels to the deacon who has just received the mission to proclaim the Gospel of Christ.

V.   WHO CAN CONFER THIS SACRAMENT?

1575   Christ himself chose the apostles and gave them a share in his mission and authority. Raised to the Father's right hand, he has not forsaken his flock but he keeps it under his constant protection through *857* the apostles, and guides it still through these same pastors who continue his work today.[61] Thus, it is Christ whose gift it is that some be apostles, others pastors. He continues to act through the bishops.[62]

1536 **1576**   Since the sacrament of Holy Orders is the sacrament of the apostolic ministry, it is for the bishops as the successors of the apostles to hand on the "gift of the Spirit,"[63] the "apostolic line."[64] Validly ordained bishops, i.e., those who are in the line of apostolic succession, validly confer the three degrees of the sacrament of Holy Orders.[65]

VI.   WHO CAN RECEIVE THIS SACRAMENT?

1577   "Only a baptized man (*vir*) validly receives sacred ordination."[66] The Lord Jesus chose men (*viri*) to form the college of the *551* twelve apostles, and the apostles did the same when they chose *861* collaborators to succeed them in their ministry.[67] The college of bishops, with whom the priests are united in the priesthood, makes *862* the college of the twelve an ever-present and ever-active reality until Christ's return. The Church recognizes herself to be bound by this choice made by the Lord himself. For this reason the ordination of women is not possible.[68]

1578   No one has a *right* to receive the sacrament of Holy Orders. Indeed no one claims this office for himself; he is called to it by *2121* God.[69] Anyone who thinks he recognizes the signs of God's call to the ordained ministry must humbly submit his desire to the authority of the Church, who has the responsibility and right to call

---

61   Cf. *Roman Missal*, Preface of the Apostles I.
62   Cf. *LG* 21; Eph 4:11.
63   *LG* 21 § 2.
64   *LG* 20.
65   Cf. DS 794 and Cf. DS 802; CIC, can. 1012; CCEO, can. 744; 747.
66   CIC, can. 1024.
67   Cf. *Mk* 3:14-19; *Lk* 6:12-16; *1 Tim* 3:1-13; *2 Tim* 1:6; *Titus* 1:5-9; St. Clement of Rome, *Ad Cor.* 42, 4; 44, 3: PG 1, 292-293; 300.
68   Cf. John Paul II, *MD* 26-27; CDF, declaration, *Inter insigniores*: AAS 69 (1977) 98-116.
69   Cf. *Heb* 5:4.

someone to receive orders. Like every grace this sacrament can be *received* only as an unmerited gift.

1579   All the ordained ministers of the Latin Church, with the exception of permanent deacons, are normally chosen from among men of faith who live a celibate life and who intend to remain *celibate* "for the sake of the kingdom of heaven."[70] Called to conse- *1618* crate themselves with undivided heart to the Lord and to "the affairs of the Lord,"[71] they give themselves entirely to God and to men. Celibacy is a sign of this new life to the service of which the Church's minister is consecrated; accepted with a joyous heart celibacy radiantly proclaims the Reign of God.[72]   *2233*

1580   In the Eastern Churches a different discipline has been in force for many centuries: while bishops are chosen solely from among celibates, married men can be ordained as deacons and priests. This practice has long been considered legitimate; these priests exercise a fruitful ministry within their communities.[73] Moreover, priestly celibacy is held in great honor in the Eastern Churches and many priests have freely chosen it for the sake of the Kingdom of God. In the East as in the West a man who has already received the sacrament of Holy Orders can no longer marry.

VII.   THE EFFECTS OF THE SACRAMENT OF HOLY ORDERS

The indelible character

1581   This sacrament configures the recipient to Christ by a special grace of the Holy Spirit, so that he may serve as Christ's instrument for his Church. By ordination one is enabled to act as a *1548* representative of Christ, Head of the Church, in his triple office of priest, prophet, and king.

1582   As in the case of Baptism and Confirmation this share in *1121* Christ's office is granted once for all. The sacrament of Holy Orders, like the other two, confers an *indelible spiritual character* and cannot be repeated or conferred temporarily.[74]

1583   It is true that someone validly ordained can, for a just reason, be discharged from the obligations and functions linked to ordination, or can be forbidden to exercise them; but he cannot become a layman again in the strict sense,[75] because the character imprinted by ordination is for ever.

---

70   *Mt* 19:12.
71   *1 Cor* 7:32.
72   Cf. *PO* 16.
73   Cf. *PO* 16.
74   Cf. Council of Trent: DS 1767; *LG* 21; 28; 29; *PO* 2.

The vocation and mission received on the day of his ordination mark him permanently.

1128 **1584**   Since it is ultimately Christ who acts and effects salvation through the ordained minister, the unworthiness of the latter does not prevent Christ from acting.[76] St. Augustine states this forcefully:

1550
> As for the proud minister, he is to be ranked with the devil. Christ's gift is not thereby profaned: what flows through him keeps its purity, and what passes through him remains clear and reaches the fertile earth. . . . The spiritual power of the sacrament is indeed comparable to light: those to be enlightened receive it in its purity, and if it should pass through defiled beings, it is not itself defiled.[77]

The grace of the Holy Spirit

1585   The grace of the Holy Spirit proper to this sacrament is configuration to Christ as Priest, Teacher, and Pastor, of whom the ordained is made a minister.

1586   For the bishop, this is first of all a grace of strength ("the governing spirit": Prayer of Episcopal Consecration in the Latin rite):[78] the grace to guide and defend his Church with strength and
2448 prudence as a father and pastor, with gratuitous love for all and a preferential love for the poor, the sick, and the needy. This grace impels him to proclaim the Gospel to all, to be the model for his flock, to go before it on the way of sanctification by identifying himself in the Eucharist with Christ the priest and victim, not fearing to give his life for his sheep:

1558
> Father, you know all hearts.
> You have chosen your servant for the office of bishop.
> May he be a shepherd to your holy flock,
> and a high priest blameless in your sight,
> ministering to you night and day;
> may he always gain the blessing of your favor
> and offer the gifts of your holy Church.
> Through the Spirit who gives the grace of high priesthood
> grant him the power
> to forgive sins as you have commanded,
> to assign ministries as you have decreed,
> and to loose from every bond by the authority which you gave to your apostles.
> May he be pleasing to you by his gentleness and purity of heart,

---

75 Cf. CIC, cann. 290-293; 1336 § 1 3°, 5°; 1338 § 2; Council of Trent: DS 1774.
76 Cf. Council of Trent: DS 1612; DS 1154.
77 St. Augustine, *In Jo. ev.* 5, 15: PL 35, 1422.
78 Cf. *Roman Pontifical*, Ordination of Bishops 26, Prayer of Consecration; cf. CD 13; 16.

> presenting a fragrant offering to you,
> through Jesus Christ, your Son. . . .[79]

1587 The spiritual gift conferred by presbyteral ordination is *1564* expressed by this prayer of the Byzantine Rite. The bishop, while laying on his hand, says among other things:

> Lord, fill with the gift of the Holy Spirit
> him whom you have deigned to raise to the rank of the priesthood,
> that he may be worthy to stand without reproach before your altar,
> to proclaim the Gospel of your kingdom,
> to fulfill the ministry of your word of truth,
> to offer you spiritual gifts and sacrifices,
> to renew your people by the bath of rebirth;
> so that he may go out to meet
> our great God and Savior Jesus Christ, your only Son,
> on the day of his second coming,
> and may receive from your vast goodness
> the recompense for a faithful administration of his order.[80]

1588 With regard to deacons, "strengthened by sacramental *1569* grace they are dedicated to the People of God, in conjunction with the bishop and his body of priests, in the service (*diakonia*) of the liturgy, of the Gospel, and of works of charity."[81]

1589 Before the grandeur of the priestly grace and office, the holy doctors felt an urgent call to conversion in order to conform their whole lives to him whose sacrament had made them ministers. Thus St. Gregory of Nazianzus, as a very young priest, exclaimed:

> We must begin by purifying ourselves before purifying others; we must be instructed to be able to instruct, become light to illuminate, draw close to God to bring him close to others, be sanctified to sanctify, lead by the hand and counsel prudently. I know whose ministers we are, where we find ourselves and to where we strive. I know God's greatness and man's weakness, but also his potential. [Who then is the priest? He is] the defender of truth, who stands with angels, gives glory with archangels, causes sacrifices to rise to the altar on high, shares Christ's priesthood, refashions creation, restores it in God's image, recreates it for the world on high *460* and, even greater, is divinized and divinizes.[82]

---

79 *Roman Pontifical,* Ordination of Bishops 26, Prayer of Consecration; cf. St. Hippolytus, *Trad. ap.* 3: SCh 11, 44-46.
80 Byzantine Liturgy, *Euchologion.*
81 *LG* 29.
82 St. Gregory of Nazianzus, *Oratio* 2, 71, 74, 73: PG 35, 480-481.

1551   And the holy Curé of Ars: "The priest continues the work of redemption on earth. . . . If we really understood the priest on earth, we would die not of fright but of love. . . . The Priesthood is the love of the heart of Jesus."[83]

IN BRIEF

1590   St. Paul said to his disciple Timothy: "I remind you to rekindle the gift of God that is within you through the laying on of my hands" (*2 Tim* 1:6), and "If any one aspires to the office of bishop, he desires a noble task." (*1 Tim* 3:1) To Titus he said: "This is why I left you in Crete, that you amend what was defective, and appoint presbyters in every town, as I directed you" (*Titus* 1:5).

1591   The whole Church is a priestly people. Through Baptism all the faithful share in the priesthood of Christ. This participation is called the "common priesthood of the faithful." Based on this common priesthood and ordered to its service, there exists another participation in the mission of Christ: the ministry conferred by the sacrament of Holy Orders, where the task is to serve in the name and in the person of Christ the Head in the midst of the community.

1592   The ministerial priesthood differs in essence from the common priesthood of the faithful because it confers a sacred power for the service of the faithful. The ordained ministers exercise their service for the People of God by teaching (*munus docendi*), divine worship (*munus liturgicum*) and pastoral governance (*munus regendi*).

1593   Since the beginning, the ordained ministry has been conferred and exercised in three degrees: that of bishops, that of presbyters, and that of deacons. The ministries conferred by ordination are irreplaceable for the organic structure of the Church: without the bishop, presbyters, and deacons, one cannot speak of the Church (cf. St. Ignatius of Antioch, *Ad Trall.* 3,1).

1594   The bishop receives the fullness of the sacrament of Holy Orders, which integrates him into the episcopal college and makes him the visible head of the particu-

---

83   St. John Vianney, quoted in B. Nodet, *Jean-Marie Vianney, Curé d'Ars*, 100.

lar Church entrusted to him. As successors of the apostles and members of the college, the bishops share in the apostolic responsibility and mission of the whole Church under the authority of the Pope, successor of St. Peter.

1595   Priests are united with the bishops in sacerdotal dignity and at the same time depend on them in the exercise of their pastoral functions; they are called to be the bishops' prudent co-workers. They form around their bishop the presbyterium which bears responsibility with him for the particular Church. They receive from the bishop the charge of a parish community or a determinate ecclesial office.

1596   Deacons are ministers ordained for tasks of service of the Church; they do not receive the ministerial priesthood, but ordination confers on them important functions in the ministry of the word, divine worship, pastoral governance, and the service of charity, tasks which they must carry out under the pastoral authority of their bishop.

1597   The sacrament of Holy Orders is conferred by the laying on of hands followed by a solemn prayer of consecration asking God to grant the ordinand the graces of the Holy Spirit required for his ministry. Ordination imprints an indelible sacramental character.

1598   The Church confers the sacrament of Holy Orders only on baptized men (*viri*), whose suitability for the exercise of the ministry has been duly recognized. Church authority alone has the responsibility and right to call someone to receive the sacrament of Holy Orders.

1599   In the Latin Church the sacrament of Holy Orders for the presbyterate is normally conferred only on candidates who are ready to embrace celibacy freely and who publicly manifest their intention of staying celibate for the love of God's kingdom and the service of men.

1600   It is bishops who confer the sacrament of Holy Orders in the three degrees.

ARTICLE 7
THE SACRAMENT OF MATRIMONY

1601   "The matrimonial covenant, by which a man and a woman establish between themselves a partnership of the whole of life, is by its nature ordered toward the good of the spouses and the procreation and education of offspring; this covenant between baptized persons has been raised by Christ the Lord to the dignity of a sacrament."[84]

I.   MARRIAGE IN GOD'S PLAN

369   **1602**   Sacred Scripture begins with the creation of man and
796   woman in the image and likeness of God and concludes with a vision of "the wedding-feast of the Lamb."[85] Scripture speaks throughout of marriage and its "mystery," its institution and the meaning God has given it, its origin and its end, its various realizations throughout the history of salvation, the difficulties arising from sin and its renewal "in the Lord" in the New Covenant of Christ and the Church.[86]

Marriage in the order of creation

1603   "The intimate community of life and love which constitutes the married state has been established by the Creator and
371   endowed by him with its own proper laws. . . . God himself is the author of marriage."[87] The vocation to marriage is written in the very nature of man and woman as they came from the hand of the
2331   Creator. Marriage is not a purely human institution despite the many variations it may have undergone through the centuries in different cultures, social structures, and spiritual attitudes. These differences should not cause us to forget its common and permanent characteristics. Although the dignity of this institution is not transparent everywhere with the same clarity,[88] some sense of the greatness of the matrimonial union exists in all cultures. "The
2210   well-being of the individual person and of both human and Christian society is closely bound up with the healthy state of conjugal and family life."[89]

---

84   CIC, can. 1055 § 1; cf. *GS* 48 § 1.
85   *Rev* 19:7, 9; cf. *Gen* 1:26-27.
86   *1 Cor* 7:39; cf. *Eph* 5:31-32.
87   *GS* 48 § 1.
88   Cf. *GS* 47 § 2.
89   *GS* 47§ 1.

1604   God who created man out of love also calls him to love –
the fundamental and innate vocation of every human being. For
man is created in the image and likeness of God who is himself
love.[90] Since God created him man and woman, their mutual love
becomes an image of the absolute and unfailing love with which   *355*
God loves man. It is good, very good, in the Creator's eyes. And
this love which God blesses is intended to be fruitful and to be
realized in the common work of watching over creation: "And God
blessed them, and God said to them: 'Be fruitful and multiply, and
fill the earth and subdue it.'"[91]

1605   Holy Scripture affirms that man and woman were created   *372*
for one another: "It is not good that the man should be alone."[92]
The woman, "flesh of his flesh," i.e., his counterpart, his equal, his
nearest in all things, is given to him by God as a "helpmate"; she
thus represents God from whom comes our help.[93] "Therefore a
man leaves his father and his mother and cleaves to his wife, and
they become one flesh."[94] The Lord himself shows that this signifies an unbreakable union of their two lives by recalling what the   *1614*
plan of the Creator had been "in the beginning": "So they are no
longer two, but one flesh."[95]

Marriage under the regime of sin

1606   Every man experiences evil around him and within himself. This experience makes itself felt in the relationships between
man and woman. Their union has always been threatened by
discord, a spirit of domination, infidelity, jealousy, and conflicts
that can escalate into hatred and separation. This disorder can
manifest itself more or less acutely, and can be more or less overcome according to the circumstances of cultures, eras, and individuals, but it does seem to have a universal character.

1607   According to faith the disorder we notice so painfully does
not stem from the *nature* of man and woman, nor from the nature   *1849*
of their relations, but from *sin*. As a break with God, the first sin
had for its first consequence the rupture of the original communion   *400*
between man and woman. Their relations were distorted by mutual recriminations;[96] their mutual attraction, the Creator's own

---

90 Cf. *Gen* 1:27; *1 Jn* 4:8, 16.
91 *Gen* 1:28; cf. 1:31.
92 *Gen* 2:18.
93 Cf. *Gen* 2:18-25.
94 *Gen* 2:24.
95 *Mt* 19:6.

gift, changed into a relationship of domination and lust;[97] and the beautiful vocation of man and woman to be fruitful, multiply, and subdue the earth was burdened by the pain of childbirth and the toil of work.[98]

55 **1608**   Nevertheless, the order of creation persists, though seriously disturbed. To heal the wounds of sin, man and woman need the help of the grace that God in his infinite mercy never refuses them.[99] Without his help man and woman cannot achieve the union of their lives for which God created them "in the beginning."

Marriage under the pedagogy of the Law

410 **1609**   In his mercy God has not forsaken sinful man. The punishments consequent upon sin, "pain in childbearing" and toil "in the sweat of your brow,"[100] also embody remedies that limit the damaging effects of sin. After the fall, marriage helps to overcome self-absorption, egoism, pursuit of one's own pleasure, and to open oneself to the other, to mutual aid and to self-giving.

1610   Moral conscience concerning the unity and indissolubility of marriage developed under the pedagogy of the old law. In the *1963* Old Testament the polygamy of patriarchs and kings is not yet *2387* explicitly rejected. Nevertheless, the law given to Moses aims at protecting the wife from arbitrary domination by the husband, even though according to the Lord's words it still carries traces of man's "hardness of heart" which was the reason Moses permitted men to divorce their wives.[101]

219 **1611**   Seeing God's covenant with Israel in the image of exclusive *2380* and faithful married love, the prophets prepared the Chosen Peo-*2361* ple's conscience for a deepened understanding of the unity and indissolubility of marriage.[102] The books of *Ruth* and *Tobit* bear moving witness to an elevated sense of marriage and to the fidelity and tenderness of spouses. Tradition has always seen in the *Song of Solomon* a unique expression of human love, a pure reflection of God's love – a love "strong as death" that "many waters cannot quench."[103]

---

96   Cf. *Gen* 3:12.
97   Cf. *Gen* 2:22; 3:16b.
98   Cf. *Gen* 1:28; 3:16-19.
99   Cf. *Gen* 3:21.
100 *Gen* 3:16,19.
101 Cf. *Mt* 19:8; *Deut* 24:1.
102 Cf. *Hos* 1-3; *Isa* 54; 62; *Jer* 2-3; 31; *Ezek* 16; 23; *Mal* 2:13-17.
103 *Song* 8:6-7.

Marriage in the Lord

1612   The nuptial covenant between God and his people Israel had prepared the way for the new and everlasting covenant in which the Son of God, by becoming incarnate and giving his life, *521* has united to himself in a certain way all mankind saved by him, thus preparing for "the wedding-feast of the Lamb."[104]

1613   On the threshold of his public life Jesus performs his first sign – at his mother's request – during a wedding feast.[105] The Church attaches great importance to Jesus' presence at the wedding at Cana. She sees in it the confirmation of the goodness of marriage and the proclamation that thenceforth marriage will be an efficacious sign of Christ's presence.

1614   In his preaching Jesus unequivocally taught the original mean- *2336* ing of the union of man and woman as the Creator willed it from the beginning: permission given by Moses to divorce one's wife was a concession to the hardness of hearts.[106] The matrimonial union of man *2382* and woman is indissoluble: God himself has determined it: "what therefore God has joined together, let no man put asunder."[107]

1615   This unequivocal insistence on the indissolubility of the mar- *2364* riage bond may have left some perplexed and could seem to be a demand impossible to realize. However, Jesus has not placed on spouses a burden impossible to bear, or too heavy – heavier than the Law of Moses.[108] By coming to restore the original order of creation disturbed by sin, he himself gives the strength and grace to live marriage in the new dimension of the Reign of God. It is by following Christ, renouncing themselves, and taking up their crosses that spouses will be able to "receive" the original meaning of marriage and live it with the help of Christ.[109] This grace of Christian marriage is a fruit of Christ's cross, the source of all Christian life. *1642*

1616   This is what the Apostle Paul makes clear when he says: "Husbands, love your wives, as Christ loved the church and gave himself up for her, that he might sanctify her," adding at once: "'For this reason a man shall leave his father and mother and be joined to his wife, and the two shall become one. This is a great mystery, and I mean in reference to Christ and the Church."[110]

---

104   *Rev* 19:7, 9; cf. *GS* 22.
105   Cf. *Jn* 2:1-11.
106   Cf. *Mt* 19:8.
107   *Mt* 19:6.
108   Cf. *Mk* 8:34; *Mt* 11:29-30.
109   Cf. *Mt* 19:11.

796 **1617** The entire Christian life bears the mark of the spousal love of Christ and the Church. Already Baptism, the entry into the People of God, is a nuptial mystery; it is so to speak the nuptial bath[111] which precedes the wedding feast, the Eucharist. Christian marriage in its turn becomes an efficacious sign, the sacrament of the covenant of Christ and the Church. Since it signifies and communicates grace, marriage between baptized persons is a true sacrament of the New Covenant.[112]

Virginity for the sake of the Kingdom

2232 **1618** Christ is the center of all Christian life. The bond with him takes precedence over all other bonds, familial or social.[113] From the very beginning of the Church there have been men and women who have renounced the great good of marriage to follow the Lamb wherever he goes, to be intent on the things of the Lord, to seek to *1579* please him, and to go out to meet the Bridegroom who is coming.[114] Christ himself has invited certain persons to follow him in this way of life, of which he remains the model:

> "For there are eunuchs who have been so from birth, and there are eunuchs who have been made eunuchs by men, and there are eunuchs who have made themselves eunuchs for the sake of the kingdom of heaven. He who is able to receive this, let him receive it."[115]

922-924 **1619** Virginity for the sake of the kingdom of heaven is an unfolding of baptismal grace, a powerful sign of the supremacy of the bond with Christ and of the ardent expectation of his return, a sign which also recalls that marriage is a reality of this present age which is passing away.[116]

1620 Both the sacrament of Matrimony and virginity for the Kingdom of God come from the Lord himself. It is he who gives them meaning and grants them the grace which is indispensable for living them out in conformity with his will.[117] Esteem of vir- *2349* ginity for the sake of the kingdom[118] and the Christian under-

---

110 *Eph* 5:25-26, 31-32; cf. *Gen* 2:24.
111 Cf. *Eph* 5:26-27.
112 Cf. DS 1800; CIC, can. 1055 § 2.
113 Cf. *Lk* 14:26; *Mk* 10:28-31.
114 Cf. *Rev* 14:4; *1 Cor* 7:32; *Mt* 25:6.
115 *Mt* 19:12.
116 Cf. *Mk* 12:25; *1 Cor* 7:31.
117 Cf. *Mt* 19:3-12.
118 Cf. *LG* 42; *PC* 12; *OT* 10.

standing of marriage are inseparable, and they reinforce each other:

> Whoever denigrates marriage also diminishes the glory of virginity. Whoever praises it makes virginity more admirable and resplendent. What appears good only in comparison with evil would not be truly good. The most excellent good is something even better than what is admitted to be good.[119]

II. THE CELEBRATION OF MARRIAGE

1621 In the Latin Rite the celebration of marriage between two Catholic faithful normally takes place during Holy Mass, because of the connection of all the sacraments with the Paschal mystery of Christ.[120] In the Eucharist the memorial of the New Covenant is *1323* realized, the New Covenant in which Christ has united himself for ever to the Church, his beloved bride for whom he gave himself up.[121] It is therefore fitting that the spouses should seal their consent to give themselves to each other through the offering of their own lives by uniting it to the offering of Christ for his Church made present in the Eucharistic sacrifice, and by receiving the *1368* Eucharist so that, communicating in the same Body and the same Blood of Christ, they may form but "one body" in Christ.[122]

1622 "Inasmuch as it is a sacramental action of sanctification, the liturgical celebration of marriage . . . must be, per se, valid, worthy, and fruitful."[123] It is therefore appropriate for the bride and groom to prepare themselves for the celebration of their marriage by receiving the sacrament of penance.   *1422*

1623 In the Latin Church, it is ordinarily understood that the spouses, as ministers of Christ's grace, mutually confer upon each other the sacrament of Matrimony by expressing their consent before the Church. In the Eastern liturgies the minister of this sacrament (which is called "Crowning") is the priest or bishop who, after receiving the mutual consent of the spouses, successively crowns the bridegroom and the bride as a sign of the marriage covenant.

---

119 St. John Chrysostom, *De virg.* 10, 1: PG 48, 540; cf. John Paul II, *FC* 16.
120 Cf. *SC* 61.
121 Cf. *LG* 6.
122 Cf. *1 Cor* 10:17.
123 *FC* 67.

1624   The various liturgies abound in prayers of blessing and epiclesis asking God's grace and blessing on the new couple, especially the bride. In the epiclesis of this sacrament the spouses receive the Holy Spirit as the communion of love of Christ and the

736   Church.[124] The Holy Spirit is the seal of their covenant, the ever-available source of their love and the strength to renew their fidelity.

III.   MATRIMONIAL CONSENT

1625   The parties to a marriage covenant are a baptized man and

1734   woman, free to contract marriage, who freely express their consent; "to be free" means:

– not being under constraint;

– not impeded by any natural or ecclesiastical law.

1626   The Church holds the exchange of consent between the

2201   spouses to be the indispensable element that "makes the marriage."[125] If consent is lacking there is no marriage.

1627   The consent consists in a "human act by which the partners mutually give themselves to each other": "I take you to be my wife" – "I take you to be my husband."[126] This consent that binds the spouses to each other finds its fulfillment in the two "becoming one flesh."[127]

1735   **1628**   The consent must be an act of the will of each of the contracting parties, free of coercion or grave external fear.[128] No human power can substitute for this consent.[129] If this freedom is lacking the marriage is invalid.

1629   For this reason (or for other reasons that render the marriage null and void) the Church, after an examination of the situation by the competent ecclesiastical tribunal, can declare the nullity of a marriage, i.e., that the marriage never existed.[130] In this case the contracting parties are free to marry, provided the natural obligations of a previous union are discharged.[131]

---

124   Cf. *Eph* 5:32.
125   CIC, can. 1057 § 1.
126   *GS* 48 § 1; *OCM* 45; cf. CIC, can. 1057 § 2.
127   *Gen* 2:24; cf. *Mk* 10:8; *Eph* 5:31.
128   Cf. CIC, can. 1103.
129   Cf. CIC, can. 1057 § 1.
130   Cf. CIC, cann. 1095-1107.
131   Cf. CIC, can. 1071.

1630   The priest (or deacon) who assists at the celebration of a marriage receives the consent of the spouses in the name of the Church and gives the blessing of the Church. The presence of the Church's minister (and also of the witnesses) visibly expresses the fact that marriage is an ecclesial reality.

1631   This is the reason why the Church normally requires that the faithful contract marriage according to the ecclesiastical form. Several reasons converge to explain this requirement:[132]

– Sacramental marriage is a liturgical act. It is therefore appropriate   *1069* that it should be celebrated in the public liturgy of the Church;

– Marriage introduces one into an ecclesial *order*, and creates rights   *1537* and duties in the Church between the spouses and towards their children;

– Since marriage is a state of life in the Church, certainty about it is necessary (hence the obligation to have witnesses);

– The public character of the consent protects the "I do" once given   *2365* and helps the spouses remain faithful to it.

1632   So that the "I do" of the spouses may be a free and responsible act and so that the marriage covenant may have solid and lasting human and Christian foundations, preparation for marriage is of prime importance.

The example and teaching given by parents and families remain   *2206* the special form of this preparation.

The role of pastors and of the Christian community as the "family of God" is indispensable for the transmission of the human and Christian values of marriage and family,[133] and much more so in our era when many young people experience broken homes which no longer sufficiently assure this initiation:

> It is imperative to give suitable and timely instruction to young people, above all in the heart of their own families, about the dignity of married love, its role and its exercise, so that, having learned the value of chastity, they will be able at a suitable age to engage in honorable courtship and enter upon a marriage of their own.[134]   *2350*

Mixed marriages and disparity of cult

1633   In many countries the situation of a *mixed marriage* (marriage between a Catholic and a baptized non-Catholic) often arises. It requires

---

132   Cf. Council of Trent: DS 1813-1816; CIC, can. 1108.
133   Cf. CIC, can. 1063.
134   *GS* 49 § 3.

particular attention on the part of couples and their pastors. A case of marriage with *disparity of cult* (between a Catholic and a non-baptized person) requires even greater circumspection.

1634   Difference of confession between the spouses does not constitute an insurmountable obstacle for marriage, when they succeed in placing in common what they have received from their respective communities, and learn from each other the way in which each lives in fidelity to Christ. But the difficulties of mixed marriages must not be underestimated. They arise from the fact that the separation of Christians has not yet been overcome. 817 The spouses risk experiencing the tragedy of Christian disunity even in the heart of their own home. Disparity of cult can further aggravate these difficulties. Differences about faith and the very notion of marriage, but also different religious mentalities, can become sources of tension in marriage, especially as regards the education of children. The temptation to religious indifference can then arise.

1635   According to the law in force in the Latin Church, a mixed marriage needs for liceity the *express permission* of ecclesiastical authority.[135] In case of disparity of cult an *express dispensation* from this impediment is required for the validity of the marriage.[136] This permission or dispensation presupposes that both parties know and do not exclude the essential ends and properties of marriage and the obligations assumed by the Catholic party concerning the baptism and education of the children in the Catholic Church.[137]

821 **1636**   Through ecumenical dialogue Christian communities in many regions have been able to put into effect a *common pastoral practice for mixed marriages.* Its task is to help such couples live out their particular situation in the light of faith, overcome the tensions between the couple's obligations to each other and towards their ecclesial communities, and encourage the flowering of what is common to them in faith and respect for what separates them.

1637   In marriages with disparity of cult the Catholic spouse has a particular task: "For the unbelieving husband is consecrated through his wife, and the unbelieving wife is consecrated through her husband."[138] It is a great joy for the Christian spouse and for the Church if this "consecration" should lead to the free conversion of the other spouse to the Christian faith.[139] Sincere married love, the humble and patient practice of the family virtues, and perseverance in prayer can prepare the non-believing spouse to accept the grace of conversion.

---

135 Cf. CIC, can. 1124.
136 Cf. CIC, can. 1086.
137 Cf. CIC, can. 1125.
138 *1 Cor* 7:14.
139 Cf. *1 Cor* 7:16.

IV.   The Effects of the Sacrament of Matrimony

1638   "From a valid marriage arises *a bond* between the spouses which by its very nature is perpetual and exclusive; furthermore, in a Christian marriage the spouses are strengthened and, as it were, consecrated for the duties and the dignity of their state *by a special sacrament.*"[140]

The marriage bond

1639   The consent by which the spouses mutually give and receive one another is sealed by God himself.[141] From their covenant arises "an institution, confirmed by the divine law, . . . even in the eyes of society."[142] The covenant between the spouses is integrated into God's covenant with man: "Authentic married love is caught up into divine love."[143]

1640   Thus *the marriage bond* has been established by God himself in such a way that a marriage concluded and consummated between baptized persons can never be dissolved. This bond, which results from the free human act of the spouses and their consummation of the marriage, is a reality, henceforth irrevocable, and gives rise to a covenant guaranteed by God's fidelity. The Church does not have the power to contravene this disposition of divine wisdom.[144]   2365

The grace of the sacrament of Matrimony

1641   "By reason of their state in life and of their order, [Christian spouses] have their own special gifts in the People of God."[145] This grace proper to the sacrament of Matrimony is intended to perfect the couple's love and to strengthen their indissoluble unity. By this grace they "help one another to attain holiness in their married life and in welcoming and educating their children."[146]

1642   *Christ is the source of this grace.* "Just as of old God encoun-   1615
tered his people with a covenant of love and fidelity, so our Savior,   796
the spouse of the Church, now encounters Christian spouses through the sacrament of Matrimony."[147] Christ dwells with them,

---

140 Cf. CIC, can. 1134.
141 Cf. *Mk* 10:9.
142 *GS* 48 § 1.
143 *GS* 48 § 2.
144 Cf. CIC, can. 1141.
145 *LG* 11 § 2.
146 *LG* 11 § 2; cf. *LG* 41.

gives them the strength to take up their crosses and so follow him, to rise again after they have fallen, to forgive one another, to bear one another's burdens, to "be subject to one another out of reverence for Christ,"[148] and to love one another with supernatural, tender, and fruitful love. In the joys of their love and family life he gives them here on earth a foretaste of the wedding feast of the Lamb:

> How can I ever express the happiness of a marriage joined by the Church, strengthened by an offering, sealed by a blessing, announced by angels, and ratified by the Father? . . . How wonderful the bond between two believers, now one in hope, one in desire, one in discipline, one in the same service! They are both children of one Father and servants of the same Master, undivided in spirit and flesh, truly two in one flesh. Where the flesh is one, one also is the spirit.[149]

V.   THE GOODS AND REQUIREMENTS OF CONJUGAL LOVE

2361   **1643**   "Conjugal love involves a totality, in which all the elements of the person enter – appeal of the body and instinct, power of feeling and affectivity, aspiration of the spirit and of will. It aims at a deeply personal unity, a unity that, beyond union in one flesh, leads to forming one heart and soul; it demands *indissolubility* and *faithfulness* in definitive mutual giving; and it is open to *fertility*. In a word it is a question of the normal characteristics of all natural conjugal love, but with a new significance which not only purifies and strengthens them, but raises them to the extent of making them the expression of specifically Christian values."[150]

The unity and indissolubility of marriage

1644   The love of the spouses requires, of its very nature, the unity and indissolubility of the spouses' community of persons, which embraces their entire life: "so they are no longer two, but one flesh."[151] They "are called to grow continually in their communion through day-to-day fidelity to their marriage promise of total mutual self-giving."[152] This human communion is confirmed, purified, and completed by communion in Jesus Christ, given through the sacrament of Matrimony. It is deepened by lives of the common faith and by the Eucharist received together.

---

147   *GS* 48 § 2.
148   *Eph* 5:21; cf. *Gal* 6:2.
149   Tertullian, *Ad uxorem.* 2, 8, 6-7: PL 1, 1412-1413; cf. *FC* 13.
150   *FC* 13.
151   *Mt* 19:6; cf. *Gen* 2:24.
152   *FC* 19.

1645   "The unity of marriage, distinctly recognized by our Lord, is made clear in the equal personal dignity which must be accorded to man and wife in mutual and unreserved affection."[153] *Polygamy* is contrary to conjugal love which is undivided and exclusive.[154]   *369*

The fidelity of conjugal love   *2364-2365*

1646   By its very nature conjugal love requires the inviolable fidelity of the spouses. This is the consequence of the gift of themselves which they make to each other. Love seeks to be definitive; it cannot be an arrangement "until further notice." The "intimate union of marriage, as a mutual giving of two persons, and the good of the children, demand total fidelity from the spouses and require an unbreakable union between them."[155]

1647   The deepest reason is found in the fidelity of God to his covenant, in that of Christ to his Church. Through the sacrament of Matrimony the spouses are enabled to represent this fidelity and witness to it. Through the sacrament, the indissolubility of marriage receives a new and deeper meaning.

1648   It can seem difficult, even impossible, to bind oneself for life to another human being. This makes it all the more important to proclaim the Good News that God loves us with a definitive and irrevocable love, that married couples share in this love, that it supports and sustains them, and that by their own faithfulness they can be witnesses to God's faithful love. Spouses who with God's grace give this witness, often in very difficult conditions, deserve the gratitude and support of the ecclesial community.[156]

1649   Yet there are some situations in which living together becomes practically impossible for a variety of reasons. In such cases the Church permits the physical *separation* of the couple and their living apart. The   *2383* spouses do not cease to be husband and wife before God and so are not free to contract a new union. In this difficult situation, the best solution would be, if possible, reconciliation. The Christian community is called to help these persons live out their situation in a Christian manner and in fidelity to their marriage bond which remains indissoluble.[157]

1650   Today there are numerous Catholics in many countries who have   *2384* recourse to civil *divorce* and contract new civil unions. In fidelity to the words of Jesus Christ – "Whoever divorces his wife and marries another, commits adultery against her; and if she divorces her husband and marries

---

153   *GS* 49 § 2.
154   Cf. *FC* 19.
155   *GS* 48 § 1.
156   Cf. *FC* 20.
157   Cf. *FC* 83; CIC, cann. 1151-1155.

another, she commits adultery"[158] – the Church maintains that a new union cannot be recognized as valid, if the first marriage was. If the divorced are remarried civilly, they find themselves in a situation that objectively contravenes God's law. Consequently, they cannot receive Eucharistic communion as long as this situation persists. For the same reason, they cannot exercise certain ecclesial responsibilities. Reconciliation through the sacrament of Penance can be granted only to those who have repented for having violated the sign of the covenant and of fidelity to Christ, and who are committed to living in complete continence.

1651   Toward Christians who live in this situation, and who often keep the faith and desire to bring up their children in a Christian manner, priests and the whole community must manifest an attentive solicitude, so that they do not consider themselves separated from the Church, in whose life they can and must participate as baptized persons:

> They should be encouraged to listen to the Word of God, to attend the Sacrifice of the Mass, to persevere in prayer, to contribute to works of charity and to community efforts for justice, to bring up their children in the Christian faith, to cultivate the spirit and practice of penance and thus implore, day by day, God's grace.[159]

2366-2367 **The openness to fertility**

1652   "By its very nature the institution of marriage and married love is ordered to the procreation and education of the offspring and it is in them that it finds its crowning glory."[160]

372

> Children are the supreme gift of marriage and contribute greatly to the good of the parents themselves. God himself said: "It is not good that man should be alone," and "from the beginning [he] made them male and female"; wishing to associate them in a special way in his own creative work, God blessed man and woman with the words: "Be fruitful and multiply." Hence, true married love and the whole structure of family life which results from it, without diminishment of the other ends of marriage, are directed to disposing the spouses to cooperate valiantly with the love of the Creator and Savior, who through them will increase and enrich his family from day to day.[161]

1653   The fruitfulness of conjugal love extends to the fruits of the moral, spiritual, and supernatural life that parents hand on to their children by education. Parents are the principal and first educators of their children.[162] In this sense the fundamental task of marriage

2231   and family is to be at the service of life.[163]

---

158 *Mk* 10:11-12.
159 *FC* 84.
160 *GS* 48 § 1; 50.
161 *GS* 50 § 1; cf. *Gen* 2:18; *Mt* 19:4; *Gen* 1:28.

1654   Spouses to whom God has not granted children can nevertheless have a conjugal life full of meaning, in both human and Christian terms. Their marriage can radiate a fruitfulness of charity, of hospitality, and of sacrifice.

VI.   THE DOMESTIC CHURCH

1655   Christ chose to be born and grow up in the bosom of the holy family of Joseph and Mary. The Church is nothing other than "the family of God." From the beginning, the core of the Church   *759* was often constituted by those who had become believers "together with all [their] household."[164] When they were converted, they desired that "their whole household" should also be saved.[165] These families who became believers were islands of Christian life in an unbelieving world.

1656   In our own time, in a world often alien and even hostile to faith, believing families are of primary importance as centers of living, radiant faith. For this reason the Second Vatican Council, using an ancient expression, calls the family the *Ecclesia domestica*.[166] It is in the bosom of the family that parents are "by word and example . . . the   *2204* first heralds of the faith with regard to their children. They should encourage them in the vocation which is proper to each child, fostering with special care any religious vocation."[167]

1657   It is here that the father of the family, the mother, children, and all members of the family exercise the *priesthood of the baptized* in a privileged way "by the reception of the sacraments, prayer and   *1268* thanksgiving, the witness of a holy life, and self-denial and active charity."[168] Thus the home is the first school of Christian life and "a   *2214-2231* school for human enrichment."[169] Here one learns endurance and the joy of work, fraternal love, generous – even repeated – forgiveness, and above all divine worship in prayer and the offering of one's life.   *2685*

1658   We must also remember the great number of *single persons* who, because of the particular circumstances in which they have to live – often not of their choosing – are especially close to Jesus' heart and therefore deserve the special affection and active solicitude of the

---

162   Cf. *GE* 3.
163   Cf. *FC* 28.
164   Cf. *Acts* 18:8.
165   Cf. *Acts* 16:31; *Acts* 11:14.
166   *LG* 11; cf. *FC* 21.
167   *LG* 11.
168   *LG* 10.
169   *GS* 52 § 1.

Church, especially of pastors. Many remain *without a human family,* often due to conditions of poverty. Some live their situation in the spirit of the Beatitudes, serving God and neighbor in exemplary fashion. The doors of homes, the "domestic churches," and of the great family which is the Church must be open to all of them. "No one 2231 is without a family in this world: the Church is a home and family for 2233 everyone, especially those who 'labor and are heavy laden.'"[170]

IN BRIEF

1659 St. Paul said: "Husbands, love your wives, as Christ loved the Church. . . . This is a great mystery, and I mean in reference to Christ and the Church" (*Eph* 5:25, 32).

1660 The marriage covenant, by which a man and a woman form with each other an intimate communion of life and love, has been founded and endowed with its own special laws by the Creator. By its very nature it is ordered to the good of the couple, as well as to the generation and education of children. Christ the Lord raised marriage between the baptized to the dignity of a sacrament (cf. CIC, can. 1055 § 1; cf. *GS* 48 § 1).

1661 The sacrament of Matrimony signifies the union of Christ and the Church. It gives spouses the grace to love each other with the love with which Christ has loved his Church; the grace of the sacrament thus perfects the human love of the spouses, strengthens their indissoluble unity, and sanctifies them on the way to eternal life (cf. Council of Trent: DS 1799).

1662 Marriage is based on the consent of the contracting parties, that is, on their will to give themselves, each to the other, mutually and definitively, in order to live a covenant of faithful and fruitful love.

1663 Since marriage establishes the couple in a public state of life in the Church, it is fitting that its celebration be public, in the framework of a liturgical celebration, before the priest (or a witness authorized by the Church), the witnesses, and the assembly of the faithful.

1664 Unity, indissolubility, and openness to fertility are essential to marriage. Polygamy is incompatible with the unity of marriage; divorce separates what God has

---

170   *FC* 85; cf. *Mt* 11:28.

joined together; the refusal of fertility turns married life away from its "supreme gift," the child (*GS* 50 §1).

1665 The remarriage of persons divorced from a living, lawful spouse contravenes the plan and law of God as taught by Christ. They are not separated from the Church, but they cannot receive Eucharistic communion. They will lead Christian lives especially by educating their children in the faith.

1666 The Christian home is the place where children receive the first proclamation of the faith. For this reason the family home is rightly called "the domestic church," a community of grace and prayer, a school of human virtues and of Christian charity.

CHAPTER FOUR
OTHER LITURGICAL CELEBRATIONS

ARTICLE 1
SACRAMENTALS

1667 "Holy Mother Church has, moreover, instituted sacramentals. These are sacred signs which bear a resemblance to the sacraments. They signify effects, particularly of a spiritual nature, which are obtained through the intercession of the Church. By them men are disposed to receive the chief effect of the sacraments, and various occasions in life are rendered holy."[171]

The characteristics of sacramentals

1668 Sacramentals are instituted for the sanctification of certain ministries of the Church, certain states of life, a great variety of circumstances in Christian life, and the use of many things helpful to man. In accordance with bishops' pastoral decisions, they can also respond to the needs, culture, and special history of the Christian people of a particular region or time. They always include a prayer, often accompanied by a specific sign, such as the laying on of hands, the sign of the cross, or the sprinkling of holy water (which recalls Baptism).   *699, 2157*

---

171 *SC* 60; cf. CIC, can. 1166; CCEO, can. 867.

784 **1669**   Sacramentals derive from the baptismal priesthood: every
2626 baptized person is called to be a "blessing," and to bless.[172] Hence
lay people may preside at certain blessings; the more a blessing
concerns ecclesial and sacramental life, the more is its administration reserved to the ordained ministry (bishops, priests, or deacons).[173]

1128 **1670**   Sacramentals do not confer the grace of the Holy Spirit in
the way that the sacraments do, but by the Church's prayer, they
prepare us to receive grace and dispose us to cooperate with it. "For
2001 well-disposed members of the faithful, the liturgy of the sacraments and sacramentals sanctifies almost every event of their lives
with the divine grace which flows from the Paschal mystery of the
Passion, Death, and Resurrection of Christ. From this source all
sacraments and sacramentals draw their power. There is scarcely
any proper use of material things which cannot be thus directed
toward the sanctification of men and the praise of God."[174]

Various forms of sacramentals

1078 **1671**   Among sacramentals *blessings* (of persons, meals, objects, and
places) come first. Every blessing praises God and prays for his gifts. In
Christ, Christians are blessed by God the Father "with every spiritual
blessing."[175] This is why the Church imparts blessings by invoking the
name of Jesus, usually while making the holy sign of the cross of Christ.

1672   Certain blessings have a lasting importance because they *consecrate* persons to God, or reserve objects and places for liturgical use. Among
those blessings which are intended for persons – not to be confused with
sacramental ordination – are the blessing of the abbot or abbess of a
monastery, the consecration of virgins, the rite of religious profession and
923, 925 the blessing of certain ministries of the Church (readers, acolytes, cate-
903 chists, etc.). The dedication or blessing of a church or an altar, the blessing
of holy oils, vessels, and vestments, bells, etc., can be mentioned as examples of blessings that concern objects.

1673   When the Church asks publicly and authoritatively in the name
of Jesus Christ that a person or object be protected against the power of the
395 Evil One and withdrawn from his dominion, it is called *exorcism.* Jesus
performed exorcisms and from him the Church has received the power
550 and office of exorcizing.[176] In a simple form, exorcism is performed at the
1237 celebration of Baptism. The solemn exorcism, called "a major exorcism,"
can be performed only by a priest and with the permission of the bishop.
The priest must proceed with prudence, strictly observing the rules estab-

---

172 Cf. *Gen* 12:2; *Lk* 6:28; *Rom* 12:14; *1 Pet* 3:9.
173 Cf. *SC* 79; *CIC,* can. 1168; *De Ben* 16, 18.
174 *SC* 61.
175 *Eph* 1:3.
176 Cf. *Mk* 1:25-26; 3:15; 6:7, 13; 16:17.

lished by the Church. Exorcism is directed at the expulsion of demons or to the liberation from demonic possession through the spiritual authority which Jesus entrusted to his Church. Illness, especially psychological illness, is a very different matter; treating this is the concern of medical science. Therefore, before an exorcism is performed, it is important to ascertain that one is dealing with the presence of the Evil One, and not an illness.[177]

Popular piety

1674   Besides sacramental liturgy and sacramentals, catechesis must take into account the forms of piety and popular devotions *2688* among the faithful. The religious sense of the Christian people has always found expression in various forms of piety surrounding the Church's sacramental life, such as the veneration of relics, visits to sanctuaries, pilgrimages, processions, the stations of the cross, religious dances, the rosary, medals,[178] etc.   *2669, 2678*

1675   These expressions of piety extend the liturgical life of the Church, but do not replace it. They "should be so drawn up that they harmonize with the liturgical seasons, accord with the sacred liturgy, are in some way derived from it and lead the people to it, since in fact the liturgy by its very nature is far superior to any of them."[179]

1676   Pastoral discernment is needed to sustain and support popular piety and, if necessary, to purify and correct the religious sense which underlies these devotions so that the faithful may advance in knowledge of the mystery of Christ.[180] Their exercise is subject to the care and   *426* judgment of the bishops and to the general norms of the Church.

> At its core the piety of the people is a storehouse of values that offers answers of Christian wisdom to the great questions of life. The Catholic wisdom of the people is capable of fashioning a vital synthesis. . . . It creatively combines the divine and the human, Christ and Mary, spirit and body, communion and institution, person and community, faith and homeland, intelligence and emotion. This wisdom is a Christian humanism that radically affirms the dignity of every person as a child of God, establishes a basic fraternity, teaches people to encounter nature and understand work, provides reasons for joy and humor even in the midst of a very hard life. For the people this wisdom is also a principle of discernment and an evangelical instinct through which they spontaneously sense when the Gospel is served in the Church and when it is emptied of its content and stifled by other interests.[181]

---

177 Cf. CIC, can. 1172.
178 Cf. Council of Nicæa II: DS 601; 603; Council of Trent: DS 1822.
179 *SC* 13 § 3.
180 Cf. John Paul II, *CT* 54.
181 CELAM, Third General Conference (Puebla, 1979), Final Document, § 448 (tr. NCCB, 1979); cf. Paul VI, *EN* 48.

IN BRIEF

1677   Sacramentals are sacred signs instituted by the Church. They prepare men to receive the fruit of the sacraments and sanctify different circumstances of life.

1678   Among the sacramentals blessings occupy an important place. They include both praise of God for his works and gifts, and the Church's intercession for men that they may be able to use God's gifts according to the spirit of the Gospel.

1679   In addition to the liturgy, Christian life is nourished by various forms of popular piety, rooted in the different cultures. While carefully clarifying them in the light of faith, the Church fosters the forms of popular piety that express an evangelical instinct and a human wisdom and that enrich Christian life.

ARTICLE 2
CHRISTIAN FUNERALS

1525 **1680**   All the sacraments, and principally those of Christian initiation, have as their goal the last Passover of the child of God which, through death, leads him into the life of the Kingdom. Then what he confessed in faith and hope will be fulfilled: "I look for the resurrection of the dead, and the life of the world to come."[182]

I.   THE CHRISTIAN'S LAST PASSOVER

1010-1014 **1681**   The Christian meaning of death is revealed in the light of the *Paschal mystery* of the death and resurrection of Christ in whom resides our only hope. The Christian who dies in Christ Jesus is "away from the body and at home with the Lord."[183]

1682   For the Christian the day of death inaugurates, *at the end of his sacramental life*, the fulfillment of his new birth begun at Baptism, the definitive "conformity" to "the image of the Son" conferred by

---

182   Niceno-Constantinopolitan Creed.
183   *2 Cor* 5:8.

the anointing of the Holy Spirit, and participation in the feast of the Kingdom which was anticipated in the Eucharist — even if final purifications are still necessary for him in order to be clothed with the nuptial garment.

1683   The Church who, as Mother, has borne the Christian sacramentally in her womb during his earthly pilgrimage, accompanies him at his journey's end, in order to surrender him "into the   *1020* Father's hands." She offers to the Father, in Christ, the child of his grace, and she commits to the earth, in hope, the seed of the body that will rise in glory.[184] This offering is fully celebrated in the   *627* Eucharistic sacrifice; the blessings before and after Mass are sacramentals.

II.   THE CELEBRATION OF FUNERALS

1684   The Christian funeral confers on the deceased neither a sacrament nor a sacramental, since he has "passed" beyond the sacramental economy. It is nonetheless a liturgical celebration of the Church.[185] The ministry of the Church aims at expressing efficacious communion with *the deceased*, at the participation in that communion of *the community* gathered for the funeral and at the proclamation of eternal life to the community.

1685   The different funeral rites express the *Paschal character* of Christian death and are in keeping with the situations and traditions of each region, even as to the color of the liturgical vestments worn.[186]

1686   The *Order of Christian Funerals (Ordo exsequiarum)* of the Roman liturgy gives three types of funeral celebrations, corresponding to the three places in which they are conducted (the home, the church, and the cemetery), and according to the importance attached to them by the family, local customs, the culture, and popular piety. This order of celebration is common to all the liturgical traditions and comprises four principal elements:

1687   *The greeting of the community.* A greeting of faith begins the celebration. Relatives and friends of the deceased are welcomed with a word of "consolation" (in the New Testament sense of the Holy Spirit's power in hope).[187] The community assembling in prayer also awaits the "words of eternal life." The death of a member of the community (or the anniversary of a death, or the seventh or fortieth day after death) is an event that should lead beyond the perspectives of "this world" and should draw the faithful into the true perspective of faith in the risen Christ.

1688   The liturgy of the Word during funerals demands very careful preparation because the assembly present for the funeral may include some faithful who rarely attend the liturgy, and friends of the deceased

---

184   Cf. *1 Cor* 15:42-44.
185   Cf. *SC* 81-82.
186   Cf. *SC* 81.
187   Cf. *1 Thess* 4:18.

who are not Christians. The homily in particular must "avoid the literary genre of funeral eulogy"[188] and illumine the mystery of Christian death in the light of the risen Christ.

1689 *The Eucharistic Sacrifice.* When the celebration takes place in church, the Eucharist is the heart of the Paschal reality of Christian death.[189] In the Eucharist, the Church expresses her efficacious communion with the departed: offering to the Father in the Holy Spirit the sacrifice of the death and resurrection of Christ, she asks to purify his child of his sins and their consequences, and to admit him to the Paschal fullness of the table of the Kingdom.[190] It is by the Eucharist thus celebrated that the community of the faithful, especially the family of the deceased, learn to live in communion with the one who "has fallen asleep in the Lord," by communicating in the Body of Christ of which he is a living member and, then, by praying for him and with him.

1690 A *farewell* to the deceased is his final "commendation to God" by the Church. It is "the last farewell by which the Christian community greets one of its members before his body is brought to its tomb."[191] The Byzantine tradition expresses this by the kiss of farewell to the deceased:

> By this final greeting "we sing for his departure from this life and separation from us, but also because there is a communion and a reunion. For even dead, we are not at all separated from one another, because we all run the same course and we will find one another again in the same place. We shall never be separated, for we live for Christ, and now we are united with Christ as we go toward him . . . we shall all be together in Christ."[192]

---

188 *OCF* 41.
189 Cf. *OCF* 1.
190 Cf. *OCF* 57.
191 *OCF* 10.
192 St. Simeon of Thessalonica, *De ordine sepulturæ.* 336: PG 155, 684.

The central section of the sarcophagus of Junius Bassus, discovered underneath the "Confessio" of the Basilica of St. Peter in Rome and dating from the year 359.

Christ in glory, portrayed very young as a sign of his divinity, is seated on the throne of heaven, with Uranus, the pagan god of heaven, as his footstool. The apostles Peter and Paul stand on either side of Christ, toward whom they are turning and from whom they receive two scrolls: the new law.

As Moses had received the old law from God on Mount Sinai, now the apostles, represented by their two leaders, receive from Christ, the Son of God, the Lord of heaven and earth, the new law, no longer written on tablets of stone, but engraved by the Holy Spirit on the hearts of believers. Christ gives the strength to live according to the "new life" (§1697). He fulfills in us what he has commanded for our benefit (cf. §2074).

PART THREE

LIFE IN CHRIST

1691   "Christian, recognize your dignity and, now that you share in God's own nature, do not return to your former base condition by sinning. Remember who is your head and of whose body you are a member. Never forget that you have been rescued *790* from the power of darkness and brought into the light of the Kingdom of God."[1]

1692   The Symbol of the faith confesses the greatness of God's gifts to man in his work of creation, and even more in redemption and sanctification. What faith confesses, the sacraments communicate: by the sacraments of rebirth, Christians have become "children of God,"[2] "partakers of the divine nature."[3] Coming to see in the faith their new dignity, Christians are called to lead henceforth a life "worthy of the gospel of Christ."[4] They are made capable of doing so by the grace of Christ and the gifts of his Spirit, which they receive through the sacraments and through prayer.

1693   Christ Jesus always did what was pleasing to the *Father*,[5] and always lived in perfect communion with him. Likewise Christ's disciples are invited to live in the sight of the Father "who sees in secret,"[6] in order to become "perfect as your heavenly Father is perfect."[7]

1694   Incorporated into *Christ* by Baptism, Christians are "dead *1267* to sin and alive to God in Christ Jesus" and so participate in the life of the Risen Lord.[8] Following Christ and united with him,[9] Chris-

---

1   St. Leo the Great, *Sermo 21 in nat. Dom.*, 3: PL 54, 192C.
2   *Jn* 1:12; *1 Jn* 3:1.
3   *2 Pet* 1:4.
4   *Phil* 1:27.
5   Cf. *Jn* 8:29.
6   *Mt* 6:6.
7   *Mt* 5:48.
8   *Rom* 6:11 and cf. 6:5; cf. *Col* 2:12.
9   Cf. *Jn* 15:5.

tians can strive to be "imitators of God as beloved children, and walk in love"[10] by conforming their thoughts, words and actions to the "mind . . . which is yours in Christ Jesus,"[11] and by following his example.[12]

1695   "Justified in the name of the Lord Jesus Christ and in the Spirit of our God,"[13] "sanctified . . . [and] called to be saints,"[14] Christians have become the temple of the *Holy Spirit*.[15] This "Spirit of the Son" teaches them to pray to the Father[16] and, having become their life, prompts them to act so as to bear "the fruit of the Spirit"[17] by charity in action. Healing the wounds of sin, the Holy Spirit renews us interiorly through a spiritual transformation.[18] He enlightens and strengthens us to live as "children of light" through "all that is good and right and true."[19]

1696   The way of Christ "leads to life"; a contrary way "leads to destruction."[20] The Gospel parable of the *two ways* remains ever
1970 present in the catechesis of the Church; it shows the importance of moral decisions for our salvation: "There are two ways, the one of life, the other of death; but between the two, there is a great difference."[21]

1697   *Catechesis* has to reveal in all clarity the joy and the demands of the way of Christ.[22] Catechesis for the "newness of life"[23] in him should be:

737 ff.   — *a catechesis of the Holy Spirit,* the interior Master of life according to Christ, a gentle guest and friend who inspires, guides, corrects, and strengthens this life;

1988 ff.   — *a catechesis of grace,* for it is by grace that we are saved and again it is by grace that our works can bear fruit for eternal life;

---

10   *Eph* 5:1-2.
11   *Phil* 2:5.
12   Cf. *Jn* 13:12-16.
13   *1 Cor* 6:11.
14   *1 Cor* 1:2
15   Cf. *1 Cor* 6:19.
16   Cf. *Gal* 4:6.
17   *Gal* 5:22, 25.
18   Cf. *Eph* 4:23.
19   *Eph* 5:8, 9.
20   *Mt* 7:13; cf. *Deut* 30:15-20.
21   *Didache* 1, 1: SCh 248, 140.
22   Cf. John Paul II, *CT* 29.
23   *Rom* 6:4.

— *a catechesis of the beatitudes,* for the way of Christ is summed up *1716 ff.*
in the beatitudes, the only path that leads to the eternal beatitude
for which the human heart longs;

— *a catechesis of sin and forgiveness,* for unless man acknowledges *1846 ff.*
that he is a sinner he cannot know the truth about himself, which
is a condition for acting justly; and without the offer of forgiveness
he would not be able to bear this truth;

— *a catechesis of the human virtues* which causes one to grasp the *1803 ff.*
beauty and attraction of right dispositions towards goodness;

— *a catechesis of the Christian virtues* of faith, hope, and charity, *1812 ff.*
generously inspired by the example of the saints;

— *a catechesis of the twofold commandment of charity* set forth in the *2067 ff.*
Decalogue;

— *an ecclesial catechesis,* for it is through the manifold exchanges of *946 ff.*
"spiritual goods" in the "communion of saints" that Christian life
can grow, develop, and be communicated.

1698   The first and last point of reference of this catechesis will *426*
always be Jesus Christ himself, who is "the way, and the truth, and
the life."[24] It is by looking to him in faith that Christ's faithful can
hope that he himself fulfills his promises in them, and that, by
loving him with the same love with which he has loved them, they
may perform works in keeping with their dignity:

> I ask you to consider that our Lord Jesus Christ is your true
> head, and that you are one of his members. He belongs to
> you as the head belongs to its members; all that is his is yours:
> his spirit, his heart, his body and soul, and all his faculties.
> You must make use of all these as of your own, to serve,
> praise, love, and glorify God. You belong to him, as members
> belong to their head. And so he longs for you to use all that
> is in you, as if it were his own, for the service and glory of
> the Father.[25]
>
> For to me, to live is Christ.[26]

---

24   *Jn* 14:6.
25   St. John Eudes, *Tract. de admirabili corde Jesu,* 1, 5.
26   *Phil* 1:21.

Section One
Man's Vocation
Life in the Spirit

1699 Life in the Holy Spirit fulfills the vocation of man (*chapter one*). This life is made up of divine charity and human solidarity (*chapter two*). It is graciously offered as salvation (*chapter three*).

Chapter One
The Dignity of the Human Person

356 **1700** The dignity of the human person is rooted in his creation in the image and likeness of God (*article 1*); it is fulfilled in his vocation to divine beatitude (*article 2*). It is essential to a human being freely to direct himself to this fulfillment (*article 3*). By his deliberate actions (*article 4*), the human person does, or does not, conform to the good promised by God and attested by moral conscience (*article 5*). Human beings make their own contribution to their interior growth; they make their whole sentient and spiritual lives into means of this growth (*article 6*). With the help of grace they grow in virtue (*article 7*), avoid sin, and if they sin they entrust
1439 themselves as did the prodigal son[1] to the mercy of our Father in heaven (*article 8*). In this way they attain to the perfection of charity.

ARTICLE 1
MAN: THE IMAGE OF GOD

359 **1701** "Christ, . . . in the very revelation of the mystery of the Father and of his love, makes man fully manifest to himself and brings to light his exalted vocation."[2] It is in Christ, "the image of the invisible God,"[3] that man has been created "in the image and likeness" of the Creator. It is in Christ, Redeemer and Savior, that the divine image, disfigured in man by the first sin, has been restored to its original beauty and ennobled by the grace of God.[4]

---

1 *Lk* 15:11-32.
2 *GS* 22.
3 *Col* 1:15; cf. 2 *Cor* 4:4.
4 Cf. *GS* 22.

1702   The divine image is present in every man. It shines forth *1878*
in the communion of persons, in the likeness of the union of the
divine persons among themselves (cf. *chapter two*).

1703   Endowed with "a spiritual and immortal" soul,[5] the hu- *363*
man person is "the only creature on earth that God has willed for
its own sake."[6] From his conception, he is destined for eternal *2258*
beatitude.

1704   The human person participates in the light and power of
the divine Spirit. By his reason, he is capable of understanding the
order of things established by the Creator. By free will, he is capable *339*
of directing himself toward his true good. He finds his perfection
"in seeking and loving what is true and good."[7]   *30*

1705   By virtue of his soul and his spiritual powers of intellect
and will, man is endowed with freedom, an "outstanding manifes- *1730*
tation of the divine image."[8]

1706   By his reason, man recognizes the voice of God which
urges him "to do what is good and avoid what is evil."[9] Everyone
is obliged to follow this law, which makes itself heard in conscience
and is fulfilled in the love of God and of neighbor. Living a moral *1776*
life bears witness to the dignity of the person.

1707   "Man, enticed by the Evil One, abused his freedom at the
very beginning of history."[10] He succumbed to temptation and did
what was evil. He still desires the good, but his nature bears the *397*
wound of original sin. He is now inclined to evil and subject to
error:

> Man is divided in himself. As a result, the whole life of men,
> both individual and social, shows itself to be a struggle, and
> a dramatic one, between good and evil, between light and
> darkness.[11]

1708   By his Passion, Christ delivered us from Satan and from *617*
sin. He merited for us the new life in the Holy Spirit. His grace
restores what sin had damaged in us.

---

5   *GS* 14 § 2.
6   *GS* 24 § 3.
7   *GS* 15 § 2.
8   *GS* 17.
9   *GS* 16.
10   *GS* 13 § 1.
11   *GS* 13 § 2.

1265 **1709** He who believes in Christ becomes a son of God. This filial adoption transforms him by giving him the ability to follow the example of Christ. It makes him capable of acting rightly and doing good. In union with his Savior, the disciple attains the perfection of charity which is holiness. Having matured in grace, the moral *1050* life blossoms into eternal life in the glory of heaven.

IN BRIEF

1710 "Christ . . . makes man fully manifest to man himself and brings to light his exalted vocation" (*GS* 22 § 1).

1711 Endowed with a spiritual soul, with intellect and with free will, the human person is from his very conception ordered to God and destined for eternal beatitude. He pursues his perfection in "seeking and loving what is true and good" (*GS* 15 § 2).

1712 In man, true freedom is an "outstanding manifestation of the divine image" (*GS* 17).

1713 Man is obliged to follow the moral law, which urges him "to do what is good and avoid what is evil" (cf. *GS* 16). This law makes itself heard in his conscience.

1714 Man, having been wounded in his nature by original sin, is subject to error and inclined to evil in exercising his freedom.

1715 He who believes in Christ has new life in the Holy Spirit. The moral life, increased and brought to maturity in grace, is to reach its fulfillment in the glory of heaven.

Article 2
OUR VOCATION TO BEATITUDE

I.   The Beatitudes

1716 The Beatitudes are at the heart of Jesus' preaching. They take up the promises made to the chosen people since Abraham. The Beatitudes fulfill the promises by ordering them no longer merely to the possession of a territory, but to the Kingdom of heaven:

> Blessed are the poor in spirit, for theirs is the kingdom of heaven.
> Blessed are those who mourn, for they shall be comforted.
> Blessed are the meek, for they shall inherit the earth.
> Blessed are those who hunger and thirst for righteousness, for they shall be satisfied.
> Blessed are the merciful, for they shall obtain mercy.
> Blessed are the pure in heart, for they shall see God.
> Blessed are the peacemakers, for they shall be called sons of God.
> Blessed are those who are persecuted for righteousness' sake,
> for theirs is the kingdom of heaven.
> Blessed are you when men revile you and persecute you
> and utter all kinds of evil against you falsely on my account.
> Rejoice and be glad,
> for your reward is great in heaven.[12]

2546

1717 The Beatitudes depict the countenance of Jesus Christ and portray his charity. They express the vocation of the faithful associated with the glory of his Passion and Resurrection; they shed light on the actions and attitudes characteristic of the Christian life; they are the paradoxical promises that sustain hope in the midst of tribulations; they proclaim the blessings and rewards already secured, however dimly, for Christ's disciples; they have begun in the lives of the Virgin Mary and all the saints.

459

1820

II.   The Desire for Happiness

1718 The Beatitudes respond to the natural desire for happiness. This desire is of divine origin: God has placed it in the human heart in order to draw man to the One who alone can fulfill it:

27, 1024

> We all want to live happily; in the whole human race there is no one who does not assent to this proposition, even before it is fully articulated.[13]

> How is it, then, that I seek you, Lord? Since in seeking you, my God, I seek a happy life, let me seek you so that my soul may live, for my body draws life from my soul and my soul draws life from you.[14]

2541

> God alone satisfies.[15]

---

12   *Mt* 5:3-12.
13   St. Augustine, *De moribus eccl.* 1, 3, 4: PL 32, 1312.
14   St. Augustine, *Conf.* 10, 20: PL 32, 791.
15   St. Thomas Aquinas, *Expos. in symb. apost.* I.

_1950_ **1719** The Beatitudes reveal the goal of human existence, the ultimate end of human acts: God calls us to his own beatitude. This vocation is addressed to each individual personally, but also to the Church as a whole, the new people made up of those who have accepted the promise and live from it in faith.

III. CHRISTIAN BEATITUDE

_1027_ **1720** The New Testament uses several expressions to characterize the beatitude to which God calls man:

– the coming of the Kingdom of God;[16]

– the vision of God: "Blessed are the pure in heart, for they shall see God";[17]

– entering into the joy of the Lord;[18]

– entering into God's rest:[19]

> There we shall rest and see, we shall see and love, we shall love and praise. Behold what will be at the end without end. For what other end do we have, if not to reach the kingdom which has no end?[20]

1721 God put us in the world to know, to love, and to serve him, and so to come to paradise. Beatitude makes us "partakers of the divine nature" and of eternal life.[21] With beatitude, man enters into _260_ the glory of Christ[22] and into the joy of the Trinitarian life.

1722 Such beatitude surpasses the understanding and powers of man. It comes from an entirely free gift of God: whence it is called _1028_ supernatural, as is the grace that disposes man to enter into the divine joy.

> "Blessed are the pure in heart, for they shall see God." It is true, because of the greatness and inexpressible glory of God, that "man shall not see me and live," for the Father cannot be grasped. But because of God's love and goodness toward us, and because he can do all things, he goes so far as to grant those who love him the privilege of seeing him. . . . For "what
> _294_ is impossible for men is possible for God."[23]

---

16 Cf. _Mt_ 4:17.

17 _Mt_ 5:8; cf. _1 Jn_ 2; _1 Cor_ 13:12.

18 _Mt_ 25:21-23.

19 Cf. _Heb_ 4:7-11.

20 St. Augustine, _De civ. Dei_ 22, 30, 5: PL 41, 804.

21 _2 Pet_ 1:4; cf. _Jn_ 17:3.

22 Cf. _Rom_ 8:18.

23 St. Irenaeus, _Adv. haeres._ 4, 20, 5: PG 7/1, 1034-1035.

1723 The beatitude we are promised confronts us with decisive moral choices. It invites us to purify our hearts of bad instincts and to seek the love of God above all else. It teaches us that true *2519* happiness is not found in riches or well-being, in human fame or power, or in any human achievement – however beneficial it may be – such as science, technology, and art, or indeed in any creature, but in God alone, the source of every good and of all love: *227*

> All bow down before wealth. Wealth is that to which the multitude of men pay an instinctive homage. They measure happiness by wealth; and by wealth they measure respectability. . . . It is a homage resulting from a profound faith . . . that with wealth he may do all things. Wealth is one idol of the day and notoriety is a second. . . . Notoriety, or the making of a noise in the world – it may be called "newspaper fame" – has come to be considered a great good in itself, and a ground of veneration.[24]

1724 The Decalogue, the Sermon on the Mount, and the apostolic catechesis describe for us the paths that lead to the Kingdom of heaven. Sustained by the grace of the Holy Spirit, we tread them, step by step, by everyday acts. By the working of the Word of Christ, we slowly bear fruit in the Church to the glory of God.[25]

IN BRIEF

1725 The Beatitudes take up and fulfill God's promises from Abraham on by ordering them to the Kingdom of heaven. They respond to the desire for happiness that God has placed in the human heart.

1726 The Beatitudes teach us the final end to which God calls us: the Kingdom, the vision of God, participation in the divine nature, eternal life, filiation, rest in God.

1727 The beatitude of eternal life is a gratuitous gift of God. It is supernatural, as is the grace that leads us there.

1728 The Beatitudes confront us with decisive choices concerning earthly goods; they purify our hearts in order to teach us to love God above all things.

---

24 John Henry Cardinal Newman, "Saintliness the Standard of Christian Principle," in *Discourses to Mixed Congregations* (London: Longmans, Green and Co., 1906) V, 89-90.

25 Cf. the parable of the sower: *Mt* 13:3-23.

1729   The beatitude of heaven sets the standards for discernment in the use of earthly goods in keeping with the law of God.

ARTICLE 3
MAN'S FREEDOM

1730   God created man a rational being, conferring on him the dignity of a person who can initiate and control his own actions. "God willed that man should be 'left in the hand of his own counsel,' so that he might of his own accord seek his Creator and
30   freely attain his full and blessed perfection by cleaving to him."[26]

> Man is rational and therefore like God; he is created with free will and is master over his acts.[27]

I.   FREEDOM AND RESPONSIBILITY

1731   Freedom is the power, rooted in reason and will, to act or not to act, to do this or that, and so to perform deliberate actions on one's own responsibility. By free will one shapes one's own life.
1721 Human freedom is a force for growth and maturity in truth and goodness; it attains its perfection when directed toward God, our beatitude.

1732   As long as freedom has not bound itself definitively to its
396   ultimate good which is God, there is the possibility of *choosing*
1849 *between good and evil*, and thus of growing in perfection or of failing and sinning. This freedom characterizes properly human acts. It is
2006 the basis of praise or blame, merit or reproach.

1803 **1733**   The more one does what is good, the freer one becomes. There is no true freedom except in the service of what is good and just. The choice to disobey and do evil is an abuse of freedom and leads to "the slavery of sin."[28]

1036 **1734**   Freedom makes man *responsible* for his acts to the extent
1804 that they are voluntary. Progress in virtue, knowledge of the good, and ascesis enhance the mastery of the will over its acts.

---

26   *GS* 17; *Sir* 15:14.
27   St. Irenaeus, *Adv. haeres.* 4, 4, 3: PG 7/1, 983.
28   Cf. *Rom* 6:17.

1735   *Imputability* and responsibility for an action can be diminished or even nullified by ignorance, inadvertence, duress, fear, habit,
inordinate attachments, and other psychological or social factors.   *597*

1736   Every act directly willed is imputable to its author: *2568*

Thus the Lord asked Eve after the sin in the garden: "What is this
that you have done?"[29] He asked Cain the same question.[30] The prophet
Nathan questioned David in the same way after he committed adultery
with the wife of Uriah and had him murdered.[31]

An action can be indirectly voluntary when it results from negligence regarding something one should have known or done: for example,
an accident arising from ignorance of traffic laws.

1737   An effect can be tolerated without being willed by its agent; for   *2263*
instance, a mother's exhaustion from tending her sick child. A bad effect
is not imputable if it was not willed either as an end or as a means of an
action, e.g., a death a person incurs in aiding someone in danger. For a bad
effect to be imputable it must be foreseeable and the agent must have the
possibility of avoiding it, as in the case of manslaughter caused by a
drunken driver.

1738   Freedom is exercised in relationships between human beings. Every human person, created in the image of God, has the
natural right to be recognized as a free and responsible being. All
owe to each other this duty of respect. The *right to the exercise of
freedom*, especially in moral and religious matters, is an inalienable
requirement of the dignity of the human person. This right must   *2106*
be recognized and protected by civil authority within the limits of
the common good and public order.[32]   *2109*

II.   HUMAN FREEDOM IN THE ECONOMY OF SALVATION

1739   *Freedom and sin.* Man's freedom is limited and fallible. In   *387*
fact, man failed. He freely sinned. By refusing God's plan of love,
he deceived himself and became a slave to sin. This first alienation
engendered a multitude of others. From its outset, human history   *401*
attests the wretchedness and oppression born of the human heart
in consequence of the abuse of freedom.

---

29   *Gen* 3:13.
30   Cf. *Gen* 4:10.
31   Cf. *2 Sam* 12:7-15.
32   Cf. *DH* 2 § 7.

2108 **1740**   *Threats to freedom.* The exercise of freedom does not imply a right to say or do everything. It is false to maintain that man, "the subject of this freedom," is "an individual who is fully self-sufficient and whose finality is the satisfaction of his own interests in the enjoyment of earthly goods."[33] Moreover, the economic, social, political, and cultural conditions that are needed for a just exercise of freedom are too often disregarded or violated. Such situations *1887* of blindness and injustice injure the moral life and involve the strong as well as the weak in the temptation to sin against charity. By deviating from the moral law man violates his own freedom, becomes imprisoned within himself, disrupts neighborly fellowship, and rebels against divine truth.

1741   *Liberation and salvation.* By his glorious Cross Christ has won salvation for all men. He redeemed them from the sin that held them in bondage. "For freedom Christ has set us free."[34] In him we *782* have communion with the "truth that makes us free."[35] The Holy Spirit has been given to us and, as the Apostle teaches, "Where the Spirit of the Lord is, there is freedom."[36] Already we glory in the "liberty of the children of God."[37]

1742   *Freedom and grace.* The grace of Christ is not in the slightest way a rival of our freedom when this freedom accords with the *2002* sense of the true and the good that God has put in the human heart. On the contrary, as Christian experience attests especially in prayer, the more docile we are to the promptings of grace, the more we grow in inner freedom and confidence during trials, such as *1784* those we face in the pressures and constraints of the outer world. By the working of grace the Holy Spirit educates us in spiritual freedom in order to make us free collaborators in his work in the Church and in the world:

> Almighty and merciful God,
> in your goodness take away from us all that is harmful,
> so that, made ready both in mind and body,
> we may freely accomplish your will.[38]

---

33 CDF, instruction, *Libertatis conscientia* 13.
34 *Gal* 5:1.
35 Cf. *Jn* 8:32.
36 *2 Cor* 17.
37 *Rom* 8:21.
38 *Roman Missal,* 32nd Sunday, Opening Prayer: *Omnipotens et misericors Deus, universa nobis adversantia propitiatus exclude, ut, mente et corpore pariter expediti, quæ tua sunt liberis mentibus exsequamur.*

IN BRIEF

1743 "God willed that man should be left in the hand of his own counsel (cf. *Sir* 15:14), so that he might of his own accord seek his creator and freely attain his full and blessed perfection by cleaving to him" (*GS* 17 § 1).

1744 Freedom is the power to act or not to act, and so to perform deliberate acts of one's own. Freedom attains perfection in its acts when directed toward God, the sovereign Good.

1745 Freedom characterizes properly human acts. It makes the human being responsible for acts of which he is the voluntary agent. His deliberate acts properly belong to him.

1746 The imputability or responsibility for an action can be diminished or nullified by ignorance, duress, fear, and other psychological or social factors.

1747 The right to the exercise of freedom, especially in religious and moral matters, is an inalienable requirement of the dignity of man. But the exercise of freedom does not entail the putative right to say or do anything.

1748 "For freedom Christ has set us free" (*Gal* 5:1).

ARTICLE 4
THE MORALITY OF HUMAN ACTS

1749 Freedom makes man a moral subject. When he acts deliberately, man is, so to speak, the *father of his acts*. Human acts, that is, acts that are freely chosen in consequence of a judgment of 1732 conscience, can be morally evaluated. They are either good or evil.

I. THE SOURCES OF MORALITY

1750 The morality of human acts depends on:

– the object chosen;

– the end in view or the intention;

– the circumstances of the action.

The object, the intention, and the circumstances make up the "sources," or constitutive elements, of the morality of human acts.

1751   The *object* chosen is a good toward which the will deliberately directs itself. It is the matter of a human act. The object chosen morally specifies the act of the will, insofar as reason recognizes and judges it to be or not to be in conformity with the true good. Objective norms of morality express the rational order of good and 1794 evil, attested to by conscience.

1752   In contrast to the object, the *intention* resides in the acting subject. Because it lies at the voluntary source of an action and determines it by its end, intention is an element essential to the moral evaluation of an action. The end is the first goal of the 2520 intention and indicates the purpose pursued in the action. The intention is a movement of the will toward the end: it is concerned with the goal of the activity. It aims at the good anticipated from the action undertaken. Intention is not limited to directing individual actions, but can guide several actions toward one and the same purpose; it can orient one's whole life toward its ultimate end. For 1731 example, a service done with the end of helping one's neighbor can at the same time be inspired by the love of God as the ultimate end of all our actions. One and the same action can also be inspired by several intentions, such as performing a service in order to obtain a favor or to boast about it.

1753   A good intention (for example, that of helping one's neighbor) does not make behavior that is intrinsically disordered, such as lying and calumny, good or just. The end does not justify the 2479 means. Thus the condemnation of an innocent person cannot be justified as a legitimate means of saving the nation. On the other 596 hand, an added bad intention (such as vainglory) makes an act evil that, in and of itself, can be good (such as almsgiving).[39]

1754   The *circumstances*, including the consequences, are secondary elements of a moral act. They contribute to increasing or diminishing the moral goodness or evil of human acts (for example, the amount of a theft). They can also diminish or increase the agent's responsibility (such as acting out of a fear of death). Cir- 1735 cumstances of themselves cannot change the moral quality of acts themselves; they can make neither good nor right an action that is in itself evil.

---

39   Cf. *Mt* 6:2-4.

II. GOOD ACTS AND EVIL ACTS

1755   A *morally good* act requires the goodness of the object, of the end, and of the circumstances together. An evil end corrupts the action, even if the object is good in itself (such as praying and fasting "in order to be seen by men").

The *object of the choice* can by itself vitiate an act in its entirety. There are some concrete acts – such as fornication – that it is always wrong to choose, because choosing them entails a disorder of the will, that is, a moral evil.

1756   It is therefore an error to judge the morality of human acts by considering only the intention that inspires them or the circumstances (environment, social pressure, duress or emergency, etc.) which supply their context. There are acts which, in and of themselves, independently of circumstances and intentions, are always gravely illicit by reason of their object; such as blasphemy and perjury, murder and adultery. One may not do evil so that good *1789* may result from it.

IN BRIEF

1757   The object, the intention, and the circumstances make up the three "sources" of the morality of human acts.

1758   The object chosen morally specifies the act of willing accordingly as reason recognizes and judges it good or evil.

1759   "An evil action cannot be justified by reference to a good intention" (cf. St. Thomas Aquinas, *Dec. praec.* 6). The end does not justify the means.

1760   A morally good act requires the goodness of its object, of its end, and of its circumstances together.

1761   There are concrete acts that it is always wrong to choose, because their choice entails a disorder of the will, i.e., a moral evil. One may not do evil so that good may result from it.

ARTICLE 5
THE MORALITY OF THE PASSIONS

1762   The human person is ordered to beatitude by his deliberate acts: the passions or feelings he experiences can dispose him to it and contribute to it.

I.   PASSIONS

1763   The term "passions" belongs to the Christian patrimony. Feelings or passions are emotions or movements of the sensitive appetite that incline us to act or not to act in regard to something felt or imagined to be good or evil.

1764   The passions are natural components of the human psyche; they form the passageway and ensure the connection between the life of the senses and the life of the mind. Our Lord called man's
368   heart the source from which the passions spring.[40]

1765   There are many passions. The most fundamental passion is love, aroused by the attraction of the good. Love causes a desire for the absent good and the hope of obtaining it; this movement finds completion in the pleasure and joy of the good possessed. The apprehension of evil causes hatred, aversion, and fear of the impending evil; this movement ends in sadness at some present evil, or in the anger that resists it.

1766   "To love is to will the good of another."[41] All other affections have their source in this first movement of the human heart
1704   toward the good. Only the good can be loved.[42] Passions "are evil if love is evil and good if it is good."[43]

II.   PASSIONS AND MORAL LIFE

1767   In themselves passions are neither good nor evil. They are morally qualified only to the extent that they effectively engage
1860   reason and will. Passions are said to be voluntary, "either because they are commanded by the will or because the will does not place

---

40 Cf. *Mk* 7:21.
41 St. Thomas Aquinas, *STh* I-II, 26, 4, *corp. art.*
42 Cf. St. Augustine, *De Trin.*, 8, 3, 4: PL 42, 949-950.
43 St. Augustine, *De civ. Dei* 14, 7, 2: PL 41, 410.

obstacles in their way."[44] It belongs to the perfection of the moral or human good that the passions be governed by reason.[45]

1768 Strong feelings are not decisive for the morality or the holiness of persons; they are simply the inexhaustible reservoir of images and affections in which the moral life is expressed. Passions are morally good when they contribute to a good action, evil in the opposite case. The upright will orders the movements of the senses it appropriates to the good and to beatitude; an evil will succumbs to disordered passions and exacerbates them. Emotions and feelings can be taken up into the *virtues* or perverted by the *vices*.   *1803, 1865*

1769 In the Christian life, the Holy Spirit himself accomplishes his work by mobilizing the whole being, with all its sorrows, fears and sadness, as is visible in the Lord's agony and passion. In Christ human feelings are able to reach their consummation in charity and divine beatitude.

1770 Moral perfection consists in man's being moved to the good not by his will alone, but also by his sensitive appetite, as in the words of the psalm: "My heart and flesh sing for joy to the living *30* God."[46]

IN BRIEF

1771 The term "passions" refers to the affections or the feelings. By his emotions man intuits the good and suspects evil.

1772 The principal passions are love and hatred, desire and fear, joy, sadness, and anger.

1773 In the passions, as movements of the sensitive appetite, there is neither moral good nor evil. But insofar as they engage reason and will, there is moral good or evil in them.

1774 Emotions and feelings can be taken up in the virtues or perverted by the vices.

---

44 St. Thomas Aquinas, *STh* I-II, 24, 1 *corp. art.*
45 Cf. St. Thomas Aquinas, *STh* I-II, 24, 3.
46 *Ps* 84:2.

1775   The perfection of the moral good consists in man's being moved to the good not only by his will but also by his "heart."

ARTICLE 6
MORAL CONSCIENCE

1776   "Deep within his conscience man discovers a law which he has not laid upon himself but which he must obey. Its voice,
1954   ever calling him to love and to do what is good and to avoid evil, sounds in his heart at the right moment.... For man has in his heart a law inscribed by God.... His conscience is man's most secret core and his sanctuary. There he is alone with God whose voice echoes in his depths."[47]

I.   THE JUDGMENT OF CONSCIENCE

1777   Moral conscience,[48] present at the heart of the person, enjoins him at the appropriate moment to do good and to avoid evil. It also judges particular choices, approving those that are good and denouncing those that are evil.[49] It bears witness to the authority of truth in reference to the supreme Good to which the human
1766   person is drawn, and it welcomes the commandments. When he
2071   listens to his conscience, the prudent man can hear God speaking.

1778   Conscience is a judgment of reason whereby the human person recognizes the moral quality of a concrete act that he is
1749   going to perform, is in the process of performing, or has already completed. In all he says and does, man is obliged to follow faithfully what he knows to be just and right. It is by the judgment of his conscience that man perceives and recognizes the prescriptions of the divine law:

> Conscience is a law of the mind; yet [Christians] would not grant that it is nothing more; I mean that it was not a dictate, nor conveyed the notion of responsibility, of duty, of a threat and a promise.... [Conscience] is a messenger of him, who, both in nature and in grace, speaks to us behind a veil, and

---

47   *GS* 16.
48   Cf. *Rom* 2:14-16.
49   Cf. *Rom* 1:32.

teaches and rules us by his representatives. Conscience is the aboriginal Vicar of Christ.[50]

1779   It is important for every person to be sufficiently present to himself in order to hear and follow the voice of his conscience. This requirement of *interiority* is all the more necessary as life often   *1886* distracts us from any reflection, self-examination or introspection:

> Return to your conscience, question it. . . . Turn inward, brethren, and in everything you do, see God as your witness.[51]

1780   The dignity of the human person implies and requires *uprightness of moral conscience.* Conscience includes the perception of the principles of morality (synderesis); their application in the given circumstances by practical discernment of reasons and goods; and finally judgment about concrete acts yet to be performed or already performed. The truth about the moral good, stated in the law of reason, is recognized practically and concretely by the *prudent judgment* of conscience. We call that man prudent who chooses in conformity with this judgment.   *1806*

1781   Conscience enables one to assume *responsibility* for the acts   *1731* performed. If man commits evil, the just judgment of conscience can remain within him as the witness to the universal truth of the good, at the same time as the evil of his particular choice. The verdict of the judgment of conscience remains a pledge of hope and mercy. In attesting to the fault committed, it calls to mind the forgiveness that must be asked, the good that must still be practiced, and the virtue that must be constantly cultivated with the grace of God:

> We shall . . . reassure our hearts before him whenever our hearts condemn us; for God is greater than our hearts, and he knows everything.[52]

1782   Man has the right to act in conscience and in freedom so as personally to make moral decisions. "He must not be forced to act contrary to his conscience. Nor must he be prevented from acting according to his conscience, especially in religious matters."[53]   *2106*

---

50 John Henry Cardinal Newman, "Letter to the Duke of Norfolk," V, in *Certain Difficulties felt by Anglicans in Catholic Teaching* II (London: Longmans Green, 1885), 248.
51 St. Augustine, *In ep Jo.* 8, 9: PL 35, 2041.
52 *1 Jn* 3:19-20.
53 *DH* 3 § 2.

II.   THE FORMATION OF CONSCIENCE

1783   Conscience must be informed and moral judgment enlightened. A well-formed conscience is upright and truthful. It formulates its judgments according to reason, in conformity with the true good willed by the wisdom of the Creator. The education of conscience is indispensable for human beings who are subjected to negative influences and tempted by sin to prefer their own *2039* judgment and to reject authoritative teachings.

1784   The education of the conscience is a lifelong task. From the earliest years, it awakens the child to the knowledge and practice of the interior law recognized by conscience. Prudent education teaches virtue; it prevents or cures fear, selfishness and pride, resentment arising from guilt, and feelings of complacency, born of human weakness and faults. The education of the conscience *1742* guarantees freedom and engenders peace of heart.

1785   In the formation of conscience the Word of God is the light for our path;[54] we must assimilate it in faith and prayer and put it into practice. We must also examine our conscience before the Lord's Cross. We are assisted by the gifts of the Holy Spirit, aided by the witness or advice of others and guided by the authoritative *890* teaching of the Church.[55]

III.   TO CHOOSE IN ACCORD WITH CONSCIENCE

1786   Faced with a moral choice, conscience can make either a right judgment in accordance with reason and the divine law or, on the contrary, an erroneous judgment that departs from them.

1787   Man is sometimes confronted by situations that make moral judgments less assured and decision difficult. But he must always seriously seek what is right and good and discern the will *1955* of God expressed in divine law.

1788   To this purpose, man strives to interpret the data of experience and the signs of the times assisted by the virtue of prudence, *1806* by the advice of competent people, and by the help of the Holy Spirit and his gifts.

---

54 Cf. *Ps* 119:105.
55 Cf. *DH* 14.

1789 Some rules apply in every case:

– One may never do evil so that good may result from it; *1756*

– the Golden Rule: "Whatever you wish that men would do to you, *1970* do so to them."[56]

– charity always proceeds by way of respect for one's neighbor and *1827* his conscience: "Thus sinning against your brethren and wounding *1971* their conscience . . . you sin against Christ."[57] Therefore "it is right not to . . . do anything that makes your brother stumble."[58]

IV.   ERRONEOUS JUDGMENT

1790 A human being must always obey the certain judgment of his conscience. If he were deliberately to act against it, he would condemn himself. Yet it can happen that moral conscience remains in ignorance and makes erroneous judgments about acts to be performed or already committed.

1791 This ignorance can often be imputed to personal responsibility. This is the case when a man "takes little trouble to find out what is true and good, or when conscience is by degrees almost *1704* blinded through the habit of committing sin."[59] In such cases, the person is culpable for the evil he commits.

1792 Ignorance of Christ and his Gospel, bad example given by *133* others, enslavement to one's passions, assertion of a mistaken notion of autonomy of conscience, rejection of the Church's authority and her teaching, lack of conversion and of charity: these can be at the source of errors of judgment in moral conduct.

1793 If – on the contrary – the ignorance is invincible, or the *1860* moral subject is not responsible for his erroneous judgment, the evil committed by the person cannot be imputed to him. It remains no less an evil, a privation, a disorder. One must therefore work to correct the errors of moral conscience.

1794 A good and pure conscience is enlightened by true faith, for charity proceeds at the same time "from a pure heart and a good conscience and sincere faith."[60]

---

56   *Mt* 7:12; cf. *Lk* 6:31; *Tob* 4:15.
57   *1 Cor* 8:12.
58   *Rom* 14:21.
59   *GS* 16.
60   *1 Tim* 5; cf. 3:9; *2 Tim* 3; *1 Pet* 3:21; *Acts* 24:16.

1751   The more a correct conscience prevails, the more do persons
                and groups turn aside from blind choice and try to be guided
                by objective standards of moral conduct.[61]

IN BRIEF

1795   "Conscience is man's most secret core, and his sanctu-
            ary. There he is alone with God whose voice echoes in
            his depths" (*GS* 16).

1796   Conscience is a judgment of reason by which the
            human person recognizes the moral quality of a con-
            crete act.

1797   For the man who has committed evil, the verdict of his
            conscience remains a pledge of conversion and of hope.

1798   A well-formed conscience is upright and truthful. It
            formulates its judgments according to reason, in con-
            formity with the true good willed by the wisdom of
            the Creator. Everyone must avail himself of the means
            to form his conscience.

1799   Faced with a moral choice, conscience can make either
            a right judgment in accordance with reason and the
            divine law or, on the contrary, an erroneous judgment
            that departs from them.

1800   A human being must always obey the certain judg-
            ment of his conscience.

1801   Conscience can remain in ignorance or make errone-
            ous judgments. Such ignorance and errors are not
            always free of guilt.

1802   The Word of God is a light for our path. We must
            assimilate it in faith and prayer and put it into practice.
            This is how moral conscience is formed.

---

61   *GS* 16.

ARTICLE 7
THE VIRTUES

1803 "Whatever is true, whatever is honorable, whatever is just, whatever is pure, whatever is lovely, whatever is gracious, if there is any excellence, if there is anything worthy of praise, think about these things."[62]

A virtue is an habitual and firm disposition to do the good. It allows the person not only to perform good acts, but to give the best of himself. The virtuous person tends toward the good with all his sensory and spiritual powers; he pursues the good and chooses it in concrete actions. *1733*

1768

The goal of a virtuous life is to become like God.[63]

I.   THE HUMAN VIRTUES

1804 *Human virtues* are firm attitudes, stable dispositions, habitual perfections of intellect and will that govern our actions, order our passions, and guide our conduct according to reason and faith. They make possible ease, self-mastery, and joy in leading a morally good life. The virtuous man is he who freely practices the good. *2500*

The moral virtues are acquired by human effort. They are the fruit and seed of morally good acts; they dispose all the powers of the human being for communion with divine love. *1827*

The cardinal virtues

1805 Four virtues play a pivotal role and accordingly are called "cardinal"; all the others are grouped around them. They are: prudence, justice, fortitude, and temperance. "If anyone loves righteousness, [Wisdom's] labors are virtues; for she teaches temperance and prudence, justice, and courage."[64] These virtues are praised under other names in many passages of Scripture.

---

62 *Phil* 4:8.
63 St. Gregory of Nyssa, *De beatitudinibus*, 1: PG 44, 1200D.
64 *Wis* 8:7.

1806   *Prudence* is the virtue that disposes practical reason to discern our true good in every circumstance and to choose the right means of achieving it; "the prudent man looks where he is going."[65] "Keep sane and sober for your prayers."[66] Prudence is *1788* "right reason in action," writes St. Thomas Aquinas, following Aristotle.[67] It is not to be confused with timidity or fear, nor with duplicity or dissimulation. It is called *auriga virtutum* (the charioteer of the virtues); it guides the other virtues by setting rule and measure. It is prudence that immediately guides the judgment of *1780* conscience. The prudent man determines and directs his conduct in accordance with this judgment. With the help of this virtue we apply moral principles to particular cases without error and overcome doubts about the good to achieve and the evil to avoid.

1807   *Justice* is the moral virtue that consists in the constant and firm will to give their due to God and neighbor. Justice toward God *2095* is called the "virtue of religion." Justice toward men disposes one to respect the rights of each and to establish in human relationships the harmony that promotes equity with regard to persons and to *2401* the common good. The just man, often mentioned in the Sacred Scriptures, is distinguished by habitual right thinking and the uprightness of his conduct toward his neighbor. "You shall not be partial to the poor or defer to the great, but in righteousness shall you judge your neighbor."[68] "Masters, treat your slaves justly and fairly, knowing that you also have a Master in heaven."[69]

1808   *Fortitude* is the moral virtue that ensures firmness in difficulties and constancy in the pursuit of the good. It strengthens the resolve to resist temptations and to overcome obstacles in the moral life. The virtue of fortitude enables one to conquer fear, even *2848* fear of death, and to face trials and persecutions. It disposes one *2473* even to renounce and sacrifice his life in defense of a just cause. "The Lord is my strength and my song."[70] "In the world you have tribulation; but be of good cheer, I have overcome the world."[71]

---

65 *Prov* 14:15.
66 *1 Pet* 4:7.
67 St. Thomas Aquinas, *STh* II-II, 47, 2.
68 *Lev* 19:15.
69 *Col* 4:1.
70 *Ps* 118:14.
71 *Jn* 16:33.

1809 *Temperance* is the moral virtue that moderates the attraction of pleasures and provides balance in the use of created goods. It ensures the will's mastery over instincts and keeps desires within the limits of what is honorable. The temperate person directs the *2341* sensitive appetites toward what is good and maintains a healthy discretion: "Do not follow your inclination and strength, walking according to the desires of your heart."[72] Temperance is often praised in the Old Testament: "Do not follow your base desires, *2517* but restrain your appetites."[73] In the New Testament it is called "moderation" or "sobriety." We ought "to live sober, upright, and godly lives in this world."[74]

> To live well is nothing other than to love God with all one's heart, with all one's soul and with all one's efforts; from this it comes about that love is kept whole and uncorrupted (through temperance). No misfortune can disturb it (and this is fortitude). It obeys only [God] (and this is justice), and is careful in discerning things, so as not to be surprised by deceit or trickery (and this is prudence).[75]

The virtues and grace

1810 Human virtues acquired by education, by deliberate acts and by a perseverance ever-renewed in repeated efforts are purified and elevated by divine grace. With God's help, they forge *1266* character and give facility in the practice of the good. The virtuous man is happy to practice them.

1811 It is not easy for man, wounded by sin, to maintain moral balance. Christ's gift of salvation offers us the grace necessary to persevere in the pursuit of the virtues. Everyone should always ask *2015* for this grace of light and strength, frequent the sacraments, cooperate with the Holy Spirit, and follow his calls to love what is good and shun evil.

---

72 *Sir* 5:2; cf. 37:27-31.
73 *Sir* 18:30.
74 *Titus* 2:12.
75 St. Augustine, *De moribus eccl.* 1, 25, 46: PL 32, 1330-1331.

2086-2094 **II.   THE THEOLOGICAL VIRTUES**
2656-2658

1812   The human virtues are rooted in the theological virtues, which adapt man's faculties for participation in the divine nature:[76] for the theological virtues relate directly to God. They dispose Christians to live in a relationship with the Holy Trinity.
1266 They have the One and Triune God for their origin, motive, and object.

1813   The theological virtues are the foundation of Christian moral activity; they animate it and give it its special character. They inform and give life to all the moral virtues. They are infused by God into the souls of the faithful to make them capable of acting as his children and of meriting eternal life. They are the pledge of the presence and action of the Holy Spirit in the faculties of the human
2008 being. There are three theological virtues: faith, hope, and charity.[77]

142-175 **Faith**

1814   Faith is the theological virtue by which we believe in God and believe all that he has said and revealed to us, and that Holy
506 Church proposes for our belief, because he is truth itself. By faith "man freely commits his entire self to God."[78] For this reason the believer seeks to know and do God's will. "The righteous shall live by faith." Living faith "work[s] through charity."[79]

1815   The gift of faith remains in one who has not sinned against it.[80] But "faith apart from works is dead":[81] when it is deprived of hope and love, faith does not fully unite the believer to Christ and does not make him a living member of his Body.

2471 **1816**   The disciple of Christ must not only keep the faith and live on it, but also profess it, confidently bear witness to it, and spread it: "All however must be prepared to confess Christ before men and to follow him along the way of the Cross, amidst the persecutions which the Church never lacks."[82] Service of and witness to the faith

---

76 Cf. *2 Pet* 1:4.
77 Cf. *1 Cor* 13:13.
78 *DV* 5.
79 *Rom* 1:17; *Gal* 5:6.
80 Cf. Council of Trent (1547): DS 1545.
81 *Jas* 2:26.
82 *LG* 42; cf. *DH* 14.

are necessary for salvation: "So every one who acknowledges me before men, I also will acknowledge before my Father who is in heaven; but whoever denies me before men, I also will deny before my Father who is in heaven."[83]

Hope

1817 Hope is the theological virtue by which we desire the kingdom of heaven and eternal life as our happiness, placing our trust in Christ's promises and relying not on our own strength, but *1024* on the help of the grace of the Holy Spirit. "Let us hold fast the confession of our hope without wavering, for he who promised is faithful."[84] "The Holy Spirit . . . he poured out upon us richly through Jesus Christ our Savior, so that we might be justified by his grace and become heirs in hope of eternal life."[85]

1818 The virtue of hope responds to the aspiration to happiness *27* which God has placed in the heart of every man; it takes up the hopes that inspire men's activities and purifies them so as to order them to the Kingdom of heaven; it keeps man from discouragement; it sustains him during times of abandonment; it opens up his heart in expectation of eternal beatitude. Buoyed up by hope, he is preserved from selfishness and led to the happiness that flows from charity.

1819 Christian hope takes up and fulfills the hope of the chosen people which has its origin and model in the *hope of Abraham*, who was blessed abundantly by the promises of God fulfilled in Isaac, and who was purified by the test of the sacrifice.[86] "Hoping against *146* hope, he believed, and thus became the father of many nations."[87]

---

83 *Mt* 10:32-33.
84 *Heb* 10:23.
85 *Titus* 3:6-7.
86 Cf. *Gen* 17:4-8; 22:1-18.
87 *Rom* 4:18.

1820   Christian hope unfolds from the beginning of Jesus'
preaching in the proclamation of the beatitudes. The *beatitudes* raise
1716 our hope toward heaven as the new Promised Land; they trace the
path that leads through the trials that await the disciples of Jesus.
But through the merits of Jesus Christ and of his Passion, God keeps
us in the "hope that does not disappoint."[88] Hope is the "sure and
steadfast anchor of the soul . . . that enters . . . where Jesus has gone
as a forerunner on our behalf."[89] Hope is also a weapon that
protects us in the struggle of salvation: "Let us . . . put on the
breastplate of faith and charity, and for a helmet the hope of
salvation."[90] It affords us joy even under trial: "Rejoice in your
hope, be patient in tribulation."[91] Hope is expressed and nourished
2772 in prayer, especially in the Our Father, the summary of everything
that hope leads us to desire.

1821   We can therefore hope in the glory of heaven promised by
God to those who love him and do his will.[92] In every circumstance,
each one of us should hope, with the grace of God, to persevere "to
2016 the end"[93] and to obtain the joy of heaven, as God's eternal reward
1037 for the good works accomplished with the grace of Christ. In hope,
the Church prays for "all men to be saved."[94] She longs to be united
with Christ, her Bridegroom, in the glory of heaven:

> Hope, O my soul, hope. You know neither the day nor the
> hour. Watch carefully, for everything passes quickly, even
> though your impatience makes doubtful what is certain, and
> turns a very short time into a long one. Dream that the more
> you struggle, the more you prove the love that you bear your
> God, and the more you will rejoice one day with your
> Beloved, in a happiness and rapture that can never end.[95]

Charity

1723 **1822**   Charity is the theological virtue by which we love God
above all things for his own sake, and our neighbor as ourselves
for the love of God.

---

88 *Rom* 5:5.
89 *Heb* 6:19-20.
90 *1 Thess* 5:8.
91 *Rom* 12:12.
92 Cf. *Rom* 8:28-30; *Mt* 7:21.
93 *Mt* 10:22; cf. Council of Trent: DS 1541.
94 *1 Tim* 2:4.
95 St. Teresa of Avila, *Excl.* 15:3.

1823 Jesus makes charity the *new commandment*.[96] By loving his 1970
own "to the end,"[97] he makes manifest the Father's love which he
receives. By loving one another, the disciples imitate the love of
Jesus which they themselves receive. Whence Jesus says: "As the
Father has loved me, so have I loved you; abide in my love." And
again: "This is my commandment, that you love one another as I
have loved you."[98]

1824 Fruit of the Spirit and fullness of the Law, charity keeps 735
the *commandments* of God and his Christ: "Abide in my love. If you
keep my commandments, you will abide in my love."[99]

1825 Christ died out of love for us, while we were still "ene- 604
mies."[100] The Lord asks us to love as he does, even our *enemies*, to
make ourselves the neighbor of those farthest away, and to love
children and the poor as Christ himself.[101]

> The Apostle Paul has given an incomparable depiction of
> charity: "charity is patient and kind, charity is not jealous or
> boastful; it is not arrogant or rude. Charity does not insist on
> its own way; it is not irritable or resentful; it does not rejoice
> at wrong, but rejoices in the right. Charity bears all things,
> believes all things, hopes all things, endures all things."[102]

1826 "If I ... have not charity," says the Apostle, "I am nothing."
Whatever my privilege, service, or even virtue, "if I . . . have not
charity, I gain nothing."[103] Charity is superior to all the virtues. It
is the first of the theological virtues: "So faith, hope, charity abide,
these three. But *the greatest of these is charity*."[104]

1827 The practice of all the virtues is animated and inspired by
charity, which "binds everything together in perfect harmony";[105]
it is the *form of the virtues*; it articulates and orders them among 815
themselves; it is the source and the goal of their Christian practice. 826
Charity upholds and purifies our human ability to love, and raises
it to the supernatural perfection of divine love.

---

96 Cf. *Jn* 13:34.
97 *Jn* 13:1.
98 *Jn* 15:9, 12.
99 *Jn* 15:9-10; cf. *Mt* 22:40; *Rom* 13:8-10.
100 *Rom* 5:10.
101 Cf. *Mt* 5:44; *Lk* 10:27-37; *Mk* 9:37; *Mt* 25:40, 45.
102 *1 Cor* 13:4-7.
103 *1 Cor* 13:1-4.
104 *1 Cor* 13:13.
105 *Col* 3:14.

1828   The practice of the moral life animated by charity gives to
the Christian the spiritual freedom of the children of God. He no
1972   longer stands before God as a slave, in servile fear, or as a merce-
nary looking for wages, but as a son responding to the love of him
who "first loved us":[106]

> If we turn away from evil out of fear of punishment, we are
> in the position of slaves. If we pursue the enticement of
> wages, . . . we resemble mercenaries. Finally if we obey for
> the sake of the good itself and out of love for him who
> commands . . . we are in the position of children.[107]

1829   The *fruits* of charity are joy, peace, and mercy; charity
demands beneficence and fraternal correction; it is benevolence; it
2540   fosters reciprocity and remains disinterested and generous; it is
friendship and communion:

> Love is itself the fulfillment of all our works. There is the goal;
> that is why we run: we run toward it, and once we reach it,
> in it we shall find rest.[108]

III.   THE GIFTS AND FRUITS OF THE HOLY SPIRIT

1830   The moral life of Christians is sustained by the gifts of the
Holy Spirit. These are permanent dispositions which make man
docile in following the promptings of the Holy Spirit.

1831   The seven *gifts* of the Holy Spirit are wisdom, understanding, counsel, fortitude, knowledge, piety, and fear of the
Lord. They belong in their fullness to Christ, Son of David.[109] They
1266, 1299   complete and perfect the virtues of those who receive them. They
make the faithful docile in readily obeying divine inspirations.

> Let your good spirit lead me on a level path.[110]

> For all who are led by the Spirit of God are sons of God . . .
> If children, then heirs, heirs of God and fellow heirs with
> Christ.[111]

---

106 Cf. *1 Jn* 4:19.
107 St. Basil, *Reg. fus. tract., prol.* 3: PG 31, 896 B.
108 St. Augustine, *In ep. Jo.* 10, 4: PL 35, 2057.
109 Cf. *Isa* 11:1-2.
110 *Ps* 143:10.
111 *Rom* 8:14, 17.

1832 The *fruits* of the Spirit are perfections that the Holy Spirit *736* forms in us as the first fruits of eternal glory. The tradition of the Church lists twelve of them: "charity, joy, peace, patience, kindness, goodness, generosity, gentleness, faithfulness, modesty, self-control, chastity."[112]

IN BRIEF

1833 Virtue is a habitual and firm disposition to do good.

1834 The human virtues are stable dispositions of the intellect and the will that govern our acts, order our passions, and guide our conduct in accordance with reason and faith. They can be grouped around the four cardinal virtues: prudence, justice, fortitude, and temperance.

1835 Prudence disposes the practical reason to discern, in every circumstance, our true good and to choose the right means for achieving it.

1836 Justice consists in the firm and constant will to give God and neighbor their due.

1837 Fortitude ensures firmness in difficulties and constancy in the pursuit of the good.

1838 Temperance moderates the attraction of the pleasures of the senses and provides balance in the use of created goods.

1839 The moral virtues grow through education, deliberate acts, and perseverance in struggle. Divine grace purifies and elevates them.

1840 The theological virtues dispose Christians to live in a relationship with the Holy Trinity. They have God for their origin, their motive, and their object – God known by faith, God hoped in and loved for his own sake.

1841 There are three theological virtues: faith, hope, and charity. They inform all the moral virtues and give life to them.

---

112 *Gal* 5:22-23 (Vulg.).

1842   By faith, we believe in God and believe all that he has revealed to us and that Holy Church proposes for our belief.

1843   By hope we desire, and with steadfast trust await from God, eternal life and the graces to merit it.

1844   By charity, we love God above all things and our neighbor as ourselves for love of God. Charity, the form of all the virtues, "binds everything together in perfect harmony" (*Col* 3:14).

1845   The seven gifts of the Holy Spirit bestowed upon Christians are wisdom, understanding, counsel, fortitude, knowledge, piety, and fear of the Lord.

ARTICLE 8
SIN

I.   MERCY AND SIN

430 **1846**   The Gospel is the revelation in Jesus Christ of God's mercy to sinners.[113] The angel announced to Joseph: "You shall call his name Jesus, for he will save his people from their sins."[114] The same *1365* is true of the Eucharist, the sacrament of redemption: "This is my blood of the covenant, which is poured out for many for the forgiveness of sins."[115]

387, 1455 **1847**   "God created us without us: but he did not will to save us without us."[116] To receive his mercy, we must admit our faults. "If we say we have no sin, we deceive ourselves, and the truth is not in us. If we confess our sins, he is faithful and just, and will forgive our sins and cleanse us from all unrighteousness."[117]

1848   As St. Paul affirms, "Where sin increased, grace abounded all the more."[118] But to do its work grace must uncover sin so as to *385* convert our hearts and bestow on us "righteousness to eternal life

---

113   Cf. *Lk* 15.
114   *Mt* 1:21.
115   *Mt* 26:28.
116   St. Augustine, *Sermo* 169, 11, 13: PL 38, 923.
117   *1 Jn* 8-9.
118   *Rom* 5:20.

through Jesus Christ our Lord."[119] Like a physician who probes the wound before treating it, God, by his Word and by his Spirit, casts a living light on sin:

> Conversion *requires convincing of sin*; it includes the interior judgment of conscience, and this, being a proof of the action of the Spirit of truth in man's inmost being, becomes at the same time the start of a new grant of grace and love: "Receive the Holy Spirit." Thus in this "convincing concerning sin" we discover *a double gift*: the gift of the truth of conscience and the gift of the certainty of redemption. The Spirit of truth is the Consoler.[120]

1433

II.   THE DEFINITION OF SIN

1849   Sin is an offense against reason, truth, and right con-   *311* science; it is failure in genuine love for God and neighbor caused by a perverse attachment to certain goods. It wounds the nature of man and injures human solidarity. It has been defined as "an utterance, a deed, or a desire contrary to the eternal law."[121]   *1952*

1850   Sin is an offense against God: "Against you, you alone,   *1440* have I sinned, and done that which is evil in your sight."[122] Sin sets itself against God's love for us and turns our hearts away from it. Like the first sin, it is disobedience, a revolt against God through   *397* the will to become "like gods,"[123] knowing and determining good and evil. Sin is thus "love of oneself even to contempt of God."[124] In this proud self-exaltation, sin is diametrically opposed to the obedience of Jesus, which achieves our salvation.[125]   *615*

1851   It is precisely in the Passion, when the mercy of Christ is about to vanquish it, that sin most clearly manifests its violence and its many forms: unbelief, murderous hatred, shunning and mockery by the leaders and the people, Pilate's cowardice and the cruelty of the soldiers, Judas' betrayal – so bitter to Jesus, Peter's   *598* denial and the disciples' flight. However, at the very hour of darkness, the hour of the prince of this world,[126] the sacrifice of   *2746, 616*

---

119   *Rom* 5:21.
120   John Paul II, *DeV* 31 § 2.
121   St. Augustine, *Contra Faustum* 22: PL 42, 418; St. Thomas Aquinas, *STh* I-II, 71, 6.
122   *Ps* 51:4.
123   *Gen* 3:5.
124   St. Augustine, *De civ. Dei* 14, 28: PL 41, 436.
125   Cf. *Phil* 2:6-9.
126   Cf. *Jn* 14:30.

Christ secretly becomes the source from which the forgiveness of
our sins will pour forth inexhaustibly.

III.   THE DIFFERENT KINDS OF SINS

1852   There are a great many kinds of sins. Scripture provides
several lists of them. The *Letter to the Galatians* contrasts the works
of the flesh with the fruit of the Spirit: "Now the works of the flesh
are plain: fornication, impurity, licentiousness, idolatry, sorcery,
enmity, strife, jealousy, anger, selfishness, dissension, factions,
envy, drunkenness, carousing, and the like. I warn you, as I warned
you before, that those who do such things shall not inherit the
Kingdom of God."[127]

1751   **1853**   Sins can be distinguished according to their objects, as can every
human act; or according to the virtues they oppose, by excess or defect; or
according to the commandments they violate. They can also be classed
according to whether they concern God, neighbor, or oneself; they can be
2067   divided into spiritual and carnal sins, or again as sins in thought, word,
deed, or omission. The root of sin is in the heart of man, in his free will,
according to the teaching of the Lord: "For out of the heart come evil
368   thoughts, murder, adultery, fornication, theft, false witness, slander. These
are what defile a man."[128] But in the heart also resides charity, the source
of the good and pure works, which sin wounds.

IV.   THE GRAVITY OF SIN: MORTAL AND VENIAL SIN

1854   Sins are rightly evaluated according to their gravity. The
distinction between mortal and venial sin, already evident in Scripture,[129] became part of the tradition of the Church. It is corrobo-
rated by human experience.

1395   **1855**   *Mortal sin* destroys charity in the heart of man by a grave
violation of God's law; it turns man away from God, who is his
ultimate end and his beatitude, by preferring an inferior good to
him.
    Venial sin allows charity to subsist, even though it offends
and wounds it.

1856   Mortal sin, by attacking the vital principle within us – that
1446   is, charity – necessitates a new initiative of God's mercy and a

---

127   *Gal* 5:19-21; cf. *Rom* 1:28-32; *1 Cor* 9-10; *Eph* 5:3-5; *Col* 3:5-8; *1 Tim* 9-10; *2 Tim*
2-5.
128   *Mt* 15:19-20.
129   Cf. *1 Jn* 16-17.

conversion of heart which is normally accomplished within the setting of the sacrament of reconciliation:

> When the will sets itself upon something that is of its nature incompatible with the charity that orients man toward his ultimate end, then the sin is mortal by its very object . . . whether it contradicts the love of God, such as blasphemy or perjury, or the love of neighbor, such as homicide or adultery. . . . But when the sinner's will is set upon something that of its nature involves a disorder, but is not opposed to the love of God and neighbor, such as thoughtless chatter or immoderate laughter and the like, such sins are venial.[130]

1857 For a *sin* to be *mortal*, three conditions must together be met: "Mortal sin is sin whose object is grave matter and which is also committed with full knowledge and deliberate consent."[131]

1858 *Grave matter* is specified by the Ten Commandments, cor- *2072*
responding to the answer of Jesus to the rich young man: "Do not kill, Do not commit adultery, Do not steal, Do not bear false witness, Do not defraud, Honor your father and your mother."[132]
The gravity of sins is more or less great: murder is graver than theft. One must also take into account who is wronged: violence against parents is in itself graver than violence against a stranger. *2214*

1859 Mortal sin requires *full knowledge* and *complete consent*. It *1734*
presupposes knowledge of the sinful character of the act, of its opposition to God's law. It also implies a consent sufficiently deliberate to be a personal choice. Feigned ignorance and hardness of heart[133] do not diminish, but rather increase, the voluntary character of a sin.

1860 *Unintentional ignorance* can diminish or even remove the *1735*
imputability of a grave offense. But no one is deemed to be ignorant of the principles of the moral law, which are written in the conscience of every man. The promptings of feelings and passions can also diminish the voluntary and free character of the offense, as can *1767*
external pressures or pathological disorders. Sin committed through malice, by deliberate choice of evil, is the gravest.

---

130 St. Thomas Aquinas, *STh* I-II, 88, 2, *corp. art.*
131 *RP* 17 § 12.
132 *Mk* 10:19.
133 Cf. *Mk* 3:5-6; *Lk* 16:19-31.

1742 **1861**   Mortal sin is a radical possibility of human freedom, as is love itself. It results in the loss of charity and the privation of sanctifying grace, that is, of the state of grace. If it is not redeemed by repentance and God's forgiveness, it causes exclusion from Christ's kingdom and the eternal death of hell, for our freedom has *1033* the power to make choices for ever, with no turning back. However, although we can judge that an act is in itself a grave offense, we must entrust judgment of persons to the justice and mercy of God.

1862   One commits *venial sin* when, in a less serious matter, he does not observe the standard prescribed by the moral law, or when he disobeys the moral law in a grave matter, but without full knowledge or without complete consent.

1394 **1863**   Venial sin weakens charity; it manifests a disordered affection for created goods; it impedes the soul's progress in the exercise of the virtues and the practice of the moral good; it merits temporal punishment. Deliberate and unrepented venial sin disposes us *1472* little by little to commit mortal sin. However venial sin does not set us in direct opposition to the will and friendship of God; it does not break the covenant with God. With God's grace it is humanly reparable. "Venial sin does not deprive the sinner of sanctifying grace, friendship with God, charity, and consequently eternal happiness."[134]

> While he is in the flesh, man cannot help but have at least some light sins. But do not despise these sins which we call "light": if you take them for light when you weigh them, tremble when you count them. A number of light objects makes a great mass; a number of drops fills a river; a number of grains makes a heap. What then is our hope? Above all, confession. . . .[135]

1864   "Whoever *blasphemes against the Holy Spirit* never has forgiveness, but is guilty of an eternal sin."[136] There are no limits to the mercy of God, but anyone who deliberately refuses to accept *2091* his mercy by repenting, rejects the forgiveness of his sins and the salvation offered by the Holy Spirit.[137] Such hardness of heart can *1037* lead to final impenitence and eternal loss.

---

134 John Paul II, *RP* 17 § 9.
135 St. Augustine, *In ep. Jo.* 1, 6: PL 35, 1982.
136 *Mk* 3:29; cf. *Mt* 12:32; *Lk* 12:10.
137 Cf. John Paul II, *DeV* 46.

V.   THE PROLIFERATION OF SIN

1865   Sin creates a proclivity to sin; it engenders vice by repeti-   *401*
tion of the same acts. This results in perverse inclinations which
cloud conscience and corrupt the concrete judgment of good and
evil. Thus sin tends to reproduce itself and reinforce itself, but it   *1768*
cannot destroy the moral sense at its root.

1866   Vices can be classified according to the virtues they oppose, or also be linked to the *capital sins* which Christian experience
has distinguished, following St. John Cassian and St. Gregory the
Great. They are called "capital" because they engender other sins,
other vices.[138] They are pride, avarice, envy, wrath, lust, gluttony,
and sloth or acedia.   *2539*

1867   The catechetical tradition also recalls that there are "*sins*   *2268*
that cry to heaven": the blood of Abel,[139] the sin of the Sodomites,[140]
the cry of the people oppressed in Egypt,[141] the cry of the foreigner,
the widow, and the orphan,[142] injustice to the wage earner.[143]

1868   Sin is a personal act. Moreover, we have a responsibility
for the sins committed by others when *we cooperate in them*:   *1736*

– by participating directly and voluntarily in them;

– by ordering, advising, praising, or approving them;

– by not disclosing or not hindering them when we have an
obligation to do so;

– by protecting evil-doers.

1869   Thus sin makes men accomplices of one another and
causes concupiscence, violence, and injustice to reign among them.
Sins give rise to social situations and institutions that are contrary
to the divine goodness. "Structures of sin" are the expression and   *408*
effect of personal sins. They lead their victims to do evil in their   *1887*
turn. In an analogous sense, they constitute a "social sin."[144]

---

138   Cf. St. Gregory the Great, *Moralia in Job*, 31, 45: PL 76, 621A.
139   Cf. *Gen* 4:10.
140   Cf. *Gen* 18:20; 19:13.
141   Cf. *Ex* 3:7-10.
142   Cf. *Ex* 20:20-22.
143   Cf. *Deut* 24:14-15; *Jas* 5:4.
144   John Paul II, *RP* 16.

IN BRIEF

1870 "God has consigned all men to disobedience, that he may have mercy upon all" (*Rom* 11:32).

1871 Sin is an utterance, a deed, or a desire contrary to the eternal law (St. Augustine, *Faust* 22: PL 42, 418). It is an offense against God. It rises up against God in a disobedience contrary to the obedience of Christ.

1872 Sin is an act contrary to reason. It wounds man's nature and injures human solidarity.

1873 The root of all sins lies in man's heart. The kinds and the gravity of sins are determined principally by their objects.

1874 To choose deliberately – that is, both knowing it and willing it – something gravely contrary to the divine law and to the ultimate end of man is to commit a mortal sin. This destroys in us the charity without which eternal beatitude is impossible. Unrepented, it brings eternal death.

1875 Venial sin constitutes a moral disorder that is reparable by charity, which it allows to subsist in us.

1876 The repetition of sins – even venial ones – engenders vices, among which are the capital sins.

CHAPTER TWO
THE HUMAN COMMUNITY

1877 The vocation of humanity is to show forth the image of *355* God and to be transformed into the image of the Father's only Son. This vocation takes a personal form since each of us is called to enter into the divine beatitude; it also concerns the human community as a whole.

ARTICLE 1
THE PERSON AND SOCIETY

I. THE COMMUNAL CHARACTER OF THE HUMAN VOCATION

1878 All men are called to the same end: God himself. There is a certain resemblance between the union of the divine persons and *1702* the fraternity that men are to establish among themselves in truth and love.[1] Love of neighbor is inseparable from love for God.

1879 The human person needs to live in society. Society is not *1936* for him an extraneous addition but a requirement of his nature. Through the exchange with others, mutual service and dialogue with his brethren, man develops his potential; he thus responds to his vocation.[2]

1880 A *society* is a group of persons bound together organically *771* by a principle of unity that goes beyond each one of them. As an assembly that is at once visible and spiritual, a society endures through time: it gathers up the past and prepares for the future. By means of society, each man is established as an "heir" and receives certain "talents" that enrich his identity and whose fruits he must develop.[3] He rightly owes loyalty to the communities of which he is part and respect to those in authority who have charge of the common good.

---

1 Cf. *GS* 24 § 3.
2 Cf. *GS* 25 § 1.
3 Cf. *Lk* 19:13, 15.

1881   Each community is defined by its purpose and consequently obeys specific rules; but "the *human person . . .* is and ought
1929 to be the principle, the subject and the end of all social institutions."[4]

1882   Certain societies, such as the family and the state, correspond more directly to the nature of man; they are necessary to
him. To promote the participation of the greatest number in the life
of a society, the creation of voluntary associations and institutions
1913 must be encouraged "on both national and international levels,
which relate to economic and social goals, to cultural and recrea-
tional activities, to sport, to various professions, and to political
affairs."[5] This "*socialization*" also expresses the natural tendency for
human beings to associate with one another for the sake of attaining objectives that exceed individual capacities. It develops the
qualities of the person, especially the sense of initiative and responsibility, and helps guarantee his rights.[6]

1883   Socialization also presents dangers. Excessive intervention
by the state can threaten personal freedom and initiative. The
teaching of the Church has elaborated the principle of *subsidiarity*,
according to which "a community of a higher order should not
interfere in the internal life of a community of a lower order,
depriving the latter of its functions, but rather should support it in
2431 case of need and help to co-ordinate its activity with the activities
of the rest of society, always with a view to the common good."[7]

1884   God has not willed to reserve to himself all exercise of
power. He entrusts to every creature the functions it is capable of
307 performing, according to the capacities of its own nature. This
mode of governance ought to be followed in social life. The way
God acts in governing the world, which bears witness to such great
regard for human freedom, should inspire the wisdom of those
who govern human communities. They should behave as ministers
302 of divine providence.

1885   The principle of subsidiarity is opposed to all forms of
collectivism. It sets limits for state intervention. It aims at harmonizing the relationships between individuals and societies. It tends
toward the establishment of true international order.

---

4   *GS* 25 § 1.
5   John XXIII, *MM* 60.
6   Cf. *GS* 25 § 2; *CA* 12.
7   *CA* 48 § 4; cf. Pius XI, *Quadragesimo anno* I, 184-186.

II. CONVERSION AND SOCIETY

1886 Society is essential to the fulfillment of the human vocation. To attain this aim, respect must be accorded to the just
hierarchy of values, which "subordinates physical and instinctual *1779*
dimensions to interior and spiritual ones:"[8]

> Human society must primarily be considered something
> pertaining to the spiritual. Through it, in the bright light of
> truth, men should share their knowledge, be able to exercise
> their rights and fulfill their obligations, be inspired to seek
> spiritual values; mutually derive genuine pleasure from the
> beautiful, of whatever order it be; always be readily disposed   *2500*
> to pass on to others the best of their own cultural heritage;
> and eagerly strive to make their own the spiritual achieve-
> ments of others. These benefits not only influence, but at the
> same time give aim and scope to all that has bearing on
> cultural expressions, economic, and social institutions, po-
> litical movements and forms, laws, and all other structures
> by which society is outwardly established and constantly
> developed.[9]

1887 The inversion of means and ends,[10] which results in giving
the value of ultimate end to what is only a means for attaining it, *909*
or in viewing persons as mere means to that end, engenders unjust
structures which "make Christian conduct in keeping with the
commandments of the divine Law-giver difficult and almost impossible."[11]   *1869*

1888 It is necessary, then, to appeal to the spiritual and moral *407*
capacities of the human person and to the permanent need for his *1430*
inner conversion, so as to obtain social changes that will really serve
him. The acknowledged priority of the conversion of heart in no
way eliminates but on the contrary imposes the obligation of
bringing the appropriate remedies to institutions and living conditions when they are an inducement to sin, so that they conform
to the norms of justice and advance the good rather than hinder
it.[12]

---

8 *CA* 36 § 2.
9 John XXIII, *PT* 36.
10 Cf. *CA* 41.
11 Pius XII, Address at Pentecost, June 1, 1941.
12 Cf. *LG* 36.

1889   Without the help of grace, men would not know how "to discern the often narrow path between the cowardice which gives in to evil, and the violence which under the illusion of fighting evil only makes it worse."[13] This is the path of charity, that is, of the
1825 love of God and of neighbor. Charity is the greatest social commandment. It respects others and their rights. It requires the practice of justice, and it alone makes us capable of it. Charity inspires a life of self-giving: "Whoever seeks to gain his life will lose it, but whoever loses his life will preserve it."[14]

IN BRIEF

1890   There is a certain resemblance between the union of the divine persons and the fraternity that men ought to establish among themselves.

1891   The human person needs life in society in order to develop in accordance with his nature. Certain societies, such as the family and the state, correspond more directly to the nature of man.

1892   "The human person ... is and ought to be the principle, the subject, and the object of every social organization" (*GS* 25 § 1).

1893   Widespread participation in voluntary associations and institutions is to be encouraged.

1894   In accordance with the principle of subsidiarity, neither the state nor any larger society should substitute itself for the initiative and responsibility of individuals and intermediary bodies.

1895   Society ought to promote the exercise of virtue, not obstruct it. It should be animated by a just hierarchy of values.

1896   Where sin has perverted the social climate, it is necessary to call for the conversion of hearts and appeal to the grace of God. Charity urges just reforms. There is no solution to the social question apart from the Gospel (cf. *CA* 3, 5).

---

13 *CA* 25.
14 *Lk* 17:33.

ARTICLE 2
PARTICIPATION IN SOCIAL LIFE

I. AUTHORITY

1897 "Human society can be neither well-ordered nor prosperous unless it has some people invested with legitimate authority to preserve its institutions and to devote themselves as far as is necessary to work and care for the good of all."[15]   *2234*

By "authority" one means the quality by virtue of which persons or institutions make laws and give orders to men and expect obedience from them.

1898 Every human community needs an authority to govern it.[16] The foundation of such authority lies in human nature. It is necessary for the unity of the state. Its role is to ensure as far as possible the common good of the society.

1899 The authority required by the moral order derives from God: "Let every person be subject to the governing authorities. For there is no authority except from God, and those that exist have been instituted by God. Therefore he who resists the authorities resists what God has appointed, and those who resist will incur judgment."[17]   *2235*

1900 The duty of obedience requires all to give due honor to authority and to treat those who are charged to exercise it with respect, and, insofar as it is deserved, with gratitude and good-will.   *2238*

> Pope St. Clement of Rome provides the Church's most ancient prayer for political authorities:[18] "Grant to them, Lord, health, peace, concord, and stability, so that they may exercise without offense the sovereignty that you have given them. Master, heavenly King of the ages, you give glory, honor, and power over the things of earth to the sons of men. Direct, Lord, their counsel, following what is pleasing and acceptable in your sight, so that by exercising with devotion and in peace and gentleness the power that you have given to them, they may find favor with you."[19]   *2240*

---

15 John XXIII, *PT* 46.
16 Cf. Leo XIII, *Immortale Dei; Diuturnum illud.*
17 *Rom* 13:1-2; cf. *1 Pet* 2:13-17.
18 Cf. as early as *1 Tim* 2:1-2.
19 St. Clement of Rome, *Ad Cor.* 61: SCh 167, 198-200.

1901   If authority belongs to the order established by God, "the choice of the political regime and the appointment of rulers are left to the free decision of the citizens."[20]

2242
The diversity of political regimes is morally acceptable, provided they serve the legitimate good of the communities that adopt them. Regimes whose nature is contrary to the natural law, to the public order, and to the fundamental rights of persons cannot achieve the common good of the nations on which they have been imposed.

1930 **1902**   Authority does not derive its moral legitimacy from itself. It must not behave in a despotic manner, but must act for the common good as a "moral force based on freedom and a sense of responsibility":[21]

1951
A human law has the character of law to the extent that it accords with right reason, and thus derives from the eternal law. Insofar as it falls short of right reason it is said to be an unjust law, and thus has not so much the nature of law as of a kind of violence.[22]

1903   Authority is exercised legitimately only when it seeks the common good of the group concerned and if it employs morally licit means to attain it. If rulers were to enact unjust laws or take
2242 measures contrary to the moral order, such arrangements would not be binding in conscience. In such a case, "authority breaks down completely and results in shameful abuse."[23]

1904   "It is preferable that each power be balanced by other powers and by other spheres of responsibility which keep it within proper bounds. This is the principle of the 'rule of law,' in which the law is sovereign and not the arbitrary will of men."[24]

II.   The Common Good

1905   In keeping with the social nature of man, the good of each
801 individual is necessarily related to the common good, which in
1881 turn can be defined only in reference to the human person:

---

20 *GS* 74 § 3.
21 *GS* 74 § 2.
22 St. Thomas Aquinas, *STh* I-II, 93, 3, *ad* 2.
23 John XXIII, *PT* 51.
24 *CA* 44.

> Do not live entirely isolated, having retreated into your-
> selves, as if you were already justified, but gather instead to
> seek the common good together.[25]

1906 By common good is to be understood "the sum total of
social conditions which allow people, either as groups or as individuals, to reach their fulfillment more fully and more easily."[26]
The common good concerns the life of all. It calls for prudence from
each, and even more from those who exercise the office of authority. It consists of *three essential elements*:

1907 First, the common good presupposes *respect for the person* 1929
as such. In the name of the common good, public authorities are
bound to respect the fundamental and inalienable rights of the
human person. Society should permit each of its members to fulfill
his vocation. In particular, the common good resides in the conditions for the exercise of the natural freedoms indispensable for the
development of the human vocation, such as "the right to act
according to a sound norm of conscience and to safeguard . . .
privacy, and rightful freedom also in matters of religion."[27]   2106

1908 Second, the common good requires the *social well-being* and
development of the group itself. Development is the epitome of all
social duties. Certainly, it is the proper function of authority to 2441
arbitrate, in the name of the common good, between various
particular interests; but it should make accessible to each what is
needed to lead a truly human life: food, clothing, health, work,
education and culture, suitable information, the right to establish
a family, and so on.[28]

1909 Finally, the common good requires *peace*, that is, the stabil- 2304
ity and security of a just order. It presupposes that authority should
ensure by morally acceptable means the *security* of society and its
members. It is the basis of the right to legitimate personal and 2310
collective defence.

1910 Each human community possesses a common good which
permits it to be recognized as such; it is in the *political community*
that its most complete realization is found. It is the role of the state 2244
to defend and promote the common good of civil society, its
citizens, and intermediate bodies.

---

25 *Ep. Barnabae*, 4, 10: PG 2, 734.
26 *GS* 26 § 1; cf. *GS* 74 § 1.
27 *GS* 26 § 2.
28 Cf. *GS* 26 § 2.

1911   Human interdependence is increasing and gradually spreading throughout the world. The unity of the human family, 2438 embracing people who enjoy equal natural dignity, implies a *universal common good*. This good calls for an organization of the community of nations able to "provide for the different needs of men; this will involve the sphere of social life to which belong questions of food, hygiene, education, . . . and certain situations arising here and there, as for example . . . alleviating the miseries of refugees dispersed throughout the world, and assisting migrants and their families."[29]

1912   The common good is always oriented towards the progress of persons: "The order of things must be subordinate to the 1881 order of persons, and not the other way around."[30] This order is founded on truth, built up in justice, and animated by love.

III.   RESPONSIBILITY AND PARTICIPATION

1913   "Participation" is the voluntary and generous engagement of a person in social interchange. It is necessary that all participate, each according to his position and role, in promoting the common good. This obligation is inherent in the dignity of the human person.

1914   Participation is achieved first of all by taking charge of the areas for which one assumes *personal responsibility*: by the care 1734 taken for the education of his family, by conscientious work, and so forth, man participates in the good of others and of society.[31]

2239 **1915**   As far as possible citizens should take an active part in *public life*. The manner of this participation may vary from one country or culture to another. "One must pay tribute to those nations whose systems permit the largest possible number of the citizens to take part in public life in a climate of genuine freedom."[32]

---

29   *GS* 84 § 2.
30   *GS* 26 § 3.
31   Cf. *CA* 43.
32   *GS* 31 § 3.

1916   As with any ethical obligation, the participation of all in realizing the common good calls for a continually renewed *conversion* of the social partners. Fraud and other subterfuges, by which *1888* some people evade the constraints of the law and the prescriptions of societal obligation, must be firmly condemned because they are incompatible with the requirements of justice. Much care should *2409* be taken to promote institutions that improve the conditions of human life.[33]

1917   It is incumbent on those who exercise authority to strengthen the values that inspire the confidence of the members of the group and encourage them to put themselves at the service of others. Participation begins with education and culture. "One is entitled to think that the future of humanity is in the hands of those who are capable of providing the generations to come with reasons for life and optimism."[34]   *1818*

IN BRIEF

1918   "There is no authority except from God, and those authorities that exist have been instituted by God" (*Rom* 13:1).

1919   Every human community needs an authority in order to endure and develop.

1920   "The political community and public authority are based on human nature and therefore . . . belong to an order established by God" (*GS* 74 § 3).

1921   Authority is exercised legitimately if it is committed to the common good of society. To attain this it must employ morally acceptable means.

1922   The diversity of political regimes is legitimate, provided they contribute to the good of the community.

1923   Political authority must be exercised within the limits of the moral order and must guarantee the conditions for the exercise of freedom.

---

33   Cf. *GS* 30 § 1.
34   *GS* 31 § 3.

1924   The common good comprises "the sum total of social conditions which allow people, either as groups or as individuals, to reach their fulfillment more fully and more easily" (*GS* 26 § 1).

1925   The common good consists of three essential elements: respect for and promotion of the fundamental rights of the person; prosperity, or the development of the spiritual and temporal goods of society; the peace and security of the group and of its members.

1926   The dignity of the human person requires the pursuit of the common good. Everyone should be concerned to create and support institutions that improve the conditions of human life.

1927   It is the role of the state to defend and promote the common good of civil society. The common good of the whole human family calls for an organization of society on the international level.

ARTICLE 3
SOCIAL JUSTICE

1928   Society ensures social justice when it provides the conditions that allow associations or individuals to obtain what is their *2832* due, according to their nature and their vocation. Social justice is linked to the common good and the exercise of authority.

I.   RESPECT FOR THE HUMAN PERSON

1881 **1929**   Social justice can be obtained only in respecting the transcendent dignity of man. The person represents the ultimate end of society, which is ordered to him:

> What is at stake is the dignity of the human person, whose defense and promotion have been entrusted to us by the Creator, and to whom the men and women at every moment of history are strictly and responsibly in debt.[35]

---

35   John Paul II, *SRS* 47.

1930 Respect for the human person entails respect for the rights that flow from his dignity as a creature. These rights are prior to society and must be recognized by it. They are the basis of the moral *1700* legitimacy of every authority: by flouting them, or refusing to *1902* recognize them in its positive legislation, a society undermines its own moral legitimacy.[36] If it does not respect them, authority can rely only on force or violence to obtain obedience from its subjects. It is the Church's role to remind men of good will of these rights and to distinguish them from unwarranted or false claims.

1931 Respect for the human person proceeds by way of respect for the principle that "everyone should look upon his neighbor *2212* (without any exception) as 'another self,' above all bearing in mind his life and the means necessary for living it with dignity."[37] No legislation could by itself do away with the fears, prejudices, and attitudes of pride and selfishness which obstruct the establishment of truly fraternal societies. Such behavior will cease only through *1825* the charity that finds in every man a "neighbor," a brother.

1932 The duty of making oneself a neighbor to others and actively serving them becomes even more urgent when it involves the disadvantaged, in whatever area this may be. "As you did it to one of the least of these my brethren, you did it to me."[38] *2449*

1933 This same duty extends to those who think or act differently from us. The teaching of Christ goes so far as to require the forgiveness of offenses. He extends the commandment of love, which is that of the New Law, to all enemies.[39] Liberation in the spirit of the Gospel is incompatible with hatred of one's enemy as *2303* a person, but not with hatred of the evil that he does as an enemy.

II. EQUALITY AND DIFFERENCES AMONG MEN

1934 Created in the image of the one God and equally endowed with rational souls, all men have the same nature and the same origin. Redeemed by the sacrifice of Christ, all are called to participate in the same divine beatitude: all therefore enjoy an equal *225* dignity.

---

36 Cf. John XXIII, *PT* 65.
37 *GS* 27 § 1.
38 *Mt* 25:40.
39 Cf. *Mt* 5:43-44.

1935 The equality of men rests essentially on their dignity as
357 persons and the rights that flow from it:

> Every form of social or cultural discrimination in fundamental personal rights on the grounds of sex, race, color, social conditions, language, or religion must be curbed and eradicated as incompatible with God's design.[40]

1879 **1936** On coming into the world, man is not equipped with everything he needs for developing his bodily and spiritual life. He needs others. Differences appear tied to age, physical abilities, intellectual or moral aptitudes, the benefits derived from social commerce, and the distribution of wealth.[41] The "talents" are not distributed equally.[42]

340 **1937** These differences belong to God's plan, who wills that each receive what he needs from others, and that those endowed
791 with particular "talents" share the benefits with those who need
1202 them. These differences encourage and often oblige persons to practice generosity, kindness, and sharing of goods; they foster the mutual enrichment of cultures:

> I distribute the virtues quite diversely; I do not give all of them to each person, but some to one, some to others. . . . I shall give principally charity to one; justice to another; humility to this one, a living faith to that one. . . . And so I have given many gifts and graces, both spiritual and temporal, with such diversity that I have not given everything to one single person, so that you may be constrained to practice charity towards one another. . . . I have willed that one should need another and that all should be my ministers in distributing the graces and gifts they have received from me.[43]

2437 **1938** There exist also *sinful inequalities* that affect millions of men and women. These are in open contradiction of the Gospel:

> Their equal dignity as persons demands that we strive for
2317 fairer and more humane conditions. Excessive economic and social disparity between individuals and peoples of the one human race is a source of scandal and militates against social justice, equity, human dignity, as well as social and international peace.[44]

---

40 *GS* 29 § 2.
41 Cf. *GS* 29 § 2.
42 Cf. *Mt* 25:14-30; *Lk* 19:11-27.
43 St Catherine of Siena, *Dial.* I, 7.
44 *GS* 29 § 3.

III.   HUMAN SOLIDARITY

1939   The principle of solidarity, also articulated in terms of *2213*
"friendship" or "social charity," is a direct demand of human and
Christian brotherhood.[45]

> An error, "today abundantly widespread, is disregard for
> the law of human solidarity and charity, dictated and im-
> posed both by our common origin and by the equality in   *360*
> rational nature of all men, whatever nation they belong to.
> This law is sealed by the sacrifice of redemption offered by
> Jesus Christ on the altar of the Cross to his heavenly Father,
> on behalf of sinful humanity."[46]

1940   Solidarity is manifested in the first place by the distribu- *2402*
tion of goods and remuneration for work. It also presupposes the
effort for a more just social order where tensions are better able to
be reduced and conflicts more readily settled by negotiation.

1941   Socio-economic problems can be resolved only with the *2317*
help of all the forms of solidarity: solidarity of the poor among
themselves, between rich and poor, of workers among themselves,
between employers and employees in a business, solidarity among
nations and peoples. International solidarity is a requirement of the
moral order; world peace depends in part upon this.

1942   The virtue of solidarity goes beyond material goods. In
spreading the spiritual goods of the faith, the Church has pro-
moted, and often opened new paths for, the development of tem- *1887*
poral goods as well. And so throughout the centuries has the Lord's
saying been verified: "Seek first his kingdom and his righteousness, and all these things shall be yours as well":[47]   *2632*

> For two thousand years this sentiment has lived and en-
> dured in the soul of the Church, impelling souls then and
> now to the heroic charity of monastic farmers, liberators of
> slaves, healers of the sick, and messengers of faith, civiliza-
> tion, and science to all generations and all peoples for the
> sake of creating the social conditions capable of offering to
> everyone possible a life worthy of man and of a Christian.[48]

---

45   Cf. John Paul II, *SRS* 38-40; *CA* 10.
46   Pius XII, *Summi pontificatus*, October 20, 1939; AAS 31 (1939) 423 ff.
47   *Mt* 6:33.
48   Pius XII, Discourse, June 1, 1941.

IN BRIEF

1943   Society ensures social justice by providing the conditions that allow associations and individuals to obtain their due.

1944   Respect for the human person considers the other "another self." It presupposes respect for the fundamental rights that flow from the dignity intrinsic of the person.

1945   The equality of men concerns their dignity as persons and the rights that flow from it.

1946   The differences among persons belong to God's plan, who wills that we should need one another. These differences should encourage charity.

1947   The equal dignity of human persons requires the effort to reduce excessive social and economic inequalities. It gives urgency to the elimination of sinful inequalities.

1948   Solidarity is an eminently Christian virtue. It practices the sharing of spiritual goods even more than material ones.

Chapter Three
God's Salvation: Law and Grace

1949   Called to beatitude but wounded by sin, man stands in need of salvation from God. Divine help comes to him in Christ through the law that guides him and the grace that sustains him:

> Work out your own salvation with fear and trembling; for God is at work in you, both to will and to work for his good pleasure.[1]

Article 1
THE MORAL LAW

1950   The moral law is the work of divine Wisdom. Its biblical meaning can be defined as fatherly instruction, God's pedagogy. It prescribes for man the ways, the rules of conduct that lead to the *53* promised beatitude; it proscribes the ways of evil which turn him *1719* away from God and his love. It is at once firm in its precepts and, in its promises, worthy of love.

1951   Law is a rule of conduct enacted by competent authority for the sake of the common good. The moral law presupposes the rational order, established among creatures for their good and to serve their final end, by the power, wisdom, and goodness of the Creator. All law finds its first and ultimate truth in the eternal law. Law is declared and established by reason as a participation in the *295* providence of the living God, Creator and Redeemer of all. "Such *306* an ordinance of reason is what one calls law."[2]

> Alone among all animate beings, man can boast of having been counted worthy to receive a law from God: as an animal endowed with reason, capable of understanding and discernment, he is to govern his conduct by using his freedom and reason, in obedience to the One who has entrusted *301* everything to him.[3]

---

1   *Phil* 2:12-13.
2   Leo XIII, *Libertas præstantissimum*: AAS 20 (1887/88), 597; cf. St. Thomas Aquinas, *STh* I-II, 90, 1.
3   Cf. Tertullian, *Adv. Marc*, 2, 4: PL 2, 288-289.

1952   There are different expressions of the moral law, all of them interrelated: eternal law – the source, in God, of all law; natural law; revealed law, comprising the Old Law and the New Law, or Law of the Gospel; finally, civil and ecclesiastical laws.

578 **1953**   The moral law finds its fullness and its unity in Christ. Jesus Christ is in person the way of perfection. He is the end of the law, for only he teaches and bestows the justice of God: "For Christ is the end of the law, that every one who has faith may be justified."[4]

I.   THE NATURAL MORAL LAW

1954   Man participates in the wisdom and goodness of the Creator who gives him mastery over his acts and the ability to govern himself with a view to the true and the good. The natural law
307 expresses the original moral sense which enables man to discern
1776 by reason the good and the evil, the truth and the lie:

> The natural law is written and engraved in the soul of each and every man, because it is human reason ordaining him to do good and forbidding him to sin . . . But this command of human reason would not have the force of law if it were not the voice and interpreter of a higher reason to which our spirit and our freedom must be submitted.[5]

1787 **1955**   The "divine and natural" law[6] shows man the way to follow so as to practice the good and attain his end. The natural law states the first and essential precepts which govern the moral
396 life. It hinges upon the desire for God and submission to him, who is the source and judge of all that is good, as well as upon the sense that the other is one's equal. Its principal precepts are expressed in
2070 the Decalogue. This law is called "natural," not in reference to the nature of irrational beings, but because reason which decrees it properly belongs to human nature:

> Where then are these rules written, if not in the book of that light we call the truth? In it is written every just law; from it the law passes into the heart of the man who does justice, not that it migrates into it, but that it places its imprint on it, like a seal on a ring that passes onto wax, without leaving the ring.[7]

---

4   *Rom* 10:4.
5   Leo XIII, *Libertas præstantissimum,* 597.
6   *GS* 89 § 1.
7   St. Augustine, *De Trin.* 14, 15, 21: PL 42, 1052.

> The natural law is nothing other than the light of understanding placed in us by God; through it we know what we must do and what we must avoid. God has given this light or law at the creation.[8]

1956 The natural law, present in the heart of each man and established by reason, is universal in its precepts and its authority extends to all men. It expresses the dignity of the person and *2261* determines the basis for his fundamental rights and duties:

> For there is a true law: right reason. It is in conformity with nature, is diffused among all men, and is immutable and eternal; its orders summon to duty; its prohibitions turn away from offense . . . . To replace it with a contrary law is a sacrilege; failure to apply even one of its provisions is forbidden; no one can abrogate it entirely.[9]

1957 Application of the natural law varies greatly; it can demand reflection that takes account of various conditions of life according to places, times, and circumstances. Nevertheless, in the diversity of cultures, the natural law remains as a rule that binds men among themselves and imposes on them, beyond the inevitable differences, common principles.

1958 The natural law is *immutable* and permanent throughout *2072* the variations of history;[10] it subsists under the flux of ideas and customs and supports their progress. The rules that express it remain substantially valid. Even when it is rejected in its very principles, it cannot be destroyed or removed from the heart of man. It always rises again in the life of individuals and societies:

> Theft is surely punished by your law, O Lord, and by the law that is written in the human heart, the law that iniquity itself does not efface.[11]

1959 The natural law, the Creator's very good work, provides the solid foundation on which man can build the structure of moral rules to guide his choices. It also provides the indispensable moral foundation for building the human community. Finally, it provides *1879* the necessary basis for the civil law with which it is connected, whether by a reflection that draws conclusions from its principles, or by additions of a positive and juridical nature.

---

8 St. Thomas Aquinas, *Dec. præc.* I.
9 Cicero, *Rep.* III, 22, 33.
10 Cf. *GS* 10.
11 St. Augustine, *Conf.* 2, 4, 9: PL 32, 678.

1960   The precepts of natural law are not perceived by everyone
clearly and immediately. In the present situation sinful man needs
2071   grace and revelation so moral and religious truths may be known
37   "by everyone with facility, with firm certainty and with no admixture of error."[12] The natural law provides revealed law and grace
with a foundation prepared by God and in accordance with the
work of the Spirit.

II.   THE OLD LAW

62   **1961**   God, our Creator and Redeemer, chose Israel for himself
to be his people and revealed his Law to them, thus preparing for
the coming of Christ. The Law of Moses expresses many truths
naturally accessible to reason. These are stated and authenticated
within the covenant of salvation.

1962   The Old Law is the first stage of revealed Law. Its moral
prescriptions are summed up in the Ten Commandments. The
2058   precepts of the Decalogue lay the foundations for the vocation of
man fashioned in the image of God; they prohibit what is contrary
to the love of God and neighbor and prescribe what is essential to
it. The Decalogue is a light offered to the conscience of every man
to make God's call and ways known to him and to protect him
against evil:

> God wrote on the tables of the Law what men did not read
> in their hearts.[13]

1963   According to Christian tradition, the Law is holy, spiritual,
and good,[14] yet still imperfect. Like a tutor[15] it shows what must
1610   be done, but does not of itself give the strength, the grace of the
Spirit, to fulfill it. Because of sin, which it cannot remove, it remains
a law of bondage. According to St. Paul, its special function is to
2542   denounce and *disclose sin*, which constitutes a "law of concupis-
2515   cence" in the human heart.[16] However, the Law remains the first
stage on the way to the kingdom. It prepares and disposes the
chosen people and each Christian for conversion and faith in the

---

12   Pius XII, *Humani generis*: DS 3876; cf. *Dei Filius* 2: DS 3005.
13   St. Augustine, *En. in Ps.* 57, 1: PL 36, 673.
14   Cf. *Rom* 7:12, 14, 16.
15   Cf. *Gal* 3:24.
16   Cf. *Rom* 7.

Savior God. It provides a teaching which endures for ever, like the Word of God.

1964   The Old Law is a *preparation for the Gospel*. "The Law is a   *122* pedagogy and a prophecy of things to come."[17] It prophesies and presages the work of liberation from sin which will be fulfilled in Christ: it provides the New Testament with images, "types," and symbols for expressing the life according to the Spirit. Finally, the Law is completed by the teaching of the sapiential books and the prophets which set its course toward the New Covenant and the Kingdom of heaven.

> There were . . . under the regimen of the Old Covenant, people who possessed the charity and grace of the Holy Spirit and longed above all for the spiritual and eternal promises by which they were associated with the New Law. Conversely, there exist carnal men under the New Covenant, still distanced from the perfection of the New Law: the fear   *1828* of punishment and certain temporal promises have been necessary, even under the New Covenant, to incite them to virtuous works. In any case, even though the Old Law prescribed charity, it did not give the Holy Spirit, through whom "God's charity has been poured into our hearts."[18]

III.   THE NEW LAW OR THE LAW OF THE GOSPEL

1965   The New Law or the Law of the Gospel is the perfection   *459* here on earth of the divine law, natural and revealed. It is the work of Christ and is expressed particularly in the Sermon on the Mount. It is also the work of the Holy Spirit and through him it becomes   *581* the interior law of charity: "I will establish a New Covenant with the house of Israel. . . . I will put my laws into their minds, and write them on their hearts, and I will be their God, and they shall be my   *715* people."[19]

1966   The New Law is the *grace of the Holy Spirit* given to the   *1999* faithful through faith in Christ. It works through charity; it uses the Sermon on the Mount to teach us what must be done and makes use of the sacraments to give us the grace to do it:

---

17   St. Irenæus, *Adv. haeres.* 4, 15, 1: PG 7/1, 1012.
18   St. Thomas Aquinas, *STh* I-II, 107, 1 *ad* 2; cf. *Rom* 5:5.
19   *Heb* 8:8, 10; cf. *Jer* 31:31-34.

> If anyone should meditate with devotion and perspicacity on the sermon our Lord gave on the mount, as we read in the Gospel of Saint Matthew, he will doubtless find there ... the perfect way of the Christian life. ... This sermon contains ... all the precepts needed to shape one's life.[20]

1967   The Law of the Gospel "fulfills," refines, surpasses, and leads the Old Law to its perfection.[21] In the Beatitudes, the New
577 Law *fulfills the divine promises* by elevating and orienting them toward the "kingdom of heaven." It is addressed to those open to accepting this new hope with faith – the poor, the humble, the afflicted, the pure of heart, those persecuted on account of Christ – and so marks out the surprising ways of the Kingdom.

1968   The Law of the Gospel *fulfills the commandments* of the Law. The Lord's Sermon on the Mount, far from abolishing or devaluing the moral prescriptions of the Old Law, releases their hidden
129 potential and has new demands arise from them: it reveals their entire divine and human truth. It does not add new external precepts, but proceeds to reform the heart, the root of human acts,
582 where man chooses between the pure and the impure,[22] where faith, hope, and charity are formed and with them the other virtues. The Gospel thus brings the Law to its fullness through imitation of the perfection of the heavenly Father, through forgiveness of enemies and prayer for persecutors, in emulation of the divine generosity.[23]

1434 **1969**   The New Law *practices the acts of religion*: almsgiving, prayer and fasting, directing them to the "Father who sees in secret," in contrast with the desire to "be seen by men."[24] Its prayer is the Our Father.[25]

1970   The Law of the Gospel requires us to make the decisive choice between "the two ways" and to put into practice the words
1696 of the Lord.[26] It is summed up in the *Golden Rule*, "Whatever you
1789 wish that men would do to you, do so to them; this is the law and the prophets."[27]

---

20 St. Augustine, *De serm. Dom.* 1, 1: PL 34, 1229-1230.
21 Cf. *Mt* 5:17-19.
22 Cf. *Mt* 15:18-19.
23 Cf. *Mt* 5:44, 48.
24 Cf. *Mt* 6:1-6; 16-18.
25 Cf. *Mt* 6:9-13; *Lk* 11:2-4.
26 Cf. *Mt* 7:13-14, 21-27.
27 *Mt* 7:12; cf. *Lk* 6:31.

The entire Law of the Gospel is contained in the *"new* 1823 *commandment"* of Jesus, to love one another as he has loved us.[28]

1971 To the Lord's Sermon on the Mount it is fitting to add the *moral catechesis of the apostolic teachings*, such as *Romans* 12-15, *1 Corinthians* 12-13, *Colossians* 3-4, *Ephesians* 4-5, etc. This doctrine hands on the Lord's teaching with the authority of the apostles, particularly in the presentation of the virtues that flow from faith in Christ and are animated by charity, the principal gift of the Holy Spirit. "Let charity be genuine. . . . Love one another with brotherly affection. . . . Rejoice in your hope, be patient in tribulation, be constant in prayer. Contribute to the needs of the saints, practice hospitality."[29] This catechesis also teaches us to deal with cases of 1789 conscience in the light of our relationship to Christ and to the Church.[30]

1972 The New Law is called a *law of love* because it makes us act 782 out of the love infused by the Holy Spirit, rather than from fear; a *law of grace*, because it confers the strength of grace to act, by means of faith and the sacraments; a *law of freedom*, because it sets us free from the ritual and juridical observances of the Old Law, inclines us to act spontaneously by the prompting of charity and, finally, lets us pass from the condition of a servant who "does not know 1828 what his master is doing" to that of a friend of Christ – "For all that I have heard from my Father I have made known to you" – or even to the status of son and heir.[31]

1973 Besides its precepts, the New Law also includes the *evan-* 2053 *gelical counsels*. The traditional distinction between God's commandments and the evangelical counsels is drawn in relation to charity, the perfection of Christian life. The precepts are intended 915 to remove whatever is incompatible with charity. The aim of the counsels is to remove whatever might hinder the development of charity, even if it is not contrary to it.[32]

1974 The evangelical counsels manifest the living fullness of charity, which is never satisfied with not giving more. They attest its vitality and call forth our spiritual readiness. The perfection of the New Law consists essentially in the precepts of love of God and 2013 neighbor. The counsels point out the more direct ways, the readier means, and are to be practiced in keeping with the vocation of each:

---

28 Cf. *Jn* 15:12; 13:34.
29 *Rom* 12:9-13.
30 Cf. *Rom* 14; *1 Cor* 5-10.
31 *Jn* 15:15; cf. *Jas* 1:25; 2:12; *Gal* 4:1-7. 21-31; *Rom* 8:15.
32 Cf. St. Thomas Aquinas, *STh* II-II, 184, 3.

[God] does not want each person to keep all the counsels, but only those appropriate to the diversity of persons, times, opportunities, and strengths, as charity requires; for it is charity, as queen of all virtues, all commandments, all counsels, and, in short, of all laws and all Christian actions, that gives to all of them their rank, order, time, and value.[33]

IN BRIEF

1975   According to Scripture the Law is a fatherly instruction by God which prescribes for man the ways that lead to the promised beatitude, and proscribes the ways of evil.

1976   "Law is an ordinance of reason for the common good, promulgated by the one who is in charge of the community" (St. Thomas Aquinas, *STh* I-II, 90, 4).

1977   Christ is the end of the law (cf. *Rom* 10:4); only he teaches and bestows the justice of God.

1978   The natural law is a participation in God's wisdom and goodness by man formed in the image of his Creator. It expresses the dignity of the human person and forms the basis of his fundamental rights and duties.

1979   The natural law is immutable, permanent throughout history. The rules that express it remain substantially valid. It is a necessary foundation for the erection of moral rules and civil law.

1980   The Old Law is the first stage of revealed law. Its moral prescriptions are summed up in the Ten Commandments.

1981   The Law of Moses contains many truths naturally accessible to reason. God has revealed them because men did not read them in their hearts.

1982   The Old Law is a preparation for the Gospel.

1983   The New Law is the grace of the Holy Spirit received by faith in Christ, operating through charity. It finds expression above all in the Lord's Sermon on the Mount and uses the sacraments to communicate grace to us.

---

33   St. Francis de Sales, *Love of God* 8, 6.

1984 The Law of the Gospel fulfills and surpasses the Old Law and brings it to perfection: its promises, through the Beatitudes of the Kingdom of heaven; its commandments, by reforming the heart, the root of human acts.

1985 The New Law is a law of love, a law of grace, a law of freedom.

1986 Besides its precepts the New Law includes the evangelical counsels. "The Church's holiness is fostered in a special way by the manifold counsels which the Lord proposes to his disciples in the Gospel" (*LG* 42 §2).

ARTICLE 2
GRACE AND JUSTIFICATION

I. JUSTIFICATION

1987 The grace of the Holy Spirit has the power to justify us, that is, to cleanse us from our sins and to communicate to us "the righteousness of God through faith in Jesus Christ" and through *734* Baptism:[34]

> But if we have died with Christ, we believe that we shall also live with him. For we know that Christ being raised from the dead will never die again; death no longer has dominion over him. The death he died he died to sin, once for all, but the life he lives he lives to God. So you also must consider yourselves as dead to sin and alive to God in Christ Jesus.[35]

1988 Through the power of the Holy Spirit we take part in Christ's Passion by dying to sin, and in his Resurrection by being born to a new life; we are members of his Body which is the Church, *654* branches grafted onto the vine which is himself:[36]

> [God] gave himself to us through his Spirit. By the participation of the Spirit, we become communicants in the divine *460* nature. . . . For this reason, those in whom the Spirit dwells are divinized.[37]

---

34 *Rom* 3:22; cf. 6:3-4.
35 *Rom* 6:8-11.
36 Cf. *1 Cor* 12; *Jn* 15:1-4.
37 St. Athanasius, *Ep. Serap.* 1, 24: PG 26, 585 and 588.

1989   The first work of the grace of the Holy Spirit is *conversion,*
effecting justification in accordance with Jesus' proclamation at the
1427 beginning of the Gospel: "Repent, for the kingdom of heaven is at
hand."[38] Moved by grace, man turns toward God and away from
sin, thus accepting forgiveness and righteousness from on high.
"Justification is not only the remission of sins, but also the sanctification and renewal of the interior man."[39]

1990   Justification *detaches man from sin* which contradicts the
love of God, and purifies his heart of sin. Justification follows upon
1446 God's merciful initiative of offering forgiveness. It reconciles man
1733 with God. It frees from the enslavement to sin, and it heals.

1991   Justification is at the same time *the acceptance of God's
righteousness* through faith in Jesus Christ. Righteousness (or "justice") here means the rectitude of divine love. With justification,
1812 faith, hope, and charity are poured into our hearts, and obedience
to the divine will is granted us.

617 **1992**   Justification has been *merited for us by the Passion of Christ*
who offered himself on the cross as a living victim, holy and
pleasing to God, and whose blood has become the instrument of
atonement for the sins of all men. Justification is conferred in
1266 Baptism, the sacrament of faith. It conforms us to the righteousness
of God, who makes us inwardly just by the power of his mercy. Its
294 purpose is the glory of God and of Christ, and the gift of eternal
life:[40]

> But now the righteousness of God has been manifested apart
> from law, although the law and the prophets bear witness to
> it, the righteousness of God through faith in Jesus Christ for
> all who believe. For there is no distinction: since all have
> sinned and fall short of the glory of God, they are justified
> by his grace as a gift, through the redemption which is in
> Christ Jesus, whom God put forward as an expiation by his
> blood, to be received by faith. This was to show God's
> righteousness, because in his divine forbearance he had
> passed over former sins; it was to prove at the present time
> that he himself is righteous and that he justifies him who has
> faith in Jesus.[41]

---

38   *Mt* 4:17.
39   Council of Trent (1547): DS 1528.
40   Cf. Council of Trent (1547): DS 1529.
41   *Rom* 3:21-26.

1993   Justification establishes *cooperation between God's grace and*   2008
man's freedom. On man's part it is expressed by the assent of faith
to the Word of God, which invites him to conversion, and in the
cooperation of charity with the prompting of the Holy Spirit who
precedes and preserves his assent:

> When God touches man's heart through the illumination of   2068
> the Holy Spirit, man himself is not inactive while receiving
> that inspiration, since he could reject it; and yet, without
> God's grace, he cannot by his own free will move himself
> toward justice in God's sight.[42]

1994   Justification is the *most excellent work of God's love* made
manifest in Christ Jesus and granted by the Holy Spirit. It is the
opinion of St. Augustine that "the justification of the wicked is a
greater work than the creation of heaven and earth," because   312
"heaven and earth will pass away but the salvation and justification of the elect . . . will not pass away."[43] He holds also that the
justification of sinners surpasses the creation of the angels in jus-   412
tice, in that it bears witness to a greater mercy.

1995   The Holy Spirit is the master of the interior life. By giving   741
birth to the "inner man,"[44] justification entails the *sanctification* of
his whole being:

> Just as you once yielded your members to impurity and to
> greater and greater iniquity, so now yield your members to
> righteousness for sanctification. . . . But now that you have
> been set free from sin and have become slaves of God, the
> return you get is sanctification and its end, eternal life.[45]

II.   GRACE

1996   Our justification comes from the grace of God. Grace is
favor, the *free and undeserved help* that God gives us to respond to
his call to become children of God, adoptive sons, partakers of the   153
divine nature and of eternal life.[46]

1997   Grace is a *participation in the life of God.* It introduces us into   375
the intimacy of Trinitarian life: by Baptism the Christian partici-   260
pates in the grace of Christ, the Head of his Body. As an "adopted

---

42 Council of Trent (1547): DS 1525.
43 St. Augustine, *In Jo. ev.* 72, 3: PL 35, 1823.
44 Cf. *Rom* 7:22; *Eph* 3:16.
45 *Rom* 6:19, 22.
46 Cf. *Jn* 1:12-18; 17:3; *Rom* 8:14-17; *2 Pet* 1:3-4.

son" he can henceforth call God "Father," in union with the only
Son. He receives the life of the Spirit who breathes charity into him
and who forms the Church.

1719 **1998**   This vocation to eternal life is *supernatural*. It depends
entirely on God's gratuitous initiative, for he alone can reveal and
give himself. It surpasses the power of human intellect and will, as
that of every other creature.[47]

1999   The grace of Christ is the gratuitous gift that God makes
to us of his own life, infused by the Holy Spirit into our soul to heal
1966 it of sin and to sanctify it. It is the *sanctifying* or *deifying grace*
received in Baptism. It is in us the source of the work of sanctification:[48]

> Therefore if any one is in Christ, he is a new creation; the old
> has passed away, behold, the new has come. All this is from
> God, who through Christ reconciled us to himself.[49]

2000   Sanctifying grace is an habitual gift, a stable and supernatural disposition that perfects the soul itself to enable it to live
with God, to act by his love. *Habitual grace*, the permanent disposition to live and act in keeping with God's call, is distinguished from
actual graces which refer to God's interventions, whether at the
beginning of conversion or in the course of the work of sanctification.

490 **2001**   The *preparation of man* for the reception of grace is already
a work of grace. This latter is needed to arouse and sustain our
collaboration in justification through faith, and in sanctification
through charity. God brings to completion in us what he has begun,
"since he who completes his work by cooperating with our will
began by working so that we might will it:"[50]

> Indeed we also work, but we are only collaborating with God
> who works, for his mercy has gone before us. It has gone
> before us so that we may be healed, and follows us so that
> once healed, we may be given life; it goes before us so that
> we may be called, and follows us so that we may be glorified;
> it goes before us so that we may live devoutly, and follows
> us so that we may always live with God: for without him we
> can do nothing.[51]

---

47 Cf. *1 Cor* 2:7-9.
48 Cf. *Jn* 4:14; 7:38-39.
49 *2 Cor* 5:17-18.
50 St. Augustine, *De gratia et libero arbitrio*, 17: PL 44, 901.
51 St. Augustine, *De natura et gratia*, 31: PL 44, 264.

2002   God's free initiative demands *man's free response*, for God has created man in his image by conferring on him, along with freedom, the power to know him and love him. The soul only *1742* enters freely into the communion of love. God immediately touches and directly moves the heart of man. He has placed in man a longing for truth and goodness that only he can satisfy. The promises of "eternal life" respond, beyond all hope, to this desire:

> If at the end of your very good works . . ., you rested on the seventh day, it was to foretell by the voice of your book that at the end of our works, which are indeed "very good" since you have given them to us, we shall also rest in you on the sabbath of eternal life.[52]

2550

2003   Grace is first and foremost the gift of the Spirit who justifies *1108* and sanctifies us. But grace also includes the gifts that the Spirit grants us to associate us with his work, to enable us to collaborate in the salvation of others and in the growth of the Body of Christ, the Church. There are *sacramental graces*, gifts proper to the differ- *1127* ent sacraments. There are furthermore *special graces*, also called *charisms* after the Greek term used by St. Paul and meaning "favor," "gratuitous gift," "benefit."[53] Whatever their character – sometimes it is extraordinary, such as the gift of miracles or of tongues – charisms are oriented toward sanctifying grace and are intended *799-801* for the common good of the Church. They are at the service of charity which builds up the Church.[54]

2004   Among the special graces ought to be mentioned the *graces of state* that accompany the exercise of the responsibilities of the Christian life and of the ministries within the Church:

> Having gifts that differ according to the grace given to us, let us use them: if prophecy, in proportion to our faith; if service, in our serving; he who teaches, in his teaching; he who exhorts, in his exhortation; he who contributes, in liberality; he who gives aid, with zeal; he who does acts of mercy, with cheerfulness.[55]

---

52   St. Augustine, *Conf.* 13, 36, 51: PL 32, 868; cf. *Gen* 1:31.
53   Cf. *LG* 12.
54   Cf. *1 Cor* 12.
55   *Rom* 12:6-8.

2005   Since it belongs to the supernatural order, grace *escapes our experience* and cannot be known except by faith. We cannot therefore rely on our feelings or our works to conclude that we are justified and saved.[56] However, according to the Lord's words – "Thus you will know them by their fruits"[57] – reflection on God's blessings in our life and in the lives of the saints offers us a guarantee that grace is at work in us and spurs us on to an ever greater faith and an attitude of trustful poverty.

> A pleasing illustration of this attitude is found in the reply of St. Joan of Arc to a question posed as a trap by her ecclesiastical judges: "Asked if she knew that she was in God's grace, she replied: 'If I am not, may it please God to put me in it; if I am, may it please God to keep me there.'"[58]

III.   MERIT

> You are glorified in the assembly of your Holy Ones, for in crowning their merits you are crowning your own gifts.[59]

1723   **2006**   The term "merit" refers in general to the *recompense owed* by a community or a society for the action of one of its members, experienced either as beneficial or harmful, deserving reward or
1807   punishment. Merit is relative to the virtue of justice, in conformity with the principle of equality which governs it.

2007   With regard to God, there is no strict right to any merit on
42   the part of man. Between God and us there is an immeasurable inequality, for we have received everything from him, our Creator.

2008   The merit of man before God in the Christian life arises from the fact that *God has freely chosen to associate man with the work*
306   *of his grace.* The fatherly action of God is first on his own initiative,
155   and then follows man's free acting through his collaboration, so
970   that the merit of good works is to be attributed in the first place to the grace of God, then to the faithful. Man's merit, moreover, itself is due to God, for his good actions proceed in Christ, from the predispositions and assistance given by the Holy Spirit.

---

56   Cf. Council of Trent (1547): DS 1533-1534.
57   *Mt* 7:20.
58   Acts of the trial of St. Joan of Arc.
59   *Roman Missal*, Prefatio I de Sanctis; *Qui in Sanctorum concilio celebraris, et eorum coronando merita tua dona coronas,* citing the "Doctor of grace," St. Augustine, *En. in Ps.* 102, 7: PL 37, 1321-1322.

2009   Filial adoption, in making us partakers by grace in the divine nature, can bestow *true merit* on us as a result of God's gratuitous justice. This is our right by grace, the full right of love, making us "co-heirs" with Christ and worthy of obtaining "the promised inheritance of eternal life."[60] The merits of our good works are gifts of the divine goodness.[61] "Grace has gone before us; now we are given what is due.... Our merits are God's gifts."[62]   *604*

2010   Since the initiative belongs to God in the order of grace, *no   1998 one can merit the initial grace* of forgiveness and justification, at the beginning of conversion. Moved by the Holy Spirit and by charity, *we can then merit* for ourselves and for others the graces needed for our sanctification, for the increase of grace and charity, and for the attainment of eternal life. Even temporal goods like health and friendship can be merited in accordance with God's wisdom. These graces and goods are the object of Christian prayer. Prayer attends to the grace we need for meritorious actions.

2011   *The charity of Christ is the source in us of all our merits* before   *492* God. Grace, by uniting us to Christ in active love, ensures the supernatural quality of our acts and consequently their merit before God and before men. The saints have always had a lively awareness that their merits were pure grace.

> After earth's exile, I hope to go and enjoy you in the father-
> land, but I do not want to lay up merits for heaven. I want
> to work for your *love alone*.... In the evening of this life, I
> shall appear before you with empty hands, for I do not ask
> you, Lord, to count my works. All our justice is blemished   *1460*
> in your eyes. I wish, then, to be clothed in your own *justice*
> and to receive from your *love* the eternal possession of *your-
> self.*[63]

---

60   Council of Trent (1547): DS 1546.
61   Cf. Council of Trent (1547): DS 1548.
62   St. Augustine, *Sermo* 298, 4-5: PL 38, 1367.
63   St. Thérèse of Lisieux, "Act of Offering" in *Story of a Soul,* tr. John Clarke (Washington DC: ICS, 1981), 277.

IV.   CHRISTIAN HOLINESS

2012   "We know that in everything God works for good with
those who love him . . . For those whom he foreknew he also
459   predestined to be conformed to the image of his Son, in order that
he might be the first-born among many brethren. And those whom
he predestined he also called; and those whom he called he also
justified; and those whom he justified he also glorified."[64]

2013   "All Christians in any state or walk of life are called to the
915, 2545   fullness of Christian life and to the perfection of charity."[65] All are
825   called to holiness: "Be perfect, as your heavenly Father is perfect."[66]

> In order to reach this perfection the faithful should use the
> strength dealt out to them by Christ's gift, so that . . . doing
> the will of the Father in everything, they may wholeheart-
> edly devote themselves to the glory of God and to the service
> of their neighbor. Thus the holiness of the People of God will
> grow in fruitful abundance, as is clearly shown in the history
> of the Church through the lives of so many saints.[67]

2014   Spiritual progress tends toward ever more intimate union
with Christ. This union is called "mystical" because it participates
774   in the mystery of Christ through the sacraments – "the holy mysteries" – and, in him, in the mystery of the Holy Trinity. God calls
us all to this intimate union with him, even if the special graces or
extraordinary signs of this mystical life are granted only to some
for the sake of manifesting the gratuitous gift given to all.

2015   The way of perfection passes by way of the Cross. There is
no holiness without renunciation and spiritual battle.[68] Spiritual
407, 2725   progress entails the ascesis and mortification that gradually lead
1438   to living in the peace and joy of the Beatitudes:

> He who climbs never stops going from beginning to begin-
> ning, through beginnings that have no end. He never stops
> desiring what he already knows.[69]

---

64   *Rom* 8:28-30.
65   *LG* 40 § 2.
66   *Mt* 5:48.
67   *LG* 40 § 2.
68   Cf. *2 Tim* 4.
69   St. Gregory of Nyssa, *Hom. in Cant.* 8: PG 44, 941C.

2016 The children of our holy mother the Church rightly hope for *the grace of final perseverance and the recompense* of God their Father for the good works accomplished with his grace in communion with Jesus.[70] Keeping the same rule of life, believers share the "blessed hope" of those whom the divine mercy gathers into the "holy city, the new Jerusalem, coming down out of heaven from God, prepared as a bride adorned for her husband."[71]

162, 1821
1274

IN BRIEF

2017 The grace of the Holy Spirit confers upon us the righteousness of God. Uniting us by faith and Baptism to the Passion and Resurrection of Christ, the Spirit makes us sharers in his life.

2018 Like conversion, justification has two aspects. Moved by grace, man turns toward God and away from sin, and so accepts forgiveness and righteousness from on high.

2019 Justification includes the remission of sins, sanctification, and the renewal of the inner man.

2020 Justification has been merited for us by the Passion of Christ. It is granted us through Baptism. It conforms us to the righteousness of God, who justifies us. It has for its goal the glory of God and of Christ, and the gift of eternal life. It is the most excellent work of God's mercy.

2021 Grace is the help God gives us to respond to our vocation of becoming his adopted sons. It introduces us into the intimacy of the Trinitarian life.

2022 The divine initiative in the work of grace precedes, prepares, and elicits the free response of man. Grace responds to the deepest yearnings of human freedom, calls freedom to cooperate with it, and perfects freedom.

2023 Sanctifying grace is the gratuitous gift of his life that God makes to us; it is infused by the Holy Spirit into the soul to heal it of sin and to sanctify it.

2024 Sanctifying grace makes us "pleasing to God." Charisms, special graces of the Holy Spirit, are oriented to sanctifying grace and are intended for the

---

70 Cf. Council of Trent (1547): DS 1576.
71 *Rev* 21:2.

common good of the Church. God also acts through many actual graces, to be distinguished from habitual grace which is permanent in us.

2025   We can have merit in God's sight only because of God's free plan to associate man with the work of his grace. Merit is to be ascribed in the first place to the grace of God, and secondly to man's collaboration. Man's merit is due to God.

2026   The grace of the Holy Spirit can confer true merit on us, by virtue of our adoptive filiation, and in accordance with God's gratuitous justice. Charity is the principal source of merit in us before God.

2027   No one can merit the initial grace which is at the origin of conversion. Moved by the Holy Spirit, we can merit for ourselves and for others all the graces needed to attain eternal life, as well as necessary temporal goods.

2028   "All Christians . . . are called to the fullness of Christian life and to the perfection of charity" (*LG* 40 § 2). "Christian perfection has but one limit, that of having none" (St. Gregory of Nyssa, *De vita Mos.*: PG 44, 300D).

2029   "If any man would come after me, let him deny himself and take up his cross and follow me" (*Mt* 16:24).

ARTICLE 3
THE CHURCH, MOTHER AND TEACHER

2030   It is in the Church, in communion with all the baptized, that the Christian fulfills his vocation. From the Church he receives the Word of God containing the teachings of "the law of Christ."[72] From the Church he receives the grace of the sacraments that sustains him on the "way." From the Church he learns the *example*
828   *of holiness* and recognizes its model and source in the all-holy Virgin Mary; he discerns it in the authentic witness of those who live it; he discovers it in the spiritual tradition and long history of the saints who have gone before him and whom the liturgy cele-
1172   brates in the rhythms of the sanctoral cycle.

72   *Gal* 6:2.

2031   *The moral life is spiritual worship.* We "present [our] bodies as a living sacrifice, holy and acceptable to God,"[73] within the Body of Christ that we form and in communion with the offering of his   *1368* Eucharist. In the liturgy and the celebration of the sacraments, prayer and teaching are conjoined with the grace of Christ to enlighten and nourish Christian activity. As does the whole of the Christian life, the moral life finds its source and summit in the Eucharistic sacrifice.

I.   MORAL LIFE AND THE MAGISTERIUM OF THE CHURCH   *85-87*
888-892

2032   The Church, the "pillar and bulwark of the truth," "has received this solemn command of Christ from the apostles to announce the saving truth."[74] "To the Church belongs the right always and everywhere to announce moral principles, including those pertaining to the social order, and to make judgments on any   *2246* human affairs to the extent that they are required by the fundamental rights of the human person or the salvation of souls."[75]   *2420*

2033   The *Magisterium of the Pastors of the Church* in moral matters is ordinarily exercised in catechesis and preaching, with the help of the works of theologians and spiritual authors. Thus from generation to generation, under the aegis and vigilance of the pastors, the "deposit" of Christian moral teaching has been handed   *84* on, a deposit composed of a characteristic body of rules, commandments, and virtues proceeding from faith in Christ and animated by charity. Alongside the Creed and the Our Father, the basis for this catechesis has traditionally been the Decalogue which sets out the principles of moral life valid for all men.

2034   The Roman Pontiff and the bishops are "authentic teachers, that is, teachers endowed with the authority of Christ, who preach the faith to the people entrusted to them, the faith to be believed and put into practice."[76] The *ordinary* and universal *Magisterium* of the Pope and the bishops in communion with him teach the faithful the truth to believe, the charity to practice, the beatitude to hope for.

---

73   *Rom* 12:1.
74   *1 Tim* 3:15; LG 17.
75   CIC, can. 747 § 2.
76   LG 25.

2035   The supreme degree of participation in the authority of Christ is ensured by the charism of *infallibility*. This infallibility extends as far as does the deposit of divine Revelation; it also extends to all those elements of doctrine, including morals, without which the saving truths of the faith cannot be preserved, explained, or observed.[77]

2036   The authority of the Magisterium extends also to the specific precepts of the *natural law*, because their observance, de-
1960 manded by the Creator, is necessary for salvation. In recalling the prescriptions of the natural law, the Magisterium of the Church exercises an essential part of its prophetic office of proclaiming to men what they truly are and reminding them of what they should be before God.[78]

2037   The law of God entrusted to the Church is taught to the faithful as the way of life and truth. The faithful therefore have the *right* to be instructed in the divine saving precepts that purify judgment and, with grace, heal wounded human reason.[79] They have the *duty* of observing the constitutions and decrees conveyed
2041 by the legitimate authority of the Church. Even if they concern disciplinary matters, these determinations call for docility in charity.

2038   In the work of teaching and applying Christian morality, the Church needs the dedication of pastors, the knowledge of theologians, and the contribution of all Christians and men of good
2442 will. Faith and the practice of the Gospel provide each person with an experience of life "in Christ," who enlightens him and makes him able to evaluate the divine and human realities according to the Spirit of God.[80] Thus the Holy Spirit can use the humblest to enlighten the learned and those in the highest positions.

---

77 Cf. *LG* 25; CDF, declaration, *Mysterium Ecclesiae* 3.
78 Cf. *DH* 14.
79 Cf. CIC, can. 213.
80 Cf. *1 Cor* 2:10-15.

2039   Ministries should be exercised in a spirit of fraternal service and dedication to the Church, in the name of the Lord.[81] At the
same time the conscience of each person should avoid confining
itself to individualistic considerations in its moral judgments of the
person's own acts. As far as possible conscience should take account of the good of all, as expressed in the moral law, natural and
revealed, and consequently in the law of the Church and in the
authoritative teaching of the Magisterium on moral questions.
Personal conscience and reason should not be set in opposition to   *1783*
the moral law or the Magisterium of the Church.

2040   Thus a true *filial spirit toward the Church* can develop among
Christians. It is the normal flowering of the baptismal grace which
has begotten us in the womb of the Church and made us members
of the Body of Christ. In her motherly care, the Church grants us
the mercy of God which prevails over all our sins and is especially
at work in the sacrament of reconciliation. With a mother's fore-
sight, she also lavishes on us day after day in her liturgy the   *167*
nourishment of the Word and Eucharist of the Lord.

II.   The Precepts of the Church

2041   The precepts of the Church are set in the context of a moral
life bound to and nourished by liturgical life. The obligatory character of these positive laws decreed by the pastoral authorities is
meant to guarantee to the faithful the indispensable minimum in
the spirit of prayer and moral effort, in the growth in love of God
and neighbor:

2042   The first precept ("You shall attend Mass on Sundays and holy
days of obligation.") requires the faithful to participate in the Eucharistic   *1389*
celebration when the Christian community gathers together on the day   *2180*
commemorating the Resurrection of the Lord.[82]

The second precept ("You shall confess your sins at least once a
year.") ensures preparation for the Eucharist by the reception of the   *1457*
sacrament of reconciliation, which continues Baptism's work of conversion and forgiveness.[83]

The third precept ("You shall humbly receive your Creator in   *1389*
Holy Communion at least during the Easter season.") guarantees as a
minimum the reception of the Lord's Body and Blood in connection with
the Paschal feasts, the origin and center of the Christian liturgy.[84]

---

81   Cf. *Rom* 12:8, 11.
82   Cf. CIC, cann. 1246-1248; CCEO, can. 881 § 1, § 2, § 4.
83   Cf. CIC, can. 989; CCEO, can. 719.
84   Cf. CIC, can. 920; CCEO, cann. 708; 881 § 3.

2043   The fourth precept ("You shall keep holy the holy days of obligation.") completes the Sunday observance by participation in the principal
2177 liturgical feasts which honor the mysteries of the Lord, the Virgin Mary,
and the saints.[85]

1387   The fifth precept ("You shall observe the prescribed days of
1438 fasting and abstinence.") ensures the times of ascesis and penance which
prepare us for the liturgical feasts; they help us acquire mastery over our
instincts and freedom of heart.[86]

1351   The faithful also have the duty of providing for the material needs
of the Church, each according to his abilities.[87]

III.   MORAL LIFE AND MISSIONARY WITNESS

2044   The fidelity of the baptized is a primordial condition for
the proclamation of the Gospel and for the *Church's mission in the*
852, 905 *world.* In order that the message of salvation can show the power
of its truth and radiance before men, it must be authenticated by
the witness of the life of Christians. "The witness of a Christian life
and good works done in a supernatural spirit have great power to
draw men to the faith and to God."[88]

753 **2045**   Because they are members of the Body whose Head is
Christ,[89] Christians contribute to *building up the Church* by the
constancy of their convictions and their moral lives. The Church
828 increases, grows, and develops through the holiness of her faithful,
until "we all attain to the unity of the faith and of the knowledge
of the Son of God, to mature manhood, to the measure of the stature
of the fullness of Christ."[90]

2046   By living with the mind of Christ, Christians *hasten the*
coming of the Reign of God, "a kingdom of justice, love, and
671, 2819 peace."[91] They do not, for all that, abandon their earthly tasks;
faithful to their master, they fulfill them with uprightness, patience, and love.

---

85 Cf. CIC, can. 1246; CCEO, cann. 881 § 1, § 4; 880 § 3.
86 Cf. CIC, cann. 1249-1251; CCEO, can. 882.
87 Cf. CIC, can. 222.
88 *AA* 6 § 2.
89 Cf. *Eph* 1:22.
90 *Eph* 4:13; cf. *LG* 39.
91 *Roman Missal*, Preface of Christ the King.

IN BRIEF

2047 The moral life is a spiritual worship. Christian activity finds its nourishment in the liturgy and the celebration of the sacraments.

2048 The precepts of the Church concern the moral and Christian life united with the liturgy and nourished by it.

2049 The Magisterium of the Pastors of the Church in moral matters is ordinarily exercised in catechesis and preaching, on the basis of the Decalogue which states the principles of moral life valid for every man.

2050 The Roman Pontiff and the bishops, as authentic teachers, preach to the People of God the faith which is to be believed and applied in moral life. It is also encumbent on them to pronounce on moral questions that fall within the natural law and reason.

2051 The infallibility of the Magisterium of the Pastors extends to all the elements of doctrine, including moral doctrine, without which the saving truths of the faith cannot be preserved, expounded, or observed.

The Ten Commandments

Exodus 20:2-17	Deuteronomy 5:6-21	A Traditional Catechetical Formula
I am the LORD your God, who brought you out of the land of Egypt, out of the house of bondage.	I am the LORD your God, who brought you out of the land of Egypt, out of the house of bondage.	1. I am the LORD your God: you shall not have strange Gods before me.
You shall have no other gods before me. You shall not make for yourself a graven image, or any likeness of anything that is in heaven above, or that is in the earth beneath, or that is in the water under the earth; you shall not bow down to them or serve them; for I the LORD your God am a jealous God, visiting the iniquity of the fathers upon the children to the third and the fourth generation of those who hate me, but showing steadfast love to thousands of those who love me and keep my commandments.	You shall have no other gods before me . . .	
You shall not take the name of the LORD your God in vain; for the LORD will not hold him guiltless who takes his name in vain.	You shall not take the name of the LORD your God in vain: . . .	2. You shall not take the name of the LORD your God in vain.
Remember the sabbath day, to keep it holy. Six days you shall labor, and do all your work; but the seventh day is a sabbath to the LORD your God; in it you shall not do any work, you, or your son, or your daughter, your manservant, or your maidservant, or your cattle, or the sojourner who is within your gates; for in six days the LORD made heaven and earth, the sea, and all that is in them, and rested the seventh day; therefore the LORD blessed the sabbath day and hallowed it.	Observe the sabbath day, to keep it holy . . .	3. Remember to keep holy the LORD'S Day.

The Ten Commandments

Exodus 20:2-17	Deuteronomy 5:6-21	A Traditional Catechetical Formula
Honor your father and your mother, that your days may be long in the land which the LORD your God gives you.	Honor your father and your mother . . .	4. Honor your father and your mother.
You shall not kill.	You shall not kill.	5. You shall not kill.
You shall not commit adultery.	Neither shall you commit adultery.	6. You shall not commit adultery.
You shall not steal.	Neither shall you steal.	7. You shall not steal.
You shall not bear false witness against your neighbor.	Neither shall you bear false witness against your neighbor.	8. You shall not bear false witness against your neighbor.
You shall not covet your neighbor's house; you shall not covet your neighbor's wife, or his manservant, or his maidservant, or his ox, or his ass, or anything that is your neighbor's.	Neither shall you covet your neighbor's wife . . . You shall not desire . . . anything that is your neighbor's.	9. You shall not covet your neighbor's wife. 10. You shall not covet your neighbor's goods.

SECTION TWO
THE TEN COMMANDMENTS

"Teacher, what must I do . . .?"

2052   "Teacher, what good deed must I do, to have eternal life?" To the young man who asked this question, Jesus answers first by invoking the necessity to recognize God as the "One there is who is good," as the supreme Good and the source of all good. Then Jesus tells him: "If you would enter life, keep the commandments." 1858 And he cites for his questioner the precepts that concern love of neighbor: "You shall not kill, You shall not commit adultery, You shall not steal, You shall not bear false witness, Honor your father and mother." Finally Jesus sums up these commandments positively: "You shall love your neighbor as yourself."[1]

2053   To this first reply Jesus adds a second: "If you would be perfect, go, sell what you possess and give to the poor, and you will have treasure in heaven; and come, follow me."[2] This reply does not do away with the first: following Jesus Christ involves keeping the Commandments. The Law has not been abolished,[3] but rather 1968 man is invited to rediscover it in the person of his Master who is its perfect fulfillment. In the three synoptic Gospels, Jesus' call to the rich young man to follow him, in the obedience of a disciple and in the observance of the Commandments, is joined to the call 1973 to poverty and chastity.[4] The evangelical counsels are inseparable from the Commandments.

2054   Jesus acknowledged the Ten Commandments, but he also showed the power of the Spirit at work in their letter. He preached 581 a "righteousness [which] exceeds that of the scribes and Pharisees"[5] as well as that of the Gentiles.[6] He unfolded all the demands of the Commandments. "You have heard that it was said to the men of old, 'You shall not kill.' . . . But I say to you that every one who is angry with his brother shall be liable to judgment."[7]

---

1   *Mt* 19:16-19.
2   *Mt* 19:21.
3   Cf. *Mt* 5:17.
4   Cf. *Mt* 19:6-12, 21, 23-29.
5   *Mt* 5:20.
6   Cf. *Mt* 5:46-47.
7   *Mt* 5:21-22.

2055   When someone asks him, "Which commandment in the
Law is the greatest?"[8] Jesus replies: "You shall love the Lord your
God with all your heart, and with all your soul, and with all your *129*
mind. This is the greatest and first commandment. And a second
is like it: You shall love your neighbor as yourself. On these two
commandments hang all the Law and the prophets."[9] The Decalogue must be interpreted in light of this twofold yet single commandment of love, the fullness of the Law:

> The commandments: "You shall not commit adultery, You
> shall not kill, You shall not steal, You shall not covet," and
> any other commandment, are summed up in this sentence:
> "You shall love your neighbor as yourself." Love does no
> wrong to a neighbor; therefore love is the fulfilling of the
> law.[10]

The Decalogue in Sacred Scripture

2056   The word "Decalogue" means literally "ten words."[11] God
revealed these "ten words" to his people on the holy mountain.
They were written "with the finger of God,"[12] unlike the other   *700*
commandments written by Moses.[13] They are pre-eminently the   *62*
words of God. They are handed on to us in the books of *Exodus*[14]
and *Deuteronomy*.[15] Beginning with the Old Testament, the sacred
books refer to the "ten words,"[16] but it is in the New Covenant in
Jesus Christ that their full meaning will be revealed.

2057   The Decalogue must first be understood in the context of
the Exodus, God's great liberating event at the center of the Old
Covenant. Whether formulated as negative commandments, pro-   *2084*
hibitions, or as positive precepts such as: "Honor your father and
mother," the "ten words" point out the conditions of a life freed
from the slavery of sin. The Decalogue is a path of life:

> If you love the LORD your God, by walking in his ways, and
> by keeping his commandments and his statutes and his
> ordinances, then you shall live and multiply.[17]

---

  8   *Mt* 22:36.
  9   *Mt* 22:37-40; cf. *Deut* 6:5; *Lev* 19:18.
 10   *Rom* 13:9-10.
 11   *Ex* 34:28; *Deut* 4:13; 10:4.
 12   *Ex* 31:18; *Deut* 5:22.
 13   Cf. *Deut* 31:9. 24.
 14   Cf. *Ex* 20:1-17.
 15   Cf. *Deut* 5:6-22.
 16   Cf. for example *Hos* 4:2; *Jer* 7:9; *Ezek* 18:5-9.
 17   *Deut* 30:16.

2170   This liberating power of the Decalogue appears, for example, in the commandment about the sabbath rest, directed also to foreigners and slaves:

> You shall remember that you were a servant in the land of Egypt, and the LORD your God brought you out thence with a mighty hand and an outstretched arm.[18]

1962 **2058**   The "ten words" sum up and proclaim God's law: "These words the Lord spoke to all your assembly at the mountain out of the midst of the fire, the cloud, and the thick darkness, with a loud voice; and he added no more. And he wrote them upon two tables of stone, and gave them to me."[19] For this reason these two tables are called "the Testimony." In fact, they contain the terms of the covenant concluded between God and his people. These "tables of the Testimony" were to be deposited in "the ark."[20]

707 **2059**   The "ten words" are pronounced by God in the midst of a theophany ("The LORD spoke with you face to face at the mountain, out of the midst of the fire."[21]). They belong to God's revelation of himself and his glory. The gift of the Commandments is the gift of
2823 God himself and his holy will. In making his will known, God reveals himself to his people.

2060   The gift of the commandments and of the Law is part of the covenant God sealed with his own. In *Exodus*, the revelation of the "ten words" is granted between the proposal of the covenant[22] and its conclusion – after the people had committed themselves to "do" all that the Lord had said, and to "obey" it.[23] The Decalogue
62 is never handed on without first recalling the covenant ("The LORD our God made a covenant with us in Horeb.").[24]

2061   The Commandments take on their full meaning within the covenant. According to Scripture, man's moral life has all its meaning in and through the covenant. The first of the "ten words" recalls that God loved his people first:

---

18 *Deut* 5:15.
19 *Deut* 5:22.
20 *Ex* 25:16; 31:18; 32:15; 34:29; 40:1-2.
21 *Deut* 5:4.
22 Cf. *Ex* 19.
23 Cf. *Ex* 24:7.
24 *Deut* 5:2.

> Since there was a passing from the paradise of freedom to the slavery of this world, in punishment for sin, the first phrase of the Decalogue, the first word of God's commandments, bears on freedom: "I am the LORD your God, who brought you out of the land of Egypt, out of the house of slavery."[25]

2086

2062 The Commandments properly so-called come in the second place: they express the implications of belonging to God through the establishment of the covenant. Moral existence is a *response* to the Lord's loving initiative. It is the acknowledgement and homage given to God and a worship of thanksgiving. It is cooperation with the plan God pursues in history.

142
2002

2063 The covenant and dialogue between God and man are also attested to by the fact that all the obligations are stated in the first person ("I am the Lord.") and addressed by God to another personal subject ("you"). In all God's commandments, the *singular* personal pronoun designates the recipient. God makes his will known to each person in particular, at the same time as he makes it known to the whole people:

878

> The Lord prescribed love towards God and taught justice towards neighbor, so that man would be neither unjust, nor unworthy of God. Thus, through the Decalogue, God prepared man to become his friend and to live in harmony with his neighbor.... The words of the Decalogue remain likewise for us Christians. Far from being abolished, they have received amplification and development from the fact of the coming of the Lord in the flesh.[26]

The Decalogue in the Church's Tradition

2064 In fidelity to Scripture and in conformity with the example of Jesus, the tradition of the Church has acknowledged the primordial importance and significance of the Decalogue.

2065 Ever since St. Augustine, the Ten Commandments have occupied a predominant place in the catechesis of baptismal candidates and the faithful. In the fifteenth century, the custom arose of expressing the commandments of the Decalogue in rhymed formulae, easy to memorize and in positive form. They are still in use today. The catechisms of the Church have often expounded Christian morality by following the order of the Ten Commandments.

---

25 Origen, *Hom. in Ex.* 8, 1: PG 12, 350; cf. *Ex* 20:2; *Deut* 5:6.
26 St. Irenaeus, *Adv. haeres.*, 4, 16, 3-4: PG 7/1, 1017-1018.

2066   The division and numbering of the Commandments have varied in the course of history. The present catechism follows the division of the Commandments established by St. Augustine, which has become traditional in the Catholic Church. It is also that of the Lutheran confessions. The Greek Fathers worked out a slightly different division, which is found in the Orthodox Churches and Reformed communities.

2067   The Ten Commandments state what is required in the love of God and love of neighbor. The first three concern love of God, 1853 and the other seven love of neighbor.

> As charity comprises the two commandments to which the Lord related the whole Law and the prophets . . . so the Ten Commandments were themselves given on two tablets. Three were written on one tablet and seven on the other.[27]

2068   The Council of Trent teaches that the Ten Commandments are obligatory for Christians and that the justified man is still 1993 bound to keep them;[28] the Second Vatican Council confirms: "The bishops, successors of the apostles, receive from the Lord . . . the mission of teaching all peoples, and of preaching the Gospel to 888 every creature, so that all men may attain salvation through faith, Baptism and the observance of the Commandments."[29]

The unity of the Decalogue

2069   The Decalogue forms a coherent whole. Each "word" refers to each of the others and to all of them; they reciprocally 2534 condition one another. The two tables shed light on one another; they form an organic unity. To transgress one commandment is to infringe all the others.[30] One cannot honor another person without blessing God his Creator. One cannot adore God without loving all men, his creatures. The Decalogue brings man's religious and social life into unity.

The Decalogue and the natural law

1955 **2070**   The Ten Commandments belong to God's revelation. At the same time they teach us the true humanity of man. They bring to light the essential duties, and therefore, indirectly, the fundamental rights inherent in the nature of the human person. The Decalogue contains a privileged expression of the natural law:

---

27 St. Augustine, *Sermo* 33, 2, 2: PL 38, 208.
28 Cf. DS 1569-1570.
29 *LG* 24.
30 Cf. *Jas* 2:10-11.

> From the beginning, God had implanted in the heart of man the precepts of the natural law. Then he was content to remind him of them. This was the Decalogue.[31]

2071   The commandments of the Decalogue, although accessible to reason alone, have been revealed. To attain a complete and *1960* certain understanding of the requirements of the natural law, sinful humanity needed this revelation:

> A full explanation of the commandments of the Decalogue became necessary in the state of sin because the light of reason was obscured and the will had gone astray.[32]

We know God's commandments through the divine revelation proposed to us in the Church, and through the voice of moral *1777* conscience.

The obligation of the Decalogue

2072   Since they express man's fundamental duties towards God and towards his neighbor, the Ten Commandments reveal, in their primordial content, *grave* obligations. They are fundamentally im- *1858* mutable, and they oblige always and everywhere. No one can *1958* dispense from them. The Ten Commandments are engraved by God in the human heart.

2073   Obedience to the Commandments also implies obligations in matter which is, in itself, light. Thus abusive language is forbidden by the fifth commandment, but would be a grave offense only as a result of circumstances or the offender's intention.

"Apart from me you can do nothing"

2074   Jesus says: "I am the vine, you are the branches. He who abides in me, and I in him, he it is that bears much fruit, for apart from me you can do nothing."[33] The fruit referred to in this saying is the *2732* holiness of a life made fruitful by union with Christ. When we believe in Jesus Christ, partake of his mysteries, and keep his commandments, the Savior himself comes to love, in us, his Father and his brethren, *521* our Father and our brethren. His person becomes, through the Spirit, the living and interior rule of our activity. "This is my commandment, that you love one another as I have loved you."[34]

---

31   St. Irenaeus, *Adv. haeres.* 4, 15, 1: PG 7/1, 1012.
32   St. Bonaventure, *Comm. sent.* 4, 37, 1, 3.
33   *Jn* 15:5.
34   *Jn* 15:12.

IN BRIEF

2075   "What good deed must I do, to have eternal life?" – "If you would enter into life, keep the commandments" (*Mt* 19:16-17).

2076   By his life and by his preaching Jesus attested to the permanent validity of the Decalogue.

2077   The gift of the Decalogue is bestowed from within the covenant concluded by God with his people. God's commandments take on their true meaning in and through this covenant.

2078   In fidelity to Scripture and in conformity with Jesus' example, the tradition of the Church has always acknowledged the primordial importance and significance of the Decalogue.

2079   The Decalogue forms an organic unity in which each "word" or "commandment" refers to all the others taken together. To transgress one commandment is to infringe the whole Law (cf. *Jas* 2:10-11).

2080   The Decalogue contains a privileged expression of the natural law. It is made known to us by divine revelation and by human reason.

2081   The Ten Commandments, in their fundamental content, state grave obligations. However, obedience to these precepts also implies obligations in matter which is, in itself, light.

2082   What God commands he makes possible by his grace.

CHAPTER ONE
"YOU SHALL LOVE THE LORD YOUR GOD
WITH ALL YOUR HEART, AND WITH ALL YOUR
SOUL, AND WITH ALL YOUR MIND"

2083   Jesus summed up man's duties toward God in this saying: *367*
"You shall love the Lord your God with all your heart, and with all
your soul, and with all your mind."[1] This immediately echoes the
solemn call: "Hear, O Israel: the LORD our God is one LORD."[2]

God has loved us first. The love of the One God is recalled   *199*
in the first of the "ten words." The commandments then make
explicit the response of love that man is called to give to his God.

ARTICLE 1
THE FIRST COMMANDMENT

> I am the LORD your God, who brought you out of the land
> of Egypt, out of the house of bondage. You shall have no
> other gods before me. You shall not make for yourself a
> graven image, or any likeness of anything that is in heaven
> above, or that is in the earth beneath, or that is in the water
> under the earth; you shall not bow down to them or serve
> them.[3]
>
> It is written: "You shall worship the Lord your God and him
> only shall you serve."[4]

I.   "YOU SHALL WORSHIP THE LORD YOUR GOD
AND HIM ONLY SHALL YOU SERVE"

2084   God makes himself known by recalling his all-powerful,
loving, and liberating action in the history of the one he addresses:
"I brought you out of the land of Egypt, out of the house of   *2057*
bondage." The first word contains the first commandment of the
Law: "You shall fear the LORD your God; you shall serve him. . . .
You shall not go after other gods."[5] God's first call and just demand
is that man accept him and worship him.   *398*

---

1   *Mt* 22:37; cf. *Lk* 10:27: ". . . and with all your strength."
2   *Deut* 6:4.
3   *Ex* 20:2-5; cf. *Deut* 5:6-9.
4   *Mt* 4:10.
5   *Deut* 6:13-14.

2085   The one and true God first reveals his glory to Israel.[6] The
revelation of the vocation and truth of man is linked to the revela-
200   tion of God. Man's vocation is to make God manifest by acting in
1701   conformity with his creation "in the image and likeness of God":

> There will never be another God, Trypho, and there has been
> no other since the world began . . . than he who made and
> ordered the universe. We do not think that our God is
> different from yours. He is the same who brought your
> fathers out of Egypt "by his powerful hand and his out-
> stretched arm." We do not place our hope in some other god,
> for there is none, but in the same God as you do: the God of
> Abraham, Isaac and Jacob.[7]

2086   "The first commandment embraces faith, hope, and charity. When we say 'God' we confess a constant, unchangeable being,
212   always the same, faithful and just, without any evil. It follows that
we must necessarily accept his words and have complete faith in
him and acknowledge his authority. He is almighty, merciful, and
infinitely beneficent. . . . Who could not place all hope in him? Who
could not love him when contemplating the treasures of goodness
and love he has poured out on us? Hence the formula God employs
2061   in the Scripture at the beginning and end of his commandments: 'I
am the LORD.'"[8]

1814-1816   **Faith**

2087   Our moral life has its source in faith in God who reveals
his love to us. St. Paul speaks of the "obedience of faith"[9] as our
143   first obligation. He shows that "ignorance of God" is the principle
and explanation of all moral deviations.[10] Our duty toward God is
to believe in him and to bear witness to him.

2088   The first commandment requires us to nourish and protect
our faith with prudence and vigilance, and to reject everything that
is opposed to it. There are various ways of sinning against faith:

157   *Voluntary doubt* about the faith disregards or refuses to
hold as true what God has revealed and the Church proposes for
belief. *Involuntary doubt* refers to hesitation in believing, difficulty

---

6 Cf. *Ex* 19:16-25; 24:15-18.
7 St. Justin, *Dial. cum Tryphone Judaeo* 11, 1: PG 6, 497.
8 *Roman Catechism* 3, 2,4.
9 *Rom* 1:5; 16:26.
10 Cf. *Rom* 1:18-32.

in overcoming objections connected with the faith, or also anxiety aroused by its obscurity. If deliberately cultivated doubt can lead to spiritual blindness.

2089   *Incredulity* is the neglect of revealed truth or the willful *162* refusal to assent to it. "*Heresy* is the obstinate post-baptismal denial *817* of some truth which must be believed with divine and catholic faith, or it is likewise an obstinate doubt concerning the same; *apostasy* is the total repudiation of the Christian faith; *schism* is the refusal of submission to the Roman Pontiff or of communion with the members of the Church subject to him."[11]

Hope   *1817-1821*

2090   When God reveals Himself and calls him, man cannot fully respond to the divine love by his own powers. He must hope that God will give him the capacity to love Him in return and to act in *1996* conformity with the commandments of charity. Hope is the confident expectation of divine blessing and the beatific vision of God; it is also the fear of offending God's love and of incurring punishment.

2091   The first commandment is also concerned with sins against hope, namely, despair and presumption:

By *despair*, man ceases to hope for his personal salvation from God, for help in attaining it or for the forgiveness of his sins. *1864* Despair is contrary to God's goodness, to his justice – for the Lord is faithful to his promises – and to his mercy.

2092   There are two kinds of *presumption*. Either man presumes upon his own capacities, (hoping to be able to save himself without help from on high), or he presumes upon God's almighty power *2732* or his mercy (hoping to obtain his forgiveness without conversion and glory without merit).

---

11   CIC, can. 751: emphasis added.

1822-1829 **Charity**

2093 Faith in God's love encompasses the call and the obligation to respond with sincere love to divine charity. The first commandment enjoins us to love God above everything and all creatures for him and because of him.[12]

2094 One can sin against God's love in various ways:

– *indifference* neglects or refuses to reflect on divine charity; it fails to consider its prevenient goodness and denies its power.

– *ingratitude* fails or refuses to acknowledge divine charity and to return him love for love.

– *lukewarmness* is hesitation or negligence in responding to divine love; it can imply refusal to give oneself over to the prompting of charity.

2733 – *acedia* or spiritual sloth goes so far as to refuse the joy that comes from God and to be repelled by divine goodness.

2303 – *hatred of God* comes from pride. It is contrary to love of God, whose goodness it denies, and whom it presumes to curse as the one who forbids sins and inflicts punishments.

II. "HIM ONLY SHALL YOU SERVE"

2095 The theological virtues of faith, hope, and charity inform and give life to the moral virtues. Thus charity leads us to render *1807* to God what we as creatures owe him in all justice. The *virtue of religion* disposes us to have this attitude.

2628 **Adoration**

2096 Adoration is the first act of the virtue of religion. To adore God is to acknowledge him as God, as the Creator and Savior, the Lord and Master of everything that exists, as infinite and merciful Love. "You shall worship the Lord your God, and him only shall you serve," says Jesus, citing *Deuteronomy*.[13]

---

12 Cf. *Deut* 6:4-5.
13 *Lk* 4:8; cf. *Deut* 6:13.

2097　To adore God is to acknowledge, in respect and absolute *2807* submission, the "nothingness of the creature" who would not exist but for God. To adore God is to praise and exalt him and to humble oneself, as Mary did in the Magnificat, confessing with gratitude that he has done great things and holy is his name.[14] The worship of the one God sets man free from turning in on himself, from the slavery of sin and the idolatry of the world.

Prayer *2558*

2098　The acts of faith, hope, and charity enjoined by the first commandment are accomplished in prayer. Lifting up the mind toward God is an expression of our adoration of God: prayer of praise and thanksgiving, intercession and petition. Prayer is an indispensable condition for being able to obey God's commandments. "[We] ought always to pray and not lose heart."[15]　*2742*

Sacrifice

2099　It is right to offer sacrifice to God as a sign of adoration and gratitude, supplication and communion: "Every action done so as to cling to God in communion of holiness, and thus achieve blessedness, is a true sacrifice."[16]　*613*

2100　Outward sacrifice, to be genuine, must be the expression of spiritual sacrifice: "The sacrifice acceptable to God is a broken spirit. . . ."[17] The prophets of the Old Covenant often denounced *2711* sacrifices that were not from the heart or not coupled with love of neighbor.[18] Jesus recalls the words of the prophet Hosea: "I desire mercy, and not sacrifice."[19] The only perfect sacrifice is the one that Christ offered on the cross as a total offering to the Father's love *614* and for our salvation.[20] By uniting ourselves with his sacrifice we *618* can make our lives a sacrifice to God.

14　Cf. *Lk* 1:46-49.
15　*Lk* 18:1.
16　St. Augustine, *De civ. Dei* 10, 6: PL 41, 283.
17　*Ps* 51:17.
18　Cf. *Am* 5:21-25; *Isa* 1:10-20.
19　*Mt* 9:13; 12:7; cf. *Hos* 6:6.
20　Cf. *Heb* 9:13-14.

Promises and vows

1237 **2101**   In many circumstances, the Christian is called to make *promises* to God. Baptism and Confirmation, Matrimony and Holy Orders always entail promises. Out of personal devotion, the Christian may also promise to God this action, that prayer, this *1064* alms-giving, that pilgrimage, and so forth. Fidelity to promises made to God is a sign of the respect owed to the divine majesty and of love for a faithful God.

2102   "A *vow* is a deliberate and free promise made to God concerning a possible and better good which must be fulfilled by reason of the virtue of religion,"[21] A vow is an act of *devotion* in which the Christian dedicates himself to God or promises him some good work. By fulfilling his vows he renders to God what has been promised and consecrated to Him. The *Acts of the Apostles* shows us St. Paul concerned to fulfill the vows he had made.[22]

1973 **2103**   The Church recognizes an exemplary value in the vows to practice the *evangelical counsels*:[23]

914   Mother Church rejoices that she has within herself many men and women who pursue the Savior's self-emptying more closely and show it forth more clearly, by undertaking poverty with the freedom of the children of God, and renouncing their own will: they submit themselves to man for the sake of God, thus going beyond what is of precept in the matter of perfection, so as to conform themselves more fully to the obedient Christ.[24]

The Church can, in certain cases and for proportionate reasons, dispense from vows and promises.[25]

The social duty of religion and the right to religious freedom

2467 **2104**   "All men are bound to seek the truth, especially in what concerns God and his Church, and to embrace it and hold on to it as they come to know it."[26] This duty derives from "the very dignity of the human person."[27] It does not contradict a "sincere respect" for different religions which frequently "reflect a ray of that truth which enlightens all men,"[28] nor the requirement of *851* charity, which urges Christians "to treat with love, prudence and

---

21 CIC, can. 1191 § 1.
22 Cf. *Acts* 18:18; 21:23-24.
23 Cf. CIC, can. 654.
24 *LG* 42 § 2.
25 Cf. CIC, cann. 692; 1196-1197.

patience those who are in error or ignorance with regard to the faith."[29]

2105   The duty of offering God genuine worship concerns man both individually and socially. This is "the traditional Catholic teaching on the moral duty of individuals and societies toward the true religion and the one Church of Christ."[30] By constantly evangelizing men, the Church works toward enabling them "to infuse *854* the Christian spirit into the mentality and mores, laws and structures of the communities in which [they] live."[31] The social duty of *898* Christians is to respect and awaken in each man the love of the true and the good. It requires them to make known the worship of the one true religion which subsists in the Catholic and apostolic Church.[32] Christians are called to be the light of the world. Thus, the Church shows forth the kingship of Christ over all creation and in particular over human societies.[33]

2106   "Nobody may be forced to act against his convictions, nor *160* is anyone to be restrained from acting in accordance with his *1782* conscience in religious matters in private or in public, alone or in *1738* association with others, within due limits."[34] This right is based on the very nature of the human person, whose dignity enables him freely to assent to the divine truth which transcends the temporal order. For this reason it "continues to exist even in those who do not live up to their obligation of seeking the truth and adhering to it."[35]

2107   "If because of the circumstances of a particular people special civil recognition is given to one religious community in the constitutional organization of a state, the right of all citizens and religious communities to religious freedom must be recognized and respected as well."[36]

2108   The right to religious liberty is neither a moral license to *1740* adhere to error, nor a supposed right to error,[37] but rather a natural right of the human person to civil liberty, i.e., immunity, within

---

26   *DH* 1 § 2.
27   *DH* 2 § 1.
28   *NA* 2 § 2.
29   *DH* 14 § 4.
30   *DH* 1 § 3.
31   *AA* 13 § 1.
32   Cf. *DH* 1.
33   Cf. *AA* 13; Leo XIII, *Immortale Dei* 3, 17; Pius XI, *Quas primas* 8, 20.
34   *DH* 2 § 1.
35   *DH* 2 § 2.
36   *DH* 6 § 3.
37   Cf. Leo XIII, *Libertas praestantissimum* 18; Pius XII, *AAS* 1953, 799.

just limits, from external constraint in religious matters by political authorities. This natural right ought to be acknowledged in the juridical order of society in such a way that it constitutes a civil right.[38]

2244 **2109**   The right to religious liberty can of itself be neither unlimited nor limited only by a "public order" conceived in a positivist or naturalist manner.[39] The "due limits" which are inherent in it must be determined for each social situation by political prudence, according to the requirements of the common good, and ratified by the civil authority in accordance with "legal principles which are in conformity with the objective *1906* moral order."[40]

III.   "YOU SHALL HAVE NO OTHER GODS BEFORE ME"

2110   The first commandment forbids honoring gods other than the one Lord who has revealed himself to his people. It proscribes superstition and irreligion. Superstition in some sense represents a perverse excess of religion; irreligion is the vice contrary by defect to the virtue of religion.

Superstition

2111   Superstition is the deviation of religious feeling and of the practices this feeling imposes. It can even affect the worship we offer the true God, e.g., when one attributes an importance in some way magical to certain practices otherwise lawful or necessary. To attribute the efficacy of prayers or of sacramental signs to their mere external performance, apart from the interior dispositions that they demand, is to fall into superstition.[41]

Idolatry

2112   The first commandment condemns *polytheism*. It requires man neither to believe in, nor to venerate, other divinities than the *210* one true God. Scripture constantly recalls this rejection of "idols, [of] silver and gold, the work of men's hands. They have mouths, but do not speak; eyes, but do not see." These empty idols make their worshippers empty: "Those who make them are like them; so

---

38 Cf. *DH* 2.
39 Cf. Pius VI, *Quod aliquantum* (1791)10; Pius IX, *Quanta cura* 3.
40 *DH* 7 § 3.
41 Cf. *Mt* 23:16-22.

are all who trust in them."[42] God, however, is the "living God"[43] who gives life and intervenes in history.

2113 Idolatry not only refers to false pagan worship. It remains a constant temptation to faith. Idolatry consists in divinizing what is not God. Man commits idolatry whenever he honors and reveres *398, 2534* a creature in place of God, whether this be gods or demons (for example, satanism), power, pleasure, race, ancestors, the state, money, etc. Jesus says, "You cannot serve God and mammon."[44] *2289* Many martyrs died for not adoring "the Beast"[45] refusing even to *2473* simulate such worship. Idolatry rejects the unique Lordship of God; it is therefore incompatible with communion with God.[46]

2114 Human life finds its unity in the adoration of the one God. The commandment to worship the Lord alone integrates man and saves him from an endless disintegration. Idolatry is a perversion of man's innate religious sense. An idolater is someone who "transfers his indestructible notion of God to anything other than God."[47]

Divination and magic

2115 God can reveal the future to his prophets or to other saints. Still, a sound Christian attitude consists in putting oneself confidently into the hands of Providence for whatever concerns the *305* future, and giving up all unhealthy curiosity about it. Improvidence, however, can constitute a lack of responsibility.

2116 All forms of *divination* are to be rejected: recourse to Satan or demons, conjuring up the dead or other practices falsely supposed to "unveil" the future.[48] Consulting horoscopes, astrology, palm reading, interpretation of omens and lots, the phenomena of clairvoyance, and recourse to mediums all conceal a desire for power over time, history, and, in the last analysis, other human beings, as well as a wish to conciliate hidden powers. They contradict the honor, respect, and loving fear that we owe to God alone.

2117 All practices of *magic* or *sorcery*, by which one attempts to tame occult powers, so as to place them at one's service and have a supernatural power over others – even if this were for the sake

---

42 *Ps* 115:4-5, 8; cf. *Isa* 44:9-20; *Jer* 10:1-16; *Dan* 14:1-30; *Bar* 6; *Wis* 13:1-15:19.
43 *Josh* 3:10; *Ps* 42:3; etc.
44 *Mt* 6:24.
45 Cf. *Rev* 13-14.
46 Cf. *Gal* 5:20; *Eph* 5:5.
47 Origen, *Contra Celsum* 2, 40: PG 11, 861.
48 Cf. *Deut* 18:10; *Jer* 29:8.

of restoring their health – are gravely contrary to the virtue of religion. These practices are even more to be condemned when accompanied by the intention of harming someone, or when they have recourse to the intervention of demons. Wearing charms is also reprehensible. *Spiritism* often implies divination or magical practices; the Church for her part warns the faithful against it. Recourse to so-called traditional cures does not justify either the invocation of evil powers or the exploitation of another's credulity.

Irreligion

2118   God's first commandment condemns the main sins of irreligion: tempting God, in words or deeds, sacrilege, and simony.

2119   *Tempting God* consists in putting his goodness and al-
394   mighty power to the test by word or deed. Thus Satan tried to induce Jesus to throw himself down from the Temple and, by this gesture, force God to act.[49] Jesus opposed Satan with the word of God: "You shall not put the LORD your God to the test."[50] The challenge contained in such tempting of God wounds the respect
2088   and trust we owe our Creator and Lord. It always harbors doubt about his love, his providence, and his power.[51]

2120   *Sacrilege* consists in profaning or treating unworthily the sacraments and other liturgical actions, as well as persons, things, or places consecrated to God. Sacrilege is a grave sin especially when committed against the Eucharist, for in this sacrament the
1374   true Body of Christ is made substantially present for us.[52]

2121   *Simony* is defined as the buying or selling of spiritual things.[53] To Simon the magician, who wanted to buy the spiritual power he saw at work in the apostles, St. Peter responded: "Your silver perish with you, because you thought you could obtain God's gift with money!"[54] Peter thus held to the words of Jesus: "You received without pay, give without pay."[55] It is impossible
1578   to appropriate to oneself spiritual goods and behave toward them as their owner or master, for they have their source in God. One can receive them only from him, without payment.

---

49   Cf. *Lk* 4:9.
50   *Deut* 6:16.
51   Cf. *1 Cor* 10:9; *Ex* 17:2-7; *Ps* 95:9.
52   Cf. CIC, cann. 1367; 1376.
53   Cf. *Acts* 8:9-24.
54   *Acts* 8:20.
55   *Mt* 10:8; cf. already *Isa* 55:1.

2122 "The minister should ask nothing for the administration of the sacraments beyond the offerings defined by the competent authority, always being careful that the needy are not deprived of the help of the sacraments because of their poverty."[56] The competent authority determines these "offerings" in accordance with the principle that the Christian people ought to contribute to the support of the Church's ministers. "The laborer deserves his food."[57]

Atheism

2123 "Many . . . of our contemporaries either do not at all perceive, or explicitly reject, this intimate and vital bond of man to God. Atheism must therefore be regarded as one of the most 29 serious problems of our time."[58]

2124 The name "atheism" covers many very different phenomena. One common form is the practical materialism which restricts its needs and aspirations to space and time. Atheistic humanism falsely considers man to be "an end to himself, and the sole maker, with supreme control, of his own history."[59] Another form of contemporary atheism looks for the liberation of man through economic and social liberation. "It holds that religion, of its very nature, thwarts such emancipation by raising man's hopes in a future life, thus both deceiving him and discouraging him from working for a better form of life on earth."[60]

2125 Since it rejects or denies the existence of God, atheism is a sin against the virtue of religion.[61] The imputability of this offense can be significantly diminished in virtue of the intentions and the 1735 circumstances. "Believers can have more than a little to do with the rise of atheism. To the extent that they are careless about their instruction in the faith, or present its teaching falsely, or even fail in their religious, moral, or social life, they must be said to conceal rather than to reveal the true nature of God and of religion."[62]

2126 Atheism is often based on a false conception of human autonomy, exaggerated to the point of refusing any dependence on God.[63] Yet, "to acknowledge God is in no way to oppose the 396 dignity of man, since such dignity is grounded and brought to 154

---

56 CIC, can. 848.
57 *Mt* 10:10; cf. *Lk* 10:7; *1 Cor* 9:5-18; *1 Tim* 5:17-18.
58 *GS* 19 § 1.
59 *GS* 20 § 1.
60 *GS* 20 § 2.
61 Cf. *Rom* 1:18.
62 *GS* 19 § 3.
63 Cf. *GS* 20 § 1.

perfection in God. . . ."[64] "For the Church knows full well that her message is in harmony with the most secret desires of the human heart."[65]

Agnosticism

2127   Agnosticism assumes a number of forms. In certain cases the agnostic refrains from denying God; instead he postulates the existence of a transcendent being which is incapable of revealing itself, and about which nothing can be said. In other cases, the
36 agnostic makes no judgment about God's existence, declaring it impossible to prove, or even to affirm or deny.

2128   Agnosticism can sometimes include a certain search for
1036 God, but it can equally express indifferentism, a flight from the ultimate question of existence, and a sluggish moral conscience. Agnosticism is all too often equivalent to practical atheism.

115-1162 **IV.**   **"YOU SHALL NOT MAKE FOR YOURSELF
                    A GRAVEN IMAGE . . ."**

2129   The divine injunction included the prohibition of every representation of God by the hand of man. *Deuteronomy* explains: "Since you saw no form on the day that the Lord spoke to you at Horeb out of the midst of the fire, beware lest you act corruptly by making a graven image for yourselves, in the form of any figure. . . ."[66] It is the absolutely transcendent God who revealed himself to Israel. "He
300 is the all," but at the same time "he is greater than all his works."[67] He
2500 is "the author of beauty."[68]

2130   Nevertheless, already in the Old Testament, God ordained or permitted the making of images that pointed symbolically toward salvation by the incarnate Word: so it was with the bronze serpent, the ark of the covenant, and the cherubim.[69]

2131   Basing itself on the mystery of the incarnate Word, the seventh ecumenical council at Nicaea (787) justified against the
476 iconoclasts the veneration of icons – of Christ, but also of the Mother of God, the angels, and all the saints. By becoming incarnate, the Son of God introduced a new "economy" of images.

---

64 *GS* 21 § 3.
65 *GS* 21 § 7.
66 *Deut* 4:15-16.
67 *Sir* 43:27-28.
68 *Wis* 13:3.
69 Cf. *Num* 21:4-9; *Wis* 16:5-14; *Jn* 3:14-15; *Ex* 25:10-22; *1 Kings* 6:23-28; 7:23-26.

2132 The Christian veneration of images is not contrary to the first commandment which proscribes idols. Indeed, "the honor rendered to an image passes to its prototype," and "whoever venerates an image venerates the person portrayed in it."[70] The honor paid to sacred images is a "respectful veneration," not the adoration due to God alone:

> Religious worship is not directed to images in themselves, considered as mere things, but under their distinctive aspect as images leading us on to God incarnate. The movement toward the image does not terminate in it as image, but tends toward that whose image it is.[71]

IN BRIEF

2133 "You shall love the Lord your God with all your heart, and with all your soul and with all your strength" (*Deut* 6:5).

2134 The first commandment summons man to believe in God, to hope in him, and to love him above all else.

2135 "You shall worship the Lord your God" (*Mt* 4:10). Adoring God, praying to him, offering him the worship that belongs to him, fulfilling the promises and vows made to him are acts of the virtue of religion which fall under obedience to the first commandment.

2136 The duty to offer God authentic worship concerns man both as an individual and as a social being.

2137 "Men of the present day want to profess their religion freely in private and in public" (*DH* 15).

2138 Superstition is a departure from the worship that we give to the true God. It is manifested in idolatry, as well as in various forms of divination and magic.

2139 Tempting God in words or deeds, sacrilege, and simony are sins of irreligion forbidden by the first commandment.

2140 Since it rejects or denies the existence of God, atheism is a sin against the first commandment.

---

70 St. Basil, *De Spiritu Sancto* 18, 45: PG 32, 149C; Council of Nicaea II: DS 601; cf. Council of Trent: DS 1821-1825; Vatican Council II: *SC* 126; *LG* 67.
71 St. Thomas Aquinas, *STh* II-II, 81, 3 *ad* 3.

2141   The veneration of sacred images is based on the mystery of the Incarnation of the Word of God. It is not contrary to the first commandment.

ARTICLE 2
THE SECOND COMMANDMENT

> You shall not take the name of the Lord your God in vain.[72]

> You have heard that it was said to the men of old, "You shall not swear falsely. . But I say to you, Do not swear at all.[73]

2807-2815 **I.   THE NAME OF THE LORD IS HOLY**

2142   The second commandment *prescribes respect for the Lord's name*. Like the first commandment, it belongs to the virtue of religion and more particularly it governs our use of speech in sacred matters.

2143   Among all the words of Revelation, there is one which is unique: the revealed name of God. God confides his name to those
203 who believe in him; he reveals himself to them in his personal mystery. The gift of a name belongs to the order of trust and intimacy. "The Lord's name is holy." For this reason man must not
435 abuse it. He must keep it in mind in silent, loving adoration. He will not introduce it into his own speech except to bless, praise, and glorify it.[74]

2144   Respect for his name is an expression of the respect owed to the mystery of God himself and to the whole sacred reality it evokes. The *sense of the sacred* is part of the virtue of religion:

> Are these feelings of fear and awe Christian feelings or not? . . .
> I say this, then, which I think no one can reasonably dispute.
> They are the class of feelings we *should* have – yes, have to an
> intense degree – if we literally had the sight of Almighty God;
> therefore they are the class of feelings which we shall have, *if*
> we realize His presence. In proportion as we believe that He is
> present, we shall have them; and not to have them, is not to
> realize, not to believe that He is present.[75]

---

72   *Ex* 20:7; *Deut* 5:11.

73   *Mt* 5:33-34.

74   Cf. *Zech* 2:13; *Ps* 29:2; 96:2; 113:1-2.

75   John Henry Cardinal Newman, *Parochial and Plain Sermons* V, 2 (London: Longmans, Green and Co., 1907) 21-22.

2145   The faithful should bear witness to the Lord's name by 2472
confessing the faith without giving way to fear.[76] Preaching and 427
catechizing should be permeated with adoration and respect for
the name of our Lord Jesus Christ.

2146   The second commandment *forbids the abuse of God's name,*
i.e., every improper use of the names of God, Jesus Christ, but also
of the Virgin Mary and all the saints.

2147   *Promises* made to others in God's name engage the divine 2101
honor, fidelity, truthfulness, and authority. They must be respected
in justice. To be unfaithful to them is to misuse God's name and in
some way to make God out to be a liar.[77]

2148   *Blasphemy* is directly opposed to the second commandment. It consists in uttering against God – inwardly or outwardly
– words of hatred, reproach, or defiance; in speaking ill of God; in
failing in respect toward him in one's speech; in misusing God's
name. St. James condemns those "who blaspheme that honorable
name [of Jesus] by which you are called."[78] The prohibition of
blasphemy extends to language against Christ's Church, the saints,
and sacred things. It is also blasphemous to make use of God's
name to cover up criminal practices, to reduce peoples to servitude,
to torture persons or put them to death. The misuse of God's name
to commit a crime can provoke others to repudiate religion.

   Blasphemy is contrary to the respect due God and his holy 1756
name. It is in itself a grave sin.[79]

2149   *Oaths* which misuse God's name, though without the intention of blasphemy, show lack of respect for the Lord. The second
commandment also forbids *magical use* of the divine name.

> [God's] name is great when spoken with respect for the
> greatness of his majesty. God's name is holy when said with
> veneration and fear of offending him.[80]

---

76   Cf. *Mt* 10:32; *1 Tim* 6:12.
77   Cf. *1 Jn* 1:10.
78   *Jas* 2:7.
79   Cf. CIC, can. 1369.
80   St. Augustine, *De serm. Dom. in monte* 2, 5, 19: PL 34, 1278.

II.   TAKING THE NAME OF THE LORD IN VAIN

2150   The second commandment *forbids false oaths*. Taking an oath or swearing is to take God as witness to what one affirms. It is to invoke the divine truthfulness as a pledge of one's own truthfulness. An oath engages the Lord's name. "You shall fear the LORD your God; you shall serve him, and swear by his name."[81]

2151   Rejection of false oaths is a duty toward God. As Creator and Lord, God is the norm of all truth. Human speech is either in 215 accord with or in opposition to God who is Truth itself. When it is truthful and legitimate, an oath highlights the relationship of human speech with God's truth. A false oath calls on God to be witness to a lie.

2476 **2152**   A person commits *perjury* when he makes a promise under oath with no intention of keeping it, or when after promising on oath he does not keep it. Perjury is a grave lack of respect for the 1756 Lord of all speech. Pledging oneself by oath to commit an evil deed is contrary to the holiness of the divine name.

2153   In the Sermon on the Mount, Jesus explained the second commandment: "You have heard that it was said to the men of old, 'You shall not swear falsely, but shall perform to the Lord what you have sworn.' But I say to you, Do not swear at all. . . . Let what you say be simply 'Yes' or 'No'; anything more than this comes from the evil one."[82] Jesus teaches that every oath involves a reference to God and that God's presence and his truth must be honored in all speech. Discretion in calling upon God is allied with 2466 a respectful awareness of his presence, which all our assertions either witness to or mock.

2154   Following St. Paul,[83] the tradition of the Church has understood Jesus' words as not excluding oaths made for grave and right reasons (for example, in court). "An oath, that is the invocation of the divine name as a witness to truth, cannot be taken unless in truth, in judgment, and in justice."[84]

---

81   *Deut* 6:13.
82   *Mt* 5:33-34, 37; cf. *Jas* 5:12.
83   Cf. *2 Cor* 1:23; *Gal* 1:20.
84   CIC, can. 1199 § 1.

2155 The holiness of the divine name demands that we neither use it for trivial matters, nor take an oath which on the basis of the circumstances could be interpreted as approval of an authority unjustly requiring it. When an oath is required by illegitimate civil authorities, it may be refused. It must be refused when it is required for purposes contrary to the dignity of persons or to ecclesial *1903* communion.

III. THE CHRISTIAN NAME

2156 The sacrament of Baptism is conferred "in the name of the *232* Father and of the Son and of the Holy Spirit."[85] In Baptism, the Lord's name sanctifies man, and the Christian receives his name in the Church. This can be the name of a saint, that is, of a disciple *1267* who has lived a life of exemplary fidelity to the Lord. The patron saint provides a model of charity; we are assured of his intercession. The "baptismal name" can also express a Christian mystery or Christian virtue. "Parents, sponsors, and the pastor are to see that a name is not given which is foreign to Christian sentiment."[86]

2157 The Christian begins his day, his prayers, and his activities with the Sign of the Cross: "in the name of the Father and of the Son and of the Holy Spirit. Amen." The baptized person dedicates *1235* the day to the glory of God and calls on the Savior's grace which lets him act in the Spirit as a child of the Father. The sign of the *1668* cross strengthens us in temptations and difficulties.

2158 God calls each one by name.[87] Everyone's name is sacred. The name is the icon of the person. It demands respect as a sign of the dignity of the one who bears it.

2159 The name one receives is a name for eternity. In the kingdom, the mysterious and unique character of each person marked with God's name will shine forth in splendor. "To him who conquers . . . I will give a white stone, with a new name written on the stone which no one knows except him who receives it."[88] "Then I looked, and Lo, on Mount Zion stood the Lamb, and with him a hundred and forty-four thousand who had his name and his Father's name written on their foreheads."[89]

---

85 *Mt* 28:19.
86 CIC, can. 855.
87 Cf. *Isa* 43:1; *Jn* 10:3.
88 *Rev* 2:17.
89 *Rev* 14:1.

IN BRIEF

2160 "O Lord, our Lord, how majestic is your name in all the earth" (*Ps* 8:1)!

2161 The second commandment enjoins respect for the Lord's name. The name of the Lord is holy.

2162 The second commandment forbids every improper use of God's name. Blasphemy is the use of the name of God, of Jesus Christ, of the Virgin Mary, and of the saints in an offensive way.

2163 False oaths call on God to be witness to a lie. Perjury is a grave offence against the Lord who is always faithful to his promises.

2164 "Do not swear whether by the Creator, or any creature, except truthfully, of necessity, and with reverence" (St. Ignatius of Loyola, *Spiritual Exercises*, 38).

2165 In Baptism, the Christian receives his name in the Church. Parents, godparents, and the pastor are to see that he be given a Christian name. The patron saint provides a model of charity and the assurance of his prayer.

2166 The Christian begins his prayers and activities with the Sign of the Cross: "in the name of the Father and of the Son and of the Holy Spirit. Amen."

2167 God calls each one by name (cf. *Isa* 43:1).

ARTICLE 3
THE THIRD COMMANDMENT

> Remember the sabbath day, to keep it holy. Six days you shall labor, and do all your work; but the seventh day is a sabbath to the Lord your God; in it you shall not do any work.[90]

> The sabbath was made for man, not man for the sabbath; so the Son of Man is lord even of the sabbath.[91]

I.   THE SABBATH DAY   *346-348*

2168   The third commandment of the Decalogue recalls the holiness of the sabbath: "The seventh day is a sabbath of solemn rest, holy to the LORD."[92]

2169   In speaking of the sabbath Scripture recalls creation: "For *2057* in six days the LORD made heaven and earth, the sea, and all that is in them, and rested the seventh day; therefore the Lord blessed the sabbath day and hallowed it."[93]

2170   Scripture also reveals in the Lord's day a *memorial of Israel's liberation* from bondage in Egypt: "You shall remember that you were a servant in the land of Egypt, and the LORD your God brought you out thence with mighty hand and outstretched arm; therefore the LORD your God commanded you to keep the sabbath day."[94]

2171   God entrusted the sabbath to Israel to keep as a *sign of the irrevocable covenant*.[95] The sabbath is for the Lord, holy and set apart for the praise of God, his work of creation, and his saving actions on behalf of Israel.

2172   God's action is the model for human action. If God "rested and was refreshed" on the seventh day, man too ought to "rest" and should let others, especially the poor, "be refreshed."[96] The *2184* sabbath brings everyday work to a halt and provides a respite. It is a day of protest against the servitude of work and the worship of money.[97]

---

90 *Ex* 20:8-10; cf. *Deut* 5:12-15.
91 *Mk* 2:27-28.
92 *Ex* 31:15.
93 *Ex* 20:11.
94 *Deut* 5:15.
95 Cf. *Ex* 31:16.
96 *Ex* 31:17; cf. 23:12.
97 Cf. *Neh* 13:15-22; *2 Chr* 36:21.

2173   The Gospel reports many incidents when Jesus was accused of violating the sabbath law. But Jesus never fails to respect
582   the holiness of this day.[98] He gives this law its authentic and
authoritative interpretation: "The sabbath was made for man, not
man for the sabbath."[99] With compassion, Christ declares the
sabbath for doing good rather than harm, for saving life rather than
killing.[100] The sabbath is the day of the Lord of mercies and a day
to honor God.[101] "The Son of Man is lord even of the sabbath."[102]

II.   THE LORD'S DAY

> This is the day which the LORD has made; let us rejoice and
> be glad in it.[103]

The day of the Resurrection: the new creation

638   **2174**   Jesus rose from the dead "on the first day of the week."[104]
Because it is the "first day," the day of Christ's Resurrection recalls
the first creation. Because it is the "eighth day" following the
349   sabbath,[105] it symbolizes the new creation ushered in by Christ's
Resurrection. For Christians it has become the first of all days, the
first of all feasts, the Lord's Day (*he kuriake hemera, dies dominica*) –
Sunday:

> We all gather on the day of the sun, for it is the first day [after
> the Jewish sabbath, but also the first day] when God, sepa-
> rating matter from darkness, made the world; and on this
> same day Jesus Christ our Savior rose from the dead.[106]

Sunday – fulfillment of the sabbath

2175   Sunday is expressly distinguished from the sabbath which
it follows chronologically every week; for Christians its ceremonial
1166   observance replaces that of the sabbath. In Christ's Passover, Sun-

---

98   Cf. *Mk* 1:21; *Jn* 9:16.
99   *Mk* 2:27.
100   Cf. *Mk* 3:4.
101   Cf. *Mt* 12:5; *Jn* 7:23.
102   *Mk* 2:28.
103   *Ps* 118:24.
104   Cf. *Mt* 28:1; *Mk* 16:2; *Lk* 24:1; *Jn* 20:1.
105   Cf. *Mk* 16:1; *Mt* 28:1.
106   St. Justin, I *Apol.* 67: PG 6, 429 and 432.

day fulfills the spiritual truth of the Jewish sabbath and announces man's eternal rest in God. For worship under the Law prepared for the mystery of Christ, and what was done there prefigured some aspects of Christ:[107]

> Those who lived according to the old order of things have come to a new hope, no longer keeping the sabbath, but the Lord's Day, in which our life is blessed by him and by his death.[108]

2176 The celebration of Sunday observes the moral commandment inscribed by nature in the human heart to render to God an outward, visible, public, and regular worship "as a sign of his universal beneficence to all."[109] Sunday worship fulfills the moral command of the Old Covenant, taking up its rhythm and spirit in the weekly celebration of the Creator and Redeemer of his people.

The Sunday Eucharist

2177 The Sunday celebration of the Lord's Day and his Eucha- *1167* rist is at the heart of the Church's life. "Sunday is the day on which the paschal mystery is celebrated in light of the apostolic tradition and is to be observed as the foremost holy day of obligation in the universal Church."[110]

"Also to be observed are the day of the Nativity of Our Lord Jesus *2043* Christ, the Epiphany, the Ascension of Christ, the feast of the Body and Blood of Christi, the feast of Mary the Mother of God, her Immaculate Conception, her Assumption, the feast of Saint Joseph, the feast of the Apostles Saints Peter and Paul, and the feast of All Saints."[111]

2178 This practice of the Christian assembly dates from the *1343* beginnings of the apostolic age.[112] The *Letter to the Hebrews* reminds the faithful "not to neglect to meet together, as is the habit of some, but to encourage one another."[113]

---

107 Cf. *1 Cor* 10:11.
108 St. Ignatius of Antioch, *Ad Magn.* 9, 1: SCh 10, 88.
109 St. Thomas Aquinas, *STh* II-II, 122, 4.
110 CIC, can. 1246 § 1.
111 CIC, can. 1246 § 2: "The conference of bishops can abolish certain holy days of obligation or transfer them to a Sunday with prior approval of the Apostolic See."
112 Cf. *Acts* 2:42-46; *1 Cor* 11:17.
113 *Heb* 10:25.

Tradition preserves the memory of an ever-timely exhortation: Come to Church early, approach the Lord, and confess your sins, repent in prayer. . . . Be present at the sacred and divine liturgy, conclude its prayer and do not leave before the dismissal. . . . We have often said: "This day is given to you for prayer and rest. This is the day that the Lord has made, let us rejoice and be glad in it."[114]

2179   "A *parish* is a definite community of the Christian faithful established on a stable basis within a particular church; the pastoral care of the parish is entrusted to a pastor as its own shepherd under the authority of the diocesan bishop."[115] It is the place where all the faithful can be gathered together for the Sunday celebration of the Eucharist. The parish initiates the Christian people into the ordinary expression of the liturgical life: it gathers them together in this celebration; it teaches Christ's saving doctrine; it practices the charity of the Lord in good works and brotherly love:

1567

2691

2226

You cannot pray at home as at church, where there is a great multitude, where exclamations are cried out to God as from one great heart, and where there is something more: the union of minds, the accord of souls, the bond of charity, the prayers of the priests.[116]

The Sunday obligation

2180   The precept of the Church specifies the law of the Lord more precisely: "On Sundays and other holy days of obligation the faithful are bound to participate in the Mass."[117] "The precept of participating in the Mass is satisfied by assistance at a Mass which is celebrated anywhere in a Catholic rite either on the holy day or on the evening of the preceding day."[118]

2042

1389

---

114   *Sermo de die dominica* 2 et 6: PG 86/1, 416C and 421C.
115   CIC, can. 515 § 1.
116   St. John Chrysostom, *De incomprehensibili* 3, 6: PG 48, 725.
117   CIC, can. 1247.
118   CIC, can. 1248 § 1.

2181 The Sunday Eucharist is the foundation and confirmation of all Christian practice. For this reason the faithful are obliged to participate in the Eucharist on days of obligation, unless excused for a serious reason (for example, illness, the care of infants) or dispensed by their own pastor.[119] Those who deliberately fail in this obligation commit a grave sin.

2182 Participation in the communal celebration of the Sunday Eucharist is a testimony of belonging and of being faithful to Christ and to his Church. The faithful give witness by this to their com- *815* munion in faith and charity. Together they testify to God's holiness and their hope of salvation. They strengthen one another under the guidance of the Holy Spirit.

2183 "If because of lack of a sacred minister or for other grave cause participation in the celebration of the Eucharist is impossible, it is specially recommended that the faithful take part in the Liturgy of the Word if it is celebrated in the parish church or in another sacred place according to the prescriptions of the diocesan bishop, or engage in prayer for an appropriate amount of time personally or in a family or, as occasion offers, in groups of families."[120]

A day of grace and rest from work

2184 Just as God "rested on the seventh day from all his work which he had done,"[121] human life has a rhythm of work and rest. *2172* The institution of the Lord's Day helps everyone enjoy adequate rest and leisure to cultivate their familial, cultural, social, and religious lives.[122]

2185 On Sundays and other holy days of obligation, the faithful are to refrain from engaging in work or activities that hinder the worship owed to God, the joy proper to the Lord's Day, the *2428* performance of the works of mercy, and the appropriate relaxation of mind and body.[123] Family needs or important social service can legitimately excuse from the obligation of Sunday rest. The faithful should see to it that legitimate excuses do not lead to habits prejudicial to religion, family life, and health.

---

119 Cf. CIC, can. 1245.
120 CIC, can. 1248 § 2.
121 *Gen* 2:2.
122 Cf. *GS* 67 § 3.
123 Cf. CIC, can. 1247.

> The charity of truth seeks holy leisure; the necessity of charity accepts just work.[124]

2186   Those Christians who have leisure should be mindful of their brethren who have the same needs and the same rights, yet cannot rest from work because of poverty and misery. Sunday is traditionally consecrated by Christian piety to good works and *2447* humble service of the sick, the infirm, and the elderly. Christians will also sanctify Sunday by devoting time and care to their families and relatives, often difficult to do on other days of the week. Sunday is a time for reflection, silence, cultivation of the mind, and meditation which furthers the growth of the Christian interior life.

2187   Sanctifying Sundays and holy days requires a common effort. Every Christian should avoid making unnecessary demands on others that would hinder them from observing the Lord's Day. Traditional activities (sport, restaurants, etc.), and social necessities (public services, etc.), re-*2289* quire some people to work on Sundays, but everyone should still take care to set aside sufficient time for leisure. With temperance and charity the faithful will see to it that they avoid the excesses and violence sometimes associated with popular leisure activities. In spite of economic constraints, public authorities should ensure citizens a time intended for rest and divine worship. Employers have a similar obligation toward their employees.

2105 **2188**   In respecting religious liberty and the common good of all, Christians should seek recognition of Sundays and the Church's holy days as legal holidays. They have to give everyone a public example of prayer, respect, and joy and defend their traditions as a precious contribution to the spiritual life of society. If a country's legislation or other reasons require work on Sunday, the day should nevertheless be lived as the day of our deliverance which lets us share in this "festal gathering," this "assembly of the first-born who are enrolled in heaven."[125]

---

124 St. Augustine, *De civ. Dei* 19, 19: PL 41, 647.
125 *Heb* 12:22-23.

IN BRIEF

2189 "Observe the sabbath day, to keep it holy" (*Deut* 5:12). "The seventh day is a sabbath of solemn rest, holy to the Lord" (*Ex* 31:15).

2190 The sabbath, which represented the completion of the first creation, has been replaced by Sunday which recalls the new creation inaugurated by the Resurrection of Christ.

2191 The Church celebrates the day of Christ's Resurrection on the "eighth day," Sunday, which is rightly called the Lord's Day (cf. *SC* 106).

2192 "Sunday . . . is to be observed as the foremost holy day of obligation in the universal Church" (CIC, can. 1246 § 1). "On Sundays and other holy days of obligation the faithful are bound to participate in the Mass" (CIC, can. 1247).

2193 "On Sundays and other holy days of obligation the faithful are bound . . . to abstain from those labors and business concerns which impede the worship to be rendered to God, the joy which is proper to the Lord's Day, or the proper relaxation of mind and body" (CIC, can. 1247).

2194 The institution of Sunday helps all "to be allowed sufficient rest and leisure to cultivate their amilial, cultural, social, and religious lives" (*GS* 67 § 3).

2195 Every Christian should avoid making unnecessary demands on others that would hinder them from observing the Lord's Day.

Chapter Two
"You Shall Love Your Neighbor as Yourself"

> Jesus said to his disciples: "Love one another even as I have loved you."[1]

2196   In response to the question about the first of the commandments, Jesus says: "The first is, 'Hear, O Israel: The Lord our God, the Lord is one; and you shall love the Lord your God with all your heart, and with all your soul, and with all your mind, and with all your strength.' The second is this, 'You shall love your neighbor as yourself.' There is no other commandment greater than these."[2]

2822   The apostle St. Paul reminds us of this: "He who loves his neighbor has fulfilled the law. The commandments, *'You shall not commit adultery, You shall not kill, You shall not steal, You shall not covet,'* and any other commandment, are summed up in this sentence, 'You shall love your neighbor as yourself.' Love does no wrong to a neighbor; therefore love is the fulfilling of the law."[3]

Article 4
THE FOURTH COMMANDMENT

> Honor your father and your mother, that your days may be long in the land which the Lord your God gives you.[4]
>
> He was obedient to them.[5]
>
> The Lord Jesus himself recalled the force of this "commandment of God."[6] The Apostle teaches: "Children, obey your parents in the Lord, for this is right. 'Honor your father and mother,' (This is the first commandment with a promise.) 'that it may be well with you and that you may live long on the earth.'"[7]

---

1   *Jn* 13:34.
2   *Mk* 12:29-31; cf. *Deut* 6:4-5; *Lev* 19:18; *Mt* 22:34-40; *Lk* 10:25-28.
3   *Rom* 13:8-10.
4   *Ex* 20:12; *Deut* 5:16.
5   *Lk* 2:51.
6   *Mk* 7:8-13.
7   *Eph* 6:1-3; cf. *Deut* 5:16.

2197 The fourth commandment opens the second table of the Decalogue. It shows us the order of charity. God has willed that, after him, we should honor our parents to whom we owe life and who have handed on to us the knowledge of God. We are obliged to honor and respect all those whom God, for our good, has vested with his authority.   *1897*

2198 This commandment is expressed in positive terms of duties to be fulfilled. It introduces the subsequent commandments which are concerned with particular respect for life, marriage, earthly goods, and speech. It constitutes one of the foundations of *2419* the social doctrine of the Church.

2199 The fourth commandment is addressed expressly to children in their relationship to their father and mother, because this relationship is the most universal. It likewise concerns the ties of kinship between members of the extended family. It requires honor, affection, and gratitude toward elders and ancestors. Finally, it extends to the duties of pupils to teachers, employees to employers, subordinates to leaders, citizens to their country, and to those who administer or govern it.

    This commandment includes and presupposes the duties of parents, instructors, teachers, leaders, magistrates, those who govern, all who exercise authority over others or over a community of persons.

2200 Observing the fourth commandment brings its reward: "Honor your father and your mother, that your days may be long in the land which the LORD your God gives you."[8] Respecting this commandment provides, along with spiritual fruits, temporal fruits of peace and prosperity. Conversely, failure to observe it *2304* brings great harm to communities and to individuals.

I. THE FAMILY IN GOD'S PLAN

The nature of the family

2201 The conjugal community is established upon the consent *1625* of the spouses. Marriage and the family are ordered to the good of the spouses and to the procreation and education of children. The love of the spouses and the begetting of children create among

---

8 *Ex* 20:12; *Deut* 5:16.

members of the same family personal relationships and primordial responsibilities.

1882 **2202**   A man and a woman united in marriage, together with their children, form a family. This institution is prior to any recognition by public authority, which has an obligation to recognize it. It should be considered the normal reference point by which the different forms of family relationship are to be evaluated.

369 **2203**   In creating man and woman, God instituted the human family and endowed it with its fundamental constitution. Its members are persons equal in dignity. For the common good of its members and of society, the family necessarily has manifold responsibilities, rights, and duties.

1655-1658 **The Christian family**

2204   "The Christian family constitutes a specific revelation and realization of ecclesial communion, and for this reason it can and *533* should be called a *domestic church*."[9] It is a community of faith, hope, and charity; it assumes singular importance in the Church, as is evident in the New Testament.[10]

1702 **2205**   The Christian family is a communion of persons, a sign and image of the communion of the Father and the Son in the Holy Spirit. In the procreation and education of children it reflects the Father's work of creation. It is called to partake of the prayer and sacrifice of Christ. Daily prayer and the reading of the Word of God strengthen it in charity. The Christian family has an evangelizing and missionary task.

2206   The relationships within the family bring an affinity of feelings, affections and interests, arising above all from the members' respect for one another. The family is a *privileged community* called to achieve a "sharing of thought and common deliberation by the spouses as well as their eager cooperation as parents in the children's upbringing."[11]

---

9   *FC* 21; cf. *LG* 11.
10 Cf. *Eph* 5:21-6:4; *Col* 3:18-21; *1 Pet* 3:1-7.
11 *GS* 52 § 1.

II. THE FAMILY AND SOCIETY

2207 The family is the *original cell of social life.* It is the natural *1880* society in which husband and wife are called to give themselves in love and in the gift of life. Authority, stability, and a life of relationships within the family constitute the foundations for freedom, *372* security, and fraternity within society. The family is the community in which, from childhood, one can learn moral values, begin to honor God, and make good use of freedom. Family life is an initiation into life in society.

2208 The family should live in such a way that its members learn to care and take responsibility for the young, the old, the sick, the handicapped, and the poor. There are many families who are at times incapable of providing this help. It devolves then on other persons, other families, and, in a subsidiary way, society to provide for their needs: "Religion that is pure and undefiled before God and the Father is this: to visit orphans and widows in their affliction and to keep oneself unstained from the world."[12]

2209 The family must be helped and defended by appropriate social measures. Where families cannot fulfill their responsibilities, other social bodies have the duty of helping them and of supporting the institution of the family. Following the principle of subsidiarity, larger communities should take care not to usurp the *1883* family's prerogatives or interfere in its life.

2210 The importance of the family for the life and well-being of society[13] entails a particular responsibility for society to support and strengthen marriage and the family. Civil authority should consider it a grave duty "to acknowledge the true nature of marriage and the family, to protect and foster them, to safeguard public morality, and promote domestic prosperity."[14]

2211 The political community has a duty to honor the family, to assist it, and to ensure especially:

– the freedom to establish a family, have children, and bring them up in keeping with the family's own moral and religious convictions;

– the protection of the stability of the marriage bond and the institution of the family;

– the freedom to profess one's faith, to hand it on, and raise one's children in it, with the necessary means and institutions;

---

12 *Jas* 1:27.
13 Cf. *GS* 47 § 1.
14 *GS* 52 § 2.

– the right to private property, to free enterprise, to obtain work and housing, and the right to emigrate;

– in keeping with the country's institutions, the right to medical care, assistance for the aged, and family benefits;

– the protection of security and health, especially with respect to dangers like drugs, pornography, alcoholism, etc.;

– the freedom to form associations with other families and so to have representation before civil authority.[15]

2212   The fourth commandment *illuminates other relationships in society.* In our brothers and sisters we see the children of our parents; in our cousins, the descendants of our ancestors; in our fellow citizens, the children of our country; in the baptized, the children of our mother the Church; in every human person, a son
225   or daughter of the One who wants to be called "our Father." In this way our relationships with our neighbors are recognized as personal in character. The neighbor is not a "unit" in the human
1931   collective; he is "someone" who by his known origins deserves particular attention and respect.

2213   Human communities are *made up of persons.* Governing them well is not limited to guaranteeing rights and fulfilling duties such as honoring contracts. Right relations between employers and employees, between those who govern and citizens, presuppose a natural good will in keeping with the dignity of human persons
1939   concerned for justice and fraternity.

III.   THE DUTIES OF FAMILY MEMBERS

The duties of children

2214   The divine fatherhood is the source of human fatherhood;[16] this is the foundation of the honor owed to parents. The respect of children, whether minors or adults, for their father and mother[17] is nourished by the natural affection born of the bond
1858   uniting them. It is required by God's commandment.[18]

2215   Respect for parents (*filial piety*) derives from *gratitude* toward those who, by the gift of life, their love and their work, have brought their children into the world and enabled them to grow in

---

15   Cf. *FC* 46.
16   Cf. *Eph* 3:14.
17   Cf. *Prov* 1:8; *Tob* 4:3-4.
18   Cf. *Ex* 20:12.

stature, wisdom, and grace. "With all your heart honor your father, and do not forget the birth pangs of your mother. Remember that through your parents you were born; what can you give back to them that equals their gift to you?"[19]

2216 Filial respect is shown by true docility and *obedience.* "My 532 son, keep your father's commandment, and forsake not your mother's teaching. . . . When you walk, they will lead you; when you lie down, they will watch over you; and when you awake, they will talk with you."[20] "A wise son hears his father's instruction, but a scoffer does not listen to rebuke."[21]

2217 As long as a child lives at home with his parents, the child should obey his parents in all that they ask of him when it is for his good or that of the family. "Children, obey your parents in everything, for this pleases the Lord."[22] Children should also obey the reasonable directions of their teachers and all to whom their parents have entrusted them. But if a child is convinced in conscience that it would be morally wrong to obey a particular order, he must not do so.

As they grow up, children should continue to respect their parents. They should anticipate their wishes, willingly seek their advice, and accept their just admonitions. Obedience toward parents ceases with the emancipation of the children; not so respect, which is always owed to them. This respect has its roots in the fear of God, one of the gifts of the Holy Spirit.   1831

2218 The fourth commandment reminds grown children of their *responsibilities toward their parents.* As much as they can, they must give them material and moral support in old age and in times of illness, loneliness, or distress. Jesus recalls this duty of gratitude.[23]

> For the Lord honored the father above the children, and he confirmed the right of the mother over her sons. Whoever honors his father atones for sins, and whoever glorifies his mother is like one who lays up treasure. Whoever honors his father will be gladdened by his own children, and when he prays he will be heard. Whoever glorifies his father will have long life, and whoever obeys the Lord will refresh his mother.[24]

---

19 *Sir* 7:27-28.
20 *Prov* 6:20-22.
21 *Prov* 13:1.
22 *Col* 3:20; cf. *Eph* 6:1.
23 Cf. *Mk* 7:10-12.
24 *Sir* 3:2-6.

> O son, help your father in his old age, and do not grieve him as long as he lives; even if he is lacking in understanding, show forbearance; in all your strength do not despise him. . . . Whoever forsakes his father is like a blasphemer, and whoever angers his mother is cursed by the Lord.[25]

2219   Filial respect promotes harmony in all of family life; it also concerns *relationships between brothers and sisters.* Respect toward parents fills the home with light and warmth. "Grandchildren are the crown of the aged."[26] "With all humility and meekness, with patience, [support] one another in charity."[27]

2220   For Christians a special gratitude is due to those from whom they have received the gift of faith, the grace of Baptism, and life in the Church. These may include parents, grandparents, other members of the family, pastors, catechists, and other teachers or friends. "I am reminded of your sincere faith, a faith that dwelt first in your grandmother Lois and your mother Eunice and now, I am sure, dwells in you."[28]

The duties of parents

2221   The fecundity of conjugal love cannot be reduced solely to the procreation of children, but must extend to their moral education and their spiritual formation. "The *role of parents in education*

1653   is of such importance that it is almost impossible to provide an adequate substitute."[29] The right and the duty of parents to educate their children are primordial and inalienable.[30]

2222   Parents must regard their children as *children of God* and respect them as *human persons.* Showing themselves obedient to the

494   will of the Father in heaven, they educate their children to fulfill God's law.

---

25 *Sir* 3:12-13, 16.
26 *Prov* 17:6.
27 *Eph* 4:2.
28 *2 Tim* 1:5.
29 *GE* 3.
30 Cf. *FC* 36.

2223   Parents have the first responsibility for the education of their children. They bear witness to this responsibility first by *creating a home* where tenderness, forgiveness, respect, fidelity, and disinterested service are the rule. The home is well suited for *education in the virtues.* This requires an apprenticeship in self-denial, sound judgment, and self-mastery – the preconditions of all   *1804* true freedom. Parents should teach their children to subordinate the "material and instinctual dimensions to interior and spiritual ones."[31] Parents have a grave responsibility to give good example to their children. By knowing how to acknowledge their own failings to their children, parents will be better able to guide and correct them:

> He who loves his son will not spare the rod. . . . He who disciplines his son will profit by him.[32]
>
> Fathers, do not provoke your children to anger, but bring them up in the discipline and instruction of the Lord.[33]

2224   The home is the natural environment for initiating a hu-   *1939* man being into solidarity and communal responsibilities. Parents should teach children to avoid the compromising and degrading influences which threaten human societies.

2225   Through the grace of the sacrament of marriage, parents receive the responsibility and privilege of *evangelizing their children.* Parents should initiate their children at an early age into the   *1656* mysteries of the faith of which they are the "first heralds" for their children. They should associate them from their tenderest years with the life of the Church.[34] A wholesome family life can foster interior dispositions that are a genuine preparation for a living faith and remain a support for it throughout one's life.

2226   *Education in the faith* by the parents should begin in the child's earliest years. This already happens when family members help one another to grow in faith by the witness of a Christian life in keeping with the Gospel. Family catechesis precedes, accompanies, and enriches other forms of instruction in the faith. Parents have the mission of teaching their children to pray and to discover their vocation as children of God.[35] The parish is the Eucharistic   *2179*

---

31   *CA* 36 § 2.
32   *Sir* 30:1-2.
33   *Eph* 6:4.
34   *LG* 11 § 2.
35   Cf. *LG* 11.

community and the heart of the liturgical life of Christian families; it is a privileged place for the catechesis of children and parents.

2013 **2227**   Children in turn contribute to the *growth in holiness* of their parents.[36] Each and everyone should be generous and tireless in forgiving one another for offenses, quarrels, injustices, and neglect. Mutual affection suggests this. The charity of Christ demands it.[37]

2228   Parents' respect and affection are expressed by the care and attention they devote to bringing up their young children and *providing for their physical and spiritual needs.* As the children grow up, the same respect and devotion lead parents to educate them in the right use of their reason and freedom.

2229   As those first responsible for the education of their children, parents have the right to *choose a school for them* which corresponds to their own convictions. This right is fundamental. As far as possible parents have the duty of choosing schools that will best help them in their task as Christian educators.[38] Public authorities have the duty of guaranteeing this parental right and of ensuring the concrete conditions for its exercise.

2230   When they become adults, children have the right and duty to *choose their profession and state of life.* They should assume their new responsibilities within a trusting relationship with their parents, willingly asking and receiving their advice and counsel. Parents should be careful not to exert pressure on their children
1625 either in the choice of a profession or in that of a spouse. This necessary restraint does not prevent them – quite the contrary – from giving their children judicious advice, particularly when they are planning to start a family.

2231   Some forgo marriage in order to care for their parents or brothers and sisters, to give themselves more completely to a profession, or to serve other honorable ends. They can contribute greatly to the good of the human family.

---

36 Cf. *GS* 48 § 4.
37 Cf. *Mt* 18:21-22; *Lk* 17:4.
38 Cf. *GE* 6.

IV. The Family and the Kingdom

2232 Family ties are important but not absolute. Just as the child grows to maturity and human and spiritual autonomy, so his unique vocation which comes from God asserts itself more clearly and forcefully. Parents should respect this call and encourage their children to follow it. They must be convinced that the first vocation of the Christian is to *follow Jesus*: "He who loves father or mother *1618* more than me is not worthy of me; and he who loves son or daughter more than me is not worthy of me."[39]

2233 Becoming a disciple of Jesus means accepting the invitation to belong to *God's family*, to live in conformity with His way of life: "For whoever does the will of my Father in heaven is my *542* brother, and sister, and mother."[40]

Parents should welcome and respect with joy and thanksgiving the Lord's call to one of their children to follow him in virginity for the sake of the Kingdom in the consecrated life or in priestly ministry.

V. The Authorities in Civil Society

2234 God's fourth commandment also enjoins us to honor all who for our good have received authority in society from God. It clarifies the duties of those who exercise authority as well as those *1897* who benefit from it.

Duties of civil authorities

2235 Those who exercise authority should do so as a service. "Whoever would be great among you must be your servant."[41] The exercise of authority is measured morally in terms of its divine origin, its reasonable nature and its specific object. No one can command or establish what is contrary to the dignity of persons *1899* and the natural law.

2236 The exercise of authority is meant to give outward expression to a just hierarchy of values in order to facilitate the exercise of freedom and responsibility by all. Those in authority should practice distributive justice wisely, taking account of the needs and *2411*

---

39 *Mt* 10:37; cf. 16:25.
40 *Mt* 12:49.
41 *Mt* 20:26.

contribution of each, with a view to harmony and peace. They should take care that the regulations and measures they adopt are not a source of temptation by setting personal interest against that of the community.[42]

2237 *Political authorities* are obliged to respect the fundamental rights of the human person. They will dispense justice humanely
357 by respecting the rights of everyone, especially of families and the disadvantaged.

The political rights attached to citizenship can and should be granted according to the requirements of the common good. They cannot be suspended by public authorities without legitimate and proportionate reasons. Political rights are meant to be exercised for the common good of the nation and the human community.

The duties of citizens

2238 Those subject to authority should regard those in authority as representatives of God, who has made them stewards of his gifts:[43]
1900 "Be subject for the Lord's sake to every human institution. . . . Live as free men, yet without using your freedom as a pretext for evil; but live as servants of God."[44] Their loyal collaboration includes the right, and at times the duty, to voice their just criticisms of that which seems harmful to the dignity of persons and to the good of the community.

1915 **2239** It is the *duty of citizens* to contribute along with the civil authorities to the good of society in a spirit of truth, justice, solidarity, and freedom. The love and service of *one's country* follow from
2310 the duty of gratitude and belong to the order of charity. Submission to legitimate authorities and service of the common good require citizens to fulfill their roles in the life of the political community.

2240 Submission to authority and co-responsibility for the common good make it morally obligatory to pay taxes, to exercise the
2265 right to vote, and to defend one's country:

> Pay to all of them their dues, taxes to whom taxes are due, revenue to whom revenue is due, respect to whom respect is due, honor to whom honor is due.[45]

---

42 Cf. *CA* 25.
43 Cf. *Rom* 13:1-2.
44 *1 Pet* 2:13, 16.
45 *Rom* 13:7.

> [Christians] reside in their own nations, but as resident aliens. They participate in all things as citizens and endure all things as foreigners. . . . They obey the established laws and their way of life surpasses the laws. . . . So noble is the position to which God has assigned them that they are not allowed to desert it.[46]

1900 The Apostle exhorts us to offer prayers and thanksgiving for kings and all who exercise authority, "that we may lead a quiet and peaceable life, godly and respectful in every way."[47]

2241 The more prosperous nations are obliged, to the extent they are able, to welcome the *foreigner* in search of the security and the means of livelihood which he cannot find in his country of origin. Public authorities should see to it that the natural right is respected that places a guest under the protection of those who receive him.

Political authorities, for the sake of the common good for which they are responsible, may make the exercise of the right to immigrate subject to various juridical conditions, especially with regard to the immigrants' duties toward their country of adoption. Immigrants are obliged to respect with gratitude the material and spiritual heritage of the country that receives them, to obey its laws and to assist in carrying civic burdens.

2242 The citizen is obliged in conscience not to follow the directives of civil authorities when they are contrary to the demands of the moral order, to the fundamental rights of persons or the teach- *1903* ings of the Gospel. *Refusing obedience* to civil authorities, when their *2313* demands are contrary to those of an upright conscience, finds its justification in the distinction between serving God and serving the political community. "Render therefore to Caesar the things that *450* are Caesar's, and to God the things that are God's."[48] "We must obey God rather than men":[49]

> When citizens are under the oppression of a public authority *1901* which oversteps its competence, they should still not refuse to give or to do what is objectively demanded of them by the common good; but it is legitimate for them to defend their own rights and those of their fellow citizens against the abuse of this authority within the limits of the natural law and the Law of the Gospel.[50]

---

46 *Ad Diognetum* 5, 5 and 10; 6, 10: PG 2, 1173 and 1176.
47 *1 Tim* 2:2.
48 *Mt* 22:21.
49 *Acts* 5:29.
50 *GS* 74 § 5.

2309 **2243**   Armed *resistance* to oppression by political authority is not
legitimate, unless all the following conditions are met: 1) there is
certain, grave, and prolonged violation of fundamental rights; 2)
all other means of redress have been exhausted; 3) such resistance
will not provoke worse disorders; 4) there is well-founded hope of
success; and 5) it is impossible reasonably to foresee any better
solution.

The political community and the Church

1910 **2244**   Every institution is inspired, at least implicitly, by a vision
of man and his destiny, from which it derives the point of reference
for its judgment, its hierarchy of values, its line of conduct. Most
societies have formed their institutions in the recognition of a
certain preeminence of man over things. Only the divinely re-
1881 vealed religion has clearly recognized man's origin and destiny in
God, the Creator and Redeemer. The Church invites political
2109 authorities to measure their judgments and decisions against this
inspired truth about God and man:

> Societies not recognizing this vision or rejecting it in the
> name of their independence from God are brought to seek
> their criteria and goal in themselves or to borrow them from
> some ideology. Since they do not admit that one can defend
> an objective criterion of good and evil, they arrogate to
> themselves an explicit or implicit totalitarian power over
> man and his destiny, as history shows.[51]

2245   The Church, because of her commission and competence,
is not to be confused in any way with the political community. She
912 is both the sign and the safeguard of the transcendent character of
the human person. "The Church respects and encourages the
political freedom and responsibility of the citizen."[52]

2246   It is a part of the Church's mission "to pass moral judgments even in matters related to politics, whenever the fundamen-
2032 tal rights of man or the salvation of souls requires it. The means,
2420 the only means, she may use are those which are in accord with the
Gospel and the welfare of all men according to the diversity of
times and circumstances."[53]

---

51   Cf. *CA* 45; 46.
52   *GS* 76 § 3.
53   *GS* 76 § 5.

IN BRIEF

2247   "Honor your father and your mother" (*Deut* 5:16; *Mk* 7:10).

2248   According to the fourth commandment, God has willed that, after him, we should honor our parents and those whom he has vested with authority for our good.

2249   The conjugal community is established upon the covenant and consent of the spouses. Marriage and family are ordered to the good of the spouses, to the procreation and the education of children.

2250   "The well-being of the individual person and of both human and Christian society is closely bound up with the healthy state of conjugal and family life" (*GS* 47 § 1).

2251   Children owe their parents respect, gratitude, just obedience, and assistance. Filial respect fosters harmony in all of family life.

2252   Parents have the first responsibility for the education of their children in the faith, prayer, and all the virtues. They have the duty to provide as far as possible for the physical and spiritual needs of their children.

2253   Parents should respect and encourage their children's vocations. They should remember and teach that the first calling of the Christian is to follow Jesus.

2254   Public authority is obliged to respect the fundamental rights of the human person and the conditions for the exercise of his freedom.

2255   It is the duty of citizens to work with civil authority for building up society in a spirit of truth, justice, solidarity, and freedom.

2256   Citizens are obliged in conscience not to follow the directives of civil authorities when they are contrary to the demands of the moral order. "We must obey God rather than men" (*Acts* 5:29).

2257   Every society's judgments and conduct reflect a vision of man and his destiny. Without the light the Gospel sheds on God and man, societies easily become totalitarian.

ARTICLE 5
THE FIFTH COMMANDMENT

You shall not kill.[54]

You have heard that it was said to the men of old, "You shall not kill: and whoever kills shall be liable to judgment." But I say to you that every one who is angry with his brother shall be liable to judgment.[55]

356   **2258**   *"Human life is sacred* because from its beginning it involves the creative action of God and it remains for ever in a special relationship with the Creator, who is its sole end. God alone is the Lord of life from its beginning until its end: no one can under any circumstance claim for himself the right directly to destroy an innocent human being."[56]

I.   RESPECT FOR HUMAN LIFE

The witness of sacred history

401   **2259**   In the account of Abel's murder by his brother Cain,[57] Scripture reveals the presence of anger and envy in man, consequences of original sin, from the beginning of human history. Man has become the enemy of his fellow man. God declares the wickedness of this fratricide: "What have you done? The voice of your brother's blood is crying to me from the ground. And now you are cursed from the ground, which has opened its mouth to receive your brother's blood from your hand."[58]

2260   The covenant between God and mankind is interwoven with reminders of God's gift of human life and man's murderous violence:

For your lifeblood I will surely require a reckoning. . . . Whoever sheds the blood of man, by man shall his blood be shed; for God made man in his own image.[59]

---

54   *Ex* 20:13; cf. *Deut* 5:17.
55   *Mt* 5:21-22.
56   CDF, instruction, *Donum vitae,* intro. 5.
57   Cf. *Gen* 4:8-12.
58   *Gen* 4:10-11.
59   *Gen* 9:5-6.

The Old Testament always considered blood a sacred sign of life.[60] This teaching remains necessary for all time.

2261 Scripture specifies the prohibition contained in the fifth commandment: "Do not slay the innocent and the righteous."[61] The deliberate murder of an innocent person is gravely contrary to the dignity of the human being, to the golden rule, and to the *1756* holiness of the Creator. The law forbidding it is universally valid: *1956* it obliges each and everyone, always and everywhere.

2262 In the Sermon on the Mount, the Lord recalls the commandment, "You shall not kill,"[62] and adds to it the proscription of anger, hatred, and vengeance. Going further, Christ asks his disciples to turn the other cheek, to love their enemies.[63] He did not defend himself and told Peter to leave his sword in its sheath.[64] *2844*

Legitimate defense

2263 The legitimate defense of persons and societies is not an exception to the prohibition against the murder of the innocent that constitutes intentional killing. "The act of self-defense can have a double effect: the preservation of one's own life; and the killing of *1737* the aggressor. . . . The one is intended, the other is not."[65]

2264 Love toward oneself remains a fundamental principle of *2196* morality. Therefore it is legitimate to insist on respect for one's own right to life. Someone who defends his life is not guilty of murder even if he is forced to deal his aggressor a lethal blow:

> If a man in self-defense uses more than necessary violence, it will be unlawful: whereas if he repels force with moderation, his defense will be lawful. . . . Nor is it necessary for salvation that a man omit the act of moderate self-defense to avoid killing the other man, since one is bound to take more care of one's own life than of another's.[66]

2265 Legitimate defense can be not only a right but a grave duty for someone responsible for another's life, the common good of the *2240* family or of the state.

---

60 Cf. *Lev* 17:14.
61 *Ex* 23:7.
62 *Mt* 5:21.
63 Cf. *Mt* 5:22-39; 5:44.
64 Cf. *Mt* 26:52.
65 St. Thomas Aquinas, *STh* II-II, 64, 7, *corp. art.*
66 St. Thomas Aquinas, *STh* II-II, 64, 7, *corp. art.*

2266   Preserving the common good of society requires rendering the aggressor unable to inflict harm. For this reason the traditional teaching of the Church has acknowledged as well-founded the
1897-1898 right and duty of legitimate public authority to punish malefactors by means of penalties commensurate with the gravity of the crime, not excluding, in cases of extreme gravity, the death penalty. For analogous reasons those holding authority have the right to repel
2308   by armed force aggressors against the community in their charge.

The primary effect of *punishment* is to redress the disorder caused by the offense. When his punishment is voluntarily ac-
1449   cepted by the offender, it takes on the value of expiation. Moreover, punishment has the effect of preserving public order and the safety of persons. Finally punishment has a medicinal value; as far as possible it should contribute to the correction of the offender.[67]

2267   If bloodless means are sufficient to defend human lives against an aggressor and to protect public order and the safety of
2306   persons, public authority should limit itself to such means, because they better correspond to the concrete conditions of the common good and are more in conformity to the dignity of the human person.

Intentional homicide

2268   The fifth commandment forbids *direct and intentional killing* as gravely sinful. The murderer and those who cooperate voluntarily in murder commit a sin that cries out to heaven for venge-
1867   ance.[68]

Infanticide,[69] fratricide, parricide, and the murder of a spouse are especially grave crimes by reason of the natural bonds which they break. Concern for eugenics or public health cannot justify any murder, even if commanded by public authority.

2269   The fifth commandment forbids doing anything with the intention of *indirectly* bringing about a person's death. The moral law prohibits exposing someone to mortal danger without grave reason, as well as refusing assistance to a person in danger.

---

67   Cf. *Lk* 23:40-43.
68   Cf. *Gen* 4:10.
69   Cf. *GS* 51 § 3.

The acceptance by human society of murderous famines, without efforts to remedy them, is a scandalous injustice and a grave offense. Those whose usurious and avaricious dealings lead to the hunger and death of their brethren in the human family indirectly commit homicide, which is imputable to them.[70]

Unintentional killing is not morally imputable. But one is **2290** not exonerated from grave offense if, without proportionate reasons, he has acted in a way that brings about someone's death, even without the intention to do so.

Abortion

2270   Human life must be respected and protected absolutely from the moment of conception. From the first moment of his existence, a human being must be recognized as having the rights **1703** of a person – among which is the inviolable right of every innocent **357** being to life.[71]

> Before I formed you in the womb I knew you, and before you were born I consecrated you.[72]

> My frame was not hidden from you, when I was being made in secret, intricately wrought in the depths of the earth.[73]

2271   Since the first century the Church has affirmed the moral evil of every procured abortion. This teaching has not changed and remains unchangeable. Direct abortion, that is to say, abortion willed either as an end or a means, is gravely contrary to the moral law:

> You shall not kill the embryo by abortion and shall not cause the newborn to perish.[74]

> God, the Lord of life, has entrusted to men the noble mission of safeguarding life, and men must carry it out in a manner worthy of themselves. Life must be protected with the utmost care from the moment of conception: abortion and infanticide are abominable crimes.[75]

---

70   Cf. *Am* 8:4-10.
71   Cf. CDF, *Donum vitae* I, 1.
72   *Jer* 1:5; cf. *Job* 10:8-12; *Ps* 22:10-11.
73   *Ps* 139:15.
74   *Didache* 2, 2: SCh 248, 148; cf. *Ep. Barnabae* 19, 5: PG 2, 777; *Ad Diognetum* 5, 6: PG 2, 1173; Tertullian, *Apol.* 9: PL 1, 319-320.
75   *GS* 51 § 3.

2272   Formal cooperation in an abortion constitutes a grave offense. The Church attaches the canonical penalty of excommunication to this crime against human life. "A person who procures a completed abortion incurs excommunication *latae sententiae*,"[76] "by the very commission of the offense,"[77] and subject to the

1463 conditions provided by Canon Law.[78] The Church does not thereby intend to restrict the scope of mercy. Rather, she makes clear the gravity of the crime committed, the irreparable harm done to the innocent who is put to death, as well as to the parents and the whole of society.

1930 **2273**   The inalienable right to life of every innocent human individual is a *constitutive element of a civil society and its legislation*:

> "The inalienable rights of the person must be recognized and respected by civil society and the political authority. These human rights depend neither on single individuals nor on parents; nor do they represent a concession made by society and the state; they belong to human nature and are inherent in the person by virtue of the creative act from which the person took his origin. Among such fundamental rights one should mention in this regard every human being's right to life and physical integrity from the moment of conception until death."[79]

> "The moment a positive law deprives a category of human beings of the protection which civil legislation ought to accord them, the state is denying the equality of all before the law. When the state does not place its power at the service of the rights of each citizen, and in particular of the more vulnerable, the very foundations of a state based on law are undermined.... As a consequence of the respect and protection which must be ensured for the unborn child from the moment of conception, the law must provide appropriate penal sanctions for every deliberate violation of the child's rights."[80]

2274   Since it must be treated from conception as a person, the embryo must be defended in its integrity, cared for, and healed, as far as possible, like any other human being.

> *Prenatal diagnosis* is morally licit, "if it respects the life and integrity of the embryo and the human fetus and is directed toward its safeguarding or healing as an individual.... It is gravely opposed to the moral law when this is done with the thought of possibly inducing an abortion, depending upon the results: a diagnosis must not be the equivalent of a death sentence."[81]

---

76   CIC, can. 1398.
77   CIC, can. 1314.
78   Cf. CIC, cann. 1323-1324.
79   CDF, *Donum vitae* III.
80   CDF, *Donum vitae* III.
81   CDF, *Donum vitae* I, 2.

2275   "One must hold as licit procedures carried out on the human embryo which respect the life and integrity of the embryo and do not involve disproportionate risks for it, but are directed toward its healing, the improvement of its condition of health, or its individual survival."[82]

"It is immoral to produce human embryos intended for exploitation as disposable biological material."[83]

"Certain attempts to *influence chromosomic or genetic inheritance* are not therapeutic but are aimed at producing human beings selected according to sex or other predetermined qualities. Such manipulations are contrary to the personal dignity of the human being and his integrity and identity"[84] which are unique and unrepeatable.

Euthanasia

2276   Those whose lives are diminished or weakened deserve *1503* special respect. Sick or handicapped persons should be helped to lead lives as normal as possible.

2277   Whatever its motives and means, direct euthanasia consists in putting an end to the lives of handicapped, sick, or dying persons. It is morally unacceptable.

Thus an act or omission which, of itself or by intention, causes death in order to eliminate suffering constitutes a murder gravely contrary to the dignity of the human person and to the respect due to the living God, his Creator. The error of judgment into which one can fall in good faith does not change the nature of this murderous act, which must always be forbidden and excluded.

2278   Discontinuing medical procedures that are burdensome, dangerous, extraordinary, or disproportionate to the expected outcome can be legitimate; it is the refusal of "over-zealous" treatment. Here one does not will to cause death; one's inability to impede it is merely accepted. The decisions should be made by the patient if he is competent and able or, if *1007* not, by those legally entitled to act for the patient, whose reasonable will and legitimate interests must always be respected.

2279   Even if death is thought imminent, the ordinary care owed to a sick person cannot be legitimately interrupted. The use of painkillers to alleviate the sufferings of the dying, even at the risk of shortening their days, can be morally in conformity with human dignity if death is not willed as either an end or a means, but only foreseen and tolerated as inevitable. Palliative care is a special form of disinterested charity. As such it should be encouraged.

---

82 CDF, *Donum vitae* I, 3.
83 CDF, *Donum vitae* I, 5.
84 CDF, *Donum vitae* I, 6.

Suicide

2280   Everyone is responsible for his life before God who has given it to him. It is God who remains the sovereign Master of life.
2258 We are obliged to accept life gratefully and preserve it for his honor and the salvation of our souls. We are stewards, not owners, of the life God has entrusted to us. It is not ours to dispose of.

2281   Suicide contradicts the natural inclination of the human being to preserve and perpetuate his life. It is gravely contrary to the just love of self. It likewise offends love of neighbor because it
2212 unjustly breaks the ties of solidarity with family, nation, and other human societies to which we continue to have obligations. Suicide is contrary to love for the living God.

2282   If suicide is committed with the intention of setting an example, especially to the young, it also takes on the gravity of
1735 scandal. Voluntary co-operation in suicide is contrary to the moral law.

Grave psychological disturbances, anguish, or grave fear of hardship, suffering, or torture can diminish the responsibility of the one committing suicide.

2283   We should not despair of the eternal salvation of persons who have taken their own lives. By ways known to him alone, God can provide the opportunity for salutary repentance. The Church
1037 prays for persons who have taken their own lives.

II.   RESPECT FOR THE DIGNITY OF PERSONS

Respect for the souls of others: scandal

2847 **2284**   Scandal is an attitude or behavior which leads another to do evil. The person who gives scandal becomes his neighbor's tempter. He damages virtue and integrity; he may even draw his brother into spiritual death. Scandal is a grave offense if by deed or omission another is deliberately led into a grave offense.

1903 **2285**   Scandal takes on a particular gravity by reason of the authority of those who cause it or the weakness of those who are scandalized. It prompted our Lord to utter this curse: "Whoever causes one of these little ones who believe in me to sin, it would be better for him to have a great millstone fastened round his neck and to be drowned in the depth of the sea."[85] Scandal is grave when

---

85   *Mt* 18:6; cf. *1 Cor* 8:10-13.

given by those who by nature or office are obliged to teach and educate others. Jesus reproaches the scribes and Pharisees on this account: he likens them to wolves in sheep's clothing.[86]

2286   Scandal can be provoked by laws or institutions, by fashion or opinion.

Therefore, they are guilty of scandal who establish laws or social *1887* structures leading to the decline of morals and the corruption of religious practice, or to "social conditions that, intentionally or not, make Christian conduct and obedience to the Commandments difficult and practically impossible."[87] This is also true of business leaders who make rules encouraging fraud, teachers who provoke their children to anger,[88] or manipu- *2498* lators of public opinion who turn it away from moral values.

2287   Anyone who uses the power at his disposal in such a way that it leads others to do wrong becomes guilty of scandal and responsible for the evil that he has directly or indirectly encouraged. "Temptations to sin are sure to come; but woe to him by whom they come!"[89]

Respect for health

2288   Life and physical health are precious gifts entrusted to us *1503* by God. We must take reasonable care of them, taking into account the needs of others and the common good.

Concern for the health of its citizens requires that society help *1509* in the attainment of living-conditions that allow them to grow and reach maturity: food and clothing, housing, health care, basic education, employment, and social assistance.

2289   If morality requires respect for the life of the body, it does *364* not make it an absolute value. It rejects a neo-pagan notion that tends to promote the *cult of the body*, to sacrifice everything for it's *2113* sake, to idolize physical perfection and success at sports. By its selective preference of the strong over the weak, such a conception can lead to the perversion of human relationships.

2290   The virtue of temperance disposes us to *avoid every kind of* *1809* *excess*: the abuse of food, alcohol, tobacco, or medicine. Those incur grave guilt who, by drunkenness or a love of speed, endanger their own and others' safety on the road, at sea, or in the air.

---

86   Cf. *Mt* 7:15.
87   Pius XII, Discourse, June 1, 1941.
88   Cf. *Eph* 6:4; *Col* 3:21.
89   *Lk* 17:1.

2291   The *use of drugs* inflicts very grave damage on human health and life. Their use, except on strictly therapeutic grounds, is a grave offense. Clandestine production of and trafficking in drugs are scandalous practices. They constitute direct co-operation in evil, since they encourage people to practices gravely contrary to the moral law.

Respect for the person and scientific research

2292   Scientific, medical, or psychological experiments on human individuals or groups can contribute to healing the sick and the advancement of public health.

159   **2293**   Basic scientific research, as well as applied research, is a significant expression of man's dominion over creation. Science and technology are precious resources when placed at the service of man and promote his integral development for the benefit of all. By themselves however they cannot disclose the meaning of existence and of human progress. Science and technology are ordered to man, from whom they take their origin and development; hence they find in the person and in his moral values both *1703*   evidence of their purpose and awareness of their limits.

2294   It is an illusion to claim moral neutrality in scientific research and its applications. On the other hand, guiding principles cannot be inferred from simple technical efficiency, or from the usefulness accruing to some at the expense of others or, even worse, from prevailing ideologies. Science and technology by their very nature require unconditional respect for *2375*   fundamental moral criteria. They must be at the service of the human person, of his inalienable rights, of his true and integral good, in conformity with the plan and the will of God.

2295   Research or experimentation on the human being cannot legitimate acts that are in themselves contrary to the dignity of *1753*   persons and to the moral law. The subjects' potential consent does not justify such acts. Experimentation on human beings is not morally legitimate if it exposes the subject's life or physical and psychological integrity to disproportionate or avoidable risks. Experimentation on human beings does not conform to the dignity of the person if it takes place without the informed consent of the subject or those who legitimately speak for him.

2296   *Organ transplants* are not morally acceptable if the donor or those who legitimately speak for him have not given their informed consent. Organ transplants conform with the moral law and can be meritorious if the physical and psychological dangers and risks incurred by the donor are proportionate to the good sought for the recipient. It is morally inadmissible directly to bring about the disabling mutilation or death of a human being, even in order to delay the death of other persons.

Respect for bodily integrity

2297 *Kidnapping* and *hostage taking* bring on a reign of terror; by means of threats they subject their victims to intolerable pressures. They are morally wrong. *Terrorism* which threatens, wounds, and kills indiscriminately is gravely against justice and charity. *Torture* which uses physical or moral violence to extract confessions, punish the guilty, frighten opponents, or satisfy hatred is contrary to respect for the person and for human dignity. Except when performed for strictly therapeutic medical reasons, directly intended *amputations, mutilations,* and *sterilizations* performed on innocent persons are against the moral law.[90]

2298 In times past, cruel practices were commonly used by legitimate governments to maintain law and order, often without protest from the Pastors of the Church, who themselves adopted in their own tribunals the prescriptions of Roman law concerning torture. Regrettable as these facts are, the Church always taught the duty of clemency and mercy. She forbade clerics to shed blood. In recent times it has become evident that *2267* these cruel practices were neither necessary for public order, nor in conformity with the legitimate rights of the human person. On the contrary, these practices led to ones even more degrading. It is necessary to work for their abolition. We must pray for the victims and their tormentors.

Respect for the dead

2299 The dying should be given attention and care to help them live their last moments in dignity and peace. They will be helped by the prayer of their relatives, who must see to it that the sick receive at the proper time the sacraments that prepare them to meet *1525* the living God.

2300 The bodies of the dead must be treated with respect and *1681-1690* charity, in faith and hope of the Resurrection. The burial of the dead is a corporal work of mercy;[91] it honors the children of God, who are temples of the Holy Spirit.

2301 Autopsies can be morally permitted for legal inquests or scientific research. The free gift of organs after death is legitimate and can be meritorious.

The Church permits cremation, provided that it does not demonstrate a denial of faith in the resurrection of the body.[92]

---

90 Cf. DS 3722.
91 Cf. *Tob* 1:16-18.
92 Cf. CIC, can. 1176 § 3.

III.   SAFEGUARDING PEACE

Peace

2302   By recalling the commandment, "You shall not kill,"[93] our
Lord asked for peace of heart and denounced murderous anger and
1765 hatred as immoral.
   Anger is a desire for revenge. "To desire vengeance in order
to do evil to someone who should be punished is illicit," but it is
praiseworthy to impose restitution "to correct vices and maintain
justice."[94] If anger reaches the point of a deliberate desire to kill or
seriously wound a neighbor, it is gravely against charity; it is a
mortal sin. The Lord says, "Everyone who is angry with his brother
shall be liable to judgment."[95]

2094 **2303**   Deliberate *hatred* is contrary to charity. Hatred of the neighbor is a sin when one deliberately wishes him evil. Hatred of the
1933 neighbor is a grave sin when one deliberately desires him grave harm.
"But I say to you, Love your enemies and pray for those who persecute
you, so that you may be sons of your Father who is in heaven."[96]

1909 **2304**   Respect for and development of human life require *peace*.
Peace is not merely the absence of war, and it is not limited to
maintaining a balance of powers between adversaries. Peace cannot be attained on earth without safeguarding the goods of persons, free communication among men, respect for the dignity of
persons and peoples, and the assiduous practice of fraternity.
1807 Peace is "the tranquillity of order."[97] Peace is the work of justice
and the effect of charity.[98]

2305   Earthly peace is the image and fruit of the *peace of Christ*,
the messianic "Prince of Peace."[99] By the blood of his Cross, "in his
1468 own person he killed the hostility,"[100] he reconciled men with God
and made his Church the sacrament of the unity of the human race
and of its union with God. "He is our peace."[101] He has declared:
"Blessed are the peacemakers."[102]

---

93 *Mt* 5:21.
94 St. Thomas Aquinas, *STh* II-II, 158, 1 *ad* 3.
95 *Mt* 5:22.
96 *Mt* 5:44-45.
97 St. Augustine, *De civ. Dei*, 19, 13, 1: PL 41, 640.
98 Cf. *Isa* 32:17; cf. *GS* 78 §§ 1-2.
99 *Isa* 9:5.
100 *Eph* 2:16 J.B.; cf. *Col* 1:20-22.
101 *Eph* 2:14.
102 *Mt* 5:9.

2306 Those who renounce violence and bloodshed and, in order to safeguard human rights, make use of those means of defense available to the weakest, bear witness to evangelical charity, pro- *2267* vided they do so without harming the rights and obligations of other men and societies. They bear legitimate witness to the gravity of the physical and moral risks of recourse to violence, with all its destruction and death.[103]

Avoiding war

2307 The fifth commandment forbids the intentional destruction of human life. Because of the evils and injustices that accompany all war, the Church insistently urges everyone to prayer and to action so that the divine Goodness may free us from the ancient bondage of war.[104]

2308 All citizens and all governments are obliged to work for the avoidance of war.

However, "as long as the danger of war persists and there is no international authority with the necessary competence and power, governments cannot be denied the right of lawful self-de- *2266* fense, once all peace efforts have failed."[105]

2309 The strict conditions for *legitimate defense by military force* *2243* require rigorous consideration. The gravity of such a decision makes it subject to rigorous conditions of moral legitimacy. At one and the same time:

– the damage inflicted by the aggressor on the nation or community of nations must be lasting, grave, and certain;

– all other means of putting an end to it must have been shown to be impractical or ineffective;

– there must be serious prospects of success;

– the use of arms must not produce evils and disorders graver than the evil to be eliminated. The power of modern means of destruction weighs very heavily in evaluating this condition.

These are the traditional elements enumerated in what is called the "just war" doctrine.

---

103 Cf. *GS* 78 § 5.
104 Cf. *GS* 81 § 4.
105 *GS* 79 § 4.

1897   The evaluation of these conditions for moral legitimacy belongs to the prudential judgment of those who have responsibility for the common good.

2310   Public authorities, in this case, have the right and duty to impose on citizens the *obligations necessary for national defense.*

2239   Those who are sworn to serve their country in the armed
1909   forces are servants of the security and freedom of nations. If they carry out their duty honorably, they truly contribute to the common good of the nation and the maintenance of peace.[106]

2311   Public authorities should make equitable provision for those who for reasons of conscience refuse to bear arms; these are
1782, 1790   nonetheless obliged to serve the human community in some other way.[107]

2312   The Church and human reason both assert the permanent validity of the *moral law during armed conflict.* "The mere fact that war has regrettably broken out does not mean that everything becomes licit between the warring parties."[108]

2313   Non-combatants, wounded soldiers, and prisoners must be respected and treated humanely.

Actions deliberately contrary to the law of nations and to its universal principles are crimes, as are the orders that command such actions. Blind obedience does not suffice to excuse those who carry them out. Thus the extermination of a people, nation, or
2242   ethnic minority must be condemned as a mortal sin. One is morally bound to resist orders that command genocide.

2314   "Every act of war directed to the indiscriminate destruction of whole cities or vast areas with their inhabitants is a crime against God and man, which merits firm and unequivocal condemnation."[109] A danger of modern warfare is that it provides the opportunity to those who possess modern scientific weapons – especially atomic, biological, or chemical weapons – to commit such crimes.

---

106 Cf. *GS* 79 § 5.
107 Cf. *GS* 79 § 3.
108 *GS* 79 § 4.
109 *GS* 80 § 3.

2315   The *accumulation of arms* strikes many as a paradoxically suitable way of deterring potential adversaries from war. They see it as the most effective means of ensuring peace among nations. This method of deterrence gives rise to strong moral reservations. The *arms race* does not ensure peace. Far from eliminating the causes of war, it risks aggravating them. Spending enormous sums to produce ever new types of weapons impedes efforts to aid needy populations;[110] it thwarts the development of peoples. *Over-armament* multiplies reasons for conflict and increases the danger of escalation.

2316   *The production and the sale of arms* affect the common good *1906* of nations and of the international community. Hence public authorities have the right and duty to regulate them. The short-term pursuit of private or collective interests cannot legitimate undertakings that promote violence and conflict among nations and compromise the international juridical order.

2317   Injustice, excessive economic or social inequalities, envy, *1938* distrust, and pride raging among men and nations constantly *2538* threaten peace and cause wars. Everything done to overcome these *1941* disorders contributes to building up peace and avoiding war:

> Insofar as men are sinners, the threat of war hangs over them and will so continue until Christ comes again; but insofar as they can vanquish sin by coming together in charity, violence itself will be vanquished and these words will be fulfilled: "they shall beat their swords into plowshares, and their spears into pruning hooks; nation shall not lift up sword against nation, neither shall they learn war any more."[111]

---

110   Cf. Paul VI, *PP* 53.
111   *GS* 78 § 6; cf. *Isa* 2:4.

IN BRIEF

2318   "In [God's] hand is the life of every living thing and the breath of all mankind" (*Job* 12:10).

2319   Every human life, from the moment of conception until death, is sacred because the human person has been willed for its own sake in the image and likeness of the living and holy God.

2320   The murder of a human being is gravely contrary to the dignity of the person and the holiness of the Creator.

2321   The prohibition of murder does not abrogate the right to render an unjust aggressor unable to inflict harm. Legitimate defense is a grave duty for whoever is responsible for the lives of others or the common good.

2322   From its conception, the child has the right to life. Direct abortion, that is, abortion willed as an end or as a means, is a "criminal" practice (*GS* 27 § 3), gravely contrary to the moral law. The Church imposes the canonical penalty of excommunication for this crime against human life.

2323   Because it should be treated as a person from conception, the embryo must be defended in its integrity, cared for, and healed like every other human being.

2324   Intentional euthanasia, whatever its forms or motives, is murder. It is gravely contrary to the dignity of the human person and to the respect due to the living God, his Creator.

2325   Suicide is seriously contrary to justice, hope, and charity. It is forbidden by the fifth commandment.

2326   Scandal is a grave offense when by deed or omission it deliberately leads others to sin.

2327   Because of the evils and injustices that all war brings with it, we must do everything reasonably possible to avoid it. The Church prays: "From famine, pestilence, and war, O Lord, deliver us."

2328 The Church and human reason assert the permanent validity of the moral law during armed conflicts. Practices deliberately contrary to the law of nations and to its universal principles are crimes.

2329 "The arms race is one of the greatest curses on the human race and the harm it inflicts on the poor is more than can be endured" (*GS* 81 § 3).

2330 "Blessed are the peacemakers, for they shall be called sons of God" (*Mt* 5:9).

ARTICLE 6
THE SIXTH COMMANDMENT

You shall not commit adultery.[112]

You have heard that it was said, "You shall not commit adultery." But I say to you that every one who looks at a woman lustfully has already committed adultery with her in his heart.[113]

369-373 I.   "MALE AND FEMALE HE CREATED THEM . . ."

2331   "God is love and in himself he lives a mystery of personal loving communion. Creating the human race in his own image . . ., God inscribed in the humanity of man and woman the *vocation,* and thus the capacity and responsibility, *of love* and commun-

1604 ion."[114]

"God created man in his own image . . . male and female he created them";[115] He blessed them and said, "Be fruitful and multiply";[116] "When God created man, he made him in the likeness of God. Male and female he created them, and he blessed them and named them Man when they were created."[117]

2332   *Sexuality* affects all aspects of the human person in the unity of his body and soul. It especially concerns affectivity, the

362 capacity to love and to procreate, and in a more general way the aptitude for forming bonds of communion with others.

2333   Everyone, man and woman, should acknowledge and accept his sexual *identity.* Physical, moral, and spiritual *difference* and *complementarity* are oriented toward the goods of marriage and the flourishing of family life. The harmony of the couple and of

1603 society depends in part on the way in which the complementarity, needs, and mutual support between the sexes are lived out.

---

112   *Ex* 20:14; *Deut* 5:18.
113   *Mt* 5:27-28.
114   *FC* 11.
115   *Gen* 1:27.
116   *Gen* 1:28.
117   *Gen* 5:1-2.

2334 "In creating men 'male and female,' God gives man and woman an equal personal dignity."[118] "Man is a person, man and *357* woman equally so, since both were created in the image and likeness of the personal God."[119]

2335 Each of the two sexes is an image of the power and tenderness of God, with equal dignity though in a different way. The *union of man and woman* in marriage is a way of imitating in the flesh the Creator's generosity and fecundity: "Therefore a man leaves his father and his mother and cleaves to his wife, and they become *2205* one flesh."[120] All human generations proceed from this union.[121]

2336 Jesus came to restore creation to the purity of its origins. *1614* In the Sermon on the Mount, he interprets God's plan strictly: "You have heard that it was said, 'You shall not commit adultery.' But I say to you that every one who looks at a woman lustfully has already committed adultery with her in his heart."[122] What God has joined together, let not man put asunder.[123]

The tradition of the Church has understood the sixth commandment as encompassing the whole of human sexuality.

II.   THE VOCATION TO CHASTITY

2337 Chastity means the successful integration of sexuality *2520* within the person and thus the inner unity of man in his bodily and spiritual being. Sexuality, in which man's belonging to the bodily and biological world is expressed, becomes personal and truly human when it is integrated into the relationship of one person to another, in the complete and lifelong mutual gift of a man and a woman.

The virtue of chastity therefore involves the integrity of the person and the integrality of the gift.

---

118   *FC* 22; cf. *GS* 49 § 2.
119   *MD* 6.
120   *Gen* 2:24.
121   Cf. *Gen* 4:1-2, 25-26; 5:1.
122   *Mt* 5:27-28.
123   Cf. *Mt* 19:6.

The integrity of the person

2338   The chaste person maintains the integrity of the powers of life and love placed in him. This integrity ensures the unity of the person; it is opposed to any behavior that would impair it. It tolerates neither a double life nor duplicity in speech.[124]

2339   Chastity includes an *apprenticeship in self-mastery* which is a training in human freedom. The alternative is clear: either man governs his passions and finds peace, or he lets himself be dominated by them and becomes unhappy.[125] "Man's dignity therefore requires him to act out of conscious and free choice, as moved and drawn in a personal way from within, and not by blind impulses in himself or by mere external constraint. Man gains such dignity when, ridding himself of all slavery to the passions, he presses

1767 forward to his goal by freely choosing what is good and, by his diligence and skill, effectively secures for himself the means suited to this end."[126]

2340   Whoever wants to remain faithful to his baptismal prom-
2015 ises and resist temptations will want to adopt the *means* for doing so: self-knowledge, practice of an ascesis adapted to the situations that confront him, obedience to God's commandments, exercise of the moral virtues, and fidelity to prayer. "Indeed it is through chastity that we are gathered together and led back to the unity from which we were fragmented into multiplicity."[127]

1809 **2341**   The virtue of chastity comes under the cardinal virtue of *temperance*, which seeks to permeate the passions and appetites of the senses with reason.

2342   Self-mastery is a *long and exacting work*. One can never consider it acquired once and for all. It presupposes renewed effort
409 at all stages of life.[128] The effort required can be more intense in certain periods, such as when the personality is being formed during childhood and adolescence.

---

124   Cf. *Mt* 5:37.
125   Cf. *Sir* 1:22.
126   *GS* 17.
127   St. Augustine, *Conf.* 10, 29, 40: PL 32, 796.
128   Cf. *Titus* 2:1-6.

2343 Chastity has *laws of growth* which progress through stages marked by imperfection and too often by sin. "Man . . . day by day builds himself up through his many free decisions; and so he knows, loves, and accomplishes moral good by stages of growth."[129]

2223

2344 Chastity represents an eminently personal task; it also involves a *cultural effort*, for there is "an interdependence between personal betterment and the improvement of society."[130] Chastity presupposes respect for the rights of the person, in particular the right to receive information and an education that respect the moral and spiritual dimensions of human life.

2525

2345 Chastity is a moral virtue. It is also a gift from God, a *grace*, a fruit of spiritual effort.[131] The Holy Spirit enables one whom the water of Baptism has regenerated to imitate the purity of Christ.[132]

1810

The integrality of the gift of self

2346 Charity is the *form* of all the virtues. Under its influence, chastity appears as a school of the gift of the person. Self-mastery is ordered to the gift of self. Chastity leads him who practices it to become a witness to his neighbor of God's fidelity and loving kindness.

1827

210

2347 The virtue of chastity blossoms in *friendship*. It shows the disciple how to follow and imitate him who has chosen us as his friends,[133] who has given himself totally to us and allows us to participate in his divine estate. Chastity is a promise of immortality.

374

Chastity is expressed notably in *friendship with one's neighbor*. Whether it develops between persons of the same or opposite sex, friendship represents a great good for all. It leads to spiritual communion.

---

129 *FC* 34.
130 *GS* 25 § 1.
131 Cf. *Gal* 5:22.
132 Cf. *1 Jn* 3:3.
133 Cf. *Jn* 15:15.

The various forms of chastity

2348   All the baptized are called to chastity. The Christian has
"put on Christ,"[134] the model for all chastity. All Christ's faithful
are called to lead a chaste life in keeping with their particular states
of life. At the moment of his Baptism, the Christian is pledged to
lead his affective life in chastity.

1620 **2349**   "People should cultivate [chastity] in the way that is suited
to their state of life. Some profess virginity or consecrated celibacy
which enables them to give themselves to God alone with an
undivided heart in a remarkable manner. Others live in the way
prescribed for all by the moral law, whether they are married or
single."[135] Married people are called to live conjugal chastity;
others practice chastity in continence:

> There are three forms of the virtue of chastity: the first is that
> of spouses, the second that of widows, and the third that of
> virgins. We do not praise any one of them to the exclusion
> of the others. . . . This is what makes for the richness of the
> discipline of the Church.[136]

1632 **2350**   Those who are *engaged to marry* are called to live chastity
in continence. They should see in this time of testing a discovery
of mutual respect, an apprenticeship in fidelity, and the hope of
receiving one another from God. They should reserve for marriage
the expressions of affection that belong to married love. They will
help each other grow in chastity.

Offenses against chastity

2351   *Lust* is disordered desire for or inordinate enjoyment of
sexual pleasure. Sexual pleasure is morally disordered when
sought for itself, isolated from its procreative and unitive purposes.

2352   By *masturbation* is to be understood the deliberate stimula-
tion of the genital organs in order to derive sexual pleasure. "Both
the Magisterium of the Church, in the course of a constant tradition, and the moral sense of the faithful have been in no doubt and
have firmly maintained that masturbation is an intrinsically and
gravely disordered action."[137] "The deliberate use of the sexual

---

134   *Gal* 3:27.
135   CDF, *Persona humana* 11.
136   St. Ambrose, *De viduis* 4, 23: PL 16, 255A.
137   CDF, *Persona humana* 9.

faculty, for whatever reason, outside of marriage is essentially contrary to its purpose." For here sexual pleasure is sought outside of "the sexual relationship which is demanded by the moral order and in which the total meaning of mutual self-giving and human procreation in the context of true love is achieved."[138]

To form an equitable judgment about the subjects' moral responsibility and to guide pastoral action, one must take into account the affective immaturity, force of acquired habit, conditions of anxiety, or other psychological or social factors that lessen or even extenuate moral culpability. *1735*

2353 *Fornication* is carnal union between an unmarried man and an unmarried woman. It is gravely contrary to the dignity of persons and of human sexuality which is naturally ordered to the good of spouses and the generation and education of children. Moreover, it is a grave scandal when there is corruption of the young.

2354 *Pornography* consists in removing real or simulated sexual *2523* acts from the intimacy of the partners, in order to display them deliberately to third parties. It offends against chastity because it perverts the conjugal act, the intimate giving of spouses to each other. It does grave injury to the dignity of its participants (actors, vendors, the public), since each one becomes an object of base pleasure and illicit profit for others. It immerses all who are involved in the illusion of a fantasy world. It is a grave offense. Civil authorities should prevent the production and distribution of pornographic materials.

2355 *Prostitution* does injury to the dignity of the person who engages in it, reducing the person to an instrument of sexual pleasure. The one who pays sins gravely against himself: he violates the chastity to which his Baptism pledged him and defiles his body, the temple of the Holy Spirit.[139] Prostitution is a social scourge. It usually involves women, but also men, children, and adolescents (The latter two cases involve the added sin of scandal.). While it is always gravely sinful to engage in prostitution, the imputability of the offense can be attenuated by destitution, blackmail, or social pressure. *1735*

---

138   CDF, *Persona humana* 9.
139   Cf. *1 Cor* 6:15-20.

2356 *Rape* is the forcible violation of the sexual intimacy of another person. It does injury to justice and charity. Rape deeply wounds the respect, freedom, and physical and moral integrity to which every person has a right. It causes grave damage that can
2297 mark the victim for life. It is always an intrinsically evil act. Graver
1756 still is the rape of children committed by parents (incest) or those
2388 responsible for the education of the children entrusted to them.

Chastity and homosexuality

2357 Homosexuality refers to relations between men or between women who experience an exclusive or predominant sexual attraction toward persons of the same sex. It has taken a great variety of forms through the centuries and in different cultures. Its psychological genesis remains largely unexplained. Basing itself on Sacred Scripture, which presents homosexual acts as acts of grave depravity,[140] tradition has always declared that "homosexual acts are intrinsically disordered."[141] They are contrary to the natural law. They close the sexual act to the gift of life. They do not
2333 proceed from a genuine affective and sexual complementarity. Under no circumstances can they be approved.

2358 The number of men and women who have deep-seated homosexual tendencies is not negligible. They do not choose their homosexual condition; for most of them it is a trial. They must be accepted with respect, compassion, and sensitivity. Every sign of unjust discrimination in their regard should be avoided. These persons are called to fulfill God's will in their lives and, if they are Christians, to unite to the sacrifice of the Lord's Cross the difficulties they may encounter from their condition.

2347 **2359** Homosexual persons are called to chastity. By the virtues of self-mastery that teach them inner freedom, at times by the support of disinterested friendship, by prayer and sacramental grace, they can and should gradually and resolutely approach Christian perfection.

---

140 Cf. *Gen* 19:1-29; *Rom* 1:24-27; *1 Cor* 6:10; *1 Tim* 1:10.
141 CDF, *Persona humana* 8.

III.   THE LOVE OF HUSBAND AND WIFE

2360   Sexuality is ordered to the conjugal love of man and woman. In marriage the physical intimacy of the spouses becomes a sign and pledge of spiritual communion. Marriage bonds be- *1601* tween baptized persons are sanctified by the sacrament.

2361   "Sexuality, by means of which man and woman give themselves to one another through the acts which are proper and exclusive to spouses, is not something simply biological, but con- *1643* cerns the innermost being of the human person as such. It is *2332* realized in a truly human way only if it is an integral part of the love by which a man and woman commit themselves totally to one another until death."[142]

> Tobias got out of bed and said to Sarah, "Sister, get up, and *1611* let us pray and implore our Lord that he grant us mercy and safety." So she got up, and they began to pray and implore that they might be kept safe. Tobias began by saying, "Blessed are you, O God of our fathers.... You made Adam, and for him you made his wife Eve as a helper and support. From the two of them the race of mankind has sprung. You said, 'It is not good that the man should be alone; let us make a helper for him like himself.' I now am taking this kinswoman of mine, not because of lust, but with sincerity. Grant that she and I may find mercy and that we may grow old together." And they both said, "Amen, Amen." Then they went to sleep for the night.[143]

2362   "The acts in marriage by which the intimate and chaste union of the spouses takes place are noble and honorable; the truly human performance of these acts fosters the self-giving they signify and enriches the spouses in joy and gratitude."[144] Sexuality is a source of joy and pleasure:

> The Creator himself ... established that in the [generative] function, spouses should experience pleasure and enjoyment of body and spirit. Therefore, the spouses do nothing evil in seeking this pleasure and enjoyment. They accept what the Creator has intended for them. At the same time, spouses should know how to keep themselves within the limits of just moderation.[145]

---

142 *FC* 11.
143 *Tob* 8:4-9.
144 *GS* 49 § 2.
145 Pius XII, Discourse, October 29, 1951.

2363   The spouses' union achieves the twofold end of marriage: the good of the spouses themselves and the transmission of life. These two meanings or values of marriage cannot be separated without altering the couple's spiritual life and compromising the goods of marriage and the future of the family.

The conjugal love of man and woman thus stands under the twofold obligation of fidelity and fecundity.

1646-1648 **Conjugal fidelity**

1603 **2364**   The married couple forms "the intimate partnership of life and love established by the Creator and governed by his laws; it is rooted in the conjugal covenant, that is, in their irrevocable personal consent."[146] Both give themselves definitively and totally to one another. They are no longer two; from now on they form one flesh. The covenant they freely contracted imposes on the spouses *1615* the obligation to preserve it as unique and indissoluble.[147] "What therefore God has joined together, let not man put asunder."[148]

2365   Fidelity expresses constancy in keeping one's given word. God is faithful. The Sacrament of Matrimony enables man and *1640* woman to enter into Christ's fidelity for his Church. Through conjugal chastity, they bear witness to this mystery before the world.

> St. John Chrysostom suggests that young husbands should say to their wives: I have taken you in my arms, and I love you, and I prefer you to my life itself. For the present life is nothing, and my most ardent dream is to spend it with you in such a way that we may be assured of not being separated in the life reserved for us. . . . I place your love above all things, and nothing would be more bitter or painful to me than to be of a different mind than you.[149]

---

146   *GS* 48 § 1.
147   Cf. CIC, can. 1056.
148   *Mk* 10:9; cf. *Mt* 19:1-12; 1 *Cor* 7:10-11.
149   St. John Chrysostom, *Hom. in Eph.* 20, 8: PG 62, 146-147.

The fecundity of marriage

1652-1653

2366 Fecundity is a gift, an *end of marriage*, for conjugal love naturally tends to be fruitful. A child does not come from outside as something added on to the mutual love of the spouses, but springs from the very heart of that mutual giving, as its fruit and fulfillment. So the Church, which "is on the side of life"[150] teaches that "each and every marriage act must remain open to the transmission of life."[151] "This particular doctrine, expounded on numerous occasions by the Magisterium, is based on the inseparable connection, established by God, which man on his own initiative may not break, between the unitive significance and the procreative significance which are both inherent to the marriage act."[152]

2367 Called to give life, spouses share in the creative power and fatherhood of God.[153] "Married couples should regard it as their proper mission to transmit human life and to educate their children; they should realize that they are thereby *cooperating with* the love of *God the Creator* and are, in a certain sense, its interpreters. They will fulfill this duty with a sense of human and Christian responsibility."[154]

2205

2368 A particular aspect of this responsibility concerns the *regulation of births*. For just reasons, spouses may wish to space the births of their children. It is their duty to make certain that their desire is not motivated by selfishness but is in conformity with the generosity appropriate to responsible parenthood. Moreover, they should conform their behavior to the objective criteria of morality:

> When it is a question of harmonizing married love with the responsible transmission of life, the morality of the behavior does not depend on sincere intention and evaluation of motives alone; but it must be determined by objective criteria, criteria drawn from the nature of the person and his acts, criteria that respect the total meaning of mutual self-giving and human procreation in the context of true love; this is possible only if the virtue of married chastity is practiced with sincerity of heart.[155]

---

150 *FC* 30.
151 *HV* 11.
152 *HV* 12; cf. Pius XI, encyclical, *Casti connubii.*
153 Cf. *Eph* 3:14; *Mt* 23:9.
154 *GS* 50 § 2.
155 *GS* 51 § 3.

2369   "By safeguarding both these essential aspects, the unitive and the procreative, the conjugal act preserves in its fullness the sense of true mutual love and its orientation toward man's exalted vocation to parenthood."[156]

2370   Periodic continence, that is, the methods of birth regulation based on self-observation and the use of infertile periods, is in conformity with the objective criteria of morality.[157] These methods respect the bodies of the spouses, encourage tenderness between them, and favor the education of an authentic freedom. In contrast, "every action which, whether in anticipation of the conjugal act, or in its accomplishment, or in the development of its natural consequences, proposes, whether as an end or as a means, to render procreation impossible" is intrinsically evil:[158]

> Thus the innate language that expresses the total reciprocal self-giving of husband and wife is overlaid, through contraception, by an objectively contradictory language, namely, that of not giving oneself totally to the other. This leads not only to a positive refusal to be open to life but also to a falsification of the inner truth of conjugal love, which is called upon to give itself in personal totality. . . . The difference, both anthropological and moral, between contraception and recourse to the rhythm of the cycle . . . involves in the final analysis two irreconcilable concepts of the human person and of human sexuality.[159]

2371   "Let all be convinced that human life and the duty of transmitting it are not limited by the horizons of this life only: their true evaluation and full significance can be understood only in
1703   reference to *man's eternal destiny.*"[160]

2372   The state has a responsibility for its citizens' well-being. In this capacity it is legitimate for it to intervene to orient the demography of the population. This can be done by means of objective and respectful information, but certainly not by authoritarian, coercive measures. The state may not legitimately usurp the initiative of spouses, who have the primary
2209   responsibility for the procreation and education of their children.[161] It is not authorized to promote demographic regulation by means contrary to the moral law.

---

156   Cf. *HV* 12.
157   *HV* 16.
158   *HV* 14.
159   *FC* 32.
160   *GS* 51 § 4.
161   Cf. *HV* 23; *PP* 37.

The gift of a child

2373 Sacred Scripture and the Church's traditional practice see in *large families* a sign of God's blessing and the parents' generosity.[162]

2374 Couples who discover that they are sterile suffer greatly. *1654* "What will you give me," asks Abraham of God, "for I continue childless?"[163] And Rachel cries to her husband Jacob, "Give me children, or I shall die!"[164]

2375 Research aimed at reducing human sterility is to be en- *2293* couraged, on condition that it is placed "at the service of the human person, of his inalienable rights, and his true and integral good according to the design and will of God."[165]

2376 Techniques that entail the dissociation of husband and wife, by the intrusion of a person other than the couple (donation of sperm or ovum, surrogate uterus), are gravely immoral. These techniques (heterologous artificial insemination and fertilization) infringe the child's right to be born of a father and mother known to him and bound to each other by marriage. They betray the spouses' "right to become a father and a mother only through each other."[166]

2377 Techniques involving only the married couple (homologous artificial insemination and fertilization) are perhaps less reprehensible, yet remain morally unacceptable. They dissociate the sexual act from the procreative act. The act which brings the child into existence is no longer an act by which two persons give themselves to one another, but one that "entrusts the life and identity of the embryo into the power of doctors and biologists and establishes the domination of technology over the origin and destiny of the human person. Such a relationship of domination is in itself contrary to the dignity and equality that must be common to parents and children."[167] "Under the moral aspect procreation is deprived of its proper perfection when it is not willed as the fruit of the conjugal act, that is to say, of the specific act of the spouses' union . . . . Only respect for the link between the meanings of the conjugal act and respect for the unity of the human being make possible procreation in conformity with the dignity of the person."[168]

---

162 Cf. *GS* 50 § 2.
163 *Gen* 15:2.
164 *Gen* 30:1.
165 CDF, *Donum vitae*. intro., 2.
166 CDF, *Donum vitae* II, 1.
167 CDF, *Donum vitae* II, 5.
168 CDF, *Donum vitae* II, 4.

2378   A child is not something *owed* to one, but is a *gift*. The "supreme gift of marriage" is a human person. A child may not be considered a piece of property, an idea to which an alleged "right to a child" would lead. In this area, only the child possesses genuine rights: the right "to be the fruit of the specific act of the conjugal love of his parents," and "the right to be respected as a person from the moment of his conception."[169]

2379   The Gospel shows that physical sterility is not an absolute evil. Spouses who still suffer from infertility after exhausting legitimate medical procedures should unite themselves with the Lord's Cross, the source of all spiritual fecundity. They can give expression to their generosity by adopting abandoned children or performing demanding services for others.

IV.   Offenses against the Dignity of Marriage

Adultery

2380   *Adultery* refers to marital infidelity. When two partners, of whom at least one is married to another party, have sexual relations – even transient ones – they commit adultery. Christ condemns even adultery of mere desire.[170] The sixth commandment and the New Testament forbid adultery absolutely.[171] The prophets denounce the gravity of adultery; they see it as an image of the sin of 1611 idolatry.[172]

2381   Adultery is an injustice. He who commits adultery fails in his commitment. He does injury to the sign of the covenant which 1640 the marriage bond is, transgresses the rights of the other spouse, and undermines the institution of marriage by breaking the contract on which it is based. He compromises the good of human generation and the welfare of children who need their parents' stable union.

---

169   CDF, *Donum vitae* II, 8.
170   Cf. *Mt* 5:27-28.
171   Cf. *Mt* 5:32; 19:6; *Mk* 10:11; 1 *Cor* 6:9-10.
172   Cf. *Hos* 2:7; *Jer* 5:7; 13:27.

Divorce

2382 The Lord Jesus insisted on the original intention of the *1614* Creator who willed that marriage be indissoluble.[173] He abrogates the accommodations that had slipped into the old Law.[174]

Between the baptized, "a ratified and consummated marriage cannot be dissolved by any human power or for any reason other than death."[175]

2383 The *separation* of spouses while maintaining the marriage *1649* bond can be legitimate in certain cases provided for by canon law.[176]

If civil divorce remains the only possible way of ensuring certain legal rights, the care of the children, or the protection of inheritance, it can be tolerated and does not constitute a moral offense.

2384 *Divorce* is a grave offense against the natural law. It claims *1650* to break the contract, to which the spouses freely consented, to live with each other till death. Divorce does injury to the covenant of salvation, of which sacramental marriage is the sign. Contracting a new union, even if it is recognized by civil law, adds to the gravity of the rupture: the remarried spouse is then in a situation of public and permanent adultery:

> If a husband, separated from his wife, approaches another woman, he is an adulterer because he makes that woman commit adultery; and the woman who lives with him is an adulteress, because she has drawn another's husband to herself.[177]

2385 Divorce is immoral also because it introduces disorder into the family and into society. This disorder brings grave harm to the deserted spouse, to children traumatized by the separation of their parents and often torn between them, and because of its contagious effect which makes it truly a plague on society.

---

173 Cf. *Mt* 5:31-32; 19:3-9; *Mk* 10:9; *Lk* 16:18; *1 Cor* 7:10-11.
174 Cf. *Mt* 19:7-9.
175 CIC, can. 1141.
176 Cf. CIC, cann. 1151-1155.
177 *St. Basil, Moralia* 73, 1: PG 31, 849-852.

2386 It can happen that one of the spouses is the innocent victim of a divorce decreed by civil law; this spouse therefore has not contravened the moral law. There is a considerable difference between a spouse who has sincerely tried to be faithful to the sacrament of marriage and is unjustly abandoned, and one who
1640 through his own grave fault destroys a canonically valid marriage.[178]

Other offenses against the dignity of marriage

2387 The predicament of a man who, desiring to convert to the Gospel, is obliged to repudiate one or more wives with whom he has shared years of conjugal life, is understandable. However
1610 *polygamy* is not in accord with the moral law. "[Conjugal] communion is radically contradicted by polygamy; this, in fact, directly negates the plan of God which was revealed from the beginning, because it is contrary to the equal personal dignity of men and women who in matrimony give themselves with a love that is total and therefore unique and exclusive."[179] The Christian who has previously lived in polygamy has a grave duty in justice to honor the obligations contracted in regard to his former wives and his children.

2356 **2388** *Incest* designates intimate relations between relatives or in-laws within a degree that prohibits marriage between them.[180] St. Paul stigmatizes this especially grave offense: "It is actually reported that there is immorality among you ... for a man is living with his father's wife.... In the name of the Lord Jesus ... you are to deliver this man to Satan for the destruction of the flesh...."[181]
2207 Incest corrupts family relationships and marks a regression toward animality.

2389 Connected to incest is any sexual abuse perpetrated by adults on children or adolescents entrusted to their care. The offense is compounded by the scandalous harm done to the physi-
2285 cal and moral integrity of the young, who will remain scarred by it all their lives; and the violation of responsibility for their upbringing.

---

178 Cf. *FC* 84.
179 *FC* 19; cf. *GS* 47 § 2.
180 Cf. *Lev* 18:7-20.
181 *1 Cor* 5:1, 4-5.

2390 In a so-called *free union*, a man and a woman refuse to give juridical and public form to a liaison involving sexual intimacy. *1631*

The expression "free union" is fallacious: what can "union" mean when the partners make no commitment to one another, each exhibiting a lack of trust in the other, in himself, or in the future?

The expression covers a number of different situations: concubinage, rejection of marriage as such, or inability to make long-term commitments.[182] All these situations offend against the dignity of marriage; they destroy the very idea of the family; they weaken the sense of fidelity. They are contrary to the moral law. *2353* The sexual act must take place exclusively within marriage. Outside of marriage it always constitutes a grave sin and excludes one from sacramental communion. *1385*

2391 Some today claim a *"right to a trial marriage"* where there is an intention of getting married later. However firm the purpose of those who engage in premature sexual relations may be, "the fact is that such liaisons can scarcely ensure mutual sincerity and fidelity in a relationship between a man and a woman, nor, especially, can they protect it from inconstancy of desires or whim."[183] Carnal union is morally legitimate only when a definitive community of life between a man and woman has been established. Human love does not tolerate "trial marriages." It demands a total *2364* and definitive gift of persons to one another.[184]

IN BRIEF

2392 "Love is the fundamental and innate vocation of every human being" (*FC* 11).

2393 By creating the human being man and woman, God gives personal dignity equally to the one and the other. Each of them, man and woman, should acknowledge and accept his sexual identity.

2394 Christ is the model of chastity. Every baptized person is called to lead a chaste life, each according to his particular state of life.

---

182 Cf. *FC* 81.
183 CDF, *Persona humana* 7.
184 Cf. *FC* 80.

2395   Chastity means the integration of sexuality within the person. It includes an apprenticeship in self-mastery.

2396   Among the sins gravely contrary to chastity are masturbation, fornication, pornography, and homosexual practices.

2397   The covenant which spouses have freely entered into entails faithful love. It imposes on them the obligation to keep their marriage indissoluble.

2398   Fecundity is a good, a gift and an end of marriage. By giving life, spouses participate in God's fatherhood.

2399   The regulation of births represents one of the aspects of responsible fatherhood and motherhood. Legitimate intentions on the part of the spouses do not justify recourse to morally unacceptable means (for example, direct sterilization or contraception).

2400   Adultery, divorce, polygamy, and free union are grave offenses against the dignity of marriage.

ARTICLE 7
THE SEVENTH COMMANDMENT

You shall not steal.[185]

2401 The seventh commandment forbids unjustly taking or keeping the goods of one's neighbor and wronging him in any way with respect to his goods. It commands justice and charity in the *1807* care of earthly goods and the fruits of men's labor. For the sake of the common good, it requires respect for the universal destination of goods and respect for the right to private property. Christian life strives to order this world's goods to God and to fraternal charity. *952*

I. THE UNIVERSAL DESTINATION AND THE PRIVATE OWNERSHIP OF GOODS

2402 In the beginning God entrusted the earth and its resources to the common stewardship of mankind to take care of them, master them by labor, and enjoy their fruits.[186] The goods of *226* creation are destined for the whole human race. However, the earth is divided up among men to assure the security of their lives, endangered by poverty and threatened by violence. The appropriation of property is legitimate for guaranteeing the freedom and dignity of persons and for helping each of them to meet his basic needs and the needs of those in his charge. It should allow for a natural solidarity to develop between men. *1939*

2403 The *right to private property*, acquired by work or received from others by inheritance or gift, does not do away with the original gift of the earth to the whole of mankind. The *universal destination of goods* remains primordial, even if the promotion of the common good requires respect for the right to private property and its exercise.

---

185 *Ex* 20:15; *Deut* 5:19; *Mt* 19:18.
186 Cf. *Gen* 1:26-29.

2404   "In his use of things man should regard the external goods he legitimately owns not merely as exclusive to himself but common to others also, in the sense that they can benefit others as well as himself."[187] The ownership of any property makes its holder a
307 steward of Providence, with the task of making it fruitful and communicating its benefits to others, first of all his family.

2405   Goods of production – material or immaterial – such as land, factories, practical or artistic skills, oblige their possessors to employ them in ways that will benefit the greatest number. Those who hold goods for use and consumption should use them with moderation, reserving the better part for guests, for the sick and the poor.

1903 **2406**   *Political authority* has the right and duty to regulate the legitimate exercise of the right to ownership for the sake of the common good.[188]

II.   Respect for Persons and Their Goods

2407   In economic matters, respect for human dignity requires the practice of the virtue of *temperance*, so as to moderate attach-
1809 ment to this world's goods; the practice of the virtue of *justice*, to
1807 preserve our neighbor's rights and render him what is his due; and
1939 the practice of *solidarity*, in accordance with the golden rule and in keeping with the generosity of the Lord, who "though he was rich, yet for your sake . . . became poor so that by his poverty, you might become rich."[189]

Respect for the goods of others

2408   The seventh commandment forbids *theft*, that is, usurping another's property against the reasonable will of the owner. There is no theft if consent can be presumed or if refusal is contrary to reason and the universal destination of goods. This is the case in obvious and urgent necessity when the only way to provide for immediate, essential needs (food, shelter, clothing . . .) is to put at one's disposal and use the property of others.[190]

---

187   *GS* 69 § 1.
188   Cf. *GS* 71 § 4; *SRS* 42; *CA* 40; 48.
189   *2 Cor* 8:9.
190   Cf. *GS* 69 § 1.

2409   Even if it does not contradict the provisions of civil law, any form of unjustly taking and keeping the property of others is against the seventh commandment: thus, deliberate retention of goods lent or of objects lost; business fraud; paying unjust wages; *1867* forcing up prices by taking advantage of the ignorance or hardship of another.[191]

The following are also morally illicit: speculation in which one contrives to manipulate the price of goods artificially in order to gain an advantage to the detriment of others; corruption in which one influences the judgment of those who must make decisions according to law; appropriation and use for private purposes of the common goods of an enterprise; work poorly done; tax evasion; forgery of checks and invoices; excessive expenses and waste. Willfully damaging private or public property is contrary to the moral law and requires reparation.

2410   *Promises* must be kept and *contracts* strictly observed to the *2101* extent that the commitments made in them are morally just. A significant part of economic and social life depends on the honoring of contracts between physical or moral persons – commercial contracts of purchase or sale, rental or labor contracts. All contracts must be agreed to and executed in good faith.

2411   Contracts are subject to *commutative justice* which regulates *1807* exchanges between persons in accordance with a strict respect for their rights. Commutative justice obliges strictly; it requires safeguarding property rights, paying debts, and fulfilling obligations freely contracted. Without commutative justice, no other form of justice is possible.

One distinguishes *commutative* justice from *legal* justice which concerns what the citizen owes in fairness to the community, and from *distributive* justice which regulates what the community owes its citizens in proportion to their contributions and needs.

2412   In virtue of commutative justice, *reparation for injustice 1459* committed requires the restitution of stolen goods to their owner:

Jesus blesses Zacchaeus for his pledge: "If I have defrauded anyone of anything, I restore it fourfold."[192] Those who, directly or indirectly, have taken possession of the goods of another, are obliged to make restitution of them, or to return the equivalent in kind or in money, if the goods have disappeared, as well as the profit or advantages their *2487* owner would have legitimately obtained from them. Likewise, all who in some manner have taken part in a theft or who have knowingly benefited from it – for example, those who ordered it, assisted in it, or received the stolen goods – are obliged to make restitution in proportion to their responsibility and to their share of what was stolen.

---

191   Cf. *Deut* 25:13-16; 24:14-15; *Jas* 5:4; *Am* 8:4-6.
192   *Lk* 19:8.

2413   *Games of chance* (card games, etc.) or *wagers* are not in themselves contrary to justice. They become morally unacceptable when they deprive someone of what is necessary to provide for his needs and those of others. The passion for gambling risks becoming an enslavement. Unfair wagers and cheating at games constitute grave matter, unless the damage inflicted is so slight that the one who suffers it cannot reasonably consider it significant.

2297 **2414**   The seventh commandment forbids acts or enterprises that for any reason – selfish or ideological, commercial, or totalitarian – lead to the *enslavement of human beings*, to their being bought, sold and exchanged like merchandise, in disregard for their personal dignity. It is a sin against the dignity of persons and their fundamental rights to reduce them by violence to their productive value or to a source of profit. St. Paul directed a Christian master to treat his Christian slave "no longer as a slave but more than a slave, as a beloved brother, . . . both in the flesh and in the Lord."[193]

Respect for the integrity of creation

226, 358 **2415**   The seventh commandment enjoins respect for the integrity of creation. Animals, like plants and inanimate beings, are by nature destined for the common good of past, present, and future humanity.[194] Use of the mineral, vegetable, and animal resources of the universe cannot be divorced from respect for moral impera-
373 tives. Man's dominion over inanimate and other living beings granted by the Creator is not absolute; it is limited by concern for the quality of life of his neighbor, including generations to come;
378 it requires a religious respect for the integrity of creation.[195]

2416   *Animals* are God's creatures. He surrounds them with his providential care. By their mere existence they bless him and give him glory.[196] Thus men owe them kindness. We should recall the
344 gentleness with which saints like St. Francis of Assisi or St. Philip Neri treated animals.

---

193   *Philem* 16.
194   Cf. *Gen* 1:28-31.
195   Cf. *CA* 37-38.
196   Cf. *Mt* 6:26; *Dan* 3:79-81.

2417 God entrusted animals to the stewardship of those whom he created in his own image.[197] Hence it is legitimate to use animals for food and clothing. They may be domesticated to help man in his work and leisure. Medical and scientific experimentation on animals, if it remains within reasonable limits, is a morally acceptable practice since it contributes to caring for or saving human lives. *2234*

2418 It is contrary to human dignity to cause animals to suffer or die needlessly. It is likewise unworthy to spend money on them that should as a priority go to the relief of human misery. One can *2446* love animals; one should not direct to them the affection due only to persons.

III. THE SOCIAL DOCTRINE OF THE CHURCH

2419 "Christian revelation . . . promotes deeper understanding *1960* of the laws of social living."[198] The Church receives from the *359* Gospel the full revelation of the truth about man. When she fulfills her mission of proclaiming the Gospel, she bears witness to man, in the name of Christ, to his dignity and his vocation to the communion of persons. She teaches him the demands of justice and peace in conformity with divine wisdom.

2420 The Church makes a moral judgment about economic and *2032* social matters, "when the fundamental rights of the person or the salvation of souls requires it."[199] In the moral order she bears a mission distinct from that of political authorities: the Church is concerned with the temporal aspects of the common good because they are ordered to the sovereign Good, our ultimate end. She *2246* strives to inspire right attitudes with respect to earthly goods and in socio-economic relationships.

2421 The social doctrine of the Church developed in the nineteenth century when the Gospel encountered modern industrial society with its new structures for the production of consumer goods, its new concept of society, the state and authority, and its new forms of labor and ownership. The development of the doctrine of the Church on economic and social matters attests the permanent value of the Church's teaching at the same time as it attests the true meaning of her Tradition, always living and active.[200]

---

197 Cf. *Gen* 2:19-20; 9:1-4.
198 *GS* 23 § 1.
199 *GS* 76 § 5.
200 Cf. *CA* 3.

2422   The Church's social teaching comprises a body of doctrine, which is articulated as the Church interprets events in the course of history, with the assistance of the Holy Spirit, in the light of the whole of what has been revealed by Jesus Christ.[201] This teaching can be more easily accepted by men of good will, the more the *2044* faithful let themselves be guided by it.

2423   The Church's social teaching proposes principles for reflection; it provides criteria for judgment; it gives guidelines for action:

> Any system in which social relationships are determined entirely by economic factors is contrary to the nature of the human person and his acts.[202]

2424   A theory that makes profit the exclusive norm and ultimate end of economic activity is morally unacceptable. The disordered desire for *2317* money cannot but produce perverse effects. It is one of the causes of the many conflicts which disturb the social order.[203]

> A system that "subordinates the basic rights of individuals and of groups to the collective organization of production" is contrary to human dignity.[204] Every practice that reduces persons to nothing more than a means of profit enslaves man, leads to idolizing money, and contributes to the spread of atheism. "You cannot serve God and mammon."[205]

2425   The Church has rejected the totalitarian and atheistic ideologies associated in modern times with "communism" or "socialism." She has *676* likewise refused to accept, in the practice of "capitalism," individualism and the absolute primacy of the law of the marketplace over human labor.[206] Regulating the economy solely by centralized planning perverts the basis of social bonds; regulating it solely by the law of the marketplace fails social justice, for "there are many human needs which cannot be satisfied by the market."[207] Reasonable regulation of the marketplace and economic initiatives, in keeping with a just hierarchy of values and a view *1886* to the common good, is to be commended.

---

201   Cf. *SRS* 1; 41.
202   Cf. *CA* 24.
203   Cf. *GS* 63 § 3; *LE* 7; 20; *CA* 35.
204   *GS* 65 § 2.
205   *Mt* 6:24; *Lk* 16:13.
206   Cf. *CA* 10; 13; 44.
207   *CA* 34.

IV. ECONOMIC ACTIVITY AND SOCIAL JUSTICE

2426   The development of economic activity and growth in production are meant to provide for the needs of human beings. Economic life is not meant solely to multiply goods produced and increase profit or power; it is ordered first of all to the service of persons, of the whole man, and of the entire human community. Economic activity, conducted according to its own proper methods, is to be exercised within the limits of the moral order, in keeping with social justice so as to correspond to God's plan for man.[208]   *1928*

2427   *Human work* proceeds directly from persons created in the   *307* image of God and called to prolong the work of creation by subduing the earth, both with and for one another.[209] Hence work   *378* is a duty: "If any one will not work, let him not eat."[210] Work honors the Creator's gifts and the talents received from him. It can also be redemptive. By enduring the hardship of work[211] in union   *531* with Jesus, the carpenter of Nazareth and the one crucified on Calvary, man collaborates in a certain fashion with the Son of God in his redemptive work. He shows himself to be a disciple of Christ by carrying the cross, daily, in the work he is called to accomplish.[212] Work can be a means of sanctification and a way of animating earthly realities with the Spirit of Christ.

2428   In work, the person exercises and fulfills in part the poten-   *2834* tial inscribed in his nature. The primordial value of labor stems from man himself, its author and its beneficiary. Work is for man,   *2185* not man for work.[213]
   Everyone should be able to draw from work the means of providing for his life and that of his family, and of serving the human community.

2429   Everyone has the *right of economic initiative;* everyone should make legitimate use of his talents to contribute to the abundance that will benefit all and to harvest the just fruits of his labor. He should seek to observe regulations issued by legitimate authority for the sake of the common good.[214]

---

208   Cf. *GS* 64.
209   Cf. *Gen* 1:28; *GS* 34; *CA* 31.
210   *2 Thess* 3:10; cf. *1 Thess* 4:11.
211   Cf. *Gen* 3:14-19.
212   Cf. *LE* 27.
213   Cf. *LE* 6.
214   Cf. *CA* 32; 34.

2430   *Economic life* brings into play different interests, often opposed to one another. This explains why the conflicts that characterize it arise.[215] Efforts should be made to reduce these conflicts by negotiation that respects the rights and duties of each social partner: those responsible for business enterprises, representatives of wage-earners (for example, trade unions), and public authorities when appropriate.

2431   The *responsibility of the state.* "Economic activity, especially the activity of a market economy, cannot be conducted in an institutional, juridical, or political vacuum. On the contrary, it presupposes sure guarantees of individual freedom and private property, as well as a stable currency and efficient public services.
1908 Hence the principal task of the state is to guarantee this security, so that those who work and produce can enjoy the fruits of their labors and thus feel encouraged to work efficiently and honestly.... Another task of the state is that of overseeing and directing the exercise of human rights in the economic sector. However, primary responsi-
1883 bility in this area belongs not to the state but to individuals and to the various groups and associations which make up society."[216]

2432   Those *responsible for business enterprises* are responsible to society for the economic and ecological effects of their opera-
2415 tions.[217] They have an obligation to consider the good of persons and not only the increase of *profits*. Profits are necessary, however. They make possible the investments that ensure the future of a business and they guarantee employment.

2433   *Access to employment* and to professions must be open to all without unjust discrimination: men and women, healthy and disabled, natives and immigrants.[218] For its part society should, according to circumstances, help citizens find work and employment.[219]

1867 **2434**   A *just wage* is the legitimate fruit of work. To refuse or withhold it can be a grave injustice.[220] In determining fair pay both the needs and the contributions of each person must be taken into account. "Remuneration for work should guarantee man the opportunity to provide a dignified livelihood for himself and his family on the material, social, cultural, and spiritual level, taking

---

215 Cf. *LE* 11.
216 *CA* 48.
217 Cf. *CA* 37.
218 Cf. *LE* 19; 22-23.
219 Cf. *CA* 48.
220 Cf. *Lev* 19:13; *Deut* 24:14-15; *Jas* 5:4.

into account the role and the productivity of each, the state of the business, and the common good."[221] Agreement between the parties is not sufficient to justify morally the amount to be received in wages.

2435 Recourse to a *strike* is morally legitimate when it cannot be avoided, or at least when it is necessary to obtain a proportionate benefit. It becomes morally unacceptable when accompanied by violence, or when objectives are included that are not directly linked to working conditions or are contrary to the common good.

2436 It is unjust not to pay the social security *contributions* required by legitimate authority.

Unemployment almost always wounds its victim's dignity and threatens the equilibrium of his life. Besides the harm done to him personally, it entails many risks for his family.[222]

V.   JUSTICE AND SOLIDARITY AMONG NATIONS

2437 On the international level, inequality of resources and *1938* economic capability is such that it creates a real "gap" between nations.[223] On the one side there are those nations possessing and developing the means of growth and, on the other, those accumulating debts.

2438 Various causes of a religious, political, economic, and financial nature today give "the social question a worldwide dimension."[224] There must be solidarity among nations which are *1911* already politically interdependent. It is even more essential when it is a question of dismantling the "perverse mechanisms" that impede the development of the less advanced countries.[225] In place of abusive if not usurious financial systems, iniquitous commercial relations among nations, and the arms race, there must be substituted a common effort to mobilize resources toward objectives of moral, cultural, and economic development, "redefining the pri- *2315* orities and hierarchies of values."[226]

---

221   *GS* 67 § 2.
222   Cf. *LE* 18.
223   Cf. *SRS* 14.
224   *SRS* 9.
225   Cf. *SRS* 17; 45.
226   *CA* 28; cf. 35.

2439 *Rich nations* have a grave moral responsibility toward those which are unable to ensure the means of their development by themselves or have been prevented from doing so by tragic historical events. It is a duty in solidarity and charity; it is also an obligation in justice if the prosperity of the rich nations has come from resources that have not been paid for fairly.

2440 *Direct aid* is an appropriate response to immediate, extraordinary needs caused by natural catastrophes, epidemics, and the like. But it does not suffice to repair the grave damage resulting from destitution or to provide a lasting solution to a country's needs. It is also necessary to *reform* international economic and financial *institutions* so that they will better promote equitable relationships with less advanced countries.[227] The efforts of poor countries working for growth and liberation must be supported.[228] This doctrine must be applied especially in the area of agricultural labor. Peasants, especially in the Third World, form the overwhelming majority of the poor.

1908 **2441** An increased sense of God and increased self-awareness are fundamental to any *full development of human society*. This development multiplies material goods and puts them at the service of the person and his freedom. It reduces dire poverty and economic exploitation. It makes for growth in respect for cultural identities and openness to the transcendent.[229]

2442 It is not the role of the Pastors of the Church to intervene directly in the political structuring and organization of social life. This task is part of the vocation of the *lay faithful*, acting on their *899* own initiative with their fellow citizens. Social action can assume various concrete forms. It should always have the common good in view and be in conformity with the message of the Gospel and the teaching of the Church. It is the role of the laity "to animate temporal realities with Christian commitment, by which they show that they are witnesses and agents of peace and justice."[230]

---

227 Cf. *SRS* 16.
228 Cf. *CA* 26.
229 Cf. *SRS* 32; *CA* 51.
230 *SRS* 47 § 6; cf. 42.

VI.   LOVE FOR THE POOR

2544-2547

2443   God blesses those who come to the aid of the poor and rebukes those who turn away from them: "Give to him who begs from you, do not refuse him who would borrow from you"; "you received without pay, give without pay."[231] It is by what they have done for the poor that Jesus Christ will recognize his chosen *786, 525* ones.[232] When "the poor have the good news preached to them," *544, 853* it is the sign of Christ's presence.[233]

2444   "The Church's love for the poor . . . is a part of her constant tradition." This love is inspired by the Gospel of the Beatitudes, of the poverty of Jesus, and of his concern for the poor.[234] Love for *1716* the poor is even one of the motives for the duty of working so as to "be able to give to those in need."[235] It extends not only to material poverty but also to the many forms of cultural and religious poverty.[236]

2445   Love for the poor is incompatible with immoderate love of *2536* riches or their selfish use:

> Come now, you rich, weep and howl for the miseries that *2547* are coming upon you. Your riches have rotted and your garments are moth-eaten. Your gold and silver have rusted, and their rust will be evidence against you and will eat your flesh like fire. You have laid up treasure for the last days. Behold, the wages of the laborers who mowed your fields, which you kept back by fraud, cry out; and the cries of the harvesters have reached the ears of the Lord of hosts. You have lived on the earth in luxury and in pleasure; you have fattened your hearts in a day of slaughter. You have condemned, you have killed the righteous man; he does not resist you.[237]

2446   St. John Chrysostom vigorously recalls this: "Not to enable the poor to share in our goods is to steal from them and deprive them of life. The goods we possess are not ours, but theirs."[238] "The demands of justice must be satisfied first of all; that which is *2402* already due in justice is not to be offered as a gift of charity":[239]

---

231   *Mt* 5:42; 10:8.
232   Cf. *Mt* 25:31-36.
233   *Mt* 11:5; cf. *Lk* 4:18.
234   *CA* 57; cf. *Lk* 6:20-22, *Mt* 8:20; *Mk* 12:41-44.
235   *Eph* 4:28.
236   Cf. *CA* 57.
237   *Jas* 5:1-6.
238   St. John Chrysostom, *Hom. in Lazaro* 2, 5: PG 48, 992.
239   *AA* 8 § 5.

> When we attend to the needs of those in want, we give them what is theirs, not ours. More than performing works of mercy, we are paying a debt of justice.[240]

1460   **2447**   The *works of mercy* are charitable actions by which we come to the aid of our neighbor in his spiritual and bodily necessities.[241] Instructing, advising, consoling, comforting are spiritual works of mercy, as are forgiving and bearing wrongs patiently. The corporal works of mercy consist especially in feeding the hungry, sheltering
1038   the homeless, clothing the naked, visiting the sick and imprisoned,
1969   and burying the dead.[242] Among all these, giving alms to the poor is one of the chief witnesses to fraternal charity: it is also a work of justice pleasing to God:[243]

> He who has two coats, let him share with him who has none; and he who has food must do likewise.[244] But give for alms those things which are within; and behold, everything is clean for you.[245] If a brother or sister is ill-clad and in lack of daily food, and one of you says to them, "Go in peace, be
1004   warmed and filled," without giving them the things needed for the body, what does it profit?[246]

    2448   "In its various forms – material deprivation, unjust oppres-
386   sion, physical and psychological illness and death – *human misery* is the obvious sign of the inherited condition of frailty and need for salvation in which man finds himself as a consequence of original sin. This misery elicited the compassion of Christ the Savior, who willingly took it upon himself and identified himself with the least of his brethren. Hence, those who are oppressed by poverty are the
1586   object of *a preferential love* on the part of the Church which, since her origin and in spite of the failings of many of her members, has not ceased to work for their relief, defense, and liberation through numerous works of charity which remain indispensable always and everywhere."[247]

---

240   St. Gregory the Great, *Regula Pastoralis*. 3, 21: PL 77, 87.
241   Cf. *Isa* 58:6-7; *Heb* 13:3.
242   Cf. *Mt* 25:31-46.
243   Cf. *Tob* 4:5-11; *Sir* 17:22; *Mt* 6:2-4.
244   *Lk* 3:11.
245   *Lk* 11:41.
246   *Jas* 2:15-16; cf. *1 Jn* 3:17.
247   CDF, instruction, *Libertatis conscientia*, 68.

2449   Beginning with the Old Testament, all kinds of juridical measures (the jubilee year of forgiveness of debts, prohibition of loans at interest and the keeping of collateral, the obligation to tithe, the daily payment of the day-laborer, the right to glean vines and fields) answer the exhortation of *Deuteronomy*: "For the poor will never cease out of the land; therefore I command you, 'You shall open wide your hand to your brother, to the needy and to the poor in the land.' "[248] Jesus makes these words his own: "The poor you always have with you, but you do not always have me."[249] In so doing he does not soften the vehemence of former oracles against "buying the poor for silver and the needy for a pair of sandals . . .," but invites us to recognize his own presence in the poor who are *1397* his brethren:[250]

> When her mother reproached her for caring for the poor and the sick at home, St. Rose of Lima said to her: "When we serve the poor and the sick, we serve Jesus. We must not fail to help our neighbors, because in them we serve Jesus.[251]   *786*

IN BRIEF

2450   "You shall not steal" (*Ex* 20:15; *Deut* 5:19). "Neither thieves, nor the greedy . . ., nor robbers will inherit the kingdom of God" (*1 Cor* 6:10).

2451   The seventh commandment enjoins the practice of justice and charity in the administration of earthly goods and the fruits of men's labor.

2452   The goods of creation are destined for the entire human race. The right to private property does not abolish the universal destination of goods.

2453   The seventh commandment forbids theft. Theft is the usurpation of another's goods against the reasonable will of the owner.

2454   Every manner of taking and using another's property unjustly is contrary to the seventh commandment. The injustice committed requires reparation. Commutative justice requires the restitution of stolen goods.

---

248 *Deut* 15:11.
249 *Jn* 12:8.
250 *Am* 8:6; cf. *Mt* 25:40.
251 P. Hansen, *Vita mirabilis* (Louvain, 1668).

2455   The moral law forbids acts which, for commercial or totalitarian purposes, lead to the enslavement of human beings, or to their being bought, sold or exchanged like merchandise.

2456   The dominion granted by the Creator over the mineral, vegetable, and animal resources of the universe cannot be separated from respect for moral obligations, including those toward generations to come.

2457   Animals are entrusted to man's stewardship; he must show them kindness. They may be used to serve the just satisfaction of man's needs.

2458   The Church makes a judgment about economic and social matters when the fundamental rights of the person or the salvation of souls requires it. She is concerned with the temporal common good of men because they are ordered to the sovereign Good, their ultimate end.

2459   Man is himself the author, center, and goal of all economic and social life. The decisive point of the social question is that goods created by God for everyone should in fact reach everyone in accordance with justice and with the help of charity.

2460   The primordial value of labor stems from man himself, its author and beneficiary. By means of his labor man participates in the work of creation. Work united to Christ can be redemptive.

2461   True development concerns the whole man. It is concerned with increasing each person's ability to respond to his vocation and hence to God's call (cf. *CA* 29).

2462   Giving alms to the poor is a witness to fraternal charity: it is also a work of justice pleasing to God.

2463   How can we not recognize Lazarus, the hungry beggar in the parable (cf. *Lk* 17:19-31), in the multitude of human beings without bread, a roof or a place to stay? How can we fail to hear Jesus: "As you did it not to one of the least of these, you did it not to me" (*Mt* 25:45)?

ARTICLE 8
THE EIGHTH COMMANDMENT

> You shall not bear false witness against your neighbor.[252]

> It was said to the men of old, "You shall not swear falsely, but shall perform to the Lord what you have sworn."[253]

2464 The eighth commandment forbids misrepresenting the truth in our relations with others. This moral prescription flows from the vocation of the holy people to bear witness to their God who is the truth and wills the truth. Offenses against the truth express by word or deed a refusal to commit oneself to moral uprightness: they are fundamental infidelities to God and, in this sense, they undermine the foundations of the covenant.

I.   LIVING IN THE TRUTH

2465 The Old Testament attests that *God is the source of all truth.*   *215* His Word is truth. His Law is truth. His "faithfulness endures to all generations."[254] Since God is "true," the members of his people are called to live in the truth.[255]

2466 In Jesus Christ, the whole of God's truth has been made manifest. "Full of grace and truth," he came as the "light of the world," he *is the Truth.*[256] "Whoever believes in me may not remain in darkness."[257] The disciple of Jesus continues in his word so as to know "the truth [that] will make you free" and that sanctifies.[258] To follow Jesus is to live in "the Spirit of truth," whom the Father sends in his name and who leads "into all the truth."[259] To his   *2153* disciples Jesus teaches the unconditional love of truth: "Let what you say be simply 'Yes or No.'"[260]

---

252   *Ex* 20:16; cf. *Deut* 5:20.
253   *Mt* 5:33.
254   *Ps* 119:90; cf. *Prov* 8:7; *2 Sam* 7:28; *Ps* 119:142; *Lk* 1:50.
255   *Rom* 3:4; cf. *Ps* 119:30.
256   *Jn* 1:14; 8:12; cf. 14:6.
257   *Jn* 12:46.
258   *Jn* 8:32; cf. 17:17.
259   *Jn* 16:13.
260   *Mt* 5:37.

2467   Man tends by nature toward the truth. He is obliged to honor and bear witness to it: "It is in accordance with their dignity
2104   that all men, because they are persons . . . are both impelled by their nature and bound by a moral obligation to seek the truth, especially religious truth. They are also bound to adhere to the truth once they come to know it and direct their whole lives in accordance with the demands of truth."[261]

2468   Truth as uprightness in human action and speech is called *truthfulness*, sincerity, or candor. Truth or truthfulness is the virtue
1458   which consists in showing oneself true in deeds and truthful in words, and in guarding against duplicity, dissimulation, and hypocrisy.

2469   "Men could not live with one another if there were not mutual confidence that they were being truthful to one an-
1807   other."[262] The virtue of truth gives another his just due. Truthfulness keeps to the just mean between what ought to be expressed and what ought to be kept secret: it entails honesty and discretion. In justice, "as a matter of honor, one man owes it to another to manifest the truth."[263]

2470   The disciple of Christ consents to "live in the truth," that is, in the simplicity of a life in conformity with the Lord's example, abiding in his truth. "If we say we have fellowship with him while we walk in darkness, we lie and do not live according to the truth."[264]

II.   To Bear Witness to the Truth

2471   Before Pilate, Christ proclaims that he "has come into the world, to bear witness to the truth."[265] The Christian is not to "be
1816   ashamed then of testifying to our Lord."[266] In situations that require witness to the faith, the Christian must profess it without equivocation, after the example of St. Paul before his judges. We must keep "a clear conscience toward God and toward men."[267]

---

261   *DH* 2 § 2.
262   St. Thomas Aquinas, *STh* II-II, 109, 3 *ad* 1.
263   St. Thomas Aquinas, *STh* II-II, 109, 3, corp. art.
264   *1 Jn* 1:6.
265   *Jn* 18:37.
266   *2 Tim* 1:8.
267   *Acts* 24:16.

2472 The duty of Christians to take part in the life of the Church impels them to act as *witnesses of the Gospel* and of the obligations that flow from it. This witness is a transmission of the faith in words *863, 905* and deeds. Witness is an act of justice that establishes the truth or makes it known.[268] *1807*

> All Christians by the example of their lives and the witness of their word, wherever they live, have an obligation to manifest the new man which they have put on in Baptism and to reveal the power of the Holy Spirit by whom they were strengthened at Confirmation.[269]

2473 *Martyrdom* is the supreme witness given to the truth of the *852* faith: it means bearing witness even unto death. The martyr bears witness to Christ who died and rose, to whom he is united by charity. He bears witness to the truth of the faith and of Christian *1808* doctrine. He endures death through an act of fortitude. "Let me become the food of the beasts, through whom it will be given me to reach God."[270] *1258*

2474 The Church has painstakingly collected the records of those who persevered to the end in witnessing to their faith. These are the acts of the Martyrs. They form the archives of truth written in letters of blood:

> Neither the pleasures of the world nor the kingdoms of this *1011* age will be of any use to me. It is better for me to die [in order to unite myself] to Christ Jesus than to reign over the ends of the earth. I seek him who died for us; I desire him who rose for us. My birth is approaching. . . .[271]

> I bless you for having judged me worthy from this day and this hour to be counted among your martyrs. . . . You have kept your promise, God of faithfulness and truth. For this reason and for everything, I praise you, I bless you, I glorify you through the eternal and heavenly High Priest, Jesus Christ, your beloved Son. Through him, who is with you and the Holy Spirit, may glory be given to you, now and in the ages to come. Amen.[272]

---

268 Cf. *Mt* 18:16.
269 *AG* 11.
270 St. Ignatius of Antioch, *Ad Rom.* 4, 1: SCh 10, 110.
271 St. Ignatius of Antioch, *Ad Rom.* 6, 1-2: SCh 10, 114.
272 *Martyrium Polycarpi* 14, 2-3: PG 5, 1040; SCh 10, 228.

III.   OFFENSES AGAINST TRUTH

2475   Christ's disciples have "put on the new man, created after the likeness of God in true righteousness and holiness."[273] By "putting away falsehood," they are to "put away all malice and all guile and insincerity and envy and all slander."[274]

2152 **2476**   *False witness and perjury.* When it is made publicly, a statement contrary to the truth takes on a particular gravity. In court it becomes false witness.[275] When it is under oath, it is perjury. Acts such as these contribute to condemnation of the innocent, exoneration of the guilty, or the increased punishment of the accused.[276] They gravely compromise the exercise of justice and the fairness of judicial decisions.

2477   *Respect for the reputation* of persons forbids every attitude and word likely to cause them unjust injury.[277] He becomes guilty:

– of *rash judgment* who, even tacitly, assumes as true, without sufficient foundation, the moral fault of a neighbor;

– of *detraction* who, without objectively valid reason, discloses another's faults and failings to persons who did not know them;[278]

– of *calumny* who, by remarks contrary to the truth, harms the reputation of others and gives occasion for false judgments concerning them.

2478   To avoid rash judgment, everyone should be careful to interpret insofar as possible his neighbor's thoughts, words, and deeds in a favorable way:

> Every good Christian ought to be more ready to give a favorable interpretation to another's statement than to condemn it. But if he cannot do so, let him ask how the other understands it. And if the latter understands it badly, let the former correct him with love. If that does not suffice, let the Christian try all suitable ways to bring the other to a correct interpretation so that he may be saved.[279]

---

273 *Eph* 4:24.
274 *Eph* 4:25; *1 Pet* 2:1.
275 Cf. *Prov* 19:9.
276 Cf. *Prov* 18:5.
277 Cf. CIC, can. 220.
278 Cf. *Sir* 21:28.
279 St. Ignatius of Loyola, *Spiritual Exercises,* 22.

2479   Detraction and calumny destroy the *reputation and honor of one's neighbor*. Honor is the social witness given to human dignity, and everyone enjoys a natural right to the honor of his name and reputation and to respect. Thus, detraction and calumny offend *1753* against the virtues of justice and charity.

2480   Every word or attitude is forbidden which by *flattery, adulation, or complaisance* encourages and confirms another in malicious acts and perverse conduct. Adulation is a grave fault if it makes one an accomplice in another's vices or grave sins. Neither the desire to be of service nor friendship justifies duplicitous speech. Adulation is a venial sin when it only seeks to be agreeable, to avoid evil, to meet a need, or to obtain legitimate advantages.

2481   *Boasting* or bragging is an offense against truth. So is *irony* aimed at disparaging someone by maliciously caricaturing some aspect of his behavior.

2482   "A *lie* consists in speaking a falsehood with the intention of deceiving."[280] The Lord denounces lying as the work of the devil: "You are of your father the devil, . . . there is no truth in him. When he lies, he speaks according to his own nature, for he is a liar and the father of lies."[281] *392*

2483   Lying is the most direct offense against the truth. To lie is to speak or act against the truth in order to lead into error someone who has the right to know the truth. By injuring man's relation to truth and to his neighbor, a lie offends against the fundamental relation of man and of his word to the Lord.

2484   The *gravity of a lie* is measured against the nature of the truth it deforms, the circumstances, the intentions of the one who lies, and the harm suffered by its victims. If a lie in itself only *1750* constitutes a venial sin, it becomes mortal when it does grave injury to the virtues of justice and charity.

2485   By its very nature, lying is to be condemned. It is a profa- *1756* nation of speech, whereas the purpose of speech is to communicate known truth to others. The deliberate intention of leading a neighbor into error by saying things contrary to the truth constitutes a failure in justice and charity. The culpability is greater when the intention of deceiving entails the risk of deadly consequences for those who are led astray.

---

280   St. Augustine, *De mendacio* 4, 5: PL 40:491.
281   *Jn* 8:44.

2486   Since it violates the virtue of truthfulness, a lie does real
violence to another. It affects his ability to know, which is a condition of every judgment and decision. It contains the seed of discord
1607   and all consequent evils. Lying is destructive of society; it undermines trust among men and tears apart the fabric of social relationships.

1459   **2487**   Every offense committed against justice and truth entails
the *duty of reparation,* even if its author has been forgiven. When it
is impossible publicly to make reparation for a wrong, it must be
made secretly. If someone who has suffered harm cannot be di-
2412   rectly compensated, he must be given moral satisfaction in the
name of charity. This duty of reparation also concerns offenses
against another's reputation. This reparation, moral and sometimes material, must be evaluated in terms of the extent of the
damage inflicted. It obliges in conscience.

IV.   RESPECT FOR THE TRUTH

1740   **2488**   The *right to the communication* of the truth is not unconditional. Everyone must conform his life to the Gospel precept of
fraternal love. This requires us in concrete situations to judge
whether or not it is appropriate to reveal the truth to someone who
asks for it.

2489   Charity and respect for the truth should dictate the response to every *request for information or communication.* The good
and safety of others, respect for privacy, and the common good are
sufficient reasons for being silent about what ought not be known
or for making use of a discreet language. The duty to avoid scandal
2284   often commands strict discretion. No one is bound to reveal the
truth to someone who does not have the right to know it.[282]

1467   **2490**   The *secret of the sacrament of reconciliation* is sacred, and
cannot be violated under any pretext. "The sacramental seal is
inviolable; therefore, it is a crime for a confessor in any way to
betray a penitent by word or in any other manner or for any
reason."[283]

---

282   Cf. *Sir* 27:16; *Prov* 25:9-10.
283   CIC, can. 983 § 1.

2491 *Professional secrets* – for example, those of political office holders, soldiers, physicians, and lawyers – or confidential information given under the seal of secrecy must be kept, save in exceptional cases where keeping the secret is bound to cause very grave harm to the one who confided it, to the one who received it or to a third party, and where the very grave harm can be avoided only by divulging the truth. Even if not confided under the seal of secrecy, private information prejudicial to another is not to be divulged without a grave and proportionate reason.

2492 Everyone should observe an appropriate reserve concern- 2522 ing persons' private lives. Those in charge of communications should maintain a fair balance between the requirements of the common good and respect for individual rights. Interference by the media in the private lives of persons engaged in political or public activity is to be condemned to the extent that it infringes upon their privacy and freedom.

V. The Use of the Social Communications Media

2493 Within modern society the communications media play a major role in information, cultural promotion, and formation. This role is increasing, as a result of technological progress, the extent and diversity of the news transmitted, and the influence exercised on public opinion.

2494 The information provided by the media is at the service of 1906 the common good.[284] Society has a right to information based on truth, freedom, justice, and solidarity:

> The proper exercise of this right demands that the content of the communication be true and – within the limits set by justice and charity – complete. Further, it should be communicated honestly and properly. This means that in the gathering and in the publication of news, the moral law and the legitimate rights and dignity of man should be upheld.[285]

---

284 Cf. *IM* 11.
285 *IM* 5 § 2.

906 **2495**   "It is necessary that all members of society meet the demands of justice and charity in this domain. They should help, through the means of social communication, in the formation and diffusion of sound public opinion."[286] Solidarity is a consequence of genuine and right communication and the free circulation of ideas that further knowledge and respect for others.

2496   The means of social communication (especially the mass media) can give rise to a certain passivity among users, making them less than *2525* vigilant consumers of what is said or shown. Users should practice moderation and discipline in their approach to the mass media. They will want to form enlightened and correct consciences the more easily to resist unwholesome influences.

2497   By the very nature of their profession, journalists have an obligation to serve the truth and not offend against charity in disseminating information. They should strive to respect, with equal care, the nature of the facts and the limits of critical judgment concerning individuals. They should not stoop to defamation.

2237 **2498**   *"Civil authorities* have particular responsibilities in this field because of the common good. . . . It is for the civil authority . . . to defend and safeguard a true and just freedom of information."[287] By promulgating *2286* laws and overseeing their application, public authorities should ensure that "public morality and social progress are not gravely endangered" through misuse of the media.[288] Civil authorities should punish any violation of the rights of individuals to their reputation and privacy. They should give timely and reliable reports concerning the general good or respond to the well-founded concerns of the people. Nothing can justify recourse to disinformation for manipulating public opinion through the media. Interventions by public authority should avoid injuring the freedom of individuals or groups.

2499   Moral judgment must condemn the plague of totalitarian states which systematically falsify the truth, exercise political control of opinion through the media, manipulate defendants and witnesses at public trials, *1903* and imagine that they secure their tyranny by strangling and repressing everything they consider "thought crimes."

---

286   *IM* 8.
287   *IM* 12.
288   *IM* 12 § 2.

VI. TRUTH, BEAUTY, AND SACRED ART

2500   The practice of goodness is accompanied by spontaneous   *1804*
spiritual joy and moral beauty. Likewise, truth carries with it the
joy and splendor of spiritual beauty. Truth is beautiful in itself.
Truth in words, the rational expression of the knowledge of created
and uncreated reality, is necessary to man, who is endowed with
intellect. But truth can also find other complementary forms of
human expression, above all when it is a matter of evoking what
is beyond words: the depths of the human heart, the exaltations of
the soul, the mystery of God. Even before revealing himself to man
in words of truth, God reveals himself to him through the universal
language of creation, the work of his Word, of his wisdom: the   *341*
order and harmony of the cosmos—which both the child and the
scientist discover—"from the greatness and beauty of created
things comes a corresponding perception of their Creator," "for the
author of beauty created them."[289]   *2129*

> [Wisdom] is a breath of the power of God, and a pure
> emanation of the glory of the Almighty; therefore nothing
> defiled gains entrance into her. For she is a reflection of
> eternal light, a spotless mirror of the working of God, and an
> image of his goodness.[290] For [wisdom] is more beautiful
> than the sun, and excels every constellation of the stars.
> Compared with the light she is found to be superior, for it is
> succeeded by the night, but against wisdom evil does not
> prevail.[291] I became enamored of her beauty.[292]

2501   Created "in the image of God,"[293] man also expresses the
truth of his relationship with God the Creator by the beauty of his
artistic works. Indeed, *art* is a distinctively human form of expression; beyond the search for the necessities of life which is common
to all living creatures, art is a freely given superabundance of the
human being's inner riches. Arising from talent given by the
Creator and from man's own effort, art is a form of practical
wisdom, uniting knowledge and skill,[294] to give form to the truth
of reality in a language accessible to sight or hearing. To the extent
that it is inspired by truth and love of beings, art bears a certain
likeness to God's activity in what he has created. Like any other   *339*

---

289   *Wis* 13:3, 5.
290   *Wis* 7:25-26.
291   *Wis* 7:29-30.
292   *Wis* 8:2.
293   *Gen* 1:26.
294   Cf. *Wis* 7:16-17.

human activity, art is not an absolute end in itself, but is ordered to and ennobled by the ultimate end of man.[295]

1156-1162 **2502**   *Sacred art* is true and beautiful when its form corresponds to its particular vocation: evoking and glorifying, in faith and adoration, the transcendent mystery of God – the surpassing invisible beauty of truth and love visible in Christ, who "reflects the glory of God and bears the very stamp of his nature," in whom "the whole fullness of deity dwells bodily."[296] This spiritual beauty of God is reflected in the most holy Virgin Mother of God, the angels, and saints. Genuine sacred art draws man to adoration, to prayer, and to the love of God, Creator and Savior, the Holy One and Sanctifier.

2503   For this reason bishops, personally or through delegates, should see to the promotion of sacred art, old and new, in all its forms and, with the same religious care, remove from the liturgy and from places of worship everything which is not in conformity with the truth of faith and the authentic beauty of *sacred* art.[297]

IN BRIEF

2504   "You shall not bear false witness against your neighbor" (*Ex* 20:16). Christ's disciples have "put on the new man, created after the likeness of God in true righteousness and holiness" (*Eph* 4:24).

2505   Truth or truthfulness is the virtue which consists in showing oneself true in deeds and truthful in words, and guarding against duplicity, dissimulation, and hypocrisy.

2506   The Christian is not to "be ashamed of testifying to our Lord" (*2 Tim* 1:8) in deed and word. Martyrdom is the supreme witness given to the truth of the faith.

2507   Respect for the reputation and honor of persons forbids all detraction and calumny in word or attitude.

---

295   Cf. Pius XII, *Musicae sacrae disciplina*; Discourses of September 3 and December 25, 1950.
296   *Heb* 1:3; *Col* 2:9.
297   Cf. *SC* 122-127.

2508 Lying consists in saying what is false with the intention of deceiving the neighbor who has the right to the truth.

2509 An offense committed against the truth requires reparation.

2510 The golden rule helps one discern, in concrete situations, whether or not it would be appropriate to reveal the truth to someone who asks for it.

2511 "The sacramental seal is inviolable" (CIC, can. 983 § 1). Professional secrets must be kept. Confidences prejudicial to another are not to be divulged.

2512 Society has a right to information based on truth, freedom, and justice. One should practice moderation and discipline in the use of the social communications media.

2513 The fine arts, but above all sacred art, "of their nature are directed toward expressing in some way the infinite beauty of God in works made by human hands. Their dedication to the increase of God's praise and of his glory is more complete, the more exclusively they are devoted to turning men's minds devoutly toward God" (SC 122).

ARTICLE 9
THE NINTH COMMANDMENT

You shall not covet your neighbor's house; you shall not covet your neighbor's wife, or his manservant, or his maidservant, or his ox, or his ass, or anything that is your neighbor's.[298]

Every one who looks at a woman lustfully has already committed adultery with her in his heart.[299]

---

298 *Ex* 20:17.
299 *Mt* 5:28.

377, 400 **2514** St. John distinguishes three kinds of covetousness or concupiscence: lust of the flesh, lust of the eyes, and pride of life.[300] In
the Catholic catechetical tradition, the ninth commandment forbids carnal concupiscence; the tenth forbids coveting another's
goods.

405 **2515** Etymologically, "concupiscence" can refer to any intense
form of human desire. Christian theology has given it a particular
meaning: the movement of the sensitive appetite contrary to the
operation of the human reason. The apostle St. Paul identifies it
with the rebellion of the "flesh" against the "spirit."[301] Concupiscence stems from the disobedience of the first sin. It unsettles man's
moral faculties and, without being in itself an offense, inclines man
to commit sins.[302]

362 **2516** Because man is a *composite being, spirit and body*, there
already exists a certain tension in him; a certain struggle of tendencies between "spirit" and "flesh" develops. But in fact this struggle
belongs to the heritage of sin. It is a consequence of sin and at the
same time a confirmation of it. It is part of the daily experience of
407 the spiritual battle:

> For the Apostle it is not a matter of despising and condemn-
> ing the body which with the spiritual soul constitutes man's
> nature and personal subjectivity. Rather, he is concerned
> with the morally *good or bad* works, or better, the permanent
> dispositions – virtues and vices – which are the fruit of
> *submission* (in the first case) or of *resistance* (in the second
> case) to *the saving action of the Holy Spirit*. For this reason the
> Apostle writes: "If we live by the Spirit, let us also walk by
> the Spirit."[303]

I. PURIFICATION OF THE HEART

368 **2517** The heart is the seat of moral personality: "Out of the heart
come evil thoughts, murder, adultery, fornication. . . ."[304] The
struggle against carnal covetousness entails purifying the heart
1809 and practicing temperance:

---

300 Cf. *1 Jn* 2:16.
301 Cf. *Gal* 5:16, 17, 24; *Eph* 2:3.
302 Cf. *Gen* 3:11; Council of Trent: DS 1515.
303 John Paul II, *DeV* 55; cf. *Gal* 5:25.
304 *Mt* 15:19.

> Remain simple and innocent, and you will be like little children who do not know the evil that destroys man's life.[305]

2518 The sixth beatitude proclaims, "Blessed are the pure in heart, for they shall see God."[306] "Pure in heart" refers to those who have attuned their intellects and wills to the demands of God's holiness, chiefly in three areas: charity;[307] chastity or sexual rectitude;[308] love of truth and orthodoxy of faith.[309] There is a connection between purity of heart, of body, and of faith: 94

> The faithful must believe the articles of the Creed "so that by believing they may obey God, by obeying may live well, by living well may purify their hearts, and with pure hearts may understand what they believe."[310] 158

2519 The "pure in heart" are promised that they will see God 2548 face to face and be like him.[311] Purity of heart is the precondition of the vision of God. Even now it enables us to see *according to* God, to accept others as "neighbors"; it lets us perceive the human body 2819 – ours and our neighbor's – as a temple of the Holy Spirit, a manifestation of divine beauty. 2501

II.   THE BATTLE FOR PURITY

2520 Baptism confers on its recipient the grace of purification 1264 from all sins. But the baptized must continue to struggle against concupiscence of the flesh and disordered desires. With God's grace he will prevail

– by the *virtue* and *gift of chastity*, for chastity lets us love with 2337 upright and undivided heart;

– by *purity of intention* which consists in seeking the true end of 1752 man: with simplicity of vision, the baptized person seeks to find and to fulfill God's will in everything;[312]

---

305 *Pastor Hermae*, Mandate 2, 1: PG 2, 916.
306 *Mt* 5:8.
307 Cf. *1 Tim* 4:3-9; *2 Tim* 2:22.
308 Cf. *1 Thess* 4:7; *Col* 3:5; *Eph* 4:19.
309 Cf. *Titus* 1:15; *1 Tim* 1:3-4; *2 Tim* 2:23-26.
310 St. Augustine, *De fide et symbolo* 10, 25: PL 40, 196.
311 Cf. *1 Cor* 13:12; *1 Jn* 3:2.
312 Cf. *Rom* 12:2; *Col* 1:10.

1762   – by *purity of vision*, external and internal; by discipline of feelings
and imagination; by refusing all complicity in impure thoughts
that incline us to turn aside from the path of God's commandments:
"Appearance arouses yearning in fools";[313]

2846   – by *prayer*:

> I thought that continence arose from one's own powers,
> which I did not recognize in myself. I was foolish enough not
> to know . . . that no one can be continent unless you grant it.
> For you would surely have granted it if my inner groaning
> had reached your ears and I with firm faith had cast my cares
> on you.[314]

2521   Purity requires *modesty*, an integral part of temperance.
Modesty protects the intimate center of the person. It means refusing to unveil what should remain hidden. It is ordered to chastity
to whose sensitivity it bears witness. It guides how one looks at
others and behaves toward them in conformity with the dignity of
persons and their solidarity.

2492   **2522**   Modesty protects the mystery of persons and their love. It
encourages patience and moderation in loving relationships; it
requires that the conditions for the definitive giving and commitment of man and woman to one another be fulfilled. Modesty is
decency. It inspires one's choice of clothing. It keeps silence or
reserve where there is evident risk of unhealthy curiosity. It is
discreet.

2354   **2523**   There is a modesty of the feelings as well as of the body. It
protests, for example, against the voyeuristic explorations of the human
body in certain advertisements, or against the solicitations of certain media
that go too far in the exhibition of intimate things. Modesty inspires a way
of life which makes it possible to resist the allurements of fashion and the
pressures of prevailing ideologies.

2524   The forms taken by modesty vary from one culture to another.
Everywhere, however, modesty exists as an intuition of the spiritual
dignity proper to man. It is born with the awakening consciousness of
being a subject. Teaching modesty to children and adolescents means
awakening in them respect for the human person.

---

313   *Wis* 15:5.
314   St. Augustine, *Conf.* 6, 11, 20: PL 32, 729-730.

2525 Christian purity requires a *purification of the social climate*. 2344
It requires of the communications media that their presentations
show concern for respect and restraint. Purity of heart brings
freedom from widespread eroticism and avoids entertainment
inclined to voyeurism and illusion.

2526 So-called *moral permissiveness* rests on an erroneous con- 1740
ception of human freedom; the necessary precondition for the
development of true freedom is to let oneself be educated in the
moral law. Those in charge of education can reasonably be expected to give young people instruction respectful of the truth, the
qualities of the heart, and the moral and spiritual dignity of man.

2527 "The Good News of Christ continually renews the life and 1204
culture of fallen man; it combats and removes the error and evil
which flow from the ever-present attraction of sin. It never ceases
to purify and elevate the morality of peoples. It takes the spiritual
qualities and endowments of every age and nation, and with
supernatural riches it causes them to blossom, as it were, from
within; it fortifies, completes, and restores them in Christ."[315]

IN BRIEF

2528 "Everyone who looks at a woman lustfully has already
committed adultery with her in his heart" (*Mt* 5:28).

2529 The ninth commandment warns against lust or carnal
concupiscence.

2530 The struggle against carnal lust involves purifying the
heart and practicing temperance.

2531 Purity of heart will enable us to see God: it enables us
even now to see things according to God.

2532 Purification of the heart demands prayer, the practice
of chastity, purity of intention and of vision.

2533 Purity of heart requires the modesty which is patience,
decency, and discretion. Modesty protects the intimate center of the person.

315 *GS* 58 § 4.

ARTICLE 10
THE TENTH COMMANDMENT

> You shall not covet . . . anything that is your neighbor's. . . .
> You shall not desire your neighbor's house, his field, or his
> manservant, or his maidservant, or his ox, or his ass, or
> anything that is your neighbor's.[316]

> For where your treasure is, there will your heart be also.[317]

2534 The tenth commandment unfolds and completes the
ninth, which is concerned with concupiscence of the flesh. It forbids coveting the goods of another, as the root of theft, robbery,
and fraud, which the seventh commandment forbids. "Lust of the
eyes" leads to the violence and injustice forbidden by the fifth
commandment.[318] Avarice, like fornication, originates in the idolatry prohibited by the first three prescriptions of the Law.[319] The
2112 tenth commandment concerns the intentions of the heart; with the
2069 ninth, it summarizes all the precepts of the Law.

I.   THE DISORDER OF COVETOUS DESIRES

2535 The sensitive appetite leads us to desire pleasant things we
do not have, e.g., the desire to eat when we are hungry or to warm
ourselves when we are cold. These desires are good in themselves;
1767 but often they exceed the limits of reason and drive us to covet
unjustly what is not ours and belongs to another or is owed to him.

2536 The tenth commandment forbids *greed* and the desire to
amass earthly goods without limit. It forbids *avarice* arising from a
2445 passion for riches and their attendant power. It also forbids the
desire to commit injustice by harming our neighbor in his temporal
goods:

> When the Law says, "You shall not covet," these words mean
> that we should banish our desires for whatever does not
> belong to us. Our thirst for another's goods is immense,
> infinite, never quenched. Thus it is written: "He who loves
> money never has money enough."[320]

---

316 *Ex* 20:17; *Deut* 5:21.
317 *Mt* 6:21.
318 Cf. *1 Jn* 2:16; *Mic* 2:2.
319 Cf. *Wis* 14:12.
320 *Roman Catechism*, III, 37; çf. *Sir* 5:8.

2537   It is not a violation of this commandment to desire to obtain things that belong to one's neighbor, provided this is done by just means. Traditional catechesis realistically mentions "those who have a harder struggle against their criminal desires" and so who "must be urged the more to keep this commandment":

> . . . merchants who desire scarcity and rising prices, who cannot bear not to be the only ones buying and selling so that they themselves can sell more dearly and buy more cheaply; those who hope that their peers will be impoverished, in order to realize a profit either by selling to them or buying from them . . . physicians who wish disease to spread; lawyers who are eager for many important cases and trials.[321]

2538   The tenth commandment requires that *envy* be banished   *2317* from the human heart. When the prophet Nathan wanted to spur King David to repentance, he told him the story about the poor man who had only one ewe lamb that he treated like his own daughter and the rich man who, despite the great number of his flocks, envied the poor man and ended by stealing his lamb.[322] Envy can lead to the worst crimes.[323] "Through the devil's envy death entered the world":[324]   *391*

> We fight one another, and envy arms us against one another. . . . If everyone strives to unsettle the Body of Christ, where shall we end up? We are engaged in making Christ's Body a corpse. . . . We declare ourselves members of one and the same organism, yet we devour one another like beasts.[325]

2539   Envy is a capital sin. It refers to the sadness at the sight of   *1866* another's goods and the immoderate desire to acquire them for oneself, even unjustly. When it wishes grave harm to a neighbor it is a mortal sin:

> St. Augustine saw envy as "*the* diabolical sin."[326] "From envy are born hatred, detraction, calumny, joy caused by the misfortune of a neighbor, and displeasure caused by his prosperity."[327]

---

321 *Roman Catechism,* III, 37.
322 Cf. *2 Sam* 12:1-4.
323 Cf. *Gen* 4:3-7; *1 Kings* 21:1-29.
324 *Wis* 2:24.
325 St. John Chrysostom, *Hom. in 2 Cor.* 27, 3-4: PG 61, 588.
326 Cf. St. Augustine, *De catechizandis rudibus* 4, 8: PL 40, 315-316.
327 St. Gregory the Great, *Moralia in Job* 31, 45: PL 76, 621.

1829 **2540**   Envy represents a form of sadness and therefore a refusal
of charity; the baptized person should struggle against it by exercising good will. Envy often comes from pride; the baptized person
should train himself to live in humility:

> Would you like to see God glorified by you? Then rejoice in
> your brother's progress and you will immediately give glory
> to God. Because his servant could conquer envy by rejoicing
> in the merits of others, God will be praised.[328]

II.   THE DESIRES OF THE SPIRIT

2541   The economy of law and grace turns men's hearts away
from avarice and envy. It initiates them into desire for the Sover-
1718 eign Good; it instructs them in the desires of the Holy Spirit who
2764 satisfies man's heart.

397   The God of the promises always warned man against
seduction by what from the beginning has seemed "good for food
. . . a delight to the eyes . . . to be desired to make one wise."[329]

1963 **2542**   The Law entrusted to Israel never sufficed to justify those
subject to it; it even became the instrument of "lust."[330] The gap
between wanting and doing points to the conflict between God's
Law which is the "law of my mind," and another law "making me
captive to the law of sin which dwells in my members."[331]

1992 **2543**   "But now the righteousness of God has been manifested
apart from law, although the law and the prophets bear witness to
it, the righteousness of God through faith in Jesus Christ for all who
believe."[332] Henceforth, Christ's faithful "have crucified the flesh
with its passions and desires"; they are led by the Spirit and follow
the desires of the Spirit.[333]

---

328   St. John Chrysostom, *Hom. in Rom.* 71, 5: PG 60, 448.
329   *Gen* 3:6.
330   Cf. *Rom* 7:7.
331   *Rom* 7:23; cf. 7:10.
332   *Rom* 3:21-22.
333   *Gal* 5:24; cf. *Rom* 8:14, 27.

III. POVERTY OF HEART

2443-2449

2544 Jesus enjoins his disciples to prefer him to everything and everyone, and bids them "renounce all that [they have]" for his sake and that of the Gospel.[334] Shortly before his passion he gave them the example of the poor widow of Jerusalem who, out of her poverty, gave all that she had to live on.[335] The precept of detachment from riches is obligatory for entrance into the Kingdom of heaven.

544

2545 All Christ's faithful are to "direct their affections rightly, lest they be hindered in their pursuit of perfect charity by the use of worldly things and by an adherence to riches which is contrary to the spirit of evangelical poverty."[336]

2013

2546 "Blessed are the poor in spirit."[337] The Beatitudes reveal an order of happiness and grace, of beauty and peace. Jesus celebrates the joy of the poor, to whom the Kingdom already belongs:[338]

1716

> The Word speaks of voluntary humility as "poverty in spirit"; the Apostle gives an example of God's poverty when he says: "For your sakes he became poor."[339]

2547 The Lord grieves over the rich, because they find their consolation in the abundance of goods.[340] "Let the proud seek and love earthly kingdoms, but blessed are the poor in spirit for theirs is the Kingdom of heaven."[341] Abandonment to the providence of the Father in heaven frees us from anxiety about tomorrow.[342] Trust in God is a preparation for the blessedness of the poor. They shall see God.

305

---

334 *Lk* 14:33; cf. *Mk* 8:35.
335 Cf. *Lk* 21:4.
336 *LG* 42 § 3.
337 *Mt* 5:3.
338 Cf. *Lk* 6:20.
339 St. Gregory of Nyssa, *De beatitudinibus* 1: PG 44, 1200D; cf. *2 Cor* 8:9.
340 *Lk* 6:24.
341 St. Augustine, *De serm. Dom. in monte* 1, 1, 3: PL 34, 1232.
342 Cf. *Mt* 6:25-34.

IV.   "I Want to See God"

2548   Desire for true happiness frees man from his immoderate
attachment to the goods of this world so that he can find his
2519 fulfillment in the vision and beatitude of God. "The promise [of
seeing God] surpasses all beatitude. . . . In Scripture, to see is to
possess. . . . Whoever sees God has obtained all the goods of which
he can conceive."[343]

2549   It remains for the holy people to struggle, with grace from
on high, to obtain the good things God promises. In order to
2015 possess and contemplate God, Christ's faithful mortify their crav-
ings and, with the grace of God, prevail over the seductions of
pleasure and power.

2550   On this way of perfection, the Spirit and the Bride call
whoever hears them[344] to perfect communion with God:

> There will true glory be, where no one will be praised by
> mistake or flattery; true honor will not be refused to the
> worthy, nor granted to the unworthy; likewise, no one un-
> worthy will pretend to be worthy, where only those who are
> worthy will be admitted. There true peace will reign, where
> no one will experience opposition either from self or others.
> God himself will be virtue's reward; he gives virtue and has
> promised to give himself as the best and greatest reward that
> could exist. . . . "I shall be their God and they will be my
> people. . . ." This is also the meaning of the Apostle's words:
> "So that God may be all in all." God himself will be the goal
> of our desires; we shall contemplate him without end, love him
> without surfeit, praise him without weariness. This gift, this
> state, this act, like eternal life itself, will assuredly be common
314 > to all.[345]

---

343   St. Gregory of Nyssa, *De beatitudinibus* 6: PG 44, 1265A.
344   Cf. *Rev* 22:17.
345   St. Augustine, *De civ. Dei*, 22, 30: PL 41, 801-802; cf. *Lev* 26:12; cf. *1 Cor* 15:28.

IN BRIEF

2551   "Where your treasure is, there will your heart be also" (*Mt* 6:21).

2552   The tenth commandment forbids avarice arising from a passion for riches and their attendant power.

2553   Envy is sadness at the sight of another's goods and the immoderate desire to have them for oneself. It is a capital sin.

2554   The baptized person combats envy through good-will, humility, and abandonment to the providence of God.

2555   Christ's faithful "have crucified the flesh with its passions and desires" (*Gal* 5:24); they are led by the Spirit and follow his desires.

2556   Detachment from riches is necessary for entering the Kingdom of heaven. "Blessed are the poor in spirit."

2557   "I want to see God" expresses the true desire of man. Thirst for God is quenched by the water of eternal life (cf. *Jn* 4:14).

Miniature from the Monastery of Dionysius on Mount Athos (codex 587), painted in Constantinople in about the year 1059.

Christ turns in prayer towards the Father (cf. §2599). He prays alone, in a deserted place. His disciples look on from a respectful distance. St. Peter, the head of the apostles, turns towards the others and points to him who is the Master and the Way of Christian prayer (cf. §2607): "Lord, teach us to pray" (*Lk* 11:1).

PART FOUR

CHRISTIAN PRAYER

SECTION ONE
PRAYER IN THE CHRISTIAN LIFE

2558   "Great is the mystery of the faith!" The Church professes this mystery in the Apostles' Creed (*Part One*) and celebrates it in the sacramental liturgy (*Part Two*), so that the life of the faithful may be conformed to Christ in the Holy Spirit to the glory of God the Father (*Part Three*). This mystery, then, requires that the faithful believe in it, that they celebrate it, and that they live from it in a vital and personal relationship with the living and true God. This relationship is prayer.

WHAT IS PRAYER?

> For me, prayer is a surge of the heart; it is a simple look turned toward heaven, it is a cry of recognition and of love, embracing both trial and joy.[1]

Prayer as God's gift

2559   "Prayer is the raising of one's mind and heart to God or the requesting of good things from God."[2] But when we pray, do we speak from the height of our pride and will, or "out of the depths" of a humble and contrite heart?[3] He who humbles himself will be exalted;[4] *humility* is the foundation of prayer. Only when we humbly acknowledge that "we do not know how to pray as we   *2613* *2763*

---

1   St. Thérèse of Lisieux, *Manuscrits autobiographiques*, C 25r.
2   St. John Damascene, *De fide orth.* 3, 24: PG 94, 1089C.
3   *Ps* 130:1.
4   Cf. *Lk* 18:9-14.

ought,"[5] are we ready to receive freely the gift of prayer. "Man is a beggar before God."[6]

2560   "If you knew the gift of God!"[7] The wonder of prayer is revealed beside the well where we come seeking water: there, Christ comes to meet every human being. It is he who first seeks us and asks us for a drink. Jesus thirsts; his asking arises from the depths of God's desire for us. Whether we realize it or not, prayer is the encounter of God's thirst with ours. God thirsts that we may thirst for him.[8]

2561   "You would have asked him, and he would have given you living water."[9] Paradoxically our prayer of petition is a response to the plea of the living God: "They have forsaken me, the fountain of living waters, and hewn out cisterns for themselves, broken cisterns that can hold no water!"[10] Prayer is the response of faith to the free promise of salvation and also a response of love to the thirst of the only Son of God.[11]

Prayer as covenant

2562   Where does prayer come from? Whether prayer is expressed in words or gestures, it is the whole man who prays. But in naming the source of prayer, Scripture speaks sometimes of the soul or the spirit, but most often of the heart (more than a thousand times). According to Scripture, it is the *heart* that prays. If our heart is far from God, the words of prayer are in vain.

2563   The heart is the dwelling-place where I am, where I live; according to the Semitic or Biblical expression, the heart is the place "to which I withdraw." The heart is our hidden center, beyond the grasp of our reason and of others; only the Spirit of God can fathom the human heart and know it fully. The heart is the place of decision, deeper than our psychic drives. It is the place of truth, *2699* where we choose life or death. It is the place of encounter, because *1696* as image of God we live in relation: it is the place of covenant.

---

5   *Rom* 8:26.
6   St. Augustine, *Sermo* 56, 6, 9: PL 38, 381.
7   *Jn* 4:10.
8   Cf. St. Augustine, *De diversis quaestionibus octoginta tribus* 64, 4: PL 40, 56.
9   *Jn* 4:10.
10 *Jer* 2:13.
11 Cf. *Jn* 7:37-39; 19:28; *Isa* 12:3; 51:1; *Zech* 12:10; 13:1.

2564　Christian prayer is a covenant relationship between God and man in Christ. It is the action of God and of man, springing forth from both the Holy Spirit and ourselves, wholly directed to the Father, in union with the human will of the Son of God made man.

Prayer as communion

2565　In the New Covenant, prayer is the living relationship of the children of God with their Father who is good beyond measure, with his Son Jesus Christ and with the Holy Spirit. The grace of the Kingdom is "the union of the entire holy and royal Trinity . . . with *260* the whole human spirit."[12] Thus, the life of prayer is the habit of being in the presence of the thrice-holy God and in communion with him. This communion of life is always possible because, through Baptism, we have already been united with Christ.[13] Prayer is *Christian* insofar as it is communion with Christ and extends throughout the Church, which is his Body. Its dimensions are those of Christ's love.[14]　　　　　　　　　　　　　　　　*792*

12　St. Gregory of Nazianzus, *Oratio*, 16, 9: PG 35, 945.
13　Cf. *Rom* 6:5.
14　Cf. *Eph* 3:18-21.

Chapter One
The Revelation of Prayer

THE UNIVERSAL CALL TO PRAYER

2566 *Man is in search of God.* In the act of creation, God calls every being from nothingness into existence. "Crowned with glory and
296 honor," man is, after the angels, capable of acknowledging "how majestic is the name of the Lord in all the earth."[1] Even after losing through his sin his likeness to God, man remains an image of his
355 Creator, and retains the desire for the one who calls him into existence.
28 All religions bear witness to men's essential search for God.[2]

2567 *God calls man first.* Man may forget his Creator or hide far from his face; he may run after idols or accuse the deity of having abandoned him; yet the living and true God tirelessly calls each
30 person to that mysterious encounter known as prayer. In prayer, the faithful God's initiative of love always comes first; our own first step is always a response. As God gradually reveals himself and
142 reveals man to himself, prayer appears as a reciprocal call, a covenant drama. Through words and actions, this drama engages the heart. It unfolds throughout the whole history of salvation.

ARTICLE 1
IN THE OLD TESTAMENT

2568 In the Old Testament, the revelation of prayer comes between the fall and the restoration of man, that is, between God's
410 sorrowful call to his first children: "Where are you? . . . What is this
1736 that you have done?"[3] and the response of God's only Son on coming into the world: "Lo, I have come to do your will, O God."[4] Prayer is bound up with human history, for it is the relationship
2738 with God in historical events.

---

1 *Ps* 8:5; 8:1.
2 Cf. *Acts* 17:27.
3 *Gen* 3:9, 13.
4 *Heb* 10:5-7.

Creation – source of prayer

2569   Prayer is lived in the first place beginning with the realities   *288*
of *creation*. The first nine chapters of Genesis describe this relationship with God as an offering of the first-born of Abel's flock, as the
invocation of the divine name at the time of Enosh, and as "walking
with God."[5] Noah's offering is pleasing to God, who blesses him   *58*
and through him all creation, because his heart was upright and
undivided; Noah, like Enoch before him, "walks with God."[6] This
kind of prayer is lived by many righteous people in all religions.

In his indefectible covenant with every living creature,[7] God
has always called people to prayer. But it is above all beginning with   *59*
our father Abraham that prayer is revealed in the Old Testament.

God's promise and the prayer of Faith

2570   When God calls him, Abraham goes forth "as the Lord had
told him";[8] Abraham's heart is entirely submissive to the Word and
so he obeys. Such attentiveness of the heart, whose decisions are   *145*
made according to God's will, is essential to prayer, while the
words used count only in relation to it. Abraham's prayer is
expressed first by deeds: a man of silence, he constructs an altar to
the Lord at each stage of his journey. Only later does Abraham's
first prayer in words appear: a veiled complaint reminding God of
his promises which seem unfulfilled.[9] Thus one aspect of the
drama of prayer appears from the beginning: the test of faith in the
fidelity of God.

2571   Because Abraham believed in God and walked in his
presence and in covenant with him,[10] the patriarch is ready to
welcome a mysterious Guest into his tent. Abraham's remarkable
hospitality at Mamre foreshadows the annunciation of the true Son   *494*
of the promise.[11] After that, once God had confided his plan,
Abraham's heart is attuned to his Lord's compassion for men and
he dares to intercede for them with bold confidence.[12]   *2635*

---

5 Cf. *Gen* 4:4, 26; *Gen* 5:24.
6 *Gen* 6:9; 8:20-9:17.
7 *Gen* 9:8-16.
8 *Gen* 12:4.
9 Cf. *Gen* 15:2 f.
10 Cf. *Gen* 15:6; 17:1 f.
11 Cf. *Gen* 18:1-15; *Lk* 1:26-38.
12 Cf. *Gen* 18:16-33.

2572   As a final stage in the purification of his faith, Abraham, "who had received the promises,"[13] is asked to sacrifice the son God had given him. Abraham's faith does not weaken ("God himself will provide the lamb for a burnt offering."), for he "considered that God was able to raise men even from the dead."[14] And so the father of believers is conformed to the likeness of the Father

603   who will not spare his own Son but will deliver him up for us all.[15] Prayer restores man to God's likeness and enables him to share in the power of God's love that saves the multitude.[16]

2573   God renews his promise to Jacob, the ancestor of the twelve tribes of Israel.[17] Before confronting his elder brother Esau, Jacob wrestles all night with a mysterious figure who refuses to reveal his name, but who blesses him before leaving him at dawn. From this account, the spiritual tradition of the Church has retained the symbol

162   of prayer as a battle of faith and as the triumph of perseverance.[18]

Moses and the prayer of the mediator

2574   Once the promise begins to be fulfilled (Passover, the Exodus, the gift of the Law, and the ratification of the covenant),

62   the prayer of Moses becomes the most striking example of intercessory prayer, which will be fulfilled in "the one mediator between God and men, the man Christ Jesus."[19]

205   **2575**   Here again the initiative is God's. From the midst of the burning bush he calls Moses.[20] This event will remain one of the primordial images of prayer in the spiritual tradition of Jews and Christians alike. When "the God of Abraham, of Isaac, and of Jacob" calls Moses to be his servant, it is because he is the living God who wants men to live. God reveals himself in order to save them, though he does not do this alone or despite them: he calls Moses to be his messenger, an associate in his compassion, his work of salvation. There is something of a divine plea in this mission, and only after long debate does Moses attune his own will to that of the Savior God. But in the dialogue in which God confides in him, Moses also learns how to pray: he balks, makes excuses, above all questions: and it is in

---

13   *Heb* 11:17.
14   *Gen* 22:8; *Heb* 11:19.
15   *Rom* 8:32.
16   Cf. *Rom* 8:16-21.
17   Cf. *Gen* 28:10-22.
18   Cf. *Gen* 32:24-30; *Lk* 18:1-8.
19   *1 Tim* 2:5.
20   *Ex* 3:1-10.

response to his question that the Lord confides his ineffable name, which will be revealed through his mighty deeds.

2576 "Thus the Lord used to speak to Moses face to face, as a man *555* speaks to his friend."[21] Moses' prayer is characteristic of contemplative prayer by which God's servant remains faithful to his mission. Moses converses with God often and at length, climbing the mountain to hear and entreat him and coming down to the people to repeat the words of his God for their guidance. Moses "is entrusted with all my house. With him I speak face to face, clearly, not in riddles," for "Moses was very humble, more so than anyone else on the face of the earth."[22]

2577 From this intimacy with the faithful God, slow to anger and abounding in steadfast love,[23] Moses drew strength and de- *210* termination for his intercession. He does not pray for himself but for the people whom God made his own. Moses already intercedes for them during the battle with the Amalekites and prays to obtain healing for Miriam.[24] But it is chiefly after their apostasy that Moses *2635* "stands in the breach" before God in order to save the people.[25] The arguments of his prayer – for intercession is also a mysterious battle – will inspire the boldness of the great intercessors among the Jewish people and in the Church: God is love; he is therefore righteous and faithful; he cannot contradict himself; he must re- *214* member his marvellous deeds, since his glory is at stake, and he cannot forsake this people that bears his name.

David and the prayer of the king

2578 The prayer of the People of God flourishes in the shadow of God's dwelling place, first the ark of the covenant and later the Temple. At first the leaders of the people – the shepherds and the prophets – teach them to pray. The infant Samuel must have learned from his mother Hannah how "to stand before the LORD" and from the priest Eli how to listen to his word: "Speak, LORD, for your servant is listening."[26] Later, he will also know the cost and consequence of intercession: "Moreover, as for me, far be it from me that I should sin against the LORD by ceasing to pray for you; and I will instruct you in the good and the right way."[27]

---

21 *Ex* 33:11.
22 *Num* 12:3, 7-8.
23 Cf. *Ex* 34:6.
24 Cf. *Ex* 17:8-12; *Num* 12:13-14.
25 *Ps* 106:23; cf. *Ex* 32:1-34:9.
26 *1 Sam* 3:9-10; cf. 1:9-18.

709 **2579**   David is par excellence the king "after God's own heart," the shepherd who prays for his people and prays in their name. His submission to the will of God, his praise, and his repentance, will be a model for the prayer of the people. His prayer, the prayer of God's Anointed, is a faithful adherence to the divine promise *436* and expresses a loving and joyful trust in God, the only King and Lord.[28] In the Psalms David, inspired by the Holy Spirit, is the first prophet of Jewish and Christian prayer. The prayer of Christ, the true Messiah and Son of David, will reveal and fulfill the meaning of this prayer.

583 **2580**   The Temple of Jerusalem, the house of prayer that David wanted to build, will be the work of his son, Solomon. The prayer at the dedication of the Temple relies on God's promise and covenant, on the active presence of his name among his People, recalling his mighty deeds at the Exodus.[29] The king lifts his hands toward heaven and begs the Lord, on his own behalf, on behalf of the entire people, and of the generations yet to come, for the forgiveness of their sins and for their daily needs, so that the nations may know that He is the only God and that the heart of his people may belong wholly and entirely to him.

Elijah, the prophets and conversion of heart

2581   For the People of God, the Temple was to be the place of their education in prayer: pilgrimages, feasts and sacrifices, the evening offering, the incense, and the bread of the Presence *1150* ("shewbread") – all these signs of the holiness and glory of God Most High and Most Near were appeals to and ways of prayer. But ritualism often encouraged an excessively external worship. The people needed education in faith and conversion of heart; this was the mission of the prophets, both before and after the Exile.

2582   Elijah is the "father" of the prophets, "the generation of those who seek him, who seek the face of the God of Jacob."[30] Elijah's name, "The Lord is my God," foretells the people's cry in response to his prayer on Mount Carmel.[31] St. James refers to Elijah in order to encourage us to pray: "The prayer of the righteous is powerful and effective."[32]

---

27   *1 Sam* 12:23.
28   Cf. *2 Sam* 7:18-29.
29   *1 Kings* 8:10-61.
30   *Ps* 24:6.
31   *1 Kings* 18:39.
32   *Jas* 5:16b-18.

2583 After Elijah had learned mercy during his retreat at the Wadi Cherith, he teaches the widow of Zarephath to believe in The Word of God and confirms her faith by his urgent prayer: God brings the widow's child back to life.[33]

The sacrifice on Mount Carmel is a decisive test for the faith of the People of God. In response to Elijah's plea, "Answer me, O LORD, answer me," the Lord's fire consumes the holocaust, *696* at the time of the evening oblation. The Eastern liturgies repeat Elijah's plea in the Eucharistic *epiclesis*.

Finally, taking the desert road that leads to the place where the living and true God reveals himself to his people, Elijah, like Moses before him, hides "in a cleft of he rock" until the mysterious presence of God has passed by.[34] But only on the mountain of the Transfiguration will Moses and Elijah behold the unveiled face of *555* him whom they sought; "the light of the knowledge of the glory of God [shines] in the face of Christ," crucified and risen.[35]

2584 In their "one to one" encounters with God, the prophets *2709* draw light and strength for their mission. Their prayer is not flight from this unfaithful world, but rather attentiveness to The Word of God. At times their prayer is an argument or a complaint, but it is always an intercession that awaits and prepares for the intervention of the Savior God, the Lord of history.[36]

The Psalms, the prayer of the assembly

2585 From the time of David to the coming of the Messiah texts appearing in these sacred books show a deepening in prayer for oneself and in prayer for others.[37] Thus the psalms were gradually *1093* collected into the five books of the Psalter (or "Praises"), the masterwork of prayer in the Old Testament.

2586 The Psalms both nourished and expressed the prayer of the People of God gathered during the great feasts at Jerusalem and each Sabbath in the synagogues. Their prayer is inseparably personal and communal; it concerns both those who are praying and all men. The Psalms arose from the communities of the Holy Land and the Diaspora, but embrace all creation. Their prayer recalls the saving events of the past, yet extends into the future, even to the

---

33 Cf. *1 Kings* 17:7-24.
34 Cf. *1 Kings* 19:1-14; cf. *Ex* 33:19-23.
35 *2 Cor* 4:6; cf. *Lk* 9:30-35.
36 Cf. *Am* 7:2, 5; *Isa* 6:5, 8, 11; *Jer* 1:6; 15:15-18; 20:7-18.
37 *Ezra* 9:6-15; *Neh* 1:4-11; *Jon* 2:3-10; *Tob* 3:11-16; *Jdt* 9:2- 14.

end of history; it commemorates the promises God has already kept, and awaits the Messiah who will fulfill them definitively. Prayed by Christ and fulfilled in him, the Psalms remain essential
1177   to the prayer of the Church.[38]

2587   The Psalter is the book in which The Word of God becomes man's prayer. In other books of the Old Testament, "the words proclaim [God's] works and bring to light the mystery they contain."[39] The words of the Psalmist, sung for God, both express and acclaim the Lord's saving works; the same Spirit inspires both God's work and man's response. Christ will unite the two. In him,
2641   the psalms continue to teach us how to pray.

2588   The Psalter's many forms of prayer take shape both in the liturgy of the Temple and in the human heart. Whether hymns or prayers of lamentation or thanksgiving, whether individual or communal, whether royal chants, songs of pilgrimage or wisdom-meditations, the Psalms are a mirror of God's marvelous deeds in the history of his people, as well as reflections of the human experiences of the Psalmist. Though a given psalm may reflect an event of the past, it still possesses such direct simplicity that it can be prayed in truth by men of all times and conditions.

2589   Certain constant characteristics appear throughout the Psalms: simplicity and spontaneity of prayer; the desire for God himself through and with all that is good in his creation; the distraught situation of the believer who, in his preferential love for the Lord, is exposed to a host of enemies and temptations, but who waits upon what the faithful God will do, in the certitude of his
304   love and in submission to his will. The prayer of the psalms is always sustained by praise; that is why the title of this collection as handed down to us is so fitting: "The Praises." Collected for the assembly's worship, the Psalter both sounds the call to prayer and sings the response to that call: *Hallelu-Yah!* ("Alleluia"), "Praise the Lord!"

> What is more pleasing than a psalm? David expresses it well: "Praise the Lord, for a psalm is good: let there be praise of our God with gladness and grace!" Yes, a psalm is a blessing on the lips of the people, praise of God, the assembly's homage, a general acclamation, a word that speaks for all, the voice of the Church, a confession of faith in song.[40]

---

38   Cf. GILH, nn. 100-109.
39   *DV* 2.
40   St. Ambrose, *In psalmum 1 enarratio*, 1, 9: PL 14, 924; *LH*, Saturday, wk 10, OR.

IN BRIEF

2590 "Prayer is the raising of one's mind and heart to God or the requesting of good things from God" (St. John Damascene, *De fide orth.* 3, 24: PG 94, 1089C).

2591 God tirelessly calls each person to this mysterious encounter with Himself. Prayer unfolds throughout the whole history of salvation as a reciprocal call between God and man.

2592 The prayer of Abraham and Jacob is presented as a battle of faith marked by trust in God's faithfulness and by certitude in the victory promised to perseverance.

2593 The prayer of Moses responds to the living God's initiative for the salvation of his people. It foreshadows the prayer of intercession of the unique mediator, Christ Jesus.

2594 The prayer of the People of God flourished in the shadow of the dwelling place of God's presence on earth, the ark of the covenant and the Temple, under the guidance of their shepherds, especially King David, and of the prophets.

2595 The prophets summoned the people to conversion of heart and, while zealously seeking the face of God, like Elijah, they interceded for the people.

2596 The Psalms constitute the masterwork of prayer in the Old Testament. They present two inseparable qualities: the personal, and the communal. They extend to all dimensions of history, recalling God's promises already fulfilled and looking for the coming of the Messiah.

2597 Prayed and fulfilled in Christ, the Psalms are an essential and permanent element of the prayer of the Church. They are suitable for men of every condition and time.

ARTICLE 2
IN THE FULLNESS OF TIME

2598   The drama of prayer is fully revealed to us in the Word who became flesh and dwells among us. To seek to understand his prayer through what his witnesses proclaim to us in the Gospel is to approach the holy Lord Jesus as Moses approached the burning bush: first to contemplate him in prayer, then to hear how he teaches us to pray, in order to know how he hears our prayer.

Jesus prays

470   **2599**   The Son of God who became Son of the Virgin learned to pray in his human heart. He learns to pray from his mother, who kept all the great things the Almighty had done and treasured them in her heart.[41] He learns to pray in the words and rhythms of the prayer of his people, in the synagogue at Nazareth and the Temple
584   at Jerusalem. But his prayer springs from an otherwise secret source, as he intimates at the age of twelve: "I must be in my Father's house."[42] Here the newness of prayer in the fullness of time begins to be revealed: his *filial prayer*, which the Father awaits
534   from his children, is finally going to be lived out by the only Son in his humanity, with and for men.

2600   The Gospel according to St. Luke emphasizes the action of the Holy Spirit and the meaning of prayer in Christ's ministry. Jesus prays *before* the decisive moments of his mission: before his
535, 554   Father's witness to him during his baptism and Transfiguration, and before his own fulfillment of the Father's plan of love by his
612   Passion.[43] He also prays before the decisive moments involving the mission of his apostles: at his election and call of the Twelve, before
858, 443   Peter's confession of him as "the Christ of God," and again that the faith of the chief of the Apostles may not fail when tempted.[44] Jesus' prayer before the events of salvation that the Father has asked him to fulfill is a humble and trusting commitment of his human will to the loving will of the Father.

---

41   Cf. *Lk* 1:49; 2:19; 2:51.
42   *Lk* 2:49.
43   Cf. *Lk* 3:21; 9:28; 22:41-44.
44   Cf. *Lk* 6:12; 9:18-20; 22:32.

2601   "He was praying in a certain place and when he had ceased, one of his disciples said to him, 'Lord, teach us to pray.'"[45] In seeing the Master at prayer the disciple of Christ also wants to pray. By *contemplating* and hearing the Son, the master of prayer, the children learn to pray to the Father.

2765

2602   Jesus often draws apart to pray *in solitude*, on a mountain, preferably at night.[46] *He includes all men* in his prayer, for he has taken on humanity in his incarnation, and he offers them to the Father when he offers himself. Jesus, the Word who has become flesh, shares by his human prayer in all that "his brethren" experience; he sympathizes with their weaknesses in order to free them.[47] It was for this that the Father sent him. His words and works are the visible manifestation of his prayer in secret.

616

2603   The evangelists have preserved two more explicit prayers offered by Christ during his public ministry. Each begins with thanksgiving. In the first, Jesus confesses the Father, acknowledges, and blesses him because he has hidden the mysteries of the Kingdom from those who think themselves learned and has revealed them to infants, the poor of the Beatitudes.[48] His exclamation, "Yes, Father!" expresses the depth of his heart, his adherence to the Father's "good pleasure," echoing his mother's *Fiat* at the time of his conception and prefiguring what he will say to the Father in his agony. The whole prayer of Jesus is contained in this loving adherence of his human heart to the mystery of the will of the Father.[49]

2673

2546

494

2604   The second prayer, before the raising of Lazarus, is recorded by St. John.[50] Thanksgiving precedes the event: "Father, I thank you for having heard me," which implies that the Father always hears his petitions. Jesus immediately adds: "I know that you always hear me," which implies that Jesus, on his part, *constantly made such petitions*. Jesus' prayer, characterized by thanksgiving, reveals to us how to ask: *before* the gift is given, Jesus commits himself to the One who in giving gives himself. The Giver is more precious than the gift; he is the "treasure"; in him abides his Son's heart; the gift is given "as well."[51]

478

---

45   *Lk* 11:1.
46   Cf. *Mk* 1:35; 6:46; *Lk* 5:16.
47   Cf. *Heb* 2:12, 15; 4:15.
48   Cf. *Mt* 11:25-27 and *Lk* 10:21-23.
49   Cf. *Eph* 1:9.
50   Cf. *Jn* 11:41-42.
51   *Mt* 6:21, 33.

2746   The priestly prayer of Jesus holds a unique place in the economy of salvation.[52] A meditation on it will conclude Section One. It reveals the ever present prayer of our High Priest and, at the same time, contains what he teaches us about our prayer to our Father, which will be developed in Section Two.

2605   When the hour had come for him to fulfill the Father's plan of love, Jesus allows a glimpse of the boundless depth of his filial prayer, not only before he freely delivered himself up (*"Abba . . .* not my will, but yours."),[53] but even in *his last words* on the Cross, where prayer and the gift of self are but one: "Father, forgive them, for they *614* know not what they do";[54] "Truly, I say to you, today you will be with me in Paradise";[55] "Woman, behold your son" – "Behold your mother";[56] "I thirst.";[57] "My God, My God, why have you forsaken me?";[58] "It is finished";[59] "Father, into your hands I commit my spirit!"[60] until the "loud cry" as he expires, giving up his spirit.[61]

403 **2606**   All the troubles, for all time, of humanity enslaved by sin and death, all the petitions and intercessions of salvation history are summed up in this cry of the incarnate Word. Here the Father *653* accepts them and, beyond all hope, answers them by raising his Son. Thus is fulfilled and brought to completion the drama of prayer in the economy of creation and salvation. The Psalter gives *2587* us the key to prayer in Christ. In the "today" of the Resurrection the Father says: "You are my Son, today I have begotten you. Ask of me, and I will make the nations your heritage, and the ends of the earth your possession."[62]

> *The Letter to the Hebrews* expresses in dramatic terms how the prayer of Jesus accomplished the victory of salvation: "In the days of his flesh, Jesus offered up prayers and supplications, with loud cries and tears, to him who was able to save him from death, and he was heard for his godly fear. Although he was a Son, he learned obedience through what he suffered, and being made perfect, he became the source of eternal salvation to all who obey him."[63]

---

52   Cf. *Jn* 17.
53   *Lk* 22:42.
54   *Lk* 23:34.
55   *Lk* 23:43.
56   *Jn* 19:26-27.
57   *Jn* 19:28.
58   *Mk* 15:34; cf. *Ps* 22:2.
59   *Jn* 19:30.
60   *Lk* 23:46.
61   Cf. *Mk* 15:37; *Jn* 19:30b.
62   *Ps* 2:7-8; cf. *Acts* 13:33.
63   *Heb* 5:7-9.

Jesus teaches us how to pray

2607   When Jesus prays he is already teaching us how to pray. *520*
His prayer to his Father is the theologal path (the path of faith,
hope, and charity) of our prayer to God. But the Gospel also gives
us Jesus' explicit teaching on prayer. Like a wise teacher he takes
hold of us where we are and leads us progressively toward the
Father. Addressing the crowds following him, Jesus builds on what
they already know of prayer from the Old Covenant and opens to
them the newness of the coming Kingdom. Then he reveals this
newness to them in parables. Finally, he will speak openly of the
Father and the Holy Spirit to his disciples who will be the teachers
of prayer in his Church.

2608   From the *Sermon on the Mount* onwards, Jesus insists on *541*
conversion of heart: reconciliation with one's brother before present- *1430*
ing an offering on the altar, love of enemies, and prayer for persecutors, prayer to the Father in secret, not heaping up empty
phrases, prayerful forgiveness from the depths of the heart, purity
of heart, and seeking the Kingdom before all else.[64] This filial
conversion is entirely directed to the Father.

2609   Once committed to conversion, the heart learns to pray in *153*
faith. Faith is a filial adherence to God beyond what we feel and *1814*
understand. It is possible because the beloved Son gives us access
to the Father. He can ask us to "seek" and to "knock," since he
himself is the door and the way.[65]

2610   Just as Jesus prays to the Father and gives thanks before
receiving his gifts, so he teaches us *filial boldness*: "Whatever you
ask in prayer, believe that you receive it, and you will."[66] Such is
the power of prayer and of faith that does not doubt: "all things are
possible to him who believes."[67] Jesus is as saddened by the "lack
of faith" of his own neighbors and the "little faith" of his own *165*
disciples[68] as he is struck with admiration at the great faith of the
Roman centurion and the Canaanite woman.[69]

2611   The prayer of faith consists not only in saying "Lord,
Lord," but in disposing the heart to do the will of the Father.[70] Jesus *2827*

---

64   Cf. *Mt* 5:23-24, 44-45; 6:7, 14-15, 21, 25, 33.
65   Cf. *Mt* 7:7-11, 13-14.
66   *Mk* 11:24.
67   *Mk* 9:23; cf. *Mt* 21:22.
68   Cf. *Mk* 6:6; *Mt* 8:26.
69   Cf. *Mt* 8:10; 15:28.
70   Cf. *Mt* 7:21.

calls his disciples to bring into their prayer this concern for cooperating with the divine plan.[71]

2612   In Jesus "the Kingdom of God is at hand."[72] He calls his
hearers to conversion and faith, but also to *watchfulness*. In prayer
672 the disciple keeps watch, attentive to Him Who Is and Him Who
Comes, in memory of his first coming in the lowliness of the flesh,
and in the hope of his second coming in glory.[73] In communion
2725 with their Master, the disciples' prayer is a battle; only by keeping
watch in prayer can one avoid falling into temptation.[74]

546 **2613**   Three principal *parables* on prayer are transmitted to us by St.
Luke:

– The first, "the importunate friend,"[75] invites us to urgent prayer: "Knock,
and it will be opened to you." To the one who prays like this, the heavenly
Father will "give whatever he needs," and above all the Holy Spirit who
contains all gifts.

– The second, "the importunate widow,"[76] is centered on one of the
qualities of prayer: it is necessary to pray always without ceasing and with
the *patience* of faith. "And yet, when the Son of Man comes, will he find
faith on earth?"

2559 – The third parable, "the Pharisee and the tax collector,"[77] concerns the
humility of the heart that prays. "God, be merciful to me a sinner!" The
Church continues to make this prayer its own: *Kyrie eleison!*

2614   When Jesus openly entrusts to his disciples the mystery of
prayer to the Father, he reveals to them what their prayer and ours
must be, once he has returned to the Father in his glorified human-
434 ity. What is new is to "ask *in his name*."[78] Faith in the Son introduces
the disciples into the knowledge of the Father, because Jesus is "the
way, and the truth, and the life."[79] Faith bears its fruit in love: it
means keeping the word and the commandments of Jesus, it means
abiding with him in the Father who, in him, so loves us that he
abides with us. In this new covenant the certitude that our petitions
will be heard is founded on the prayer of Jesus.[80]

---

71   Cf. *Mt* 9:38; *Lk* 10:2; *Jn* 4:34.
72   *Mk* 1:15.
73   Cf. *Mk* 13; *Lk* 21:34-36.
74   Cf. *Lk* 22:40, 46.
75   Cf. *Lk* 11:5-13.
76   Cf. *Lk* 18:1-8.
77   Cf. *Lk* 18:9-14.
78   *Jn* 14:13.
79   *Jn* 14:6.
80   Cf. *Jn* 14:13-14.

2615 Even more, what the Father gives us when our prayer is *728* united with that of Jesus is "another Counselor, to be with you for ever, even the Spirit of truth."[81] This new dimension of prayer and of its circumstances is displayed throughout the farewell discourse.[82] In the Holy Spirit, Christian prayer is a communion of love with the Father, not only through Christ but also *in him*: "Hitherto you have asked nothing in my name; ask, and you will receive, that your joy may be full."[83]

Jesus hears our prayer

2616 Prayer *to Jesus* is answered by him already during his ministry, through signs that anticipate the power of his death and Resurrection: Jesus hears the prayer of faith, expressed in words (the leper, *548* Jairus, the Canaanite woman, the good thief)[84] or in silence (the bearers of the paralytic, the woman with a hemorrhage who touches his clothes, the tears and ointment of the sinful woman).[85] The urgent request of the blind men, "Have mercy on us, Son of David" or "Jesus, Son of David, have mercy on me!" has been renewed in the traditional prayer to Jesus known as the *Jesus Prayer*: "Lord Jesus Christ, Son of God, have mercy on me, a sinner!"[86] Healing infirmities or forgiving *2667* sins, Jesus always responds to a prayer offered in faith: "Your faith has made you well; go in peace."

> St. Augustine wonderfully summarizes the three dimensions of Jesus' prayer: "He prays for us as our priest, prays in us as our Head, and is prayed to by us as our God. Therefore let us acknowledge our voice in him and his in us."[87]

---

81 *Jn* 14:16-17.
82 Cf. *Jn* 14:23-26; 15:7, 16; 16:13-15; 16:23-27.
83 *Jn* 16:24.
84 Cf. *Mk* 1:40-41; 5:36; 7:29; Cf. *Lk* 23:39-43.
85 Cf. *Mk* 2:5; 5:28; *Lk* 7:37-38.
86 *Mt* 9:27; *Mk* 10:48.
87 St. Augustine, *En. in Ps.* 85, 1: PL 37, 1081; cf. GILH 7.

The prayer of the Virgin Mary

148 **2617**   Mary's prayer is revealed to us at the dawning of the fullness of time. Before the incarnation of the Son of God, and before the outpouring of the Holy Spirit, her prayer cooperates in a unique way with the Father's plan of loving kindness: at the *494* Annunciation, for Christ's conception; at Pentecost, for the formation of the Church, his Body.[88] In the faith of his humble handmaid, the Gift of God found the acceptance he had awaited from the *490* beginning of time. She whom the Almighty made "full of grace" responds by offering her whole being: "Behold I am the handmaid of the Lord; let it be [done] to me according to your word." "*Fiat*": this is Christian prayer: to be wholly God's, because he is wholly ours.

2674 **2618**   The Gospel reveals to us how Mary prays and intercedes in faith. At Cana,[89] the mother of Jesus asks her son for the needs of a wedding feast; this is the sign of another feast – that of the wedding of the Lamb where he gives his body and blood at the request of the Church, his Bride. It is at the hour of the New Covenant, at the foot of the cross,[90] that Mary is heard as the *726* Woman, the new Eve, the true "Mother of all the living."

2619   That is why the Canticle of Mary,[91] the *Magnificat* (Latin) or *Megalynei* (Byzantine) is the song both of the Mother of God and of the Church; the song of the Daughter of Zion and of the new People of God; the song of thanksgiving for the fullness of graces *724* poured out in the economy of salvation and the song of the "poor" whose hope is met by the fulfillment of the promises made to our ancestors, "to Abraham and to his posterity for ever."

IN BRIEF

2620   Jesus' filial prayer is the perfect model of prayer in the New Testament. Often done in solitude and in secret, the prayer of Jesus involves a loving adherence to the will of the Father even to the Cross and an absolute confidence in being heard.

2621   In his teaching, Jesus teaches his disciples to pray with a purified heart, with lively and persevering faith,

---

88 Cf. *Lk* 1:38; *Acts* 1:14.
89 Cf. *Jn* 2:1-12.
90 Cf. *Jn* 19:25-27.
91 Cf. *Lk* 1:46-55.

with filial boldness. He calls them to vigilance and invites them to present their petitions to God in his name. Jesus Christ himself answers prayers addressed to him.

2622   The prayers of the Virgin Mary, in her Fiat and Magnificat, are characterized by the generous offering of her whole being in faith.

ARTICLE 3
IN THE AGE OF THE CHURCH

2623   On the day of Pentecost, the Spirit of the Promise was *731* poured out on the disciples, gathered "together in one place."[92] While awaiting the Spirit, "all these with one accord devoted themselves to prayer."[93] The Spirit who teaches the Church and recalls for her everything that Jesus said[94] was also to form her in the life of prayer.

2624   In the first community of Jerusalem, believers "devoted *1342* themselves to the apostles' teaching and fellowship, to the breaking of bread, and the prayers."[95] This sequence is characteristic of the Church's prayer: founded on the apostolic faith; authenticated by charity; nourished in the Eucharist.

2625   In the first place these are prayers that the faithful hear and read in the Scriptures, but also that they make their own – especially those of the Psalms, in view of their fulfillment in Christ.[96] The Holy Spirit, who thus keeps the memory of Christ alive in his *1092* Church at prayer, also leads her toward the fullness of truth and inspires new formulations expressing the unfathomable mystery of Christ at work in his Church's life, sacraments, and mission. These formulations are developed in the great liturgical and spiritual traditions. The *forms of prayer* revealed in the apostolic and *1200* canonical Scriptures remain normative for Christian prayer.

---

92   *Acts* 2:1.
93   *Acts* 1:14.
94   Cf. *Jn* 14:26.
95   *Acts* 2:42.
96   Cf. *Lk* 24:27, 44.

I.   BLESSING AND ADORATION

1078 **2626**   *Blessing* expresses the basic movement of Christian prayer: it is an encounter between God and man. In blessing, God's gift and man's acceptance of it are united in dialogue with each other. The prayer of blessing is man's response to God's gifts: because God blesses, the human heart can in return bless the One who is the source of every blessing.

1083 **2627**   Two fundamental forms express this movement: our prayer *ascends* in the Holy Spirit through Christ to the Father – we bless him for having blessed us;[97] it implores the grace of the Holy Spirit that *descends* through Christ from the Father – he blesses us.[98]

2096-2097 **2628**   *Adoration* is the first attitude of man acknowledging that he is a creature before his Creator. It exalts the greatness of the Lord who made us[99] and the almighty power of the Savior who sets us free from evil. Adoration is homage of the spirit to the "King of Glory,"[100] respectful silence in the presence of the "ever greater" God.[101] Adoration of the thrice-holy and sovereign God of love *2559* blends with humility and gives assurance to our supplications.

II.   PRAYER OF PETITION

2629   The vocabulary of supplication in the New Testament is rich in shades of meaning: ask, beseech, plead, invoke, entreat, cry out, even "struggle in prayer."[102] Its most usual form, because the most spontaneous, is petition: by prayer of petition we express awareness of our relationship with God. We are creatures who are *396* not our own beginning, not the masters of adversity, not our own last end. We are sinners who as Christians know that we have turned away from our Father. Our petition is already a turning back to him.

2630   The New Testament contains scarcely any prayers of lamentation, so frequent in the Old Testament. In the risen Christ the Church's *2090* petition is buoyed by hope, even if we still wait in a state of expectation and must be converted anew every day. Christian petition, what St. Paul calls "groaning," arises from another depth, that of creation "in labor pains" and that of ourselves "as we wait for the redemption of our bodies.

---

97   Cf. *Eph* 1:3-14; *2 Cor* 1:3-7; *1 Pet* 1:3-9.
98   Cf. *2 Cor* 13:14; *Rom* 15:5-6, 13; *Eph* 6:23-24.
99   Cf. *Ps* 95:1-6.
100 *Ps* 24, 9-10.
101 Cf. St. Augustine, *En. in Ps.* 62, 16: PL 36, 757-758.
102 Cf. *Rom* 15:30; *Col* 4:12.

For in this hope we were saved."[103] In the end, however, "with sighs too deep for words" the Holy Spirit "helps us in our weakness; for we do not know how to pray as we ought, but the Spirit himself intercedes for us with sighs too deep for words."[104]

2631   The first movement of the prayer of petition is *asking forgiveness*,   *2838* like the tax collector in the parable: "God, be merciful to me a sinner!"[105] It is a prerequisite for righteous and pure prayer. A trusting humility brings us back into the light of communion between the Father and his Son Jesus Christ and with one another, so that "we receive from him whatever we ask."[106] Asking forgiveness is the prerequisite for both the Eucharistic liturgy and personal prayer.

2632   Christian petition is centered on the desire and *search for*   *2816* *the Kingdom to come*, in keeping with the teaching of Christ.[107] There is a hierarchy in these petitions: we pray first for the Kingdom, then for what is necessary to welcome it and cooperate with its coming.   *1942* This collaboration with the mission of Christ and the Holy Spirit, which is now that of the Church, is the object of the prayer of the apostolic community.[108] It is the prayer of Paul, the apostle par excellence, which reveals to us how the divine solicitude for all the churches ought to inspire Christian prayer.[109] By prayer every   *2854* baptized person works for the coming of the Kingdom.

2633   When we share in God's saving love, we understand that   *2830* *every need* can become the object of petition. Christ, who assumed all things in order to redeem all things, is glorified by what we ask the Father in his name.[110] It is with this confidence that St. James and St. Paul exhort us to pray *at all times*.[111]

III.   PRAYER OF INTERCESSION

2634   Intercession is a prayer of petition which leads us to pray as Jesus did. He is the one intercessor with the Father on behalf of all men, especially sinners.[112] He is "able for all time to save those   *432* who draw near to God through him, since he always lives to make

---

103   *Rom* 8:22-24.
104   *Rom* 8:26.
105   *Lk* 18:13.
106   *1 Jn* 3:22; cf. 1:7-2:2.
107   Cf. *Mt* 6:10, 33; *Lk* 11:2, 13.
108   Cf. *Acts* 6:6; 13:3.
109   Cf. *Rom* 10:1; *Eph* 1:16-23; *Phil* 1:9-11; *Col* 1:3-6; 4:3-4, 12.
110   Cf. *Jn* 14:13.
111   Cf. *Jas* 1:5-8; *Eph* 5:20; *Phil* 4:6-7; *Col* 3:16-17; *1 Thess* 5:17-18.
112   Cf. *Rom* 8:34; *1 Jn* 2:1; *1 Tim* 2:5-8.

intercession for them."[113] The Holy Spirit "himself intercedes for us . . . and intercedes for the saints according to the will of God."[114]

2571 **2635** Since Abraham, intercession – asking on behalf of another – has been characteristic of a heart attuned to God's mercy. In the age of the Church, Christian intercession participates in Christ's, as an expression of the communion of saints. In intercession, he who prays looks "not only to his own interests, but also to the interests of others,"
2577 even to the point of praying for those who do him harm.[115]

2636 The first Christian communities lived this form of fellowship intensely.[116] Thus the Apostle Paul gives them a share in his ministry of preaching the Gospel[117] but also intercedes for them.[118] The intercession of Christians recognizes no boundaries: "for all
1900 men, for kings and all who are in high positions," for persecutors,
1037 for the salvation of those who reject the Gospel.[119]

IV.   Prayer of Thanksgiving

224 **2637** Thanksgiving characterizes the prayer of the Church which, in celebrating the Eucharist, reveals and becomes more fully
1328 what she is. Indeed, in the work of salvation, Christ sets creation free from sin and death to consecrate it anew and make it return to the Father, for his glory. The thanksgiving of the members of the
2603 Body participates in that of their Head.

2638 As in the prayer of petition, every event and need can become an offering of thanksgiving. The letters of St. Paul often begin and end with thanksgiving, and the Lord Jesus is always present in it: "Give thanks in all circumstances; for this is the will of God in Christ Jesus for you"; "Continue steadfastly in prayer, being watchful in it with thanksgiving."[120]

---

113 *Heb* 7:25.
114 *Rom* 8:26-27.
115 *Phil* 2:4; cf. *Acts* 7:60; *Lk* 23:28, 34.
116 Cf. *Acts* 12:5; 20:36; 21:5; *2 Cor* 9:14.
117 Cf. *Eph* 6:18-20; *Col* 4:3-4; *1 Thess* 5:25.
118 Cf. *2 Thess* 1:11; *Col* 1:3; *Phil* 1:3-4.
119 *1 Tim* 2:1; cf. *Rom* 12:14; 10:1.
120 *1 Thess* 5:18; *Col* 4:2.

V.   PRAYER OF PRAISE

2639   Praise is the form of prayer which recognizes most immediately that God is God. It lauds God for his own sake and gives him glory, quite beyond what he does, but simply because HE IS. It shares in the blessed happiness of the pure of heart who love God *213* in faith before seeing him in glory. By praise, the Spirit is joined to our spirits to bear witness that we are children of God,[121] testifying to the only Son in whom we are adopted and by whom we glorify the Father. Praise embraces the other forms of prayer and carries them toward him who is its source and goal: the "one God, the Father, from whom are all things and for whom we exist."[122]

2640   St. Luke in his gospel often expresses wonder and praise at the marvels of Christ and in his *Acts of the Apostles* stresses them as actions of the Holy Spirit: the community of Jerusalem, the invalid healed by Peter and John, the crowd that gives glory to God for that, and the pagans of Pisidia who "were glad and glorified the word of God."[123]

2641   "[Address] one another in psalms and hymns and spiritual songs, singing and making melody to the Lord with all your heart."[124] Like the inspired writers of the New Testament, the first Christian communities read the Book of Psalms in a new way, singing in it the mystery of Christ. In the newness of the Spirit, they also composed hymns and canticles in *2587* the light of the unheard-of event that God accomplished in his Son: his Incarnation, his death which conquered death, his Resurrection, and Ascension to the right hand of the Father.[125] Doxology, the praise of God, arises from this "marvelous work" of the whole economy of salvation.[126]

2642   The *Revelation* of "what must soon take place," the *Apocalypse*, is borne along by the songs of the heavenly liturgy[127] but also by the intercession of the "witnesses" (martyrs).[128] The prophets and the saints, *1137* all those who were slain on earth for their witness to Jesus, the vast throng of those who, having come through the great tribulation, have gone before us into the Kingdom, all sing the praise and glory of him who sits on the throne, and of the Lamb.[129] In communion with them, the Church on earth also sings these songs with faith in the midst of trial. By means of petition and intercession, faith hopes against all hope and gives thanks to the "Father of lights," from whom "every perfect gift" comes down.[130] Thus faith is pure praise.

---

121   Cf. *Rom* 8:16.
122   *1 Cor* 8:6.
123   *Acts* 2:47; 3:9; 4:21;13:48.
124   *Eph* 5:19; *Col* 3:16.
125   Cf. *Phil* 2:6-11; *Col* 1:15-20; *Eph* 5:14; *1 Tim* 3:16; 6:15-16; *2 Tim* 2:11-13.
126   Cf. *Eph* 1:3-14; *Rom* 16:25-27; *Eph* 3:20-21; *Jude* 24-25.
127   Cf. *Rev* 4:8-11; 5:9-14; 7:10-12.
128   *Rev* 6:10.
129   Cf. *Rev* 18:24; 19:1-8.
130   *Jas* 1:17.

2643   The Eucharist contains and expresses all forms of prayer:
it is "the pure offering" of the whole Body of Christ to the glory of
God's name[131] and, according to the traditions of East and West, it
1330   is *the* "sacrifice of praise."

IN BRIEF

2644   The Holy Spirit who teaches the Church and recalls to
her all that Jesus said also instructs her in the life of
prayer, inspiring new expressions of the same basic
forms of prayer: blessing, petition, intercession,
thanksgiving, and praise.

2645   Because God blesses the human heart, it can in return
bless him who is the source of every blessing.

2646   Forgiveness, the quest for the Kingdom, and every
true need are objects of the prayer of petition.

2647   Prayer of intercession consists in asking on behalf of
another. It knows no boundaries and extends to one's
enemies.

2648   Every joy and suffering, every event and need can
become the matter for thanksgiving which, sharing in
that of Christ, should fill one's whole life: "Give thanks
in all circumstances" (*1 Thess* 5:18).

2649   Prayer of praise is entirely disinterested and rises to God,
lauds him, and gives him glory for his own sake, quite
beyond what he has done, but simply because HE IS.

---

131   Cf. *Mal* 1:11.

CHAPTER TWO
THE TRADITION OF PRAYER

2650   Prayer cannot be reduced to the spontaneous outpouring
of interior impulse: in order to pray, one must have the will to pray.
Nor is it enough to know what the Scriptures reveal about prayer:
one must also learn how to pray. Through a living transmission
(Sacred Tradition) within "the believing and praying Church,"[1] the *75*
Holy Spirit teaches the children of God how to pray.

2651   The tradition of Christian prayer is one of the ways in which *94*
the tradition of faith takes shape and grows, especially through the
contemplation and study of believers who treasure in their hearts the
events and words of the economy of salvation, and through their
profound grasp of the spiritual realities they experience.[2]

ARTICLE 1
AT THE WELLSPRINGS OF PRAYER

2652   The Holy Spirit is the *living water* "welling up to eternal life"[3] *694*
in the heart that prays. It is he who teaches us to accept it at its source:
Christ. Indeed in the Christian life there are several wellsprings where
Christ awaits us to enable us to drink of the Holy Spirit.

The Word of God

2653   The Church "forcefully and specially exhorts all the Chris- *133*
tian faithful . . . to learn 'the surpassing knowledge of Jesus Christ'
(Phil 3:8) by frequent reading of the divine Scriptures. . . . Let them
remember, however, that prayer should accompany the reading of
Sacred Scripture, so that a dialogue takes place between God and
man. For 'we speak to him when we pray; we listen to him when *1100*
we read the divine oracles.'"[4]

2654   The spiritual writers, paraphrasing *Matthew* 7:7, summarize in this way the dispositions of the heart nourished by the word
of God in prayer: "Seek in reading and you will find in meditating;

---

1   *DV* 8.
2   Cf. *DV* 8.
3   *Jn* 4:14
4   *DV* 25; cf. *Phil* 3:8; St. Ambrose, *De officiis ministrorum* 1, 20, 88: PL 16, 50.

knock in mental prayer and it will be opened to you by contemplation."[5]

The Liturgy of the Church

1073 **2655**   In the sacramental liturgy of the Church, the mission of Christ and of the Holy Spirit proclaims, makes present, and communicates the mystery of salvation, which is continued in the heart
368 that prays. The spiritual writers sometimes compare the heart to an altar. Prayer internalizes and assimilates the liturgy during and after its celebration. Even when it is lived out "in secret,"[6] prayer is always prayer *of the Church*; it is a communion with the Holy Trinity.[7]

1812-1829 **The theological virtues**

2656   One enters into prayer as one enters into liturgy: by the narrow gate of *faith*. Through the signs of his presence, it is the Face of the Lord that we seek and desire; it is his Word that we want to hear and keep.

2657   The Holy Spirit, who instructs us to celebrate the liturgy in expectation of Christ's return, teaches us to pray in *hope*. Conversely, the prayer of the Church and personal prayer nourish hope in us. The psalms especially, with their concrete and varied language, teach us to fix our hope in God: "I waited patiently for the LORD; he inclined to me and heard my cry."[8] As St. Paul prayed: "May the God of hope fill you with all joy and peace in believing, so that by the power of the Holy Spirit you may abound in hope."[9]

2658   "Hope does not disappoint us, because God's *love* has been poured into our hearts by the Holy Spirit who has been given to us."[10] Prayer, formed by the liturgical life, draws everything into the love by which we are loved in Christ and which enables us to
826 respond to him by loving as he has loved us. Love is the source of

---

5   Guigo the Carthusian, *Scala Paradisi*: PL 40, 998.
6   Cf. *Mt* 6:6.
7   GILH 9.
8   *Ps* 40:2.
9   *Rom* 15:13.
10   *Rom* 5:5.

prayer; whoever draws from it reaches the summit of prayer. In the words of the Curé of Ars:

> I love you, O my God, and my only desire is to love you until the last breath of my life. I love you, O my infinitely lovable God, and I would rather die loving you, than live without loving you. I love you, Lord, and the only grace I ask is to love you eternally. . . . My God, if my tongue cannot say in every moment that I love you, I want my heart to repeat it to you as often as I draw breath.[11]

"Today"

2659   We learn to pray at certain moments by hearing the Word   *1165*
of the Lord and sharing in his Paschal mystery, but his Spirit is
offered us at all times, in the events of *each day*, to make prayer   *2837*
spring up from us. Jesus' teaching about praying to our Father is
in the same vein as his teaching about providence:[12] time is in the
Father's hands; it is in the present that we encounter him, not   *305*
yesterday nor tomorrow, but today: "O that *today* you would
hearken to his voice! Harden not your hearts."[13]

2660   Prayer in the events of each day and each moment is one
of the secrets of the kingdom revealed to "little children," to the
servants of Christ, to the poor of the Beatitudes. It is right and good   *2546*
to pray so that the coming of the kingdom of justice and peace may   *2632*
influence the march of history, but it is just as important to bring the
help of prayer into humble, everyday situations; all forms of prayer
can be the leaven to which the Lord compares the kingdom.[14]

IN BRIEF

2661   By a living transmission –Tradition – the Holy Spirit
in the Church teaches the children of God to pray.

2662   The Word of God, the liturgy of the Church, and the
virtues of faith, hope, and charity are sources of
prayer.

---

11   St. John Vianney, *Prayer.*
12   Cf. *Mt* 6:11, 34.
13   *Ps* 95:7-8.
14   Cf. *Lk* 13:20-21.

ARTICLE 2
THE WAY OF PRAYER

1201 **2663**   In the living tradition of prayer, each Church proposes to its faithful, according to its historic, social, and cultural context, a language for prayer: words, melodies, gestures, iconography. The Magisterium of the Church[15] has the task of discerning the fidelity of these ways of praying to the tradition of apostolic faith; it is for pastors and catechists to explain their meaning, always in relation to Jesus Christ.

Prayer to the Father

2664   There is no other way of Christian prayer than Christ. Whether our prayer is communal or personal, vocal or interior, it *2780* has access to the Father only if we pray "in the name" of Jesus. The sacred humanity of Jesus is therefore the way by which the Holy Spirit teaches us to pray to God our Father.

Prayer to Jesus

2665   The prayer of the Church, nourished by the Word of God and the celebration of the liturgy, teaches us to pray to the Lord *451* Jesus. Even though her prayer is addressed above all to the Father, it includes in all the liturgical traditions forms of prayer addressed to Christ. Certain psalms, given their use in the Prayer of the Church, and the New Testament place on our lips and engrave in our hearts prayer to Christ in the form of invocations: Son of God, Word of God, Lord, Savior, Lamb of God, King, Beloved Son, Son of the Virgin, Good Shepherd, our Life, our Light, our Hope, our Resurrection, Friend of mankind. . . .

2666   But the one name that contains everything is the one that *432* the Son of God received in his incarnation: JESUS. The divine name may not be spoken by human lips, but by assuming our humanity The Word of God hands it over to us and we can invoke it: "Jesus," "YHWH saves."[16] The name "Jesus" contains all: God and man and *435* the whole economy of creation and salvation. To pray "Jesus" is to invoke him and to call him within us. His name is the only one that contains the presence it signifies. Jesus is the Risen One, and

---

15   Cf. *DV* 10.
16   Cf. *Ex* 3:14; 33:19-23; *Mt* 1:21.

whoever invokes the name of Jesus is welcoming the Son of God who loved him and who gave himself up for him.[17]

2667   This simple invocation of faith developed in the tradition of prayer under many forms in East and West. The most usual formulation, transmitted by the spiritual writers of the Sinai, Syria, and Mt. Athos, is   *2616* the invocation, "Lord Jesus Christ, Son of God, have mercy on us sinners." It combines the Christological hymn of *Philippians* 2:6-11 with the cry of the publican and the blind men begging for light.[18] By it the heart is opened to human wretchedness and the Savior's mercy.

2668   The invocation of the holy name of Jesus is the simplest way of   *435* praying always. When the holy name is repeated often by a humbly attentive heart, the prayer is not lost by heaping up empty phrases,[19] but holds fast to the word and "brings forth fruit with patience."[20] This prayer is possible "at all times" because it is not one occupation among others but the only occupation: that of loving God, which animates and transfigures every action in Christ Jesus.

2669   The prayer of the Church venerates and honors the *Heart of Jesus*   *478* just as it invokes his most holy name. It adores the incarnate Word and his Heart which, out of love for men, he allowed to be pierced by our sins. Christian prayer loves to follow *the way of the cross* in the Savior's steps. The stations from the Praetorium to Golgotha and the tomb trace the way   *1674* of Jesus, who by his holy Cross has redeemed the world.

"Come, Holy Spirit"

2670   "No one can say 'Jesus is Lord' except by the Holy Spirit."[21]   *683* Every time we begin to pray to Jesus it is the Holy Spirit who draws us on the way of prayer by his prevenient grace. Since he teaches us   *2001* to pray by recalling Christ, how could we not pray to the Spirit too? That is why the Church invites us to call upon the Holy Spirit every day, especially at the beginning and the end of every important action.   *1310*

> If the Spirit should not be worshiped, how can he divinize me through Baptism? If he should be worshiped, should he not be the object of adoration?[22]

2671   The traditional form of petition to the Holy Spirit is to invoke the Father through Christ our Lord to give us the Consoler Spirit.[23] Jesus insists on this petition to be made in his name at the very moment

---

17   *Rom* 10:13; *Acts* 2:21; 3:15-16; *Gal* 2:20.
18   Cf. *Mk* 10:46-52; *Lk* 18:13.
19   Cf. *Mt* 6:7.
20   Cf. *Lk* 8:15.
21   *1 Cor* 12:3.
22   St. Gregory of Nazianzus, *Oratio*, 31, 28: PG 36, 165.
23   Cf. *Lk* 11:13.

when he promises the gift of the Spirit of Truth.[24] But the simplest and most direct prayer is also traditional, "Come, Holy Spirit," and every liturgical tradition has developed it in antiphons and hymns.

> Come, Holy Spirit, fill the hearts of your faithful and enkindle in them the fire of your love.[25]

> Heavenly King, Consoler Spirit, Spirit of Truth, present everywhere and filling all things, treasure of all good and source of all life, come dwell in us, cleanse and save us, you who are All-Good.[26]

695 **2672**   The Holy Spirit, whose anointing permeates our whole being, is the interior Master of Christian prayer. He is the artisan of the living tradition of prayer. To be sure, there are as many paths of prayer as there are persons who pray, but it is the same Spirit acting in all and with all. It is in the communion of the Holy Spirit that Christian prayer is prayer in the Church.

In communion with the holy Mother of God

689 **2673**   In prayer the Holy Spirit unites us to the person of the only Son, in his glorified humanity, through which and in which our filial prayer unites us in the Church with the Mother of Jesus.[27]

494 **2674**   Mary gave her consent in faith at the Annunciation and maintained it without hesitation at the foot of the Cross. Ever since, her motherhood has extended to the brothers and sisters of her Son "who still journey on earth surrounded by dangers and difficulties."[28] Jesus, the only mediator, is the way of our prayer; Mary, his mother and ours, is wholly transparent to him: she "shows the way" (*hodigitria*), and is herself "the Sign" of the way, according to the traditional iconography of East and West.

970 **2675**   Beginning with Mary's unique cooperation with the working of the Holy Spirit, the Churches developed their prayer to the holy Mother of God, centering it on the person of Christ manifested *512* in his mysteries. In countless hymns and antiphons expressing this prayer, two movements usually alternate with one another: the *2619* first "magnifies" the Lord for the "great things" he did for his lowly

---

24   Cf. *Jn* 14:17; 15:26; 16:13.
25   *Roman Missal*, Pentecost, Sequence.
26   Byzantine Liturgy, Pentecost Vespers, Troparion.
27   Cf. *Acts* 1:14.
28   *LG* 62.

servant and through her for all human beings;[29] the second entrusts the supplications and praises of the children of God to the Mother of Jesus, because she now knows the humanity which, in her, the Son of God espoused.

2676 This twofold movement of prayer to Mary has found a privileged expression in the *Ave Maria:*

Hail Mary [or Rejoice, Mary]: the greeting of the angel Gabriel 722 opens this prayer. It is God himself who, through his angel as intermediary, greets Mary. Our prayer dares to take up this greeting to Mary with the regard God had for the lowliness of his humble servant and to exult in the joy he finds in her.[30]

Full of grace, the Lord is with thee: These two phrases of the angel's 490 greeting shed light on one another. Mary is full of grace because the Lord is with her. The grace with which she is filled is the presence of him who is the source of all grace. "Rejoice . . . O Daughter of Jerusalem . . . the Lord your God is in your midst."[31] Mary, in whom the Lord himself has just made his dwelling, is the daughter of Zion in person, the ark of the covenant, the place where the glory of the Lord dwells. She is "the dwelling of God . . . with men."[32] Full of grace, Mary is wholly given over to him who has come to dwell in her and whom she is about to give to the world.

Blessed art thou among women and blessed is the fruit of thy womb, 435 *Jesus.* After the angel's greeting, we make Elizabeth's greeting our own. "Filled with the Holy Spirit," Elizabeth is the first in the long succession of generations who have called Mary "blessed."[33] "Blessed is she who believed. . . ."[34] Mary is "blessed among women" because she believed in the fulfillment of the Lord's word. Abraham, because of his faith, became 146 a blessing for all the nations of the earth.[35] Mary, because of her faith, became the mother of believers, through whom all nations of the earth receive him who is God's own blessing: Jesus, the "fruit of thy womb."

2677 *Holy Mary, Mother of God:* With Elizabeth we marvel, "And why 495 is this granted me, that the mother of my Lord should come to me?"[36] Because she gives us Jesus, her son, Mary is Mother of God and our mother; we can entrust all our cares and petitions to her: she prays for us as she prayed for herself: "Let it be to me according to your word."[37] By entrusting ourselves to her prayer, we abandon ourselves to the will of God together with her: "Thy will be done."

---

29 Cf. *Lk* 1:46-55.
30 Cf. *Lk* 1:48; *Zeph* 3:17b.
31 *Zeph* 3:14, 17a.
32 *Rev* 21:3.
33 *Lk* 1:41, 48.
34 *Lk* 1:45.
35 Cf. *Gen* 12:3.
36 *Lk* 1:43.
37 *Lk* 1:38.

Pray for us sinners, now and at the hour of our death: By asking Mary to pray for us, we acknowledge ourselves to be poor sinners and we address ourselves to the "Mother of Mercy," the All-Holy One. We give ourselves over to her now, in the Today of our lives. And our trust broadens further, already at the present moment, to surrender "the hour of our death" wholly to her care. May she be there as she was at her son's death on the cross. May she welcome us as our mother at the hour of our passing[38] to lead us to her son, Jesus, in paradise.

1020

971, 1674   **2678**   Medieval piety in the West developed the prayer of the rosary as a popular substitute for the Liturgy of the Hours. In the East, the litany called the *Akathistos* and the *Paraclesis* remained closer to the choral office in the Byzantine churches, while the Armenian, Coptic, and Syriac traditions preferred popular hymns and songs to the Mother of God. But in the *Ave Maria*, the *theotokia*, the hymns of St. Ephrem or St. Gregory of Narek, the tradition of prayer is basically the same.

967   **2679**   Mary is the perfect *Orans* (pray-er), a figure of the Church. When we pray to her, we are adhering with her to the plan of the Father, who sends his Son to save all men. Like the beloved disciple we welcome Jesus' mother into our homes,[39] for she has become the mother of all the living. We can pray with and to her. The prayer of the Church is sustained by the prayer of Mary and united with it in hope.[40]

972

IN BRIEF

2680   Prayer is primarily addressed to the Father; it can also be directed toward Jesus, particularly by the invocation of his holy name: "Lord Jesus Christ, Son of God, have mercy on us sinners."

2681   "No one can say 'Jesus is Lord', except by the Holy Spirit" (*1 Cor* 12:3). The Church invites us to invoke the Holy Spirit as the interior Teacher of Christian prayer.

2682   Because of Mary's singular cooperation with the action of the Holy Spirit, the Church loves to pray in communion with the Virgin Mary, to magnify with her the great things the Lord has done for her, and to entrust supplications and praises to her.

---

38   Cf. *Jn* 19:27.
39   Cf. *Jn* 19:27.
40   Cf. *LG* 68-69.

ARTICLE 3
GUIDES FOR PRAYER

A cloud of witnesses

2683   The witnesses who have preceded us into the kingdom,[41] especially those whom the Church recognizes as saints, share in the living tradition of prayer by the example of their lives, the transmission of their writings, and their prayer today. They contemplate God, praise him and constantly care for those whom they have left on earth. When they entered into the joy of their Master,   *956* they were "put in charge of many things."[42] Their intercession is their most exalted service to God's plan. We can and should ask them to intercede for us and for the whole world.

2684   In the communion of saints, many and varied *spiritualities*   *917* have been developed throughout the history of the churches. The personal charism of some witnesses to God's love for men has been handed on, like "the spirit" of Elijah to Elisha and John the Baptist,   *919* so that their followers may have a share in this spirit.[43] A distinct spirituality can also arise at the point of convergence of liturgical and theological currents, bearing witness to the integration of the faith into a particular human environment and its history. The   *1202* different schools of Christian spirituality share in the living tradition of prayer and are essential guides for the faithful. In their rich diversity they are refractions of the one pure light of the Holy Spirit.

> The Spirit is truly the dwelling of the saints and the saints are for the Spirit a place where he dwells as in his own home, since they offer themselves as a dwelling place for God and are called his temple.[44]

Servants of prayer

2685   The *Christian family* is the first place of education in prayer.   *1657* Based on the sacrament of marriage, the family is the "domestic church" where God's children learn to pray "as the Church" and to persevere in prayer. For young children in particular, daily family prayer is the first witness of the Church's living memory as awakened patiently by the Holy Spirit.

---

41   Cf. *Heb* 12:1.
42   Cf. *Mt* 25:21.
43   Cf. *2 Kings* 2:9; *Lk* 1:1; PC 2.
44   St. Basil, *De Spiritu Sancto*, 26, 62: PG 32, 184.

1547 **2686**   *Ordained ministers* are also responsible for the formation in prayer of their brothers and sisters in Christ. Servants of the Good Shepherd, they are ordained to lead the People of God to the living waters of prayer: the Word of God, the liturgy, the theologal life (the life of faith, hope, and charity), and the Today of God in concrete situations.[45]

916 **2687**   Many *religious* have consecrated their whole lives to prayer. Hermits, monks, and nuns since the time of the desert fathers have devoted their time to praising God and interceding for his people. The consecrated life cannot be sustained or spread without prayer; it is one of the living sources of contemplation and the spiritual life of the Church.

2688   The *catechesis* of children, young people, and adults aims at teaching them to meditate on The Word of God in personal prayer, practicing it in liturgical prayer, and internalizing it at all times in order to bear fruit in a new life. Catechesis is also a time
1674 for the discernment and education of popular piety.[46] The memorization of basic prayers offers an essential support to the life of prayer, but it is important to help learners savor their meaning.

2689   *Prayer groups*, indeed "schools of prayer," are today one of the signs and one of the driving forces of renewal of prayer in the Church, provided they drink from authentic wellsprings of Christian prayer. Concern for ecclesial communion is a sign of true prayer in the Church.

2690   The Holy Spirit gives to certain of the faithful the gifts of wisdom, faith and discernment for the sake of this common good which is prayer (*spiritual direction*). Men and women so endowed are true servants of the living tradition of prayer.

> According to St. John of the Cross, the person wishing to advance toward perfection should "take care into whose hands he entrusts himself, for as the master is, so will the disciple be, and as the father is so will be the son." And further: "In addition to being learned and discreet a director should be experienced. . . . If the spiritual director has no experience of the spiritual life, he will be incapable of leading into it the souls whom God is calling to it, and he will not even understand them."[47]

---

45 Cf. *PO* 4-6.
46 Cf. *CT* 54.
47 St. John of the Cross, *The Living Flame of Love*, stanza 3, 30, in *The Collected Works of St. John of the Cross*, eds K. Kavanaugh OCD and O. Rodriguez OCD (Washington DC: Institute of Carmelite Studies, 1979), 621.

Places favorable for prayer

2691   The church, the house of God, is the proper place for the *1181* liturgical prayer of the parish community. It is also the privileged *2097* place for adoration of the real presence of Christ in the Blessed *1379* Sacrament. The choice of a favorable place is not a matter of indifference for true prayer.

– For personal prayer, this can be a "prayer corner" with the Sacred Scriptures and icons, in order to be there, in secret, before our Father.[48] In a Christian family, this kind of little oratory fosters prayer in common.

– In regions where monasteries exist, the vocation of these commu- *1175* nities is to further the participation of the faithful in the Liturgy of the Hours and to provide necessary solitude for more intense personal prayer.[49]

– Pilgrimages evoke our earthly journey toward heaven and are *1674* traditionally very special occasions for renewal in prayer. For pilgrims seeking living water, shrines are special places for living the forms of Christian prayer "in Church."

IN BRIEF

2692   In prayer, the pilgrim Church is associated with that of the saints, whose intercession she asks.

2693   The different schools of Christian spirituality share in the living tradition of prayer and are precious guides for the spiritual life.

2694   The Christian family is the first place for education in prayer.

2695   Ordained ministers, the consecrated life, catechesis, prayer groups, and "spiritual direction" ensure assistance within the Church in the practice of prayer.

2696   The most appropriate places for prayer are personal or family oratories, monasteries, places of pilgrimage, and above all the church, which is the proper place for liturgical prayer for the parish community and the privileged place for Eucharistic adoration.

---

48 Cf. *Mt* 6:6.
49 Cf. *PC* 7.

CHAPTER THREE
THE LIFE OF PRAYER

2697 Prayer is the life of the new heart. It ought to animate us at every moment. But we tend to forget him who is our life and our all. This is why the Fathers of the spiritual life in the Deuteronomic and prophetic traditions insist that prayer is a remembrance of God often *1099* awakened by the memory of the heart: "We must remember God more often than we draw breath."[1] But we cannot pray "at all times" if we do not pray at specific times, consciously willing it. These are the special times of Christian prayer, both in intensity and duration.

1168 **2698** The Tradition of the Church proposes to the faithful certain rhythms of praying intended to nourish continual prayer. Some are daily, such as morning and evening prayer, grace before *1174* and after meals, the Liturgy of the Hours. Sundays, centered on the *2177* Eucharist, are kept holy primarily by prayer. The cycle of the liturgical year and its great feasts are also basic rhythms of the Christian's life of prayer.

2699 The Lord leads all persons by paths and in ways pleasing to him, and each believer responds according to his heart's resolve and the personal expressions of his prayer. However, Christian Tradition has retained three major expressions of prayer: vocal, meditative, and contemplative. They have one basic trait in com-
2563 mon: composure of heart. This vigilance in keeping the Word and dwelling in the presence of God makes these three expressions intense times in the life of prayer.

ARTICLE 1
EXPRESSIONS OF PRAYER

I.   VOCAL PRAYER

1176 **2700** Through his Word, God speaks to man. By words, mental or vocal, our prayer takes flesh. Yet it is most important that the heart should be present to him to whom we are speaking in prayer: "Whether or not our prayer is heard depends not on the number of words, but on the fervor of our souls."[2]

---

1   St. Gregory of Nazianzus, *Orat. theo.*, 27, 1, 4: PG 36, 16.
2   St. John Chrysostom, *Ecloga de oratione* 2: PG 63, 585.

2701   Vocal prayer is an essential element of the Christian life. To his disciples, drawn by their Master's silent prayer, Jesus teaches a vocal prayer, the Our Father. He not only prayed aloud the liturgical prayers of the synagogue but, as the Gospels show, *2603* he raised his voice to express his personal prayer, from exultant blessing of the Father to the agony of Gesthemani.[3]   *612*

2702   The need to involve the senses in interior prayer corresponds to a requirement of our human nature. We are body and spirit, and we experience the need to translate our feelings exter- *1146* nally. We must pray with our whole being to give all power possible to our supplication.

2703   This need also corresponds to a divine requirement. God seeks worshippers in Spirit and in Truth, and consequently living prayer that rises from the depths of the soul. He also wants the external expression that associates the body with interior prayer, for it renders him that perfect homage which is his due.   *2097*

2704   Because it is external and so thoroughly human, vocal prayer is the form of prayer most readily accessible to groups. Even interior prayer, however, cannot neglect vocal prayer. Prayer is internalized to the extent that we become aware of him "to whom we speak."[4] Thus vocal prayer becomes an initial form of contemplative prayer.

II.   Meditation

2705   Meditation is above all a quest. The mind seeks to understand *158* the why and how of the Christian life, in order to adhere and respond to what the Lord is asking. The required attentiveness is difficult to sustain. We are usually helped by books, and Christians do not want for them: the Sacred Scriptures, particularly the Gospels, holy icons, liturgical texts of the day or season, writings of the spiritual fathers, *127* works of spirituality, the great book of creation, and that of history – the page on which the "today" of God is written.

2706   To meditate on what we read helps us to make it our own by confronting it with ourselves. Here, another book is opened: the book of life. We pass from thoughts to reality. To the extent that we are humble and faithful, we discover in meditation the move-

---

3   Cf. *Mt* 11:25-26; *Mk* 14:36.
4   St. Teresa of Jesus, *The Way of Perfection* 26, 9 in *The Collected Works of St. Teresa of Avila*, tr. K. Kavanaugh, OCD, and O. Rodriguez, OCD (Washington DC: Institute of Carmelite Studies, 1980), II, 136.

ments that stir the heart and we are able to discern them. It is a question of acting truthfully in order to come into the light: "Lord, what do you want me to do?"

2690 **2707**   There are as many and varied methods of meditation as there are spiritual masters. Christians owe it to themselves to develop the desire to meditate regularly, lest they come to resemble the three first kinds of soil in the parable of the sower.[5] But a *2664* method is only a guide; the important thing is to advance, with the Holy Spirit, along the one way of prayer: Christ Jesus.

2708   Meditation engages thought, imagination, emotion, and desire. This mobilization of faculties is necessary in order to deepen our convictions of faith, prompt the conversion of our heart, and strengthen our will to follow Christ. Christian prayer tries above all to meditate on the mysteries of Christ, as in *lectio divina* or the *516* rosary. This form of prayerful reflection is of great value, but *2678* Christian prayer should go further: to the knowledge of the love of the Lord Jesus, to union with him.

III.   CONTEMPLATIVE PRAYER

2709   What is contemplative prayer? St. Teresa answers: "Contemplative prayer [*oración mental*] in my opinion is nothing else *2562-2564* than a close sharing between friends; it means taking time frequently to be alone with him who we know loves us."[6]
Contemplative prayer seeks him "whom my soul loves."[7] It is Jesus, and in him, the Father. We seek him, because to desire him is always the beginning of love, and we seek him in that pure faith which causes us to be born of him and to live in him. In this inner prayer we can still meditate, but our attention is fixed on the Lord himself.

2710   The choice of the *time and duration of the prayer* arises from a determined will, revealing the secrets of the heart. One does not *2726* undertake contemplative prayer only when one has the time: one makes time for the Lord, with the firm determination not to give up, no matter what trials and dryness one may encounter. One cannot always meditate, but one can always enter into inner prayer, independently of the conditions of health, work, or emo-

---

5 Cf. *Mk* 4:4-7, 15-19.
6 St. Teresa of Jesus, *The Book of Her Life*, 8, 5 in *The Collected Works of St. Teresa of Avila*, tr. K.Kavanaugh, OCD, and O. Rodriguez, OCD (Washington DC: Institute of Carmelite Studies, 1976), I, 67.
7 *Song* 1:7; cf. 3:1-4.

tional state. The heart is the place of this quest and encounter, in poverty and in faith.

2711   *Entering into contemplative prayer* is like entering into the Eucharistic liturgy: we "gather up" the heart, recollect our whole being under the prompting of the Holy Spirit, abide in the dwelling *1348* place of the Lord which we are, awaken our faith in order to enter into the presence of him who awaits us. We let our masks fall and turn our hearts back to the Lord who loves us, so as to hand ourselves over to him as an offering to be purified and transformed. *2100*

2712   Contemplative prayer is the prayer of the child of God, of the forgiven sinner who agrees to welcome the love by which he is loved and who wants to respond to it by loving even more.[8] But he knows that the love he is returning is poured out by the Spirit in his heart, for everything is grace from God. Contemplative prayer is the poor and humble surrender to the loving will of the Father in ever deeper union with his beloved Son.   *2822*

2713   Contemplative prayer is the simplest expression of the *2559* mystery of prayer. It is a *gift*, a grace; it can be accepted only in humility and poverty. Contemplative prayer is a *covenant* relationship established by God within our hearts.[9] Contemplative prayer is a *communion* in which the Holy Trinity conforms man, the image of God, "to his likeness."

2714   Contemplative prayer is also the pre-eminently *intense time* of prayer. In it the Father strengthens our inner being with power through his Spirit "that Christ may dwell in [our] hearts through faith" and we may be "grounded in love."[10]

2715   Contemplation is a *gaze* of faith, fixed on Jesus. "I look at him and he looks at me": this is what a certain peasant of Ars used to say to his holy curé about his prayer before the tabernacle. This focus on Jesus is a renunciation of self. His gaze purifies our heart; the light of the countenance of Jesus illumines the eyes of our heart and teaches us to see everything in the light of his truth and his compassion for all men. Contemplation also turns its gaze on the *521* mysteries of the life of Christ. Thus it learns the "interior knowledge of our Lord," the more to love him and follow him.[11]

---

8   Cf. *Lk* 7:36-50; 19:1-10.
9   Cf. *Jer* 31:33.
10 *Eph* 3:16-17.
11 Cf. St. Ignatius of Loyola, *Spiritual Exercises*, 104.

2716   Contemplative prayer is *hearing* the Word of God. Far from being passive, such attentiveness is the obedience of faith, the
494   unconditional acceptance of a servant, and the loving commitment of a child. It participates in the "Yes" of the Son become servant and the *Fiat* of God's lowly handmaid.

533   **2717**   Contemplative prayer is *silence*, the "symbol of the world to come"[12] or "silent love."[13] Words in this kind of prayer are not speeches; they are like kindling that feeds the fire of love. In this silence, unbearable to the "outer" man, the Father speaks to us his incarnate Word, who suffered, died, and rose; in this silence the
498   Spirit of adoption enables us to share in the prayer of Jesus.

2718   Contemplative prayer is a union with the prayer of Christ insofar as it makes us participate in his mystery. The mystery of Christ is celebrated by the Church in the Eucharist, and the Holy Spirit makes it come alive in contemplative prayer so that our charity will manifest it in our acts.

2719   Contemplative prayer is a communion of love bearing Life for the multitude, to the extent that it consents to abide in the night
165   of faith. The Paschal night of the Resurrection passes through the night of the agony and the tomb – the three intense moments of the Hour of Jesus which his Spirit (and not "the flesh [which] is weak") brings to life in prayer. We must be willing to "keep watch with
2730 [him] one hour."[14]

IN BRIEF

2720   The Church invites the faithful to regular prayer: daily prayers, the Liturgy of the Hours, Sunday Eucharist , the feasts of the liturgical year.

2721   The Christian tradition comprises three major expressions of the life of prayer: vocal prayer, meditation, and contemplative prayer. They have in common the recollection of the heart.

2722   Vocal prayer, founded on the union of body and soul in human nature, associates the body with the interior prayer of the heart, following Christ's example of

---

12 Cf. St. Isaac of Nineveh, *Tract. myst.* 66.
13 St. John of the Cross, *Maxims and Counsels*, 53 in *The Collected Works of St. John of the Cross*, tr. K. Kavanaugh, OCD, and O. Rodriguez, OCD (Washington DC: Institute of Carmelite Studies, 1979), 678.
14 Cf. *Mt* 26:40.

praying to his Father and teaching the Our Father to his disciples.

2723   Meditation is a prayerful quest engaging thought, imagination, emotion, and desire. Its goal is to make our own in faith the subject considered, by confronting it with the reality of our own life.

2724   Contemplative prayer is the simple expression of the mystery of prayer. It is a gaze of faith fixed on Jesus, an attentiveness to the Word of God, a silent love. It achieves real union with the prayer of Christ to the extent that it makes us share in his mystery.

ARTICLE 2
THE BATTLE OF PRAYER

2725   Prayer is both a gift of grace and a determined response on our part. It always presupposes effort. The great figures of prayer of the Old Covenant before Christ, as well as the Mother of God, the saints, and he himself, all teach us this: prayer is a battle. Against whom? Against ourselves and against the wiles of the tempter who *2612* does all he can to turn man away from prayer, away from union with *409* God. We pray as we live, because we live as we pray. If we do not want to act habitually according to the Spirit of Christ, neither can we pray habitually in his name. The "spiritual battle" of the Christian's new life is inseparable from the battle of prayer. *2015*

I.   OBJECTIONS TO PRAYER

2726   In the battle of prayer, we must face in ourselves and around us *erroneous notions of prayer*. Some people view prayer as a simple psychological activity, others as an effort of concentration to reach a mental void. Still others reduce prayer to ritual words and postures. Many Christians unconsciously regard prayer as an occupation that is incompatible with all the other things they have to do: they "don't have the time." Those who seek God by prayer *2710* are quickly discouraged because they do not know that prayer comes also from the Holy Spirit and not from themselves alone.

2727 We must also face the fact that certain attitudes deriving from the *mentality* of "this present world" can penetrate our lives if we are not vigilant. For example, some would have it that only

37 that is true which can be verified by reason and science; yet prayer is a mystery that overflows both our conscious and unconscious lives. Others overly prize production and profit; thus prayer, being unproductive, is useless. Still others exalt sensuality and comfort as the criteria of the true, the good, and the beautiful; whereas prayer, the "love of beauty" (*philokalia*), is caught up in the glory

2500 of the living and true God. Finally, some see prayer as a flight from the world in reaction against activism; but in fact, Christian prayer is neither an escape from reality nor a divorce from life.

2728 Finally, our battle has to confront what we experience as *failure in prayer*: discouragement during periods of dryness; sadness that, because we have "great possessions,"[15] we have not given all to the Lord; disappointment over not being heard according to our own will; wounded pride, stiffened by the indignity that is ours as sinners; our resistance to the idea that prayer is a free and unmerited gift; and so forth. The conclusion is always the same: what good does it do to pray? To overcome these obstacles, we must battle to gain humility, trust, and perseverance.

II.   HUMBLE VIGILANCE OF HEART

Facing difficulties in prayer

2729 The habitual difficulty in prayer is *distraction*. It can affect words and their meaning in vocal prayer; it can concern, more profoundly, him to whom we are praying, in vocal prayer (liturgical or personal), meditation, and contemplative prayer. To set about hunting down distractions would be to fall into their trap, when all that is necessary is to turn back to our heart: for a

2711 distraction reveals to us what we are attached to, and this humble awareness before the Lord should awaken our preferential love for him and lead us resolutely to offer him our heart to be purified. Therein lies the battle, the choice of which master to serve.[16]

2730 In positive terms, the battle against the possessive and dominating self requires *vigilance*, sobriety of heart. When Jesus insists on vigilance, he always relates it to himself, to his coming

2659 on the last day and every day: *today*. The bridegroom comes in the

---

15 Cf. *Mk* 10:22.
16 Cf. *Mt* 6:21, 24.

middle of the night; the light that must not be extinguished is that of faith: "'Come,' my heart says, 'seek his face!'"[17]

2731 Another difficulty, especially for those who sincerely want to pray, is *dryness*. Dryness belongs to contemplative prayer when the heart is separated from God, with no taste for thoughts, memories, and feelings, even spiritual ones. This is the moment of sheer faith clinging faithfully to Jesus in his agony and in his tomb. "Unless a grain of wheat falls into the earth and dies, it remains alone; but if it dies, it bears much fruit."[18] If dryness is due to the lack of roots, because the word has fallen on rocky soil, the battle requires conversion.[19]   *1426*

Facing temptations in prayer

2732 The most common yet most hidden temptation is our *lack of* *2609* *faith*. It expresses itself less by declared incredulity than by our actual preferences. When we begin to pray, a thousand labors or cares *2089* thought to be urgent vie for priority; once again, it is the moment of truth for the heart: what is its real love? Sometimes we turn to the Lord as a last resort, but do we really believe he is? Sometimes we enlist the Lord as an ally, but our heart remains presumptuous. In each case, our lack of faith reveals that we do not yet share in the disposition of a humble heart: "Apart from me, you can do *nothing*."[20]   *2092, 2074*

2733 Another temptation, to which presumption opens the *2094* gate, is *acedia*. The spiritual writers understand by this a form of depression due to lax ascetical practice, decreasing vigilance, carelessness of heart. "The spirit indeed is willing, but the flesh is weak."[21] The greater the height, the harder the fall. Painful as discouragement is, it is the reverse of presumption. The humble are not surprised by their distress; it leads them to trust more, to *2559* hold fast in constancy.

III.   FILIAL TRUST

2734 Filial trust is tested – it proves itself – in tribulation.[22] The principal difficulty concerns the *prayer of petition*, for oneself or for *2629* others in intercession. Some even stop praying because they think

---

17 *Ps* 27:8.
18 *Jn* 12:24.
19 Cf. *Lk* 8:6, 13.
20 *Jn* 15:5.
21 *Mt* 26:41.
22 Cf. *Rom* 5:3-5.

their petition is not heard. Here two questions should be asked: Why do we think our petition has not been heard? How is our prayer heard, how is it "efficacious"?

Why do we complain of not being heard?

2735   In the first place, we ought to be astonished by this fact: when we praise God or give him thanks for his benefits in general, we are not particularly concerned whether or not our prayer is acceptable to him. On the other hand, we demand to see the results of our petitions. What is the image of God that motivates our prayer: an instrument to
2779   be used? or the Father of our Lord Jesus Christ?

2559   **2736**   Are we convinced that "we do not know how to pray as we ought"?[23] Are we asking God for "what is good for us"? Our Father knows what we need before we ask him,[24] but he awaits our
1730   petition because the dignity of his children lies in their freedom. We must pray, then, with his Spirit of freedom, to be able truly to know what he wants.[25]

2737   "You ask and do not receive, because you ask wrongly, to spend it on your passions."[26] If we ask with a divided heart, we are "adulterers";[27] God cannot answer us, for he desires our well-being, our life. "Or do you suppose that it is in vain that the scripture says, 'He yearns jealously over the spirit which he has made to dwell in us?'"[28] That our God is "jealous" for us is the sign of how true his love is. If we enter into the desire of his Spirit, we shall be heard.

> Do not be troubled if you do not immediately receive from God what you ask him; for he desires to do something even greater for you, while you cling to him in prayer.[29]

> God wills that our desire should be exercised in prayer, that we may be able to receive what he is prepared to give.[30]

---

23   *Rom* 8:26.
24   Cf. *Mt* 6:8.
25   Cf. *Rom* 8:27.
26   *Jas* 4:3; cf. the whole context: *Jas* 4:1-10; 1:5-8; 5:16.
27   *Jas* 4:4.
28   *Jas* 4:5.
29   Evagrius Ponticus, *De oratione* 34: PG 79, 1173.
30   St. Augustine, *Ep.* 130, 8, 17: PL 33, 500.

How is our prayer efficacious?

2738   The revelation of prayer in the economy of salvation teaches us that faith rests on God's action in history. Our filial trust is enkindled by his supreme act: the Passion and Resurrection of *2568* his Son. Christian prayer is cooperation with his providence, his *307* plan of love for men.

2739   For St. Paul, this trust is bold, founded on the prayer of the *2778* Spirit in us and on the faithful love of the Father who has given us his only Son.[31] Transformation of the praying heart is the first response to our petition.

2740   The prayer of Jesus makes Christian prayer an efficacious petition. He is its model, he prays in us and with us. Since the heart of the Son seeks only what pleases the Father, how could the prayer of the children of adoption be centered on the gifts rather than the Giver?   *2604*

2741   Jesus also prays for us – in our place and on our behalf. All our petitions were gathered up, once for all, in his cry on the Cross and, in his Resurrection, heard by the Father. This is why he never *2606* ceases to intercede for us with the Father.[32] If our prayer is resolutely united with that of Jesus, in trust and boldness as children, we obtain all that we ask in his name, even more than any particular *2614* thing: the Holy Spirit himself, who contains all gifts.

IV.   PERSERVERING IN LOVE

2742   "Pray constantly . . . always and for everything giving *2098* thanks in the name of our Lord Jesus Christ to God the Father."[33] St. Paul adds, "Pray at all times in the Spirit, with all prayer and supplication. To that end keep alert with all perseverance making supplication for all the saints."[34] For "we have not been commanded to work, to keep watch and to fast constantly, but it has been laid down that we are to pray without ceasing."[35] This tireless fervor can come only from love. Against our dullness and laziness, the battle of prayer is that of humble, trusting, and persevering *love*. This love opens our hearts to three enlightening and life-giving *162* facts of faith about prayer.

---

31   Cf. *Rom* 10:12-13; 8:26-39.
32   Cf. *Heb* 5:7; 7:25; 9:24.
33   *1 Thess* 5:17; *Eph* 5:20.
34   *Eph* 6:18.
35   Evagrius Ponticus, *Pract.* 49: PG 40, 1245C.

2743   *It is always possible to pray:* The time of the Christian is that of the risen Christ who is with us always, no matter what tempests may arise.[36] Our time is in the hands of God:

> It is possible to offer fervent prayer even while walking in public or strolling alone, or seated in your shop, . . . while buying or selling, . . . or even while cooking.[37]

2744   *Prayer is a vital necessity.* Proof from the contrary is no less convincing: if we do not allow the Spirit to lead us, we fall back into the slavery of sin.[38] How can the Holy Spirit be our life if our heart is far from him?

> Nothing is equal to prayer; for what is impossible it makes possible, what is difficult, easy. . . . For it is impossible, utterly impossible, for the man who prays eagerly and invokes God ceaselessly ever to sin.[39]

> Those who pray are certainly saved; those who do not pray are certainly damned.[40]

2745   Prayer and *Christian life* are *inseparable,* for they concern the same love and the same renunciation, proceeding from love; the same filial and loving conformity with the Father's plan of love; the same transforming union in the Holy Spirit who conforms us more and more to Christ Jesus; the same love for all men, the love with which *2660* Jesus has loved us. "Whatever you ask the Father in my name, he [will] give it to you. This I command you, to love one another."[41]

> He "prays without ceasing" who unites prayer to works and good works to prayer. Only in this way can we consider as realizable the principle of praying without ceasing.[42]

---

36   Cf. *Mt* 28:20; *Lk* 8:24.
37   St. John Chrysostom, *Ecloga de oratione* 2: PG 63, 585.
38   Cf. *Gal* 5:16-25.
39   St. John Chrysostom, *De Anna* 4, 5: PG 54, 666.
40   St. Alphonsus Liguori, *Del gran mezzo della preghiera.*
41   *Jn* 15:16-17.
42   Origen, *De orat.* 12: PG 11, 452C.

ARTICLE 3
THE PRAYER OF THE HOUR OF JESUS

2746   When "his hour" came, Jesus prayed to the Father.[43] His prayer, the longest transmitted by the Gospel, embraces the whole economy of creation and salvation, as well as his death and Resurrection. The prayer of the Hour of Jesus always remains his own, *1085* just as his Passover "once for all" remains ever present in the liturgy of his Church.

2747   Christian Tradition rightly calls this prayer the "priestly" prayer of Jesus. It is the prayer of our high priest, inseparable from his sacrifice, from his passing over (Passover) to the Father to whom he is wholly "consecrated."[44]

2748   In this Paschal and sacrificial prayer, everything is reca- *518* pitulated in Christ:[45] God and the world; the Word and the flesh; eternal life and time; the love that hands itself over and the sin that betrays it; the disciples present and those who will believe in him by their word; humiliation and glory. It is the prayer of unity. *820*

2749   Jesus fulfilled the work of the Father completely; his prayer, like his sacrifice, extends until the end of time. The prayer of this hour fills the end-times and carries them toward their consummation. Jesus, the Son to whom the Father has given all things, has given himself wholly back to the Father, yet expresses himself with a sovereign freedom[46] by virtue of the power the Father has given him over all flesh. The Son, who made himself Servant, is Lord, the *Pantocrator.* Our high priest who prays for us is also the one who prays in us and the God who hears our prayer. *2616*

2750   By entering into the holy name of the Lord Jesus we can *2815* accept, from within, the prayer he teaches us: "Our Father!" His priestly prayer fulfills, from within, the great petitions of the Lord's Prayer: concern for the Father's name;[47] passionate zeal for his kingdom (glory);[48] the accomplishment of the will of the Father, of his plan of salvation;[49] and deliverance from evil.[50]

---

43   Cf. *Jn* 17.
44   Cf. *Jn* 17:11, 13, 19.
45   Cf. *Eph* 1:10.
46   Cf. *Jn* 17:11, 13, 19, 24.
47   Cf. *Jn* 17:6, 11, 12, 26.
48   Cf. *Jn* 17:1, 5, 10, 22, 23-26.
49   Cf. *Jn* 17:2, 4, 6, 9, 11, 12, 24.
50   Cf. *Jn* 17:15.

2751   Finally, in this prayer Jesus reveals and gives to us the "knowledge," inseparably one, of the Father and of the Son,[51] which is the very mystery of the life of prayer.

240

IN BRIEF

2752   Prayer presupposes an effort, a fight against ourselves and the wiles of the Tempter. The battle of prayer is inseparable from the necessary "spiritual battle" to act habitually according to the Spirit of Christ: we pray as we live, because we live as we pray.

2753   In the battle of prayer we must confront erroneous conceptions of prayer, various currents of thought, and our own experience of failure. We must respond with humility, trust, and perseverance to these temptations which cast doubt on the usefulness or even the possibility of prayer.

2754   The principal difficulties in the practice of prayer are distraction and dryness. The remedy lies in faith, conversion, and vigilance of heart.

2755   Two frequent temptations threaten prayer: lack of faith and acedia – a form of depression stemming from lax ascetical practice that leads to discouragement.

2756   Filial trust is put to the test when we feel that our prayer is not always heard. The Gospel invites us to ask ourselves about the conformity of our prayer to the desire of the Spirit.

2757   "Pray constantly" (*1 Thess* 5:17). It is always possible to pray. It is even a vital necessity. Prayer and Christian life are inseparable.

2758   The prayer of the hour of Jesus, rightly called the "priestly prayer" (cf. *Jn* 17), sums up the whole economy of creation and salvation. It fulfills the great petitions of the Our Father.

---

51   Cf. *Jn* 17:3, 6-10, 25.

SECTION TWO
THE LORD'S PRAYER
"OUR FATHER!"

2759 Jesus "was praying at a certain place, and when he ceased, one of his disciples said to him, 'Lord, teach us to pray, as John taught his disciples.'"[1] In response to this request the Lord entrusts to his disciples and to his Church the fundamental Christian prayer. St. Luke presents a brief text of five petitions,[2] while St. Matthew gives a more developed version of seven petitions.[3] The liturgical tradition of the Church has retained St. Matthew's text:

> **Our Father who art in heaven,**
> **hallowed be thy name.**
> **Thy kingdom come.**
> **Thy will be done on earth, as it is in heaven.**
> **Give us this day our daily bread,**
> **and forgive us our trespasses,**
> > **as we forgive those who trespass against us,**
> **and lead us not into temptation,**
> **but deliver us from evil.**

2760 Very early on, liturgical usage concluded the Lord's Prayer with a doxology. In the *Didache,* we find, "For yours are the power and the glory for ever."[4] The *Apostolic Constitutions* add to the beginning: "the kingdom," and this is the formula retained to our day in ecumenical prayer.[5] The Byzantine tradition adds after "the glory" the words "Father, Son, and Holy Spirit." The *Roman Missal* develops the last petition in the explicit perspective of "awaiting our blessed hope" and of the Second Coming of our Lord Jesus Christ.[6] Then comes the assembly's acclamation or the repetition of the doxology from the *Apostolic Constitutions.* **2855**

2854

---

1 *Lk* 11:1.
2 Cf. *Lk* 11:2-4.
3 Cf. *Mt* 6:9-13.
4 *Didache* 8, 2: SCh 248, 174.
5 *Apostolic Constitutions,* 7, 24, 1: PG 1, 1016.
6 *Titus* 2:13; cf. *Roman Missal* 22, Embolism after the Lord's Prayer.

ARTICLE 1
"THE SUMMARY OF THE WHOLE GOSPEL"

2761 The Lord's Prayer "is truly the summary of the whole gospel."[7] "Since the Lord . . . after handing over the practice of prayer, said elsewhere, 'Ask and you will receive,' and since everyone has petitions which are peculiar to his circumstances, the regular and appropriate prayer [the Lord's Prayer] is said first, as the foundation of further desires."[8]

I. AT THE CENTER OF THE SCRIPTURES

2762 After showing how the psalms are the principal food of Christian prayer and flow together in the petitions of the Our Father, St. Augustine concludes:

> Run through all the words of the holy prayers [in Scripture], and I do not think that you will find anything in them that is not contained and included in the Lord's Prayer.[9]

102 **2763** All the Scriptures – the Law, the Prophets, and the Psalms – are fulfilled in Christ.[10] The Gospel is this "Good News." Its first proclamation is summarized by St. Matthew in the Sermon on the Mount;[11] the prayer to our Father is at the center of this proclamation. It is in this context that each petition bequeathed to us by the Lord is illuminated:

> The Lord's Prayer is the most perfect of prayers. . . . In it we
2541 ask, not only for all the things we can rightly desire, but also in the sequence that they should be desired. This prayer not only teaches us to ask for things, but also in what order we should desire them.[12]

1965 **2764** The Sermon on the Mount is teaching for life, the Our Father is a prayer; but in both the one and the other the Spirit of the Lord gives new form to our desires, those inner movements that animate our lives. Jesus teaches us this new life by his words; *1969* he teaches us to ask for it by our prayer. The rightness of our life in him will depend on the rightness of our prayer.

---

7 Tertullian, *De orat.* 1: PL 1, 1155.
8 Tertullian, *De orat.* 10: PL 1, 1165; cf. *Lk* 11:9.
9 St. Augustine, *Ep.* 130, 12, 22: PL 33, 503.
10 Cf. *Lk* 24:44.
11 Cf. *Mt* 5-7.
12 St. Thomas Aquinas, *STh* II-II, 83, 9.

II. "THE LORD'S PRAYER"

2765 The traditional expression "the Lord's Prayer" – *oratio Dominica* – means that the prayer to our Father is taught and given to us by the Lord Jesus. The prayer that comes to us from Jesus is truly unique: it is "of the Lord." On the one hand, in the words of this prayer the only Son gives us the words the Father gave him:[13] *2701* he is the master of our prayer. On the other, as Word incarnate, he knows in his human heart the needs of his human brothers and sisters and reveals them to us: he is the model of our prayer.

2766 But Jesus does not give us a formula to repeat mechanically.[14] As in every vocal prayer, it is through the Word of God that the Holy Spirit teaches the children of God to pray to their Father. Jesus not only gives us the words of our filial prayer; at the same time he gives us the Spirit by whom these words become in us "spirit and life."[15] Even more, the proof and possibility of our filial prayer is that the Father "sent the Spirit of his Son into our hearts, crying, '*Abba!* Father!'"[16] Since our prayer sets forth our desires before God, it is again the Father, "he who searches the hearts of men," who "knows what is the mind of the Spirit, because the Spirit intercedes for the saints according to the will of God."[17] The prayer to Our Father is inserted into the mysterious mission of the Son and *690* of the Spirit.

III. THE PRAYER OF THE CHURCH

2767 This indivisible gift of the Lord's words and of the Holy Spirit who gives life to them in the hearts of believers has been received and lived by the Church from the beginning. The first communities prayed the Lord's Prayer three times a day,[18] in place of the "Eighteen Benedictions" customary in Jewish piety.

2768 According to the apostolic tradition, the Lord's Prayer is essentially rooted in liturgical prayer:

> [The Lord] teaches us to make prayer in common for all our brethren. For he did not say "my Father" who art in heaven, but "our" Father, offering petitions for the common Body.[19]

---

13 Cf. *Jn* 17:7.
14 Cf. *Mt* 6:7; *1 Kings* 18:26-29.
15 *Jn* 6:63.
16 *Gal* 4:6.
17 *Rom* 8:27.
18 Cf. *Didache* 8, 3: SCh 248, 174.
19 St. John Chrysostom, *Hom. in Mt.* 19, 4: PG 57, 278.

In all the liturgical traditions, the Lord's Prayer is an integral part of the major hours of the Divine Office. In the three sacraments of Christian initiation its ecclesial character is especially in evidence:

2769   In *Baptism* and *Confirmation*, the handing on (*traditio*) of the Lord's Prayer signifies new birth into the divine life. Since Christian prayer is our speaking to God with the very word of God, those who are "born anew . . . through the living and abiding word of God"[20] learn to invoke their Father by the one Word he always hears. They can henceforth do so, for the seal of the Holy Spirit's anointing is indelibly placed on their hearts, ears, lips, indeed their whole filial being. This is why most of the patristic commentaries on the Our Father are addressed to catechumens and neophytes. When the Church prays the Lord's Prayer, it is always the people made up of the "new-born" who pray and obtain mercy.[21]

1243

1350 **2770**   In the *Eucharistic liturgy* the Lord's Prayer appears as the prayer of the whole Church and there reveals its full meaning and efficacy. Placed between the *anaphora* (the Eucharistic prayer) and the communion, the Lord's Prayer sums up on the one hand all the petitions and intercessions expressed in the movement of the *epiclesis* and, on the other, knocks at the door of the Banquet of the kingdom which sacramental communion anticipates.

2771   In the Eucharist, the Lord's Prayer also reveals the *eschatological* character of its petitions. It is the proper prayer of "the end-time," the time of salvation that began with the outpouring of the Holy Spirit and will be fulfilled with the Lord's return. The petitions addressed to our Father, as distinct from the prayers of the old covenant, rely on the mystery of salvation already accomplished, once for all, in Christ crucified and risen.

1403

1820 **2772**   From this unshakeable faith springs forth the hope that sustains each of the seven petitions, which express the groanings of the present age, this time of patience and expectation during which "it does not yet appear what we shall be."[22] The Eucharist and the Lord's Prayer look eagerly for the Lord's return, "until he comes."[23]

---

20   *1 Pet* 1:23.
21   Cf. *1 Pet* 2:1-10.
22   *1 Jn* 3:2; cf. *Col* 3:4.
23   *1 Cor* 11:26.

IN BRIEF

2773 In response to his disciples' request "Lord, teach us to pray" (*Lk* 11:1), Jesus entrusts them with the fundamental Christian prayer, the Our Father.

2774 "The Lord's Prayer is truly the summary of the whole gospel,"[24] the "most perfect of prayers."[25] It is at the center of the Scriptures.

2775 It is called "the Lord's Prayer" because it comes to us from the Lord Jesus, the master and model of our prayer.

2776 The Lord's Prayer is the quintessential prayer of the Church. It is an integral part of the major hours of the Divine Office and of the sacraments of Christian initiation: Baptism, Confirmation, and Eucharist. Integrated into the Eucharist it reveals the eschatological character of its petitions, hoping for the Lord, "until he comes" (*1 Cor* 11:26).

ARTICLE 2
"OUR FATHER WHO ART IN HEAVEN"

I. "WE DARE TO SAY"

2777 In the Roman liturgy, the Eucharistic assembly is invited to pray to our heavenly Father with filial boldness; the Eastern liturgies develop and use similar expressions: "dare in all confidence," "make us worthy of. . . ." From the burning bush Moses heard a voice saying to him, "Do not come near; put off your shoes from your feet, for the place on which you are standing is holy ground."[26] Only Jesus could cross that threshold of the divine holiness, for "when he had made purification for sins," he brought us into the Father's presence: "Here am I, and the children God has given me."[27]

---

24 Tertullian, *De orat.* 1:PL 1, 1251-1255.
25 St. Thomas Aquinas, *STh* II-II, 83, 9.
26 *Ex* 3:5.
27 *Heb* 1:3; 2:13.

> Our awareness of our status as slaves would make us sink
> into the ground and our earthly condition would dissolve
> into dust, if the authority of our Father himself and the Spirit
> of his Son had not impelled us to this cry . . . 'Abba, Father!'
> . . . When would a mortal dare call God 'Father,' if man's
> innermost being were not animated by power from on
> high?"[28]

270

2778   This power of the Spirit who introduces us to the Lord's
Prayer is expressed in the liturgies of East and of West by the
beautiful, characteristically Christian expression: *parrhesia,*
2828 straightforward simplicity, filial trust, joyous assurance, humble
boldness, the certainty of being loved.[29]

II.   "FATHER!"

2779   Before we make our own this first exclamation of the
Lord's Prayer, we must humbly cleanse our hearts of certain false
images drawn "from this world." *Humility* makes us recognize that
"no one knows the Son except the Father, and no one knows the
Father except the Son and anyone to whom the Son chooses to
reveal him," that is, "to little children."[30] The *purification* of our
hearts has to do with paternal or maternal images, stemming from
our personal and cultural history, and influencing our relationship
with God. God our Father transcends the categories of the created
239 world. To impose our own ideas in this area "upon him" would be
to fabricate idols to adore or pull down. To pray to the Father is to
enter into his mystery as he is and as the Son has revealed him to us.

> The expression God the Father had never been revealed to
> anyone. When Moses himself asked God who he was, he
> heard another name. The Father's name has been revealed
> to us in the Son, for the name "Son" implies the new name
> "Father."[31]

240 **2780**   We can invoke God as "Father" because *he is revealed to us*
by his Son become man and because his Spirit makes him known
to us. The personal relation of the Son to the Father is something
that man cannot conceive of nor the angelic powers even dimly see:
and yet, the Spirit of the Son grants a participation in that very
relation to us who believe that Jesus is the Christ and that we are
born of God.[32]

---

28 St. Peter Chrysologus, *Sermo* 71, 3: PL 52, 401CD; cf. *Gal* 4:6.
29 Cf. *Eph* 3:12; *Heb* 3:6; 4:16; 10:19; *1 Jn* 2:28; 3:21; 5:14.
30 *Mt* 11:25-27.
31 Tertullian, *De orat.* 3: PL 1, 1155.
32 Cf. *Jn* 1:1; *1 Jn* 5:1.

2781   When we pray to the Father, we are *in communion with him*   *2665*
and with his Son, Jesus Christ.[33] Then we know and recognize him
with an ever new sense of wonder. The first phrase of the Our
Father is a blessing of adoration before it is a supplication. For it is
the glory of God that we should recognize him as "Father," the true
God. We give him thanks for having revealed his name to us, for
the gift of believing in it, and for the indwelling of his Presence in
us.

2782   We can adore the Father because he has caused us to be
reborn to his life by *adopting* us as his children in his only Son: by
Baptism, he incorporates us into the Body of his Christ; through   *1267*
the anointing of his Spirit who flows from the head to the members,
he makes us other "Christs."

> God, indeed, who has predestined us to adoption as his sons,
> has conformed us to the glorious Body of Christ. So then you
> who have become sharers in Christ are appropriately called
> "Christs."[34]

> The new man, reborn and restored to his God by grace , says
> first of all, "Father!" because he has now begun to be a son.[35]

2783   Thus the Lord's Prayer *reveals us to ourselves* at the same   *1701*
time that it reveals the Father to us.[36]

> O man, you did not dare to raise your face to heaven, you
> lowered your eyes to the earth, and suddenly you have received
> the grace of Christ: all your sins have been forgiven. From being
> a wicked servant you have become a good son. . . . Then raise
> your eyes to the Father who has begotten you through Baptism,
> to the Father who has redeemed you through his Son, and say:
> "Our Father. . . ." But do not claim any privilege. He is the Father
> in a special way only of Christ, but he is the common Father of
> us all, because while he has begotten only Christ, he has created
> us. Then also say by his grace, "Our Father," so that you may
> merit being his son.[37]

2784   The free gift of adoption requires on our part continual   *1428*
conversion and *new life*. Praying to our Father should develop in
us two fundamental dispositions:

First, *the desire to become like him*: though created in his
image, we are restored to his likeness by grace; and we must   *1997*
respond to this grace.

---

33   Cf. *1 Jn* 1:3.
34   St. Cyril of Jerusalem, *Catech. myst.* 3, 1: PG 33, 1088A.
35   St. Cyprian, *De Dom. orat.* 9: PL 4, 525A.
36   Cf. *GS* 22 § 1.
37   St. Ambrose, *De Sacr.* 5, 4, 19: PL 16:450-451.

> We must remember . . . and know that when we call God "our Father" we ought to behave as sons of God.[38]

> You cannot call the God of all kindness your Father if you preserve a cruel and inhuman heart; for in this case you no longer have in you the marks of the heavenly Father's kindness.[39]

> We must contemplate the beauty of the Father without ceasing and adorn our own souls accordingly.[40]

2562 **2785** Second, *a humble and trusting heart* that enables us "to turn and become like children":[41] for it is to "little children" that the Father is revealed.[42]

> [The prayer is accomplished] by the contemplation of God alone, and by the warmth of love, through which the soul, molded and directed to love him, speaks very familiarly to God as to its own Father with special devotion.[43]

> Our Father: at this name love is aroused in us . . . and the confidence of obtaining what we are about to ask. . . . What would he not give to his children who ask, since he has already granted them the gift of being his children?[44]

III.   "OUR" FATHER

443 **2786**   "Our" Father refers to God. The adjective, as used by us, does not express possession, but an entirely new relationship with God.

2787   When we say "our" Father, we recognize first that all his promises of love announced by the prophets are fulfilled in the *new* *782* *and eternal covenant* in his Christ: we have become "his" people and he is henceforth "our" God. This new relationship is the purely gratuitous gift of belonging to each other: we are to respond to "grace and truth" given us in Jesus Christ with love and faithfulness.[45]

---

38 St. Cyprian, *De Dom. orat.* 11: PL 4:526B.

39 St. John Chrysostom, *De orat Dom.* 3: PG 51, 44.

40 St. Gregory of Nyssa, *De orat. Dom.* 2: PG 44, 1148B.

41 *Mt* 18:3.

42 Cf. *Mt* 11:25.

43 St. John Cassian, *Coll.* 9, 18: PL 49, 788C.

44 St. Augustine, *De serm. Dom. in monte* 2, 4, 16: PL 34, 1276.

45 *Jn* 1:17; cf. *Hos* 2:21-22; 6:1-6.

2788   Since the Lord's Prayer is that of his people in the "end-time," this "our" also expresses the certitude of our hope in God's ultimate promise: in the new Jerusalem he will say to the victor, "I will be his God and he shall be my son."[46]

2789   When we pray to "our" Father, we personally address the Father of our Lord Jesus Christ. By doing so we do not divide the Godhead, since the Father is its "source and origin," but rather confess that the Son is eternally begotten by him and the Holy Spirit   *245* proceeds from him. We are not confusing the persons, for we confess that our communion is with the Father and his Son, Jesus Christ, in their one Holy Spirit. The *Holy Trinity* is consubstantial and indivisible. When we pray to the Father, we adore and glorify   *253* him together with the Son and the Holy Spirit.

2790   Grammatically, "our" qualifies a reality common to more than one person. There is only one God, and he is recognized as Father by those who, through faith in his only Son, are reborn of him by water and the Spirit.[47] The *Church* is this new communion   *787* of God and men. United with the only Son, who has become "the firstborn among many brethren," she is in communion with one and the same Father in one and the same Holy Spirit.[48] In praying "our" Father, each of the baptized is praying in this communion: "The company of those who believed were of one heart and soul."[49]

2791   For this reason, in spite of the divisions among Christians,   *821* this prayer to "our" Father remains our common patrimony and an urgent summons for all the baptized. In communion by faith in Christ and by Baptism, they ought to join in Jesus' prayer for the unity of his disciples.[50]

2792   Finally, if we pray the Our Father sincerely, we leave individualism behind, because the love that we receive frees us from it. The "our" at the beginning of the Lord's Prayer, like the "us" of the last four petitions, excludes no one. If we are to say it truthfully, our divisions and oppositions have to be overcome.[51]

---

46   *Rev* 21:7.
47   Cf. *1 Jn* 5:1; *Jn* 3:5.
48   *Rom* 8:29; cf. *Eph* 4:4-6.
49   *Acts* 4:32.
50   Cf. *UR* 8; 22.
51   Cf. *Mt* 5:23-24; 6:14-15.

2793   The baptized cannot pray to "our" Father without bringing before him all those for whom he gave his beloved Son. God's
604 love has no bounds, neither should our prayer.[52] Praying "our"
Father opens to us the dimensions of his love revealed in Christ:
praying with and for all who do not yet know him, so that Christ
may "gather into one the children of God."[53] God's care for all men
and for the whole of creation has inspired all the great practitioners
of prayer; it should extend our prayer to the full breadth of love
whenever we dare to say "our" Father.

IV.   "WHO ART IN HEAVEN"

326 **2794**   This biblical expression does not mean a place ("space"),
but a way of being; it does not mean that God is distant, but
majestic. Our Father is not "elsewhere": he transcends everything
we can conceive of his holiness. It is precisely because he is thrice-
holy that he is so close to the humble and contrite heart.

> "Our Father who art in heaven" is rightly understood to
> mean that God is in the hearts of the just, as in his holy
> temple. At the same time, it means that those who pray
> should desire the one they invoke to dwell in them.[54]

> "Heaven" could also be those who bear the image of the
> heavenly world, and in whom God dwells and tarries.[55]

2795   The symbol of the heavens refers us back to the mystery of
the covenant we are living when we pray to our Father. He is in
heaven, his dwelling place; the Father's house is our homeland. Sin
has exiled us from the land of the covenant,[56] but conversion of
1024 heart enables us to return to the Father, to heaven.[57] In Christ, then,
heaven and earth are reconciled,[58] for the Son alone "descended
from heaven" and causes us to ascend there with him, by his Cross,
Resurrection, and Ascension.[59]

---

52 Cf. *NA* 5.
53 *Jn* 11:52.
54 St. Augustine, *De serm. Dom. in monte* 2, 5, 18: PL 34, 1277.
55 St. Cyril of Jerusalem, *Catech. myst.* 5:11: PG 33, 1117.
56 Cf. *Gen* 3.
57 *Jer* 3:19-4:1a; *Lk* 15:18, 21.
58 Cf. *Isa* 45:8; *Ps* 85:12.
59 *Jn* 3:13; 12:32; 14:2-3; 16:28; 20:17; *Eph* 4:9-10; *Heb* 1:3; 2:13.

2796 When the Church prays "our Father who art in heaven," she is professing that we are the People of God, already seated "with him in the heavenly places in Christ Jesus" and "hidden with Christ in God;"[60] yet at the same time, "here indeed we groan, and *1003* long to put on our heavenly dwelling."[61]

> [Christians] are in the flesh, but do not live according to the flesh. They spend their lives on earth, but are citizens of heaven.[62]

IN BRIEF

2797 Simple and faithful trust, humble and joyous assurance are the proper dispositions for one who prays the Our Father.

2798 We can invoke God as "Father" because the Son of God made man has revealed him to us. In this Son, through Baptism, we are incorporated and adopted as sons of God.

2799 The Lord's Prayer brings us into communion with the Father and with his Son, Jesus Christ. At the same time it reveals us to ourselves (cf. *GS* 22 § 1).

2800 Praying to our Father should develop in us the will to become like him and foster in us a humble and trusting heart.

2801 When we say "Our" Father, we are invoking the new covenant in Jesus Christ, communion with the Holy Trinity, and the divine love which spreads through the Church to encompass the world.

2802 "Who art in heaven" does not refer to a place but to God's majesty and his presence in the hearts of the just. Heaven, the Father's house, is the true homeland toward which we are heading and to which, already, we belong.

---

60 *Eph* 2:6; *Col* 3:3.
61 *2 Cor* 5:2; cf. *Phil* 3:20; *Heb* 13:14.
62 *Ad Diognetum* 5: PG 2, 1173.

ARTICLE 3
THE SEVEN PETITIONS

2803   After we have placed ourselves in the presence of God our Father to adore and to love and to bless him, the Spirit of adoption stirs up in our hearts seven petitions, seven blessings. The first three, more theologal, draw us toward the glory of the Father; the last four, as ways toward him, commend our wretchedness to his grace. "Deep calls to deep."[63]

2627

2804   The first series of petitions carries us toward him, for his own sake: *thy* name, *thy* kingdom, *thy* will! It is characteristic of love to think first of the one whom we love. In none of the three petitions do we mention ourselves; the burning desire, even anguish, of the beloved Son for his Father's glory seizes us:[64] "hallowed be thy name, thy kingdom come, thy will be done...." These three supplications were already answered in the saving sacrifice of Christ, but they are henceforth directed in hope toward their final fulfillment, for God is not yet all in all.[65]

2805   The second series of petitions unfolds with the same movement as certain Eucharistic epicleses: as an offering up of our expectations, that draws down upon itself the eyes of the Father of mercies. They go up from us and concern us from this very moment, in our present world: "give *us* . . . forgive *us* . . . lead *us* not . . . deliver *us*. . . ." The fourth and fifth petitions concern our life as such – to be fed and to be healed of sin; the last two concern our battle for the victory of life – that battle of prayer.

1105

2806   By the three first petitions, we are strengthened in faith, filled with hope, and set aflame by charity. Being creatures and still sinners, we have to petition for us, for that "us" bound by the world and history, which we offer to the boundless love of God. For through the name of his Christ and the reign of his Holy Spirit, our Father accomplishes his plan of salvation, for us and for the whole world.

2656-2658

---

63   *Ps* 42:7.
64   Cf. *Lk* 22:44; 12:50.
65   Cf. *1 Cor* 15:28.

I. "HALLOWED BE THY NAME"

2142-2159

2807 The term "to hallow" is to be understood here not primarily in its causative sense (only God hallows, makes holy), but above all in an evaluative sense: to recognize as holy, to treat in a holy way. And so, in adoration, this invocation is sometimes under- *2097* stood as praise and thanksgiving.[66] But this petition is here taught to us by Jesus as an optative: a petition, a desire, and an expectation in which God and man are involved. Beginning with this first petition to our Father, we are immersed in the innermost mystery of his Godhead and the drama of the salvation of our humanity. Asking the Father that his name be made holy draws us into his plan of loving kindness for the fullness of time, "according to his purpose which he set forth in Christ," that we might "be holy and blameless before him in love."[67]

2808 In the decisive moments of his economy God reveals his name, but he does so by accomplishing his work. This work, then, is realized for us and in us only if his name is hallowed by us and in us.

2809 The holiness of God is the inaccessible center of his eternal *203, 432* mystery. What is revealed of it in creation and history, Scripture calls "glory," the radiance of his majesty.[68] In making man in his *293* image and likeness, God "crowned him with glory and honor," but by sinning, man fell "short of the glory of God."[69] From that time on, God was to manifest his holiness by revealing and giving his *705* name, in order to restore man to the image of his Creator.[70]

2810 In the promise to Abraham and the oath that accompanied it,[71] God commits himself but without disclosing his name. He begins to reveal it to Moses and makes it known clearly before the eyes of the whole people when he saves them from the Egyptians: "he has triumphed gloriously."[72] From the covenant of Sinai onwards, this people is "his own" and it is to be a "holy (or "consecrated": the same word is used for both in Hebrew) nation,"[73] because the name of God dwells in it. *63*

---

66 Cf. *Ps* 111:9; *Lk* 1:49.
67 *Eph* 1:9, 4.
68 Cf. *Ps* 8; *Isa* 6:3.
69 *Ps* 8:5; *Rom* 3:23; cf. *Gen* 1:26.
70 *Col* 3:10.
71 Cf. *Heb* 6:13.
72 *Ex* 15:1; cf. 3:14.
73 Cf. *Ex* 19:5-6.

2143   **2811**   In spite of the holy Law that again and again their Holy God gives them – "You shall be holy, for I the LORD your God am holy" – and although the Lord shows patience for the sake of his name, the people turn away from the Holy One of Israel and profane his name among the nations.[74] For this reason the just ones of the old covenant, the poor survivors returned from exile, and the prophets burned with passion for the name.

434   **2812**   Finally, in Jesus the name of the Holy God is revealed and given to us, in the flesh, as Savior, revealed by what he is, by his word, and by his sacrifice.[75] This is the heart of his priestly prayer: "Holy Father . . . for their sake I consecrate myself, that they also may be consecrated in truth."[76] Because he "sanctifies" his own name, Jesus reveals to us the name of the Father.[77] At the end of Christ's Passover, the Father gives him the name that is above all names: "Jesus Christ is Lord, to the glory of God the Father."[78]

2013   **2813**   In the waters of Baptism, we have been "washed . . . sanctified . . . justified in the name of the Lord Jesus Christ and in the Spirit of our God."[79] Our Father calls us to holiness in the whole of our life, and since "he is the source of [our] life in Christ Jesus, who became for us wisdom from God, and . . .sanctification,"[80] both his glory and our life depend on the hallowing of his name in us and by us. Such is the urgency of our first petition.

> By whom is God hallowed, since he is the one who hallows? But since he said, "You shall be holy to me; for I the LORD am holy," we seek and ask that we who were sanctified in Baptism may persevere in what we have begun to be. And we ask this daily, for we need sanctification daily, so that we who fail daily may cleanse away our sins by being sanctified continually. . . . We pray that this sanctification may remain in us.[81]

2814   The sanctification of his name among the nations depends
2045   inseparably on our *life* and our *prayer*:

> We ask God to hallow his name, which by its own holiness saves and makes holy all creation . . . . It is this name that gives salvation to a lost world. But we ask that this name of God should be hallowed in us through our actions. For God's

---

74   *Ezek* 20:9, 14, 22, 39; cf. *Lev* 19:2.
75   Cf. *Mt* 1:21; *Lk* 1:31; *Jn* 8:28; 17:8; 17:17-19.
76   *Jn* 17:11, 19.
77   Cf. *Ezek* 20:39; 36:20-21; *Jn* 17:6.
78   *Phil* 2:9-11.
79   *1 Cor* 6:11.
80   *1 Cor* 1:30; cf. *1 Thess* 4:7.
81   St. Cyprian, *De Dom. orat.* 12: PL 4, 527A; *Lev* 20:26.

name is blessed when we live well, but is blasphemed when we live wickedly. As the Apostle says: "The name of God is blasphemed among the Gentiles because of you." We ask then that, just as the name of God is holy, so we may obtain his holiness in our souls.[82]

When we say "hallowed be thy name," we ask that it should be hallowed in us, who are in him; but also in others whom God's grace still awaits, that we may obey the precept that obliges us to pray for everyone, even our enemies. That is why we do not say expressly "hallowed be thy name 'in us,'" for we ask that it be so in all men.[83]

2815   This petition embodies all the others. Like the six petitions that follow, it is fulfilled by *the prayer of Christ*. Prayer to our Father is our prayer, if it is prayed *in the name* of Jesus.[84] In his priestly *2750* prayer, Jesus asks: "Holy Father, protect in your name those whom you have given me."[85]

II.   "THY KINGDOM COME"

2816   In the New Testament, the word *basileia* can be translated *541* by "kingship" (abstract noun), "kingdom" (concrete noun) or "reign" (action noun). The Kingdom of God lies ahead of us. It is *2632* brought near in the Word incarnate, it is proclaimed throughout the whole Gospel, and it has come in Christ's death and Resurrection. The Kingdom of God has been coming since the Last Supper *560* and, in the Eucharist, it is in our midst. The kingdom will come in *1107* glory when Christ hands it over to his Father:

It may even be . . . that the Kingdom of God means Christ himself, whom we daily desire to come, and whose coming we wish to be manifested quickly to us. For as he is our resurrection, since in him we rise, so he can also be understood as the Kingdom of God, for in him we shall reign.[86]

2817   This petition is *"Marana tha,"* the cry of the Spirit and the *451, 2632* Bride: "Come, Lord Jesus." *671*

Even if it had not been prescribed to pray for the coming of the kingdom, we would willingly have brought forth this speech, eager to embrace our hope. In indignation the souls of the martyrs under the altar cry out to the Lord: "O Sovereign Lord, holy and true, how long before you judge and avenge our blood on those who dwell upon the earth?" For

82   St. Peter Chrysologus, *Sermo* 71, 4: PL 52:402A; cf. *Rom* 2:24; *Ezek* 36:20-22.
83   Tertullian, *De orat*. 3: PL 1:1157A.
84   Cf. *Jn* 14:13; 15:16; 16:24, 26.
85   *Jn* 17:11.
86   St. Cyprian, *De Dom. orat*. 13: PL 4, 528A.

their retribution is ordained for the end of the world. Indeed, as soon as possible, Lord, may your kingdom come![87]

769 **2818**   In the Lord's Prayer, "thy kingdom come" refers primarily to the final coming of the reign of God through Christ's return.[88] But, far from distracting the Church from her mission in this present world, this desire commits her to it all the more strongly. Since Pentecost, the coming of that Reign is the work of the Spirit of the Lord who "complete[s] his work on earth and brings us the fullness of grace."[89]

2046 **2819**   "The kingdom of God [is] righteousness and peace and joy in the Holy Spirit."[90] The end-time in which we live is the age of 2516 the outpouring of the Spirit. Ever since Pentecost, a decisive battle has been joined between "the flesh" and the Spirit.[91]

2519   Only a pure soul can boldly say: "Thy kingdom come." One who has heard Paul say, "Let not sin therefore reign in your mortal bodies," and has purified himself in action, thought, and word will say to God: "Thy kingdom come!"[92]

2820   By a discernment according to the Spirit, Christians have to distinguish between the growth of the Reign of God and the 1049 progress of the culture and society in which they are involved. This distinction is not a separation. Man's vocation to eternal life does not suppress, but actually reinforces, his duty to put into action in this world the energies and means received from the Creator to serve justice and peace.[93]

2746 **2821**   This petition is taken up and granted in the prayer *of* Jesus which is present and effective in the Eucharist; it bears its fruit in new life in keeping with the Beatitudes.[94]

---

87 Tertullian, *De orat.* 5: PL 1, 1159A; cf. *Heb* 4:11; *Rev* 6:9; 22:20.
88 Cf. *Titus* 2:13.
89 *Roman Missal*, Eucharistic Prayer IV, 118.
90 *Rom* 14:17.
91 Cf. *Gal* 5:16-25.
92 St. Cyril of Jerusalem, *Catech. myst.* 5, 13: PG 33, 1120A; cf. *Rom* 6:12.
93 Cf. *GS* 22; 32; 39; 45; *EN* 31.
94 Cf. *Jn* 17:17-20; *Mt* 5:13-16; 6:24; 7:12-13.

III. "Thy Will Be Done on Earth as It Is in Heaven"

2822 Our Father "desires all men to be saved and to come to the *851* knowledge of the truth."[95] He "is forbearing toward you, not wishing that any should perish."[96] His commandment is "that you love one another; even as I have loved you, that you also love one *2196* another."[97] This commandment summarizes all the others and expresses his entire will.

2823 "He has made known to us the mystery of his will, accord- *59* ing to his good pleasure that he set forth in Christ . . . to gather up all things in him, things in heaven and things on earth. In Christ we have also obtained an inheritance, having been destined according to the purpose of him who accomplishes all things according to his counsel and will."[98] We ask insistently for this loving plan to be fully realized on earth as it is already in heaven.

2824 In Christ, and through his human will, the will of the *475* Father has been perfectly fulfilled once for all. Jesus said on entering into this world: "Lo, I have come to do your will, O God."[99] Only Jesus can say: "I always do what is pleasing to him."[100] In the prayer of his agony, he consents totally to this will: "not my will, but yours be done."[101] For this reason Jesus "gave himself for our *612* sins to deliver us from the present evil age, according to the will of our God and Father."[102] "And by that will we have been sanctified through the offering of the body of Jesus Christ once for all."[103]

2825 "Although he was a Son, [Jesus] learned obedience through what he suffered."[104] How much more reason have we sinful creatures to learn obedience – we who in him have become children of adoption. We ask our Father to unite our will to his Son's, in order to fulfill his will, his plan of salvation for the life of *615* the world. We are radically incapable of this, but united with Jesus and with the power of his Holy Spirit, we can surrender our will to him and decide to choose what his Son has always chosen: to do what is pleasing to the Father.[105]

---

95 *1 Tim* 2:3-4.
96 *2 Pet* 3:9; cf. *Mt* 18:14.
97 *Jn* 13:34; cf. *1 Jn* 3; 4; *Lk* 10:25-37.
98 *Eph* 1:9-11.
99 *Heb* 10:7; *Ps* 40:7.
100 *Jn* 8:29.
101 *Lk* 22:42; cf. *Jn* 4:34; 5:30; 6:38.
102 *Gal* 1:4.
103 *Heb* 10:10.
104 *Heb* 5:8.
105 Cf. *Jn* 8:29.

> In committing ourselves to [Christ], we can become one spirit with him, and thereby accomplish his will, in such wise that it will be perfect on earth as it is in heaven.[106]

> Consider how [Jesus Christ] teaches us to be humble, by making us see that our virtue does not depend on our work alone but on grace from on high. He commands each of the faithful who prays to do so universally, for the whole world. For he did not say "thy will be done in me or in us," but "on earth," the whole earth, so that error may be banished from it, truth take root in it, all vice be destroyed on it, virtue flourish on it, and earth no longer differ from heaven.[107]

2826   By prayer we can discern "what is the will of God" and obtain the endurance to do it.[108] Jesus teaches us that one enters the kingdom of heaven not by speaking words, but by doing "the will of my Father in heaven."[109]

2611   **2827**   "If any one is a worshiper of God and does his will, God listens to him."[110] Such is the power of the Church's prayer in the name of her Lord, above all in the Eucharist. Her prayer is also a communion of intercession with the all-holy Mother of God[111] and all the saints who have been pleasing to the Lord because they willed his will alone:

796
> It would not be inconsistent with the truth to understand the words, "Thy will be done on earth as it is in heaven," to mean: "in the Church as in our Lord Jesus Christ himself"; or "in the Bride who has been betrothed, just as in the Bridegroom who has accomplished the will of the Father."[112]

---

106   Origen, *De orat.* 26: PG 11, 501B.
107   St. John Chrysostom, *Hom. in Mt.* 19, 5: PG 57, 280.
108   *Rom* 12:2; cf. *Eph* 5:17; cf. *Heb* 10:36.
109   *Mt* 7:21.
110   *Jn* 9:31; cf. *1 Jn* 5:14.
111   Cf *Lk* 1:38, 49.
112   St. Augustine, *De serm. Dom.* 2, 6, 24: PL 34, 1279.

IV. "GIVE US THIS DAY OUR DAILY BREAD"

2828   *"Give us"*: The trust of children who look to their Father for   *2778*
everything is beautiful. "He makes his sun rise on the evil and on
the good, and sends rain on the just and on the unjust."[113] He gives
to all the living "their food in due season."[114] Jesus teaches us this
petition, because it glorifies our Father by acknowledging how
good he is, beyond all goodness.

2829   "Give us" also expresses the covenant. We are his and he
is ours, for our sake. But this "us" also recognizes him as the Father
of all men and we pray to him for them all, in solidarity with their   *1939*
needs and sufferings.

2830   *"Our bread"*: The Father who gives us life cannot but give
us the nourishment life requires – all appropriate goods and blessings, both material and spiritual. In the Sermon on the Mount, Jesus   *2633*
insists on the filial trust that cooperates with our Father's providence.[115] He is not inviting us to idleness,[116] but wants to relieve
us from nagging worry and preoccupation. Such is the filial surrender of the children of God:

> To those who seek the kingdom of God and his righteous-
> ness, he has promised to give all else besides. Since every-
> thing indeed belongs to God, he who possesses God wants   *227*
> for nothing, if he himself is not found wanting before
> God.[117]

2831   But the presence of those who hunger because they lack
bread opens up another profound meaning of this petition. The
drama of hunger in the world calls Christians who pray sincerely
to exercise responsibility toward their brethren, both in their personal behavior and in their solidarity with the human family. This
petition of the Lord's Prayer cannot be isolated from the parables
of the poor man Lazarus and of the Last Judgment.[118]   *1038*

---

113   *Mt* 5:45.
114   *Ps* 104:27.
115   Cf. *Mt* 6:25-34.
116   Cf. *2 Thess* 3:6-13.
117   St. Cyprian, *De Dom. orat.* 21: PL 4, 534A.
118   Cf. *Lk* 16:19-31; *Mt* 25:31-46.

2832   As leaven in the dough, the newness of the kingdom
should make the earth "rise" by the Spirit of Christ.[119] This must
1928 be shown by the establishment of justice in personal and social,
economic and international relations, without ever forgetting that
there are no just structures without people who want to be just.

2790 **2833**   "Our" bread is the "one" loaf for the "many." In the
2546 Beatitudes "poverty" is the virtue of sharing: it calls us to communicate and share both material and spiritual goods, not by coercion
but out of love, so that the abundance of some may remedy the
needs of others.[120]

2428 **2834**   "Pray and work."[121] "Pray as if everything depended on
God and work as if everything depended on you."[122] Even when
we have done our work, the food we receive is still a gift from our
Father; it is good to ask him for it with thanksgiving, as Christian
families do when saying grace at meals.

2835   This petition, with the responsibility it involves, also applies to another hunger from which men are perishing: "Man does
not live by bread alone, but . . . by every word that proceeds from
the mouth of God,"[123] that is, by the Word he speaks and the Spirit
he breathes forth. Christians must make every effort "to proclaim
2443 the good news to the poor." There is a famine on earth, "not a
famine of bread, nor a thirst for water, but of hearing the words of
the LORD."[124] For this reason the specifically Christian sense of this
fourth petition concerns the Bread of Life: The Word of God
1384 accepted in faith, the Body of Christ received in the Eucharist.[125]

1165 **2836**   *"This day"* is also an expression of trust taught us by the
Lord,[126] which we would never have presumed to invent. Since it
refers above all to his Word and to the Body of his Son, this "today"
is not only that of our mortal time, but also the "today" of God.

> If you receive the bread each day, each day is today for you.
> If Christ is yours today, he rises for you every day. How can
> this be? "You are my Son, today I have begotten you."
> Therefore, "today" is when Christ rises.[127]

---

119 Cf. *AA* 5.
120 Cf. *2 Cor* 8:1-15.
121 Cf. St. Benedict, *Regula*, 20, 48.
122 Attributed to St. Ignatius Loyola, cf. Joseph de Guibert, SJ, *The Jesuits: Their
     Spiritual Doctrine and Practice*, (Chicago: Loyola University Press, 1964), 148, n. 55.
123 *Deut* 8:3; *Mt* 4:4.
124 *Am* 8:11.
125 Cf. *Jn* 6:26-58.
126 Cf. *Mt* 6:34; *Ex* 16:19.
127 St. Ambrose, *De Sacr.* 5, 4, 26: PL 16, 453A; cf. *Ps* 2:7.

2837   *"Daily"* (*epiousios*) occurs nowhere else in the New Testa- *2659*
ment. Taken in a temporal sense, this word is a pedagogical repetition of "this day,"[128] to confirm us in trust "without reservation."
Taken in the qualitative sense, it signifies what is necessary for life, *2633*
and more broadly every good thing sufficient for subsistence.[129]
Taken literally (*epi-ousios*: "super-essential"), it refers directly to the
Bread of Life, the Body of Christ, the "medicine of immortality," *1405*
without which we have no life within us.[130] Finally in this connection, its heavenly meaning is evident: "this day" is the Day of the
Lord, the day of the feast of the kingdom, anticipated in the *1166*
Eucharist that is already the foretaste of the kingdom to come. For
this reason it is fitting for the Eucharistic liturgy to be celebrated
each day.   *1389*

> The Eucharist is our daily bread. The power belonging to this
> divine food makes it a bond of union. Its effect is then
> understood as unity, so that, gathered into his Body and
> made members of him, we may become what we receive. . . .
> This also is our daily bread: the readings you hear each day
> in church and the hymns you hear and sing. All these are
> necessities for our pilgrimage.[131]

> The Father in heaven urges us, as children of heaven, to ask
> for the bread of heaven. [Christ] himself is the bread who,
> sown in the Virgin, raised up in the flesh, kneaded in the
> Passion, baked in the oven of the tomb, reserved in churches,
> brought to altars, furnishes the faithful each day with food
> from heaven.[132]

V.   "AND FORGIVE US OUR TRESPASSES, AS WE FORGIVE THOSE WHO TRESPASS AGAINST US"

2838   This petition is astonishing. If it consisted only of the first *1425*
phrase, "And forgive us our trespasses," it might have been included, implicitly, in the first three petitions of the Lord's Prayer,
since Christ's sacrifice is "that sins may be forgiven." But, accord- *1933*
ing to the second phrase, our petition will not be heard unless we
have first met a strict requirement. Our petition looks to the future,
but our response must come first, for the two parts are joined by *2631*
the single word "as."

---

128   Cf. *Ex* 16:19-21.
129   Cf. *1 Tim* 6:8.
130   St. Ignatius of Antioch, *Ad Eph.* 20, 2: PG 5, 661; *Jn* 6:53-56.
131   St. Augustine, *Sermo* 57, 7: PL 38, 389.
132   St. Peter Chrysologus, *Sermo* 67: PL 52, 392; cf. *Jn* 6:51.

And forgive us our trespasses . . .

2839   With bold confidence, we began praying to our Father. In begging him that his name be hallowed, we were in fact asking him that we ourselves might be always made more holy. But though 1425 we are clothed with the baptismal garment, we do not cease to sin, 1439 to turn away from God. Now, in this new petition, we return to him like the prodigal son and, like the tax collector, recognize that we are sinners before him.[133] Our petition begins with a "confession" of our wretchedness and his mercy. Our hope is firm because, in his Son, "we have redemption, the forgiveness of sins."[134] We find the efficacious and undoubted sign of his forgiveness in the 1422 sacraments of his Church.[135]

2840   Now – and this is daunting – this outpouring of mercy cannot penetrate our hearts as long as we have not forgiven those who have trespassed against us. Love, like the Body of Christ, is indivisible; we cannot love the God we cannot see if we do not love the brother or sister we do see.[136] In refusing to forgive our brothers and sisters, our hearts are closed and their hardness makes them 1864 impervious to the Father's merciful love; but in confessing our sins, our hearts are opened to his grace.

2841   This petition is so important that it is the only one to which the Lord returns and which he develops explicitly in the Sermon on the Mount.[137] This crucial requirement of the covenant mystery is impossible for man. But "with God all things are possible."[138]

. . . as we forgive those who trespass against us

2842   This "as" is not unique in Jesus' teaching: "You, therefore, must be perfect, *as* your heavenly Father is perfect"; "Be merciful, even *as* your Father is merciful"; "A new commandment I give to you, that you love one another, even *as* I have loved you, that you also love one another."[139] It is impossible to keep the Lord's commandment by imitating the divine model from outside; there 521 has to be a vital participation, coming from the depths of the heart, in the holiness and the mercy and the love of our God. Only the

---

133   Cf. *Lk* 15:11-32; 18:13.
134   *Col* 1:14; *Eph* 1:7.
135   Cf. *Mt* 26:28; *Jn* 20:23.
136   Cf. *1 Jn* 4:20.
137   Cf. *Mt* 6:14-15; 5:23-24; *Mk* 11:25.
138   *Mt* 19:26.
139   *Mt* 5:48; *Lk* 6:36; *Jn* 13:34.

Spirit by whom we live can make "ours" the same mind that was in Christ Jesus.[140] Then the unity of forgiveness becomes possible and we find ourselves "forgiving one another, *as* God in Christ forgave" us.[141]

2843   Thus the Lord's words on forgiveness, the love that loves to the end,[142] become a living reality. The parable of the merciless servant, which crowns the Lord's teaching on ecclesial communion, ends with these words: "So also my heavenly Father will do to every one of you, if you do not forgive your brother from your heart."[143] It is there, in fact, "in the depths of the *heart*," that everything is bound and loosed. It is not in our power not to feel *368* or to forget an offense; but the heart that offers itself to the Holy Spirit turns injury into compassion and purifies the memory in transforming the hurt into intercession.

2844   Christian prayer extends to the *forgiveness of enemies*,[144] *2262* transfiguring the disciple by configuring him to his Master. Forgiveness is a high-point of Christian prayer; only hearts attuned to God's compassion can receive the gift of prayer. Forgiveness also bears witness that, in our world, love is stronger than sin. The martyrs of yesterday and today bear this witness to Jesus. Forgiveness is the fundamental condition of the reconciliation of the children of God with their Father and of men with one another.[145]

2845   There is no limit or measure to this essentially divine *1441* forgiveness,[146] whether one speaks of "sins" as in *Luke* (11:4), or "debts" as in *Matthew* (6:12). We are always debtors: "Owe no one anything, except to love one another."[147] The communion of the Holy Trinity is the source and criterion of truth in every relationship. It is lived out in prayer, above all in the Eucharist.[148]

> God does not accept the sacrifice of a sower of disunion, but commands that he depart from the altar so that he may first be reconciled with his brother. For God can be appeased only by prayers that make peace. To God, the better offering is peace, brotherly concord, and a people made one in the unity of the Father, Son, and Holy Spirit.[149]

---

140   Cf. *Gal* 5:25; *Phil* 2:1, 5.
141   *Eph* 4:32.
142   Cf. *Jn* 13:1.
143   Cf. *Mt* 18:23-35.
144   Cf. *Mt* 5:43-44.
145   Cf. *2 Cor* 5:18-21; John Paul II, *DM* 14.
146   Cf. *Mt* 18:21-22; *Lk* 17:3-4.
147   *Rom* 13:8.
148   Cf. *Mt* 5:23-24; *1 Jn* 3:19-24.
149   St. Cyprian, *De Dom. orat.* 23: PL 4, 535-536; cf. *Mt* 5:24.

VI.   "And Lead Us Not into Temptation"

2846   This petition goes to the root of the preceding one, for our sins result from our consenting to temptation; we therefore ask our
164   Father not to "lead" us into temptation. It is difficult to translate the Greek verb used by a single English word: the Greek means both "do not allow us to enter into temptation" and "do not let us yield to temptation."[150] "God cannot be tempted by evil and he himself tempts no one";[151] on the contrary, he wants to set us free from evil. We ask him not to allow us to take the way that leads to
2516   sin. We are engaged in the battle "between flesh and spirit"; this petition implores the Spirit of discernment and strength.

2847   The Holy Spirit makes us *discern* between trials, which are necessary for the growth of the inner man,[152] and temptation, which leads to sin and death.[153] We must also discern between
2284   being tempted and consenting to temptation. Finally, discernment unmasks the lie of temptation, whose object appears to be good, a "delight to the eyes" and desirable,[154] when in reality its fruit is death.

> God does not want to impose the good, but wants free beings. . . . There is a certain usefulness to temptation. No one but God knows what our soul has received from him, not even we ourselves. But temptation reveals it in order to teach us to know ourselves, and in this way we discover our evil inclinations and are obliged to give thanks for the goods that temptation has revealed to us.[155]

2848   "Lead us not into temptation" implies a *decision of the heart*: "For where your treasure is, there will your heart be also. . . . No one can serve two masters."[156] "If we live by the Spirit, let us also walk by the Spirit."[157] In this assent to the Holy Spirit the Father gives us strength. "No testing has overtaken you that is not com-
1808   mon to man. God is faithful, and he will not let you be tempted beyond your strength, but with the temptation will also provide the way of escape, so that you may be able to endure it."[158]

---

150   Cf. *Mt* 26:41.
151   *Jas* 1:13.
152   Cf. *Lk.* 8:13-15; *Acts* 14:22; *Rom* 5:3-5; *2 Tim* 3:12.
153   Cf. *Jas* 1:14-15.
154   Cf. *Gen* 3:6.
155   Origen, *De orat.* 29: PG 11, 544CD.
156   *Mt* 6:21, 24.
157   *Gal* 5:25.
158   *1 Cor* 10:13.

2849 Such a battle and such a victory become possible only through prayer. It is by his prayer that Jesus vanquishes the tempter, both at the outset of his public mission and in the ultimate struggle of his agony[159] In this petition to our heavenly Father, Christ unites us to his battle and his agony. He urges us to *vigilance*   540, 612 of the heart in communion with his own. Vigilance is "custody of the heart," and Jesus prayed for us to the Father: "Keep them in   2612 your name."[160] The Holy Spirit constantly seeks to awaken us to keep watch.[161] Finally, this petition takes on all its dramatic meaning in relation to the last temptation of our earthly battle; it asks for *final perseverance*. "Lo, I am coming like a thief! Blessed is he who is awake."[162]   162

VII. "But Deliver Us from Evil"

2850 The last petition to our Father is also included in Jesus' prayer: "I am not asking you to take them out of the world, but I ask you to protect them from the evil one."[163] It touches each of us personally, but it is always "we" who pray, in communion with the whole Church, for the deliverance of the whole human family. The Lord's Prayer continually opens us to the range of God's economy of salvation. Our interdependence in the drama of sin and death is turned into solidarity in the Body of Christ, the "commun-   309 ion of saints."[164]

2851 In this petition, evil is not an abstraction, but refers to a person, Satan, the Evil One, the angel who opposes God. The devil (*dia-bolos*) is the one who "throws himself across" God's plan and   391 his work of salvation accomplished in Christ.

2852 "A murderer from the beginning, . . . a liar and the father of lies," Satan is "the deceiver of the whole world."[165] Through him sin and death entered the world and by his definitive defeat all creation will be "freed from the corruption of sin and death."[166] Now "we know that anyone born of God does not sin, but He who was born of God keeps him, and the evil one does not touch him.

---

159 Cf. *Mt* 4:1-11; 26:36-44.
160 *Jn* 17:11; cf. *Mk* 13:9, 23, 33-37; 14:38; *Lk* 12:35-40.
161 Cf. *1 Cor* 16:13; *Col* 4:2; *1 Thess* 5:6; *1 Pet* 5:8.
162 *Rev* 16:15.
163 *Jn* 17:15.
164 Cf. *RP* 16.
165 *Jn* 8:44; *Rev* 12:9.
166 *Roman Missal*, Eucharistic Prayer IV, 125.

We know that we are of God, and the whole world is in the power of the evil one."[167]

> The Lord who has taken away your sin and pardoned your faults also protects you and keeps you from the wiles of your adversary the devil, so that the enemy, who is accustomed to leading into sin, may not surprise you. One who entrusts himself to God does not dread the devil. "If God is for us, who is against us?"[168]

677 **2853**   Victory over the "prince of this world"[169] was won once for all at the Hour when Jesus freely gave himself up to death to give us his life. This is the judgment of this world, and the prince of this world is "cast out."[170] "He pursued the woman"[171] but had no hold on her: the new Eve, "full of grace" of the Holy Spirit, is *490* preserved from sin and the corruption of death (the Immaculate *972* Conception and the Assumption of the Most Holy Mother of God, Mary, ever virgin). "Then the dragon was angry with the woman, and went off to make war on the rest of her offspring."[172] Therefore the Spirit and the Church pray: "Come, Lord Jesus,"[173] since his coming will deliver us from the Evil One.

2854   When we ask to be delivered from the Evil One, we pray as well to be freed from all evils, present, past, and future, of which he is the author or instigator. In this final petition, the Church brings before the Father all the distress of the world. Along with deliverance from the evils that overwhelm humanity, she implores the precious gift of peace and the grace of perseverance in expec-
2632 tation of Christ's return. By praying in this way, she anticipates in humility of faith the gathering together of everyone and everything in him who has "the keys of Death and Hades," who "is and who was and who is to come, the Almighty."[174]

---

167   1 *Jn* 5:18-19.
168   St. Ambrose, *De Sacr.* 5, 4, 30: PL 16, 454; cf. *Rom* 8:31.
169   *Jn* 14:30.
170   *Jn* 12:31; *Rev* 12:10.
171   *Rev* 12:13-16.
172   *Rev* 12:17.
173   *Rev* 22:17, 20.
174   *Rev* 1:8, 18; cf. *Rev* 1:4; *Eph* 1:10.

Deliver us, Lord, we beseech you, from every evil and grant us peace in our day, so that aided by your mercy we might be ever free from sin and protected from all anxiety, as we await the blessed hope and the coming of our Savior, Jesus Christ.[175]

1041

ARTICLE 4
THE FINAL DOXOLOGY

2855 The final doxology, "For the kingdom, the power and the *2760* glory are yours, now and forever," takes up again, by inclusion, the first three petitions to our Father: the glorification of his name, the coming of his reign, and the power of his saving will. But these prayers are now proclaimed as adoration and thanksgiving, as in the liturgy of heaven.[176] The ruler of this world has mendaciously attributed to himself the three titles of kingship, power, and glory.[177] Christ, the Lord, restores them to his Father and our Father, until he hands over the kingdom to him when the mystery of salvation will be brought to its completion and God will be all in all.[178]

2856 "Then, after the prayer is over you say 'Amen,' which *1061-1065* means 'So be it,' thus ratifying with our 'Amen' what is contained in the prayer that God has taught us."[179]

IN BRIEF

2857 In the Our Father, the object of the first three petitions is the glory of the Father: the sanctification of his name, the coming of the kingdom, and the fulfillment of his will. The four others present our wants to him: they ask that our lives be nourished, healed of sin, and made victorious in the struggle of good over evil.

---

175 *Roman Missal,* Embolism after the Lord's Prayer, 126: *Libera nos, quæsumus, Domine, ab omnibus malis, da propitius pacem in diebus nostris, ut, ope misericordiæ tuæ adiuti, et a peccato simus semper liberi, et ab omni perturbatione securi: expectantes beatam spem et adventum Salvatoris nostri Iesu Christi.*

176 Cf. *Rev* 1:6; 4:11; 5:13.

177 Cf. *Lk* 4:5-6.

178 *1 Cor* 15:24-28.

179 St. Cyril of Jerusalem, *Catech. myst.* 5, 18: PG 33, 1124; cf. Cf. *Lk* 1:38.

2858   By asking "hallowed be thy name" we enter into God's plan, the sanctification of his name – revealed first to Moses and then in Jesus – by us and in us, in every nation and in each man.

2859   By the second petition, the Church looks first to Christ's return and the final coming of the Reign of God. It also prays for the growth of the Kingdom of God in the "today" of our own lives.

2860   In the third petition, we ask our Father to unite our will to that of his Son, so as to fulfill his plan of salvation in the life of the world.

2861   In the fourth petition, by saying "give us," we express in communion with our brethren our filial trust in our heavenly Father. "Our daily bread" refers to the earthly nourishment necessary to everyone for subsistence, and also to the Bread of Life: the Word of God and the Body of Christ. It is received in God's "today," as the indispensable, (super-) essential nourishment of the feast of the coming Kingdom anticipated in the Eucharist .

2862   The fifth petition begs God's mercy for our offences, mercy which can penetrate our hearts only if we have learned to forgive our enemies, with the example and help of Christ.

2863   When we say "lead us not into temptation" we are asking God not to allow us to take the path that leads to sin. This petition implores the Spirit of discernment and strength; it requests the grace of vigilance and final perseverance.

2864   In the last petition, "but deliver us from evil," Christians pray to God with the Church to show forth the victory, already won by Christ, over the "ruler of this world," Satan, the angel personally opposed to God and to his plan of salvation.

2865   By the final "Amen," we express our "fiat" concerning the seven petitions: "So be it."

INDEX OF CITATIONS

The arabic number(s) following the citation refers to the text paragraph number(s); the asterisk following a text paragraph number indicates that the citation has been paraphrased.

SACRED SCRIPTURE

OLD TESTAMENT

Genesis

1:1-2:4	337
1:1	268,* 279, 280, 290
1:2-3	292*
1:2	243,* 703,* 1218*
1:3	298*
1:4	299
1:10	299
1:12	299
1:14	347*
1:18	299
1:21	299
1:26-29	2402*
1:26-28	307*
1:26-27	1602*
1:26	36,* 225, 299,* 343,*2501, 2809
1:27	355, 383, 1604,* 2331
1:28-31	2415*
1:28	372, 373, 1604, 1607,* 1652, 2331, 2427*
1:31	299, 1604*
2:1-3	345
2:2	314,* 2184
2:7	362, 369,* 703*
2:8	378*
2:15	378
2:17	376,* 396, 396, 400,* 1006,* 1008*
2:18-25	1605*
2:18	371, 1652
2:19-20	371, 2417*

2:22	369,* 1607*
2:23	371
2:24	372, 1627,* 1644,* 2335
2:25	376*
3	390,* 2795*
3:1-5	391*
3:1-11	397*
3:3	1008*
3:5	392, 398,* 399,* 1850
3:6	2541, 2847
3:7	400*
3:8-10	29*
3:9-10	399*
3:9	410,* 2568
3:11-13	400*
3:11	2515
3:12	1607*
3:13	1736, 2568
3:14-19	2427*
3:15	70,* 410,* 489*
3:16-19	1607*
3:16	376,* 400,* 1609
3:16b	1607*
3:17-19	378*
3:17	400*
3:19	376,* 400, 400,* 1008,* 1609
3:20	489*
3:21	1608*
3:24	332*
4:1-2	2335*
4:3-15	401*
4:3-7	2538*
4:4	2569*
4:8-12	2259*
4:10-11	2259

Leviticus

Numbers

Deuteronomy

Romans

1 Corinthians

James

1:5-8	2633,* 2737*
1:13	2846
1:14-15	2847*
1:17	212, 2642
1:25	1972*
1:27	2208
2:7	432,* 2148
2:10-11	2069,* 2079*
2:10	578
2:12	1972*
2:14-26	162*
2:15-16	2447
2:26	1815
4:1-10	2737*
4:2-3	2737
4:4	2737
4:5	2737
5:1-6	2445
5:4	1867,* 2409,* 2434*
5:12	2153*
5:14-15	1510, 1511,* 1526
5:14	1519
5:15	1519,* 1520
5:16	2737*
5:16b-18	2582
5:20	1434*

1 Peter

1	2627*
1:3-9	2627*
1:3	654*
1:7	1031*
1:10-12	719
1:18-20	602
1:18-19	517*
1:18	622
1:19	613*
1:23	1228,* 2769
2:1-10	2769*
2:1	2475
2:4-5	1141,* 1179
2:4	552
2:5	756,* 901, 1268, 1330,* 1546*
2:7	756*
2:9	709,* 782, 803, 1141, 1268, 1546*
2:13-17	1899*
2:13	2238

2:16	2238
2:21	618
2:24	612
3:1-7	2204*
3:9	1669*
3:18-19	632*
3:20-21	845*
3:20	1219
3:21	128,* 1094,* 1794*
4:6	634
4:7	670,* 1806
4:8	1434
4:14	693
4:17	672*
5:3	893, 1551*
5:4	754*
5:7	322
5:8	409,* 2849*

2 Peter

1:3-4	1996*
1:4	406, 1129,* 1265, 1692, 1721, 1812*
1:16-18	554*
2:4	392*
3:9	1037, 2822
3:11-12	671*
3:12-13	677*
3:13	1043, 1405*

1 John

1:1-4	425
1:3-7	1108*
1:3	2781*
1:5	214
1:6	2470
1:7-2:2	2631*
1:8-10	827*
1:8-9	1847
1:8	1425
1:10	2147*
2:1-2	1460*
2:1	519, 692,* 2634*
2:2	605,* 606
2:16	377,* 2514,* 2534*
2:18	670, 672,* 675*
2:20	91,* 695*
2:22	675*
2:23	454*

PROFESSIONS OF FAITH

(Cited by DS numbers)

ECUMENICAL COUNCILS

(Cited by DS numbers, except for Vatican II)

VATICAN I (1869-1870)

VATICAN II (1962-1965)

Sacrosanctum concilium
(December 4, 1963)

Orientalium ecclesiarum
(November 21, 1964)

Unitatis redintegratio
(November 21, 1964)

PARTICULAR COUNCILS AND SYNODS

(cited by DS number)

PONTIFICAL DOCUMENTS

JOHN PAUL II (1978-)

ECCLESIASTICAL DOCUMENTS

CANON LAW

LITURGY

LATIN RITE

Canticle

Evening Prayer, Saturday
461*

Prayers

Ave Maria   1014, 2676, 2677
O sacrum convivium
1342
Veni sancte Spiritus
2671
Litany of the saints
1014

EASTERN RITES

Liturgy of St. John Chrysostom

Cherubic Hymn   335*
Anaphora   42, 1137
Preparation for Communion
1386

Byzantine Liturgy

1166
consecratory Preface of the Ordination of Bishops
1541
consecratory Prayer of the Ordination of Deacons
1543
consecratory Prayer of the Ordination of Prebyters
1542

Troparia

O monogenes   469
of the feast of the Dormition (August 15)
966
of Easter   638
of Sunday Matins, second mode
703
of Vespers, Pentecost
291, 732, 2671

Kontakia

of the feast of the Transfiguration
555
of Romanos the
Melodist   525

Euchologion

formula of
absolution   481
Prayer of
ordination   1587

Syriac Liturgy

of Antioch, epiclesis of
consecration of
the holy chrism   1297

Fanqîth

Syriac Office of Antioch,
vol. 6, summer,
p. 193B   1167
Syriac Office of Antioch,
vol. 1, commons,
p. 237A-B   1391

ECCLESIASTICAL WRITERS

Anselm of Canterbury, St.

Proslogion

proemium: PL 153, 225A   158

Aristides

Apologia

16, 6   760*

Athanasius of Alexandria, St.

De incarnatione

54, 3   PG 25, 192B   460

Epistula festivalis

329   PG 26, 1366A   1169

Epistulae ad Serapionem

1, 24   PG 26, 588   1988

Augustine, St.   695

Confessiones

1, 1, 1	PL 32, 659-661	30
2, 4, 9	PL 32, 678	1958
3, 6, 11	PL 32, 688	300
6, 11, 20	PL 32, 729-730	2520
7, 7, 11	PL 32, 739	385
9, 6, 14	PL 32, 769-770	1157
9, 11, 27	PL 32, 775	1371
10, 20, 29	PL 32, 791	1718
10, 28, 39	PL 32, 795	45
10, 29, 40	PL 32, 796	2340
13, 36, 51	PL 32, 868	2002

Contra epistulam Manichaei quam vocant fundamenti

5, 6   PL 42, 176   119

Contra Faustum manichaeum

| 22 | PL 42, 418 | 1849 |
| 22 | PL 42, 418 | 1871 |

De catechizandis rudibus

| 3, 5 | PL 40, 256 | 281* |
| 4, 8 | PL 40, 315-316 | 2539 |

De civitate Dei

10, 6	PL 41, 224	1372, 2099
14, 7	PL 41, 410	1766
14, 28	PL 41, 436	1850
18, 51	PL 41, 614	769
19, 13	PL 41, 640	2304
19, 19	PL 41, 647	2185
22, 17	PL 41, 779	1118
22, 30	PL 41, 804	1720, 2550

De diversis quaestionibus octoginta tribus

64, 4   PL 40, 56   2560*

De fide et symbolo

10, 25   PL 40, 196   2518

De Genesi contra Manichaeos

1, 2, 4   PL 35, 175   338

De gratia et libero arbitrio

17   PL 44, 901   2001

De libero arbitrio

1, 1, 1   PL 32, 1221-1223   311*

De mendacio

4, 5   PL 40, 491   2482

De moribus ecclesiae catholicae

| 1, 3, 4 | PL 32, 1312 | 1718 |
| 1, 25, 46 | PL 32, 1330-1331 | 1809 |

De natura et gratia

31   PL 44, 264   2001

De sancta virginitate

| 3 | PL 40, 398 | 506 |
| 6 | PL 40, 399 | 963 |

Benedict, St.

Regula

20		2834*
43, 3	PL 66, 675-676	347
48		2834

Bernard of Clairvaux, St.

Homilia super missus est

4, 11	PL 183, 86B	108

In Canticum sermones

27, 14	PL 183, 920D	771

Bonaventure, St.

In libros sententiarum

2, 1, 2, 2, 1		293
4, 37, 1, 3		2071

Caesaria the Younger, St.

To St. Richildis and St. Radegunde

	SCh 345, 480	127

Caesarius of Arles, St.

Expositio symboli (sermo 9)

	CCL 103, 47	232

Catherine of Siena, St.

dialogues

1, 7		1937
4, 13	*LH,* OR, week 19, Sunday	356
4, 138		313

Clement of Alexandria

Paedagogus

1, 6, 27	PG 8, 281	760, 813

Clement of Rome, St.

Epistula ad Corinthios

7, 4	PG 1, 224	1432
42, 4	PG 1, 292-293	1577
42, 44	PG 1, 291-300	861*
44, 3	PG 1, 300	1577
61, 1-2	SCh 167, 198-200	1900

Cyprian of Carthage, St.   1290

De ecclesiae catholicae unitate

	PL 4 (1891), 509-536	846
6	PL 4 (1891), 519	181

De Dominica oratione

9	PL 4 (1891), 525A	2782
11	PL 4 (1891), 526B	2784
12	PL 4 (1891), 527A	2813
13	PL 4 (1891), 528A	2816
21	PL 4 (1891), 551	2803
23	PL 4 (1891), 535-536	
		810, 2845

Epistulae

58, 10, 1	PL 4 (1891), 368	1028
73, 21	PL 3, 1169	846

Cyril of Alexandria, St.

Commentarius in johannem

12, 11	PG 74, 560-561	738

In Lucam

22, 19	PG 72, 921B	1381

Cyril of Jerusalem, St.

Catecheses illuminandorum

5, 12	PG 33, 521-524	186
18, 29	PG 33, 1049	
LH, OR, week 17, Thursday		1050

Ignatius of Loyola, St.

Irenaeus of Lyons, St.

Isaac of Niniveh, St.

Jerome, St.

Joan of Arc, St.

Thomas More, St.

Letter from Prison

SUBJECT INDEX

Prefatory Note to Index

The main entry words are printed in bold type as are references to definitions or exact descriptions (for example, **Angels; demons: 327-330**). References to "In Brief" texts are printed in italics (for example, **Angels; demons:** *350*). The sub-headings that follow main entries provide additional information about the same or closely related topics (for example: **Abraham:** call of Abraham: 59, 72, 762). Cross references with "see" or "see also" supply information about relevant main entry words. The primary objective in constructing this index was to provide the most comprehensive survey possible of the contents, not the most complete listing of all references to a given subject.

Abortion: 2270-75

condemnation in the early Church: 2271
excommunication as penalty: 2272
inalienable right to life: 2273
protection of human life from the moment of conception: 2270, *2319*, *2322-23*

Abraham

call of Abraham: 59, *72*, *762*
faith of Abraham: 144-46, 165, 1080, 2676
hope of Abraham: 1819
in the Muslim religion: 841
prayer of Abraham: 2570-72, *2592*, 2635
promise to Abraham: 705-6, 762, 1222, 1716, 2810
  fulfillment of the promises: 422, *1725*, 2619

Absolution: see Penance, sacrament of: as liturgical celebration

Acedia: (spiritual sloth)

as capital sin: 1866
as sin against love: 2094
as temptation in prayer: 2733

Act; action

beatitude as meaning and end: 1719, 1723
circumstances and consequences: 1754

end does not justify the means: 1753, *1759*
intention and goal: 1752-53
judgment as good or bad: 1749-50, 1755-56, *1757*, *1760*
object: 1751, *1758*

Adoration

and blessing: 1078, 2628, 2781
and respect for God's name: 2143, 2145
and sacred art: 2502
of the Blessed Sacrament: 1178, 1183, 1378-81, *1418*, 2691, *2696*
prayer as expression of: 2098
sacrifice as sign of: 2099
worship of God by the Church: 1083
see also: Worship

Adultery: 2380-81

as grave sin: 1756, 1856, 1858, *2400*
importance of conjugal fidelity: 1646, 2364-65, *2397*
in Jesus' preaching: 2336

Advent: 524, 1095

see also Liturgy: liturgical seasons

Agnosticism

as practical atheism: 2128
forms: 2127

Alcohol

abuse: 2290

Almsgiving

as act of religion: 1969
as expression of penance: 1434, 1438
as form of piety: 575, 2101
as witness to fraternal charity: 2447,
2462
on behalf of the dead: 1032

Altar: 1181-82, 1383, 2570

Amputation: see Medical
treatment

Analogy

between Creator and creature: 41
of faith: 114

Anamnesis

in the Eucharistic celebration: 1354,
1362
in the general liturgical celebration:
1103
in the sacramental celebration: 1106

Angels; demons: 327-330, *350*

as servants of Christ: 331, *351*, 1034,
1038
"fall" of angels:
as irrevocable sin: 392-93, *414*
by their free decision: 391-92
Satan as a "fallen angel": 391, *414*
given intelligence and free will: 311
guardian angels: 336
heaven as "place" of angels: 326, 1023
in salvation history: 332-33
significance for the Church: 334-35, *352*
"son of God" as title for angels: 441

Anger; wrath

as passion: 1765
as sin:
consequence of original sin: 2259
desire for vengeance: 2302
forbidden in Sermon on the Mount:
2262
mortal sin: 1866, 2302

Animals

experimentation on: 2417
exploitation forbidden: 2415, 2418
place in creation: 2415-16
relationship to man: 2417-18, *2457*

Anointing

Anointing of the Sick: 1523
as sign of the Holy Spirit: 695
Baptism: 1237
Confirmation: 1289, 1293-96
ordination of priests and bishops: 1574

Anointing of the Sick

administration by priests and bishops:
1516, *1530*
as a sacrament:
one of the seven sacraments: 1113,
1210
"sacrament of the dying": 1523
since the beginning of the Church:
1510
liturgical celebration: 1517
elements of the celebration:
1518-19, *1531*
main effects: 1520-23, *1532*
comfort, peace, and courage: 1520
forgiveness of sins: 1520
preparation for death: 1523
sanctification of the Church: 1522
union with the Passion of Christ:
1521
purpose: 1499, 1511, *1526-27*
reception:
Eucharist as "viaticum": 1517,
1524-25
preparation: 1516-17
reception recommended: 1515, *1528*
recipient: 1514
repeated reception: 1515, *1529*
rite: 1513
tradition of "Extreme Unction": 1512

Antichrist: 675

see also: Jesus: Second Coming

Anxiety: 2088

Apostasy: 2089, 817

Apostles

apostolic teaching as way to heaven:
75-77, 1724
called by Jesus to follow him: 1506
Church built on the foundation of the
apostles: 857, 860
commissioned by Jesus: 2, 858-60
power of the keys: 981
preach the Paschal mystery: 571

sin as offense against God: 1850
speaking about God: 39-43, *48*
special salvific actions:
    calls Israel: 62-64, 218-19, 2085
    inspires the authors of Holy
    Scripture: 105-6
    New Covenant: 64
    reveals himself to Moses: 205
    saves Israel from sin: 431
    sends his Son: 422

Good

in judging an action: 1755-56

Goodness

as fruit of the Holy Spirit: 736, 1832

Good News: see Gospel

Gospel

and the Law of the Old Covenant: 1963
as Good News: 571
as revelation of God's mercy: 1846
command to proclaim: 2
formation: 126
place and significance in the New
    Testament: 125-27
record of Jesus' life: 514-15, 534, 573
two ways of recording Jesus' message:
    76

Grace

as God's gift:
    as charism: 2003
    as gift of the Holy Spirit: 2003
    as God's gratuitous help: 1996, *2021*
effects:
    as uniting with Christ in active
    love: 2011
    forges the human character: 1810
    justification: 654, 1987, 1989
    parent-child relationship with God:
    1997
    participation in the life of God: 1997
    sanctification: 824, 1999, *2023-24*
    vocation to eternal life: 1998
faith as grace: 153-55
graces of state: 2004
habitual and actual grace: 2000
reception:
    and human experience: 2005
    meriting grace: 2010, *2025-27*
    readiness to receive: 2001
    requirements: 2002

unbelief as refusal of grace: 678
    within man's earthly life: 1021
role of grace in the man-God
    relationship: 35, *2022*
sacramental grace: 2003

Greed: see Desires, disordered

Habits

and the imputability of an act: 1735

Hail Mary: 435, 2676-78

Happiness

substance of true happiness: 1723
virtue of hope and desire for
    happiness: 1818

Hatred

as grave sin: 2303
as passion: 1765
forbidden in Sermon on the Mount:
    2262

Health

and the virtue of temperance: 2290
and use of drugs: 2291
and worship of the body: 2289
duty of concern for health: 2288

Heart of Jesus, adoration of: 2669,
1439

Heaven:

as "place of God": 326
as "place of the deceased": 1023-29
"seen and unseen" world: 325
see World; Creation

Hell: 1033

as consequence of mortal sin: 1861
as location of the damned: 633
God predestines no one to damnation:
    1037
in Jesus' preaching: 1034
in the teaching of the Church: 1035
teaching about hell as admonition: 1036

Heresy: 2089, 817

Hierarchy

of truths: see Truth; Dogma
in the Church: see Church: structure

Holiness; sanctity; saints

holiness:
  all Christians called to holiness:
  2013-14, *2028-29*
  entails asceticism: 2015
  God wants man to be glorified: 2012
  taught by the Church: 2030
saints:
  and the Holy Spirit's activity
  in the Church: 688
  and the Holy Spirit's activity
  in men: 686
  as companions in prayer: 2683-2684
  as example of Christian holiness:
  1717, 2030
  as patrons: 2156
  communion of saints: 946-59
  intercession of saints: 956
  significance of canonization: 828

Holy Days of Obligation:

2042-43, 2177, 2180, 2185, 2187-88,
2192, 2193

Holy Spirit

acts:
  in all mankind:
    animates all creation: 703
    awakens faith: 684
    comes unceasingly into the
    world: 732
    enables communication
    with Christ: 683
    grants gifts to all: 2003
    helps man grow in spiritual
    freedom: 1742
    master and source of prayer:
    741, 2652
    "principal author" of Holy
    Scripture: 304
    restores the divine likeness: 734
    reveals God: 687
    reveals the Trinity: 244, 684
    source of all holiness: 749
  in the Church:
    brings about the unity of the
    Church: 813
    Church as temple of the Holy
    Spirit: 797-98
    directs and supports the
    Church: 768, 747
    in the liturgy of the Church:
    1091-1109

    living memory of the Church:
    1099
    mission in the Church: 737, 739
    responsible for the Church's
    mission: 852
consubstantial with the Father and the
  Son: 685, 689
faith in the Holy Spirit: 14, 152, 202, 742
gifts of the Holy Spirit: 768, 798-801,
  1830
  at Confirmation: 1303
  first gift is love: 733, 735
  fruits of the Spirit: 736, 1832
  in Baptism: 1266
  in the Anointing of the Sick: 1520
  in the charism of healing: 1508
  in the sacrament of Holy Orders:
  1585-89
  in the sheltering of sinners: 827
  the seven gifts: 1831, 1845
in God's work of salvation:
  in the preaching of Jesus: 714, 728
  in the theophanies of the Old
  Testament: 707
  Jesus gives the Holy Spirit: 730
  John the Baptist and the preparation
  of the people: 718, 720
  Mary's conception and the birth
  of the Son of God: 723
  outpouring on Pentecost: 731
  place in the economy of salvation:
  685-86
  preparation for the Messiah: 702
  preparation of Mary: 722, 725, *744*
  prophetic texts: 715
  the promised coming of the Holy
  Spirit: 706, 729
joint mission with the Son: 689-90, 727,
  743
life "in the Holy Spirit": 740, 1699, *2017*
  conversion: 1433
  forgiveness of sins: 976
  sin of "blaspheming against
  the Holy Spirit": 1864
manifestation as a divine Person: 731
names:
  "Holy Spirit": 691
  in the Acts of the Apostles and
  Letters of the New Testament: 693
  "Paraclete": 692
  "Spirit of Truth": 692
self-revelation: 687
symbols:
  cloud and light: 697
  "Finger of God": 700

John the Baptist

Baptism of Jesus: 535-37
Baptism of repentance: 720, 1224
filled with the Holy Spirit in his
    mother's womb: 717
fire of the Holy Spirit glows in him:
    696, 718
role in salvation history: 523, 719
witness given to Jesus: 608

Journalists: 2497

Joy: 301, 523, 1829

as fruit of the Holy Spirit: 736, 1832
see also: Happiness

Judgment, rash: 2477

Justice: 1807

legal commutative and distributive:
    2411
as cardinal virtue: 1805
see also: Virtues: cardinal virtues

Justification: 1987, *2018-19*

as most excellent work of God's love:
    1994
as receiving of God's justice: 1991
as sanctification of the whole human
    being: 1995
collaboration between God's grace
    and man's freedom: 1993
conferred through Baptism: 1266, 1992
grace of conversion precedes
    justification: 1989
in the Paschal mystery: 654
made possible by God's grace: 1987
merited by Christ's Passion: 1992, *2020*
possibility to rediscover grace of
    justification in Penance: 1446

Kidnapping: 2297

Killing

concern for eugenics never justifies:
    2268
failure to give assistance: 2277
forbidden in Jesus' preaching: 2262
forbidden in the Old Testament: 2261
legitimate defense: 2263-67
murder as sin that cries out to heaven:
    2268

stopping or omitting medical
    treatment: 2278
suicide: 2280-83, *2325*
unintentional killing, 2269

Kindness

as fruit of the Holy Spirit: 736, 1832
God's kindness: see God: attributes

Knowledge

as gift of the Holy Spirit: 1831

Knowledge of God

and human soul: 33
God lets himself be known: 31, 34,
    54-55
    in historical circumstances: 37
    natural knowledge of God: 32, 47
    through grace: 35
    through reason: 35, 36
    through revelation: 35, 38

Laity: 897

civil duties: 912
importance:
    in catechesis: 906
    in governing the Church: 911
    in secular institutes: 928-29
    in the Church's teaching office: 906
    in the mass media: 906
    in the preaching of the Gospel: 900,
        905
mission in the Church and in the
    world: 873-75
participation in Christ's kingly office:
    908-13
participation in Christ's priestly office:
    901-3
participation in Christ's prophetic
    office: 904
right and duty to manifest opinions:
    907
vocation: 898

Last Judgment: see Jesus Christ: Second Coming

Last Supper: see Jesus Christ: life of Jesus

influence of love on the other passions: 1766

love as most fundamental passion: 1765, *1772*

moral perfection: 1770, *1775*

moral determination of: 1767, *1773*, 2552

Passover of Christ; Paschal mystery: 571

as foundation of Christ's Reign: 671

as center of Christ's Good News: 571-72

for the salvation of men: 1067

fullness in the outpouring of the Holy Spirit: 731

Passover of Israel: 1164

Sunday as the fulfillment of Christ's Passover: 2175

see also: Easter

Patience

as one of the fruits of the Holy Spirit: 736, 1832

Patriarch: 61, 205, 707

Patriarchate: 887

Peace: 2304

as fruit of the Holy Spirit: 736, 1832

as fruit of love: 1829

disorders threatening freedom to be eliminated: 2317

earthly peace as "image of the peace of Christ": 2305

Penance: see Penance, sacrament of; Contrition

Penance, sacrament of; Confession

acts of reconciliation in daily life: 1435

and Baptism: 1425-26, 1427, 1429

and the Eucharist: 1436

as liturgical celebration:
  absolution:
      does not dispense from reparation: 1459
      formula of absolution: 1449
      in danger of death: 1483
      of sins: 1424
  confession of sins: 1456, 1458

essential parts: *1491*

fundamental structure: 1480

historically: 1447-48

penance imposed by the confessor: 1460, *1494*

preparation: 1454

as sacrament of reconciliation with God and the Church: 980, 1440, *1486*

called:
    "sacrament of confession": 1424
    "sacrament of conversion": 1423
    "sacrament of forgiveness": 1424
    "sacrament of Penance": 1423
    "sacrament of reconciliation": 1424

effects:
    basic effects: 1422, *1496*
    reconciliation with God: 980, 1468
    reconciliation with the Church: 980, 1469

eschatological sense: 1470

further means to obtain forgiveness of sins: 1434
    prayer and the reading of Scripture: 1437

in communal celebration: 1482

instituted by Christ: 1446, *1485*

meaning of contrition: 1430-33, 1452-53, *1492*

minister:
    through the bishop and priest: 1461, *1495*

necessity for salvation:
    as liturgical expression of conversion and forgiveness: 1440
    for reconciliation with God and the Church: 1484
    for forgiveness of mortal sin: 1395
    for satisfaction: 1459
    for preparation to receive Communion: 1385
    to attain the grace of justification: 1446

obligation to receive: 1457, *1493*, 2042

sacramental seal of confession: 1467, 2490

Penance, works of

conversion as precondition: 1430

meaning: 1460

on behalf of the dead: 1032

Pentateuch: 702

in the liturgy of the Old Covenant: 2588
People of God as expressed in the
    Psalms: 716
Psalms as book of the Old Testament:
    2585
"Psalms of David": 2579

Punishment

death penalty:
    imposition according to the
    traditional teaching of the Church:
    2266
    nonaggression as mark of love:
    2306
    preference for punishment without
    bloodshed: 2267
limitations on punishment: 2267
meaning and effect: 2266
right of society to protect itself: 2265
see also: Torture

Purgatory: 1030-32

Purity of heart: 2518

demands purification of the social
    atmosphere: 2525
goal: 2519, *2531*
in the struggle against carnal desires:
    2517, *2530*
means for preserving purity: 2520, *2532*
requires modesty: 2521, *2533*

Rape: 2356

Readers: 1143

Reason

and faith: 156-59, 286
and Law: 1951
as ability of man: 286
sin as offense against: 1849

Redemption

as center of the Christian message: 571,
    601
as source of Christ's authority over the
    Church: 669
continues in the liturgy: 1069
meaning ascertainable only in faith: 573
requires perseverance in charity: 837

Religion, virtue of

duty of religious worship: 2105

oaths as lack of respect for God: 2149
offenses against virtue of religion:
    2118-22:
    sacrilege: 2120
    simony: 2121
    tempting God: 2119
respect for God's name: 2143
use of words with respect to holy
    things: 2142

Religious life; religious: see
Church: structure; Evangelical
counsels

Reparation

in the New Testament: 2412, *2424*
for offenses against the truth: 2487,
    2509

Reproduction: see Matrimony:
purpose

Resistance

against unjust authority: 2242
with force of arms: 2243

Responsibility

and participation in the common
    good: 1914
for the sins of others: 1868
imputability: 1735-36
in virtue of man's freedom: 1734
role of conscience: 1781

Resurrection of Christ: see Jesus
Christ: Resurrection of Jesus

Resurrection of the dead:
988-1004

already risen with Christ in Baptism:
    1002-4
and Jesus: 994-95, *1019*
as work of the Trinity: 989
in Christianity: 991
in the Old Testament: 992-93
on the last day: 1001
"resurrection of the flesh": 686, 990,
    1015, 1017
the transfigured body of the
    resurrected: 999-1000

Revelation

can appear obscure: 157

ABBREVIATIONS

The following are abbreviations cited in the text:

AA	*Apostolicam actuositatem*	FC	*Familiaris consortio*
AAS	*Acta Apostolicae Sedis*	GCD	General Catechetical
AF	J. B. Lightfoot, ed.,		Directory
	The Apostolic Fathers	GE	*Gravissimum educationis*
	(New York: Macmillan,	GILH	General Introduction
	1889-1890)		to LH
AG	*Ad gentes*	GIRM	General Instruction
Ben	*de Benedictionibus*		to RomM
CA	*Centesimus annus*	GS	*Gaudium et spes*
Catech. R.	*Catechismus Romanus*	HV	*Humanae vitae*
CCEO	Corpus Canonum	ICEL	International Commission
	Ecclesiarum		on English in the Liturgy
	Orientalium	IM	*Inter mirifica*
CCL	Corpus Christianorum,	LE	*Laborem exercens*
	Series Latina	LG	*Lumen gentium*
	(Turnhout, 1953-)	LH	*Liturgy of the Hours*
CD	*Christus Dominus*	LXX	Septuagint
CDF	Congregation for the	MC	*Marialis cultus*
	Doctrine of the Faith	MD	*Mulieris dignitatem*
CELAM	Consejo Episcopal	MF	*Mysterium fidei*
	Latinoamericano	MM	*Mater et magistra*
CIC	Codex Iuris Canonici	NA	*Nostra aetate*
CL	*Christifideles laici*	NCCB	National Conference
COD	*Conciliorum*		of Catholic Bishops
	oecumenicorum decreta		(U.S.A.)
CPG	*Solemn Profession of Faith*:	ND	Neuner-Dupuis,
	Credo of the People		*The Christian Faith*
	of God		*in the Doctrinal*
CSEL	Corpus Scriptorum		*Documents of the*
	Ecclesiasticorum		*Catholic Church*
	Latinorum	OBA	*Ordo baptismi adultorum*
	(Vienna, 1866-)	OC	*Ordo confirmationis*
CT	*Catechesi tradendae*	OCF	Order of Christian
DeV	*Dominum et Vivificanum*		Funerals
DH	*Dignitatis humanae*	OCM	*Ordo celebrandi*
DM	*Dives in misericordia*		*Matrimonium*
DS	Denzinger-Schönmetzer,	OCV	*Ordo consecrationis*
	Enchiridion Symbolorum,		*virginum*
	definitionum et	OE	*Orientalium ecclesiarum*
	declarationum de rebus	OP	*Ordo paenitentiae*
	fidei et morum (1965)	OR	Office of Readings
DV	*Dei Verbum*	OT	*Optatam totius*
EN	*Evangelii nuntiandi*	PC	*Perfectae caritatis*
EP	Eucharistic Prayer		

PG	J. P. Migne, ed., Patrologia Graeca (Paris, 1857-1866)	RCIA	*Rite of christian initiation of adults*
		RH	*Redemptor hominis*
PL	J. P. Migne, ed., Patrologia Latina (Paris: 1841-1855)	RomM	*Roman Missal*
		RMat	*Redemptoris Mater*
		RMiss	*Redemptoris Missio*
PLS	J. P. Migne, ed., Patrologia Latina Supplement	RP	*Reconciliatio et paenitentia*
		SC	*Sacrosanctum concilium*
		SCG	Summa Contra Gentiles
PO	*Presbyterorum ordinis*	SCh	Sources Chrétiennes (Paris: 1942-)
PP	*Populorum progressio*		
PT	*Pacem in terris*	SRS	*Sollicitudo rei socialis*
RBC	*Rite of Baptism of Children*	STh	Summa Theologiae
		UR	*Unitatis redintegratio*

The following abbreviations are used for the books of the Bible cited in the text:

Gen	Genesis	*Am*	Amos
Ex	Exodus	*Jon*	Jonah
Lev	Leviticus	*Mic*	Micah
Num	Numbers	*Zeph*	Zephaniah
Deut	Deuteronomy	*Zech*	Zechariah
Josh	Joshua	*Mal*	Malachi
Judg	Judges	*Mt*	Matthew
1 Sam	1 Samuel	*Mk*	Mark
2 Sam	2 Samuel	*Lk*	Luke
1 Kings	1 Kings	*Jn*	John
2 Kings	2 Kings	*Acts*	Acts of the Apostles
1 Chr	1 Chronicles	*Rom*	Romans
2 Chr	2 Chronicles	*1 Cor*	1 Corinthians
Ezra	Ezra	*2 Cor*	2 Corinthians
Neh	Nehemiah	*Gal*	Galatians
Tob	Tobit	*Eph*	Ephesians
Jdt	Judith	*Phil*	Philippians
Esth	Esther	*Col*	Colossians
2 Macc	2 Maccabees	*1 Thess*	1 Thessalonians
Job	Job	*2 Thess*	2 Thessalonians
Ps	Psalms	*1 Tim*	1 Timothy
Prov	Proverbs	*2 Tim*	2 Timothy
Eccl	Ecclesiastes	*Titus*	Titus
Song	Song of Solomon	*Philem*	Philemon
Wis	Wisdom	*Heb*	Hebrews
Sir	Sirach	*Jas*	James
Isa	Isaiah	*1 Pet*	1 Peter
Jer	Jeremiah	*2 Pet*	2 Peter
Lam	Lamentations	*1 Jn*	1 John
Bar	Baruch	*2 Jn*	2 John
Ezek	Ezekiel	*3 Jn*	3 John
Dan	Daniel	*Jude*	Jude
Hos	Hosea	*Rev*	Revelation
Joel	Joel